THE ORIGINS OF PEACE

THE ORIGINS
OF PEACE

A Study of Peacemaking and the Structure
of Peace Settlements

ROBERT F. RANDLE

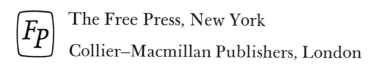

The Free Press, New York
Collier–Macmillan Publishers, London

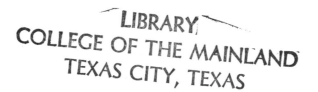

The Free Press
A Division of The Macmillan Company
866 Third Avenue, New York, New York 10022

Collier–Macmillan Canada Ltd., Toronto, Ontario

Library of Congress Catalog Card Number: 72–80078

printing number
1 2 3 4 5 6 7 8 9 10

for C H R I S and M I K E

. . . infin che il Veltro verrà. . . .

INSTITUTE OF WAR AND PEACE STUDIES

The Origins of Peace is one of a series of studies sponsored by the Institute of War and Peace Studies of Columbia University. Among those Institute studies also dealing with war, peace, and national security are *Defense and Diplomacy* by Alfred Vagts; *Man, the State and War* by Kenneth N. Waltz; *The Common Defense* by Samuel P. Huntington; *Strategy, Politics and Defense Budgets* by Warner R. Schilling, Paul Y. Hammond, and Glenn H. Snyder; *The Politics of Military Unification* by Demetrios Caraley; *NATO and the Range of American Choice* by William T. R. Fox and Annette Baker Fox; *The Politics of Policy Making in Defense and Foreign Affairs* by Roger Hilsman; *Inspection for Disarmament* edited by Seymour Melman; and *To Move a Nation* by Roger Hilsman, jointly sponsored with the Washington Center of Foreign Policy Research, Johns Hopkins University. Institute studies now in press include *German Nuclear Weapons Policy* by Catherine Kelleher; *Planning, Prediction and Policy-making in Foreign Affairs* by Robert L. Rothstein; and *European Security and the Atlantic System,* edited by Warner R. Schilling and William T. R. Fox.

Preface

In this book, I have sought to contribute to the ever-growing body of peace literature. Although I have dealt with a number of aspects of peacemaking, I have concentrated mainly upon the structure and content of *peace settlements*. My interest in this subject goes back to the year 1965, when I had planned to do an historical study of the great peace conferences of Westphalia, Utrecht, Vienna, and Versailles, regarding their work-products as constitutions of the European state system. I set this project temporarily aside, however, in order to make a detailed historical and legal study of the settlement of the Franco-Vietminh War. This work eventuated in a book, *Geneva 1954: The Settlement of the Indochinese War*,[1] the analyses in which prefigure some of the ideas of this study. Returning to the general program of research and reading in the area of peacemaking, I gradually came to see that nothing less than a thorough survey of modern wars and their settlements and a detailed study of some of the latter would do justice to this vast and important topic. My earlier interests in the "great" settlements became enveloped in a wider effort to view them in analytical perspective in relation to less great settlements, seeking to understand what, if any, concepts and processes were common to them all.

I have thought to apply what I believe are the still valid historical

1 Princeton, 1969.

methods of Machiavelli and Clausewitz[2] to the study of the peacemaking process. Thus, the generalizations made in the text are, for the most part, based upon a study of past wars, the diplomatic histories of their peace settlements, and their peace treaties and related documents. My students and I have, over the past two years, collected some 500 wars from 1500 to 1971. We started with the tables of wars that appear in Wright's *A Study of War*,[3] in *The Statistics of Deadly Quarrels* by Lewis F. Richardson,[4] and in Pitirim A. Sorokin's *Social and Cultural Dynamics*.[5] We reviewed and edited these tables, comparing them with information gathered in our own historical surveys. We then supplemented our war list with summary data on war outcomes and peace settlements. I selected about 60 of the settlements for closer study, 46 of which are analyzed in some detail in this book. My choice of wars for analysis was dictated in part, by what I call *structural criteria:* the number and types of belligerents and the way they were involved in the war. The classification system offered here is based upon this structure, forming a kind of "Periodic Table" of peace settlements. As the character of a war determines the character of its settlement, I propose that the resolutions of major wars can be best understood by investigating the settlements first of the simplest, and then of progressively more complicated, wars. While the most complex wars pose unique analytical problems, the scheme presented in this book will show that wars—and their settlements—do indeed have common elements, whether a war between two states or among several scores of states, whether a Sino-Japanese War or a Second World War. In short, I intended to provide both a framework for the analysis of wars and their settlements and a method employing certain analytical building blocks for a study of their structure.

As I have indicated, the conclusions of this book are based upon history, especially upon a study of peace settlements of the past. To be thorough, however—that is, to cover all the essential aspects of peacemaking and to show the various possibilities for settlement inherent in a specific situation for a particular combination of belligerents—it was often necessary to elaborate peacemaking scenarios. This valid and useful technique is employed by policymakers and their advisors and by strategic theorists in thinking about various unthinkable futures.

At the end of Chapters 2, 3, 5, and 6 and in Chapter 10, I have provided

2 Or Aristotle and the *Federalist Papers;* more recently, Quincy Wright, *A Study of War* (Chicago: University of Chicago Press, 1942), or Karl Deutsch *et al., Political Community and the North Atlantic Area* (Princeton: Princeton University Press, 1957) —among others.

3 *Op. cit.,* Vol. 1, pp. 636–51 (Appendix XX: Wars from 1500 to 1940).

4 Pittsburgh: The Boxwood Press, 1960, pp. 32–127 (wars from 1820 to 1953).

5 New York: American Book Co., 1937, Vol. 4 (entitled *War and Revolution*), pp. 543–619 (wars from 500 B.C. to 1925).

summaries of peace settlements of most of the wars I have studied. The format of my analysis dictated that I should arrange these summaries as I have done, including them at the ends of the chapters that dealt in general terms with the settlement of a particular category of wars. Of course, steps taken toward peace and the modes and elements of settlement of multilateral wars (Chapter 9) are often similar and even identical to those for simple external wars (Chapter 2). Conversely, the generalizations I have made in the early chapters can be supported by the histories of the settlements of the more complex wars analyzed in the later chapters. I have attempted to show this connection between the early generalizations and the later evidence by cross-reference footnotes. A study of all the wars discussed in the text provides a basis for the theoretical discussion of peacemaking throughout the book. As it stands, containing historical summaries of wars along with hypothetical scenarios, conclusions supported by evidence along with pure speculation, this work demonstrates the efficacy of a systematic analysis of the sort advanced by the author. It shows that the very structure of a war and its contemporary political, economic, and social milieu set limits upon what policymakers and peace planners may do. Within these limits, it also shows what peacemakers can do, and what possibilities for settlement exist.

I have sought to keep *The Origins of Peace* a descriptive work; and in this sense, it will be *descriptive* of what happened during peace efforts of the past and what could happen in hypothetical situations of the future. Where prescription has crept in, I would hope that the historical evidence and the argument convince the reader of the potential of the prescribed programs of settlement or peace policies. Continued study of the approximately 500 war terminations of the period surveyed by my students and me could enable us to *prescribe* with greater assurance, having additional corroborations (or disconfirmations) of my hypotheses and conclusions. However, the further studies I am currently pursuing have the object of enlarging my sample, testing my conclusions, and generating new hypotheses.

There are at least two objections a critic might raise to this historically oriented study. First, he might ask whether the advent of nuclear weapons has not so changed the rules of war that it has become unhelpful to examine wars and their terminations from 1500 to 1945. I would deny the cogency of this criticism. I have no doubt that were we to experience the catastrophe of a nuclear war, peacemakers might have to deal with utterly novel problems in moving toward a settlement.[6] I would nonetheless argue that the principal elements of the peacemaking process de-

6 See Herman Kahn's "Issues of Thermonuclear War Termination," in W. T. R. Fox (ed.), *How Wars End, The Annals of the American Academy of Political and Social Science,* Vol. 392 (November, 1970), pp. 133–72.

scribed in the text will be applicable to the settlements of such wars. In any event, barring the utopia of eternal peace, we can quite realistically expect to see the outbreak of conventional wars in the future, even though a number of states possess thermonuclear weapons—just as, since the first use of the atomic bomb against Japan, there have been at least 18 wars between states and 55 civil wars, in some of which other states actively intervened. As far as the pathological state system is concerned, it is "business as usual." Thus, I would argue, the conclusions and schema of this book will remain valid even as we move farther into an age of technologically assured mass destruction. Writing of peace settlements, one does assume that there will be future wars to settle. If there were no wars, there would be no need for peace settlements; and my efforts here would then appear to have been only a curious intellectual exercise. The reader will undoubtedly share with the author the fervent hope that this work will become obsolete: In the absence of wars, peacemaking studies would become academic. But the prospects of this happening are unfortunately slight.

There is a second, and in my view a more substantial, criticism: that the author has ignored the peacemaking practices of cultures other than the Western European. It is no answer to this objection to assert that I have considered wars involving non-European states (the Ottoman Empire, for example, or China, Japan, or Iraq). In the survey period (1500–1970), Europe and the West were in the ascendant. Peace settlements were Europeanized, as it were; thus, the settlements considered by the author are bound to have a bias toward European concepts and methods. Only further study can remove or substantiate the grounds of this objection. Were such an investigation to be undertaken, it ought to include pure, non-Western wars as well as wars before 1500. If the reader will permit me a generalization (prejudice, if you will), I would venture to say that in ending wars, policymakers and peace planners of non-Western cultures behaved in much the same way as their Western counterparts and that this generalization has become more and more true since 1500. This book, then, purports to describe the peacemaking process in a period when Western culture, for better or for worse, became globally influential. As it is likely to remain so for many years to come, it is not impossible that the concepts and conclusions of my study will be helpful to the peacemaker and student of the future.

Contributions of others to the completion of this study are gratefully acknowledged. I owe my greatest debt to William T. R. Fox, Director of the Institute of War and Peace Studies, and James T. Shotwell Professor of International Relations at Columbia University. My intellectual obligations to him pre-date this work, going back to my graduate-student days. For this long-standing debt, I express my gratitude. In respect of this project, I thank him for his and the Institute's support. Columbia arranged for me a one semester's leave under a Chamberlain Fellowship, and its Office of the Dean of the Graduate School of Arts and Sciences furnished funds partially to defray typing expenses, as did the Institute of War and Peace studies. I want to express my appreciation to my seminar students, Columbia College seniors, who helped me prepare the lists of wars and peace settlements: David Aborn, Stevan C. Adelman, A. Regis Boff, Eric Brown, Spencer M. Cowan, Robert Douglas, Rafael Epstein, and Philip Zegarelli. Mitchell Orfuss assisted in the editing of Chapter 11; and my research assistant for 1970–71, Jeffrey Golden, helped me with a review of the historical survey and the bibliography and made a number of helpful criticisms of the next-to-last draft of the manuscript. To both of them, I offer my thanks. I wish to acknowledge with gratitude the permission given me by The American Academy of Political and Social Science to incorporate in Chapter 10 my essay, "The Domestic Origins of Peace," which appeared in the November 1970 issue of *The Annals*.[7] Finally, I thank Professor James N. Rosenau for his valuable suggestions for the improvement of the manuscript.

—Robert F. Randle
Perth Amboy and New York City

7 Cited in the preceding note.

Contents

1. Some General Considerations   1

The Structure of Wars
Outcomes of War
Stages of Peace Negotiations
Factors Influencing Peace Negotiations
The State System and Peacemaking

2. The Settlement of Simple External Wars   24

The Simple External War: Preliminaries
Military Settlement
Wars and War Aims
Elements of the Political Settlement
Bargaining Strength, War Aims, and the Political Settlement
Summaries of Settlements of Some Simple External Wars

3. The Settlement of Simple Internal Wars   84

Preliminaries
The Military Settlement
Political Settlement of an Internal War for Control of the
    Polity

Political Settlement of a War for Independence
Summaries of Settlements of Some Simple Internal Wars

4. Alliances and Peacemaking   116

Alliance Cohesiveness
Effects of Defeat
Reduced Alliance Effectiveness
Peace Policy Formulation and Policy Differences
Preliminary Phase of Peacemaking
The Military Settlement Phase
The Political Settlement Phase
The Settlement of Some Complex External Wars

5. The Settlement of Complex Internal Wars   181

Classification
General Outcome and Modes of Settlement
Summaries of Settlements of Some Complex Internal Wars

6. War-Oriented Actors in the Political Environment of War   244

The Interests of War-Oriented Actors
Great Powers
Nonbelligerent Allies
Regional and Border War-Oriented States
International Organizations as War-Oriented Actors

7. War-Oriented Actors and Peacemaking   270

The "Presence" of the War-Oriented Actor in the
    Peacemaking Process
Promotion or Prevention of Peace Negotiations
War Aims of the War-Oriented Actor and the Elements
    of a Settlement
Conferences of War-Oriented States
Proxy Internal Wars and Their Settlement

8. Multilateral Wars and Their Settlement   307

Form and Analysis of Multilateral Wars
Multilateral War: A System-Transforming War
Termination of the Multilateral War
Comprehensive Settlement by a Single Conference

Piecemeal Settlement by Separate Conferences
Preliminaries to Negotiations and the Military Phase
   of the Settlement
The Political Settlement: A Constitution for the State System

9. Multilateral War Settlements in Modern History   337

Wars of the First Group
Wars of the Second Group

10. Domestic Politics and Peacemaking   430

The Domestic Origins of Peace
Transnational Pressures in the Domestic Peacemaking Process
Domestic Politics in the Negotiation of a Peace Settlement

11. Planning for Peace   457

Coordinated Peace Planning
Peace Plans
Ideologies and Peace Plans
The Content of Peace Plans
Military Operations and Peace Plans
De-escalation
Preparing the Polity for Peace

12. The Failure of Peace Settlements   481

Kinds of Inadequacies
Failures Deriving from Causes Other than Inadequate
   Settlements
Remedies for a Failing Settlement
Improved Settlements

Epilogue   502

APPENDIX I. Disagreements over the Structure of War   508

APPENDIX II. Relative Compatibility of War Aims   511

Bibliography   517

Index   537

THE ORIGINS OF PEACE

Some General Considerations

Wars appear to be inevitable in the state system as we know it. They appear to have been equally inevitable in the state systems of the past. But all wars, whether started by accident or by design, must end; and they end almost exclusively by design. Statesmen and diplomats agree, at least tacitly, upon the terms of an armistice. Further negotiations, if undertaken at all, usually result in a peace settlement, the nature of which depends primarily upon two factors: the kind of war currently being fought and the structure of the state system, which is in part the political environment of the warring states.

The Structure of Wars

Wars can be classified according to their level of violence (nuclear wars, limited and general conventional wars, and so forth). They can also be classified according to the purposes for which they were fought: wars of imperial expansion, colonial wars, wars for independence, religious wars, and the like. We will find it convenient to classify wars in yet another way, according to the number of actors involved and the manner of their involvement in the war in which they are engaged. From this point of view, there are two basic types of wars: wars between states and wars within states. Since the latter are internal with respect to the political system of a given state, we shall call them *internal wars;* and since wars between states are correspondingly external to the state's political system, we shall call them *external wars.* In the simplest form of external war, state A is in conflict with state B. Frequently, more than two belligerent states are involved: state A may be allied with several other states, and the adversary state B may also have allies. The allies of either A or B may be their cobelligerents, or some allies may be cobelligerents while others remain merely sympathetic but nonbelligerent, providing arms or some form of financial support. In external wars in which the actors in conflict are partners in alliances, the character of the peace settlement will depend not only upon the political interaction between the belligerents $(A$ or $B)$, but also upon the relations among all allies who might conceivably find themselves at odds over the conduct of the war and the collective aims to be pursued in any negotiations leading to a cease-fire and a peace settlement.

In the simplest type of *internal war,* a faction x is in conflict with another faction y. One faction is usually the incumbent government of the state, and the opposing faction is in rebellion against the incumbent. As in the case of external wars, the form of the internal war can become quite complex. Either of the factions may be allied to or supported by other states, in which case the internal war has become internationalized. State A may recognize the state of belligerency between the factions x and y; or A may even recognize the insurgent faction as the legitimate government of the state affected by the war. In either case, the legal step of recognition alone can have an important effect upon the course of the war. Allies can, of course, provide more than mere legal support. Thus, the relationship between state A and faction x may be that of a genuine wartime coalition, with state A supplying money, weapons, or even troops to assist faction x in the war effort. If faction y, on the other hand, were allied to another state B, then the internal war would indeed have important international ramifications of a type that we shall have to examine in detail. Through its support of faction y, state B puts itself into a relationship of conflict with state A (supporting faction x); and the internal war (x vs. y) becomes a "proxy" external war between state A and state B. If both A and B were to send troops to support their factions, the internal war would take on the character of an external war. We could envisage further complexities when one or both factions are tied to an alliance of several states. In all cases of faction-state alliances, intra-alliance relations often play as important a part in the peace settlement as the war aims of the primary belligerents (factions x and y).

The most complex wars are those in which the external war is widespread, where many states are involved, or where one or more internal wars are being fought in the context of a complicated array of alliances of states and factions. We shall call these multilateral wars. The two World Wars of this century are examples of this kind. Needless to say, the sheer complexity of the multilateral war renders peacemaking a really formidable task.

Our discussion thus far may be summarized as shown in Table 1–1.[1]

Having presented the classification scheme used in this book, we undertake in the remainder of this chapter to adumbrate several of the variables, other than the type of war, that enable us to characterize peace settlements. See Figure 1–1.

TABLE 1–1. Classification of wars according to how the actively belligerent parties are engaged.

Type of war	Form	Examples
External (between states)		
Simple	state *A* vs. state *B*	*Indian-Pakistan Wars (1965)* *Russo-Finnish War (1939–40)*
Complex	states *A, M, N* vs. state *B*	*Suez War of 1956* (Egypt vs. France, Britain, Israel) *Crimean War, 1853–56* (Russia vs. France, Britain, Turkey, Sardinia)
	states *A, M, N* vs. states *B, O, P*	*Austro-Prussian War of 1866* (Prussia & Italy vs. Austria, Saxony, Bavaria, Hanover, Baden, Nassau, Hesse-Kassel, Hesse-Darmstadt)

1 In attempting to classify wars, it is often difficult to distinguish between a complex and a multilateral war. If we consider structure alone, the Seven Years' War (1756–1763: Prussia, Britain, Hanover vs. Austria, Russia, Spain, Sweden, Saxony) could be classified as a complex external war. I prefer to regard it as a multilateral war (and I have treated it as such in Chapter 9) because of the number of great powers involved and the impact of the war upon the relations of European states. Historical context thus cannot be ignored when we classify wars. The following chapters will, of course, assist the reader in comprehending the structure of wars and should therefore make classification easier. As a war can often be subsumed under more than one category, Appendix I has been included to point up the analytical consequences of such a situation.

Also, I have not indicated the extent to which the simple wars listed here were internationalized as a result of the existence of what I call war-oriented actors (see Chapters 6 and 7 for a discussion of the role of such actors in the peacemaking process). Nonetheless, internationalization did not take the form of active involvement of the war-oriented states in hostilities. Hence, these wars may be classified as simple internal wars.

TABLE 1-1. (continued)

Type of war	Form	Examples
Internal (between factions within a state)		
Simple	faction x vs. faction y in state R	T'ai p'ing Rebellion, 1851–64 (Ch'ing dynasty vs. T'ai p'ings) Cuban Civil War, 1956–59 (Batista regime vs. insurgents) Kurdish Civil War, 1961–1967+ (Iraq gov't. vs. Kurdish nationalists)
Complex	faction x and state A vs. faction y;	War of the Three Henrys, 1585–1598 (French Huguenots vs. French Catholics and Spain) American Revolution, 1775–83 (Amer. colonists & France (from 1778) & Spain (from 1779) & Netherlands (from 1780) vs. Britain)
	faction x and state A vs. faction y and state B	Korean War, 1950–53 (DRNK & CPR vs. ROK, US and 15 members of the UN) Yemeni Civil War, 1962–69+ (Yemen Republic & Egypt vs. Yemen Royalists & Saudi Arabia)
Multilateral wars	many possible combinations of external wars, often coupled with internal war situations	First world War, 1914–1919+ Second World War, 1939–1945+

For wars that end with negotiations, a number of analytical inputs (shown in boxes numbered 1 through 6) impinge upon the settlement process during all its stages. Points T_1 to T_3 represent thresholds of settlement. A "threshold" is a point in the settlement process where, after the parties have made crucial decisions—and perhaps compromises—

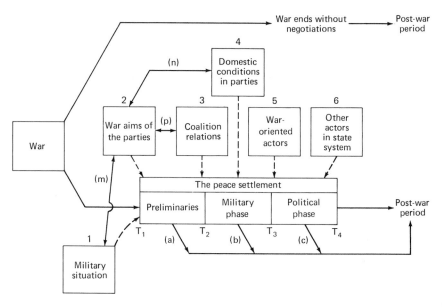

FIGURE 1–1. The peace settlement process.

affecting their war aims and interests, they may proceed to the next stage of peace negotiations, and ultimately toward a more complete settlement. The settlement threshold concept is heuristic. Although Figure 1–1 shows thresholds before and between stages of negotiations, they may also be regarded as demarking the limits of the major issues (or issue areas) in the negotiations. An incomplete settlement results when all thresholds of settlement have not been crossed. Arrows *a, b* and *c* indicate that the settlement process remains incomplete, and the parties move into the postwar period without having resolved all the war issues. The arrows *m, n,* and *p* are intended to show that certain of the input variables are interrelated. We shall explore these interrelations later.

Outcomes of War

An internal war may end in the complete defeat of one of the factions.[2] Obliterated, that faction not only ceases to be an effective political and military entity, it also ceases to exist. In an external war, one state may conquer an adversary and then annex the defeated state, after

2 Indeed, George Modelski has shown that most recent internal wars have ended in this way: In 100 such wars (1900–1962), 78 ended with victory for either the insurgents or the incumbents. See "International Settlement of Internal Wars," in J. N. Rosenau, *International Aspects of Civil Strife* (Princeton: Princeton University Press, 1964).

dissolving its government and demobilizing its armed forces. Comparatively little can be said about this sort of "peacemaking." See Figure 1–2, outcome 1.

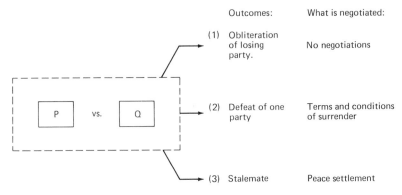

FIGURE 1–2.   Possible outcomes of war between parties P and Q.

In a war that ends with the destruction of one party, the victor consults no one and negotiates with no one. But having made this bald assertion, we must recognize that an important exception exists: When the victor is allied with other states or factions, it must consult these parties. Such consultation may take the form of hard bargaining among the coalition partners and may eventuate in a variation, even an amelioration, of the conditions of conquest imposed by the victor.

If a war ends in the surrender of one of the belligerents, the terms of that surrender will have to be agreed upon by the principals and by some or all of the allies of the primary parties, if there are allies involved. If the surrender is to be conditional, then the substance of the conditions must be negotiated. Should the surrender be unconditional, we have a situation identical or analogous to a conquest in which the victorious allies need consult only among themselves. On the other hand, an ostensibly unconditional surrender may include at least implicit conditions. Whenever the defeated state or faction continues in juridical existence, an unconditional surrender will invariably require the winning state or alliance to negotiate with the defeated state in order to impose the terms of surrender and obtain a promise of compliance. In such negotiations, the victors often accept conditions; in this case, the "unconditional surrender" will have to be treated as a particular form of conditional surrender. In 1943, for example, the Italian government surrendered unconditionally to the Allies but extracted a promise from the English and the Americans: Italian post-armistice cooperation was to accrue to Italy's favor when accounts were finally settled at a peace conference. In late 1943, the Badoglio Government declared war on Germany, and the

Allies recognized Italy as a cobelligerent. During subsequent peace negotiations (1945–47), Italy not only was given a hearing, but also managed to influence peace proposals in her favor through traditional diplomatic channels. Germany's axis satellites in Southeastern Europe also benefitted from a mitigation of the unconditional surrender policy. And, in 1945, the Allies agreed to a condition in the "unconditional surrender" of the Japanese, namely, to respect the sovereignty of the Emperor. Thus, in all these cases, there was bargaining between the victorious Allies and the defeated states.

Where war has not resulted in the decisive defeat or either side, absent the intervention of third-party belligerents or the introduction of startlingly effective and novel weapons, the way may be said to be stalemated. Perceiving the stalemate, the belligerents may agree that a continuation of hostilities would result in no gains to themselves. But even if one party were perceived to be losing, the adversary might be willing to agree to a cease-fire because of war weariness or because it expected to obtain as much at the negotiating table as it could obtain in combat. Continuing hostilities could be costly, in terms of men, time, or money, even for the belligerent who knows he has won, or will eventually win, a military victory. Having determined to end the war, for whatever reasons, the antagonists must negotiate the terms of a cease-fire and any subsequent political settlement; in these circumstances, there is likely to be much hard bargaining between the negotiators. Negotiations will undoubtedly be more protracted than in the case of the war that has ended in the defeat of one belligerent and thereby deprived that party of bargaining strength.

This study is concerned, in part, with the process of peacemaking. That process is best exemplified by negotiations leading to a peace settlement or by a cessation of hostilities and ultimately a political settlement through the acquiescence of a defeated party in a *conditional surrender* or a *conditioned* "unconditional surrender" (Fig. 1–2. Outcomes 2 and 3). In this sense, wars that end in the obliteration of a defeated faction or the destruction and elimination of a state will not interest us. Wars without at least an implicit peace settlement are not our concern.

Stages of Peace Negotiations

A peace settlement is usually achieved in two stages. The first, the resolution of military questions, includes the cessation of hostilities and the subsequent deployment of the armed forces of the belligerents during a period, sometimes an extended period, after the truce. The second stage, that of the political settlement, is usually the stage of the peace conference or, more generally, the stage of negotiations whose aim is agreement upon political, legal, and economic terms for some form of a restoration of peaceful relations between the belligerents. As we shall see later in this study, this emphasis upon the two-stage nature of peace settlements does not exclude other eventualities: 1. Other kinds of agreements may be concluded between the belligerents (e.g., protocols on procedures, treaties of alliance, and collective security or collective defense agreements). 2. There may also be agreements negotiated among wartime allies relating, for example, to coalition action in the final stages of the war or at the peace conference. 3. The military settlement may not be achieved until as late a time as the final political settlement, meaning that during negotiations dealing with political terms military operations continue.

The latter considerations serve to emphasize an important point. The conduct of military operations dramatically affects the processes of the peace settlement, certainly in its military settlement phase, but frequently in the political phase as well. A change in the military position of one of the belligerents will affect its bargaining position and hence its peace policy (see Fig. 1–1). The military ascendency of one party over the other often determines what the stronger party will demand and what it will be willing to accept in terms of a settlement. A battle won or lost may cause the negotiators of the state or faction to alter their war aims and even result in one party's breaking off negotiations entirely.

It is often the policy of one belligerent to require a cease-fire as a condition for agreeing to peace talks. In this way, the military situation is frozen, and the peace negotiations can proceed without concern for the possibility that military gains or losses could radically influence the bargaining process. In 1961, the United States, providing equipment, weapons, and noncombatant personnel for the right-wing Laotian faction under Prince Boun Oum and Phoumi Nosavan, refused to agree to a reconvening of the Geneva Conference on Indochina to settle the Laotian Civil War until the Pathet Lao first agreed to a cease-fire. The precondition was substantially met, and the conference was convened. While the negotiations were protracted, the battlefield situation was frozen as of mid–1961 and consequently, there were no changes in the military situation after that time to affect the bargaining in Geneva and Zurich. There are, of course, a number of considerations that enter into the question of whether or not to demand (or accept) a cease-fire before agreeing to further negotiations, not the least of which is the military position of the belligerents at the time the decision is made. More will be said about this later.

Factors Influencing Peace Negotiations

It is possible to categorize, in general terms, the major factors that influence the course of negotiations for peace. We have already mentioned one factor, the military situation at the time negotiations begin and the changes, if any, in that situation as the peace talks progress. The domestic political situation in each of the major state actors is also crucially important (see Fig. 1–1). In the democratic polity, public opinion and the attitudes of the attentive elites and elected representatives toward the war will influence both the conduct of the war by that polity's government and the peace policies of the democratic state's negotiators. In more authoritarian or in totalitarian polities, public opinion will usually count for little in shaping peace policy, but domestic elite opinion might have a more marked effect as, for example, the anti-Turk war party in the Czar's court affected Russia's policy toward the Ottoman Empire in the nineteenth century, demanding and often obtaining the Czar's agreement to rigorous peace terms after successful wars against the Turks; or as oligarchical or military elites in the developing countries of the twentieth century have influenced the peace negotiations in which their states have been engaged.

Changes in the composition of wartime coalitions will also affect negotiations. Hence, the analyst must study the nature and internal political behavior of the relevant alliances. He must also determine to what extent matters of concern to particular pairs of the allies might influence peace talks. Let us suppose that we are examining an external war between states A, B, and C, on the one hand, and states M and N, on the other (see Fig. 1–3).

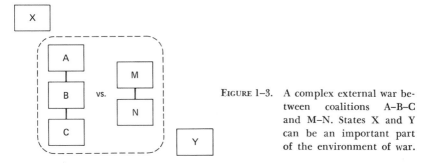

FIGURE 1–3. A complex external war between coalitions A–B–C and M–N. States X and Y can be an important part of the environment of war.

All five states are engaged in peace negotiations, in either the military or political settlement phase. In the absence of an agreement on a cease-fire, the military balance of power (that is, the relative military strengths and weaknesses of the five states) will affect the course and outcome of the negotiations. Moreover, the domestic political situations in A, B, C, M, and N will inevitably figure into the bargaining equations; and the analyst will have to determine what political and social events in the five states have influenced, or may influence, peace negotiations. He will also have to look into the coalition relations A-B-C and M-N and consider the interaction among the allied state pairs *A-B, B-C,* and *A-C* of the triangular alliance *A-B-C.* Since it is rarely adequate to describe the relationship of belligerents to each other as one of total hostility (and to stop there), it will also be necessary to consider the policy interaction between all other pairings of states: *A-M, A-N, B-M, B-N, C-M,* and *C-N.* This is particularly the case as the end of a war approaches when, in anticipation of peace and of new relations between the former belligerents, coalition members adopt new policies that frequently conflict with the policies of their partners.

States, factions, or international organizations not previously involved in the conflict may play an important role in peace negotiations. They may act as mediators or adjudicators, or they may impose a settlement upon the belligerents. It is even possible to envisage a wholly non-involved state adopting a policy that has no apparent relationship to the issues in dispute between the belligerents, but that nevertheless affects the course of the peace talks. Thus, in the external war of *A-B-C* with *M-N,* in which the parties are negotiating a settlement, another state, *X,* might declare war on still another state, *Y;* or *X* and *Y* might conclude a commercial agreement that will considerably improve their economic position and hence enhance their power positions relative to the belligerents. Events such as these could indeed affect the settlement of the external war. Whether they do depends upon the relations and capabilities of the pairs *A-X, A-Y, B-X, B-Y,* and so forth.

Values—Ideological and Power Political

A peace settlement is more difficult to achieve when the emotions of the negotiators, the elites, or the relevant publics are stirred by the issues of the war. In general terms, we say that states or factions go to war because their policymakers, and perhaps also their peoples, attach great weight to certain values which they deem worth defending. Establishing a calculus of values would be a formidable undertaking, but for our purposes it is unnecessary. We can limit our remarks to merely qualitative and general statements.

The values attached to the conduct of war are of two kinds: ideological and power political. *Ideological values* are those based upon or derived from more or less formal postulates of belief. Thus, religions such as Catholicism, Protestantism, or Islam or secular theologies such as Maoism, Marxism, Pan-Slavism, and certain forms of democratic capitalism, when shared by significant influential segments of the peoples of states or factions, give rise to the ideological values that form the basis for war aims. Both religious and secular ideologies are usually based upon a limited number of precepts that have been elaborated and developed by *ideologues.* From these precepts, the systems of belief purport to yield norms of conduct deductively in many, if not all, real world situations.

Power political values derive from one fundamental value: the preservation and well-being of the state. They are, in short, values that follow from the doctrine of *raison d'état* and are not limited by time and circumstance to immediate threats to a state's integrity such as exist when, for example, an invasion force stands poised on a state's frontiers. Power political values also include ends served by any efforts to enhance the *security* of the state, even in times of peace when no immediate threat to the state's existence is apparent. The stateman's attempts to insure the future security of his state through the use of force, acquisition of territory, collective and bilateral defense agreements, control of client states, and treaty guarantees are efforts designed to secure "values" based ultimately on *raison d'état*.

Power political values are equally important in the case of an internal war. The incumbent regime naturally regards itself as "the state." Insurgents aspire to be "the state"; and they treat their movement as an end in itself, making it the equivalent of a state in terms of the values of the members of the insurgent faction. Thus, whether in an external or an internal war, the belligerents are sure to seek the continued existence of the political entity of which they are members. This principle of preserving the polity has many corollaries, often only remotely related to the goal of self-preservation, corollaries that find expression in the various policies that states or factions pursue in the name of security.

The struggle to preserve or to gain ideological or power political values is evident in the stages just before a declaration of war, and that struggle continues throughout the war and during all phases of the negotiations for peace. Indeed, the struggle may be intense enough to prevent agreement upon even minimum terms of a settlement. In fact, all cases where belligerents refuse to consider a movement towards peace or are unable to agree upon peace terms after negotiations have begun can usually be ascribed to such intensely espoused ideological or power political values. The war issues have become too intensely *ideologized;* and if the parties are to achieve even a partial settlement, the war must become *de-ideologized.* The values that the leaders of the states or factions had hoped to gain must be *devalued.* Qualitatively (for that is the only way we can describe it for the present), the competition for values must diminish in intensity below a certain level before peace will be possible. With respect to ideological values, de-ideologization can occur under the following circumstances:

1. The ideological values over which the war was being fought may be repudiated. This drastic change could occur if there were a change in government in one of the belligerent states or if some or all the ruling elites of a state or faction were replaced. The new government or new elites might attach much less importance to the ideological values and be more willing to make peace on terms theretofore unacceptable.

2. The ruling elites of the state or faction could decide that peace was

essential. That decision might be based upon power political considerations, perhaps upon the most fundamental consideration of all, the survival of the state (or merely the survival of the elites as a class or as leaders of the polity). When the state's existence is in the balance, ideological values may well have to be sacrificed, at least temporarily. But the discarding of an ideology usually has to be made palatable even to the most sophisticated practitioner of *realpolitik*. Hence, an effort is made to divorce the symbols and concepts of the ideology from the issues of the war. The content and intensity of war propaganda is then changed, and the public and attentive elites are reeducated.

3. The de-ideologization may be less a consciously adopted policy than a barely perceptible trend, less a decision made within a limited time period than one made gradually or incrementally over months. This process may occur by means of a social or political change within the belligerent actor or through a change in the international environment. Changes of this sort may result in the displacement, however slowly, of the ideological values by other, more attractive ideological or power political values (peace, economic development, reconstruction, and the like). As people become interested in other, often mundane, matters, the war may be perceived as redundant, interfering with other desirable goals, or simply uninteresting, irrational, or irrelevant to the current style.

Where the question of the survival of the state is so pressing as to be evident to even the most uninformed persons, there is no need to find ideological grounds for war. But often, when the basis for a particular war policy is obscure and remote from considerations of the state's security, when in fact that question does not even arise in the context of the war, then consciously or unconsciously war aims sometimes become ideologized. Policymakers feel impelled to rationalize war aims in terms of an official or prevailing ideology, which makes it difficult to distinguish the ideological from the power political bases of a war, because leaders often do cloak power political values in ideology.

There are also difficulties in disentangling the complex motives policymakers have for declaring, waging, and ending wars. These problems were nowhere more prominent than in the international system that was Germany of the sixteenth century, particularly during the years of the religious wars, 1521 to 1555. Then, the rival ideologies were essentially Catholicism on the one hand and Protestantism (including Lutheranism, Calvinism, and Anabaptism) on the other. The Landgrave Philip of Hesse and Albert of Hohenzollern (First Duke of Prussia) secularized their principalities. They professed Protestantism, but their espousal of the cause of the Schmalkaldic League was based upon the desire to secure autonomy within the Empire and to increase their revenues through the dissolution of religious orders and the severance of ties with the Papacy.

Emperor Charles V was unquestionably a sincere Roman Catholic, and he waged war against the Protestant princes in the name of Catholicism. But his German policies were also determined by his desire to maintain Habsburg imperial supremacy, to secure Burgundy and limit the power of the Valois, and to contain Ottoman incursions against his eastern territories. There were, on the other hand, instances where policy orientation was dictated almost exclusively by ideology: Elector John Frederick of Saxony, for example, joined the Schmalkaldic League because he was a Lutheran and supported the Lutheran cause. When defeated by the Emperor in 1547, he chose to remain a Lutheran and lose his principality, rather than to renounce his faith and retain his holdings. Reference to the entire context of official policy statements expressing a rationale for particular war policies or for peacemaking can help the analyst assess the relative importance of the ideological and power political components of the policies of a state or faction. There will, of course, be a residue of uncertainty, and there are often ample grounds for dispute as to the primacy of this or that motive or war aim.

In addition to the de-ideologization process, a complete settlement will be impossible to achieve unless a similar (or analogous) devaluation of relevant power political values also takes place. It could come about for the same reasons de-ideologization occurred: change in government or composition of the ruling elites, replacement or displacement of one group of power political values by another group, evolution of the state system, or changes in the internal political situation of one of the belligerent states or factions that render the power political values for which the war is being fought irrelevant or outmoded. Devaluation of power political values will be more dramatically brought about by a worsening of the military situation than will de-ideologization. Leaders and other influential elites are more apt to be willing to bargain away certain nonvital power political values than those ideological values to which they or their publics are emotionally committed. De-ideologization, like its opposite, the proselytization of an ideology and intensification of the commitment to ideological values, requires a particular kind of education—and this takes time. Hence, during peace negotiations, diplomats will find that they have more flexibility to bargain with non-vital power political values than they have with ideological values. Of course, a severe battlefield defeat or an internal crisis that suddenly caused the attentive elites or even the public to doubt the wisdom of a war policy, however unwelcome either eventuality might be for the state's negotiators, could enable them to bargain more pragmatically, unrestricted by the exigencies of ideological precepts. This is perhaps only another way of saying that a military or political catastrophe can suddenly diminish the intensity of a value conflict over which the war is being fought. What must be emphasized, however, is that before peace is possible, both the ideological and power political values of at least one of the belligerents must become less intensely supported.

Devaluation or de-ideologization, taking place gradually and incrementally, will not necessarily permit a peace settlement. There may be a series of thresholds of settlement for each of the *major issues* of the war. We can use a more convenient, and reasonably valid, simplification, however: Treat the situation of conflict as if there were three thresholds, one for agreement to begin peace negotiations, another for a military settlement, and the third, for a political settlement. (See Figure 1–1). Devaluation may proceed far enough to allow the belligerents to reach an accord on the terms of a cease-fire and supplementary technical terms (assuming they have crossed the first threshold, the decision to negotiate). Without further devaluation, the antagonists may have to be content with a more or less hostile technical state of war, without fighting. The threshold for a political settlement is usually more difficult to cross than the threshold for a military settlement. The parties may be willing to pay the price in values of a cease-fire; but they might not want to accept, nor indeed feel they must accept, the more burdensome costs of a complete settlement, one that restores peace in fact and in law. On three occasions (in 1949, 1956, and 1970), the Israelis and certain of their Arab adversaries agreed to armistices following wars they had fought. While the war issues were sufficiently de-ideologized to permit tenuous military settlements, continued bitterness prevented the states from crossing political settlement thresholds. The issues of the Korean War had become de-ideologized and devalued enough by July, 1953, to permit a military settlement but not a political one. And in the Indonesian War for Independence (1945–1949), military settlements were arranged three times: in 1946, 1947, and 1949. Hostilities were resumed in 1947 and 1948 because an adequate settlement had not been achieved, in great part because of insufficient de-ideologization and deevaluation. The political settlement threshold was finally crossed in late 1949, and the Dutch formally recognized the independence of the United States of Indonesia and executed settlement documents embodying the formal transfer of sovereignty.

Orientation of States Toward the War

Earlier, we referred to the international environment as a major factor influencing the course of peace negotiations and the character of the peace settlement. Let us make an attempt to characterize this international environment in greater detail. Apart from the belligerents, we define two classes of actors (i.e., states, factions, or organizations): those whose policies and interests are oriented toward the issues of the war, the *war-oriented actors,* and those actors with no direct interest in the war. It is possible to elaborate upon the characteristics of the first class of actors. All others will (by definition) fall into the second class (see Fig. 1–1).

War-oriented actors include:

1. allies of the belligerents.
2. the great powers.
3. regional states, including middle-range powers in regions affected by the war and any states or factions on the frontiers of one of the belligerents.
4. international organizations whose aim is to prevent war or to conciliate differences between states at war, or international organizations to which any of the belligerents belong.

Allies of the belligerents might, of course, be belligerents, in which case according to my definition, they are not "war-oriented actors." But allies might also be non-belligerents (category 1), an invariably important category of war-oriented actor.

Great powers are states that have that status at the time the war is being fought and the peace settlement negotiated. A great power is a state with broad and versatile capabilities (or, to use the phrase most common in the field, with great *national power*). But while possession of ample capabilities is a necessary condition of great power status, it is not a sufficient condition, for the state must see itself in that role and the leaders of other states must perceive it and treat it as a great power. Thus, as an additional requirement of great power status, the state's policymakers must perceive their state as playing a political and economic role on a global scale, limited to no one particular geographical region. The policymakers of other states (and factions) must usually always apprise themselves of a great power's policies and often compensate for them in formulating policies for their own polities.

A brief analysis of two wars, in terms of the ways in which the various parties are involved, will illustrate the meaning of *war-oriented status*. In the First Balkan War of 1912, the belligerents were Turkey on the one side and, on the other, the Balkan League comprising Bulgaria, Serbia, Greece, and Montenegro. The great powers (Austria, Britain, France, Germany, and Russia) were war-oriented states. In an effort to preserve the *status quo*, they played an unusually active peacemaking role through the mechanism of a conference of ambassadors in London and through traditional diplomatic channels. The only other war-oriented state was Roumania, a regional state.

In the French Indochina War (1945–1954),[3] the situation was a bit more complicated and can be outlined very briefly as follows.

3 My study, *Geneva, 1954: The Settlement of the Indochinese War* (Princeton: Princeton University Press, 1969), treats this peace settlement in detail.

A. *Belligerents*
   1. Principals: France vs. the Vietminh (Democratic Republic of Vietnam or DRVN)
   2. Belligerent allies:
      a. of France: State of Vietnam, Royal Laotian Government, Royal Cambodian Government
      b. of the DRVN: Pathet Lao, Khmer Issarak
B. *War-oriented actors*
   1. Great powers: Britain and the United States supporting France; the Soviet Union and the People's Republic of China (CPR) supporting the DRVN
   2. Nonbelligerent allies:
      a. of France: Britain and the US through NATO
      b. of the DRVN: The terms of their alliances are unknown, but there were certainly *de facto* alliances with the CPR and the Soviet Union.
   3. Regional states: CPR, India, Thailand, Australia, New Zealand
   4. International organizations: the U.N. (in a very peripheral role)

Through the process of devaluation, the elites of a *war-oriented actor* will change their attitudes and policy toward the war. Their policymakers then become increasingly interested in peacemaking; and because of their interest in the issues of the war, they often envisage themselves as playing a part in the peace negotiations. They will want to be consulted; and they will want to attend the peace conference, if one is to be held. If the war-oriented state has been actively engaged in hostilities or has provided technicians, volunteers, or material resources (as opposed to merely verbal support), it will undoubtedly demand a voice in the settlement and may attempt to veto terms it does not favor. The interest of the nonbelligerent war-oriented actor in the outcome of the war and the peace negotiations can be either pragmatic or ideological. The determination of its policymakers to be consulted is a consequence of their desire to insure that the settlement will provide for the security of their state and possibly compensate them for the assistance they had rendered one of the belligerents. These compensations may, as we have said, take the form of security guarantees, but they do occasionally appear in the form of ostensibly unselfish demands. Thus, in addition to guarantees of its own territories, the war-oriented state may ask for a strengthened collective security system, an improved international legal system, or a concert of states designed to prevent war and conciliate differences before they become intense value conflicts. In any case, whether its aims are idealistic (or ideological) or pragmatic, the policymakers of a nonbelligerent war-oriented state will want to be in a position to influence peace negotiations in the direction their own policies are tending. In addition to consultation and active participation in the peacemaking process, war-oriented states may want to act as mediators of a conflict. States with no direct interest in the war would be the ideal "honest brokers"; and if a particular war-oriented state has not become too closely identified with either of the protagonists or with the issues of the war, its offer of mediation may be accepted. The state's intensity of support for the values (or ideology) of either side is likely to be in inverse relation to that state's desire to mediate and to the willingness of one or both belligerents to submit to the proffered good offices.

It is, of course, conceivable that a nonbelligerent war-oriented actor might want the war to continue rather than see peace restored on terms unfavorable to itself. This is particularly the case where certain allies of the belligerent states have assumed some war costs and feel they could not be adequately repaid unless the war were to continue until a more favorable military situation enabled their belligerent ally to demand and receive compensations. In this case, the war-oriented state's policymakers would attempt to prevent a settlement. Whether or not they succeeded would depend upon the desires of the belligerents' policymakers for peace and the influence of those war-oriented states that wanted a settlement.

A thorough analysis of the peacemaking process will require us to examine not only the policy interaction between pairs of states or factions actively engaged in war, but also pairs of *nonbelligerent* war-oriented actors. Thus, in an external war where the allies A-M were at war with the allies B-N, for example, we would in the course of our analysis consider the policies of the pairs A-M, B-N, A-B, A-N, B-M, and M-N and the reciprocal effects of such policies upon the belligerent actors

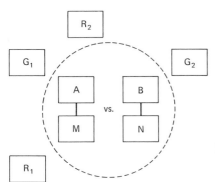

FIGURE 1–4. A complex external war in the context of several war-oriented states.

in each pair (see Fig. 1–4). In the same fashion, we would examine the interaction of the relevant war-oriented actors—among themselves and between them and the belligerents. In the case of A-M vs. B-N, let us assure that the war-oriented states comprise two nonbelligerent great powers, G_1 and G_2, and two regional states, R_1 and R_2. A thorough analysis requires us to look at the policies and behavior of the pairs, A-G_1,

$B\text{-}G_1$, $A\text{-}R_1$, $B\text{-}R_1$, $R_1\text{-}R_2$, $G_1\text{-}G_2$, and so on, through all the permutations of pairs of states.[4]

The State System and Peacemaking

We have placed all non-war-oriented actors in one category, without distinguishing among the several types of states (or factions or international organizations) that make up this class. This practice has the advantage of simplicity; and, in our case, it is not likely to lead to unsophisticated analysis or error, as we will not forget to investigate, in more general terms, the structure of the state system of which both war-oriented and non-war-oriented actors are a part.

It has been said that the state system is the *permissive cause* of wars—that the structure and operation of the state system does not inevitably or invariably lead to war, but merely makes war possible and even likely when other forces operate to bring it about.[5] In the peacemaking process, the state system is also permissive of the peace settlement eventually achieved. It establishes limits for the peacemaking process. Several solutions are likely to be possible within those limits. But possible solutions are not necessarily solutions that are acceptable to the belligerents; and our definitions must be more refined, our analysis more thorough, if we are to specify acceptable solutions. Nonetheless, reference to the structure of the state system and to the character of the war being fought (in terms of how the actors are involved, which is a way of considering the war from a system perspective) is a way first to understand what was (or is) possible for peace negotiators.

We distinguish between the statics and the dynamics of the state system. By *statics*, we refer to the way in which the state system is stratified in terms of the capabilities of *power position* of each state. Almost every basic text in international relations emphasizes the components of a state's capabilities—what one writer has called the *power inventory*[6]—which includes human and material resources, state of technology, industrial capacity, size and capabilities of the armed forces, state of the economy, and the quality and efficiency of the government and its conduct of foreign relations. It is also customary to include in the power inventory some assessment of geographical parameters (location, size,

4 Permuting pairs of belligerent and war-oriented actors in this fashion will undoubtedly reveal that some pairs are uninteresting; policy interaction between them may be minimal or their relations may have no relevance to, and consequently no impact upon, peacemaking.

5 K. N. Waltz, *Man, the State and War* (New York: Columbia University Press, 1959), Chapters VI and VII.

6 S. B. Jones, "The Power Inventory and National Strategy," *World Politics* (1954), pp. 421–452.

topography, and climate). An evaluation of a state's capabilities is difficult to make and subject to a wide margin of error, not the least because there is little agreement among authorities respecting the relative weights to be assigned to the elements of national power or the more basic problem of quantifying factors such as location and quality of government. Nevertheless, we do grade things (whether apples or states), and we continue to attempt to refine our tools for more accurate grading. We do recognize that there are great powers, middle-range states and small states. We can safely categorize most states in gross terms. It is when we try to compare states within the same general class that we have difficulty. Thus, we classify with relative ease the Soviet Union and the United States as great powers; Belgium and Cambodia as small states. But we have greater difficulty in comparing the *power* (capabilities) of states within the same general category. In spite of the problems and pitfalls of this sort of analysis, an appreciation of the statics of the state system, as we have described them, and of the manner in which states are stratified according to their capabilities is justifiably regarded as essential by most students of international affairs. One reason is that political leaders base their foreign policy decisions upon an assessment of the capabilities of their allies as well as their antagonists; another, that ranking of states is, in one way or another, important for theoretical discourse.

An even more formidable task is to describe the *dynamics* of the state system: how the pattern of state relationships changes over the course of time. A starting point for analysing dynamics is to determine the current pattern, deriving from the power positions of the component states of the system. (This, as we have seen, is an uncertain starting point.) One possible next step is to project the probable power position of the state at some future time, after which we determine (in the form, perhaps, of hypothetical scenarios) ways in which each state can go from where it is to where the power projection says it will be in x years. Projections of this kind are not impracticable and are valuable, within their margins of error, for determining the limits of probable state policy within the time span covered by the estimate. Adequate analysis requires something more, however—something even more subjective, even more difficult, if not impossible, to quantify, namely, consideration of the image the people of a given state have of themselves as a collectivity, the role they view themselves as playing in the world, and to what position they aspire relative to other states and peoples.

A state may, of course, use its national power or capabilities for any number of policies. Hence, it is always necessary for us to ask for what purposes its capabilities will be used. They will, of course, be used in support of policies the policymaking elites have chosen, which in turn depend upon the aspirations and ambitions those elites entertain for their state's status in a world of competing states. Thus, policymaking elites will strive to use the capabilities of their state most generally for fulfilling their conception of the role they want their state to play in world affairs. (I do not mean to suggest that other, more specific purposes do not assume primacy in the day-to-day operations of the state's foreign office. These specific purposes must be understood, for they are indeed controlling in particular situations—and that is all we ever have, "particular situations.") The elites' perceptions of their own role and their state's role in the world does serve to indicate the probable trend of a state's foreign policies over a period of years. These aspirations and this self-image assume the form of an internal ideology, an often implicit value structure. An understanding of those values is essential to an understanding of the dynamics of a particular state's power position.

A state may not use its capabilities effectively in the choice or execution of its foreign policy. In other words, available power may be used inefficiently. Thus, it is not really the gross or aggregate national capabilities that are important in policy analysis, but rather effective power or simply the "effectiveness" of the state. Here, too, we must ask, "effectiveness for what purpose?"; and the answer depends upon the purposes of the policymaking elites in particular situations. Those purposes, however, are generated with reference to values that constitute the aspirations of the elites and their peoples for a regional or world role. In the context of war and the peacemaking process, the purposes of the policymakers are termed *war aims;* and we shall deal with these in greater detail in subsequent chapters. During the negotiations leading to a peace settlement, the capabilities and effectiveness of the adversaries (whether states or factions) and their elites' perceptions of these qualities are of very great importance; the same factors are only slightly less significant for other war-oriented actors, for these factors determine nothing less than the capacity and will of the belligerents to wage war.

In the absence of a cease-fire agreement before peace talks begin, the visible weaknesses and war weariness of the warring state may lead an opponent to hope for military gains or even victory and may thereby render him less willing to make peace. War, of course, requires great expenditures of a belligerent's capabilities. Losses can affect morale and ultimately lead to a revision of an elite's self-image. Thus, especially toward the end of a war, the changed capabilities of a state will have an influence upon its bargaining position during peace negotiations and upon its ability to carry out the terms of the agreed settlement.

The longer a war lasts or the greater the number of states that become involved (i.e., the greater the internationalization of the war), the greater will be the impact of the war upon the state system, particularly upon the states with no direct interest in the war. These latter states are likely to have diplomatic and commercial dealings with the belligerents and other war-oriented states. When a war becomes extensively internationalized, these relations will be affected. Non-war-oriented states will find it hard to avoid commitment to war issues. Their trade may be reduced or their goods seized, and there will be an increased probability that one or more of the belligerents will make demands upon uninvolved states that the latter will find difficult to accept. Thus, extensive internationalization of the war works to transform states with no direct interest in the war into war-oriented states. It does more: any war changes both the absolute and the relative level of a state's capabilities and effectiveness. States not actively engaged in the conflict may maintain their capabilities at the prewar level, or their capabilities may actually increase as a result of increased trade in essential military supplies and foodstuffs. In either case, in the last stages of the war and in the postwar period the relative power position of all states in the state system will have changed. It is essential that the negotiators of the peace settlement appreciate the extent and significance of these changes (particularly in the case of an extensively internationalized war). A peace settlement must be realistic in the context of the state system as it exists at the war's end and as the system is likely to be in the early postwar years.[7] If peacekeeping institutions have been created, the problem of what role other states will play in such a scheme should be faced, especially for states whose power position has been enhanced by the war.

War, moreover, can demonstrate the adequacy of an ideology. Success on the battlefield confirms the precepts of the victor's value system and often leads to an attitude of inflexible moral self-righteousness at the peace talks. When that ideology has resulted in the more efficient use of the state's resources (where, in other words, it has improved the state's effectiveness) peace negotiators will have to assess the consequences of the possibly increased attraction of the ideology for others. The new, ideologically based effectiveness may indeed prevent a settlement altogether. The belligerent actor's elites might feel that they would benefit by continuing the war on the assumption that their ideology-in-action will lead to further gains. War-oriented states that share the "proved" ideology may prevent a settlement, if possible, or they may insist upon terms more favorable to them than attainable at an earlier time. Such states may also take advantage of the instability generated by the war to proselytize, eventually internationalizing the war more extensively. An ideology that has shown success in improving state effectiveness will attract followers in other states, whether or not they are involved in a particular war. An extreme result of this proselytization might be the outbreak of one or more internal wars, precipitated by insurgent groups who challenge the incumbents and their ideology.

It is the task of the peacemakers to settle the original war *and all*

---

7 An unrealistic settlement is usually an inadequate settlement. See Chapter 12.

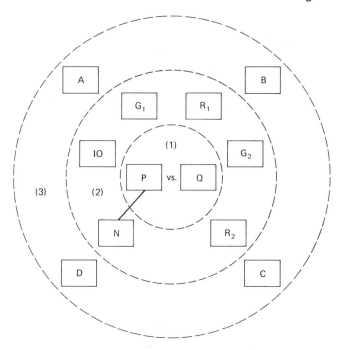

FIGURE 1-5.   The context of war and peace negotiations.

related wars, if they are able to do so. They have the formidable task of attempting to contain the conflicts, perhaps by preventing proselytization of the ideology that seems to be their cause, as after the Napoleonic Wars the conservative powers of the Concert of Europe attempted to forestall the spread of revolutions by measures including the Concert, the Holy Alliance, and the Troppau Protocol. Peacemakers may also attempt to contain or prevent war by establishing rules for the peaceful adoption of the ideology by other states, as for example, the German princes of the Empire agreed to do in the Peace of Augsburg with the rule, "cuius regio, eius religio" ("he who rules a territory determines its religion"). Whatever the final content of the settlement, they must revise radically their estimates of the capabilities of the state that has recently made more effective use of its ideology.

The discussion in this chapter has centered upon the proposition that the character of a peace settlement depends upon the character of the war terminated by that settlement. We characterize a war by the following factors:

1. the structure of the war (the belligerent parties and how they are involved in the war).

2. the war aims of the parties.

3. the domestic political situations within the polities of the belligerents.

4. the coalition relations among them.

5. the military situation at or approaching the war's end.

Factors 3, 4, and 5 in part determine the relative power positions of the belligerents and therefore their bargaining power during negotiations. A sixth factor is the extent to which the issues of the war have become de-ideologized or devalued (what ideological thresholds have been crossed and the completeness of the settlement that can be achieved).

The war, moreover, is in the "context" of the state system (see Fig. 1–1 and Fig. 1–5).

In Figure 1–5, the first circle includes the primary belligerents. The six factors just enumerated characterize the war between the parties P and Q and the possible peace settlement. Circle 2 includes the war-oriented actors G_1, G_2 (great powers), R_1, R_2 (regional states), N (a nonbelligerent ally of P), and IO (an international organization). Other actors in the state system (A, B, C, D) are shown in circle 3. As (and if) the war becomes extensively internationalized, circles 1 and 2 expand at the expense of circle 3. It shall be our task to investigate, in greater detail, the character of wars, their context or environment, and the relationships among the factors discussed in this chapter. We may then come to understand the peacemaking process better than heretofore.

The Settlement of
Simple External Wars

CHAPTER 2

We first consider how wars between states came to an end: in this chapter, the termination of *simple* external wars, the prototype of all external wars. We shall then characterize such wars by classifying them according to the issues over which the war is fought, that is, according to the war aims of the belligerents. This we do in order to understand both the form and the content of the political settlement.

The Simple External War: Preliminaries

We assume that one belligerent has not completely destroyed the adversary state. In consequence, the latter is in a position, however weak, to bargain over at least some of the terms of a settlement. This means either that the war in effect has reached a stalemate or that although one belligerent surrenders to the other, it will nevertheless be able to condition the surrender in some way during a phase of the peace negotiations.

The settlement process begins with what we shall call a *preliminary stage* (see Table 2–1), which includes a *peace feeler* phase in which the belligerents determine each others' willingness to negotiate a cease-fire or a lower level of violence on one or more battle fronts, and under what conditions it can be done. Peace feelers may also be made by nonbelligerent third parties, either by completely disinterested states (states disinterested in the issues of that war and probably not allied with either belligerent) or by a war-oriented state, including one or more of the nonbelligerent allies of the primary belligerents. The decision to inquire

TABLE 2-1.   The preliminary bargaining phase in settlements of external wars:
examples of procedural and substantive elements.

Element of the preliminary phase	Some examples
peace feelers launched by belligerents	Britain in the War of 1812 (pp. 63–4) ; France in the Franco-Prussian War (pp. 68–70) ; Russia in the Crimean War (pp. 165–9) ; Denmark in the War over Schleswig-Holstein of 1864 (pp. 169–71) ; France in the War of the Spanish Succession (pp. 357–66) ; China in the Boxer Rebellion (pp. 175–7) ; Finland in the Russo-Finnish War (pp. 79–81) .
peace feelers launched by third parties	Britain in the War of the Pacific (pp. 171–3) ; American states in the Chaco War (pp. 76–9) ; Sweden in the Franco-Dutch War of 1672–1679 (pp. 340–7) and in the European War of 1683–1700 (pp. 347–57) ; the Pope in the Thirty Years' War (pp. 379–92) .
peace feelers rejected because they appear to a party to be propagandistic	France rejected the Pope's peace feelers in the Thirty Years' War (pp. 379–92) ; the U.S. rejected DRVN peace proposals (and vice versa) in the Vietnam War (1965–?) ; France rejected Ho Chi Minh's feeler in late 1953 in the Franco-Vietminh War of 1946–1954; the Allies rejected the feelers of Prince Sixte de Bourbon during the First World War (pp. 405–28) .
conditions attached to feelers as prerequisites of further peace talks	Opium war (pp. 64–6) ; Mexican-American War (pp. 66–8) ; Franco-Prussian War (pp. 68–70) ; Russo-Finnish War (pp. 79–81) ; Crimean War (pp. 165–9) ; War of the Pacific (pp. 71–3) ; Thirty Years' War (pp. 379–92) ; the First World War (pp. 405–28) .
secret feelers and preliminary negotiations	France and Holland in the War of the Spanish Succession (pp. 357–66) .
negotiations over site of talks	Second Anglo-Dutch War (pp. 160–3) ; Franco-Spanish War, ending with the Peace of the Pyrenees in 1659 (See Thirty Years' War, pp. 379–92) .
agenda questions	War of 1812 (pp. 63–4) ; Korean War (pp. 233–6) ; Laotian Civil War (pp. 236–40) ; Thirty Years' War (pp. 379–92) ; Seven Years' War (pp. 374–9) .

TABLE 2-1 (continued)

Elements of the preliminary phase	Some examples
procedures for peace talks	Thirty Years' War (pp. 379–92) ; Conferences of Chatillon and Troyes in the Napoleonic Wars (pp. 392–405) ; the 1855 conference during the Crimean War (pp. 165–9) ; the First World War (pp. 405–28) . In the Russo-Polish War (pp. 73–6) and the Second Anglo-Dutch War (pp. 160–3) , preliminary peace treaties were actually concluded that contained the basic agreements later inserted in the definitive peace treaties.
third-party sponsorship of peace talks	Chaco War (pp. 76–9) ; Second War over Schleswig-Holstein (pp. 169–71) ; the Danish King mediated the Hamburg Conference during the Thirty Years' War (pp. 379–92) .

about the possibility of peace or the decision to respond to such an inquiry can be made only after the policymakers of the state answer the question, "Shall we negotiate?" If these policymakers believe that a military victory can still be won, then no peace feeler will be made (or the response to others' overtures will be negative). If they believe that the feelers of the other party are not sincere, but have been launched only to affect the morale of the troops of either side or to influence elite or public opinion in third-party states, the reaction to the feelers will usually be negative.

The question, "Shall we negotiate?" must be coupled with a second question: "What conditions should we formulate as a prerequisite to our agreeing to negotiate?" It is here that the belligerent in the superior military position may have a good deal of latitude in imposing conditions of both a military and a political nature. Unwillingness of the weaker belligerent to accept such conditions can lead either to a negative reaction to the peace feeler or to further negotiations over the conditions prerequisite to negotiations. In the case of a near stalemate, there is unlikely to be acceptance by either belligerent of stringent preconditions. Both sides will want to begin their talks for the most part unrestricted. The decision of a disinterested third party to initiate peace feelers might be a consequence of the fact that the latter state had perceived more clearly than the belligerents the possibilities and need for peace negotiations in the circumstances then subsisting either on the battlefield or somewhere in the relevant domestic political environment.

Peace feelers may be kept secret, or they may be publicized. The domestic political situation within the polity of one of the parties might entirely prevent efforts to make peace, even the most preliminary efforts;

or it might merely require that peace feelers be made privately and discretely. The latter will usually be the case where one segment of the elites wants to continue hostilities and others want peace. Those desiring peace seek to get a peace effort moving and thus confront the militants with a *fait accompli*. Secret peace feelers may also be deemed preferable when the effect of such a move upon the armed forces might be adverse.

If the belligerents decide to discuss the possibility of their negotiating a peace, they will send representatives to a mutually satisfactory meeting place. The preliminary talks open with a discussion of the agenda or of conditions to further negotiations that one or the other party seeks to impose. Assuming that conditions do not result in a breakdown of the talks, the representatives could then turn to important procedural matters concerning the form of peace negotiations: how formal the conference should be, who will be invited, what topics will be on the agenda, and in what order. Agreement upon these matters is frequently embodied in a *protocol of conference procedure.*

During this stage, the role of the third-party states becomes a bit clearer. They may offer their good offices to conciliate, mediate, or adjudicate the dispute and can serve as important brokers between representatives of the belligerents during the preliminary talks. Indeed, for this reason the belligerents often decide that the presence of representatives of third-party states at the peace conference is essential. In certain cases, the initiatives of third-party states require their actually sponsoring the peace conference while they pursue actively the task of keeping preliminary and principal peace talks going. An international organization (such as the League of Nations or the United Nations) might also fill this role of the disinterested third party.

Military Settlement

In practice, there is usually a hiatus between preliminary negotiations and the actual negotiations for a cease-fire; the latter are often treated formally and symbolically as the beginning of peace talks. Occasionally however, the transition between phases is less well marked. The terms and conditions of an armistice and certain ultimate political questions (relating to the substance of the final political settlement) may of course be discussed at the preliminary talks, which could be gradually transformed into primary talks.

The first and major issue in the *military settlement phase* (see Table 2–2) is the cessation of hostilities. The parties will undoubtedly spend some time discussing the *conditions* of a cease-fire: those agreements or understandings the parties deem essential before they agree to the terms of the settlement. A number of technical questions must also be resolved. When shall the cease-fire become effective, and in what theater of opera-

TABLE 2–2. The military settlement phase of peacemaking: examples of elements of a settlement.

Element of military settlement	Some examples
terms and conditions of an armistice	Russo-Polish War (pp. 73–6); Franco-Prussian War (pp. 68–70); Napoleonic Wars (pp. 392–405); First World War (pp. 405–28).
commission appointed to spell out details of an armistice	British commanders in the Opium War (pp. 64–6); Franco-Prussian War (pp. 68–70); War of the Austrian Succession (pp. 366–74); First World War (pp. 405–28).
technical questions relating to implementation of cease-fire	Mexican-American War (pp. 66–8); Franco-Prussian War (pp. 68–70); Thirty Years' War (pp. 379–92); Franco-Vietminh War of 1949–1954.
movement of troops	Opium War (pp. 64–6); Russo-Polish War (pp. 73–6); Russo-Finnish War (pp. 79–81); Franco-Dutch War of 1672–1679 (pp. 340–7); War of the Austrian Succession (pp. 366–74).
exacuation of wounded	Franco-Prussian War (pp. 68–70); Franco-Vietminh War.
prisoners of war	War of 1812 (pp. 63–4); Mexican-American War (pp. 66–8); Franco-Prussian War (pp. 68–70); Italo-Abyssinian War (pp. 72–3); Crimean War (pp. 165–9); War of the Spanish Succession (pp. 357–66); Seven Years' War (pp. 374–9).
military administration of occupied areas	Franco-Prussian War (pp. 68–70); Mexican-American War (pp. 66–8); Franco-Tunisian War of 1881 (pp. 71–2).
supervision of procedures of a military settlement	Chaco War (pp. 76–9); Russo-Polish War (pp. 73–6). International Control Commissions after the Franco-Vietminh War; supervisory commissions after the Korean War (pp. 233–6).
demilitarization provisions	Chaco War (pp. 76–9); Russo-Finnish War (pp. 79–81); Last War of the Habsburg-Valois Rivalry (pp. 157–60); Crimean War (pp. 165–9); Boxer Rebellion (pp. 175–7); the Peace of Carlowitz ending the war in the Eastern Theater: the European War of 1683–1700 (pp. 347–57). After the First World War (pp. 405–28), the Central Powers were disarmed.
neutralization	Savoy in the European War of 1683–1700 (pp. 347–57); Switzerland in the Thirty Years' War (pp. 379–92) and the Napoleonic Wars (pp. 392–405); Laos after the Laotian Civil War (pp. 236–40).

tions? Shall it be a permanent or a temporary cease-fire? If temporary, for what period of time? And by what means shall the cease-fire be implemented? The post-armistice disposition of the armed forces of the belligerents is a second major area of discussion. What procedures will be followed for the disengagement of combat troops? How will guerrillas or partisans be managed? Will the troops, regular and irregular, withdraw from the entire theater of combat or from particular areas only? How shall the withdrawal be implemented? The naval and air forces of the belligerents may be moved to bases outside the immediate theater of combat. Troops may have to be moved to temporary assembly or regroupment areas and then withdrawn. They may be withdrawn all at once by a date fixed by the negotiators or withdrawn in stages.

In many military settlements, the armistice agreement contains only the most general provisions. Agreement upon details is left to a commission whose presence in the combat zone will permit an *ad hoc* solution of problems as they arise. Usually, the commission is made up of officers of the armed forces of the belligerents, who maintain close contact with their respective commanders and function as a liaison group for supervising joint operations required for proper implementation. The belligerent commanders must, of necessity, coordinate their plans for the cease-fire and the withdrawal of troops between themselves and with their governments and the peace negotiators.

Often, the belligerents will have to agree upon additional technical questions to insure the security of their forces and any civilians in or near the areas through which their forces move. Provisions for the protection of property will undoubtedly be made a part of the armistice agreement, as will methods for the removal of weapons, mines, unexploded shells, and bombs. Responsibility for these tasks and general responsibility for the protection of persons and property is usually assigned to the commanders in charge of executing the cease-fire, as execution is a military function. Also negotiated at this time are provisions for the evacuation of wounded, burial of the dead, and the release and exchange of prisoners and interned civilians. Prisoner exchange may be scheduled to take place by a fixed date or in echelons on dates fixed by the peace negotiators or by a military commission. The obligation to provide transportation and food for the wounded and for prisoners may be imposed by the provisions of the armistice agreement upon one or both parties. Indeed, it may be necessary for the negotiators to discuss the question of food supply and transportation in considerable detail. The threat of starvation and the inadequacy of shelter and transportation facilities in combat zones (or in the entire territory of one of the belligerent states) may require immediate attention. The problem of food supply could, of course, become an element in the hard bargaining between the parties and may not be settled immediately.

Terms for the military administration of areas controlled by the armed forces of one or both of the belligerents are usually made a part of the armistice agreement. Again, the details can be worked out by the military commission in the combat zones, subject to the guidelines of the armistice agreement. When the armed forces of one of the belligerents begin to withdraw from a given area, originally part of state A's territory, administrative competence is usually assigned to military or civil authorities of state B if there is to be an occupation regime, to state A if the area is to be recovered by A. This is a matter that can be finally resolved only in the political settlement phase. Pending such a settlement, the former belligerents might nonetheless have to agree upon some disposition of territories for purposes of military administration. If the question of whose army is to exercise administrative jurisdiction in a specific area is the subject of disagreement, then power to administer might be granted to military or civilian authorities of a third, disinterested state or to an international organization.

Procedures for withdrawal of troops and other related technical military provisions are usually supervised either by an independent commission made up of representatives of an international organization or by third-party states. The competence of this commission depends upon the mandate granted it by the former adversaries. However, third-party states may succeed in inducing the belligerents to grant wide supervisory powers to the commission, powers that would enable it to control the execution of cease-fire procedures. Needless to say, the decision to establish such a commission and the question of its composition and competence will be the subject of negotiations between the belligerents. Experience has shown that states are extremely reluctant to grant supervisory commissions powers much beyond those of *observing* the conduct of the armed forces of the parties after the cease-fire and reporting upon what has been accomplished. Policymakers of formerly belligerent states are eager to establish a date for ending the commission's mandate to function within their borders, as they usually regard it as an institution that, in however small a way, compromises their states' sovereignty.

There will inevitably be violations, or at least complaints of violations, of the cease-fire agreement; and the belligerents will have to agree early upon procedures for disposing of these complaints and ameliorating the consequences of an actual violation. Otherwise hostilities could resume. To this end, the military commission or the independent supervisory commission may be given the authority to investigate all charges of violation of the cease-fire or the provisions of the armistice agreement. Disposition of the findings and reports of either of the commissions varies. The commissioners themselves may attempt an *ad hoc* solution to the complaint, or they may refer it to the peace negotiators, to other representatives of the belligerents, or to third parties. The longterm preservation of peace is more properly a political question relating to peacekeeping as opposed to peacemaking. One incident, one alleged violation, can of course cause a breakdown in the peace talks and a resumption of hostilities. If the belligerents are convinced, or can be convinced, that it is in their interests to maintain the armistice, then the dispute growing out of the violation can be conciliated, either directly between the parties or with the help of a distinterested third party. On the other hand, cease-fire agreements are tenuous things, and one violation can result in a renewal of the war. Certainly, a flagrant violation that compromised the security of the armed forces of one of the parties or, more generally, resulted in a substantial shift in the relative bargaining positions of the parties, is likely to lead to a renewal of the fighting.

The disarmament, demilitarization, and neutralization terms of an armistice agreement are another major area of negotiations in the military settlement phase of the peacemaking process. The parties may agree upon a mutual reduction of armaments, including a reduction in the number of aircraft and naval vessels each may possess. What is more likely is a compulsory or quasicompulsory unilateral reduction forced on one of the parties when that party is in a disadvantageous bargaining position as a result of a military defeat. But in the event of a stalemate, disarmament terms are usually the subject of lengthy talks, and agreement is doubtful at best. The belligerents may, however, agree to dismantle certain bases and to demilitarize certain areas of their states; they may agree to limit the size of their reserves and even reduce the recruiting and training programs for their armed forces. Naturally, the extent of the demilitarization is a matter for agreement between the parties. As non-belligerents could be affected by demilitarization or neutralization, such states might want to express their views and present demands for the guarantee of their own security.

The term *neutralization* refers to the demilitarization of a given area, usually a third state whose policies are in some way related to the reasons for the outbreak of hostilities between the primary belligerents. Neutralization is, however, more than mere demilitarization, since it also requires both the belligerents and other states to pursue (or to forebear pursuing) certain policies relative to the neutralized state. Thus, while demilitarization is a military problem (with political implications), neutralization is more clearly both a political and a military problem. The parties undertake a longterm political program of refraining from making any decisions about a particular state that would incorporate that state in an alliance or, more generally, involve it in any cooperative enterprise with one of the former belligerents for the maintenance of that belligerent's security. Neutralization is a problem with enough political implications to be considered later when we discuss the political phase of the peacemaking process.

The belligerents themselves may agree, as part of their policies for defusing their conflict, not to join alliances directed against the other party or alliances designed to pursue collectively the values that had brought them to war. But here again, we have a political question (albeit closely related to military questions). Military questions, as they manifest themselves in peace settlements, do have political implications; and political questions indeed have their military aspects.

Wars and War Aims

It is no doubt true that states go to war in order to attain valued ends, either power political or ideological. It is also true that any particular war is a unique event, one that has never occurred before and will not occur again; and the policymakers of the states involved have purposes that are specific and unique to that war. If we accept only the implications of this latter point of view, comparisons between wars and generalizations about them would be impossible to make. However, the issues of war and settlements of wars, as with other questions of political science, can in fact be discussed. In discussing them, we fix our discourse at one or more levels of analysis. Provided that we know the level of analysis of our discourse, provided that we do not confuse levels and try always to keep in mind the limitations of analysis for answering certain questions, it is perfectly valid for us to choose arbitrarily one level of analysis. Again we make one proviso—that we do not exclude the perspective of other levels. Such an approach is not only valid, but it may be the only approach possible. And so, in order to list the reasons that states fight wars, that is, to catalogue the issues of external wars, we shall select a level of analysis somewhere between that which says issues are always unique and one that in a reductionist fashion regards war policies as motivated simply by either power political or ideological ends.

We postulate that in a simple external war between state A and state B, the policymakers of the belligerents will be motivated by one or a combination of war aims. Even in the simplest case, we are apt to find a number of war aims intertwined, as policymakers usually have mixed motives for any policy. Independent observers might be inclined to argue over the primacy of this or that war aim or whether state A's leaders based a policy upon one particular war aim as opposed to others. For the moment, these problems need not concern us. For we need only inquire, at this point, what the most common war aims are of policymakers who have gone to war. The following is offered as a generalized list of external wars characterized according to war aims or war issues.[1] Such a list is

1 This categorization of war aims is based upon an analysis of the aims of the belligerents of the wars studied by the author, particularly those whose settle-

necessary because, in order to understand how the content of a peace settlement is determined, we must first understand the nature of the possible war aims of the belligerent actors.

1. There is first the war by state A to gain dominance over other states, particularly the adversary, state B. This is often called a *hegemonial war*. It is worthwhile to distinguish several types in this category:

a. A war to acquire territory, either the territory of state B or territory in another state or region.

b. A war to acquire resources in state B or in other states or regions. This will usually entail the acquisition of territory by state A in order to secure resources such as mines, raw materials, stockpiles of minerals, or weapons; but it is conceivable that state A might want merely to secure a resource and then withdraw.

c. A war to acquire influence or control over the policies of another state (either state B or a third state). In this case no permanent occupation is intended, and possibly only a limited invasion, that is, just enough military pressure to persuade the policymakers of state B (or the third state) to acquiesce in the demands of the policymakers of state A for the right to exercise influence in the formulation of policy. A successful war of this sort may have a multiplier effect: States other than state B would tend to comply with state A's demand for similar rights on their territories were state A to defeat state B or to threaten war against them.

A dynastic war would be subsumed under one or more of these subcategories. In such a war, a monarch seeks to enhance the status of his family through the acquisition of domains in another state. Although sometimes an arranged marriage can achieve peaceful dynastic aggrandizement, the monarch must often resort to war: a war for dominance of his own state or a war for his or his family's dominance abroad, with the monarch acting as if he were the state. With the passing of absolute monarchies, such wars have now become rare.

2. A second kind of external war is the war to consolidate the state in fulfillment of some *legitimating principle*. The war to bring all the people comprising the *nation* of state A under the authority and jurisdiction of A's government is the most common war of this type in the modern era. State A makes war upon state B because it is alleged that people with nationality A, living in state B, desire to be governed by the authorities of A. Here, the legitimating principle is *national self-determination*. It is possible that some other principle justifying a war for the consolidation of state A might be operative, as once were grants from a

---

ments are summarized at the end of this chapter and in Chapters 3, 4, 5, and 9. In these summaries, I have explicitly, albeit briefly, described the war aims of the principal belligerents to permit the reader to test the adequacy of my classification.

Pope, a Holy Roman Emperor, or the Sultan, any of whom exercised vague supranational authority or suzerainty over subordinate or tributary states at various times in the past.[2]

3. A third category is the war to preserve the *status quo*.

a. There is the war in which state A seeks to maintain its dominant position relative to state B and other states. This kind of war is state A's forceful response to policies of state B that are intended by the latter to win a position of dominance for state B at the expense of A.

b. There is also the war in which state A seeks to maintain its position—not necessarily a paramount position—against state B. This and the preceding types of war are often called wars to preserve an *existing balance of power*.

c. Finally, there is the *status quo* defensive war in which state A seeks to preserve its territory, resources, or weapons from takeover by state B. In short, it is a war to defend state A.

4. Wars waged for a *secular or religious ideology* are a fourth category. Thus, an ideology to which the policymakers of state A adhere might require a holy war against state B and the occupation and subjugation of its people. Or the ideology might simply justify a war to convert the people of state B, in order to increase the number of ideological adherents or to bring the benefits of the culture of which the ideology is a part to a benighted people.

Ideological wars are also waged to prevent the spread of an ideology. In the modern era, it is also possible to regard such wars as having the purpose of preventing a state from gaining dominance. In earlier times, however, we do see counter-ideological wars waged without primary regard to the territories involved.

In the case of either ideological or counter-ideological wars, the particular ideology could be either universal or intranational. An ideology might purport to be timeless and to appeal to all people irrespective of their race or nationality (hence, universal); or it might only be the formalized structure of precepts, beliefs, and symbols of the people and elites of one particular state. Marxism is an example of a universal ideology; *manifest destiny*, an example of an intranational ideology.

5. Wars are also waged for *retribution and punishment*. State B might provoke A, perhaps by the persecution of A's nationals or by interference with A's trade. State A's policymakers might then deem the situation so intolerable that they respond with a declaration of war.

6. There are also *wars of opportunity*, in which a state seeks to take

---

2 The reader may object that the war for consolidation of the state is really a war to acquire territory (with some elements of the ideological type of war we will also consider). Even so, this type of war has been (and is) so significant as to warrant separate consideration even at the risk of redundancy.

advantage of an existing situation to achieve some advantage that can usually be won quickly. Thus, in a late stage of a war between states B and C in which B is about to surrender, state A might declare war on B in order to put itself in a formal state of war with B, thereby hoping to secure an invitation to the peace conference or at least some gain for being on the winning side. State A might take advantage of B's weakness to declare war and seize part of B's territory or resources, thus confronting the future peace negotiators with a *fait accompli*. Needless to say, a state enters a war of opportunity in the expectation that there will, in fact, be no appreciable losses. The state's policymakers expect the war to be a short one with a very small probability that human and material costs will exceed some estimated low figure. Sometimes this expectation is not fulfilled. The state that enters a war of opportunity may find itself threatened with disaster as the course of the war alters in the enemy's favor.

It must be emphasized that there are often several issues involved in any war, and the policymakers of the belligerents may themselves be at a loss to identify what issue was uppermost in their formulation of a war policy. Moreover, the war issues of one belligerent certainly need not be identical to those of the other belligerent. It is possible for state A and state B to go to war because both seek territory or resources in state C or because both adhere to antagonistic ideologies and actively proselytize. On the other hand, it is more likely that state A will go to war for reasons different from those of state B: state A might seek territorial acquisitions from state C, for example; state B would then declare war on A to preserve the status quo. Or state A might declare war on state C in order to convert the people of C to A's ideology. State B would see this as A's design ultimately to attain dominance over B and would therefore declare war on A to preserve the status quo.

The war aims of states often change during the war. Hence, by the time peace negotiations are about to begin, a belligerent's war aims may not be the same as those at the outbreak of the war. Won or lost battles, sustained losses, and the exigencies of coalition policy, among other things, will affect the aims of any belligerent. As we noted in the first chapter, the values of the key decision-makers often change during the war in response to a number of conditions; and indeed, the persons making the decisions also often change. De-ideologization or devaluation might occur, thus permitting a peaceful settlement. A change in war aims that worked against a peace settlement would also be possible: new war aims might be advanced while old ones became of lesser importance, and the net effect of these transformations would be a prolongation of hostilities until all war aims were satisfied or the policymakers became convinced that the war aims could not be satisfied.

Elements of the Political Settlement

In external wars, there are a number of key problem areas over which peace negotiators must bargain in order to effect a settlement. (Certain problems are common to a particular kind of external war only, and they will be considered later in the chapter. Finally, those problems unique to the particular war being waged we will not presently investigate.) The problem areas with which we shall deal are: territory, persons affected by the war, resumption of relations between the belligerents, guarantees of security, the future adjustment of disputes, and penalties.

The parties' war aims in part determine the terms of a peace settlement. In the schematic diagram of Figure 2–1, we indicate that the

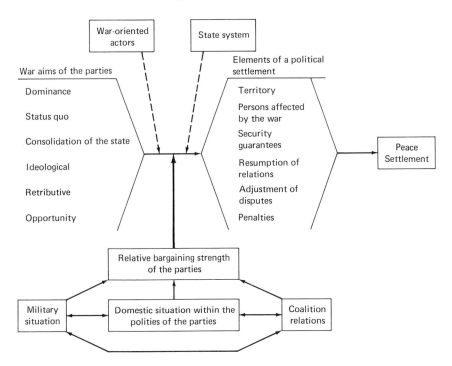

FIGURE 2–1. Determinants of the content of a political settlement.

content of a peace settlement expresses the war aims of the belligerent parties to the degree that the parties' bargaining strength prmits satisfaction of those aims. The elements of a political settlement are those issues over which the belligerent parties usually negotiate. The relative bargaining power of the belligerents is shaped by the military situation at the war's end, by coalition relations, and by domestic political conditions within the polities of the parties. These factors, as well as the number and character of the war-oriented actors and the events and conditions in the state system as a whole, form the context of the war and, in turn, affect the way in which (and the extent to which) the parties' war aims become provisions in a peace settlement (see also Figs. 1–1 and 1–5). The military situation affects both the coalition relations of the parties and their domestic politics. Indeed, there is an interaction among these three factors that we shall have to study in greater detail. We cannot, of course, envisage the nature of a political settlement until we have appraised all (or most) of the factors depicted in Figure 2–1. We shall undertake to characterize the context of war in this and in subsequent chapters. In the remainder of this chapter, we shall deal with the relationship between war aims and the elements of a political settlement, after a discussion of the nature of those elements.

Territory

The acquisition of territory may not be the primary aim of either belligerent in a simple external war, but war is effectively prosecuted only by military operations upon the territories of either antagonist, their allies, or a third state. Hence, territorial questions almost always arise at some point in peace negotiations. But we should also emphasize that the acquisition of territory either for itself alone or for security reasons is indeed very often an aim of the belligerents. The negotiations for a political settlement then hinge largely on the question of who shall be awarded particular areas under the control of the belligerents or other states? Although the issues of many negotiating situations can often be reduced quite fairly to the one issue of the terms of a territorial award, its resolution is generally difficult. We can supply some schemes for resolution, but negotiations over territorial questions are often protracted and emotionally charged. The negotiators may envisage possible solutions, but they often fail to agree upon an acceptable solution.

In the brief discussion here, we shall arbitrarily exclude cases in which the territories of allies or third states are in any way the subject of belligerent bargaining. This is, of course, an artificial situation; but it does reduce the external war to its simplest form for purposes of the present analysis. We will deal with alliances and war-oriented state relations in later chapters.

Because, as we have noted, combat operations usually have the objective of securing the territory of an opponent state, territorial questions impose upon the parties at the peace talks the task of defining the limits of areas that have changed hands. Thus, the final boundaries of the belligerent states or of any other territory over which the primary belligerents have fought must be delimited and agreed upon. The negotiators usually discuss the location of the boundaries in only very general terms, leaving it to commissions of experts at the conference and on the scene to fix accurately the delimiting line between jurisdictions. However, if the boundary in certain areas has become a highly politicized (and publicized) question, the peace negotiators may attend to the details of delimitation themselves. One of the first matters to be discussed will be the question of whether the cease-fire line shall be a political frontier. The armistice agreement will no doubt make some provision for the withdrawal of troops from the line of contact to prevent incidents that might lead to the resumption of hostilities. It is quite possible that this line of contact will later become a boundary between the belligerents or between a belligerent and an involved third state.

Certain areas could be made subject to a *special regime,* governed by a statute incorporated in the peace treaty. The negotiators must not only delimit the area of the regime, but must also define its character and determine the length of time the regime will last. A statute formulated during peace talks usually constitutes its basic law. There are three types of special regimes:

1. A *zone of occupation:* Here, the military success of one of the belligerents has resulted in the defeat of the other, and the latter acquiesces in the more or less temporary occupation of a portion of its territory. During the occupation period, the nationals of the defeated belligerent initially will be under the jurisdiction of a military government, which might or might not evolve into a government of civilians controlled wholly or in part by the government of the defeated state. The occupation agreement often determines what law will apply to crimes and to the matters ordinarily subject to a civil code. The nationals of the defeated state within the zone may be governed by the laws of that state, but occupation troops may either be entirely governed by the laws of the victor state or be made subject to the military code of the victor state for crimes, but to the civil laws of the defeated state. It would be most unusual for occupation forces to be made subject to the defeated state's criminal laws in the early stages of the occupation.

The occupation agreement might also stipulate that the defeated state must bear the costs of the occupation and specify the manner in which reimbursement is to be made. Provision may be made for terminating the regime and for the withdrawal of occupation troops. Currency and economic questions are also common subjects covered by the occupation agreement.

2. The *plebiscite regime:* A second kind of special regime is an area set aside for a plebiscite. The belligerents agree that they will abide by the will of the inhabitants of the particular area, as that will is expressed in a plebiscite whose date and procedures are specified in the peace treaty. Before the plebiscite, the area will either be placed under the jurisdiction

TABLE 2–3. Examples of disposition of territory in peace settlements.

Cessions: The Karelian Isthmus to the Soviet Union after the Russo-Finnish War; Hong Kong to Britain after the Opium War; Tarapaca (from Peru) and Antofagasta (from Bolivia) to Chile after the War of the Pacific; the Duchies to Austria and Prussia after the Second War over Schleswig-Holstein; Alsace-Lorraine to Germany after the Franco-Prussian War; American southwest territories to the U.S. after the Mexican-American War; Black Sea territories to Russia after the Russo-Turkish War of 1768–74; reciprocal cessions among Britain, France, and Spain after the War for American Independence; Silesia to Prussia after the War of the Austrian Succession; Transylvania and Hungarian territories to Austria after the European War of 1683–1700; North American territories to Britain from France after the War of the Spanish Succession and the Seven Years' War; reciprocal cessions between Spain and France in the region of the Spanish Netherlands after the Franco-Dutch War of 1672–9.

Status quo ante bellum: The settlements of the War of 1812, the Italo-Abyssinian War of 1894–6, the Austro-Russian War against Turkey (1787–92) in respect of Austria and Turkey (but not Russia and Turkey) ; for France and Spain after the Dutch Revolt; between Britain and Holland, and France and Denmark, after the Franco-Dutch War of 1672–9; and between France and Holland, and France and England, after the European War of 1683–1700.

Independence and the running of boundaries for new states: Poland after the First World War and the Russo-Polish War; Texas after the Texas Revolt; the Irish Free State and Northern Ireland after the Irish Rebellion (also an instance of partition) ; the U.S. after the War for American Independence; Greece after the War for Greek Independence; several Balkan states after the Russo-Turkish War of 1877–8; the German Confederation after the Wars of France against Europe; the Baltic states (in treaties with the Soviet Union) and the succession states of the Habsburg and Ottoman Empire after the First World War. [In the latter case, boundaries, of course, had to be described as well for the parent states, Austria, Hungary, and Turkey, and for Germany.] The Principalities after the Greek Revolt, and Bulgaria after the Russo-Turkish War of 1877–8 were given autonomy; and boundaries for them were also delineated.

Plebiscite regimes: Tacna and Arica after the War of the Pacific; and the Saar, Silesia, East Prussia, Schleswig, and Klagenfurt after the First World War.

Free territory: The four French cities reserved for the Huguenots after the Third Huguenot War; the free ports of China after the Opium War; the Free Territory of Cracow after the Napoleonic Wars; Danzig and the Saar (under League of Nations Trusteeship) after the First World War.

Occupation regimes: Calais after the Last War of the Habsburg-Valois Rivalry; Peru during the War of the Pacific; parts of France after the Franco-Prussian War; the Rhine bridgeheads after the First World War; the French Protectorate for Tunisia after the Franco-Tunisian War; mandates after the First World War; and the Boer Republics after the Boer War.

Easements: British use of Irish ports after the Irish Rebellion; Bolivian rights of transit across Chilean territory after the War of the Pacific; French right of troop transit across Lorraine after the European War of 1683–1700; and across Münster after the Franco-Dutch War of 1672–9.

Other territorial arrangements: fishing rights for Americans and wood-cutting rights in Spanish Honduras for Englishmen after the War for American Independence; lease of the Hango Peninsula to the Soviet Union after the Russo-Finnish War; and the Chaco arbitral area after the Chaco War.

of the state controlling the area at the time of the cease-fire or be governed by a special administration furnished by a third state or an international organization acceptable to the belligerents. Agreement of the negotiators upon the need for a plebiscite is not always easy to obtain: either party will be loath to lose territory, especially if a former enemy might gain thereby. Another hotly disputed question is the procedure for dividing the plebiscite area into election districts. Gerrymandering is indeed possible; and either party might be convinced that the apportionment plan favored by the other will produce results adverse to its interests. The plebiscite may be supervised by a commission composed of representatives of the belligerent states, third states, or international organizations.

3. The *free territory:* A new political entity with sovereign or quasi-sovereign powers is a third kind of special regime. The parties might not be able to agree upon the disposition of disputed territory because they will simply not accept control of that territory by the other party, certainly not by a former or a traditional enemy. A strategically valuable area such as a port and its environs, an industrial area, or a large city would be an example of such a territory. The solution then, the only acceptable solution, is to refrain from awarding the territory to any existing state; and to create a new political entity, with all or most of the characteristics of an independent sovereign. The statute of the quasi-sovereign state or free territory, either as part of or accompanying the peace treaty, will function as the territory's constitution. It may envisage a plebiscite at some future time, when the people of the free territory could decide whether they want to remain independent or annex themselves to one or the other of the former belligerents (or a third state). The statute may, however, prohibit any solution that does not have the approval of the signatories of the peace treaty, irrespective of the desires of the inhabitants of the area. The sovereignty of the free territory might also be encumbered with provisions establishing rights for the belligerents and other states; for example, rights to transport goods across the territory, to use ports and port facilities, to ship goods on canals or rivers, perhaps free of customs duties and other impositions. The territorial integrity and security of the free territory are frequently guaranteed by the signatories of the peace treaty (and others).

Persons Affected by the War

The cease-fire agreement will usually contain provisions for the exchange of prisoners of war and the release and repatriation of interned civilians. The peace treaty is also likely to contain procedures for the transfer of peoples and the repatriation of displaced persons. The territorial settlement may result in the forced dispossession of inhabitants of particular areas; and certain persons, fearing the consequences of invasion and occupation by the enemy, may voluntarily leave their homes. At the time of the cease-fire, and possibly later, when the peace treaty is being negotiated, the existence of large numbers of displaced persons will pose often severe problems for the administrators of the areas of combat operations and for the peacemakers and their governments. Arrange-

TABLE 2–4. Provisions in peace settlements relating to persons affected by the war.

Free movement: Mexican-American War; Second Anglo-Dutch War; and the Dutch Revolt. In the settlements of the First World War and the Dutch-Spanish conflict of the Thirty Years' War, persons were given the right to return to their prewar domiciles.

Provisions relating to the transfer or repatriation of peoples: transfer required for Tartars in Moldavia after the European War of 1683–1700; Austria permitted to transfer Hungarians internally after the latter war; transfer and restitution of Acadians after Second Anglo-Dutch War of 1664–7; other transfer provisions in settlements of the First World War, Russo-Polish, and Korean Wars (and although not analyzed in this study, the Second World War and the Franco-Vietminh War of 1946–54).

Nationality provisions: Mexican-American War; Russo-Polish War; Struggle for Tunisian Independence; Russo-Turkish War of 1877–8; First World War.

Amnesty: for the insurgents after the Cuban Revolt; the Third Huguenot War and the Hungarian Rebellion of 1703–11; for subjects of the Porte in the Balkans after the Austro-Russian War against Turkey of 1787–92; reciprocal amnesty for U.S. and British citizens after the War for American Independence; and the First Peace of Paris after the Napoleonic Wars.

Restitution of property: Mexican-American War; Autro-Russian War against Turkey of 1787–92; War of the Polish Succession; for Russian citizens in the Ottoman Empire after the Greek Revolt; for English creditors in America after the War for American Independence; for Dutch and Spanish citizens after the Dutch Revolt; for French and Dutch citizens after the Franco-Dutch War of 1672–9; Thirty Years' War; and the War of the Austrian Succession.

General guarantees of civil liberties: Dutch Revolt; Franco-Dutch War of 1672–9; for Indians after the War of 1812 and the War of the Spanish Succession; for minorities in the succession states of Hapsburg Empire after the First World War; for subjects of the Porte in the Principalities after the Crimean War, and for his subjects in the Balkans after the Russo-Turkish War of 1877–8.

Guarantees of religious liberties: Third Huguenot War; for British and Dutch citizens after the Dutch Revolt; for Dutch citizens and German princes after the Thirty Years' War.

Public debts apportioned: Thirty Years' War; Wars of France against Europe (1792–1815); and the First World War.

Legal provisions (concerning contracts, debts, judgments, sentences, etc.) Franco-Prussian War; Russo-Polish War; Struggle for Tunisian Independence; Last War of the Habsburg-Valois Rivalry; Second Anglo-Dutch War; Dutch Revolt (Franco-Spanish settlement); Thirty Years' War; Wars of France against Europe, First World War (including the abrogated Treaties of Brest-Litovsk and Bucharest).

ments will have to be made to feed and shelter such persons. Procedures for their repatriation will have to be adopted, and the expenses of these procedures must be apportioned to one or both belligerents.

Whether or not the armistice agreement so provides, the peace treaty is likely to contain terms pursuant to which the signatories agree to respect the civil rights and liberties of persons subject to their jurisdiction. Promises to refrain from prosecuting individuals who sympathized with the opposing side may also be included. Such provisions are almost certainly to be made a part of a settlement in which territories of one of the belligerents or a third state are awarded to the other belligerent. Such areas may be inhabited by nationals of the former or by minority groups whose rights the latter and interested third parties will be anxious to protect. In addition to the guarantees of the lives and property of individuals, there is sometimes (in more enlightened times) explicit recognition of the rights of all peoples to participate equally in the political processes of the signatories (either as voters or as candidates for public office), to practice their religions without interference, and to engage in all forms of business activity and the professions freely on the same basis as nationals of the former belligerents.

When a territorial settlement transfers areas of one of the belligerents to the other, nationality provisions are essential. There must be agreement upon the attribution of nationality to all persons whose nationality is doubtful or undetermined as a result of the war, the prospective peace, and the transfer of territories. Procedures for expatriation and for acquiring the nationality and eventually the status of citizen of one of the former belligerent states are established by the peace treaty, along with provisions concerning the legal consequences for the individual of a change in nationality, specifying, for example, when his property is subject to taxation, when he is subject to the laws of his new state, the effects of his remaining a national of state A while residing in an area under the jurisdiction of state B, whether his newly acquired nationality is subject to restrictions while the future of a territory under a special regime is determined by its inhabitants, and many other similar questions.

Resumption of Relations Between Belligerents

The rupture of formal diplomatic relations that a war has brought about must be repaired by the peace settlement. The state of war is officially ended when a formal peace treaty comes into effect. Diplomatic relations are then restored, although the parties may in fact have established extensive informal relations since the cessation of hostilities. The peace treaty also specifies which prewar treaties will again become operative. Or in lieu of such a provision, the settlement will provide for future meetings at which the treaty regime between the former belligerents can be clarified. Although de-ideologization and devaluation of the war issues may not have proceeded far enough to permit the parties to sign a treaty of friendship and commerce, they will nevertheless want at least to adumbrate the basis for their future commercial and economic relations. Each must agree to revise domestic legislation that prohibited trade with the other during the war, and they will want to reconsider prohibitions on the travel of their nationals to areas under the jurisdiction of the other. Public opinion permitting, they might agree to extend "most favored nation" treatment to each other's trade and commerce and to refrain from imposing discriminatory duties or quotas on each other. Of course, agreement on these matters may be achieved only after the ratification of the peace treaty, or not at all if the former belligerents continue to regard each other as enemies in fact (if not in law).

The signatories might also want to reach agreement upon the legal consequences of the war and the peace settlement for judgments, debts, and claims (causes of action) of persons against either state or against individuals of the other state. Legal relations suspended during (and because of) the war are often held to be reinstated as of a date fixed by the parties, and debts acquired in the prewar period are often treated as if war had not intervened. Also, execution upon judgments rendered before the war is usually made possible. The problem of the effect of the war and the peace settlement upon contracts is a complex one about which few generalizations can be made. The parties might be compelled to determine whether the contracts of their nationals with nationals of the other belligerent have been rendered void by the war of, if still

TABLE 2–5.   Peace settlement provisions relating to the resumption of relations between belligerents.

Supplementary treaties of commerce concluded: War of 1812; Franco-Dutch War of 1672-9; War of the Spanish Succession; War of the Austrian Succession; and for the Dutch after Thirty Years' War. (The bilateral treaties recognizing the Soviet Union after the First World War contained commercial terms.)

Prewar treaties confirmed: Franco-Prussian War; Franco-Tunisian War; Italo-Abyssinian War of 1894-6; Last War of the Habsburg-Valois Rivalry; Crimean War; Second War over Schleswig-Holstein; Greek Revolt; War of the Polish Succession; and most major peace treaties of the multilateral wars discussed in Chapter 9. (All prior treaties were abolished in the settlement of the Russian conflict against Turkey in the Austro-Russian War against Turkey of 1787-92.)

Consular relations: Struggle for Tunisian Independence; Crimean War.

New bases for international relations: in respect of maritime rights after the Crimean War; consular precedence, slavery and the public law of rivers after the Napoleonic Wars; in the multifarious innovations of the League of Nations after the First World War; and the law of rivers and air space after the latter war.

operative, in what ways the terms of the contracts should be varied in the public interests of the signatories of the peace treaty, or how the war shall be deemed to have affected the subject matter of the contracts. The claims of one state against the other (or of nationals of one state against the other) might be annulled. Or the duty to pay restitution, if such a duty is subsequently established, might be assumed by either state, that is, each state agrees to satisfy the established claims of its own nationals. There is quite a variation in practice, however. If one of the belligerents can be said to have won the war, it may obtain the promise of the losing state to satisfy its claims and the claims of its nationals without granting reciprocal rights.

Guarantees of Security

As we have seen, the armistice agreement often provides for the demilitarization or neutralization of certain areas of one or both of the belligerents, and these arrangements frequently find their way into the peace treaty, where they are likely to be expanded or clarified. Either belligerent, having just agreed to end a war, would like to assure for itself an adequate defense in the event that its former adversary decides to renew hostilities. Both may even be disposed to try to *prevent* the outbreak of a new war; in this event, their terms for insuring security through demilitarization are likely to be more generously and faithfully respected, if not more extensive and sophisticated.

It may be that the *territorial settlement* will be deemed to provide either state sufficient security. On the other hand, hostile feelings, fear, and distrust might be so intense that no possible guarantees will provide security that will be deemed sufficient, particularly where the states share a common frontier or are historical enemies. In any event, the form security guarantees take will depend upon two factors: the relative bargaining positions of the representatives of the belligerents at the armistice and peace negotiations and the degree to which either state fears and distrusts the other. If state A were in a strong bargaining position and profoundly distrusted state B, we would expect A to require B to adhere to a rather elaborate scheme for the demilitarization of large areas within B, and perhaps also to disarm. If A were in a weak bargaining position, it would simply have to tolerate some measure of insecurity, as A's representatives would probably not be able to obtain sufficient guarantees at the peace talks. Should the two states have near equal bargaining power and should distrust be minimal, the peace treaty would probably contain minimal security guarantees. If the level of hostility and distrust were high, the parties would obviously submit proposals for what they regarded as adequate and sufficient guarantees; but whether agreement could be achieved is another matter. Even if the peace treaty contained elaborate guarantees, a high level of hostility would tend to work toward an early violation of its terms, if not actually to a resumption of hostilities.

Apart from the security derived from the cession of territory to one of the belligerents or the creation of a newly independent and demilitarized buffer state or a free territory, the most common form of security insurance is the demilitarization of some areas, particularly the frontier areas, of either or both belligerents. In such a scheme, the peace treaty provides for the withdrawal of troops from defined areas, the dismantling of fortifications and military bases, and the permanent prohibition of troop movements and military exercises. The secured zones may also include bodies of water and air space.

Disarmament is another form of insurance. The parties may agree to disarm either partially or completely. Unilateral disarmament, in whatever form or degree, can usually be imposed only by a victor on a defeated state. In a partial disarmament program, the disarming state would reduce the size of its navy and air force. The treaty often prescribes the types of naval vessels and aircraft that are to be scrapped and may even require the disarming state to hand over such craft to the adversary. The size of the armed forces of the disarming state would also be regulated, as would the maximum size of the reserves, police, and paramilitary forces. Restrictions on the numbers, character, and size of military schools, clubs, and other organizations that might conceivably be used to train troops could also be imposed.

The parties might agree that one or both shall cease the manufacture and importation of weapons, ammunition, and other war material, or limit the quantities of such weapons manufactured to the minimum essential for the maintenance of the internal security of the state. They might also agree merely to repair or replace but not augment the weapons of those military or paramilitary forces permitted to exist under the terms of the treaty. Often, special weapons that can be used only for large-scale or offensive war or weapons that have come to be accepted as especially dangerous or inhumane are entirely prohibited to one or both parties.

A disarmament scheme can foster a sense of security only when the treaty provides procedures for inspection. Where one party has surrendered to the other, the former will almost certainly be required to permit inspection if the victor *imposed* disarmament. However, while short-term inspection might be possible in the aftermath of the war, long-term inspection is another matter. Here, the cooperation of the state to be inspected is essential. A defeated party will become increasingly loath to permit inspection as it recovers from its defeat, particularly if the inspecting state evidenced an unwillingness or an inability to impose sanctions. A state can hardly be expected to cooperate with inspection teams when the arrangement is not reciprocal: the scheme would be regarded as an infringement of the sovereignty of the inspected state, which, as time passes, will find ways to rearm in spite of the terms of the peace treaty. The situation might be different if the two former belligerents could reach agreement in the postwar period for mutual disarmament and reciprocal rights of inspection. History has shown that states may seem willing to disarm, but rarely do—and almost never permit inspection except under conditions of duress.

Another form of a security guarantee is the neutralization of territory, usually that set aside for a plebiscite or the subject of a special free territorial regime. The neutralized state is forbidden to enter a collective defense alliance, especially where its purpose is to provide for joint defense against a former adversary of the neutralized state. The latter also agrees not to invite the armed forces of another state into areas under its jurisdiction and agrees further not to permit the establishment of bases designed for possible use by third powers. Of course, standard demilitarization provisions are the basis for neutralization; and thus the neutralized state could be required to reduce its armed forces to a level sufficient to preserve domestic stability only. But as neutralization concerns the relations of the subject state with third powers, neutralization, to be effective, must be recognized and respected by third states. In other words, it must effect a modification in the relations of third-party states. If only state A recognized the neutralized status of state B, our state system is such that we might expect states C, D, and E to attempt to persuade or compel state B to violate the peace treaty provisions defining that status whenever it was in their interest to do so. If state B had been neutralized pursuant to a formal agreement of states A, C, D and E, all would be deterred to some extent by the legal obligation to respect the neutralization agreement. This discussion is not meant to imply that unless third states are involved, neutralization is not a device for the political settlement of a simple external war. As we have said, the representatives of states A and B may create a neutralized entity out of parts of the territory of either or both states, at the same time vesting this entity with independence (in the case of a free territory).

The bargaining position of one of the former belligerents might be so strong, and its fears for its future security so deep, that the stronger state might secure the right to intervene with its armed forces in the affairs of the weaker state. Such intervention would be conditioned on the occurrence of some domestic or foreign event that the stronger state deemed a threat to its security: for example, a *coup d'état* that brought a hostile faction to power in the weaker state, armed intervention by a third state, or the alliance of the weaker state with a third state. The weaker state's independence would be illusory if the intervention provision were broadly drawn. Indeed, the right to intervene militarily might even be coupled with other rights to interfere in a most direct way in the political processes of the weaker state. This takes us close to the limit of the assumption we made earlier that, as a result of the war, both belligerents emerged intact as sovereign entities. (Recall that we earlier assumed that the war did not end in the obliteration of one of the states.) It has not been unknown for puppet states to emerge from external wars. However, if these states preserved the myth of sovereignty, together with a modicum of independence in at least domestic political affairs, then it would be possible for them eventually to become independent again in their handling of external affairs as well. This could occur if the stronger state could find guarantees of its security through other means or if the dominant state were to become weak.

TABLE 2–6. Provisions in peace settlements relating to security guarantees.

Demilitarization: prohibitions of British forts in Scotland after the Last War of the Habsburg-Valois Rivalry; demilitarization of the Rhineland after the Thirty Years' War, the European War of 1683–1700, and the First World War; demilitarized zone on the Dutch frontier after the Dutch Revolt, and around Perekop after the European War of 1683–1700; partial disarming and demilitarization of Germany, Austria and Hungary after the First World War.

Forts and bases permitted: Russo-Turkish War of 1768–74; Russo-Finnish War; Last War of the Habsburg-Valois Rivalry; the "Barrier" after the War of the Spanish Succession.

Neutralization: the Black Sea and the Straits after the Crimean War; Laos after the Laotian Civil War; Savoy after the European War of 1683–1700; Switzerland after the Thirty Years' War.

Non-intervention: Russo-Polish Wars; Laotian Civil War.

Reciprocal promises of aid: Russia and Turkey after the First War of Mehemet Ali; France and Austria after the War of the Spanish Succession; Prussia and Austria after the Seven Years' War.

Collective guarantees: for the Ottoman Empire after the Crimean War; for the peace settlement of the War of the Polish Succession; joint guarantee of Saxony after the Napoleonic Wars (and the First and Second Peace of Paris after the same wars) ; guarantee of Silesia to Prussia after the Seven Years' War.

Dynastic guarantees: contracts of marriage after the Last War of the Habsburg-Valois Rivalry, the Franco-Dutch War of 1672–9, and the Peace of the Pyrenees (1659), ending the Franco-Spanish War that had begun with France's intervention in the Thirty Years' War in 1635; confirmation of the Pragmatic Sanction after the War of the Austrian Succession; recognition of the Hanoverian succession in England after the Wars of the Spanish and Austrian Successions; eternal separation of the Crowns of Spain and France after the War of the Spanish Succession; settlement of titles and territories after the War of the Polish Succession; and French recognition of the Protestant succession in Britain after the European War of 1683–1700.

Use of hostages: Last War of the Habsburg-Valois Rivalry; War of the Austrian Succession; and the European War of 1683–1700.

The belligerents may be able to agree upon the terms of written guarantees of each other's territorial integrity, coupled with the promise to refrain from interfering in the internal affairs of the other. Of a similar nature is the promise of the two states to renounce the use of force or threats of force in their mutual relations. Guarantees of this sort have not yet been effective in assuring leaders of states that they may rely solely or, in the face of a crisis, even partly upon them to provide sufficient security. States signatory to charters of regional and worldwide collective security organizations such as the League of Nations and the United Nations have made such commitments. If the belligerents in our hypothetical external war were members of such organizations, they would be bound by those guarantees in the postwar period. If fear and distrust are widespread at the end of an external war, however, promises to respect territorial integrity do little to allay suspicion. And if one of the states were in a strong bargaining position, it would invariably seek to extract an agreement from the weaker state to cede territory, to demilitarize, or to disarm. Only when "sufficient" security has been obtained will leaders of states that have promised to respect the territorial integrity of each other feel that those promises have any real value. The exchange of such promises are not really the means to obtain sufficient security, but rather are indications that it has already been obtained by other means.

Adjustments of Disputes

Even after the most ideologized of wars, belligerent states sometimes adopt procedures for the resolution of the future disputes that will invariably arise out of the implementation of either the military or political terms of the peace settlement. A commission composed of representatives of the belligerents or of third states is empowered by the terms of the peace agreements to observe or supervise the execution of its terms. In the event that a party complains of a violation, the commission will make an investigation. When it has collected and studied the facts of an alleged violation, it will propose terms for the settlement of the dispute, provided that its competence extends to mediation of this sort. Otherwise, it will merely forward a report of its findings to the governments of the two states, and it will be left to those governments to settle the matter between themselves. Adoption of such procedures indicates that the belligerents have implicitly agreed not to resume hostilities until after the investigatory commission fully performs its function, whether that be mediation of the dispute on the scene or reporting to the governments of the belligerents. If they have exchanged explicit promises not to resort to force, either in the peace treaty or by their adherence to the charter of an international organization such as the U.N., and if the matter involved in the dispute does not affect their vital national interests, then they will very likely find some acceptable solution short of war. The efficacy of third-party mediation or conciliation should not be discounted. Not only will a third party be able to look more dispassionately at the facts of a dispute, it may be able to propose solutions that are more acceptable from it than if proposed by one or the other of the belligerents. Acceptance by one state of a solution proposed by the other might be regarded as the equivalent of surrender by the elites or the people of the accepting state. In any case, should the dispute affect vital security interests of the parties, no amount of mediation by a third state is likely to prevent the outbreak of hostilities.

The peace treaty might also provide for the adjudication of legal disputes arising out of the settlement. The states must consent to the referral of such a dispute to an independent body of jurists, and they must also consent to be bound by the judgment of that body, or the adjudication procedure would be quite meaningless. Some disputes are susceptible of being adjudicated; others are not, just as some disputes can be arbitrated, while others cannot. *Arbitration* can be efficacious for disputes involving a quantifiable factor such as time, money, or a commodity. As in the case of mediation, conciliation, and adjudication, the states must consent to be bound by arbitration.

The peace negotiators would also be wise to include in the peace treaty provisions for the interpretation of its terms. Disputes over the meaning

TABLE 2–7. Provisions for the adjustment of disputes between belligerents included in a peace settlement.

General provisions for the adjustment of disputes were included in the settlements of the Mexican-American War, the Chaco War, and the First World War, and in the Covenant of the League of Nations.

Limited, special purpose procedures for the adjustment of disputes were instituted after a number of the wars analyzed in this and subsequent chapters:

Type of dispute to be adjusted	*War*
boundary disputes	War of 1812
disputes concerning the Chaco area (to be mediated by the Peace Conference)	Chaco War
war pension arbitration	Irish Rebellion
arbitration of the claims of nationals	War of the Pacific
trade débâcles	Franco-Dutch War of 1672–9
arbitration of questions pertaining to the Duchy of Lorraine	Thirty Years' War
adjudication of questions relating to international river law	Napoleonic Wars (further elaborated in the settlements of the Crimean and First World Wars).
arbitration of economic and financial disputes	First World War

of terms are as apt to arise as disputes relating to the performance of offensive acts. In fact, the two are closely related; and adjustment of a dispute requires the interpretation of a treaty provision as well as the determination of the facts of an alleged violation.

It is worthwhile to emphasize again that in our consideration of these elements common to most settlements of external wars, we are dealing now only with simple external wars. Allies of either belligerent and war-oriented states are, by our hypothesis, not involved. Naturally, the form of a settlement of even the simplest external war will be influenced by what else is happening in the state system (see Fig. 2–1). A state that sought to obtain some guarantee of its security from a peace settlement, some cession of territory, the establishment of a special territorial regime, or some mode of dispute adjustment that could prevent the resumption of hostilities, will find that the nature of its proposals for the form of the settlement will be influenced by the behavior of other states. Even in the absence of threats to either of the former belligerents, an unstable state system will in itself pose a threat to them and affect the kind of peace settlement achieved. Wars, or the possibility of wars, between other states over issues unrelated to the particular issues that were the basis of the war between the two belligerents may delay or prevent a peace settlement. The sense of insecurity bred by the behavior and policies of other states may make the attainment of sufficient security between the two belligerents impossible.

Penalties

Penalty provisions will not appear as a matter of course in all treaties of peace, but only in those concluded by states one of which can be said either to have lost the war or to occupy a weak position as a result of major battlefield losses. Having lost a war, a state will have to acquiesce in quite severe penalties. Penalty provisions in the peace treaty are usually an indication that one of the signatories was in a measurably inferior bargaining position. The weaker the position, the more rigorous are likely to be the penalty clauses.

If the war was intensely ideologized and resulted in severe losses, the party in the stronger bargaining position will attempt to extract reparations, restitution, or an indemnity from the weaker party. There is a problem with respect to the definition of these terms. Restoration in kind of articles, commodities, and other identifiable objects removed from the territory of one state to another state is generally called *restitution*. The return of works of art, rolling stock, monetary gold, objects of historical or archaeological value, and property removed by force or duress is subject to restitution; and the peace treaty frequently provides for it.

The treaty might also include provisions for the payment by the state in the weaker bargaining position of compensation for *direct cost* of damage done to private and public property in the territory of the other state. The stronger party might also force the state in the weaker bargaining position to agree to pay for the *indirect costs* of the war, such as veteran's pensions, losses sustained because of the interruption of business, and war costs. The latter include expenditures of the victorious state for defense and for the prosecution of the war. Needless to say, only if one of the parties has lost the war and surrendered to the other party will there be any likelihood that such extreme penalties can be exacted, and in a stalemated external war the states are apt to waive even demands for direct damages. The term *reparations* should be used in the restricted sense, to designate only direct damages; but it has, unfortunately, also been used to cover some forms of indirect damages; and it also has come to mean any payments, of whatever nature, the peace treaty requires one state to make to the other state. We will use it here in the restricted sense.

Implicit in the demand for reparations is a judgment that one party was responsible for the war, at least more responsible than the other state. The treaty may quite explicitly require the state in the weaker bargaining position to admit that it committed aggression. Because of public opinion and the intensity of feeling generated by a war, the peace negotiators for the victorious state may feel compelled to require the defeated state to admit its guilt in order to justify the exaction of reparations. The admission is, in itself, a penalty, one that is likely to be bitterly resented by the attentive public of the supposedly guilty state.

If reparations will be paid, other questions arise: How much shall be paid? In what form shall payment be made (in gold, currency or goods) ; in how many installments and by what dates? What will be the consequences of a default in payment? The negotiators may agree upon a fixed sum, usually after much haggling. They might, however, defer computation to a later date and establish a commission of experts to fix the total amount of payments and to resolve other related technical economic matters. Payments might be in gold; but they might also be payable in deliveries from current industrial production or in capital goods. The party in the stronger bargaining position might be intent upon crippling the economy of the defeated state, which could be done by requiring large reparations payments. If the victor state, in its own interests, wanted the defeated state to remain (or to become) a viable economic entity, then a cautious reparations policy would be necessary: the defeated state must be permitted to resume the production of goods, at least, to be able to make deliveries to the victor from current production. An economically healthy state, even though a former enemy, might be necessary for the growth of the trade and commerce of the victor. The peace treaty cannot, of course, provide for every detail. Much will have to be left to the subsequent agreement of the parties (for example, specification of the exact type and quality of goods to be delivered). Provision must, however, be made for the adjustment of disputes over reparations.

Penalties might also take the form of seizure of goods and property of nationals of the defeated state, goods that are situated in the victor state. Often the latter requires the defeated state to recognize the legitimacy of that seizure and to accept the obligation to pay its own nationals for any claims arising therefrom. The defeated state might also be required to arrest and surrender up individuals defined by the peace treaty as war criminals. This is, of course, an extraordinary provision, and one not likely to be included unless the war has left a very profound legacy of bitterness.

The cession of territory to the stronger state is another form of penalty; and the territory ceded may be some or all of the colonies of ths weaker state or perhaps even a part of the state proper. The defeated state could be required to dissolve political organizations ideologically antagonistic to the victor state. It might also be required to renounce economic benefits under certain prewar treaties; and it might be forced to withdraw its representatives from banks, corporations, and other economic or financial organizations engaged in or regulating international business.

TABLE 2–8.   Penalty provisions in peace settlements.

Penalties requiring cash payments were imposed upon these nations after the wars named:

Defeated Party	War
China	Opium War
France	Franco-Prussian War
Ashanti	Ashanti War
Certain Tunisian tribes	Franco-Tunisian War
Soviet Union	Russo-Polish War
Ottoman Empire (to Russia)	Greek Revolt
Ottoman Empire (to Russia)	Russo-Turkish War of 1877–8
United Provinces to Great Britain	Franco-Dutch War of 1672–9

In addition to a cash penalty in the Boxer Rebellion, China was required to apologize to the Powers, erect expiatory monuments, punish individuals, and prohibit the formation of antiforeign organizations. Pursuant to the settlement of the First World War, Germany was required to admit war guilt, agree in principle to the trial of its "war criminals," and pay reparations.

Bargaining Strength, War Aims, and the Political Settlement

The political settlement of an external war is determined in part, by interbelligerent power positions, the parties' *bargaining positions* as they exist at the war's end and during the course of peace negotiations (see

Fig. 2–1). If a state can be said to have won the war or if it has otherwise put itself in a strong bargaining position because of favorable military developments, it will be able very nearly to attain the objects for which it had fought. Conversely, having lost the war or finding itself in a weak bargaining position because of battle losses, a state will fail (or nearly fail) to attain its war aims. Yet, many other factors than bargaining strength enter into a "two-person" bargaining situation, not the least of which will be the constraints of domestic and world politics. Even in a hypothetically isolated simple external war, an analyst could conceive of attitudes on the part of the peace negotiators incommensurate with their position of military strength or weakness: In the interests of better long-term relations, the stronger state might forego all or part of a value for which it had fought;[3] skillful diplomacy might ameliorate the condition in which the negotiators of the weaker state find themselves;[4] or the latter might be able to bargain with values other than those directly involved in the war (e.g., trade or raw materials) and hence cut its losses of the values at issue in the war (e.g., territory or a right to intervene).[5] It is difficult to make any valid generalizations at this level of analysis other than to say that bargaining strength influences the outcome of peace talks and that the stronger party tends to achieve the objects for which it fought the war, but does not always do so. Without specification of the environment of an external war, a discussion of a political settlement will be incomplete; and only the complete analysis will enable us to discern why the strength of its negotiating position has not favorably influenced the outcome for the stronger party or why it has not fully achieved its objectives. For the time being, however, let us deal only with the settlement of the war issues of the general type listed earlier in the chapter. The following discussions are in the nature of scenarios supported, to some extent, by the historical examples cited in the notes.

3 True of France with respect to Russia in the Crimean War (pp. 165–9): Russia relative to China in the Boxer Rebellion (pp. 175–7); and Britain with respect to the Boer colonies after the Boer War (pp. 173–5).

4 Such was the case of Great Britain during the negotiations for peace settling the War for American Independence (pp. 217–22), and earlier in the late stages of the Dutch Revolt (pp. 208–14). France in the Franco-Dutch War (pp. 340–7) was able to dissolve the coalition against Louis XIV and to retain a relatively strong bargaining position at Nijmegen.

5 The Pope was defeated in the Last War of the Habsburg-Valois Rivalry (pp. 157–60), but he was able to bargain effectively with his neutrality and his power to forgive the French monarch. Louis XIV often bargained with his willingness to recognize a dynasty, as in the European War of 1683–1700 (pp. 347–57). Territories in the New World could be regarded as "other values" vis-à-vis the settlements of the European wars of the eighteenth century.

War for Dominance

If the acquisition of territory was the primary war objective of the state that sought dominance, the disposition of territory will be the most important element of the settlement. It may take any of the forms discussed in the preceding section. The state in the stronger bargaining position may obtain all the territory it demanded,[6] or it might obtain territory together with other values (resources, commercial privileges, and the like).[7] It may also succeed in penalizing the weaker state and obtaining what it deems an adequate guarantee of its security.[8] But the state that initially sought a position of dominance could find itself in the weaker position at the war's end. It will then have to pay in territory and other values.[9] In a situation where the states are in approximately equal bargaining positions, the territorial element is still important in the political settlement, as are guarantees of security. The parties might return to the *status quo ante*,[10] or there may be some trade-offs in values, including territories.[11]

In a war for dominance through the acquisition of resources, territory will also loom large when, as in most cases, the resources are on or under the earth. The stronger state might, however, demand deliveries of the resource rather than the occupation of territory because the costs of occupation or acquisition of territory would outweigh the risks involved

6 Russia in the Austro-Russian War against Turkey of 1787–92 (pp. 163–5) ; Britain after the Seven Years' War (pp. 374–9) ; Chile after the War of the Pacific (pp. 171–3) .

7 In the Opium War (pp. 64–6) , Britain secured trading enclaves in Chinese cities and recognition of her trading rights in China. In the War of the Austrian Succession (pp. 366–74) , Britain obtained formal rights to engage in the slave trade.

8 The Powers secured territory and a guarantee of the eternal separation of the Crowns of Spain and France in the War of the Spanish Succession (pp. 357–66) .

9 Russia in the Levant at the settlement of the Crimean War (pp. 165–9) ; Spain during the Dutch Revolt (pp. 208–14) ; the Emperor after the Thirty Years' War (pp. 379–92) ; and France after the War of the Spanish Succession (pp. 357–66) .

10 Last War of the Habsburg-Valois Rivalry (pp. 157–60) ; for Britain and the United Provinces in the Franco-Dutch War of 1672–79 and the European War of 1683–1700 (pp. 340–57) ; and for Austria and Turkey in the Austro-Russian War against Turkey of 1787–92 (pp. 163–5).

11 Great Britain and the United Provinces in the Second Anglo-Dutch War of 1664–67 (pp. 160–3) ; Britain and France in the War of American Independence (pp. 217–22) .

in relying upon a promise for future deliveries of the resource.[12] If the settlement does require delivery of resources, the quantities required will depend upon how effective the weaker party is in resisting the demands of the stronger.

Finally, in settling a war for dominance in which one state sought (short of outright annexation) to control or influence the policies of another state, the moving state might seek territory, the right to intervene militarily, the right to construct bases, perhaps even some form of veto or other means for influencing legislation, or commercial arrangements favorable to its nationals.[13] In a position short of victory, the stronger state might receive some of these rights in more or less limited form. A state that had not been defeated would probably not grant such important concessions as the right to intervene, to veto or control legislation, or to construct bases.[14] In a very weak bargaining position, it would probably cede some territory and agree to the delivery of resources and the payment of an indemnity. Insistence by the stronger on a right to intervene politically or militarily will, in certain situations, result in the renewal of hostilities.[15]

War to Preserve the Status Quo

The war to preserve the status quo is the complement of the war for dominance. One state seeks dominance, and the other seeks to preserve the status quo, either to defend itself or to maintain its own position relative to the adversary or third states. A successful defensive war may subsequently evolve into a war for dominance by the state that originally sought to preserve the status quo.[16]

12 This element in the German policy relative to Russia in 1918 led to the arrangement for the Ukraine in the Treaties of Brest-Litovsk. (See the First World War, pp. 405–28.)

13 France obtained a Protectorate over Tunisia in the Franco-Tunisian War (pp. 71–2); Russia secured bases from Finland in the Russo-Finnish War (pp. 79–81); and Britain and other powers obtained extraterritorial rights in China: see the Opium War (pp. 64–6) and the Boxer Rebellion (pp. 175–7).

14 See the cases of Turkey after the First World War (pp. 405–28), and France after the Franco-Prussian War (pp. 68–70). In the wars between Russia and Turkey in the nineteenth century, the great powers were able to prevent excessive Russian influence upon the Porte and the partitioning of the Ottoman Empire.

15 The Tory demands for intervention rights in Spain and France prolonged the War of the Spanish Succession (pp. 357–66). Sweden and France claimed the right to intervene in the Holy Roman Empire on behalf of "German Liberties." This prolonged the Thirty Years' War (pp. 379–92).

16 This happened in the Austro-Turkish conflict of the European War of 1683–1700 (pp. 347–57).

In the case of a defensive war, a successful defense means the denial of territory to the attacker. At the peace talks, the successful defender may simply demand an indemnity and guarantees of security;[17] or it may demand the cession of territory from the state that attempted to alter the status quo, as a form of territorial insurance for its future security.[18] If the costs of the war have been high or the defender has carried the war to the initiating state, a demand for territory would almost certainly be made, particularly if, at the time of the cease-fire, the defender retains possession of some territory. As in the case of the war for dominance, an approximately balanced bargaining position could lead to the trade-off of territories with other values.[19]

The state that was successful in a war to maintain its position relative to an aggressive state will seek guarantees of its security and at least implicit assurance that the latter will not again attempt to alter the status quo.[20] If the defender's bargaining position were very strong, it might be able to impose penalties which would prevent the aggressive state from again mustering the capabilities for waging another war for dominance.[21] In the event that both states were in about the same bargaining position, the adversaries might have to content themselves merely with promises to settle their differences by peaceful means.[22] The state intent upon altering the status quo could hope that with the passage of time its disabilities would be cured and it would be able to resume hostilities against the defending state.

War to Consolidate the State

The territorial element figures large in the settlement of a war to consolidate the state. If the state that seeks to consolidate itself is victorious, then it will be awarded the territory for which it fought.[23] If it

17 The Powers demanded both of France in the Second Peace of Paris (Napoleonic Wars, pp. 392–405). Compare the policy of the Emperor of Abyssinia after the Italo-Abyssinian War (pp. 72–3).

18 Holland obtained "The Barrier" in the War of the Spanish Succession (pp. 357–66).

19 See the Franco-Dutch War of 1672–79 (pp. 340–7).

20 The Great Powers obtained such assurances from Russia during the Greek Revolt (pp. 222–5) and the Crimean War (pp. 165–9).

21 The Allies penalized Germany in the settlement of the First World War (pp. 405–28), in part, to prevent future "aggression." Compare the Second Peace of Paris, a part of the settlement of the Napoleonic Wars (pp. 392–405).

22 True of Russia and Turkey after the European War of 1683–1700 (pp. 347–57); and France and Austria guaranteed the peace established to end the War of the Polish Succession (pp. 214–7).

23 U.S. in the Mexican-American War (pp. 66–8); Prussia in the War of the Austrian Succession (pp. 366–74); and Russia in the Russo-Turkish War of

loses, it may find itself resisting the territorial demands of the adversary.[24] A state that opposes the aspirations of another state to consolidate may decide to acquiesce in some demands even if it is in a favorable bargaining position at the peace conference, if it finds that the cost of retaining certain territories might be too high.[25] Thus, for example, state A might seek to annex that portion of the territory of state B containing persons of A nationality. Although B might successfully resist such a war aim on the part of A, the policymakers of B might then decide to permit a plebiscite in portions of the territory in dispute, create a free territory, or cede the territory to A outright: the presence of aroused A nationals within B's polity could constitute a serious threat to its internal security. Having reached this decision, however, the policymakers of state B would very likely seek a *quid pro quo* at the peace talks in the form of concessions of other values from state A.[26]

Ideological War

In an ideological war, a state seeks by means of force to impose its ideology upon an adversary state. Often, the latter's response just prior to the outbreak of hostilities and its policies during the war are also conditioned by an ideology, as the aggressive ideology of one party often gives rise to a counter-ideology on the part of another.[27] A war of this sort has momentous domestic consequences for each belligerent and usually entails large-scale re-education of the people, suppression of organizations sympathetic to the opposing ideology, censorship, or formalized official propaganda. But even the most pragmatic state will take measures similar to those of the ideologized state in order to prevent possible adverse effects of the alien ideology upon its war effort.

The state against whom an ideological war is waged may regard it as a war for dominance.[28] The peace settlement could then take on the

---

1768–74 (pp. 61–2). Poland obtained territory and an indemnity from Russia after the Russo-Polish War (pp. 73–6).

24 Denmark, in the Second War over Schleswig-Holstein (pp. 169–71), had to surrender up the Duchies.

25 That was certainly true for Prussia in respect of France in the Franco-Prussian War (pp. 68–70).

26 The Chaco War (pp. 76–9) provides an instance of this.

27 Examples are the French response to Spanish intervention in the War of the Three Henries (1585–98) and, generally, the wars of the Reformation and Counter-Reformation. One might also recall the evolution of anti-communist ideology in the U.S. in the 1940s and 1950s.

28 French leaders embarked upon an ideological war after 1792, but the other European Powers regarded it as an attempt to establish a French Imperium (pp. 392–405). In the Thirty Years' War (pp. 379–92), the motives of Fer-

character of the settlement of a war for dominance. But ideologies are not restricted to specific territories, nor will territorial guarantees prevent their spread. The peace negotiators will therefore attempt to promote or inhibit, extol or discredit, the ideology and its principles, insofar as possible.[29]

Victory in an ideological war will mean at least a change in the official propaganda of the defeated state and perhaps also a change in its ideology, even the conversion of its people to a new ideology. If the state that waged the ideological war is defeated, and the adversary decides not to carry the war into the territory of the defeated state, territorial questions may not assume importance, but the ideological issues certainly will. The consequences of the original attempt, however abortive, by the defeated state to spread the ideology would have to be faced at the peace talks. Thus we would expect to see provisions in the peace treaty designed to limit the effects of the alien ideology.[30] In addition to the usual guarantees of security, organizations that proselytize the ideology would undoubtedly be forbidden to exist.[31] There might be an attempt to include provisions for censoring newspapers, magazines, radio broadcasts, and political pamphlets. If the ideologically aggressive state had not been defeated but was merely in the weaker bargaining position, the stronger state might seek promises from the other state's leaders that they would refrain from directing their propaganda against it and would take steps to reduce the intensity of the ideological war.[32] The content of the treaty provisions will depend, as we have said, upon the relative bargaining strengths of the belligerents. When they are approximately equal, we would expect to see efforts by each state's leaders to check the influence of the alien ideology within their own polities to see to it that their citizens were minimally influenced.

Peace settlements of ideological wars are often unsatisfactory. First, it is more difficult to prevent the spread of ideas than to stop armies; and second, as the ideological threshold will of necessity be high in an ideological war, peace will barely be possible and will be tenuous at

---

dinand II were, in part, ideological, as were those of his adversaries, although the latter suspected that ideology cloaked his designs to become dominant in Central Europe.

29 This was attempted after the Thirty Years' War (pp. 379–92) and the Napoleonic Wars (pp. 392–405) .

30 The Allies, in effect, treated "German militarism" as an "alien ideology" in the First World War (pp. 405–28) . The Versailles Treaty's extensive demilitarization clauses could then be regarded as measures designed to destroy that ideology.

31 The de-nazification program for Germany after the Second World War is an example.

32 See the settlement of the Russo-Polish War (pp. 73–6)

best.[33] If *both* states have ideologized the war, settlement will be especially difficult, and domestic efforts to prevent further spread of the alien ideology more stringent. In such a case it is doubtful whether more than a cease-fire be agreed upon.[34] Emotions may run too high for the negotiators even to attempt a political settlement. Realizing the inadequacy of the peace settlement for the prevention of the spread of the ideology, the state's policymakers will more readily resume hostilities in order to insure their ideological integrity.[35]

War for Retribution

In a war for retribution, the state initiating the war seeks to punish the state that provoked it. If the initiating state were to win the war, the peace settlement would probably penalize the provoking state in some way[36] and in addition would extract security guarantees (and cause the provocation to be removed). Generally, the character of the settlement depends on the nature of the original provocation. If persecution of the nationals of the initiating state were at issue, the victor might seek both guarantees and perhaps legislation to prevent reoccurrences, together with compensation for its affected nationals.[37] If the troops of the provoking state had invaded the territory of the initiating state, creation of a buffer zone through the acquisition of territory by the victor or demilitarization of the provoking state's frontiers would probably effect an adequate solution.[38]

A state may stage a provocation to elicit an aggressive response as a pretext for waging an ideological war or a war for dominance. In such a case, the initiating state's aim is still retribution. The only difference is that the provoking state expects, indeed hopes for, the adversary to respond with force and may be better prepared for war and therefore

33 Examples include the Franco-Prussian War (pp. 68–70), the Laotian Civil War (pp. 236–40), the Huguenot Wars, and the settlement of the First World War (pp. 405–28).

34 See the Korean War (pp. 233–6). Religious principles forbade the Sultan to conclude anything more than a cease-fire with the Christian infidel before 1700.

35 Chaco War (pp. 76–9), the Huguenot Wars, and the Indochina settlements of 1954.

36 Austria penalized Turkey at the end of the European War of 1683–1700 (pp. 347–57).

37 Compare the settlement for the Boxer Rebellion (pp. 175–7).

38 Compare the Korean War (pp. 233–6) and the 1918–19 war between Hungary and Roumania (the First World War: pp. 405–28). The mere existence of the Kaunitz coalition provoked Prussia in the Seven Years' War (pp. 374–9). The confirmation of the cession of Silesia provided the solution.

more likely to win.[39] The loss of a war for retribution by the initiating state could lead to the loss of territory or other values.[40] And when the belligerents have approximately equal bargaining strength, the state that had been provoked would still undoubtedly endeavor to prevent the reoccurrence of the provocation through appropriate terms in the peace treaty.[41]

War of Opportunity

As defined, the war of opportunity is one in which a state seeks to secure very specific, limited values by going to war, in the expectation of achieving its aims without significant losses. Presumably, if it seeks to secure the territory or resources of a weakened or weaker state, it would not have gone to war unless its policymakers were fairly sure they could secure these items at low cost. The peace settlement, in the case of a successfully opportunistic state, would provide for the transfer of the property to the victor.[42] If the predictions of its policymakers turn out to be incorrect, the opportunistic state may be willing to accept a settlement that merely cut its losses.[43] Or if the opportunistic state were placed in a poor bargaining position by defeats on the battlefield, it might find itself giving up its own territory or resources, providing guarantees for the other state, and paying an indemnity as well.

A state may declare war on another simply to put itself formally in a state of war and thus be eligible for an invitation to the peace conference.[44] It may hope to secure values there without committing troops

39 Hitler staged the attack upon the Gleiwitz transmitter (by German soldiers dressed in Polish uniforms) to provide himself with a pretext and justification for attacking Poland in 1939.

40 Münster in the Second Anglo-Dutch War of 1664–7 (pp. 160–3) ; China in the Boxer Rebellion (pp. 175–7) ; and France in the Franco-Prussian War (pp. 68–70) .

41 The guarantees secured by the Powers from Russia in the settlement of the Crimean War (pp. 165–9) were of this sort, as were those of the Korean War (pp. 233–6) . In the War of 1812 (pp. 63–4) , however, the question of the impressment of American seamen by the British was not resolved: it had been one of the matters that had provoked the U.S.

42 Territory was secured by Savoy in the War of the Spanish Succession (pp. 357–66) , Prussia in the Second War over Schleswig-Holstein (pp. 169–71) , Russia during the Greek Revolt (pp. 222–5) , and Austria in the Austro-Russian War against Turkey of 1787–92 (pp. 163–5) .

43 True of Cologne and Münster in the Franco-Dutch War of 1672–79 (pp. 340–7) , Sweden in the Seven Years' War (pp. 374–9) , and Prussia during the Napoleonic Wars (pp. 392–405) .

44 Certain states of Latin America did this during both the First and Second World Wars, as did Sardinia in the Crimean War (pp. 165–9) .

to any campaigns. Although it might secure the aim to which it aspired, other states would be loath to concede too much to a state that had not made sacrifices in the war effort. Correspondingly, if the state that had put itself formally at war with another found itself on the losing side, the victor would probably not demand so much from it as from those that had carried the burden of the war effort and caused most of the victor's losses. On the other hand, the victor might be vindictive against all enemies, formal or otherwise; and the state that went to war for purely formal reasons might lose as much as the more active belligerents.

Summaries of Settlements of Some Simple External Wars

The wars summarized below constitute a representative sample of some simple external wars in the modern era.

RUSSO-TURKISH WAR (1768–1774)

PARTIES' WAR AIMS: Russia's aim was to secure warm-water ports on the Black Sea littoral and further consolidate the Russian Empire. Turkey's fear of Russian expansion led the Porte to declare war to maintain the status quo.

OUTCOME: After military victories late in the war, Russia secured most of her objectives.

WAR-ORIENTED STATES: France, Britain, and especially Prussia and Austria wanted to maintain a balance of power and thus prevent the partitioning of the Ottoman Empire. Austria and Prussia sought—and later obtained—part of Poland after the Russians suppressed the Polish Rebellion. Sweden was also war-oriented.

FACTORS TENDING TO PROMOTE PEACE: For Turkey, it was the defeat of her forces and the prospect of losses of territory; for Russia, it was the costs of the war, the Pugachev Rebellion, fear of war with Austria and Prussia, the Polish problem, and the prospect of competition and war from a recently revived Sweden.

THE SETTLEMENT: PRELIMINARIES: Negotiations in 1772 broke down because of excessive Russian territorial demands in the Crimea. Those of late 1772 and early 1773 also failed because of Russian demands respecting the Black Sea and the Straits. Successful campaigns in the spring of 1774 induced the Porte to ask for peace talks. These culminated in the Treaty of Kutchuk Kainarji, signed on 10 July 1774.[45]

MILITARY SETTLEMENT: A cease-fire was to be effective on the date of the signature of the treaty. The parties agreed not to take the offensive if

45 Martens, G. F. von, *Recueil de Traités,* Vol. 2 (Göttingen, Librarie Dieterich, 1817), pp. 287–322. The reader is referred to the bibliography for additional works relating to the peace settlements summarized in this section. These supplement the documents and studies cited in the footnotes.

hostilities were to break out after signature; and if the war did resume, any gains resulting therefrom would be nullified, and restitution made. The parties retained the right to construct forts anywhere within their territories. The fortress at the mouth of the Dnieper was given to Russia; but the Russians were to evacuate Moldavia, Wallachia, Bessarabia, Bulgaria, and Georgia on dates and according to procedures specified in the Treaty.

POLITICAL SETTLEMENT:[46] Russia was ceded territory on the Black Sea between the Bug and the Dnieper, the districts of Kertsh and Jenicale together with their fortresses, and the northern coast of the Sea of Azov. Turkey recognized the independence of the peoples of the Kuban, the Crimea, and other areas (although the Porte was given the right to invest the Khan of Crimea). Turkey also guaranteed free passage of Russian pilgrims to Jerusalem. Russia was given the right to navigate freely on the Black Sea and in the Straits and was to be permitted to build an Orthodox Church in Constantinople. She understook to protect Christians in the Ottoman Empire and to make representations to the Porte on their behalf.

There was to be an amnesty for all political prisoners; and the civil and religious rights of persons in Bessarabia, Moldavia, and Wallachia were to be observed by the Porte. The rights of merchants were specified and recognized by the Porte. Provision was also made for the release of prisoners of war and slaves.

There were no security guarantee provisions except a general and vague promise to the effect that the parties would not entertain inimical designs toward each other. (Of course, the forts and territories acquired by Russia provided her with certain guarantees against her adversary.)

All prior treaties were abolished. Russia was to send a minister to Constantinople; and Russian consulates were to be established in major Ottoman ports. Turkey was also to help Russsia establish commercial relations with Algiers, Tunis, and Tripoli.

The parties agreed to consult about frontier disputes, through either appointed commissioners or accredited ministers. Otherwise the Treaty was silent on the question of adjusting disputes.

By secret treaty, the Porte agreed to pay an indemnity to Russia.

COMMENTS: The settlement of *Kutchuk Kainarji* opened the "Eastern Question," a series of recurrent crises grounded on the fear of the consequences of the dissolution of the Ottoman Empire for the balance of power in Europe and in the Levant. This Levantine problem was to remain the concern of the Great Powers until 1923.

46 In the short descriptions of the political settlements of this and other wars analyzed in this book, I have tried to adhere to one general outline, taking up the elements of settlement in this order: territory, persons affected by the war, security guarantees, resumption of relations, adjustment of disputes, and penalties.

THE WAR OF 1812 (1812–1814) United States vs. Great Britain

PARTIES' WAR AIMS: Britain sought supremacy on the seas and the preservation of the economic and juridical integrity of its North American possessions. The U.S. fought in defense of its neutrality and its trading rights, for consolidation through westward expansion, and in defense of the concept of American (as distinct from British) nationality.

OUTCOME: The outcome was ambiguous with no clear victory for either belligerent. Peace came with the ratification of the Treaty of Ghent, signed on 24 December 1814.[47]

WAR-ORIENTED STATES: Russia, whose offer of mediation was declined by Britain, was a war-oriented state, as were other European states, preoccupied with the final stages of the Napoleonic Wars of which this war was an outgrowth.

FACTORS FOR PEACE: For the U.S., the costs of the war were high. There were defeats and unsuccessful military operations against Canada, and Washington had been burned. Britain wanted to wind up the war in America along with the European wars in order to enjoy a period of recovery and peace. The threat of renewed hostilities on the continent persuaded the British to give up their demands for control of the Great Lakes and an Indian state in the Ohio region. This concession was also induced by American victories near Baltimore, at Plattsburg, Fort Erie, and on Lake Champlain that adversely affected the British bargaining position at the Congress of Vienna.

THE SETTLEMENT: PRELIMINARIES: Negotiations began in August, 1814, after an offer by the British Foreign Minister, Castlereagh, for direct negotiations. The American commissioners arrived in early 1814, but had to wait until August before negotiations began. Resolution of agenda questions took over a month.

MILITARY SETTLEMENT: A cease-fire was to come with ratification of the Treaty. Vessels seized after a 12-day period of grace in North American waters were to be restored. There were similar provisions for other areas of the high seas, but with different periods of grace. The parties were to end hostilities with the Indians and restore to them the privileges to which they had been entitled in 1811. The Treaty said nothing about the impressment of seamen, which had been one of the issues leading to war. Prisoners of war were to be returned after they paid the debts they had incurred in captivity. The prisoners' own states were to pay for their maintenance.

POLITICAL SETTLEMENT: All territories were to be restored to the party that had exercised prewar sovereignty over them. In other words, there was to be a return to the *status quo ante bellum*—with certain minor

47 Hertslet, Lewis, *A Complete Collection of the Treaties and Conventions . . . between Great Britain and Foreign Powers*, Vol. 1 (London, Henry Butterworth, 1827), pp. 378 f.

exceptions. Property in the restored territories was to be left intact, and archives and records were to be returned. Boundary commissions were set up to mark and run the boundaries between the U.S. and Canada from Nova Scotia to the Lake of the Woods. The question of Britain's right to navigate the Mississippi River had arisen in the negotiations, but was not resolved.

Both parties agreed to seek the abolition of slavery. Persons whose rights were affected by the decisions of the boundary commissions were protected in specified ways.

Nothing was said about the resumption of relations between the parties, although it was understood that negotiations to that end would continue. They did, in fact, eventuate in a Convention of Commerce, dated 3 July 1815, establishing commercial relations between the countries on a free-trade, most favored nation basis. In the Treaty of Ghent, nothing was said about neutral rights, Britain tacitly reserving the right to seize vessels on the high seas in war time. The controversy over fisheries was substantially resolved by a convention in 1818.[48]

No guarantees of security were exchanged. There were, moreover, no provisions for the settlement of future disputes, except that procedures in the event of disagreement between the commissioners of the boundary commissions wre outlined. No penalties were exacted.

COMMENTS: The settlement eventually opened the West to American expansion, in part because of Britain's concession early in the negotiations not to demand an Indian state in Ohio. The Treaty was quite short; and many of what we have called the "elements of a settlement" were omitted, as the parties realized that negotiations must continue after ratification, when other questions could then hopefully be resolved.

THE OPIUM WAR or THE ANGLO-CHINESE WAR of 1841–1842

PARTIES' WAR AIMS: Britain sought to promote her commercial dominance in the East by opening up China to trade and by a revision of the commercial and juridical bases of trade with China. China, on the other hand, sought to defend her internal sovereignty and maintain the status quo in her relations with other states.

OUTCOME: Chinese forces were defeated on land and sea. The Treaty of Nanking, signed on 29 August 1842, ended the war.[49]

FACTORS FOR PEACE: For China, defeat; for Britain, the achievement of limited objectives by military and ultimately diplomatic means.

THE SETTLEMENT: PRELIMINARIES: After much debate, the Emperor sent

48 *Ibid.,* pp. 386 f.

49 Bernhardt, Gaston de, *Handbook of Treaties relating to Commerce and Navigation between Great Britain and Foreign Powers* (London: His Majesty's Stationery Office, 1912) , pp. 83–87.

the Viceroy of Chihli to Canton to negotiate peace. When he agreed to the hard British terms (particularly the cession of Hong Kong), the Chinese emissary was recalled and condemned to death. (He was later reprieved.) The war was renewed; and the British took Amoy, Ningpo, and Nanking, after which the Chinese again agreed to negotiate.

MILITARY SETTLEMENT: The Treaty declared that the parties would deal with each other on the basis of peace and friendship. Withdrawal of British troops from Nanking and the Grand Canal was to take place when the Chinese paid the first installment of the indemnity. Certain islands would be held by the British until the "treaty ports" were opened to trade. It was a measure of Chinese weakness that the military provisions of the Treaty were so sketchy and left so much to the discretion of British military commanders.

POLITICAL SETTLEMENT: Hong Kong was ceded to Britain in perpetuity. British subjects were permitted to reside and trade in Canton, Amoy, Foochow, Ningpo, and Shanghai; and a British superintendent was appointed for each port to deal with the Chinese government on all matters pertaining to commerce. China agreed to abolish the practice of licensing certain (Hong) merchants to deal exclusively with the British: Chinese merchants would henceforth be free to deal with whomsoever they pleased. China would also establish a fair and regular tariff for foreign trade at all ports and for the movement of goods inland.

The subjects of each party were to enjoy full protection for their persons and property in the dominions of the other party. China also agreed to the unconditional release of all British subjects and to an amnesty for all Chinese who had been imprisoned for dealing with or serving the British. By supplementary agreement, Britain was given the right to try, under British law, all its subjects accused of having committed a crime on Chinese territory.

Article II of the Peace Treaty established in very general terms the procedural basis for future diplomatic relations between the countries. There were no provisions for the adjustment of disputes or for security guarantees.

The Emperor was to pay $6 million for the opium of British subjects delivered up as ransom to the Chinese in 1839, $3 million for debts owed British subjects by Hong merchants, and $12 million to defray the costs of the British military expedition to China. Dates of payments were specified.

COMMENTS: France and the United States were war-oriented in the sense that they were eager to extract roughly similar commercial concessions from the Chinese. Normal relations with China (as the West conceived of them) were still impossible, travel by foreigners within the interior of China was forbidden, and diplomatic relations were to be handled principally by a commissioner in Canton. Hence, contact with the capital was minimal and often nonexistent. The Treaty was silent on ways to normalize diplomatic relations after the war.

THE MEXICAN-AMERICAN WAR (1845–1848)

PARTIES' WAR AIMS: The United States wanted dominance on the continent, consolidation of the state, and fulfillment of its "manifest destiny." The Mexicans fought in defense of Greater Mexico and because they resented the U.S. annexation of Texas.

OUTCOME: Mexico capitulated and was required to cede about 40 per cent of her territory to the U.S. (including the present southwestern states and California).

FACTORS FOR PEACE: For Mexico, defeat; for the U.S., the prospect of satisfying its goals through negotiations after military victories.

THE SETTLEMENT: PRELIMINARIES: After the landing of a U.S. force at Vera Cruz and the rout of the Mexican Army in 1847, armistice negotiations were begun. But these collapsed after two weeks because the Mexican government could not bring itself to accept the American demands. U.S. forces entered Mexico City in September, and negotiations were started once again.

MILITARY SETTLEMENT: *The Treaty of Guadelupe Hidalgo,* signed on 2 February 1848, proclaimed that there would be peace between the parties.[50] After the signature of the Treaty, a convention for a provisional suspension of hostilities was to be negotiated between a delegate of the U.S. General-in-Chief and one appointed by the Mexican government. As the circumstances permitted, constitutional order would be re-established "as regards the political, administrative, and judicial branches." U.S. forces would be ordered not to destroy weapons, forts, or public property in Mexico.

Subsequent to the exchange of ratifications (completed by 4 July 1848), the U.S. was to order the end of the blockade, the evacuation of U.S. troops from the interior to the coasts (with the assistance and facilities of the Mexican government), and the restoration of forts and certain territories to Mexico. Evacuation of Mexico City was to be completed within one month after the order therefor. The U.S. would then hand over customs houses to the Mexican government, render an account of all duties collected, and pay Mexico the sum of customs receipts (less expenses) within three months. Prisoners were to be returned as soon as practicable after the exchange of ratifications. Final evacuation of the Mexican coastal areas was to be completed within three months; but if this was not possible and the troops had to remain during the "sickly

50 Malloy, W. M., *Conventions, International Acts, Protocols and Agreements between the U.S.A. and other Powers, 1776–1909;* Vol. 1 (Washington, D.C.: U.S. Government Printing Office, 1910), pp. 1107–1121.

season," Mexico was to provide billets for them. Supplies and provisions for the U.S. forces were to be allowed to enter Mexico duty-free. The U.S. would take steps to prevent smuggling. The right of the parties to fortify any point on their territory was also recognized.

If war were to break out between the parties at any time after signature of the Treaty, certain rules were to be observed: merchants were to be permitted to remain unmolested on the adversary's territory for 12 months. If the troops of one country invaded the other, women, children, clergy, scholars, farmers, artisans, merchants, fishermen, and all persons whose "occupations are for the subsistence and benefit of mankind," were to be unmolested. Property rights would be respected, and if confiscations were necessary, payments would be made. The Treaty also contained rather detailed rules for the care of prisoners of war, and it declared that a state of war between the parties would not nullify the effect of these provisions.

POLITICAL SETTLEMENT: A boundary between Mexico and the U.S. was defined, and a commission was established to mark and run it from San Diego to the mouth of the Rio Grande. The U.S. was to pay $15 million for the cession of territory north of the boundary.

United States vessels had the right of free passage in the Gulf of California, and vessels of both countries were permitted to navigate the Rio Grande.

Mexican citizens in the U.S. (and in territories ceded to the U.S.) were to be secure in their lives and property. They could emigrate with their property without hindrance. If they chose to reside in the U.S., they must elect U.S. citizenship within one year from the exchange of ratifications. The U.S. would assume the obligation to pay claims of Americans against the Mexican government. A commission was established to examine such claims, and Mexico agreed to cooperate by providing the necessary records and documents. (Articles concerning Indian problems were included, but were abrogated in 1853.)

The Treaty of Friendship and Commerce of 5 April 1831 was revived for 8 years. The only provision for guarantees was a single sentence: that each party would respect the boundary defined by the boundary commission, and change it only by mutual consent. There were no penalty provisions.

The parties agreed to negotiate their differences in the future and to seek mediation of a "friendly nation" if necessary. If, in a dispute, either party proposed negotiations or mediation, the other must accede "unless deemed by it altogether incompatible with the nature of their difference, or the circumstance of the case."

COMMENTS: The exception to the provision for peacefully settling future disputes would have permitted the use of force because of its very breadth. But most such provisions have had implicit reservations of this kind, until the advent of the Kellogg-Briand Pact and the U.N. Charter, whose signatories renounced the use of force in their relations with other states. Even in these cases, however, the practices of states since 1945 show that recourse has been had to force all too frequently.

FRANCO-PRUSSIAN WAR (1870–1871)

WAR AIMS: France wanted to punish Prussia for insults to French honor, to maintain the dominance of France relative to the German states, and to maintain the status quo relative to Prussia. Prussia sought to consolidate the German states into a single German Empire under a Prussian King-Emperor, with Prussian supremacy in Germany. Prussia also sought to punish France and reduce her ability to threaten Germany.

OUTCOME: The French armies were defeated, and France capitulated to the German Empire (proclaimed on 18 January 1871). The (Second) French Empire collapsed and a new Republic was proclaimed in September, 1870. The establishment of the Paris Commune was contemporaneous with negotiations for the Treaty of Peace of Frankfort, signed on 10 May 1871.[51] The Commune was suppressed in May, 1871.

FACTORS FOR PEACE: For France, the realization that foreign assistance would not be forthcoming and the desire of many Frenchmen for political stability after the collapse of the Empire; for Prussia: victory that would bring with it satisfaction of war aims and substantial reimbursement for the costs of the war and fear of foreign intervention if the war were prolonged or if Prussia demanded the permanent occupation or control of France.

WAR-ORIENTED STATES: Britain, Russia, Austria, and Italy were preoccupied with other matters but interested in the outcome of the war.

THE SETTLEMENT: PRELIMINARIES: The Imperialist Emigrés, including the Empress Eugénie and the Emperor himself, proposed to negotiate peace in the winter of 1870–1871. General Trochu, head of the government of National Defense, asked for an armistice on 20 January 1871, but Bismarck refused. Favre, delegate of the Government, negotiated the general plan of an armistice and peace settlement, the most important element of which was French agreement to hold general elections for a National Assembly to resolve the question of peace. These elections were held in February and demonstrated the desire of the French people to end the war and to re-establish order within the country.

MILITARY SETTLEMENT: It is important to note the formal framework of the settlement. It comprised an Armistice, signed at Versailles, on 28 January 1871;[52] the Preliminaries of Peace, dated 26 February 1871;[53]

51 Martens, *Nouveau Recueil Général de Traités*, Vol. 19 (Göttingen: Librairie de Dieterich, 1874), pp. 688 f.
52 *Ibid.*, pp. 626 f.
53 *Ibid.*, pp. 653 f, 667 f.

the Treaty of Peace, signed at Frankfort, 10 May;[54] and the shorter, technical and supplementary agreements negotiated between April and December, 1871.[55] A Franco-German conference to consider the manifold problems arising out of the execution of the peace agreements met from July to December, 1871.

A cease-fire was set for Paris for the date on which the Armistice was signed and for other parts of France on slightly later dates. A demarcation line between French and German forces was defined, and a buffer zone of 10 kilometers on each side of that line was established. The military commanders were to administer the areas they occupied. Provision was also made for a naval cease-fire and the restoration of vessels seized thereafter. The siege of Belfort and operations in other specified areas of France were to continue. The purpose of the armistice was declared to be that of permitting the French to elect a National Assembly to determine whether the war was to be ended. The German army would assist in the elections. Special provisions were negotiated for the garrisoning of the Paris forts by the Germans, who were not to enter Paris during the term of the Armistice agreements. The French Army was to disarm and *Francs-Tireurs* were to be dissolved, but the French National Guard was to remain armed in order to maintain order in Paris. The German Army would assist in provisioning Paris as soon as the ring of outer forts had been turned over to the Germans. Movement of persons through the demarcation lines was prohibited except with the permission of the military commanders. The French would begin to release German prisoners. Additional technical conventions were subsequently negotiated (relating to the evacuation of the wounded, telegraphic and postal services, and the like).

In the Preliminaries of Peace (26 February), it was declared that German evacuation from Paris would begin immediately after the ratification of that agreement by the National Assembly, which had been elected in early February and had assembled at Bordeaux. The French government had the duty to feed all occupation troops, but the Germans were to make no requisitions. Prisoner exchange would proceed, and the administration of French territories held by the German Army was to be handed over to the French government after ratification. In the final Treaty of Peace, many of these provisions were repeated with the additional promise by France not to concentrate troops on the right bank of the Loire.

POLITICAL SETTLEMENT: In the Preliminaries of Peace, France renounced in perpetuity all right and title to Alsace and Lorraine, ceding them to the German Empire. The bounds of the cession were set out; and

54 *Ibid.,* pp. 688 f.
55 *Ibid.,* Vol. 20, pp. 781 f, 799 f, 847 ff.

a commission was established to run the new boundary. The Treaty of Frankfort modified this grant slightly and also provided for equal rights of navigation on the Moselle and certain canals in France and Germany.

The civil rights of inhabitants of the Alsace-Lorraine were to be regulated on as favorable a basis as possible when peace was restored. There were to be no obstacles to emigration. Nationality provisions were included in the final Treaty of Peace, as well as a guarantee that no persons were to be prosecuted for wartime activities that had favored either of the former enemies. These matters were further elaborated in the postwar period. Rights of nationals were guaranteed.

Treaties of commerce between France and the individual states that now made up the German Empire were declared to be void. The parties would negotiate a new treaty of commerce on a most favored nation basis. A commercial treaty for the Alsace-Lorraine was concluded shortly after the peace settlement, when other technical conventions were also negotiated to normalize the relations of the parties as they pertained to economic and juridical relations in and for the Alsace-Lorraine. In addition, religious connections of that territory to France were severed. Apart from the provisions concerning the transferred provinces and the "promise" to negotiate a commercial treaty sometime in the future, there were no important terms for the normalization of Franco-German relations.

Beyond the provisions described above, there was no exchange of guarantees, although the disarming of the French troops was certainly a guarantee for Germany, as was the occupation, which lasted in parts of France until 1873. There were no terms for the resolution of future disputes.

A 5-billion-franc indemnity was imposed on France, payable in installments. Progressive and gradual evacuation of German troops was scheduled to coincide with each installment. The payment of this huge indemnity was completed 2 years ahead of schedule (September, 1873), and the last of the German troops were then evacuated.

COMMENTS: The approximately two dozen agreements that comprised the settlement of the Franco-Prussian War were exceptionally detailed in all respects. The paucity of provisions for guarantees can be attributed to the superior military strength of Germany, then needing no guarantees from a weakened France, the latter being too weak to obtain guarantees from Germany. The bitterness of feeling between the peoples of the antagonists and the humiliation of the French no doubt prevented the parties' negotiating provisions for settling future differences or adopting terms for normalizing their relations on a basis of friendship and cooperation.

THE ASHANTI WAR (1873–1874) Great Britain vs. the Ashantis

PARTIES' WAR AIMS: Britain sought to obtain control of the Guinea Coast. The Ashanti sought both to obtain tribute from tribes in the area and to preserve local supremacy over them. They also sought gains through their attacks on British merchants, whenever the opportunity presented itself.

OUTCOME: The Ashanti were defeated, and their capital of Kumasi destroyed. (Britain did not formally annex Ashanti until 1902.)

FACTORS FOR PEACE: For the Ashanti, their defeat; for the British the ability to achieve their aims without further hostilities.

THE SETTLEMENT: PRELIMINARIES: The British Commander seized Kumasi and offered terms to the King, who accepted them.

MILITARY SETTLEMENT: A state of perpetual peace was proclaimed, and the King of the Ashanti was to withdraw his troops from the coast.[56]

POLITICAL SETTLEMENT: The King renounced all rights over tribes on the coast, in effect dissolving the Ashanti Confederation. He agreed to keep a key road open in order to encourage commerce between the British and the tribes of the area. The King also recognized the right of the British to trade freely with the Ashanti.

The subjects of the King and those of Queen Victoria were proclaimed to be friends. The King agreed to check the practice of human sacrifice and to pay an indemnity to the Queen for the expense "he has occasioned Her Majesty by the late war."

COMMENTS: The simplicity of the peace settlement was commensurate with the limited objectives of the British and in keeping with their conception of the primitiveness of their adversary.

THE FRANCO-TUNISIAN WAR (1881)

PARTIES' WAR AIMS: France's aim was to expand her empire, dominate North Africa, and defend Algeria against bandits. Tunisia's aim was her own defense.

OUTCOME: French military successes compelled the Bey of Tunis to accept a protectorate status for Tunisia.

WAR-ORIENTED STATES: Italy, which had aspirations of her own in the Maghreb, and Spain, with interests in neighboring Morocco, were war-oriented.

FACTORS FOR PEACE: For Tunisia, occupation of their country by the French; for France, reasonable prospects of securing its aims at low cost through negotiations.

THE SETTLEMENT: PRELIMINARIES: After occupation, which had progressed without substantial opposition, the French delivered an ultimatum to the Bey, requiring him to negotiate a peace treaty and threatening to recognize a Pretender if he did not do so.

MILITARY SETTLEMENT: There were no explicit cease-fire provisions. However the treaty (known as the Treaty of Kasr-Said or the Treaty of Bardo, dated 12 May 1881) quite clearly implied that peace was to be

56 Hertslet, *op. cit.* (London: Butterworth, 1880), pp. 22–24.

restored between the Bey and France;[57] but since the Bey evidently had little control over certain tribes, he could not commit himself to a formal cease-fire for all of his domains, and France could not rely upon such a commitment. Thus Tunisia (the Bey) consented to the French occupation of certain points in the realm so that the superior arms of France could re-establish order and guarantee the security of the frontiers and the seacoast. This occupation would cease when the parties agreed that local administrations were capable of maintaining order. Tunisia agreed to prohibit the introduction of arms through Djerba, Gabès, and the ports of southern Tunisia.

POLITICAL SETTLEMENT: By virtue of the Treaty arrangements, Tunisia assumed the status of a protectorate of France.

The only provision concerning individuals related to the rights of creditors in Tunisia, the parties agreeing that they would negotiate the basis for the financial organization of the realm, for servicing its national debt, and for guaranteeing the rights of creditors.

All prior treaties between the parties, including treaties of peace, friendship, and commerce, were confirmed. France was to be represented in Tunis by a resident minister who would oversee the execution of the Treaty and function as a liaison official. French diplomats and consuls in other countries were charged with the protection of Tunisian nationals and Tunisian interests. The Bey agreed not to conclude any act of an international character without notice to France or without giving France a chance to make representations. France would answer for (*se porter garant*) the implementation of treaties between Tunisia and other European powers.

France undertook to guarantee the security of the Bey against all dangers to his person and his dynasty and against all threats to the tranquillity of the state.

No indemnity was imposed upon the Bey directly, but a *contribution de guerre* was to be imposed upon unruly tribes of the seacoast and the frontiers. The Bey was responsible for its collection. A treaty was to be negotiated specifying the amount and means of collection.

COMMENTS: The treaty establishing a protectorate is a special kind of peace treaty. The Bey retained some powers over the internal adminstration of his realm but relatively few powers to conduct his affairs with other states independently of French intermediation. There were no provisions for the settlement of future disputes.

ITALO-ABYSSINIAN WAR (1894–1896)

PARTIES' WAR AIMS: Italy sought to create an empire in East Africa on the Red Sea, and this required suzerainty over Ethiopia. Ethiopia's aim was her defense.

57 Martens, *Nouveau Recueil Général de Traités*, 2° Série, Vol. 6 (Göttingen: Librairie de Dieterich, 1881), pp. 507–8.

OUTCOME: Italian forces were defeated and routed at Adowa in March, 1896. Ethiopia maintained its independence; and the Italian colony of Eritrea was somewhat reduced in size.

WAR-ORIENTED STATES: Great Britain, Austria, and France.

FACTORS FOR PEACE: For Italy, its shocking defeat at Adowa; for Ethiopia, achievement of its objectives of defending its independence and territorial integrity.

THE SETTLEMENT: PRELIMINARIES: The government of the Italian Prime Minister collapsed. His successor asked the Emperor to negotiate peace, and he agreed to do so.

MILITARY SETTLEMENT: The state of war was declared at an end. In a separate Convention, Italy was granted the right to maintain troops at Gueldessa. Italian prisioners were to be freed (when the Treaty was ratified) and handed over to an Italian official at Harar. Italy would pay the expenses Ethiopia incurred in repatriating the prisoners.[58]

POLITICAL SETTLEMENT: Italy recognized the independence of the Abyssinian Empire. Within one year, representatives of the parties were to establish the frontiers of Eritrea and Ethiopia. Until then, the *status quo ante* was to be observed. Both parties were to be prohibited from crossing the provisional frontier (defined in the Treaty). Until a boundary was established, Italy was not to cede any territory to another power (only to Ethiopia).

There were no provisions concerning persons affected by the war. The parties agreed to negotiate a commercial treaty. The Treaty of Outchalé (or Uccialli), of 2 May 1889, was annulled. (In that Treaty, Italy had acquired some extraterritorial rights in Ethiopia; and in the Italian version thereof, only Italy was empowered to act as the intermediary between the Emperor of Abyssinia and other powers.)

No penalties were imposed on Italy, and no guarantees exchanged (except that perpetual peace was declared to exist between the parties). There were no provisions for the adjustment of future differences.

COMMENTS: While Italy retained a substantial warmaking capability, the defeat at Adowa persuaded many Italians of the utter mindlessness of the pursuit of empire in so remote a region as Abyssinia. The Emperor of Abyssinia, moreover, was willing to permit the Italians to remain in Eritrea unmolested on not unfavorable terms.

THE RUSSO-POLISH WAR of 1920–1921[59]

PARTIES' WAR AIMS: The Poles sought to consolidate their state by the acquisition of territories in the East. The war was also fought with reli-

---

58 The relevant documents of the settlement appear in Martens, *Nouveau Recueil Général de Traités,* 2° Série, Vol. 25 (Leipzig: Librairie Dieterich, 1900), pp. 59–61.

59 This war was an outgrowth of the First World War, whose settlement is discussed in Chapter 9 (pp. 405–28). It illustrates the point made subsequently

gious fervor by some Poles out of hatred for the Russians, their traditional enemies. The Soviet Union's aim was defense, but with successes in
mid-1920, her leaders sought retribution and the acquisition of territories; after reverses in 1921, their aim was defense once again.

OUTCOME: The Soviet advance toward Warsaw was stopped, and a
Polish counteroffensive drove deep into the Ukraine and White Russia.
The frontier, established according to the terms of the Treaty of Riga[60]
(18 March 1921), was considerably to the east of the Curzon Line, which
the Allied peacemakers had agreed at Versailles to be the new Poland's
eastern frontier.

WAR-ORIENTED STATES: France, which wanted a strong Poland between
Germany and the Soviet Union, urged the Poles to make war on the
Bolsheviks and sent a military advisory mission to Warsaw. Britain and
Italy were also war-oriented.

FACTORS FOR PEACE: For the Soviets, defeat and military weakness, fear
for the loss of additional territory, and the desire to consolidate internally; for Poland, the near achievement of her objective of securing the
boundary of 1772 and some pressure from the Allies.

THE SETTLEMENT: PRELIMINARIES: A Preliminary Treaty of Peace was
signed on 12 October 1920, an Annex to which delineated in some detail
the conditions of an armistice.[61] The Preliminary Treaty represented the
agreement of the parties on the general nature of a future territorial
settlement, an agreement the Poles evidently wanted before negotiating
the armistice. It was attached as a separate document to the Treaty.

MILITARY SETTLEMENT: The cease-fire was to be effective on 18 October
1921. The Polish troops were to remain in position, but the Russian
troops were to withdraw a distance of 15 kilometers from the Polish lines.
The buffer zone was to be neutralized and administered by the party to
whom the territory was to be ceded. Further movements were required to
enlarge the buffer zone. Liaison officers were to be appointed, as was a
mixed military commission to assist in the execution of the armistice
agreement. During evacuation, there were to be no reprisals, and property was to be left intact. The truce would last 21 days and could be
denounced with 48 hours' notice. However, if neither party denounced it,
the truce would be extended automatically until the Peace Treaty was
signed.

The Preliminary Treaty established a mixed commission to supervise
the exchange of prisoners, hostages, and political internees and to organize the repatriation of exiles, refugees, and emigrés.

The permanent treaty, Treaty of Riga, required the troops of the

---

that multilateral wars often comprise a number of smaller wars that can be
(and sometimes must be) settled separately.

60 Martens, *Nouveau Recueil Général de Traités*, 3° Série, Vol. 13 (Leipzig:
Librairie Theodor Weicher, 1924), pp. 141 f.

61 *Ibid.*, pp. 120 ff.

parties to withdraw to the defined frontiers. Additional provisions for the repatriation of prisoners of war were included. Terms of the Preliminary Treaty were incorporated by reference.

POLITICAL SETTLEMENT: In many of its articles, the Preliminary Treaty indicated that the parties would undertake negotiations concerning specified elements of a settlement, looking toward agreement, failing which hostilities could be resumed. The Preliminary Treaty also declared that the parties recognized the independence of the Ukraine and White Russia (which, by 1920, were *de facto* part of the Soviet Union). It specified approximately the frontiers they would respect, renounced rights to territories awarded to the opposite party, and purported to establish relations on the basis of respect for the sovereignty of the other party and on the basis of promises to refrain from intervening in the internal affairs of the other. The Treaty of Riga defined the frontier and prescribed the duties of a mixed boundary commission established by the Preliminary Treaty. The parties were to enjoy rights of free navigation on rivers that crossed the frontier. The Soviets declared that the matter of the Polish-Lithuanian border was solely the concern of Poland and Lithuania. The nonintervention provisions were considerably detailed: the parties even agreed not to create, and indeed would prohibit, any organizations which aimed to abolish the government of the other, resume the war between them, or provide a government-in-exile for the other party.

Trophies of war, archives, records, libraries, "goods of state," rolling stock, ships, and other property were to be restored. The terms for restitution were very detailed and tended to favor Poland.

Nationality provisions were incorporated in the Treaty of Riga, as were religious guarantees and guarantees of the civil rights of the nationals of one party residing in the other's territory. There was to be an amnesty for all political crimes or for acts committed during the war by nationals of the other party. The Soviets recognized their obligation to make restitution on the same basis as for citizens of third-party states, to Polish citizens (and corporations) for damages sustained during the Revolution and the civil wars. Other terms related to financial arrangements for individuals, corporations, banks, and the like. Annexes spelled out in even greater detail other nationality terms.

Diplomatic relations between the parties were to be re-established immediately after ratification. And within 6 weeks, negotiations would open for a commercial treaty. The declarations of noninterference and respect for sovereignty also provided a basis for the resumption of relations. There were no additional terms for guarantees or for the adjustment of future disputes.

The Soviets were to pay Poland an indemnity of 30 million Roubles in compensation for the active role Poles had played in the economic life of the Russian Empire. The cession of territory and the requirements for the restitution of property were onerous enough to be considered a penalty, at least by the Soviet Union.

COMMENTS: In terms of form, the most noteworthy aspect of these agreements is the painstakingly detailed drafting of the provisions relating to nationality, restitution of property, and financial arrangements. With the frontier well east of the Curzon Line, many persons not of Polish nationality were included in the Polish state, and there was otherwise much shifting of peoples as a result of the war. Thus, extensive provisions relating to persons affected by the war were absolutely essential.

The procedure followed by the belligerents of first negotiating a formal preliminary treaty of peace (including both military and political terms) has been a common enough practice. (Refer to the Franco-Prussian War discussed in this chapter and the wars discussed subsequently: the Second War over Schleswig-Holstein (pp. 169–71), the War of the Pacific (pp. 171–3), the War of the Polish Succession (pp. 214–7), the War for American Independence (pp. 217–22), and the Russo-Turkish War of 1877–78 (pp. 228–33). A party would probably regard such a procedure as desirable (assuming its bargaining position was strong), if it wanted to extract concessions from its adversary in exchange for a cease-fire. However, there might be circumstances in which all the belligerents would agree to negotiate a preliminary treaty prior to the definitive treaty: if, for example, the war involved many parties and many issues and some simplification was desirable, or if an immediate settlement of some of the resolvable issues was necessary.

THE CHACO WAR (1928–1938) Bolivia vs. Paraguay

PARTIES' WAR AIMS: The dispute was over the possession of Chaco Boreal, where oil had recently been discovered. Both sides claimed to be defending their interests and territory; and both sides sought to consolidate their states by the acquisition of the Chaco. Bolivia's claim rested upon the terms of the Audencias of Charcas and Guairas. (The geopolitical fact that she was a landlocked state furnished an impetus for her claims.) Paraguay also relied upon the Audencias and upon the fact that she had colonized the Chaco (about 50,000 Paraguayans had settled there). The war was ideologized because of intense nationalist sentiments on each side.

OUTCOME: The military fortunes of the parties shifted during the war. Both were exhausted by the time the fighting stopped in 1935. The final award required Bolivia to renounce jurisdiction over most of the Chaco (some 100,000 square miles), but she retained certain oil fields.

WAR-ORIENTED ACTORS: The United States and Argentina were the principal movers for mediation. Chile, Brazil, Peru, and Uruguay also played an important role in mediation, as did the League of Nations.

FACTORS FOR PEACE: The exhaustion of the belligerents was a factor, as was the influence of a few enlightened Paraguayan and Bolivian leaders. Pressures from the war-oriented actors, particularly the embargo on arms shipments, were also significant.

THE SETTLEMENT: PRELIMINARIES: The final settlement of the Chaco War was simple and straightforward; the efforts to achieve that settlement were complex and fascinating, a lesson in the difficulties confronting peacemakers as they attempt to reach agreement merely to begin peace talks.

A Conference on Conciliation and Arbitration, meeting in Washington in early 1928, tendered its good offices to the belligerents. A Treaty on Conciliation had reached the final draft stage by early 1929, and a special Protocol was signed on 3 January 1929, creating a Commission of Inquiry and Conciliation to investigate the facts of the Chaco dispute and report back to the Conference. The Commission (composed of representatives of Argentina, Brazil, Chile, Uruguay, and the U.S.) was able to arrange a repatriation of prisoners in mid-1929 and to induce the belligerents to accept terms settling the quarrels stemming from the border incidents of 1928. Although the matter was beyond its competence, the Commission tried to resolve the question of sovereignty over the Chaco, but failed.

Hostilities were resumed in 1932 on a larger scale. Mediation efforts were complicated by U.S.–Argentine rivalry and competition between the two major mediating groups: the ABCP group (Argentina, Brazil, Chile, and Peru) and the Commission. Proposals for a cease-fire were rejected throughout 1932 and 1933. In May 1933, Paraguay formally declared war on Bolivia.

The League of Nations had discussed the Chaco War on several occasions, but remained on the periphery because of Western Hemisphere mediation efforts and because of U.S. opposition to League action. With the formal declaration of war, however, the League took formal cognizance of the dispute in 1933 and dispatched a Commission of Inquiry in November. A cease-fire in December collapsed in January, 1934. The League recommended an arms embargo. This was adopted, the U.S. complying in May. That same month, Bolivia appealed for League Mediation under Article XV of the Covenant; and the Assembly's Committee recommended a peace plan. Bolivia accepted the plan, but Paraguay did not. Her forces were on the offensive and had occupied the Chaco and even some Bolivian territory. As a sanction, the League lifted the arms embargo for Bolivia, whereupon Paraguay withdrew from the League in February, 1935. The ABCP states, together with the U.S. and Paraguay, moved again to mediate; and in May the belligerents agreed to accept that mediation. Negotiations collapsed in June. (Bolivia favored merely a truce during negotiations; Paraguay, an immediate truce coupled with demobilization and demilitarization of the Chaco. This dispute caused the parties to break off their talks.) When talks resumed again within a week, they almost failed once again over the question of guarantees and the size of the area in the Chaco that was to be subject to arbitration (the parties having by then accepted arbitration as a means to end the dispute). A draft protocol was signed on 12 June 1935, and with it came a cease-fire.[62] Diplomatic relations were not resumed until 1937; the peace treaty was signed on 21 July 1938 and ratified in August.

MILITARY SETTLEMENT: The Protocol of 12 June 1935 contained the principal provisions for the cease-fire and its implementation. A Neutral Commission composed of representatives of the mediating states was authorized to fix a line of separation between forces of the belligerents. A 12-day truce was set for this purpose. The Neutral Commission was to hear and accept proposals from the belligerents' military commanders; when the Commission had agreed upon a line, the armistice would come into effect. Thereafter, the parties would begin demobilization until their respective armed forces had an aggregate strength of not more than 5000 men. Bolivia and Paraguay also agreed not to make new purchases of war material until the conclusion of a treaty of peace. The Neutral Commission was charged with supervising and observing the truce, the line of separation between the armies of the Parties, and security procedures. Exchange of prisoners of war was undertaken pursuant to agreements reached in early 1936; and transit regulations for military and paramilitary forces in the Chaco were promulgated in 1937.

POLITICAL SETTLEMENT: The frontiers of the parties in the Chaco were to be determined by an arbitration commission composed of representatives of Argentina, Brazil, Chile, Peru, Uruguay, and the U.S. This line would be fixed within the bounds of an area described in the treaty. The arbitrators were to decide *ex aequo et bono*, on the basis of the experience accumulated by the Peace Conference and its military advisors, handing down their decision within two months after ratification. After the announcement of the award, the parties were to name a mixed commission to run and mark the boundary. The parties would implement the terms of the award within 90 days of ratification, under the supervision of the Peace Conference (ABCP powers, the U.S., and Uruguay). Paraguay guaranteed free transit through its territory for goods going to and from Bolivia, the latter being given the right of access to the sea through Puerto Casado, where Bolivia could construct depots and establish customs agents.

Within 30 days after ratification, the parties would formally exchange accredited diplomatic representatives. Economic and commercial treaties were to be negotiated at a later date. Both renounced all claims arising

---

62 *The Chaco Peace Conference* (Washington: U.S. Government Printing Office, 1940).

out of the war. There were no specific provisions concerning persons affected by the war, nor were there formal guarantees of security.

The belligerents agreed to renew their nonaggression pact and renounced the use of force to resolve their disputes. They agreed further that if they were unable themselves to resolve their differences, they would have recourse to the conciliation and arbitration procedures prescribed by international law or by the relevant Pan American agreements. Disputes over the Chaco award were to be resolved by the Peace Conference.

Ratification was to be accomplished by means of a plebiscite in Paraguay, and by a National Constitutional Convention in Bolivia.

COMMENTS: As is evident, the preliminary phase of negotiations for peace was drawn out over the entire length of the war; the League of Nations and many states of the Western Hemisphere were involved in conciliation efforts. Due to the ideologization of issues, a political settlement was not achieved until 3 years after the cease-fire. Even then, it was incomplete: the questions that were left unresolved continued to plague the former belligerents' relations after 1938.

RUSSO-FINNISH WAR (THE WINTER WAR) (1939–1940)

WAR AIMS: The Soviet Union sought to improve its security in the Baltic by acquiring bases and portions of Finnish territory, being impelled to do so by the threat posed to them by the war among Germany, England, and France. The Soviets sought maximally to convert Finland into a client state. Finland fought in its own defense.

OUTCOME: By the early spring of 1940, the Soviets had penetrated the Mannerheim Line, but only after overcoming the unexpectedly tenacious resistance of the Finns. Finland was then obliged to accede to Soviet demands, but it did retain its independence.

WAR-ORIENTED ACTORS: Britain, France, Sweden, Norway, and Hungary contemplated giving aid to the Finns; the U.S. offered mediation and a loan. The League of Nations expelled the Soviet Union for violating its treaty obligations. Germany's attitude was ambiguous but certainly not friendly towards Finland. Italy was also war-oriented.

FACTORS FOR PEACE: For the Soviets, high war costs were a factor, as well as fear of hostilities with France and Britain—or at least concern for the consequences were the latter to send aid to Finland. The Soviets had also achieved their more limited objective of acquiring bases and territory; but they apparently gave up the aim of transforming Finland into a satellite when they failed to support their creation, the Finnish Democratic Government under O. W. Kuusinen. In the case of Finland, defeat, the prospects of further loss of territory, and the refusal of Sweden to permit transit of troops across her territory induced the Finns to move for peace.

THE SETTLEMENT: PRELIMINARIES: Finland sought to learn of Soviet peace terms directly, but failed. Then she tried through intermediaries, first Germany and then a friend of the Russian Minister in Stockholm. These overtures also failed. When the Swedish Foreign Minister offered mediation, it was accepted by the Soviets, who asked to know what territorial concessions the Finns would make. The concessions offered were refused. Finally, in late February, Molotov made known the Soviets' demands. Finland regarded them as unacceptable and again sought Swedish permission for the transit of British or French troops and arms. Sweden refused. Russia also sought to use Britain as an intermediary, but the British government regarded the terms as too harsh and refused to transmit them. Russia then demanded Finnish acceptance of the terms. Helsinki replied through a Swedish intermediary, asking for a more precise definition of the territories demanded by the Soviets. Moscow replied with only slightly less harsh terms. On 5 March, Finland agreed to accept the terms as a basis for negotiations. The Soviets refused a Swedish proposal for a truce during negotiations, which began on 8 March.

MILITARY SETTLEMENT: There was to be a cease-fire on the day the Treaty of Peace was signed (12 March 1940).[63] The Treaty contained the Soviet agreement to withdraw Russian troops from Petsamo and a limitation upon Finnish naval vessels and bases in Arctic waters. A protocol contained more detailed stipulations respecting implementation of the truce. Immediately, the armies were to separate from each other a distance of one kilometer. Withdrawal behind the new frontiers was to be effected according to the schedules provided, and measures were to be taken by the commanders of the withdrawing troops to preserve property. The parties agreed to terms for the exchange of prisoners of war. The commanders of the armies of the parties were given full powers to resolve questions arising under the terms of the Protocol.

POLITICAL SETTLEMENT: Finland ceded to the Soviet Union the entire Karelian Isthmus with the city of Viipuri, the bay of Viipuri (and islands), and the northern and western shores of Lake Ladoga. The exact boundary was to be fixed by a commission to be set up within 10 days of the signing of the Treaty. The Hango Peninsula was to be leased for 30 years in order to permit the Soviets to construct a naval base "designed to guard entry to the Gulf of Finland from aggression." The Soviets were also permitted to station troops and an air force on Hango. The Soviets agreed to pay Finland 8 million Finnish Marks per year as rent. Through the Petsamo district to Norway and across Finland to Sweden, the Soviet Union was given the right of free transit.

There were no provisions concerning persons affected by the war, nor were penalties imposed (other than the loss of territory). The parties

63 Martens, *Nouveau Recueil Général de Traités*, 3° Série, Vol. 38 (Greifswald: Librairie Julius Abel, 1941), pp. 323–27.

would resume economic relations when the Treaty entered into force, and would negotiate a new commercial treaty. The two states were to cooperate in constructing a railroad across Finland to Sweden.

The parties also agreed to refrain from attacking one another or from concluding an alliance with a third state directed against either party.

COMMENTS: In slightly over a year's time, the German invasion of the Soviet Union nullified the settlement. Finland declared war on the Soviets in 1941. She was forced out of the war in 1944 and signed a peace treaty with the Allies in 1947. It is significant that although in a position to extract very harsh peace terms from the defeated Finns in 1940, the Soviet Union did not do so because of pressure from the war-oriented states and the Soviet leaders' unwillingness to sustain the costs of an occupation of Finland and the probable repercussions of such an occupation for the Russo-German alliance. The role of war-oriented states in the preliminary phase of negotiations was thus significant.

In terms of outcome and relative bargaining strength, we have seen examples of wars in which one of the belligerents was defeated and had minimal leverage in determining the terms of the settlement (the Opium War, Mexican-American War, Ashanti War, Franco-Tunisian War); we have seen others that ended in a virtual draw (the Chaco War, the War of 1812); and still others in which a defeated belligerent still retained, for various reasons, an important modicum of influence during negotiations (Russo-Finnish War, Russo-Polish War, Italo-Abyssinian War).[64]

64 The reader should also refer to the settlements of the wars described in subsequent chapters to find support for the generalizations made in this chapter. Cross-reference footnotes in the text and in Tables 2–1 to 2–8 should simplify this process. The notion of *war-oriented* status is developed in Chapters 6 and 7, to which the reader is urged to refer.

In the settlements later summarized, we include examples of the impact of bargaining strength upon the course and outcome of peace negotiations:

a. cases in which a belligerent is defeated and has little bargaining power: Mexico in the Texas Revolt (pp. 106–7), Britain in the Second Anglo-Dutch War: 1664–7 (pp. 160–3), Denmark in the Second War over Schleswig-Holstein (pp. 169–71), Peru and Bolivia in the War of the Pacific, 1879–83 (pp. 171–3), and China in the Boxer Rebellion (pp. 175–7).

b. wars ending in a draw: Last War of the Habsburg-Valois Rivalry, 1557–9 (pp. 157–60), the Franco-Dutch War, 1672–9 (pp. 340–7), and the conflict between France and Austria in the multilateral European War of 1683–1700 (pp. 347–57).

c. where a belligerent, although defeated, retains some measure of bargaining power: the rebels in the Hungarian Rebellion, 1703–11 (pp. 104–5) and the Cuban Revolt, 1869–78 (pp. 107–8); the Ottman Empire in the Austro-Russian War against Turkey, 1787–92 (pp. 163–5) and in the Greek War for Independence, 1821–30 (pp. 222–5), and France in 1708 during the War of the Spanish Succession (pp 357–66) as well as in 1814 after the Napoleonic Wars (pp. 392–405).

The sample also demonstrates the extent to which the war aims of each belligerent were achieved. The settlement summaries illustrate the general pattern of simple external war settlements described earlier. They are too brief, of course, to do justice to the intricate, often intriguing, diplomacy surrounding the peace talks. But they suggest which aspects of particular wars are interesting for our purposes. For example, the thoroughness and technical detail of the settlements of the Franco-Prussian and Russo-Polish Wars is most striking;[65] and the preliminary bargaining phases of the Chaco War and the War of 1812 settlements, each a case study in itself, point up the importance of preconference negotiations and agreements for the final settlement.[66] A war ending in a clear defeat of one belligerent and an ultimatum from the victor allows the loser little time or opportunity to bargain over preconditions for peace talks. In such a case, the preliminary phase is usually of little interest (as in the Ashanti War or the Franco-Tunisian War).

Some elements of a settlement are missing from many of the wars summarized. There are reasons for these omissions: insufficient de-ideologization of the war issues (in the Franco-Prussian War or the incomplete settlements of the Chaco dispute up to 1938) ;[67] a decision, in the face of

65 The detailed settlements of the Crimean War (infra, pp. 165–9), the War of the Polish Succession, 1733–5 (pp. 214–7), the Russo-Turkish War of 1877–8 (pp. 228–33) and the Struggle for Tunisian Independence, 1949–56 (pp. 111–2) are also examples, as are the settlements of the Napoleonic Wars (pp. 392–405) and the First World War (pp. 405–28). There were quite detailed military settlements for the Franco-Prussian and Russo-Polish Wars summarized in this chapter, and for the War of the Polish Succession, the Korean War (pp. 233–6), the Wars of the Spanish (pp. 357–66) and Austrian (pp. 366–74) Successions, and the Franco-Vietminh War of 1946–1954 (see the author's Geneva 1954: The Settlement of the Indochinese War, op. cit.). When the analyst takes into consideration the supplementary negotiations and agreements that took place during and after the peace talks for the Thirty Years' War (pp. 379–92), the Napoleonic Wars, and the First World War, he will find other evidence and examples of the form of the military settlements of wars described herein and the ways in which these came about.

66 This is also the case for the settlements of the Struggle for Tunisian Independence (infra, pp. 111–2), the Last War of the Habsburg-Valois Rivalry (pp. 157–60), the Crimean War (pp. 165–9), the Second War over Schleswig-Holstein (pp. 169–71), War of the Polish Succession (pp. 214–7) and the multilateral wars analyzed in Chapter 9—although, in the last days of the First World War, neither Bulgaria nor Austria-Hungary were able to bargain for terms during the preliminary negotiating phase. In most of these wars, the preliminary negotiations were intricate and interesting, many extending over months and even years.

67 See also the settlements of the Third Huguenot War, 1568–70 (infra, pp. 101–3), Irish Rebellion, 1919–21 (pp. 109–10), Dutch Revolt, 1566–1609 (pp. 208–14), Korean War (pp. 233–6), and Laotian Civil War (pp. 236–40).

a stalemate, to leave the unresolved problems to future negotiations (War of 1812) ;[68] the realization that broaching certain issues might exacerbate relations between the negotiators or raise too many other thorny questions; or simply a conclusion by the belligerents' policy-makers that some matters are not important in the context of negotiations (for the British in the Opium War, matters other than the security of their trade were of this sort). Perhaps a victor has achieved his limited objectives, and a relatively simple settlement is thought to be sufficient (as in the Ashanti War or the Franco-Tunisian War).[69] When a victorious belligerent has obtained security guarantees through the acquisition of territory and feels sufficiently secure to avoid considering problems of future conflict resolution, provisions of this kind will be omitted (the Russo-Turkish War).[70] Whatever the reason, the incompleteness or inadequacy of a settlement will in most instances lead to difficulties, even to war, unless the parties cure the defects in the agreements that establish between them the rules of their relations in the postwar period.[71]

68 True also of elements of the settlements of the War for American Independence (*infra*, pp. 217–22), the War of the Spanish Succession (pp. 357–66), Thirty Years' War (pp. 379–92), and the Dutch Revolt (pp. 208–14).

69 Other examples of settlements in which elements have been omitted, either because the victor virtually achieved his war aims in their entirety or the war itself was regarded by a party as simple, involving one or two issues that were (or could be) easily resolved, include the Struggle for Egyptian Independence (*infra*, pp. 110–1), the Kurdish Insurrection (pp. 112–3), the Austro-Russian War against Turkey, 1787–92 (pp. 163–5), War of the Pacific (pp. 171–3), the Boxer Rebellion (pp. 175–7), and the settlements with many minor states in the multilateral wars analyzed in Chapter 9.

70 In the settlement of the Second War over Schleswig-Holstein (*infra*, pp. 169–71), the disposition of territories acquired by the victorious allies (Prussia and Austria) was unclear and eventually led to war between them.

71 A final note on the classification of elements of a political settlement: It could be argued that both economic and financial terms are of such importance in peacemaking that each deserves to be singled out as an element of settlement. The major treaties making up the settlement of the First World War, for example, contained sections specifically entitled *Economic Clauses* and *Financial Clauses*. In the earliest wars within our period of analysis, a nonpenalty cash payment was often agreed to be a necessary part of the settlement for what we would call economic reasons (see the Thirty Years' War, the European War of 1683–1700, and the Franco-Dutch War of 1672–9). In spite of the very definite importance of economic questions—and indeed without denying their importance—I have preferred to subsume economic and financial matters under other elements of settlement, to wit: resumption of relations, persons (individual and corporate) affected by the war, and penalties. I have also subsumed religious and dynastic problems under other elements (see Tables 2–1 to 2–8).

The Settlement of
Simple Internal Wars

In most internal wars, the insurgents fight to achieve some measure of control over their government. If they seek to replace the incumbent regime and take over the state entirely, we have an internal *war for control of the polity*. If the insurgents want only autonomy or independence for their group, they may seek to control only a part of the territory and people of the state. We shall call this second type of internal war a *war for independence*.[1] Both types of internal war are fought to establish the right of the insurgents to govern, whether all or part of the state; and in both types, the insurgents' objective is to be wholly or partially free of the incumbent governmental authority. On occasion, insurgents have fought to obtain goals less sweeping than the right of self-government, for example, the right to practice a particular religion, to obtain certain commercial privileges, or to be relieved of economic burdens such as taxes (or even to prevent persons of a different race or nationality from settling in a region). When conflicts of this sort are serious enough to be regarded as internal wars—or variously as civil wars, rebellions, revolts, or insurrections—as opposed to riots or other civil disturbances of a relatively minor kind, we do not err too greatly if we subsume such wars under either category, at least for purposes of considering the structure of peace settlements.

1 Another kind of war for independence is one in which the insurgents move to secede from the parent state in order to become part of another state. For a discussion of several theoretical aspects of internal wars, see Harry Eckstein (ed.), *Internal War* (New York: Free Press of Glencoe, 1964).

Preliminaries

Let us assume that the factions in an internal war, both the insurgents (x) and the incumbents (y), desire a peace settlement.[2] By this assumption, we exclude the usual outcome of an internal war for control of the polity, namely, the complete defeat and destruction of one faction and the vesting of control of the apparatus of state authority in the victorious faction.[3] Thus, we are to assume that the factions recognize that neither will be able to liquidate the other, at least for the present. The factions desire negotiations, for the same reasons that state belligerents in an external war desire negotiations: either they genuinely want peace (permanently or for the time being) or they believe that a manifest willingness to negotiate coupled with ostensibly real moves to bring a peace conference into being will have propaganda value. In the case of the stalemated internal war, the factions could conclude that the competition between them will eventually be by peaceful political means, the success of which depends upon the ability of the factions to win the support of the enfranchised population or the elites of the polity. Moves toward peace could have a very significant effect upon peaceful political competition during and after negotiations.

In the simple internal war, the stage preliminary to negotiations will be analogous, if not similar, to the same stage in the settlement of the *simple external* war. There will probably be peace feelers, either secretly brought to the attention of the other side or publicized widely. There will be talks about talks, consideration of preconditions of negotiations, and agreements upon procedures such as the form of the conference, invitees, agenda, and conference procedures—any one of which may slow up negotiations or manifest insurmountable difficulties that could prolong the war. There is finally the possibility that a disinterested third state might play the role of a broker in mediating the dispute between the parties. In most cases, the incumbent faction will regard the peace efforts of a third-party state (or an international organization) as an undesirable interference in its state's domestic affairs. Nonetheless, it is conceivable that in a stalemate, a third party acceptable to both factions just might be found.

The Military Settlement

In the military phase of negotiations for the settlement of a war for control over the apparatus of state, the approach to the problems of the

2 See Table 3–1 for historical examples of the preliminaries to negotiations discussed in this section. See also Table 2–1 in Chapter 2.
3 Modelski, *op. cit.* (Chapter 1).

cessation of hostilities and the immediate disposition of the troops of each faction will be, in most respects, similar to that for the military settlement of a simple external war.[4] Technically the problems are identical: to stop the fighting and to provide for the peaceful disengagement of troops and for their withdrawal from the areas of combat operations. In the case of the internal war, too, the object is to separate the former combatants to prevent incidents that might lead to the resumption of hostilities.

The problem of the ultimate disposition of the troops of the factions will be unique for this type of war, however. The troops of one faction, usually the incumbents, will remain in existence (provided that they were not totally defeated), although the settlement might require their partial demobilization. They will thus remain administratively the national force of the particular state. But the troops of the insurgents are another matter, and the question of their continued existence will require the particular attention of the negotiators. Insurgent forces can be treated in a number of ways, assuming their status is negotiable—that they have not been wholly destroyed or even completely victorious. They may be demobilized, with guarantees for their civil liberties and perhaps also promises of the same opportunities for pay, promotions, and assignments as persons in the incumbents' armed forces; they may be incorporated in the national armed forces of the state, again with guarantees; or finally, they may be permitted to remain in existence as an independent armed force within a particular area of the state, The terms of the last solution would have to be formulated carefully by the negotiators. Unless jurisdictional questions respecting the authority and competence of national and insurgent forces are raised and answered at the peace conference or institutional means are provided for resolving such questions at a later time, the existence of two forces in the same country is likely to result in the future outbreak of hostilities. Ultimately, the question of the long-term disposition of the insurgents' armed forces is a political question: it depends upon the sort of political settlement the negotiators conclude.

The armistice agreement may also contain provisions for the protection of persons and property in zones of combat or areas used by the forces of either faction for regroupment and withdrawal. It may also provide for the removal or destruction of mines, bombs, and other weapons; and it may contain provisions for the temporary military administration of territories of the state, although this is likely to be a political question that must wait upon the political settlement for its resolution.

The armistice terms may be supervised by a military commission

4 See Table 3–1 for historical examples of the elements of a military settlement of internal wars. See also Table 2–2 in Chapter 2.

TABLE 3–1. The preliminary negotiating and military settlement phases of an internal war: some examples of the elements of these phases in historical peace settlements.

Element	Some examples
peace feelers	Soviet Union in the Korean War (pp. 233–6) ; Britain in the Irish Rebellion (pp. 109–10) ; both parties in the Dutch Revolt (pp. 208–14) .
preliminary talks	Hungarian Rebellion of 1703–11 (pp. 104–5) ; Irish Rebellion (pp. 109–10) ; Struggles for Egyptian (pp. 110–11) and Tunisian (pp. 111–2) Independence; Thirty Years' War (pp. 379–92) ; War of the Spanish Succession (pp. 357–66) .
preconditions to further negotiations	Russo-Turkish War of 1877–78 (pp. 228–33) .
procedures for peace talks	Kurdish Insurrection (pp. 112–3) ; Korean War (pp. 233–6) ; Thirty Years' War (pp. 379–92) .
third-party mediation	Great Powers in the Greek War for Independence (pp. 222–5) ; France in the Wars of Mehemet Ali (pp. 225–8) ; Britain refused third-party mediation several times during the War for American Independence (pp. 217–22) .
cease-fire	See the summaries of internal wars in this chapter and in Chapters 5 and 9. There was a unilateral U.N. cease-fire during the Korean War (pp. 233–6) .
prisoners of war provided for	Texas Revolt (pp. 106–7) ; Dutch Revolt (pp. 208–14) ; American Revolution (pp. 217–22) ; Korean War (pp. 233–6) ; Laotian Civil War (pp. 236–40) .
demobilization of incumbent's troops	Irish Revolt (pp. 109–10) ; Thirty Years' War (pp. 379–92) .
demobilization of insurgent's troops (with guarantees)	Hungarian Rebellion (pp. 104–5) ; Cuban Revolt (pp. 107–8) .
movement and security of troops	Texas Revolt (pp. 160–7) ; Dutch Revolt (pp. 208–14) ; War of the Polish Succession (pp. 214–7) ; Second War of Mehemet Ali (pp. 226–8) ; Korean War (pp. 233–6) .
incorporation of insurgent troops into the incumbent's army	This was the ultimate intention of the peacemakers in respect of the Laotian phase of the Franco-Vietminh (French Indochina) War, ending in 1954.

TABLE 3–1 (continued)

Element	Some examples
insurgents allowed an independent army	Third Huguenot War (pp. 101–3) ; Second War of Mehemet Ali (pp. 226–8) ; and the Pathet Lao were permitted to have an army in two provinces of Laos in 1954; but they were subsequently to integrate this army into the Royal Government's. They did not do so.
independent army for a newly independent state	Irish Rebellion (pp. 109–10) ; Tunisian Independence (pp. 111–2) ; American Revolution (pp. 217–22) ; and many others.
protection of persons and property during cease-fire	Kurdish Insurrection (pp. 112–3) ; Irish Rebellion (pp. 109–10) ; War of the Polish Succession (pp. 214–7) .
military administration of occupied areas	Great Powers in the Greek Revolt (pp. 222–5) .
detailed technical terms in a cease-fire agreement	Russo-Turkish War of 1877–78 (pp. 228–33) ; Korean War (pp. 233–6) ; War of the Polish Succession (pp. 214–7) .
supervision of cease-fire	ISC in Laotian Civil War (pp. 236–40) ; party and third-party supervision in the Korean War (pp. 233–6) .
neutralization	Laos after the Laotian Civil War (pp. 236–40) .

composed of officers of the factions, who will also double as a commission for resolving technical questions as they arise on the scene. On the other hand, the factions might agree to invite representatives of third states or an international organization to serve as observers or supervisors on the armistice control commission. The powers of that commission will be the subject of negotiation between the factions; but if third states are asked to provide officers for this task, it is possible that they could demand and obtain a commission of wider competence than the factions might, at first, have been willing to establish. If the factions attached a high enough value to supervision by third parties, they may well feel compelled to acquiesce in the demands of those parties.[5]

5 Just as the disposition of troops after a cease-fire is unique for an internal war, so is the *supervision* of the cease-fire, where formidable difficulties can arise for the control commissions, particularly if the war has been fought by a multiplicity of guerrilla groups. There will be no single "main line of resistance," and thus no single demarcation line between the combatants. Supervision in such a situation would require a control commission with a large staff and extensive technical capabilities.

The handling of violations and complaints of violations are subjects of importance. As in the case of the simple external war, they may be considered by an armistice commission, a military commission, *ad hoc* investigating teams, or by a committee of representatives of the factions in the capital of the state.

Political Settlement of an Internal War for Control of the Polity

If there has been sufficient devaluation and de-ideologization, that is, if the factions come to adhere less intensely to their power political and ideological values, they will want to agree upon more than just a cease-fire. A political settlement will also be possible if the requisite power political and ideological thresholds have been crossed.

In a simple internal war for political control of the polity, the following solutions are possible:

1. The insurgents agree to disarm and disband. With guarantees for their lives and property, they return to their former places of residence and resume their prewar status. They may be permitted to form their own political party and take part in the peaceful competition of political parties.

2. The insurgent faction is authorized to remain in existence as a separate political (and perhaps military) movement, with the understanding that they will be guaranteed a fixed minimum number of posts in the government of the state. This is the *coalition government* solution. The peace compact will probably also contain provisions guaranteeing the civil liberties of all parties.

3. The factions agree that the military and political forces of each shall remain in existence, but shall be physically separated from each other. This is the *partition* solution, of which there are two general types:

a. division of the state arbitrarily into two areas, one of which is assigned to the insurgents, the other to the incumbents.

b. division of the state into a multiplicity of areas congruent with the areas controlled by the factions when a cease-fire comes into effect. In this case, the state becomes, in effect, a federation of the separate areas under the control of the factions.

Whichever mode of partition is agreed upon, the assignment of territories is likely to be the subject of intense negotiations. Each faction will want to continue to maintain its authority in areas controlled by it at the time of the cease-fire, and each will want to obtain control over areas that will enhance its future political position (for example, cities, ports, territories with rich natural resources, and areas that provide natural defenses). The factions, in short, will have to think about the possible future resumption of hostilities and will therefore seek to place themselves in a position that will not compromise their security.

In the partition solution, the problem of the assignment of territories can be reduced, in part, to the related problem of the determination of boundaries of the assigned zones. Boundaries must be fixed in the settlement agreement, and for that purpose a boundary commission is usually constituted. The boundary might be the line of contact of the opposing troops at the time of the cease-fire; it might be a wholly different line. In the latter case, the factions must arrange to have their troops withdraw into the areas delimited by the new boundaries. A buffer zone on each side of the new boundaries might be the subject of a special regime defined by the factions in the armistice agreement or in the overall peace compact. The buffer zone will probably be demilitarized or otherwise subject to special supervision in order to minimize the chances of an outbreak of hostilities at the boundary where the zones (and, in the absence of provisions to remove them) the armed forces of the factions are contiguous. If the antagonists remain bitterly divided, the buffer zone regime and the inter-zonal boundary could assume importance for a longer period, comparable to a demilitarized boundary between independent states, until the factions, either in the peace compact or by a subsequent agreement, agree to modify the regime, to undo the partition, and unite the polity under a single national authority.

The *dissolution* of the insurgent movement will be possible only if the insurgents are in an extremely weak position militarily or politically, a position nevertheless that the incumbents cannot, for some reason, exploit by continuing hostilities until the defeat of the insurgents. Moreover, to accept the dissolution of their faction, the insurgent leaders would have to be impressed with the extent of their weakness and conclude that dissolution with guarantees was more acceptable than continuing to fight, at the risk of complete destruction. The *coalition government* solution would probably be adopted when the factions have about equal bargaining power, when the leaders of either faction concluded that they must tolerate the inconvenience of cooperating with the adversary rather than bear the costs of continued fighting that promised no dramatic alteration in the relative power position of the antagonists. Either party might also suppose that, in due course, the other could be eliminated from the coalition, through peaceful political competition or subversion. The *partition* solution might be the only one possible if the factions are still hostile and cannot bring themselves to cooperate within a coalition. Physical separation will then be necessary, unless the factions decided to resume hostilities. The faction leaders will not look kindly upon a division of their state and will probably regard the partition solution as temporary, until combat can be resumed at some time after a respite or until a future conference can somehow resolve the question of the unity of the state.

It may be agreed in the event of either a coalition government or the dissolution of the insurgent movement that the political future of the state is to be resolved by elections at some fixed date; if elections are deemed undesirable in an authoritarian polity, the faction negotiators may simply provide for a conference of the state's elites. The task of this conference would be to determine the constitution of the state after a period of time had passed and emotions generated by the war had cooled. Elections, however, have become the generally accepted mode for resolution of the fundamental questions relating to the future of states. They may be "democratic" in the sense that a widely enfranchised segment of the population would freely express its political preferences, or they may be limited to only a small proportion of the people of a state, or they may be guided and the results foreordained. The symbolic value of elections of whatever form, in an era when self-determination has become the paramount political principle, cannot be discounted. If elections are the means through which the temporary regime created at the peace conference is to be ended, the negotiators generally establish certain rules for them. A specific date is set; and provision is usually made for supervision of the elections: either by teams composed of representatives of the factions or by persons delegated by a third-party state or an international organization. As in the case of the armistice commission, the competence of this elections supervisory commission would be determined by the factions. It may be that the duties of the armistice commission also include elections supervision, and the functional life of the armistice commission would be extended to permit it to accomplish this political task. Generally, the elections supervisory commission observes the conduct of the campaign, the registration of parties and of voters, the operation of polling places on election day, and the counting of ballots. It is usually guided by the terms—often vague—of the compact of peace between the factions.

As in the case of violations of the cease-fire agreement, violations of the electoral provisions of a peace compact could be treated in a number of different ways. The commission might be empowered to investigate alleged violations, assess responsibility for them, and make recommendations on the spot or to a committee of the factions. Disposition of complaints or of recommended solutions depends upon the political situation in the state in the postwar period. Unsatisfactory handling of disputes could lead to the breakup of the coalition government (or to a remobilization of the recently demobilized insurgents) and ultimately to a renewal of hostilities.

Should the factions adopt the partition solution, they will frequently stipulate that division of the country is to be regarded as temporary, to be replaced by a new and more permanent political regime legitimized by elections or by a conference of representatives of the factions. Partition can become permanent in fact, if not in law, if the factions make no mention of the future of the state in the peace compact, or if they remain mutually hostile over the course of months or years but yet refuse to renew military activity to unite the state. The latter course is always possible, of course, but the balance of military power of the factions may remain about equal in the postwar years; without a desire to compromise on the part of the faction leaders, even to achieve highly valued unification, partition will persist. But if elections were eventually accepted as the means for ending partition, the factions must usually schedule consultations in order to agree upon election procedures. Here such important technical questions will arise as: Will elections be held simultaneously in all zones, or will they be held at different times for different zones? Will representatives of one faction be permitted to observe or supervise elections in the other faction's zone? What standards of conduct shall apply before and during elections? And, after elections, how shall amalgamation of the zones actually be accomplished? The factions must, of course, agree to accept the results of the elections: The losing faction must acquiesce in the other's victory. The loser must not resort to force in order to reverse the results of the election or to maintain its authority within its zone. The victor most probably must guarantee the safety and the civil rights of the members of the losing faction. Presumably, these matters would have been discussed at the interfaction consultations earlier. The effects of an election loss for one of the zonal authorities might be mitigated by a transition to a provisional coalition government, the tenure of which could be limited by the date either of the next national elections or the coming into effect of a new constitution.

There are a number of paths the factions might take toward the adoption of a new constitution.[6] In the case of the coalition government solution, areas of the state could remain under temporary military administration until the peace compact was signed. That compact would provide for a provisional government of the state and for the drafting of the constitution. When the constitution had been drafted and approved by a committee appointed by the factions (on a date fixed in the compact or by supplementary agreement), elections for a constituent assembly would be held. The draft of the constitution might be submitted to the assembly which may or may not have the power to amend the draft or adopt a wholly new constitution. Subsequently, elections would be held under the new constitution, and a permanent political regime with a functioning government would come into existence. The constituent assembly phase might be omitted, in which case the constitutional drafting committee of the factions or the faction leaders themselves would

6 The discussion of procedures for the adoption of a constitution is in the nature of a scenario based generally upon the history of the world after the Second World War. But see the English Revolution (pp. 103–4), the early years of the Dutch Revolt (pp. 208–14) and the Russo-Turkish War of 1877–8 in respect of Bulgaria and Rumelia (pp. 228–33).

reach agreement on the final form of the constitution, after which general elections conducted in accordance with that constitution could be held. The composition of the constitutional drafting committee would certainly be a major question at the peace conference. Control by one of the factions of the drafting process would invariably lead to a constitution favorable to the political position of that faction, which might then be able to win in peace what it could not win on the battlefield. Equally difficult to resolve would be the question of the composition, structure, and powers of the provisional government for the state, questions upon which much negotiating time would no doubt be spent.

In the case of a partitioned state, presumably each of the factions will establish their own provisional governments in their assigned zones. The longer partition lasts, the more characteristics of permanence will the zonal governments acquire. Each faction may even adopt a constitution for its zone, and each zone might become a going concern in its own right, establishing commercial and even diplomatic relations with third states. This will complicate the process of ending the temporary regime, simply because the internal problems of the state have become internationalized. Other states may have come to accept the status quo of the partitioned state, and they might have become interested in the issues that divide the factions.

After they agree to amalgamation, the faction leaders could appoint a constitutional drafting committee, and the resulting document could be approved by the leaders or by the people of the state in a referendum. There are also the questions of whether to amalgamate before or after the promulgation of the constitution and the additional technical legal and political questions that follow from either alternative.

As we have seen, when the factions agree to a partition solution, they will provide for boundaries between zones and often a buffer zone on either side of the boundaries. But the factions might further agree to demilitarize other areas of their zones, to reduce the overall strength of their armed forces, to forbid the manufacture and importation of munitions and certain weapons, and to close down some military bases. If, at the time of the armistice agreement or peace compact, the factions or a third-party broker anticipate that the provisionally partitioned regime will eventually be transformed into a unified state, then demilitarization provisions could be made a part of the interfaction agreements of peace with the belief (or perhaps merely the hope) that they would actually be implemented. Naturally, in adopting such provisions neither faction would want to render its state defenseless in the face of actual or potential threats from other states or render themselves defenseless against each other. If the factions had reservations about the possibilities of permanent peace between themselves (that is, if they believed that peace was only a respite to allow resupply and rearmament), or if a violation after the cease-fire so altered the balance of military or political power of the

TABLE 3–2. Internal war for control of the polity: some examples of elements of a political settlement.

Element	Some examples
coalition government	Laotian Civil War (pp. 236–40). The settlement of the Cyprus War for Independence (1955–59) was also kind of coalition government solution.*
partition	Greek War for Independence: in respect of The Principalities (pp. 222–5); Korean War (pp. 233–6); Wars of Mehemet Ali (pp. 225–8).
boundaries of partitioned zones	Irish Rebellion (pp. 109–10); Korean War (pp. 233–6); temporary boundary for divided Vietnam after the Franco-Vietminh War that ended in 1954.
dissolution of insurgent's army	Khmer Issarak and Pathet Lao after the Franco-Vietminh War; army of the Greek Communist party in the Greek Civil War that ended in 1945.
elections	Korean War (pp. 233–6); Cyprus War for Independence; and Franco-Vietminh War.
constitutional amendment subsequent to an internal war	English Revolution of 1688 (pp. 103–4); War of the Polish Succession (pp. 214–7); Thirty Years' War (pp. 379–92): the Imperial Constitution was amended by the settlements of 1635 and 1648.
demilitarization	Second War of Mehemet Ali (pp. 226–8).
neutralization	Laotian Civil War (pp. 236–40).

* See Foley, Charles, *Legacy of Strife: Cyprus from Rebellion to Civil War* (Harmondsworth, Middlesex, England: Penguin Press, 1964); Royal Institute of International Affairs, *Cyprus: The Dispute and the Settlement* (London: Oxford University Press, 1959); Stegenga, J. A., *The United Nations Force in Cyprus* (Columbus: Ohio State University Press, 1968).

factions, then demilitarization provisions would be of little value, for they would simply not be observed. While hostilities might not be renewed, the factions would remain fully armed and fortified in their zones, and the state would remain divided.

Political Settlement of a War for Independence

The war for independence is an internal war in the sense that the conflict begins internally, within a state. The insurgent faction is in rebellion against an incumbent government (perhaps a colonial power), which the rebels regard as alien. The basis for this judgment is the cultural, religious, or national differences between the incumbent governors and the insurgent leaders and between the elites and peoples that support each faction. The internal war for independence may end in the complete destruction of the forces of the insurgents. It usually does; and if the matter ended there, the situation would be uninteresting for our analysis. If, however, the insurgent faction gains independence, or even forces the incumbent government to grant it some measure of local autonomy, we will have a peace settlement.

The stage preliminary to peace talks in a war for independence will be similar to that for either the simple external war or the simple internal war for control of the polity. The preconditions to negotiations may be different, of course, relating as they might to the ultimate aim of independence that distinguished this kind of war. A cease-fire will be concluded in the military phase of negotiations, although one party might press for agreement on the terms of the complete peaceful settlement before agreeing to suspend hostilities. When the cease-fire has been put into effect, the armed forces of the factions will disengage, regroup, and withdraw from the theater of combat operations. Provision for the security of those forces and for the civilian population in the areas through which the troops move would no doubt be made. The negotiators will also seek to reach an accord concerning the exchange of prisoners of war and interned civilians, guarantees of the life and property of persons bearing allegiance to either faction, and the means for supervising the cease-fire and the withdrawal of troops. The character of the military settlement will depend in large part upon the relative power positions of the factions at the time negotiations began and during their progress.

The political settlement could take on one of several forms:

1. Independence for the insurgent faction. A part of the territory of the state will be assigned in perpetuity to the insurgents. This territory will become a new, independent successor state, governed by the insurgent faction at first, but fundamentally free to determine its own form of government.

2. Autonomy for the insurgent faction. An area of the state will be assigned to the insurgents, who are given the right to govern themselves. Formally, the insurgents are not sovereign and independent. Their "state" is associated in some way (delineated in the peace treaty) with the state of the incumbent government. The insurgent faction might be given the right to determine its own domestic policies, while foreign affairs and defense policy remain with the incumbent government. The unitary state as it existed before the war would be transformed into a federative or confederative state by the peace treaty and accompanying legislation.

3. A third possible solution entails granting political concessions to the

insurgent faction and to the people that supported them. The incumbent faction might have succeeded in putting down the rebellion, but at a cost that compelled them to take steps to alleviate domestic discontent. In the wake of this sort of victory, elites of the incumbent government might feel that some political concessions were necessary merely to appease the insurgents and to return the state to a condition of peace. In time, the war issues would be forgotten. Others in the incumbent government (and the insurgent faction leaders) might regard concessions at the war's end as the first in a series, leading eventually to the insurgent's autonomy or independence. The insurgents might plan to renew hostilities when they were able to do so, if this evolution toward autonomy did not take place. In any event, this solution (granting concessions short of autonomy) follows from the fact that although the insurgents have not placed themselves in a strong bargaining position as a result of military operations (and may even have lost the war), the incumbents wish to eliminate internal discontent by concessions of a political, economic, or cultural nature.

Let us consider the sort of political settlement required by the solution of *complete independence*. The factions must, of course, agree upon the formal grant of independence. Even at as late a time as the negotiations over political questions, the incumbent faction may not yet have reconciled itself to losing a part of its polity, even a distant colonial domain. Thus, the incumbents might seek to condition the grant, converting it to local autonomy rather thas the complete independence demanded by the insurgent faction.

Assuming that the insurgents have obtained a promise of full independence before or during the negotiations, the peace treaty will contain a clause pursuant to which the parent state, governed by the incumbent faction, unconditionally grants the newly established successor state (governed in all likelihood, at least provisionally, by the leaders of the insurgent faction) full and complete independence and sovereignty. Questions might arise respecting the government of the new state, apparently a matter solely of a domestic political kind, but the peace treaty might very well deal with it. The parent state might, in fact, succeed in extracting promises and concessions from the insurgents relating to how they will govern the successor state. Thus, the peace treaty might provide for the creation of a constitutional drafting committee with a composition fixed by its terms; it might provide for the election of a constituent assembly and establish procedures for such elections, including the creation of an elections supervisory commission. The peace treaty could even provide for the creation of a provisional government of a specified composition. The presence of such clauses in the treaty would demonstrate that as the parent state had at least minimally determined the nature of the regime for the successor state, it had the bargaining power to secure the concessions.

If it had enough bargaining power, the parent state could succeed in securing additional favorable terms, such as special rights for its nationals in the territory of the successor state. Such rights might be commercial in nature, or even juridical in the sense that a special regime of law may be created for parent-state nationals. In circumstances of internal instability or an external threat to the existence of the successor state the parent state may be given the right to station troops within the successor state. Moreover, the insurgents may also agree to adhere to a bilateral security pact in association with the parent state or to a collective defense pact in a coalition with the latter and its allies. A threat to the insurgent faction (and to the successor state), whether internal or external, might thus permit its leaders to overcome their antipathy toward the incumbents, even in the relatively short time required to negotiate a peace settlement, and persuade them to allow troops of the parent state to remain on their soil. Put another way, there would have to be relatively rapid de-ideologization; and the external threat would have to be severe enough to induce it.

On the other hand, the insurgents may be able to extract certain concessions from the incumbents of the parent state, for example, the right to use rivers or canals through its territories or to transport goods across the parent state under equal or more favorable terms than granted to others. The parent state might even assume the debt of the successor state (that is, it would agree not to allocate a portion of its postwar national debt to the successor state). The parent state could also relinquish all claims against the insurgents and its nationals; or it could agree to transfer, without charge, title to equipment, factories, inventories, and installations owned by it. The successor state might even succeed in winning a promise of aid from the parent state in the form of foodstuffs, armaments, and technical or financial assistance. All such concessions are likely to be the result of a decision on the part of policymakers of the parent state to normalize relations with the successor state as quickly as possible after ratification of the peace treaty.

Even though the incumbents may well fail to secure commercial, juridical, or military rights from the insurgents, they will no doubt insist upon provisions in the peace treaty designed to protect the lives and properties of parent-state nationals still residing in the successor state. These will include a promise by the insurgents to refrain from reprisals and to protect foreign nationals from attacks or seizures in the successor state. There may also be a clause requiring the latter to reimburse parent-state nationals for all property seized during hostilities and guaranteeing them the right to conduct business and engage in skilled or professional occupations on the same basis as the nationals of the successor state. The negotiators may also agree that special provisions were required to protect the rights of minorities other than nationals of the parent state. Clauses to protect minorities in the practice of their businesses or religions would be an enlightened addition to the peace treaty, although they are frequently omitted. The question of minorities may be deemed by the insurgents to be of no concern to the incumbent government after independence, and the insurgents may be loath to have their sovereign prerogatives hampered by guarantees for minorities.

As a result of the war, many persons will have changed their places of residence. After the declaration of independence by the successor state, there will be some individuals who will leave for the parent state, preferring not to remain in what might become an increasingly hostile environment; and there will be some who will depart for the successor state to become citizens there. The peace treaty will usually contain provisions defining the status of the *national* of the parent and the successor states and delineating procedures for change of nationality. Guarantees of civil and personal liberties of nationals and minorities (to which we have already alluded) would be particularly necessary during the period when persons are attempting to change their residence and citizenship status. The policymakers of a state might be willing to tolerate the presence of foreign nationals, especially if they benefitted the economy; but they might not show a similarly beneficent attitude toward persons who intended to depart with their goods and capital. The nationality terms of the treaty of peace and independence may also include guarantees for the property of departing nationals or rules for the sale or disposal of such properties (and the allocation of the proceeds of the sale) to insure just compensation. These are likely to be thorny issues, occasioning much discussion during the peace talks. Disputes between departing and resident nationals (and departing nationals and the state) may attend the efforts of the emigrants to move their property to another state. In view of the probability that these disputes will continue on into the postwar period, the negotiators may constitute a special arbitral tribunal to handle property claims of the persons and their governments. In the absence of such a tribunal, controversies of this kind would undoubtedly be settled later, on an *ad hoc* basis—if they are settled at all. In respect of the settlement of disputes, the treaty of peace after a war for independence (an internal war) takes on some of the attributes of a treaty of peace for the political settlement of an external war. Indeed, other "elements of settlement" of the external war that we have discussed may also be included in the treaty of peace and independence.

The peace treaty will also contain clauses defining the boundaries of the insurgents' new state. One or several *ad hoc* boundary commissions may be established to work out the exact location of boundaries and to settle disputes of a minor kind. In the event of serious disagreements over boundaries, the leaders of the two factions will undoubtedly want the right finally to decide and not delegate such a right to a technical commission. The fixing of a boundary may be further complicated by the fact that minorities inhabit border areas. While strategic and security con-

TABLE 3–3. Internal war for independence: some examples of elements of a political settlement.

Element	Some examples
independence of the insurgents	Texas Revolt (pp. 106–7) ; Irish Rebellion (pp. 109–10) —but with partition and some formal ties to the Crown; Egyptian (pp. 110–1) and Tunisian (pp. 111–2) Independence; Dutch Revolt (pp. 208–14) ; War for American Independence (pp. 217–22) .
autonomy for insurgents	Third Huguenot War (pp. 101–3) ; Kurdish Insurrection (pp. 112–3) ; Bosnia and Herzegovina after the Peace of San Stefano in the Russo-Turkish War of 1877–78 (pp. 228–33) .
concession to insurgents	Emperor to German Princes in the Thirty Years' War (pp. 379–92) . See also Third Huguenot War (pp. 101–3) ; Cuban Revolt (pp. 107–8) ; Hungarian Rebellion (pp. 104–5) .
parent state reserved rights	Egyptian (pp. 110–1) and Tunisian (pp. 111–2) Independence; the great power reserved their rights as well as those of the Ottoman Empire in the settlement of the Greek Revolt (pp. 222–5) ; and see also Irish Rebellion (pp. 109–10) .
regime or guarantees for nationals of parent state	Tunisian Independence (pp. 111–2) ; American Revolution (pp. 217–22) ; Kurdish Insurrection (pp. 112–3) .
insurgents win independence *and* rights in parent state	Dutch Revolt (pp. 208–14) ; American Revolution (pp. 217–22) ; succession states to the Habsburg Empire after First World War (pp. 405–28) .
arbitral tribunals	Irish Rebellion (pp. 109–10) ; Tunisian Independence (pp. 111–2) .
boundaries of new states: technical details	American Revolution (pp. 217–22) ; Greek War for Independence (pp. 222–5) ; Russo-Turkish War of 1877–78 (pp. 228–33) ; First World War (pp. 405–28) —boundaries sometimes had to wait for a plebiscite.

siderations will be paramount in the negotiations, the factions may finally have to acquiesce in a plebiscite in order to determine the disposition of territories upon which the minority peoples reside. It should be noted that, even when legally obligated to protect the rights of minorities, states have often resorted to force to solve their minorities problems, particularly where border areas are involved. During peace negotiations, the factions may find themselves so irremediably divided over the disposition of territories and the location of the boundary that they disregard the question of minority rights and indeed define a boundary that divides minority-inhabited areas. Or they may assign those areas to the state least likely to sympathize with the desires of the minority. In all fairness, we should recognize that the resolution of minority problems is a very difficult task.

If the political solution of the war for independence is to be a grant of autonomy to the insurgent faction (i.e., a grant short of independence), then the compact of settlement will in effect amend the constitution of the state. A concession of the power to govern assigned territories, even if restricted to authority over local matters, is an important one. Its most dramatic and far-reaching constitutional effect is the conversion of a unitary state to a confederation. If the state of the incumbents previously was a federation, the peace compact will add a separate and domestically autonomous polity to it, which would undoubtedly have state-wide ramifications for future intrastate relations. The peace compact must then be framed with the understanding that the factions are not merely ending an internal war, but are also drafting a constitution for their state. The compact will therefore contain the formal grant of autonomy and define the boundaries of the territories to be assigned to the formerly

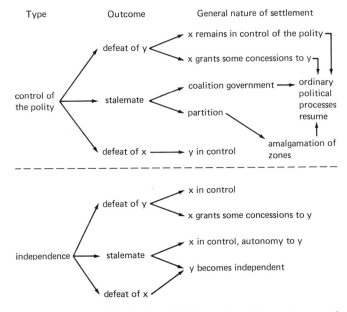

FIGURE 3-1. A simplified schematic illustration of the outcome and settlement of a simple internal war between the incumbent faction, x, and the insurgent faction, y.

insurgent faction. The limits of autonomy will be defined, that is, the powers granted to the new "state" will be adumbrated, as well as the powers reserved by the central government. Nationality questions will probably not arise, since all prewar citizens will retain that status after the war, although a hybrid citizenship status might be formulated for some residents of the new "state," for purposes relating to internal administration. Provision may also be made (and should be made) for settling future political and legal disputes arising out of the confederal relation between the central, principal state and the future autonomous province.

A summary of our discussion with respect to the outcome and settlement of simple internal wars is depicted schematically in Figure 3–1.

As we have seen, a simple internal war can end with the defeat of either faction or in a stalemate. The outcome determines the form and indeed, the content, of a possible settlement; as in the external war, *outcome* describes the military situation at or approaching the war's end (see Fig. 2–1). We shall return to an analysis of the *context* of internal wars and other variables influencing the peacemaking process in Chapter 5.

Summaries of Settlements of Some Simple Internal Wars

Only one simple internal war for control of the polity is listed in the summaries below, the English Revolution of 1688–1689. This singularity is hardly representative, as there have been many such internal wars in modern times. But it is significant that most of them have ended without negotiations, with the complete suppression of the insurgents. For our purposes, this outcome is an uninteresting end to war; the paucity of wars for control in our sample can be defended on the basis of the sheer unavailability of negotiated settlements of such wars.[7]

THIRD HUGUENOT WAR (1568–1570)

French Protestants (Huguenots) vs. French Monarch

AIM OF INSURGENTS: The Huguenots sought religious liberty and recognition of their autonomy in predominantly Reformed Protestant regions. (The autonomy actually enjoyed in certain areas often bordered on complete independence of the French Crown.)

7 Other wars for control of the polity discussed in subsequent summaries of settlements include the Korean War (*infra,* pp. 233–6), the Laotian Civil War (pp. 236–40), War of the Polish Succession (pp. 214–7), the Grisons Struggle during the Thirty Years' War (pp. 379–92), the Russian Revolution and Civil Wars, and the Finnish Civil War during and after the First World War (pp. 405–28), and the Peninsular War (after 1808) with Spanish rebels pitted against French troops during the Napoleonic Wars (pp. 392–405).

OUTCOME: A tenuous peace came with the settlment embodied in the Edict of St. Germain, 8 August 1570.[8]

FACTORS FOR PEACE: Divisions within the French nobility (many loyalists did not want the total ruin of the Huguenots), the financial weakness of the Crown, and the military stalemate induced the parties to move toward peace.

WAR-ORIENTED STATES: England, Spain.

MILITARY SETTLEMENT: With the publication of the Edict, all persons in the realm were to lay down their arms. All officials were to swear to obey the Edict, and all subjects were enjoined to act peacefully as brothers on pain of being treated as disturbers of the peace. Prisoners were to be released.

POLITICAL SETTLEMENT: The Edict declared that the memory of past troubles was erased: It was unlawful to mention them or litigate questions arising out of them. The leaders of the Huguenots were to declare themselves subjects of the King. General and specific amnesties were proclaimed. In all cities and villages of the realm, the King's subjects were to live without inquiry or molestation, nor be compelled to do anything against their conscience in respect of matters of religion, provided the subjects conducted themselves according to the terms of the Edict. Searching of homes was also prohibited. The exercise of the Reformed religion was permitted in specified areas but forbidden in others. Roman Catholics were to be allowed to practice their religion everywhere, and their property seized during the war was to be returned. Protestants were neither to be excluded from universities, schools, and hospitals nor prevented from holding office. Protestant exiles were permitted to return and would be recompensed for the confiscation of their goods. Ransoms would be arbitrated. Judgments and process against Protestants by reason of their religion were revoked and annulled. There was to be equal taxation of all subjects.

The cities of Rochelle, Montauban, Cognac, and La Charité were granted to the Protestants for 2 years as places "of private repose." They were to be returned to the King undamaged and unchanged. Roman Catholics were to enjoy the right to practice their religion in these cities.

Commerce among all parts of the realm was to be restored and move freely. Detailed procedures for settling disputes between subjects of different religions were set forth "to ensure fairness and remove suspicion."

The *Parlements* were instructed to enregister the Edict immediately without modification. All officers were to obey its letter and spirit. Violations would be punishable by death.

8 Du Mont, Jean, *Corps Universel Diplomatique du Droit des Gens,* Vol. 5 (Amsterdam: Brunel, 1728), pp. 180 f. The reader is referred to the bibliography for additional works supplementing the studies and documents cited in this section.

COMMENTS: This was one of a number of wars internal to France between Huguenots and Catholic Loyalists. The eighth such war was complicated by the intervention of Spain and by the existence for a time of not two, but rather three, factions. It was known as the War of the Three Henrys. The preceding seven Huguenot Wars were simple internal wars. The settlement of this war could have been made to work, but the issues were too ideologized and distrust was too widespread. In a case such as this, even the most technically adequate settlement cannot establish permanent peace.

THE ENGLISH ("GLORIOUS") REVOLUTION OF 1688–1689[9]

English elites vs. James II

AIM OF INSURGENTS: The Revolution's goal was to gain effective parliamentary control of the polity by limiting the King's prerogatives.

OUTCOME: After minor battle action, it became clear that the English nobles and people would not support the King, who then fled to France. The principal insurgent leaders had invited William of Orange to intervene. Having done so successfully, William became joint sovereign with his wife Mary, a daughter of James II.

FACTORS FOR PEACE: Defeat of the incumbent forces was the principal factor for peace.

WAR-ORIENTED STATES: The Netherlands, France.

THE SETTLEMENT:[10] The problem of legitimizing the Revolution was foremost in the minds of England's leaders and was the subject of intense parliamentary debate in early 1689. In December, 1688, a Convention Parliament was summoned by William at the request of the Peers and former members of the House of Commons. Elections were held, and the Convention met in January, 1689. The difficulty confronting the Parliament was to rationalize its own legitimacy. After James had fled, England had no King; and according to the English Constitution, Parliament could not function legitimately without a King. By what right therefore did William summon a Parliament? And by what right did the Convention Parliament promulgate laws, particularly the laws fixing the succession? The solution was a compromise between the Tory principle of

---

9 It could be argued that this war was really a complex internal war (see Chapter 5), with the Dutch supporting the rebellious English nobles against King James II. However, the war-oriented states played virtually no part in the settlement, the Dutch armed forces played a minimal role in the Revolution, and The Netherlands was not formally—and barely functionally—a belligerent. I have therefore treated this war as a simple internal war. Naturally, a thorough analysis of the settlement would require us to consider the policies and influence of the war-oriented allies of the factions. See Appendix I for a discussion of the multiple modes of analyzing wars that are difficult to classify.

10 Macaulay, T. B., *The History of England from the Accession of James II*, Vol. 2 (London: J. M. Dent, 1906), pp. 159 f.

Divine Right and the Lockean theories of the Whigs. By an Act of Parliament, it was declared that by fleeing England, James II had abdicated. The throne being vacant, William and Mary were to be vested with joint sovereignty (administration vested in William alone). It was further declared that no Roman Catholic could wear the Crown. In the interview between Parliament and William in February, 1689, the latter accepted the Crown and the limitations Parliament had imposed upon the sovereign's powers. The Convention was then made a Parliament *de jure*. The leaders of the Revolution, and others, were required to swear an oath of allegiance to William as King *de facto,* but not as King *de jure.* (Some Tories remained profoundly disturbed about the constitutionality of the settlement.)

By a series of acts, including the Declaration of Right, Parliament adumbrated a political settlement of the Revolution. A law could be promulgated or altered only if a statute were passed by both houses with the consent of the King. Judges were to have tenure during "their good behavior"; the King could no longer arbitrarily remove judges. The interpretation of the laws of the realm was entrusted solely to the judiciary. Dissenters were to enjoy free public worship, although their civil disabilities remained. The maintenance of the army was legal for one year only, renewable each year by Parliament. In the spirit of the Glorious Revolution, the Licensing Act was allowed to expire in 1695, thus permitting freedom of the press except for libel and sedition. In 1701, the succession was fixed in the House of Hanover.

COMMENTS: In an internal war for control of the polity, successful insurgents must legitimize their rule. And efforts by them to remedy the political and economic discontinuities caused by the war are, in effect, a settlement of it. There was no military settlement for the Revolution, as the King's forces had collapsed and disintegrated.

THE HUNGARIAN REBELLION (1703–1711)
Hungarian rebels vs. Habsburg Empire

AIM OF INSURGENTS: The rebels fought for the restoration of ancient Hungarian liberties, reduction of taxes, and religious toleration.

OUTCOME: Defeats weakened the rebels' forces, and concessions granted by Joseph I (King of Hungary and Holy Roman Emperor) won over some of the Hungarian leaders, who accepted the Peace of Szatmar, 30 June 1711.[11]

FACTORS FOR PEACE: For the Hungarians, defeat, depopulation from the plague and the rebellion, divisions within the leadership, and the not unreasonable terms offered by the Emperor; for the Emperor, the desire

---

11 Macartney, C. A., *Hungary: A Short History* (Edinburgh: University Press, 1962), pp. 89 f.

to pacify his realm without further embittering the Hungarians, and certainly without massacring them.

WAR-ORIENTED STATES: The Rebellion took place during the War of the Spanish Succession,[12] and Habsburg policy (as well as military plans for the suppression of the revolt) can be understood only in relation to that war and to the Habsburg successes and failures in it. The Great Powers involved in the multilateral Succession War were war-oriented in respect of the rebellion within the Habsburg realm.

THE SETTLEMENT: PRELIMINARIES: Informal talks between leaders of the Rebellion and Habsburg officials took place at various times during the war. These talks were exploratory in nature, designed to determine whether the leaders would accept a peace settlement and what terms they would accept.

MILITARY SETTLEMENT: There was to be an armistice in which the rebels would put down their arms. An amnesty was to be given to anyone who within three weeks took an oath of loyalty to the Crown. All except the Rákóczi family accepted the amnesty.

POLITICAL SETTLEMENT: The King promised to convoke a Diet to hear complaints. The constitutional and religious position of 1687–1689 was confirmed (these were less favorable terms than were offered the insurgents in 1706). Hereditary succession in the male line of the Habsburgs was recognized. The King promised to observe Hungary's laws and privileges "as the King and the assembled Estates shall agree on the interpretation thereof;"[13] and the *jus resistendi* was abolished (this was the right to resist the King without imputation of treason if he violated certain feudal privileges of the Hungarian nobles).

At a Diet at Pozsony in 1712, the King swore to respect the national rights and liberties of Hungary and to rule Hungary according to its laws only, not according to the pattern of rule in other provinces of the Habsburg realm. The Diet of 1723 confirmed this oath and further stipulated that the Diet was to meet every three years. The King promised to defend the integrity of Hungary and not incorporate it into his dominions. A standing army, one third of which was to be Hungarians, was to be stationed in the Kingdom and controlled by a Council of State to which Hungary would send representatives. The Diet accepted Maria Theresa as the legitimate Empress and Queen of Hungary, conceding that only if the Habsburg line were extinguished would Hungary recover the right to elect its own monarch.

COMMENTS: Although the Rebellion failed militarily, the insurgents did succeed in obtaining significant concessions from the incumbents.

12 See Chapter 9 for an analysis of the settlement of The War of the Spanish Succession.
13 Macartney, *op. cit.*, p. 89.

THE TEXAS REVOLT (1835–1836) Texas settlers vs. Mexican Government

AIM OF INSURGENTS: In response to a Mexican attempt belatedly to exercise real authority in its Texas province, the insurgents revolted and proclaimed their independence.

OUTCOME: Military successes resulted in *de facto* Mexican recognition of Texas independence in the two Treaties of Velasco of 14 May 1836.[14]

FACTORS FOR PEACE: For Mexico, defeat and inability to administer Texas; for the Texans, achievement of their objectives.

THE SETTLEMENT: PRELIMINARIES: Santa Anna, President of Mexico and commander of the Mexican forces in Mexico, was captured after the Battle of San Jacinto. He was induced to acquiesce in Texas terms for a settlement.

MILITARY SETTLEMENT: An immediate cease-fire was proclaimed. The Mexican army was to move south of the Rio Grande; and in this move, no Mexican soldiers or officers were to use or take the property of any person without their consent and just indemnification. The forces of the parties were to separate at least five leagues. All property taken by Mexicans during the war was to be returned to the Commander of the Texas forces or to the Texas Government. Prisoners were to be freed, the Mexican Government being billed for the cost of prisoner maintenance.

POLITICAL SETTLEMENT: Santa Anna agreed not to take up arms again against the people of Texas. Texas independence was not mentioned in the Treaty. But Santa Anna, in a secret agreement, obligated himself to prepare "things in the Cabinet of Mexico that a mission sent thither by the government of Texas may be well received and by means of negotiations all differences might be settled and independence acknowledged."[15] Subsequent actions of Mexican officials, including Santa Anna, indicated that Mexico recognized at least the *de facto* independence of Texas. Indeed, this view is confirmed by the fact that in 1843, Santa Anna (again dictator after domestic upheavals) offered a plan to Texas officials for the "reincorporation" of Texas in Mexico. In March, 1837, the United States appointed a Chargé d'Affaires to Texas. Annexation to the United States occurred in 1845.

COMMENTS: The settlement embodied in the two rather short Treaties of Velasco was a simple one. The Texans, after all, had been functionally independent for many years before the Revolt occurred, and there were few symbols of Mexican sovereignty in this northern province. The Texas negotiators therefore sought a Mexican pronouncement on complete independence and military provisions ensuring Texas security. Other

14 Maillard, N. D., *The History of the Republic of Texas* (London: Smith, Elder & Co., 1842), pp. 112–114.

15 Wharton, C. R., *Texas Under Many Flags*, Vol. 1 (Chicago: The American Historical Society, 1930), p. 298.

matters could be resolved by the Texans themselves without deliberating upon them at the peace talks, just as they had been taken care of before and during the Revolt.

THE CUBAN REVOLT (1869–1878) Cuban insurgents vs. Spain

AIM OF INSURGENTS: independence.

OUTCOME: The rebels were induced to lay down their arms and accept the Treaty of Zanjon (15 February 1878) to end revolt.[16]

FACTORS FOR PEACE: For Spain, the costs of war, and the likelihood that guerilla war could not be ended without making concessions were factors for peace; for the rebels, war weariness after sustaining defeats and the attractiveness of some of the concessions from Spain.

WAR-ORIENTED STATES: The United States, which almost intervened and which sought twice to mediate on terms favorable to the rebels, was war-oriented.

THE SETTLEMENT: PRELIMINARIES: The Military Governor of Cuba (Martinez-Campos) issued decrees rescinding banishment of rebels, raising embargoes, reducing taxes and tariffs, and ordering the return of some confiscated properties (1877). In the face of these concessions, the rebel leadership was divided, but most of them ultimately decided to negotiate peace.

MILITARY SETTLEMENT: There was to be a cease-fire, and the rebels were to deposit their arms at specified places. The Commander-in-Chief of the Spanish armies would furnish transportation to the insurgents so that they could capitulate at these places. All rebels thus surrendering were given amnesty, and no person was to be compelled to render military service until peace was established over the whole of Cuba.

POLITICAL SETTLEMENT: The political, organic, and administrative laws of Puerto Rico were established for Cuba. This change gave Cubans the same constitutional rights as all Spaniards, at least in theory. There was to be freedom for slaves and Asiatic Coolies. Persons desiring to leave Cuba would be permitted to do so with the assistance of Spanish authorities. A reported secret agreement promised representation of Cuba in the *Cortes*. It also promised elections, a new militia composed of Cubans as well as Spanish, abolition of slavery within 5 years, inclusion of the war debt in the public estimates of the island, and recognition of the military rank of the insurgent officers.

COMMENTS: Although many of the terms of the Treaty were frequently disregarded by both sides, the bulk of the rebels surrendered on 26 February, and the island was gradually pacified after that. Although Cuba did obtain representation in the Cortes, the delegates were ap-

16 Johnson, W. F., *The History of Cuba*, Vol. 3 (New York: B. F. Buck & Co., 1920), pp. 297 f.

pointed by a Spanish Governor-General who retained virtually dictatorial powers after the war. Slavery was abolished in 1886. Taxation was oppressive, however, as were tariffs and other trade restrictions. The reader should compare this internal war with the Hungarian Rebellion; in both, the rebels' resistance petered out with the promise of concessions by the incumbents. Thus, the wars did not end simply, on a specific date; rather, fighting gradually died out. This process is often characteristic of internal wars.

THE PHILIPPINE INSURRECTION (1898–1902)

Filipino insurgents vs. U.S.

AIM OF INSURGENTS: independence.

OUTCOME: The insurrection collapsed with the capture of the rebel leader Aguilnaldo in 1901. The islands were substantially pacified by 1902.

THE SETTLEMENT: Although the insurrection was suppressed, the United States, by means of internal law, promulgated a settlement. By a series of Executive Orders, the President established a Philippine Commission in 1900 with authority to govern the Islands. The Commission was at first composed of 3 U.S. citizens; three Filipinos were subsequently appointed. In the Act of 1 July 1902,[17] Congress permitted Philippine representation in the House of Representatives (2 resident commissioners to the U.S., without vote). The Act also placed property acquired from Spain pursuant to the Peace Treaty of 10 December 1898 under the control of the Government of the Philippines. Preference was to be given to settlers and occupants of the land in selling and granting lands in the public domain. The Act also included detailed provisions concerning mineral rights, municipal bonds, coinage, and franchises. Congress also promulgated a Bill of Rights for the Philippines and ordered a census after which the President was to direct the Philippine Commission to call general elections for a Philippine Assembly.[18] That Assembly was to act conjointly with the Commission in governing the Islands. It was inaugurated in 1907. Under the Wilson Administration, rapid Filipinization of the government apparatus was carried out.

COMMENTS: We have an example here of the suppression of a rebellion followed by legislation of the incumbent regime granting significant concessions to the people in whose name the insurgents warred for independence. It is difficult to say what the United States would have done had there been no insurrection; but as it had occurred, many American leaders (but not all) were convinced of the necessity of granting complete independence to the Filipinos eventually and taking steps to give them autonomy within a very short space of time.

17 *U.S. Statutes at Large* (1901–1903), 57th Congress, Vol. 32, Part 1, Chap. 1369
    (Washington: U.S. Government Printing Office, 1903), pp. 691–712.
18 *Ibid.,* p. 693.

THE IRISH REBELLION (1919–1921)

Irish insurgents vs. Great Britain

AIM OF INSURGENTS: independence.

OUTCOME: Ireland was partitioned; commonwealth status was given to an Irish Free State later the Republic of Ireland, while the six northern counties became Northern Ireland, with a separate government.

FACTORS FOR PEACE: The British policymakers realized that the rebellion could not be suppressed at a reasonable cost in lives and matériel. The desire for a peace of reconciliation, pressures from the U.S. and Commonwealth States, and division of opinion at home were additional inducements for peace. For the Irish, the war costs, division of opinion in Ireland, war weariness, and possibly the British threat of "immediate and terrible war" were factors for peace.

WAR-ORIENTED ACTORS: States within the British Commonwealth and the United States.

THE SETTLEMENT: PRELIMINARIES: British peace feelers originated with a speech by the King at Belfast in June, 1921, and a letter from Lloyd George to the Irish leader Eamon de Valera,[19] who had been released from arrest to engage in negotiations. After an exchange of letters between the leaders, a truce for 11 July was arranged, De Valera having concluded that before talks could begin a truce was necessary. He had difficulty persuading some of the Irish republicans. Throughout August and September, the leaders of the two sides negotiated over the preconditions and procedures of a peace conference, which finally began in October.

MILITARY SETTLEMENT: The truce agreement came into effect on 11 July.[20] The British agreed to refrain from sending more troops to Ireland, staging provocative displays of force, and pursuing Irish insurgents. They were also to forego all surveillance activity and not interfere with the movements of the insurgents. The Irish Army would stop its attacks on all Crown Forces and civilians and refrain from interfering with Government operations or with private property. The Irish would also try to prevent any activity that might disturb the peace.

POLITICAL SETTLEMENT: The Articles of Agreement were signed on 6 December 1921 and came into effect in January 1922.[21] Ireland was to have the same status as Canada, New Zealand, Australia, and the Union of South Africa in the British Commonwealth. A new political entity, called the *Irish Free State*, was created with a parliament responsible for making laws and seeing to their execution. The relation of the Free State to the Imperial Crown in Ireland was to be the same as that for Canada, and the representative of the Crown in Ireland was to be appointed in

19 Macardle, Dorothy, *The Irish Republic* (London: Gollancz, 1937), p. 466.
20 *Ibid.*, pp. 475–6.
21 *Ibid.*, pp. 953 f.

the same manner as the Governor-General of Canada. The Members of Parliament of the Free State were to take an oath of allegiance to the Irish Free State and to His Majesty the King.

Northern Ireland was to be a separate entity; and a boundary commission was established to determine the line of partition. Laws against the free exercise of religion in either part of Ireland were forbidden. A provisional government of the Free State was to be established immediately, and the British would transfer powers to it.

The Irish Free State was responsible for the public debt of Britain in Ireland and for the payment of war pensions. Arbitration was provided in the event of disagreement. The Free State was also responsible for the salaries of certain officials who might be retired as a result of the change of government.

The ports of Ireland were open for the use of the parties. Facilities at specified ports were to be provided for British use.

The British undertook to defend Ireland. This provision was to be reviewed in 5 years. The size of the Irish Army was not to exceed a prescribed level.

COMMENTS: Dissatisfaction with the terms of the Agreement led to a split within the Sinn Fein and to civil war, which dragged on for years (until at least 1932). That was another war, however, with another settlement. The settlement of 1922 does show that an internal war for independence can end with a partition of territories, much like the solution described for a war for control of the polity.

THE STRUGGLE FOR EGYPTIAN INDEPENDENCE (1919–1922)
Egyptian nationalists vs. Britain

AIM OF INSURGENTS: Independence.

OUTCOME: Britain unilaterally declared the independence of Egypt.

FACTORS FOR PEACE: The weakness of Britain after the First World War was certainly a major factor. Costs of suppression were high, and Britain desired to maintain tolerably good relations with Egyptian nationalists and still retain some privileges in Egypt.

THE SETTLEMENT: PRELIMINARIES: The Milner Mission left Egypt in 1920 convinced of the need to accommodate Egyptian nationalism. Zaghlul, a nationalist leader, refused to negotiate a treaty with Britain, however. He did not want to commit himself in writing to the terms the British were willing to grant, in part because he wanted more of a free hand to exploit, for his own ends, the weaknesses of the British juridical position before and after independence; in part, because he did not like the British terms (the Sudan would not be a part of Egypt, and the British would have the right to maintain bases on Egyptian soil). Negotiations continued with frequent interruptions throughout 1921 and 1922. Finally, the British decided to give Egypt its independence by means of a unilateral declaration.

POLITICAL SETTLEMENT: The protectorate was ended and Egyptian independence proclaimed as of 28 February 1922. Martial law was to be withdrawn when Parliament had passed an Act of Indemnity. Britain reserved for future discussion and agreement the security and communications of the Empire in Egypt, defense of Egypt against "foreign aggression or interference, direct or indirect," protection of foreign interests and minorities, and the Sudan. "Pending the conclusion of such agreements the status quo in these matters shall remain intact."[22]

COMMENTS: This was an unusual case in which the parent state could not get the insurgents to bargain on the terms of the independence that the parent state intended to grant. Future negotiations remedied this to some extent.

THE STRUGGLE FOR TUNISIAN INDEPENDENCE (1949–1956)
Tunisian nationalists vs. France

AIM OF INSURGENTS: Independence.

OUTCOME: Independence was granted in the Treaties of 3 June 1955 and in the Protocol of 20 March 1956.

FACTORS FOR PEACE: France's inability—financial and military—to retain control over Tunisia, the desire for a peace of reconciliation to lay the basis for good post-independence relations, and pressure from allies were the principal inducements for peace.

WAR-ORIENTED ACTORS: United States, Britain, Egypt, Morocco, Spain, Libya, and the United Nations.

THE SETTLEMENT: PRELIMINARIES: Premier Mendès-France, in July, 1954, recognized the need to give Tunisia internal autonomy. Bourguiba, the Tunisian nationalist leader, was released; and negotiations concerning the status of Tunisia were opened, lasting until complete independence was obtained. The French, however, were willing to grant Tunisia only internal autonomy; hence the very detailed treaties of 3 June 1955 accomplished only that. In the Protocol of 20 March 1956, France recognized the complete independence of Tunisia, externally as well as internally.

MILITARY SETTLEMENT: In the 1955 Treaties, both parties recognized their solidarity respecting matters of security and defense.[23] Tunisia would undertake, on France's demand, to implement measures to permit France to carry out its obligations for the defense of the "Free World." Tunisia would assume gradual control over police forces according to the schedules provided. However, France would retain some police powers at the frontiers and in ports. The Protocol of 1956 abrogated all provisions contrary to the status of complete independence; presumably, residual

22 Marlowe, John, *Anglo-Egyptian Relations, 1800–1953* (London: Cresset Press, 1954), p. 248.

23 *Conventions entre La France et La Tunisie, Signés à Paris, Le 3 Juin 1955* (Paris: Imprimerie National, 1955).

French police powers were thereby nullified.[24] Tunisia was then free to establish its own army.

POLITICAL SETTLEMENT: In the 1956 Protocol, France recognized Tunisian independence and abrogated the Bardo Treaty of 12 May 1881.[25] The Treaties of 3 June 1955 were not entirely abrogated, and they did define post-independence Franco-Tunisian relations in important ways. For our purposes, they are important as negotiated agreements for the settlement of a war for independence. Thus, the Treaties of 3 June 1955 provided that: a. France recognized the internal autonomy of Tunisia but would retain authority in areas of foreign affairs and defense; b. Tunisia recognized the Universal Declaration of Human Rights and would undertake to protect the civil rights of all persons within its territory; c. France was to nominate Tunisia to membership in international organizations; d. the Bey of Tunis was to be kept informed of international negotiations concerning Tunisia; e. Tunisia would promulgate internal laws for the purpose of fulfilling treaties; f. Arabic was the official language of Tunisia, but French was not to be regarded as a foreign language; g. a French High Commissioner to Tunisia was appointed with duties and immunities specified; and h. an arbitral tribunal was established to interpret the Treaty and consider violations thereof. Other treaties of the same date provided, in detail, for the nationality of persons affected by the change in Tunisia's juridical status, for administrative and technical cooperation during the transition to internal autonomy, and for cultural relations, judicial administration, and financial and economic arrangements. Only those provisions of the 1955 Treaties were abrogated that were inconsistent with Tunisian independence. After 1956, the parties were to "perfect the modalities of interdependence by organizing cooperation, particularly in defense and foreign relations;"[26] and negotiations were to proceed in order to determine what aid France would give to the Tunisian National Army.

COMMENTS: The internal war in this instance (as in the case of the struggle for Egyptian independence) consisted of the often violent agitation of the nationalists and guerilla warfare. The settlement was, in its entirety, thorough and logical.

THE KURDISH INSURRECTION (1961–1967; 1970)

Kurdish nationalists vs. Iraq

AIM OF INSURGENTS: Autonomy, not independence.

OUTCOME: Negotiated agreements defined the status of the Kurds in Iraq.

24 Frankland, Noble, *Documents on International Affairs* (London: Oxford University Press, 1959), pp. 692–3.
25 See the Franco-Tunisian War, *supra.*
26 Frankland. *op. cit.,* p. 693.

FACTORS FOR PEACE: For Iraq, preoccupation with foreign problems, costs of attempting to suppress the rebellion; for the Kurds, war weariness and the prospect of securing their goals through negotiations.

WAR-ORIENTED STATES: Iran and Turkey.

THE SETTLEMENT: Frequently interrupted negotiations have continued from 1965 to the time of this writing.[27] In June 1966, the Kurds agreed to a peace plan that promised coequal status for the Arab and Kurdish languages, decentralization of the government administration, elections, proportional representation of the Kurds in the National Assembly of Iraq, representation in the Cabinet and in the judiciary, civil service, and armed forces, and recognition by Iraq of the Kurdish right to organize a political party and establish a Kurdish press. In July, 1966, Kurdish leaders ordered a cease-fire, although there was no agreement on the division of royalties for oil produced from oil fields in Kurdish areas. It was not until May, 1967, that President Arif of Iraq formed a Cabinet with 2 Kurds. In October, 1967, Iraq began to move Arab tribesmen away from Erbil to placate the Kurds. In December, 1968, renewed clashes between the parties occurred, followed by new peace offers from the central government in May, 1969. They led to a second agreement in October, according to which the Kurdish language was to be taught in secondary schools and universities in Kurdish areas. Schools were to get Kurdish names, and Kurdish authors were to be allowed to publish their writings. A third agreement followed in March, 1970: Iraq recognized the autonomy of the Kurds within a defined area in northern Iraq. A new Iraqi constitution would be drafted and was to proclaim that Iraq was a country of 2 nationalities: Kurd and Iraqi. The Kurd army was to remain intact. Iraq would have the right to all oil, although it was not certain that Kirkuk (within the oil fields) would be included in the area recognized as Kurdish. By the end of March, 1970, the Iraq government was reconstituted with increased Kurdish representation. Kurdish armed forces were legalized, and the Government began to move its troops from the north. A new constitution had been drafted, recognizing the cultural and economic rights of the Kurds.

COMMENTS: The settlement process of this unusual war has extended over 4 years and cannot yet be considered terminated.

The internal wars for independence summarized here ended in several ways. The insurgents were victorious in the Texas Revolt and the war

27 See the following issues of *The New York Times:* for 1966: 29 June, 12 July; for 1967: 3 October; 1968; 21 March, 24 June, 22 July, 4 and 19 August, 19 November; 1969: 30 March, 21 and 24 May, 12 October; and for 1970: 30 March.

and agitation for Tunisian Independence;[28] they were defeated in the Philippine Insurrection, but the parent state made concessions to the rebels' aspirations for greater autonomy. In the Cuban Rebellion (ended 1878) and the Hungarian Rebellion (ended 1711), the rebels, quite close to defeat, were induced to lay down their arms by promises of amnesty and political rights.[29] In the Huguenot, Irish, and Kurdish internal wars, neither side was willing or able to settle the issue solely by military means, and settlements not entirely pleasing to the factions were negotiated.[30] We even have an example of an internal war for independence in which disagreements among the rebel leaders prompted the parent state (Great Britain) to grant independence (to Egypt) unilaterally without adequately negotiating the basis of the separation.

In respect to the thoroughness of the settlements, we have the rather detailed treaties between France and Tunisia at one extreme[31] and the incomplete settlement embodied in the Treaty of Velasco ending the Texas Revolt, at the other. We had one war that ended with the partition of the successor state, the Irish Rebellion. (There also were Egyptian nationalists who regarded the retention of the Sudan by Britain as an unjustified partition of Egyptian lands when the independence of Egypt was promulgated in 1922).[32]

28 Insurgents were also successful in the Dutch Revolt (infra, pp. 208–14), the War for American Independence (pp. 217–22), the Greek War for Independence (pp. 222–5), in several Balkan states in the Russo-Turkish War of 1877–8 (pp. 228–33) and in the Hejaz in the First World War (pp. 405–28).
29 Insurgents seeking independence failed utterly in the Bohemian Revolt of the Thirty Years' War (infra, pp. 379–92) and the Armenian Revolt in the First World War (pp. 405–28). Induced by Great Britain, Spain granted the Catalonian rebels amnesty after the rebellion of the latter had failed during the War of the Spanish Succession (pp. 357–66).
30 The Korean War (infra, pp. 233–6) was a war for control of the polity that ended in a draw; and the internal war that afflicted the Holy Roman Empire during the Thirty Years' War (pp. 379–92) was more or less resolved by a compromise peace that was a recognition of the military stalemate within the Empire. In both cases, none of the parties was pleased with the settlement.
31 See also note 65 in Chapter 2 for other examples.
32 The Palatinate was partitioned in the Peace of Westphalia, ending the Thirty Years' War (infra, pp. 379–92). The Netherlands was partitioned during the Dutch Revolt (pp. 208–14), the Walloon provinces being retained by Spain. Korea after the Korean War (pp. 233–6), British North America after the War for American Independence (pp. 217–22), and the Arab-Levantine provinces of the Ottoman Empire after the First World War (pp. 405–28) were also partitioned. In the last case, the Middle Eastern states that originated from the partition were mandated to Britain and France (but not the Hejaz which became wholly independent). A similar partition-protectorate solution was implemented in the final settlement of the Russo-Turkish War of 1877–8

In the Huguenot War and the Hungarian and Kurdish Rebellions, the insurgents fought for autonomy in the exercise of certain rights and privileges and for recognition by the incumbent regime of those rights, as they concerned the rebels' religion, nationality, or culture. While the aim of the insurgents was not independence, as we understand it, the settlements of these wars resemble the settlements of wars for independence.[33] In the English Revolution, we see an example of a settlement that was a compromise between the Whigs and Tories, a kind of coalition government solution. We shall have to wait until the chapter on complex internal wars (Chapter 5) to find additional examples of settlements of wars for control of the polity and instances of partition or coalition government solutions of such wars.[34]

---

for Bosnia and Herzegovina, which were assigned to Austria-Hungary for administration.

33 The German Protestant princes fought for greater religious and political autonomy in the Thirty Years' War (infra, pp. 379–92). Bulgarian leaders sought and obtained greater autonomy from the Porte in the Russo-Turkish War of 1877–8 (pp. 228–33); and the Pasha of Egypt sought to expand his domain of control, subject to the Sultan, in the First and Second Wars of Mehemet Ali (pp. 225–8).

34 The coalition government solution was employed in the settlement of the Laotian Civil War (infra, pp. 236–40). Great-power administration of Eastern Rumelia and Bulgaria was a kind of coalition government solution; it was adopted by the signatories of the Peace of Berlin, ending the Russo-Turkish War of 1877–8 (pp. 228–33). A listing of other wars for control of the polity may be found in note 7.

Alliances and Peacemaking

CHAPTER 4

Alliance Cohesiveness

When alliances of states become involved in war, peacemaking gains yet another dimension, and the settlement process becomes still more complex. It is not just a matter of there being more than two parties, each an adversary of the other, although that is surely important. There are also the *intra-alliance relations* that affect the conduct of the war and the course of the peace negotiations in crucial ways.

An alliance is an associaton of states or of states and factions. We will be chiefly concerned with wartime alliances and hence with alliances that are directed to the achievement of one or several war aims. We shall also deal with alliances during peace negotiations and thus with allies more or less collectively interested in the settlement of complex wars—and to the extent the partners want peace, variously intent upon bringing about a settlement that comports with their interests as well as the interests of the alliance. The form of the alliance, its rules of operation, and the purposes to which it is dedicated and for which it was constituted are usually spelled out in an agreement between the coalition partners that most often take the form of a formal treaty of alliance. Reference to the treaty and to agreements concluded pursuant to it enable us to discern some of the allies' war aims.

The purposes of an alliance are its reasons-for-being. The allies' agreement or acquiescence in these purposes provides for cohesiveness between them; and indeed, without at least tacit agreement about such purposes, the alliance would never have been formed, or if formed, would it long have held together. Certainly war is a major incentive for alliance formation, because war poses most starkly the threat to the single state's existence, inducing its policymakers to seek the cooperation of other states that feel threatened so that they may share resources for prosecuting the war against a common enemy. The pervasive and fundamental purpose of wartime alliances is the security of the component states or factions; survival of each partner is the key motivation. There are, of course, alliances in which some partners are not even remotely threatened with extinction as formal political organizations. And the policymakers of threatened states might themselves believe that their chances of survival are high. Yet they enter an alliance to secure a variety of ideological or power political values they deem important. In the Crimean War, it was Turkey whose territorial integrity was threatened by Russia. Turkey's allies (France and Britain) fought to prevent partition of the Ottoman Empire and to preserve a balance of power in Europe and in the Middle East, not because there was an immediate danger in their own security. In the Suez War of 1956, Israel's policymakers believed that the threat to the continued existence of their state from Egypt was real and pressing. The leaders of Israel's allies in the venture (France and Britain) never believed that Egypt constituted a threat to their states' existence. They could, and did, argue that seizure of the Suez Canal might cut vital communications links. But only a few policymakers convinced themselves that Nasser ultimately posed as serious a threat to their more extensively conceived national interests as he did to Israel's. The survival of the state or faction remains an important reason for seeking allies. It is not the only reason, of course, although political leaders often rationalize or justify alliance policies by warning of the dangers of continuing to act alone.

The members of an *effective* alliance often treat it as an end in itself; that is, they regard it as an entity whose survival must assume primacy in the formation and execution of their policies. One need only recall the extent to which Allied war policies in the Second World War were advertised in American and British newspapers as the policies not of the individual countries, but of the Alliance itself; or how often British and American political leaders justified their decisions in terms of the exigencies of that Alliance. At base, this attitude is derived from the belief that the alliance is essential to the achievement of the war aims of *each* ally and from the recognition that each must proceed upon the assumption that the alliance *as an alliance* also has a vital survival value. Such a perspective promotes the cohesiveness that makes an alliance more effective in accomplishing its objectives. But the policymaker, as a servant of his state, rarely permits rhetoric proclaiming the primacy of alliance objectives to obscure the fact that the alliance is merely an *instrument* for the achievement of his own state's war aims. He will cooperate with the other states' policymakers only so far and so long as cooperation pays off.

The most important variable to which we direct our attention in analyzing intracoalition cooperation is the degree of cohesiveness between members of the alliance.[1] Agreement among the allies about the purposes of the alliance and the methods for achieving them produces cohesiveness. Disagreements produce strains and may result in the dissolution of the alliance. The allies may disagree because their war aims are intrinsically incompatible or because they cannot agree whose aims (and which aims) are primary. They may also disagree about methods for conducting war operations, the implementation of war policies (assuming agreement on the ends of those policies), or bargaining tactics at the peace conference. As long as they agree about their coalition's *objectives,* disagreements about methods or means, while frequently bitter, will probably not result in dissolution—although there have been exceptions.

Two special cases of disagreement over war aims should be distinguished. The first occurs when one of the allies realizes that in spite of the past utility of the alliance, it can more quickly and completely achieve its aims outside the partnership (either during the war or at the peace talks). In 1540, Venice left the coalition of the Pope and Emperor Charles V, then at war with the Ottoman Empire, and sued for a separate peace because her allies would not supply the assistance needed to protect her possessions nor help to lessen the impact of an increasingly costly war. The Emperor's aims were limited to securing the Western Mediterranean against Algerian pirates; Venice's were more broadly conceived. When the incompatibility of aims became manifest and the shortage of grain brought the danger home to the Signoria, continued coalition action was deemed valueless. Venice accepted the hard but necessary peace offered by the Turks.

If some allies discover that their partners have made moves toward peace without consulting them, they will undoubtedly pursue a more independent path, perhaps abandoning the alliance altogether. Thus, in the Seven Years' War, Frederick the Great, hearing of his British ally's secret peace overtures to Austria (allegedly including an offer to make territorial concessions at Prussia's expense), decided to accept an alliance with Russia and provide the latter military assistance in a war against Denmark. Britain thereupon declined to pay Prussia a subsidy; and the alliance, in effect, ended. However, from the very beginning of the war, the war aims of Britain and Prussia had diverged; and ultimately, it was

1 Liska, George, *Nations in Alliance: The Limits of Interdependence* (Baltimore: Johns Hopkins Press, 1968), Chapter 2.

this fact that caused the break. For, by 1760, British aims had largely been secured (against France in North America, in the West Indies, and in India), while Frederick's aims in Central Europe had not. Britain was not disposed to continue to pay for Prussia's territorial ambitions. In the Seven Years' War, the coalition against Frederick the Great also had its difficulties. Of this coalition, created by the Austrian Chancellor Count Kaunitz-Rittberg, Walter L. Dorn has written:[2]

> Kaunitz's masterpiece, the great coalition, so irresistible on paper, suffered from all the defects of most eighteenth-century combinations. It was inspired by no common ideology, no deep-seated community of sentiment. . . . The coalition was a union of courts and as such was subject to the influence of cabals, to the corruption of ministers and generals, above all to the limited financial resources and divergent interests and war aims of its members. . . .
>
> To some extent these defects were of Kaunitz's own making. Had the Austrian chancellor been less close-fisted with his allies and less exclusively preoccupied with purely Austrian interests, had he abandoned in time his stubborn refusal to make commitments regarding the division of spoils, he would in all probability have received more cordial cooperation from France and Russia. It was a mistake to offer France so paltry a reward for the disproportionately heavy burden she had contracted to assume.

Where allies want the same thing, their leaders are likely to withdraw from the alliance. In the War of the Polish Succession (1733–1735), France's allies, Spain and Sardinia, both wanted control of Milan, particularly the fortress at Mantua; and when Cardinal Fleury, Minister to Louis XV, would promise it to neither state, they both refused their cooperation. The alliance had functionally dissolved.

Another special case of disagreement is suggested by the example of Britain in the Seven Years' War. When an ally actually attains its objectives, its leaders often conclude that the alliance will no longer be worth support. In the Franco-Dutch War (1672–1679), after achieving her aims of supremacy on the seas and the defense and security of her territories, the United Netherlands moved to make peace with France. Toward their allies, Spain, Brandenburg, the Empire and others, the Dutch assumed an attitude of indifference: they were welcome to sign a treaty of peace if they were so disposed. The wars between Holland and France and Spain and France were ended with the Peace of Nijmegen. The Emperor fought on for six more months but eventually abandoned the Elector of Brandenburg to make peace in February, 1679. Thus, the alliance was sacrificed by its principal partners, as soon as they had either achieved their aims or discovered that they could do so only by risking more serious losses. In the War of the League of Augsburg (the European war

2 *Competition for Empire, 1740–1763* (New York: Harper, 1940), p. 326.

of 1683–1700), Louis XIV induced the Duke of Savoy to defect from the Grand Alliance and accept peace in 1696. He accomplished this by satisfying the Duke's opportunistic war aims through concessions made formally in the Treaty of Turin. The Duke had learned that the allies had approached France, seeking peace and very probably intending to sacrifice his interests for theirs. Indeed, some of the allies had been negotiating with the French, among them William III of England. When Louis agreed to recognize the Protestant Succession in England and to satisfy demands for the promotion of English commercial interests, William's aims were also satisfied; like the Duke of Savoy, he deserted the alliance and moved to make peace with France. The other partners were thereupon impelled to make peace, spurred on by several appropriately timed French concessions to Spain and the Netherlands during the peace negotiations (Ryswick, 1697). England again deserted her coalition partners in the War of the Spanish Succession (1701–1714). The aims of her major allies were, in some cases, largely unsatisfied. In the peace settlement of Utrecht, England took the greatest share of the spoils. As these examples show, where the utility of an alliance for one partner has decreased, dissolution of the alliance usually ensues, leaving the partners to continue the war and achieve peace without the support of the states or factions that have withdrawn. The latter will remain formally at war until they conclude a separate peace.

For convenience of analysis, we can distinguish three conditions of a wartime coalition. There is first, the healthy coalition, characterized by high cohesiveness among the partners who agree with each other about the primary war aims. Objectively (from the point of view of the independent observer), each party has compatible or nearly compatible war aims. Subjectively, the policymakers of the member states see the alliance as the best means for the achievement of those aims. The Triple Alliance (Britain, Prussia, and the United Provinces), formed in 1788, was just such a healthy coalition, as was the alliance in the First World War known as the Allied and Associated Powers. This is not to say that there were no disagreements; indeed there were. But they were subordinated to the interests of the cooperation needed to fulfill the overall purposes of the alliance and thus directly satisfy the compatible goals of the partners.

At the other extreme, there is the alliance-in-dissolution, where disagreement, for whatever reasons, has resulted in the breakup of the coalition. The consequences of dissolution are usually momentous, both for the conduct of the war and for the peace settlement. After dissolution, the war against the opposing states or factions may continue, with all the former allies remaining belligerents. There may also be a series of separate peace settlements, or a realignment of the parties may take place, the withdrawing states forming a coalition with the former adversary and declaring war on the parties that remain joined in the alliance. Any of these eventualities will obviously affect the character of the peace settlement. The First Coalition against France (1793–1795) dissolved when the allies discovered that they could not easily achieve their opportunistic aims of dismembering revolutionary France. The diverging war aims of the Allies in the Second World War became manifest when they began to discuss plans for the postwar order. After Germany's unconditional surrender and with it the annihilation of Nazism, the principal goal upon which the Allies did agree had been achieved, and a force for alliance cohesion disappeared. Faced with the task of political and economic reconstruction, the coalition dissolved. The resulting conflict between the former allies long delayed the peace settlements and had prevented an adequate settlement for Germany altogether. And in the negotiations to end the War for American Independence, the conflicting aims of the French and American allies prompted the American Commissioners, contrary to their instructions from the Congress, to negotiate a separate peace with England. The Preliminary Treaty of Peace was signed in November, 1782; the Definitive Treaty in September, 1783. Happy to exploit the differences between the allies, the British made peace, on not unfavorable terms, with the French and Spanish in January, 1783.

A third and intermediate condition of the wartime coalition is possible, in which the allies come to disagree over aims and methods, but manage to preserve the alliance until after the peace settlement. After limited victory, the English-Dutch alliance was on the verge of breaking up in 1707 (in the War of the Spanish Succession), when each became suspicious of the other's intentions with respect to the acquisition of the spoils of war. But when Louis XIV rejected the peace terms of the allies in 1708 and renewed the war against them, the allies were able to cure the ills of the alliance for the time being and prosecute the war in close cooperation from 1710 until 1713, when the coalition again began to dissolve.

The characteristics of the strained alliance will vary, depending on the nature and seriousness of the disagreements and on the kind of intraalliance compromises reached to preserve at least the facade of unity. While there may be difficulties in characterizing alliances as healthy or strained, it is valuable for our purposes to do so and to regard alliances as arrayed along a cohesiveness spectrum. At one end, we have a highly cohesive alliance. As we move toward the other end of the spectrum, cohesiveness decreases until the alliance dissolves. Near the midpoint, disagreements will sharply highlight intracoalition relations, and we will see instances of power political and ideological conflicts among the partners. Of course, there is competition in an alliance with a high degree of cohesiveness. But its intensity is much lower, and certainly less visible.

Intrinsic incompatibility of the allies' war aims is the most fundamental source of the disagreements that produce strains in an alliance

and reduce its cohesiveness. War aims of allies are intrinsically incompatible if satisfaction of the aims of one of them will preclude satisfaction of
the aims of the others or adversely affects their national interests. In order
to anticipate when such a state of affairs might arise, we can contrast, in a
systematic way, one of the types of war aims we delineated in the second
chapter with the other types. Recall that we classified war aims as follows:
dominance, consolidation of the state, status quo, ideological, retributive,
and opportunistic. A comparison would reveal the possibilities for conflicts among allies that seek to fulfill their aims; it would show which
aims were compatible and which intrinsically incompatible.[3] For example, in an external war involving the alliance of A and B, if both
partners sought dominance in a particular region, conflict would surely
arise; the aims of A and B are intrinsically incompatible. If one partner
sought to consolidate at the expense of a third-party state, while its allies
favored the status quo, the effect of acquisition would so alter the local
balance of power that the other partners would want to resist.

It is essential to remember that during a complex external war in
which at least one alliance is involved, the war aims of each of the allies
may be transformed by the impact of domestic and world political events
and particularly by successes and failures in the war and at the peace
talks. By the time the belligerents are ready to discuss cease-fire terms, the
war aims of each member of the coalition may be different from its aims
at the time the coalition was formed or the war began. Moreover, new
war aims might be formulated by each state and come to occupy as
important a place as the original war aims. Thus, while intra-alliance
cooperation was possible at the time the alliance was established, external
causes might alter the situation, modify original war aims, and introduce
new ones with far-reaching consequences for the war and peace.

It is not uncommon for a state to have more than one war aim. When
we consider that the two or more states of a wartime coalition might have
many aims, the complexities of the situation will be readily appreciated.
Moreover, the war aims of a single state often conflict with one another:
in other words, the aims of a state might be internally inconsistent and
their implementation vacillating, making coalition relations even more
difficult than they are ordinarily. No matter how complicated the situation, in the multiplicity of war aims of alliance partners, analysis should
start with an estimate of the relative incompatibility of those aims.

Another complicating factor in complex external wars is the existence
of alliances on both sides; the war could take the form of states A, B, and
C against states X, Y, and Z. There is also a possibility that the alliance,
as a collectivity or as individuals, may have different war aims for each of
the belligerents in the enemy alliance. For example, states A and B might

3 Such a systematic comparison is made in Appendix II.

have the same war aim relative to states X and $Y;$ they might have different war aims relative to state $Z;$ and state C might have still another war aim relative to $X, Y, Z.$[4]

Effects of Defeat

There is nothing like military defeat to promote disagreements among coalition partners. It shifts the perspectives of the actors, affects their individual and collective capabilities for waging war, induces disagreements over methods for conducting the war, and transforms the war aims of the allies. In an external war of A and B vs. X, if state X were to defeat the alliance or inflict severe losses upon the allies, disagreements between A and B would tend to become more severe, and the relative incompatibility of their war aims would probably become more evident. Aware of this, state X's policymakers might try to persuade either A or B to make a separate peace. It is clear that if state A, for example, has waged a war for opportunity, defeat will be so at variance with the expectations of A's policymakers that they could indeed be wooed away from the alliance by state X. In other wars, defeat might persuade one or both allies to cut their losses and make peace. When only one does so, the alliance usually dissolves. In the Great Northern War (1700–1721), Sweden invaded Saxony, forced peace upon the Elector, and thereby disassociated him from the alliance. Sometimes the mere threat of invasion is sufficient: one after another of the Italian Principalities deserted the Italian League in 1494 and surrendered to Charles VIII of France, often without a fight, as they feared the ravages that might be visited upon them if they resisted. For long periods of time, Louis XIV and Napoleon were able to prevent the formation of adversary coalitions or the effective functioning of the anti-French coalitions that had been formed, by playing upon the mutual jealousies and suspicions of the European Powers. They frequently pursued a strategy that enabled them to concentrate their forces against one ally, defeat him, and by judicious, often moderate, peace terms induce the ally to desert the adversary coalition.

What does the possibility of defeat of the alliance mean for our analysis? It means that we must look again at our comparison of the war aims of the allies, but only after we have considered how the defeat has affected the original (or earlier) aims. A state that has embarked upon a war for dominance may, after battlefield defeats, find itself forced to fight a war for the status quo, for example. After we have determined in what way, if at all, the military situation has transformed the war aims of the allies, then we may proceed to examine the relative incompatibility of the war aims in the face of military adversity. While states fighting wars

4 Note the structure of the First World War (pp. 405–28), for example.

of opportunity are apt to desert the losing alliance, states fighting status-quo defensive wars against a formidable enemy might become so preoccupied with the defense of their own territories that they have few capabilities to spare for their partners. Then the coalition would functionally, although perhaps not formally, dissolve; and one ally might sue for peace to cut its losses. Alliance partners fighting an ideological war and sharing the same ideology will tend to cooperate even in defeat, probably to the extent of concerted peace moves.

Factors other than defeat—a domestic political or economic crisis, for example, or the exigencies of wartime strategy—could change a state's war aims, as could world events in the international political environment of the war.[5] In order to obtain the support of Portugal in the War of the Spanish Succession and to persuade her to join their alliance against Louis XIV, Britain and the Netherlands had to agree to place a candidate on the Spanish throne who would be friendly to Portugal. In making this agreement in 1703, the allies had to revise their war aims substantially, in order to win over a state whose contribution to the war effort they needed and on whose territory they wished to establish a naval base. As the Crimean War dragged on through 1855, the British adopted increasingly rigorous and demanding peace terms from Russia. By the end of the year, the British came to want the surrender of Russian territory in Bessarabia and the neutralization of the Black Sea, rather than the admittedly vague aim of maintaining a balance of power in the Levant, which was one of their primary original aims. This revision of aims can be attributed to the bitterness engendered by hostilities and to the growing confidence of Britain and France as Austria and Prussia moved to ally with them.

The dynamics of war-aim transformation are interesting, of course, as the forces or factors that influence that process can also affect peacemaking. An appreciation of the possibility of such transformations also points up the need to identify the allies' war aims in the late stages of a war, especially at crucial times during peace negotiations. Having identified them, we can then assess their compatibility with each other.

Reduced Alliance Effectiveness

A successful wartime coalition is one in which intra-alliance relations in no way inhibit the effectiveness of the collective effort to wage war or make peace. Such will be the case where the allies have relatively compatible war aims; or where, if their war aims are incompatible, a *particular issue* has not as yet presented itself over which the allies might differ, that is, the incompatibility is not evident because the potentially incompatible war aims are inchoate or unexpressed (while the *compatible* war

5 See Fig. 2–1 in Chapter 2 and Fig. 1–1 in Chapter 1.

aims have been more clearly enunciated or particular coalition problems have been solved on the basis of an agreement upon compatible aims). Alliance effectiveness can be reduced by factors other than an incompatibility of war aims: for example, an inability to coordinate operations or failure to agree upon the means for achieving a mutual aim. Truly effective cooperation aganst Napoleon was impossible for the Third Coalition (1805) because the war aims of the allies, Russia, Austria, and Britain (later joined for one month by Prussia), were not only incompatible but diffuse; the war aims were only those of the individual allies, and these were never transformed into *alliance war aims*. In circumstances such as these, Napoleon was able to wreck the Coalition by his usual combination of military success (against Austria and Prussia at Austerlitz) and bribery (the cession of Hanover to Prussia). After the death of Zwingli at Cappel in 1531, the members of the Schmalkaldic League (founded in February, 1531) were able to settle their differences and organize their forces. The League so impressed the Catholics that their League of Nuremburg (1538) was patterned after it. Nevertheless, in the war of 1546–1547, the Protestant allies were unable to coordinate their operations, nor had they adequately solved problems of leadership and control. They were defeated by the Catholic League, principally by the forces of Charles V. And in 1508, Maximilian committed the Empire to a war against Venice in joining the League of Cambrai (an alliance of France, Spain, and the Pope). The Reichstag refused to vote him the money or the army he needed. The Estates were not interested in the war, nor did they favor an alliance with France, the traditional enemy of the Empire. The war was fought without a substantial Imperial force and without achieving Maximilian's aims in Italy. Thus, for domestic political reasons, an ally, while remaining formally in the alliance, was forced to act as if it were not an ally. For the actively belligerent partners, the Empire had functionally abandoned the League.

We are more interested in the compatibility of war aims here, however, as disagreements about these fundamental questions more frequently lead to a reduction in the effectiveness of the alliance during peace negotiations. But, what does reduced alliance effectiveness mean? Given disagreement among the allies over incompatible war aims, we will often find that no decisions defining particular or general aims can be made; hence, there will be no alliance policies respecting certain areas of operations or negotiations. After the naval victory at Lepanto in October, 1571, the allies of the Holy League (Spain, Venice, and the Pope) were unable to agree over where the next move against the Turks should be made. They wasted a whole sailing season arguing; and when Cyprus fell to the Turks, Venice left the League and made peace in March, 1573. The Venetians reasoned, as they had in 1540, that the alliance could not preserve their territories against Turkish attacks. Indeed, although continued fighting might have brought the League some limited victories, without the Spanish navy in the Eastern Mediterranean, Venice's territory could not be secured. Thus, divergent war aims prevented the League from acting effectively after Lepanto and led to its dissolution after the fall of Cyprus.

The effects of disagreement may even spill over into policy areas where there may have been some limited agreement on ends. Strains in the alliance may prevent the partners from deciding how to achieve ends upon which they have agreed, and thus there will be no implementation (or poor implementation) of alliance policies. Should allies be able to reach decisions they claim to be alliance decisions, but which not all partners support, alliance action will have only the most lukewarm support (if that) of the nonacquiescing states. Again, coordinated action on the part of the alliance partners will suffer. SEATO (formed in 1954) has not functioned as it was intended. Neither France nor Great Britain, NATO allies of the United States, has participated in the Vietnam War (1965–1971+), nor has Pakistan. In fact, these states have expressed their opposition to U.S. policies in Indochina. Although SEATO meetings continue to be held, it could be said to have functionally dissolved (it has certainly been functionally modified) insofar as its Charter's Article IV collective defense measures are concerned.

Inability to agree upon war aims may lead not only to reduced alliance effectiveness, but also reduce the effectiveness of the policies of the *individual* allies. Here, the alliance will become a burden to its members. So disgusted was Frederick the Great with what appeared to him to be the military incompetence of his French ally that he made a separate peace with Austria in 1742, ending one phase of the War of the Austrian Succession. Prussia was in a difficult position financially; and, through the efforts of a British mediator, Maria Theresa had made major concessions to her enemy Frederick. Not being one to be deterred by alliance ties in any event, the Prussian leader, pocketing the Austrian concessions, quickly came to see that the alliance with France had become a burden, restricting his ambitious diplomacy, and must therefore be abandoned.

Attempts to cooperate in the face of difficulties in the definition of war aims may prove costly to allies: Allocation of resources to an ineffective alliance are poor investments for the state making them, as they are costs for which few benefits are returned. Discord that reduces the effectiveness of an alliance will increase the relative effectiveness of the enemy's policies. The policymakers of the adversary state may find that their situation has improved. They may be able to obtain more values than they had anticipated, as Britain obtained more from France at Paris in 1783 in the negotiations that ended the war for American independence. They might find that the alliance cannot make decisions; or making them, cannot implement them. This will offer the adversary policymakers opportunities for the promotion of their own peace policies. If the strains in the alliance are serious enough, the adversary may be able to induce one or more of the allies to break away from their partners and conclude a separate peace. The enemy state's power position is then improved to the degree that the alliance's capabilities are reduced by the loss of the capabilities of the defecting states. The policymakers of the adversary may even be able to persuade one or more of the former allies to form a coalition with their state, thus *adding* the capabilities of the defecting state to their own. As we have seen, leaders like Louis XIV and Napoleon were masters of this art. Any changes of status of the belligerents will be reflected in corresponding changes in bargaining positions at the peace talks.

Peace Policy Formulation and Policy Differences

When alliances are involved, the concrete, often difficult questions of policy that arise during peacemaking must be resolved in three rather than the usual two steps. Any policy, with or without an alliance, must work its way through the policymaking machinery of a particular state; having been formulated and modified to meet the demands of domestic political groups and interests, a policy will then be subjected to the bargaining process at the peace conference where the adversary seeks further modifications or abandonment in favor of his own policies. When an alliance is party to an external war, the interallied consultation and negotiating process constitutes yet another challenge to one particular state's policies, intermediate between the domestic policy process and the conference bargaining process (see Fig. 4–1).

Alliance policy is hammered out at interallied meetings, and it is there that the incompatibilities of the allies' war aims become manifest in each member's response to the particular questions of prosecuting war or making peace. Now, differences between allies do not occur because the war

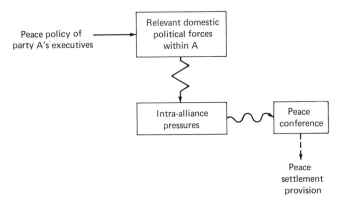

FIGURE 4–1. Some key bargaining centers where a peace policy is modified.

aims of one are theoretically incompatible with those of another. They do not arise, in other words, from the mere possibility of incompatibility. Differences arise over specific questions, the solution to which requires a state's policymakers to take a definite policy position, to make concrete proposals based upon and oriented by a theretofore implicit war aim. Until the representatives of a state, whether in a peace conference or in a war council, take a position on an issue, the allies of that state can treat the expressions of its war aims as abstract rhetoric, perhaps propaganda for domestic consumption; or they may officially ignore the expressions because the exigencies of a cooperative alliance policy in watime requires this. They may even delude themselves into believing that their allies do not mean what they say or assume that the war aims of their partners can be modified by hard interallied bargaining.

In this chapter, we consider the questions that are likely to arise in each phase of the settlement of a complex external war and show how, and with what consequences, disagreements and conflicts between allies can occur when the coalition is forced to confront the incompatible war aims of its members as they attempt to secure the peace. We should indicate at the outset the four possible general modes of settlement of the complex external war, remembering that policy disagreements in each of the modes listed might arise at any of the stages of the peace settlement.

Let us suppose the war has the form, *ABC* vs. *X,* where only one alliance is involved, that comprised of the states *A, B,* and *C* (see Fig. 4–2).

1. *ABC* determines its policies collectively and arranges a cease-fire and a settlement of the war with state *X.* Whatever disagreements may arise

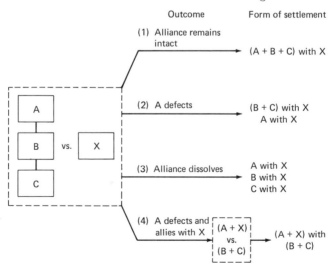

FIGURE 4–2. General modes of settlement of a complex external war.

within the coalition are resolved, enabling the allies to take common negotiating positions.

2. State *A* defects from the coalition, leaving *BC* allied, still determined to pursue common policies. State X must deal with state *A* and alliance *BC* separately in concluding a peace settltment. However, during the peace talks it may be necessary for *A*, *BC*, and X to reach common agreement on matters arising out of state *A's* former alliance ties.

3. The alliance *ABC* could dissolve because of differences among the allies. The individual states *A*, *B*, and *C* must then reach a settlement with state X.

4. At least one state, *A*, leaves the alliance *ABC*. State *A* reaches an agreement with state X and enters a coalition with state X against *BC*, the war then assuming the form, *AX* vs. *BC*.[6]

Preliminary Phase of Peacemaking[7]

Peace Feeler Stage: Whether to Negotiate or Continue to Fight

The cluster of problems presented in this stage usually arises in one of two situations: when the alliance *A-B-C* has decided to propose peace

6 In the wars involving coalitions analyzed in some detail in this book, we shall find four patterns of settlement: a. Those in which the alliances remained intact throughout the peacemaking process—the Crimean War, Second War over Schleswig-Holstein, Boer War, Boxer Rebellion, Korean War, Russia and her Balkan allies in the Russo-Turkish War of 1877–8, and the internal alliances of the Dutch Revolt and the American Colonies in the War for American Independence. b. Those in which an ally defects, leaving the alliance in being —Russia and Sweden left the Versailles Alliance against Prussia in the Seven Years' War; Savoy deserted the Grand Alliance in the European War of 1687–1700; Russia left her allies during the First World War; the Empire deserted the Second Grand Alliance at the end of the War of the Spanish Succession. c. Those in which the alliances dissolved completely—the external alliances of the Dutch Revolt (France, Britain, and the Dutch Rebels) ; the First, Second, and Third Coalitions against France in the Wars of France against Europe (the Napoleonic Wars) ; the War of the Pacific; the alliance of the Pope with France in the Last War of the Habsburg-Valois Rivalry; the Anglo-Münster alliance of the Second Anglo-Dutch War; and the Austro-Russian alliance of the Austro-Russian War against Turkey of 1787–92. d. Those in which a party leaves an alliance and joins the adversary, declaring war on its former allies— Savoy and Portugal deserted France and joined the Second Grand Alliance against her in the War of the Spanish Succession; Savoy abandoned her alliance with France and went to war with Prussia, France's ally in the War of the Austrian Succession; in the Laotian Civil War, the centrist faction of Souvanna Phouma was an enemy of the Pathet Lao until the revolt of the right-wing faction and Phoumi Nosavan's seizure of the capital in 1960, at which time Souvanna allied himself functionally with the Pathet Lao.

7 Refer to Table 2–1 in Chapter 2 for historical examples.

negotiations to the other side or when the adversary state of alliance has proposed them and the alliance *A-B-C* must decide upon a response. The proposal for peace talks poses most starkly the question whether the states should continue waging war or agree to a cease-fire and talks, the object of which will be to determine whether a complete peace settlement can be reached. Generally speaking, the central issue at this stage, expressed in power political terms, is this: Would a state gain more (and sustain fewer losses) by fighting or by negotiating? A state that has achieved its war aims or whose policymakers conclude that further fighting would probably win no additional values will want to negotiate.[8] Further, the state that has lost a great deal and anticipates more losses will want to negotiate.[9] But the state that still hopes to make gains in the war and estimates that such gains would outweigh the losses (according to whatever calculus the state's policymakers use) will want to continue the war.[10] Rarely is the matter so simple or so clear, even for the single state (as opposed to a coalition of states). In deciding whether to fight or to negotiate, the policymaker must consider not only the gains and losses from war operations *per se,* but he must also determine what gains or losses there will be at home or in other areas of the world in which his state has interests. Thus, the question calls for a rather complex analysis, and answers are not obvious. The situation becomes even more complex when a coalition is confronted with the question of whether to talk about a peace settlement. Incompatibilities of war aims, and the existence of war aims that some states have fulfilled and other states have not, frequently lead to disagreements and conflict.[11]

8 True of Austria in the Austro-Russian War against Turkey of 1787–92 (pp. 163–5); the United Provinces in the Franco-Dutch War of 1672–9 (pp. 340–7); and Prussia in the War of the Austrian Succession (pp. 366–74). In the War for American Independence (pp. 217–22), the Colonies and France were willing to make peace with England (and did so), even though they were obligated to continue the war until Spain's aims were achieved. Savoy concluded a separate peace with France during the European War of 1683–1700 (pp. 347–57) because he was promised the return of territories lost during the war and also because he feared his allies would betray him. In the Franco-Dutch War of 1672–9, France and Britain both wanted peace by 1679 because they had come to believe that a continuation of the war was not worth the costs.

9 Münster in the Second Anglo-Dutch War (pp. 160–3); Bavaria in the War of the Austrian Succession (pp. 366–74); Sweden in the Seven Years' War (pp. 374–9); and Russia in the Wars of the Second and Third Coalitions during the Wars for French Hegemony in Europe (pp. 392–405).

10 Austria in the War of the Spanish Succession (pp. 357–66); Bolivia in the War of the Pacific (pp. 171–3); and Great Britain during the Napoleonic Wars (pp. 392–405).

11 The following discussion is in the nature of a series of scenarios based in part upon the historical evidence of alliance relationships in wartime and at peace

States waging a retributive war or a war of opportunity will be willing to open peace negotiations if the values they seek will be unobtainable by continued fighting, or if reduction in their quality or quantity will probably result from further fighting. Allies that insist at this juncture upon continuing the war will find themselves at odds with partners such as these. The state with the unfulfilled war aim of consolidation or dominance or with ideological war aims might be opposed to peace negotiations if war still offered them the opportunity to achieve their aims. States waging a purely status quo war are apt to be persuaded to accept what can be obtained by talking rather than by fighting, should a phase of the war be reached where their own territories have been more or less successfully defended or their relative power positions maintained. Should the enemy occupy the territory of a state fighting a defensive status quo war, its policymakers would probably be unwilling to enter into peace negotiations unless the enemy agreed to withdraw. And a state that had engaged in a war to maintain its position may, like the state waging a war for dominance, refuse to negotiate without additional efforts to realize its objectives, until further defeats persuade its leaders that these objectives cannot be realized. The ally with satisfied war aims or decidedly unsatisfiable war aims will find itself in disagreement with this sort of ally. A complete analysis for a particular war would require us to examine every war aim of each ally, determine whether the ally had achieved its aims and to what extent, and then consider the relationship between the degree of war-aim satisfaction and the position of each ally on the question of whether to fight or negotiate.

It is well to note at this point that a decision by the policymakers of a state or an alliance to agree to negotiations does not necessarily mean that they expect a peace settlement to result. They may believe that talking and fighting (or even talking after a cease-fire had been ar-

---

conferences briefly discussed in the settlement summaries at the end of this Chapter and in Chapters 5 and 9, and in part upon a comparison of the relative compatibilities of the war aims of partners in alliance (see Appendix II). Scenarios are necessary for a complete consideration of these aspects of peacemaking, because my sample is simply not large enough to provide empirical support for all my generalizations. It would, in any event, be difficult to make generalizations in this area to fit every case (or indeed, most cases), at this level of analysis. Nonetheless, having been warned of the limitations of the following analyses, the student of peace settlements may still profit from a systematic approach to describing the effects of compatible and incompatible war aims and policies of allies upon the movement toward peace. For one thing, they are suggestive of problems and conflicts that are likely to arise in certain (even recurring) circumstances; and for another, they provide a starting point for the analysis of peacemaking in complex external and multilateral wars.

ranged) might yield higher returns than simply fighting. The hope or expectation of peace may be there, but it need not be.[12] Often belligerents enter negotiations for tactical reasons, in the belief that talks will assist their efforts on the battlefield or will produce value payoffs in negotiations that can be obtained only at a higher cost in battle. If peace should result from talks begun for tactical motives, it would be another payoff, desired more by some states than by others, no doubt with compromises and with costs to all. But however fortuitous, it would be peace.

If the allies agree either to continue the war or to negotiate with the enemy, without substantial disagreement, the alliance will act as a unit *after* the decision is made; and we could treat the situation as equivalent to a simple external war (assuming there is no alliance involved on the other side). If, however, the allies disagree, several alternatives would be foreseeable: In one case, some of the allies could continue to fight, while others indicate their willingness to talk to enemy representatives: functionally (although perhaps not formally), the coalition would be dissolved.[13] In another, the alliance might retain its integrity, but the allies that dissent might act automatically within the alliance, rendering coalition policymaking very much more difficult. States that preferred to negotiate could reduce the resources allocated to the war effort and raise obstacles to the continued prosecution of the war. These states could continue to cooperate in the war effort, but just barely; their actions would reduce the effectiveness of the coalition. On the other hand, the states that preferred to fight might raise difficulties for the negotiators; they could insist upon more stringent armistice conditions, cause delays during the talks, and even stage pretexts for breaking with the enemy. Such states might participate in the peace talks, but grudgingly and offering resistance to almost all compromises. The coalition would thus have reduced effectiveness as a peacemaking entity; the peace desired by other members of the coalition would be delayed and might even fail to materialize.

If the decision to negotiate has been made, a number of questions follow in train. When should the peace feelers be made? Through what channels, and to whom? Shall the feelers be made directly to the enemy or through a third party? If a third party, which one and with what instructions? What form should the feelers take (secret note or oral approach, a news broadcast, a newspaper release)? In the event the enemy has made the first approach, how should a response be made, in what form, and to whom? How should preliminary talks be arranged

12 This was possibly the motive of the Chinese and North Koreans in the Korean War (pp. 233–6) and of most parties in the Laotian Civil War (pp. 236–40).

13 Refer to Fig. 4–2.

(talks to discuss the procedures for the more formal peace talks)? Where will these talks be held, and when? What states ought to be invited, and what rank and status should their representatives be? Lastly, what preconditions to talks or to a cease-fire should be imposed or proposed?

Preconditions of Peace Talks

The first major decision likely to produce intracoalition discussion, not to say disagreement, is the choice between conditioned and unconditioned talks. Policymakers having reasons for wanting talks to start immediately and to proceed without delay will prefer unconditioned talks, simply because conditions require agreement at several levels, domestically, within the alliance, and between the belligerents; and such negotiations will of course take time. Other members of the alliance might support unconditioned talks for propagandistic or tactical reasons; if their interests are too deeply engaged, they will demand conditions, the substance of which we now consider.

Among the most important conditions are those connected with the cease-fire; the choice faced is this: shall there be a cease-fire before substantive peace talks begin, or shall the peace talks begin and the cease-fire be arranged as the talks proceed (perhaps at as late a time as the signing of the peace treaty or the date the peace treaty takes effect)? The choice is important for reasons discussed earlier. Within an alliance, states that expect to obtain most from a superior (and improving) military situation would probably prefer to have the talks begin before a cease-fire in anticipation of military victories that would add to the bargaining strength of the coalition. States that only reluctantly went along with the decision of the coalition to negotiate will be found to be supporters of an armistice later in the peace talks.

States that have obtained the values for which they waged war and achieved their war aims will generally want an early cease-fire, on the theory that in further fighting they could only lose part or all of what they have acquired. Included in this category would be states waging a war for retributive or opportunity values or a war for the consolidation of the state. For certain states (e.g., those waging a war for dominance and, on occasion, the greedy state fighting a war for opportunity values), the desire to supplement what they already have amply achieved may prompt them to press for a postponement of the cease-fire until well after the peace talks have begun.

Those allies that anticipate greater losses the longer hostilities continue will press for an early armistice. Thus, states waging defensive or position-maintaining status quo wars, whose forces were losing battles, or whose territories were about to be invaded will want a quick cease-fire.

Once the alliance as such has collectively decided to talk rather than continue to wage war, the issue of when to press for the cease-fire will probably not result in a dissolved coalition. Getting the enemy to agree might be the problem. Of course, allies may not support the collective decision with equal enthusiasm, but that is not an issue over which an alliance is dissolved. This is not the case with other possible conditions to peace talks upon which some of the allies might insist. For some states, there are absolutely non-negotiable matters, usually concerning territorial integrity and the security of the state. Were the coalition to attempt to broach such subjects in a peace offer or otherwise indicate their negotiability, the coalition would find itself in crisis. A situation is conceivable where all but one state in an alliance agreed to the contents of peace feelers. The dissenting state will not acquiesce because the feelers imply a condition of settlement, perhaps that the rights of its navy to seize vessels on the high seas or mutual guarantees under a collective defense pact with a third state will be negotiable subjects at future peace talks. Were these feelers to be presented to the opposing state or alliance and accepted as the basis for negotiations, the dissenting state might find that it would not only have to withdraw from the alliance but also reverse its decision to agree to peace talks and continue hostilities alone. However, it could continue negotiating with its former allies and the enemy until a compromise was agreed upon, after which the participation of the dissenting state in the peace talks would be assured. If the matter were judged sufficiently vital, the dissenting state would not compromise unless forced to do so (usually after severe reverses on the battlefield or by a change of government within). The question of what matters are non-negotiable and excluded from talks, preliminary or otherwise, will be unique for each state and could reflect the unique historical character and geographical position of that state.

The problem of what is to be included in the peace offer (or in the response to an offer) will certainly be as important as what is excluded. A state may, in the very early stages of the peace settlement process, be able to obtain concessions of profound importance from the enemy. The enemy might, in order to satisfy preconditions to the talks, agree to substantive grants of rights for the possession or control of territory, privileges of a commercial or legal kind for nationals of the demanding state, or guarantees of security and penalties. In short, the enemy could grant concessions relating to the most important issues of a military and political settlement. The state seeking to obtain these concessions as preconditions to peace talks will attempt early in the bargaining process, to preclude the opponent procedurally from later raising and negotiating the values obtained when the opponent accepted the preconditions. What is important here, insofar as the demanding state is concerned, are possession of relative bargaining strength at the peace feeler stage and the existence of an opponent that was pressed sufficiently to prejudice its case at so early a stage of the settlement process.

An alliance of high cohesiveness can obtain satisfaction of preconditions more easily than one riddled with conflict. Correspondingly, the alliance of whom an enemy demands the satisfaction of preconditions can more effectively resist such demands if its cohesiveness were high.

Procedural Questions

Belligerents must agree upon the kind of conference they will hold for negotiating peace. The situation is not different when one or more alliances are involved in the war. If anything, the decision regarding the mode of negotiation will be more important then, as more parties will want to be in a position to exchange their views and accept or reject the peace settlement. Members of a coalition must agree among themselves upon the form of conference before submitting a proposal for peace talks to the enemy or after submitting the proposal, during the period of the interchange of notes leading to the talks. Of course, any arrangement that excludes one of the allies will be looked upon as an effort to make peace without that ally. This could result in dissolution of the alliance and eventually to separate peace talks between the enemy and each of the former allies.

It is inevitable that all belligerent members of the coalition will want to attend the peace conference. But what other states should be invited? Who will issue the invitations; and what will be the form of the invitations? If a third, disinterested state has involved itself in efforts to promote a settlement, this state is likely to take the initiative in choosing participants and sending out invitations. The allies must, however, accept this third party as a mediator. In a multilateral war involving many states and many issues and covering a wide geographical area, there will be few disinterested states; and a mediator acceptable to some allies may not be acceptable to all. The critical question is whether mediation by a particular third state would prejudice the case of any one of the allies, or whether it might adversely affect the achievement of values it hoped to obtain during the peace negotiations. Perhaps it is more accurate to say that the question is whether the ally thinks the mediator may be prejudiced. If what is involved were issues regarded as vital by the objecting state, third-party mediation would probably be refused by the alliance as a whole in the interests of alliance cohesiveness, unless another third party were available to fill that role.

If there were a plurality of states at war with the alliance, some of the allies might object to the presence of one or more enemy states at the peace talks. Yet if these states have in fact taken part in the war, an adequate peace cannot be achieved unless all belligerent parties are present. The adversary may want puppet states, subdivisions of the states, or states that had been merely formally at war to be present at the conference; but the allies will undoubtedly object to the presence of inactive or puppet belligerents.[14]

At the preliminary peace talks, the belligerents, whether individual states or alliances, must agree on other procedural matters before the main conference or the principal negotiations can begin: What form should the minutes of the conference sessions take? What records should be preserved? Should the sessions be public or restricted? If restricted, how should communiqués or press releases be prepared? What seating arrangements will be made? How will the chairman and officers of the conference be selected? In what order will formal speeches be made? Questions of precedence (seating, order of speaking, and the like) may lead to intra-alliance disputes if, because of historical rivalries or sensitiveness to world or regional positions, one of the allies insists upon precedence over another ally. (A similar problem presents itself when the question of the official languages of the conference arises.) Early agreement or quick resolution of controversies of this sort smooths alliance relations during the peace talks, just as a prolongation of the dispute exacerbates those relations.[15]

Agreement on the agenda the allies proposed to the adversary could cause problems for the alliance. The agenda question is two-fold: What subjects shall be inscribed on the agenda? And in what order shall those subjects be discussed by the negotiators? If the subjects that some allies want to exclude from the agenda affect the interests and security of other allies, then the stage will be set for a major intra-alliance dispute. Given agreement on matters to be excluded, the allies must then agree upon matters to be included. It is safe to say that the allies would want any question relating to any war aim on the agenda, except those that were agreed to be non-negotiable. If the coalition is not to be disrupted at the critical stage preliminary to the peace talks, any "inclusion-exclusion" agenda controversy must be resolved by a compromise: A subject might be put on the agenda with an explicit reservation of rights by the dissent-

---

14 It is more likely that this question would produce a dispute between the belligerents rather than among the allies. Some allies might object to sending invitations to other members of their own alliance, to states that had played a minimal role in the war effort, or to states that had declared war recently in order to obtain some opportunity value. Should these latter states acquiesce in the objections and absent themselves from the conference, the controversy would end there. The actively belligerent members of the coalition would probably not permit a controversy of this sort to disrupt the coalition. It is possible that the inactive allies will acquiesce in being "represented" at the conference by their more active partners. We will have more to say about nonbelligerent allies as war-oriented actors in Chapters 6 and 7.

15 As in the case of conference invitees, questions of precedence and prestige usually assume greater importance between belligerents than among allies.

ing state, or a subject might be omitted with the understanding that it will be negotiated later. If the allies do not settle the question before the agenda proposal is made to the enemy representatives, they will certainly have to settle it afterwards, when the issue might become more complicated when the enemy makes his counter-proposals in the face of intra-alliance discord. The matter of the order of the agenda will be of greater importance between belligerents than among allies. Order of discussion may affect the substance of the negotiations, as decisions on certain questions early in the talks could prevent their being raised later (according to a principle analogous to the legal principle of *res adjudicata*).

Procedural questions will, of course, arise during the course of the peace negotiations. One particularly important one is the form the final act of the conference will take. As the answer will be determined in part by the character of the political settlement, the parties may not be able to decide the question until a later time. Yet a complete peace settlement requires that most, if not all, belligerents be obligated in specific ways to perform acts necessary to end hostilities and bring about the resumption of normal relations. Thus, the final act usually assumes the form of a peace treaty requiring the signature of the representatives of the belligerents and, subsequently, the ratification of the treaty by the constitutional processes of each of the signatories. It is possible that one of the allies might not want its obligations spelled out clearly; it might want the peace treaty equivocal on certain matters. Ambiguous provisions in the peace treaty are frequently accepted to mask disagreements between belligerents or among allies and yet achieve the other objectives of a settlement that all parties want (a cease-fire, for example). It is also done to deceive or confuse domestic opposition to the treaty and thus assist its ratification.

The Military Settlement Phase

The Cease-Fire

The question of when the cease-fire is to come into effect often highlights the disagreement among allies over the efficacy of negotiating for peace.[16] Some allies, not willing to be delayed by reluctant partners, may be able to persuade the enemy to accept a truce on the fronts in which they alone are engaged. It would be left to the other allies to negotiate separate truces later. If war operations are severable in this way and the adversaries are willing to accept separate truces, then the reluctance of some of the allies to conclude a simultaneous truce ought not immediately disrupt the alliance. The holdouts could then wait the days, or at

16 The reader should refer to Table 2–2 in Chapter 2 and Table 3–1 in Chapter 3.

most a week or two, until the adversaries have met their preconditions or until they have reconciled themselves to their inability to obtain better terms. A long delay is apt to interfere with the peacemaking efforts of other allies, who will undoubtedly become increasingly exasperated with partners that are holding out for better terms on their war fronts. Should the impatience increase to the point where the allies that had agreed to an armistice approached the enemy with the view to beginning talks on subjects affecting all the belligerents, then the coalition could be strained to the point where dissolution is likely. The allies desiring a settlement are likely to conclude that the holdouts do not want a settlement, and they may then negotiate a separate peace after dissolving the alliance (see Fig. 4–2).

Troop Disposition

Assuming that we have agreement on a simultaneous cease-fire on all fronts of the war, a number of now familiar questions follow: Where will the cease-fire line be located? Will the troops of the belligerents remain deployed at that line until a political settlement is reached, or will they withdraw? If the troops withdraw, how will they do so and to what areas? Ordinarily, the cease-fire line is the line of contact between the belligerent troops at the time the cease-fire comes into effect. The terms of the armistice agreement might, however, require withdrawals of one of the parties before its terms become fully effective, although this would be most unusual, as it could result in increased casualties among the withdrawing forces. These technical questions of troop emplacement and withdrawal are apt to occasion controversy among allies only if the arrangements are deemed prejudicial to the security and integrity of the ally and its forces. Thus, if an opponent were occupying part of the territory of one of the allies, the latter might accept an armistice agreement that allows the enemy troops to remain very briefly upon its soil, but it would almost surely want those troops withdrawn eventually. Should its partners not provide adequate support during negotiations for its position on quick withdrawal of enemy forces, there is a danger that the coalition will be disrupted. An ally might also be anxious about the presence of *allied* troops within its territories and seek to obtain assurances from its partners that these troops will withdraw in due course, after a condition of stability had been established in areas that had been theaters of war. If the troops of the allies were stationed in or were traversing the territories of other allies, it would be in the interest of the alliance to encourage the negotiation of more or less formal agreements respecting allied troop status, including the conditions pursuant to which the troops would be withdrawn. A state fighting a war for dominance would, no doubt, have to be circumspect in its dealings with allies as concerns the disposition of its armed forces on their territory. Allies would fear for their own security unless the dominant state gave them rather specific guarantees. In the absence of such guarantees, the dominant state might find that its lack of concern for the qualms of its allies had resulted in the dissolution of the alliance, or if the dominant ally were especially cavalier, in the realignment of the former allies with the enemy.

Military Administration of Areas in the Combat Zone

The coalition will also have to agree upon policies relating to the administration, if only temporary, of areas of the adversary state under their control at the time of the cease-fire. Usually, areas occupied by the armed forces of one of the allies will be administered by that ally. In the event military operations had been conducted by two or more allies jointly, then it will be most important for those allies to work out a scheme for the military government of occupied areas, including procedures for eventually handing over administration to civilian authorities of the former enemy, or otherwise as the peace conference may direct. There is, of course, the possibility of conflict between allies in joint occupation, particularly if one ally's leaders felt that their state's prestige had been damaged by its being given too small a role in the military government, or if its assessment for the costs of the occupation were too high, or if the state wanted to remain permanently in control of the territory, but its allies (and eventually the peace conference) had decided otherwise. The permanent occupation or annexation of an adversary's territory is more likely to lead to disruptive conflicts among allies than temporary occupation since, as we have seen, this kind of disposition of territory affects quite directly the future security of all the allies.

The Political Settlement Phase

Territory

How much, and to whom granted? These are the two major questions respecting the disposition of territory at the end of an external war.[17] Even if the annexation of territory is not contemplated, the establishment of a particular regime or the award to one party of certain rights within the territories of the other party still raises the questions of how much territory is to be affected by the new regime (or within what areas will a party be given special rights) and what party will be awarded the

17 See Tables 2–3 to 2–8 for historical examples of the elements of a political settlement discussed here. See also note 11 with reference to the scenario-like discussion that follows.

rights or secure the benefits of the new regime? These questions, as we indicated earlier, must be answered during the political phase of the peace settlement process. And even before interbelligerent negotiations, they will first have to be answered by the members of a wartime coalition.[18]

It is the state waging a war for dominance that is most apt to find its policies in conflict with those of its allies.[19] No matter to what extent the subordinate allies acquiesced in their positions relative to the dominant ally during the wartime emergency, with the approach of peace, the policymakers of the subordinate allies find that they have reservations about the dominant partner's war aims. First, there will be the fear that too much strength possessed by the dominant state will in and of itself constitute a threat to their security, simply because a statesman can never know when strength may be used against him, however friendly wartime relations have been with the possessor thereof. There is the lurking suspicion among policymakers that a state having superior power will be tempted to use it to increase its superiority. Secondly, the leaders of the subordinate states may have been willing to forego the usual amenities of interstate relations during the war—the amenities that require, in theory, all states to treat each other on the basis of complete equality and respect. But they will want normal relations to resume at the war's end. They will demand, however cautiously, that the dominant state respect the territorial integrity of their states and refrain from interfering in their internal affairs. States that were once dominant or centers of culture will be particularly sensitive to the drive to paramountcy of their dominant partner. Thus, when the peace conference attends to the disposition of territory, the subordinate states will bargain hard with their coalition partners for the adoption of their policies as the policies of the entire coalition.

The dominant ally may seek to annex territory from the enemy. If the subordinate allies support the dominant partner, there will be no conflict. However, they may completely oppose all territorial claims or oppose some claims and support others, meanwhile advancing their own territorial ambitions. The motive for opposing the dominant state may be fear for what that ally's increased capabilities might mean to their own state's security. But the motive may also be *self-aggrandizement*. Knowing that only a certain number of square miles of territory is available for annexation, the subordinate allies will want their shares. In

18 See Fig. 4-1.

19 I remind the reader that by *dominance* I mean either a position of unquestionable superiority or the striving after dominance by a state with sufficient capabilities to persuade its policymakers that a position of paramountcy is attainable. In discussing the dominance of a state, we must be careful to describe the context, that is, dominance in what region and relative to which states.

either case, opposition to the claims of the dominant ally (and to each other's claims) for territory creates a classic bargaining situation that may either be resolved by compromise or lead to the dissolution of the alliance and conflict. Dissolution might allow the enemy to come out with a better bargain or, as we have noted earlier with such disruptive problems, it might also lead to a reversal of alliances and the resumption of hostilities.

The dominant ally need not be interested in annexations, but only in special rights within the territories of the enemy. Here too, subordinate allies might either acquiesce or resist. In the intracoalition bargaining that ensues, a compromise may be reached in which the allies trade off territories and special rights in the traditional *balance-of-power* practice of compensations. One subordinate state might not get all the territory its representatives demanded, but it might get a small piece of territory together with commercial or legal rights in the remainder. In the event an intracoalition dispute over the disposition of territories cannot be resolved by the technique of compensations or value trade-offs, the allies may permit the enemy to retain the territory. They could, of course, create a special regime that would deny each of them and the enemy the opportunity to exploit the area or to influence its political future. In order to settle a territorial dispute, the allies could agree to establish a "free territory" in an area they each had wanted to control. The alliance could also agree to permit the people of an area to decide their political future by plebiscite, although the outcome of such a process can often be anticipated. Nevertheless, the plebiscite solution postpones disposition of the territory until some later time, and this decision could permit the coalition to function more effectively during the ongoing peace talks. Naturally, either of these solutions (free territory or plebiscite) might be proposed on its own merits rather than as a technique for resolving an intra-alliance dispute over the spoils of war.

The state waging a war for consolidation according to the principle of nationality will claim territory inhabited by its nationals. Any ally also advancing claims for the same territory will naturally be in direct conflict with the consolidating state. If there are nationals of the state in territories under the jurisdiction of some of the allies, then the latter can with justification expect that the principle of national self-determination will eventually result in the consolidating state's making claims against them. The state seeking consolidation will probably accept a plebiscite in areas it claims if it can be sure of a favorable outcome, if its nonresident nationals can be counted upon to vote in its favor. Outright annexation at the conclusion of the peace conference would be preferred, of course, as the outcome of a plebiscite is never completely certain and may indeed be uncertain if there is a welter of peoples inhabiting an area. The consolidating state will bitterly oppose its allies' claims to the same terri-

tory and resist any effort to establish a special regime whose effect would
be to deny its claim. The consolidating state might also oppose a plebiscite if the outcome were in doubt. In that event, it could attempt to
guarantee a favorable outcome by influencing the apportionment of
electoral districts, by the appointment of its nationals to election supervisory commissions, and by the promulgation of election rules that would
bring about the sought after results.

Although the allies may decide not to annex all the territories of a
defeated enemy, they may establish an occupation regime; and while this
would presumably be a temporary arrangement, the allies will have to
determine among themselves which states will be assigned which areas.
Occupation laws and interzone regulations for trade and commerce,
movement of persons, and currency will also have to be established,
probably during the peace-conference period, if not before. All these
matters may occasion disputes. On the one hand, occupation will have
certain costs, most of which the occupying states will attempt to assess
against the occupied state. On the other hand, occupation does offer the
occupying power an opportunity to exploit the resources of the former
enemy and to control its internal politics by means of a governing regime
friendly to the occupying state. Finally, there is always the chance that
the occupation will not end; the occupying power may not leave.

Allies concerned about the relative dominance of other allies will seek
to obtain the largest and richest zone of occupation possible, with maximum freedom of action therein. They will want to limit the gains of
their partners, if these gains threaten their own share of the war values or
their security.

States waging either a retributive war or a defensive war are not likely
to have large claims to territory, and they may have no claims at all,
except to the extent that they demand demilitarization of the former
enemy. They will, however, be concerned with the territorial demands of
other allies. The state fighting the defensive war will not want the peace
settlement to occasion future threats to its security by a state striving for
dominance; and its policymakers may recognize that an inadequate,
punitive territorial settlement, leaving the enemy and some allies dissatisfied, would provide the basis for future wars.

The war aims of the state waging an ideological war are apt to be
treated as identical to those of a state waging a war for dominance, even
by states of the same or sympathetic ideologies. After all, the ideological
state will want sufficient influence within the enemy state to promote its
ideology, and this would require, in effect, a territorial settlement. If all
the allies have the same ideology, then all their claims against the enemy
state will very probably have the same ideological basis. Undoubtedly,
the coalition would then want to establish an occupation regime for a
defeated enemy to allow time and opportunity for indoctrination of the

enemy's citizens, and this could give rise to some of the problems we discussed. An adversary in a fairly strong bargaining position at the end of a war might be able to resist the ideological demands of the alliance, in which case all of the allies will fail equally to obtain their ideological objectives.

A war for opportunity values may be fought solely or in part for the acquisition of territory. Not having expended resources in the war effort, the state seeking opportunity values in the form of territory could find its claims discounted by its allies; and in bargaining with them, it might have to accept compensation in some other form.

The allies will undoubtedly realize that there is some merit in the proposition that a state should be compensated from war spoils in proportion to the human and material costs it sustained during the war. Hence, while they might admit the justice of a superior partner's claims against an enemy, they would still not want to deprive themselves of sufficient security by awarding too large areas to the dominant state, simply because the latter had sustained the highest costs. There are, of course, situations where they will be unable to deny the territorial claims of their dominant ally, either because the ally is too strong to resist or because, being in possession of the territory in question, the dominant state can be ousted only by the use of force, force which the allies might not want, and perhaps could not afford, to apply. Nevertheless, the subordinate states might still seek to persuade the dominant ally to moderate its demands and take compensation in other than territorial values. Or they might propose to establish a special regime in the territory and, because of other commitments or preoccupations, the dominant state might not be in a position to resist such a program.

The allies might want to regulate rivers, canals, and other transportation and communication links used by several states. Certainly, this question will arise where the adversary's territories are crossed by international rivers and canals. The most acceptable solution appears to be the one that allows all users access on equal terms, except in time of war. A regulatory commission will usually be established with the competence to establish technical rules and rates. The allies could differ over the question of the composition of such a commission. Naturally, those states whose territories are crossed by the transportation artery will demand representation as of right. But whether other states will also be represented could occasion some dispute. In the case of rivers, for example, riverine states have invariably been represented on international commissions for the supervision of the regime for that river. As a riverine state, a former enemy will also be entitled to representation, unless that state is penalized in the settlement and its sovereignty over the river suspended. It is difficult to envisage how this state of affairs could be anything but temporary. Among allies, the question of commission composition might cause disagreement, especially where the allies not traversed by the transportation link demand representation. As this demand could be part of an effort to extend a state's influence, the demands of a nonriverine dominant state would undoubtedly be resisted. A disagreement of this sort could embitter intracoalition relations, but it is not likely to lead to disruption of the alliance. Hence, as a compromise, particularly when other more weighty issues are in dispute, the allies might agree to the demands for representation of their partners on the theory that use of the river will affect the interests of them all.

Persons Affected by the War

Theories for ascribing nationality to persons, for dealing with refugees and displaced persons, and for protecting the personal and commercial rights of nationals of the belligerent states are, for the most part, technical and relatively unpoliticized. In their application, they may indeed become politicized; but these difficulties usually arise in the postwar period. Thus, the allies should have fewer problems among themselves in reconciling their views with respect to persons affected by the war than would the allies on the one hand and the opponent states on the other. The allies might disagree over the protection and guarantees to be offered to minorities and nationals of other allies in territories they acquired at the end of the war. The difficulty could be removed by a declaration that citizens belonging to a racial or religious minority will have the same rights as other citizens of the declarant; that allied nationals will have the same rights as citizens or, minimally, the same rights as aliens, who will in any case be guaranteed their personal civil liberties.

Proclaiming these principles is one thing, implementing them another. An ally (state A) will be opposed to the cession of territory inhabited by A's nationals to another ally (state B). Spokesmen for state A will insist that A has a right to exercise jurisdiction over persons having A nationality—and this presumes, probably correctly, that A nationals would be more willing to be governed by conationals than by non-nationals. If there were a large number of persons of A nationality in the territory coming under B's control, then B would probably be inviting bad relations with state A, and possibly internal troubles. Disagreement over such a question could result in the disruption of an alliance of A and B. If state A's security required that a given territory be taken from the enemy, it should, in the interest of alliance harmony, agree to a plebiscite or perhaps even an outright cessation to state B. The real problem would arise if A wanted to deprive B of that area.

The allies will also have to reach agreement over the status of debts and contracts of their nationals or citizens whose contractual relations have been disrupted. Such matters can be troublesome, and the negotiations tedious, but they are usually settled without serious disagreement.

Guarantees of Security

Collective Defense

An ally, having experienced the beneficial results of a wartime coalition, might decide that its security could best be maintained in peacetime by continued coordinated action with other allies. The wartime coalition would then be converted to a *collective defense* alliance. Its purpose is to provide security for the allies against a threat from the enemy of the war that has just ended. As long as that threat seemed real and credible, the peacetime alliance would be useful and characterized by high cohesiveness. Intra-alliance discord and a lessening of the tensions between the former adversaries (and with it, a corresponding decrease in the probability that the former enemy will continue to pose a threat) usually results in decreasing cohesiveness, and perhaps the eventual dissolution of the alliance. The behavior of states in a collective defense coalition cannot be discussed here. That is a separate subject.[20] What is important is the fact that during the late stages of a complex external war, or during the peace talks, the allies might attempt to transform their wartime coalition into a peacetime alliance in order to guarantee themselves the sufficient security they deemed vital. Each ally would then have to determine whether it intends to seek that security solely through its own efforts or collectively with other allies. Of course, it would never abandon traditional guarantees if it could get them; but, having decided to form a collective defense pact, it could regard the pact as a supplement to those guarantees.

Having determined that purely unilateral security efforts will not have the efficacy of collective efforts, a state's policymakers must then face the question of what form the defense alliance shall take. This depends upon the kind of threat anticipated, as well as the policy goals of each individual ally. By *kind of threat,* I envisage two significant parameters: the nature of the potential enemy (whether a single state or an alliance, what sort of state, and its capabilities and intentions) and a judgment of the nature of the threat. To make that judgment, we pose several ques-

---

20 Wolfers, Arnold, *Discord and Collaboration* (Baltimore: Johns Hopkins Press, 1962), pp. 167 f, 181 f, 205 f.; Liska, George, *Nations in Alliance, op. cit.;* Beer, F. A. (ed.), *Alliances: Latent War Communities in the Contemporary World* (New York: Holt, Rinehart & Winston, 1970); Rothstein, R. L., *Alliances and Small Powers* (New York: Columbia University Press, 1968); Osgood, R. E., *Alliances and American Foreign Policy* (Baltimore: Johns Hopkins Press, 1968); Fox, W. T. R. & Fox, A. B., *NATO and the Range of American Choice* (New York: Columbia University Press, 1967).

tions: What do the allies have to fear from the potential enemy? Will it be direct or indirect aggression, and in what region? Will the threat be commercial or economic in nature, rather than military? Or will the enemy use propaganda against one or more of the allies? In other words, will the threat be a military one or political or ideological? Answers to these questions will dictate the optimum form of the collective defense organization, as briefly indicated in Table 4–1. This table is by no means complete; but it will serve to adumbrate the general relationship between the parameters and the very practical questions each raises for the allies, were they to attempt to transform their wartime coalition into a collective defense pact. Many of these questions will have been answered for wartime coalition planning. Now, they must be projected for an indefinite period in the postwar era.

The allies will have to agree upon the form of organization that will best fulfill their aims. What organization, given the nature of the enemy and the threat, will provide the optimum coordination of joint efforts? What organization will be necessary to insure proper command and deployment of the alliance's armed forces? The solution of problems such as these will be based upon the experiences of the allies in the recent war and in the peacemaking efforts at the end of the war. Since attempts to

TABLE 4–1.   The design of a collective defense organization in the postwar period.

parameter	organizational problem posed by parameter
1. capabilities of the enemy	How will each ally allocate specific resources to the alliance; in what quantities, how produced, and how paid for?
2. the threatened region	Where will the resources be placed and the armed forces deployed? Where will fortifications be located and other defense efforts made?
3. direct or indirect aggression	What type of military forces are required, and what types of weapons are likely to be used in an attack? Where shall the armed forces of the alliance be deployed?
4. weapons and technology	What individual and coordinated programs for weapons production shall be established? How shall research be budgeted among allies?
5. economic	How strengthen the economies of the allies and improve the economic position of the allies relative to non-allies? How shall techniques be rationalized to prevent disruptive commercial disagreements among allies?
6. ideological	What coordinated counter-ideological efforts should be made to reduce the effectiveness of the enemy's ideology?

transform the alliance into a collective defense organization could occur during the peace talks, the substance of the intra-allied dialogue respecting that transformation could affect peace negotiations.

States that had fought a pure *opportunity war* are not likely to be persuaded of the need to cooperate with allies after the war, unless the costs of the future joint efforts will be outweighed by the probable acquisition of additional opportunity or security values. The same could be said for the state that had waged a *retributive war,* but for other reasons. The rationale for defense against the punished state might be absent, unless it was in a position to repeat the provocation. That would be an inducement for the state that had moved against the provocateur to participate in the postwar alliance. In either case, if the policymakers of the states had determined that the former enemy constituted a real threat to their states' security, then, of course, a collective defense pact would be attractive.

States that had fought a status quo war might regard the continuation of the alliance as a necessity, as the former enemy could attempt to revise its power position relative to the allies. But status quo states would find it difficult to continue cooperation with an ally that had fought the war to achieve dominance and then, in the postwar period, pressed its drive for dominance. In that event, the coalition would probably not last. The status quo states might find themselves in a coalition directed against the former ally, even if this meant realigning with the former enemy.

Each of the allies will want to minimize the quantity of its resources allocated to the joint defense and to lessen or avoid indirect costs such as the presence of allied troops on its territories or economic dislocations. It may not like being a target of the enemy or may barely tolerate the need to consult, rather than to act unilaterally. Disputes over these questions could prevent formation of the collective pact and embitter the relations of the allies. Thus, the effects of having attempted and failed to form a collective defense pact may not be confined merely to the failure to form such a pact. The allies may become so estranged in the process that the wartime coalition will not last through the peace negotiations.

In addition to the traditional guarantees of security (e.g., disarmament or demilitarization of the former enemy or prohibitions against the manufacture of certain weapons), the allies might seek to prevent the enemy from joining a collective defense alliance directed against themselves. This would preclude their opponent's pooling his resources with that of other states and deny him the benefits of coordinated action for as long as the prohibition can be maintained.

Each ally will have its unique conceptions of the sufficient security the peace settlement should provide. Each ally will seek to obtain the requisite guarantees and will expect sympathetic support from its partners. Were this expectation to be disappointed, and were its allies actively to oppose the security demands of one state, then the intra-alliance disagreements could become serious enough to delay negotiations or disrupt the alliance. If the allies have won the war or are otherwise in a strong bargaining position, their demands will be high and are likely to be met by the adversary. If they lost the war, or nearly lost it, demands will be made of them. In a situation where the belligerents are of nearly equal bargaining power, the most each side can obtain will be promises to refrain from the use of force against the other. Disputes would arise when the allies attempted to agree upon the specific demands to be presented to the enemy. The geography of the region of the belligerents may be such that any demilitarization of territory would primarily benefit only one ally, leaving other allies to face a fully fortified frontier. Disarmament, even if the opposing states could be forced to accept it, will not be a welcome form of demilitarization to the state striving for dominance. But allies of this state, particularly small states, will recognize that only in disarmament can they find security. In this situation, a controversy among the allies will result. Thus, in addition to the usual sources of disagreement—unequal sharing in benefits or values and, in this case, the sharing of security values—there is a further source: One or more allies are unwilling even to request the particular forms of security guarantees other allies deem necessary. The motives of the reluctant allies could then come under a cloud of suspicion, resulting not only in the disruption of the alliance but also in that essential mistrust out of which reversal of alliances results.

If the allies were in a relatively weak bargaining position at the peace talks, then the opponents would demand security guarantees of each of the allies. One obvious demand would be the dissolution of the wartime coalition, although the opponents of the alliance could not seriously entertain such a proposal unless the allies had lost (or very nearly lost) the war or unless the alliance was in any event on the verge of dissolution for other reasons. Successfully met, however, a demand to dissolve the alliance would prevent, for a time at least, the formation of a collective defense pact among the former allies. Defeat removes the reason-for-being of a wartime coalition and can prompt its dissolution. In fact, each ally might strive to prove itself less responsible for the war than the others, leave the alliance, and then pursue wholly unilateral policies at the peace talks, hoping to come away with a better settlement than might be expected had it remained tied to the "more guilty" parties.

There will be situations where the allies will be asked to provide security guarantees for the former enemy states, and it is conceivable that some of the allies will request that other allies provide those guarantees. As in the case of the victorious ally that refused to request guarantees from a weaker adversary, disagreements could arise if one ally refused to hamper its future freedom of action by providing the requested guarantees (assuming that it is in a position to refuse them). Thus, while some allies might be willing to recognize the neutrality of a third state, another ally might not be willing to forego the future gains it could obtain by dealing with the third state as a nonneutral (with the latter supporting the ally's policies or allowing intervention, for example). The ally might refuse to disarm or to refrain from producing certain kinds of weapons, while other allies were willing to do so. Or the great-power ally, having extensive commitments and responsibilities, might decide that it could not satisfy its allies' demands for the demilitarization or disarmament that would hamper fulfillment of its worldwide obligations. Indeed, if the world were unsettled at the time of the peace conference, it would in any case be difficult for any state to achieve an acceptable level of security. More than this, however, the great power with diplomatic connections in areas far removed from the region of the recent external war (and the region with which the peace conference was concerned) would be loath deliberately to reduce its capabilities when they might shortly be needed elsewhere and if to do so might invite aggression by the removal of its deterrent power. While policymakers of those allies requesting guarantees might well understand the reasons for their partner's refusing to give them, they might nonetheless decide that the alliance will not provide them with adequate benefits unless these partners make the concessions they deem necessary for their security. In fact, if a great-power ally were involved in other crises, this might in itself provide the basis for the other allies' concluding that the wartime alliance no longer had any efficacy, as their connection to the great power could result in their becoming embroiled in disorders and war in remote regions. In this case, the alliance would be a negative security guarantee; and the allies with limited interests would probably feel themselves doing well to leave the alliance and would certainly refuse to join a collective defense pact with the great power.

Collective Security

There is another form of a security guarantee the belligerents might attempt to secure: the *collective security guarantee* within an international organization where each member agrees to act in concert with others against any "aggressor" state. After the losses of the recent war, either side might decide that only by establishing effective interstate cooperation against the use of force can future wars be prevented. When such a decision is made at the end of a war, the precise form of the collective security organization may become a topic for discussion at the peace conference.

How will the wartime coalition be affected by the prospect of the establishment of a collective security organization? For reasons we have noted above, the allies may want to dissolve their coalition at the war's end. States that had decided to go their own way in the postwar period might prefer to remain outside any organization that would in any way place inhibitions upon their policies. Yet, the costs of membership in security organizations of the past have not been onerous; and they have often been outweighed by the prestige costs, and sometimes the economic and security costs, of nonmembership. Of course, it is easy to conceive of an organization in one's imagination that would demand more of its members than historical collective security organizations. Thus, a future organization might require the surrender of the right to declare war unilaterally. It might demand the disarmament or demilitarization of its members, with inspection by an international inspectorate. It might be empowered to impose collective mandatory sanctions against states that have been declared aggressors or that have otherwise violated the constitution of the organization. Some states would be reluctant to become participants in such a broadly conceived collective security scheme and might indeed prefer to "go it alone."

Coalition partners that sought to convert their wartime coalition into a collective defense pact during the peace negotiations might react differently to various proposals for a collective security organization. Their responses depend upon a number of factors, including the aspirations of their policymakers or peoples and the stability of the international environment. Thus, there might be some states that will come to regard the *collective security organization* as their salvation and the means to prevent their involvement in future wars. These states will have to reappraise their roles in the wartime coalition if it were transformed into a collective defense pact, as they may regard such a commitment as incompatible with an effective international security regime. They could decide to leave the alliance and rely solely on the guarantees that a collective security organization could provide. If this occurred during the peace talks, the bargaining positions of the adversaries would be altered, and the settlement might take on a quite different character. If it occurred after the settlement had been reached, the implementation of the terms of the peace treaty could conceivably be affected, in so far as coalition action was required for that implementation. However, there will be some states that would not want to rely entirely upon collective security guarantees. They might, however, regard them as worthwhile supplements to the other guarantees that could be extracted from a weak or a defeated enemy. And a *collective defense pact* among the war-time coalition partners could also be regarded by its members as a guarantee supplementary to those provided by the collective security organization— however irreconcilable in theory the two might be. (As Wolfers has shown,[21] if one of the defense pact members is branded an "aggressor" by the collective security organization, the other members of the defense pact will face a painful choice: either to support the security organization and the principle of collective security, and thereby offend an ally and

21 Wolfers, *op. cit.*, pp. 181–204.

perhaps irreparably damage the defense pact; or support the ally in order to preserve the defense pact against a still dangerous common enemy and thereby irreparably harm the security organization by failing to support with positive measures the principle of collective security.)

States that regard the defense pact as fully compatible with the collective security organization will remain in the alliance. They would (and could) support the organization unless it attempted to deny them the guarantees they hoped to obtain from other sources. If a conflict arose between the security policies of member states that belonged to a collective defense pact and the principles of the collective security organization, the organization would either have to acquiesce in the security policies of the members of the defense pact or oppose their policies. If the latter course were adopted, the defense pact states might leave the organization; and the members of the organization would then have to enforce their decision. Or failing to oppose the defense pact states, the organization would experience a decline in its credibility and effectiveness. Either eventuality would be unfortunate for the maintenance of peace. But as this problem is related to the beginning of a new war and not to the end of an old one, it is more properly a problem of peacekeeping rather than peacemaking, and one with which we cannot yet deal.

At the end of an external war, a state might join an existing collective security organization, in which case it would be fairly clear to its policy-makers what obligations they were undertaking and what benefits they would receive. On the other hand, that state, along with others, might decide to create a wholly new security organization, either to supersede or supplement pre-existing organizations or simply to establish one where there was none before. In the latter case, the allies would have to agree, if they could, upon the purposes and structure of the organization and determine how the former enemy states would fit into the scheme they were elaborating. States that had fought status quo wars will want to establish an organization that will preserve the status quo. If such states appreciate the inevitability of change, they will at least seek to create an organization that would provide for peaceful change, one that will redirect the forces of change toward other states or toward issues that would not appreciably affect the status quo. States that have fought an ideological war or a war for dominance will want an organization that will promote their expansive ideological or power political aims. As a first step, they may seek to dominate the organization. The ideologically oriented state might even attempt to incorporate its own ideology in the constitution of the organization.

The conflicts between allies that arise during the formative period of a security organization will be analogous, if not identical, to the conflicts that arose during the war. In the event of serious discord, the organization may not come into existence, or dissenting states may simply refuse to join it. A collective security organization is not likely to be effective (that is, to offer adequate guarantees to its members) if important states, particularly great powers, remain aloof. Should the disagreements over the aims and structure of a collective security organization become manifest during the peacemaking process, several consequences are conceivable:

1. Allies obstructed in their efforts to obtain what they deem adequate security guarantees from the international organization might become more obdurate in their determination to obtain them from the former enemy. Their demands for guarantees will, in other words, become more stringent, perhaps to the extent that neither the enemy nor their allies will be willing to support them. This could lead to a dissolution of the alliance or a failure of the peace talks.

2. The part that an ally plays in the discussions concerning the establishment of the organization may create or confirm suspicions the partners have of that ally's motives, which could lead them to a reappraisal of the value of the alliance, to its dissolution, and to the protraction and embitterment of the negotiations for peace.

3. A final settlement might be impossible to achieve; or if achieved, it might be an inadequate settlement for some (or all) of the parties. Having obtained acceptable guarantees from neither the enemy nor a collective security organization, some states might refuse to accept the settlement; or agreeing to it, they might attach reservations the effect of which would be to render the settlement incomplete. Unless there were some agreement later in the postwar period, this state of affairs could lead to war.

The allies must decide what role the "other side" is to play in a collective security regime. The former enemy might be excluded, in which case the regime would actually take on the attributes of a collective defense scheme. If the enemy state were a great power or an important regional state, it would be folly to exclude it; the organization would be a rather poorer guarantor of the peace. The enemy state may be asked to join, immediately upon the establishment of the organization or after a lapse of time. It might be asked to present proposals for a proposed constitution for a new organization. Allies seeking a peace of reconciliation will advocate consulting the former enemy. Allies determined to punish the adversary, but accepting the need and desirability of his becoming a member, will want to impose conditions upon that membership or at least exclude him from the discussions that will shape the organization and determine its purposes and form.

Penalties

If, in fact, the situation at the war's end permits the imposition of a penalty by states that were allied during the war, the allies must first decide whether to impose a penalty and, in addition, what other demands are to be made of the former enemy. This question is not likely to occasion serious discord in the alliance. But other related questions are indeed likely to do so: How will the indemnity or the reparations be shared by the allies? When shall the reparations or indemnity be made payable? And what steps shall be taken in the event of default?

Each ally may attempt to offset the costs and damages of the war by extracting compensatory values from the enemy and will seek to guarantee a share of the reparations for itself, unless because of the economic relations of the ally with other states and the enemy, its policymakers conclude that the costs of reparations might eventually be borne by them. A state could not be expected to subsidize reparations for its allies. But even assuming the allies agreed in principle that the enemy must pay part of these costs, in the course of peace negotiations, some of the allies might come to the realization that an enemy made to pay reparations would be a burden upon them, requiring supportive loans and technical assistance. The alternatives would be default by the former adversary and a further weakening of its economic position, reducing it to a state of economic dependency or leading to a deterioration in the standard of living of the enemy's citizens (perhaps even resulting in starvation) as the victors forced delivery of staples and essential resources.

It is difficult to correlate war aims with the controversies that are apt to arise among allies over questions of penalties. States that have fought retributive wars will seek a penalty. Those that have fought opportunity wars will want to secure their opportunity values; but as these values may not be regarded by them as a sufficient penalty, they may demand more, particularly if the size of the reparations of other allies interfere with their obtaining the retributive or opportunity values. States that have waged a defensive war may regard an indemnity as a justifiable way to weaken the enemy and preventing him from renewing his aggression at an early date. They could also be motivated by the desire to punish the aggressor. On the other hand, these states and others might not want to impose penalties, or what they regard as excessive penalties. For the state bent upon paramountcy in a given region, the incorporation of a penalty provision in a peace treaty could furnish an assist in its drive for dominance. But some of the allies may prefer to promote their postwar policies by other means. As penalties could give rise to a desire for revenge on the part of the elites of the enemy, allies hoping for a peace of reconciliation may oppose them.

There will be states that have suffered from the war, and they will expect reparations as a matter of right. Small states with relatively small gross national products will attach great importance to penalties, because an indemnity or reparations could have an important positive effect upon their economies. Hence, small states would expect sympathetic support for their reparations demands from allies to whom reparations might be of lesser importance. Failing to obtain their support, the states seeking penalties might desert the alliance.

The allies, whatever their views, are not likely to permit the issue of reparations to disrupt the alliance completely. After all, reparations and other penalties do not usually affect the ultimate interests of the recipient states. Hence we would expect that although intra-alliance bargaining may be "hard," a compromise will be found.

We have dealt above with the case where the alliance is in a strong enough bargaining position to be able to impose penalties. Should the alliance and its enemy be in approximately equal bargaining positions, then penalties will not be imposed, simply because neither side would be weak enough to acquiesce in demands for a penalty. Finally, if the enemy were in the strong bargaining position, then the allies might find themselves required to pay an indemnity. Usually such a penalty would be imposed on an individual basis. Hence, if the alliance outlasted the military defeats that had placed its members in a weak position, a penalty as such would probably not cause the dissolution of the alliance. In the unlikely case in which the enemy simply presents one demand for an indemnity to the alliance as a whole, then the allies must decide the share of payments each must bear, and this may occasion serious disputes.

Resumption of Relations

The decision to resume relations with a former enemy, and the conditions of such resumption, are usually not matters for collective decision. It is within the prerogative of individual states to determine whether to establish diplomatic and commercial relations with other states; and this determination includes the question of the degree of normalization of relations between former belligerents. Allies might coordinate their policies, however, especially after a war which had been not only a break in the diplomatic relations of a multiplicity of states, but also an extensive and thorough interruption in legal, commercial, and economic relations. The peace settlement should then provide rational methods for bringing all states as near to normal relations as possible.

During the peace negotiations, technical procedures for resuming relations with the enemy will not ordinarily produce serious disagreement among allies. But in one area in particular conflict is possible. Should a state create the impression that it intends to favor the enemy more than its allies are willing to favor him, the allies may conclude that that state is attempting an early realignment of powers, to the prejudice of the aims and ideals of the alliance. Indeed, because of disagreements over other aspects of the settlement, a state might be prompted to seek a "soft" peace and the immediate resumption of relations with the enemy, under favorable conditions. This is a kind of insurance against whatever ambitions they suspect the other allies have. And a state may also seek a "hard" settlement by which it would secure territory or resources from the enemy, so improving its power position that other allies would be justified in suspecting it of seeking dominance over the former enemy and eventually over themselves. Those allies could counter their ambitious ally's demands for a "hard" peace with their own attempts at quick reconciliation and resumption of relations with the enemy on favorable terms.

In considering the question of resuming relations with the former adversary, the policymakers of the allies must determine when relations shall be resumed. Other related problems include the status of treaties (i.e., the legal relations of the states) and the normalization of trade and other commercial and economic relations between the belligerents. In the case of treaties, the states must decide which shall again become operative and which shall be void. The war will have created wholly novel conditions that the allies will want to regulate formally by means of new written agreements. Renewed trade and other economic relations will usually be based upon a new or a reactivated treaty of commerce, with the necessary detailed terms negotiated over a period of time after the peace settlement. Essential to the restoration of normalized trade relations will be the disposition of claims of nationals of either belligerent against the other. All these matters could be of interest to the allies *collectively;* and they will want to consult together about the general approach to resuming commercial relations with the enemy. If the alliance is a viable one, they will agree upon and coordinate the legal and diplomatic terms of renewed relations, making such terms a part of the peace treaty.

Another matter for discussion might be the reconstruction and rehabilitation of adversary states that have sustained severe war damage. Of course, the war damage of the allies will have priority over those of the enemy; but it might be necessary to provide for the reconstruction of the enemy state, perhaps for humanitarian reasons or for the very practical reason that an entire region affected by the war must recover *in toto* for any one part of it to become politically and economically sound. Finally, insofar as it is within their power to decide, the allies might invite (or refuse to invite) the enemy state to become a member of a collective security organization. Diplomatic dealings within such an organization would facilitate the resumption of diplomatic relations and perhaps promote commercial ties as well.

On any of these matters, the allies may disagree; but as we said earlier, the disagreements should not aggravate alliance relations unless they give rise to suspicions that one or more of the allies intend to cultivate a former adversary for purposes that could not be reconciled with the aims of the alliance or the national interests of the other allies. Then, within the general area of the question of resuming relations with the enemy, there will probably occur a series of highly technical disputes relating to the details of this element of the settlement, details that mask more serious questions of a state's vital interests.

Adjustment of Disputes

Allies that decide to establish institutionalized means for the adjustment of disputes may regard their alliance as the necessary basis for mediation, arbitration, or adjudication. They will then create mechanisms within the alliance for settling disputes. Such steps will be taken only if the allies intend to maintain the alliance. At the end of a war, the transformation of the wartime coalition into a collective defense alliance may supply a sufficient reason for reducing *intra-alliance* frictions. In fact, the act of establishing a collective defense alliance implies that the allies feel the international system is not stable enough to allow them to rely wholly upon general *interstate* mechanisms for the adjustment of disputes. It suggests that the enemy will remain an enemy in the postwar era; it implies that his relations with the allies will not be friendly and might indeed be motivated by revenge or the desire to revise the outcome of the war and the peace settlement. In that event, only disputes among trusting allies could be settled amicably according to rules established by them. There might still be good reasons for wanting to settle disputes with the former enemy by peaceful means; but there would be little incentive to create formal, institutional methods for doing so.

Yet, the situation may not be as stark as this. Leaders of the belligerents could come to realize that peace was essential, at least for the present, and during the peace conference attempt to agree upon means for settling disputes that could eventuate in a new war. The allies would adopt intra-alliance conciliation procedures to supplement general, interstate methods. Should the former belligerents create a collective security organization to guarantee all its members a modicum of security, undoubtedly that organization would be empowered, in a variety of ways, to achieve the peaceful settlement of disputes. Whatever the design of the plan for the adjustment of disputes, the allies would probably consult first among themselves—simply because the existing alliance made consultation easier among its partners—and afterward they would attempt to work out a scheme of mediation at the peace talks with the former enemy state.

The principal source of intra-alliance friction in this area will be differential support of procedures for the peaceful settlement of disputes. Thus, if some of the allies prefer to preserve their freedom of action and not be hampered by what they regard as restrictive institutions for conciliation, and if other allies, particularly the small states, conclude that their security would be more efficaciously guaranteed by giving such institutions broad competence, then a basis for intra-alliance disagreement will be present. States supporting sophisticated methods for mediation may come to suspect the motives of the allies that opposed them; and these suspicions, reinforced perhaps by the policies and ambitions of these states as revealed during the peace talks, could lead to the disruption of the alliance.

The Settlement of Some Complex External Wars

The wars selected for brief analysis here provide some illustrations of the settlement of complex external wars and of the relationship between alliances and peacemaking.[22]

LAST WAR OF THE HABSBURG-VALOIS RIVALRY (1557–1559)
Spain (Habsburgs) and England vs. France and the Pope

WAR AIMS: France and Spain sought to increase the prestige of their dynasties and to achieve dominance in Europe. The Pope hated the Habsburgs and feared they would dominate the Church; hence, his principal aim was to defend Church interests and Church lands. Queen Mary of England was devoted to her husband, Philip II of Spain. She was willing to defend Spanish interests but also looked for gains at the expense of France.

OUTCOME: England lost Calais to France. The *status quo ante bellum* was restored in Italy. Spain and France agreed to peace, since both states were near bankruptcy. The *Treaties of Câteau-Cambrésis,* 2–3 April 1559, ended the war.

WAR-ORIENTED STATES: German Princes, Venice, and Turkey.

FACTORS FOR PEACE: For England, defeat at Calais and her perception of the error of the Spanish alliance were factors for peace; for France and Spain, war weariness, financial exhaustion, and the burdensome costs of the war; for the Pope, defeat at the hands of Spain and the offer of a conciliatory peace.

ALLIANCES: The war had begun when Henry II of France came to the aid of Pope Paul IV, who had provoked the Duke of Alva (of Spain) into occupying Papal domains. The French King would not countenance a change in the Italian status quo, particularly not in favor of his rival, Spain. In September, 1557, Alva surrounded Rome and offered favorable terms for peace to the Pope, who accepted them. The peace terms included restitution of all Papal lands and submission of Philip to the Holy See, in return for which the Pope agreed to make peace, to remain

22 Additional studies that deal with the peace settlements summarized in this section can be found in the Bibliography.

neutral in the ongoing war, and to forgive Philip. Thus, the Papal-French alliance, based upon calculations of self-interest and the Pope's hatred of Spain, did not survive defeat of the Pope's forces and the offer of a peace settlement acceptable to Rome.

The Anglo-Spanish alliance was based on the marital tie between Mary Tudor and Philip II (and Mary's continuing hope for a child). The alliance remained intact through the settlement, although Mary died during the peace talks. The allies did not coordinate their operations to any significant extent. After the loss of Calais, it is doubtful that the alliance would have lasted had Spain not agreed to talk peace.

THE SETTLEMENT: PRELIMINARIES: Negotiations opened at Lille in October 1558 and were then moved to the Abbey of Cercamp in Cambrésis, but they were interrupted by the death of Mary Tudor and Philip's proposal of marriage to Elizabeth, the consequences of which were too important not to affect the peace talks. Ultimately, the proposal was turned down. An agreement on the suspension of hostilities in the low countries was reached in December and renewed in February, to last as long as the negotiations continued.[23] An area was set aside for Elizabeth's negotiators, to which merchants and couriers were to be given free access.

MILITARY SETTLEMENT: The cease-fire of late 1558 was converted to a permanent peace. Violations would not provide a pretext for renewal of hostilities, but the perpetrators were to be punished. Prisoners were also to be exchanged. The parties promised not to invade the territories of the other nor to aid anyone who intended to commit an act of aggression. The ships of war of one party were to give security to port officers of the other party and do no injury, on pain of having the ships confiscated. England agreed to construct no forts in Scotland and to demolish identified forts. Letters of marque would no longer be issued. (Generally, details on the implementation of the cease-fire were sparse.)

POLITICAL SETTLEMENT: There were two treaties of peace, one between Spain and France and the other between France and England.

1. The Treaty of France and England, signed 2 April 1558, proclaimed a perpetual peace between the signatories.[24] Calais and environs were ceded to France for 8 years, after which the area was to be restored to England. As surety for this cession, France would have her merchants provide 500,000 gold crowns and send hostages to England, who would be bound by oath to remain there but be free to move throughout the realm. France could change the hostages every 2 months. Neither party would

23 Bernard, Jacques, *Recueil des Traitez de Paix,* Vol. 2 (Amsterdam: Henry et la Veuve de T. Boom, 1700), p. 283. The reader is again reminded that other works about this and other complex external wars are to be found in the Bibliography.

24 Great Britain, *General Collection of Treatys,* 2nd Ed., Vol. 2 (London: Knapton, Darby *et al.,* 1732), pp. 46 f.

attempt to change the terms of the settlement by force of arms. If France did so, Calais was to be delivered to England immediately or, failing this, the surety would be payable to England by the hostages. If the Queen tried to innovate, France's obligation to return Calais and pay the surety was abolished.

The subjects of either monarch were free to travel or do business in the other's domains. It was further agreed that all future disputes would be resolved amicably. Neither would receive rebels or traitors.

2. By the Treaty between France and Spain, signed 3 April 1559, the parties renounced all acts incompatible with the peace that was proclaimed in the treaty.[25] Flanders and Artois were to remain in the Spanish Netherlands, and the peoples of the provinces were to enjoy all the rights the French King had granted them. France was to evacuate Savoy and the Piedmont, but retain the fortresses at Turin, Saluzzo, and Pignerol. Corsica was ceded to Genoa. Metz, Toul, and Verdun were to go to France. Florence (the Medici) was to take Sienna *in fief;* and Lombardy was divided, the west given to Savoy and the south and east to Farnese and Gonzaga. France renounced all claims in Italy (but refused to admit the validity of Spanish claims in the New World). Elizabeth of Valois (elder daughter of Henry II) was to marry Philip II; and Henry's sister Marguerite was to marry the Duke of Savoy. When this latter marriage was consummated, Spain would withdraw from Savoy. The Duke of Savoy was not to molest any citizens after assuming control of the lands ceded to him. The judgments and acts of the French King in those lands were to be respected by the Duke.

Subjects of the signatories were permitted to travel and do business in the domains of the other. There was to be an amnesty, and all prewar debts were declared to be valid. Treaties in force in 1551 were to continue in force. The parties recognized that other parties to the treaty were bound thereby: the Pope, the Holy Roman Emperor, Portugal, Poland, Savoy, Lorraine, Venice, and Florence. Others could adhere with the consent of the parties. There were no separate provisions for guarantees or the adjustment of disputes, although the territorial changes, the contracts of marriage, and the retention by France of the Italian fortresses could be regarded as guarantees. The parties also agreed to call a Council for the establishment of a "true union" of Roman Catholics and employ their good offices on behalf of Christianity. (The Pope was not at all happy about this provision.) No penalties were imposed.

COMMENTS: France was surrounded by Spanish territories but remained dominant in Italy and allied *de facto* with the Pope. We should remember that by Charles V's resignation in 1555, the Habsburg realm was thenceforth divided between Spain and the Empire of central and

25 Bernard, *op. cit.,* Vol. 2, pp. 287 f.

eastern Europe. Thus, the years 1555 to 1559 saw territorial settlements of far-reaching importance.

SECOND ANGLO-DUTCH WAR (1664–1667)
England and Bishop of Münster vs. France, The United Netherlands, Denmark, Brandenburg, and Brunswick-Lüneburg

WAR AIMS: Commercial rivalry between Britain and Holland was the reason for their hostilities, and each sought superiority over the other. Münster made war on Holland because the Dutch refused to recognize the Bishop's claim to Borkelo; and the latter was determined to redress this wrong. France and the other states wanted to maintain their positions relative to their adversaries and other states, and hence they were fighting a defensive war. Yet Louis XIV's motives were also more grandiose. He had designs on the Spanish Netherlands and wanted the benevolent neutrality of the Dutch in order to prevent their obstructing his schemes, hence his alliance with them.

OUTCOME: France drove Münster from Holland. Threatened by Brandenburg and France, the Bishop made peace in April, 1666.[26] With Swedish mediation, the war was settled at Breda, 21 and 31 July 1667, but not before the Dutch made a surprise attack on English naval stations (and substantially improved the Dutch bargaining position).

WAR-ORIENTED STATE: Sweden.

FACTORS FOR PEACE: For Holland, the costs of the war had been high and the returns small; for England, the costs had also been high, and the plague and Great Fire presented additional burdens for Charles II, along with his domestic troubles in England and Scotland. Both Holland and England were alarmed by the French King's claims to the Spanish Netherlands—rights Louis XIV claimed had devolved upon his wife, the Spanish Infanta, Maria Theresa. These claims impelled the King to protract the Anglo-Dutch war and to preoccupy his Dutch ally-adversary. The other states (Denmark, Brandenburg, and Brunswick) achieved their limited goals and were willing to acquiesce in peace.

ALLIANCES: The alliance between Britain and Münster was of the most tenuous sort; the grievance of the Bishop over Borkelo and his desire to seek retribution temporarily fitted in with Britain's plans. Britain provided the Bishop with a subsidy in return for his promise to invade Holland.[27] With the intervention of France, the defeat of his forces, and the threat from France and Brandenburg, the Bishop made peace. His ally England, after all, could not help him in his difficult position in April, 1666, when he made peace. This left England without allies. Only

---

26 *Ibid.,* Vol. 4, pp. 156, 163.
27 Nussbaum, F. L., *The Triumph of Science and Reason, 1660–1685* (New York: Harper & Row, 1953), pp. 154–5.

Sweden remained England's friend, and she would not go to war. She merely offered to mediate between the antagonists.

France and Holland formed their alliance before the war in April, 1662, each party agreeing to defend the other if attacked by another power.[28] It was pursuant to the terms of this treaty that Louis XIV declared war on England in January, 1666. Holland's position was further strengthened by separate alliances with Denmark and with Brandenburg in February, 1666, and by the Quadruple Alliance of October, 1666, between Holland, Denmark, Brandenburg, and Brunswick-Lüneburg.[29] Under the terms of this treaty, each party agreed to come to the defense of the others if attacked. The armed forces to be contributed by the parties were specified, and each promised not to enter into any agreement incompatible with the purposes of the alliance and to refrain from making a separate peace.

Just as France and England were not the bitterest enemies in this war, France and Holland were not the closest allies. Their war aims were compatible until the very latest stages of the war (1667), when Louis XIV declared his claim to the Spanish inheritance. His claim worried the Dutch, because French acquisition of the Spanish Netherlands would put a strong France on their borders. The alliance lasted through the peace settlement, but just barely. Indeed, later that same year (in the War of the Devolution) Holland, allied with England, was at war with France!

THE SETTLEMENT: PRELIMINARIES: Preliminary peace negotiations between England and France began at St. Albans in January, 1667. These led to an understanding that France would return her conquests in the West Indies to England, in return for which Charles II promised he would refrain for one year from forming any alliances inimical to France. By March, it was agreed that Breda would be the site of the peace talks.[30]

There were three treaties of peace: one between France and England, signed on 21 July 1667[31]; a second between Holland and England, signed on 31 July 1667[32]; and a third between Denmark and England, signed on the same day.[33]

MILITARY SETTLEMENT: A cessation of hostilities was declared, and letters of marque annulled. Reparations for ships seized as prizes was to be made for seizures after dates set forth in a schedule in the treaties. The

28 Garden, Guillaume, le Comte de, *Histoire Générale des Traités de Paix,* Vol. 3 (Paris: Amyot, 1848–87), pp. 41 f.
29 Bernard, *op. cit.,* Vol. 4, pp. 171 f. (the Treaty of the Quadruple Alliance) ; Garden, *op. cit.,* pp. 48–9.
30 Garden, *op. cit.,* pp. 50 f.
31 Great Britain, *General Collection of Treatys, op. cit.,* Vol. 1, pp. 127 f.
32 Bernard, *op. cit.,* Vol. 4, pp. 211 f.
33 *Ibid.,* pp. 222 f.

Danish treaty set the cease-fire for different times in different areas of combat.

POLITICAL SETTLEMENT: 1. In the treaty between France and England, peace was proclaimed, all past offenses were to be forgotten, from whatever cause, and the parties promised to refrain from all acts of hostility. Britain ceded St. Christopher to France; and France retroceded Acadia, Antigua, Montserrat, and all the other islands England had possessed before the war had begun.

There was to be restitution to persons driven out of Acadia by the British; and persons that had lawfully obtained property in conquered territories were to be protected in their rights. Within one year of the treaty, all persons desiring to leave the territory of one party for that of the other were free to do so. Prisoners were to be freed without ransom. There were also provisions for the freedom of slaves and indentured servants.

Navigation and commerce between the signatories was declared free, and all edicts contrary to this declaration were nullified. Sweden was incorporated as a party to the settlement. There were no further provisions (guarantees, penalties, or the resolution of future disputes, for example).

2. According to the terms of the peace treaty between Holland and England, the parties were to retain the territories acquired by the other before 20 May 1667. Thus, England retained New Netherlands (renamed New York); Holland retained Pularoon and Surinam. All other territories acquired after that date were to be restored pursuant to a schedule provided in the treaty.

Holland and England formed a defensive alliance and agreed to return rebels and traitors. Holland acquired the substantial right to import into England in her own ships all goods originating in the Rhine basin. She was to salute British ships only in the English Channel. Nothing was said about the other honors due the flag of England or the competition for trade in the East Indies and in West Africa, where the rivalry of the "allies" was to intensify. There were few provisions respecting persons affected by the war.

3. The treaty between Denmark and England was the simplest of the three. Peace was to bring with it freedom for the subjects of either to trade with each other and on each other's territories. Compensation for goods and property seized during the war was to be provided. British subjects were given the right to recover by legal process all goods seized in Denmark during the war. Special protocols were attached for The Sound tolls and the Orkney Islands.

COMMENTS: Differing dates for a cease-fire were necessary because hostilities were widespread, and communications with distant forces difficult. This was, moreover, a war in which domestic forces (particularly within The Netherlands and England) were an important factor in the decisions of the actors to move to make peace. The reader is referred to Chapter 10 for a discussion of domestic politics and peacemaking.

AUSTRO-RUSSIAN WAR against TURKEY (1787–1792)

Russia and Austria (1788–91) vs. Turkey and Sweden (a belligerent against Russia from 1788, in alliance with Turkey from 1789)

WAR AIMS: Russia and Austria sought the acquisition of territories from the Ottoman Empire, the foundation of a "Greek Empire," and the establishment of a Russian client state in the Principalities. Austria cooperated because of the good personal relations between Emperor Joseph II and Catherine the Great. The former also wanted to secure whatever gains might be offered by another "inevitable" war between the Porte and Russia. Turkey's aims were her defense, ending of Russian provocations (consisting of a number of activities of Russian consuls in the Empire that were unacceptable to the Porte), and the prevention of Russian expansion in the Caucasus.

OUTCOME: Austria deserted the alliance and made peace at Sistova in August, 1791.[34] The strength of Russian arms and the weakness of the Ottoman Empire were balanced by the remonstrances of war-oriented states who were fearful of the consequences of the break-up of Turkey. Russia agreed to a somewhat advantageous peace at *Jassy,* on January 1792.[35]

WAR-ORIENTED STATES: Great Britain, Prussia, United Provinces, France, Sweden, and Denmark. The latter, honoring the terms of a Russo-Danish alliance, was at war with Sweden for one month in 1788, but she was forced to make peace by the remonstrances of Britain and the threats of Russia.

FACTORS FOR PEACE: The deaths of the Sultan and Joseph II brought to the thrones of Turkey and Austria rulers who were more amenable to a settlement and, in the case of Austria, less willing to accept Catherine's "Grand Plan." Austria was troubled by domestic unrest, Russia by the costs of the war; Turkey simply wanted peace because she anticipated further defeats. The complex environment that was the state system of the period brought a variety of pressures for peace to bear on the belligerents and the war-oriented states, not the least of which was domestic turmoil in Holland and revolution in France. Both Britain and Prussia pressed Catherine to make peace; and Prussia entered into a alliance with Turkey, agreeing to enter the war in the spring of 1791. Austria, not wanting war with Prussia, accepted the mediation of Britain, Prussia and the United Provinces.

34 Martens, *Recueil de Traités,* Vol. 5 (Göttingen: Librairie de Dieterich, 1826), pp. 244 f.

35 *Ibid.,* pp. 291 f.

ALLIANCES: The alliance between Russia and Austria resulted from two private interviews and the private correspondence of Catherine and Joseph II in June, 1781. Both parties were agreed on the desirability of securing Ottoman territories, although there was some disagreement over the size and quality of the shares. The offensive alliance lasted until Leopold II (Joseph's successor) decided to improve his relations with Prussia and to terminate a war that, in the circumstances, could not bring Austria substantial benefits without excessive costs. The Swedish-Turkish alliance was concluded rather late in the war (July, 1789). It brought no benefits to Sweden, although the Swedish war against Russia certainly helped the Porte. In violation of the terms of the alliance, Sweden made a separate peace with Russia at Verela on 14 August 1790.

THE SETTLEMENTS: 1. In the *Peace of Sistova* of 4 August 1791 between Austria and Turkey, there were few military terms. The parties, proclaiming a perpetual peace and a perfect union of their countries, agreed to the status quo of February, 1788. Austria was to return the areas in Moldavia and Wallachia conquered by her forces. A boundary commission was to be established after ratification of the treaty to fix the boundary for the Principalities, Bosnia, Serbia, and Ostrava.

An amnesty for all inhabitants of the Balkan provinces of the Ottoman Empire was proclaimed. The Porte guaranteed Austrian merchants against Algerian and Tunisian pirates, agreed to facilitate commerce and trade and to adopt measures to insure the tranquillity of border areas. Prisoners of war were to be freed, except those that had embraced the religion of the other party; and these were free to remain in the land of their internment. Expatriates' rights were recognized; and dual citizens were granted the right to choose either nationality.

Prewar treaties between the parties were declared to be in effect. The prewar rights of merchants were also restored. Subjects of either of the signatories could move freely in the territories of the other, with no taxes or other hindrances not also imposed upon the party's own subjects. The Porte confirmed the rights of Roman Catholics in Turkey.

There were no penalty provisions, no guarantees, and no provisions for the settlement of future disputes. The mediators (Britain, Prussia, and Holland) signed the treaty *as mediators*.

2. In the Peace of Jassy, 9 January 1792, Russia and Turkey agreed to dispatch orders to their commanders in the field to cease hostilities. Prisoners of war and slaves were to be released without ransom. Provision was made for the evacuation of Russian troops from territories that were not annexed by Russia.

The Dniester was to be the new boundary between the parties. The Porte recognized the prewar annexation of the Crimea by Russia. Moldavia was returned to Turkey with stipulations: Turkey would not exact any contributions from the inhabitants of the Principality for war costs, but would permit them to make claims for damages for two years; and persons were to be allowed to leave with their property for 14 months after ratification of the peace treaty. Certain rights of persons within Moldavia (and within the Crimea and lands east of the Dniester) were protected by the treaty. An amnesty was proclaimed.

Specific prewar treaties were declared valid and in force. Commerce was to be re-established on a completely free and unencumbered basis. Turkey was to give surety for the Barbary corsairs. Procedures for the exchange of ambassadors were briefly adumbrated.

COMMENTS: By the Treaties of Kutchuk-Kainarji[36] and Jassy and the Convention Explicative (respecting the Crimea), Russia became firmly ensconced on the Black Sea, with her frontier at the Dniester. In the areas between the Dniester and the Danube, the hold of Turkey was made more tenuous still by the rights of the inhabitants secured for them by Russian arms and by Russian diplomats in the peace settlements. The other powers of Europe were more interested in the terms of the settlement at Jassy than that of Kutchuk-Kainarji. Henceforth, that interest would grow.

THE CRIMEAN WAR (1854–1856)

Russia vs. Britain, France, Turkey and Sardinia

WAR AIMS: Turkey fought to defend her lands. Sardinia sought an opportunity to participate in the war with the Allies, win an invitation to the peace conference, and present the "Italian Question" for consideration by the Powers. Russia fought to protect Orthodox communicants in the Ottoman Empire and to secure territories from the Porte. Britain and France wanted to defend the integrity of the Ottoman Empire and preserve a balance of power in Europe. In the course of the war, the aims of the *Allies* became both more specific and demanding, to wit, retrocession of Bessarabia to Turkey and the restriction of the rights of the Russians to maintain warships on the Black Sea.

OUTCOME: The allies won some victories in the Crimea at very great costs. Although Russia withdrew from the Danubian Principalities in July, 1854, and accepted the Four Points as the basis of a negotiated settlement in November, 1854, the war went on for another 15 months, further embittering the belligerents. A conference of the Powers in Vienna from March to June, 1855, was unsuccesful. Finally in early 1856, the Congress of Paris was convened and eventuated in a peace settlement by the end of March. Russia became an enemy of the status quo and cool to Austria, her former partner in the Concert and in the Holy Alliance.

WAR-ORIENTED STATES: Austria, Prussia, and Sweden.

FACTORS FOR PEACE: Austria, a nonbelligerent ally of France and Britain, worked assiduously for peace. Czar Nicholas died in 1855, and

36 See the settlement of the Russo-Turkish War of 1768–74 (pp. 61–2).

the new Czar, Alexander II, was more amenable to accepting the terms of the Allies. France was beset with domestic problems; the costs of the war had been high and the gains slight, with a less than noteworthy performance on the part of the French army. Moreover, French elites favored an easy peace with Russia in order to establish friendly ties with her and thus end the Concert of Powers (of 1814) aimed at curbing French revisionism. The British Court and the army wanted to continue the war, but pressure from allies, the desire to get on with the business of trade without the hindrances posed by war, and the substantial achievement of her war aims induced Britain to negotiate for peace.

ALLIANCES: 1. An alliance of Britain, France and Turkey was formed on 12 March 1854 to meet Russian aggression against the Ottoman Empire.[37] Britain and France promised to send a naval squadron to Constantinople and ground troops to the Empire. The parties further agreed to transmit to each other any Russian proposals and were to make no separate peace. A further convention between France and Britain (10 April 1854) made definite the intention of the allies to restore territories to the Sultan (i.e., Moldavia and Wallachia). They declared they had gone to war to maintain the balance of power, and for no other advantage.

2. Austria and Prussia formed an alliance in April, 1854, each agreeing to defend the territories of the other against an attack from any source.[38] The parties proclaimed the priority of German rights and interests.

3. In June, 1854, Austria allied itself to Turkey, promising to secure Russian evacuation of the Principalities.[39] In July, Russia did evacuate Moldavia and Wallachia; and in November, Austrian troops moved in to guarantee the Principalities against attack.

4. France, Britain, and Austria formed an alliance in December, 1854.[40] This was a true "diplomatic revolution"; thenceforth, Russian and Austrian relations would be cool, and eventually hostile. By the terms of the alliance, the parties agreed not to conclude a separate peace (if Austria were to become a belligerent). They agreed to consult before entering into any arrangement with Russia and to defend the Principalities.

5. Sardinia joined the Anglo-French alliance in January 1855, agreeing to provide 15,000 troops.[41] The Powers guaranteed Sardinia against attack during the war, and Britain agreed to advance a loan of one million pounds. Sardinia joined the alliance with Turkey in March.

37 Martens, *Nouveau Recueil de Traités,* Vol. 15 (Göttingen: Librairie de Dieterich, 1857), pp. 565 f.
38 *Ibid.,* pp. 572, 578, 598.
39 *Ibid.,* pp. 594–95.
40 *Ibid.,* pp. 600–602.
41 *Ibid.,* pp. 606, 609–11, 623–24.

6. In November, Britain and Sweden entered into a secret alliance, according to which the latter promised to make no cessions to Russia nor grant any other rights to the Czar. Sweden would also communicate all proposals from the Russians to the British and French, who were to cooperate to resist Russian demands.

These alliances remained viable during the war and at the Congress of Paris.

THE SETTLEMENT: PRELIMINARIES: We have mentioned the failure of the conference at Vienna in early 1855.[42] After the fall of Sebastopol to the Allies in September, 1855, peace feelers were aired and informal talks over peace terms began in December. On February 1, the Czar formally agreed to the Four Points: 1. the Russian guarantee of the Principalities was to be replaced with a European guarantee; 2. the Danube was to be free; 3. the regime of the Black Sea was to be revised and the Sea "neutralized"; and 4. Russia must renounce the "right" to protect Christians in the Ottoman Empire and cooperate with the Powers in implementing reforms.[43] The Preliminaries of Peace embodying these points were agreed to, and a cease-fire was declared. Sardinia adhered to the Protocol of Vienna (i.e., the Four Points), and formal peace talks began on 25 February 1856.[44]

MILITARY SETTLEMENT: The cease-fire was to be effective until the peace congress ended. Troops of the belligerents were to hold their positions but refrain from all aggressive acts. The blockade of Russia was to continue, however, but the navies of the allies would commit no hostile acts.

The General Treaty of Peace, 30 March 1856, proclaimed peace from the date of the exchange of ratifications.[45] Prisoners of war were to be rendered up to the appropriate states. The Black Sea was open to the merchant ships of all nations, but warships were prohibited, with the exception of those necessary to service the coasts. Russia and Turkey concluded a separate convention, approved by the Powers, limiting their Black Sea navies to 6 steam ships of 800 tons and 4 steam or sail ships of no more than 200 tons. Each signatory was also permitted to station 2 light warships at the mouth of the Danube. The Sultan promised to establish as a law for the Empire that no foreign warships were to be permitted in the Straits in peacetime, except for light warships serving the legations of the Powers. Russia and Turkey agreed to refrain from building arsenals on the littoral of the Black Sea. The Powers also obligated themselves to evacuate all occupied territories. To this end, special arrangements were to be negotiated.

42 *Ibid.*, pp. 633 f.
43 *Ibid.*, pp. 702–4.
44 *Ibid.*, pp. 700 f.
45 *Ibid.*, pp. 770 f. The revisions of the 1841 Straits Convention is on pp. 782 f.

POLITICAL SETTLEMENT: Russia retroceded Kars and all other Turkish territory in her possession to Turkey and agreed to the rectification (by the Powers) of the Bessarabian frontier. Territory formerly part of Bessarabia would be attached to Moldavia, which was to be under the suzerainty of the Porte (along with Wallachia). The Ionian Isles were placed under British protection. In Asia, Turkey and Russia agreed to the *status quo ante*. The two would be joined by France and Britain in fixing a boundary. France and Britain restored Sebastopol, Balaklava, Kertch, Kinburn, Jenikaleh, and other cities to Russia. It was also agreed that Serbia would continue as a dependency of the Porte, although under a guarantee of the Powers. Turkey had the right to garrison Serbia. But the right to intervene in Serbia by any state, including Turkey, required the consent of the Powers.

There was to be an amnesty for all subjects of the parties, particularly those who had entered the service of another belligerent. In vague terms, the Sultan promised to issue a firman "consecrating his generous intentions" with respect to his Christian subjects. (The Powers declared that in no case would the matter of Christians in Turkey give rise to an individual or collective right to intervene.) The Sultan promised to recognize the liberties of subjects in the Principalities and in Serbia. Special provisions for the administration of the Principalities were included. A commission of the Powers was to meet at Bucharest to revise the laws of Moldavia and Wallachia.

Turkey was declared to be a member of the European Concert and to be entitled to the benefit of the public law of Europe. All agreed to respect her independence and territorial integrity. In a separate treaty of guarantee among Austria, Britain, and France (10 April 1856), this provision was supported by the promise that any infraction of the General Treaty of Peace would be regarded as a cause for war.[46] If the security of the Principalities was in any way threatened, Turkey would meet with the Powers to determine what course of action to take. There was to be no intervention without the preliminary agreement of all the Powers.

Until revisions were undertaken, prewar treaties were to remain in effect. Russia and Turkey would admit consuls to ports on the Black Sea (in conformity with international legal practices), and the Black Sea was to be open for the favorable development of commerce.[47]

On 16 April 1856, the former belligerents (and Austria and Prussia) concluded a Convention on Maritime Rights, which declared privateering abolished. It further stipulated that a blockade must be effective to be legal; that a neutral flag protected enemy goods, with the exception of contraband; and that neutral goods (except contraband) could not be

46 *Ibid.*, pp. 790–1.
47 *Ibid.*, pp. 786–8.

seized from enemy ships.[48] The parties agreed to communicate this Convention to other governments.

COMMENTS: Cavour was permitted to speak at the Congress and thus champion "Italian rights" against Austria, Naples, and the Papal States, but Sardinia received no territory. The settlement was a thorough one, drafted with care and precision (where precision was possible). It made the best of a bad situation (namely, the decline of the Ottoman Empire) and went beyond it to consider and resolve questions of European public law.

SECOND WAR OVER SCHLESWIG-HOLSTEIN (1864)

Austria and Prussia vs. Denmark

WAR AIMS: Denmark's aim was to consolidate the state by normalizing the relationship of the Duchies in federation with the Crown by the proclamation of a new constitution (thereby acquiescing in the demands of Danish nationalists). Austria wanted a confederation of the Duchies, with substantial autonomy for them relative to Denmark, particularly for the resident Germans (thus supporting the position of the German nationalists in the German Confederation and enhancing Austria's status in the Bund). Prussia sought the acquisition of the Duchies.

OUTCOME: Denmark was defeated in the Duchies, which were ceded to the allies to dispose of as they determined.

WAR-ORIENTED STATES: France, Great Britain, German Confederation, Russia, and Sweden.

FACTORS FOR PEACE: The allies achieved their war aims; Denmark was defeated, and her policymakers concluded that further resistance was useless.

ALLIANCES: Prussia and Austria, former competitors in the *Bund* and future enemies in the Austro-Prussian War (1886), became allies in this war against Denmark.[49] Had the Austrians known Bismarck's intention eventually to annex the Duchies to Prussia, they would never have cooperated. But such was the style of his diplomacy, coupled with the fact that pro-Prussian ministers were in the ascendancy in Vienna, that the war aims of the partners appeared compatible and the differences between them only differences over means. During military operations, Austria tended to be cautious, fearing the intervention of the other European powers. Indeed, she opposed the invasion of Jutland altogether. The alliance survived the peace settlement and the Gastein Convention (14 August 1865), but within a year the former allies were at war. It should be mentioned that the alliance was an occasional *ad hoc* one, based mainly on agreements of a military nature.

48 *Ibid.*, pp. 791–2.
49 Steefel, L. D., *The Schleswig-Holstein Question* (Cambridge: Harvard University Press, 1932), pp. 102 f.

THE SETTLEMENT: PRELIMINARIES: The Conference of London, comprising belligerent and war-oriented states, met from April to June, 1864, and while agreeing on the future status of the Duchies and their relations to Denmark, was unable to agree on the Schleswig-Holstein frontier. It ended in failure.[50] The Conference had arranged a six-week cease-fire; but fighting was resumed after the collapse of the talks. Further Prussian successes brought about a change of government in Copenhagen and proposals for an armistice, which began on 20 July. The Preliminaries of Peace were signed in Vienna on 1 August, this document sketching the terms of a final peace settlement which the Danes accepted.[51]

MILITARY SETTLEMENT: The Preliminaries and an annexed Protocol embodied the terms of the military settlement. A cease-fire was proclaimed for the period of time required to negotiate a peace treaty. The belligerents were to retain possession of all territories occupied by them as of 2 August. If negotiations were not complete by 15 September, any party could denounce the truce with 6 weeks notice prior to resuming the war. Denmark agreed to raise the blockade of Prussian ports. The allies were permitted to maintain their troops in Jutland in numbers sufficient to guarantee their security, the expenses for this (except salaries) being borne by Denmark. Prisoners were to be released; but Danish prisoners could not again serve in the Danish army unless hostilities were renewed. There were to be no further seizures of goods or property.

POLITICAL SETTLEMENT: The Treaty of Peace of Vienna was signed on 30 October 1864. It restored peace.[52] Denmark renounced sovereignty and all claims to Schleswig and Holstein in favor of Austria and Prussia and agreed to recognize their disposition of the Duchies. The boundaries of the cession were defined in general terms, and a commission was appointed to run and mark the boundary.

The public debt of the Duchies and Denmark was fixed, and procedures for its discharge were provided. Denmark would offer restitution for ships of commerce and for buildings in the Duchies damaged or destroyed during the war. A commission with its seat at Copenhagen was to determine the size of the Danish indemnity, with deductions for confiscations by the allies. The new governments in the Duchies were to assume the obligations and contract rights for public administration.

All subjects of Denmark from the Duchies serving in the Danish army were to be discharged. All residents could leave with their property during the period running for 6 years from the ratification. No person was to be molested for his opinions or conduct during the war. The troops of the allies were to be evacuated within 3 weeks of ratification.

50 Martens, *Nouveau Recueil de Traités*, Vol. 17, Part 2 (Göttingen: Librairie de Dieterich, 1869) , pp. 347 f.
51 *Ibid.*, pp. 470 f.
52 *Ibid.*, pp. 474 f. See also *ibid.*, Vol. 18, pp. 1, 8 f.

Treaties in force before the war were declared valid. Commerce was to be restored between the parties on a most favored nation basis. There were no provisions for adjustments of disputes or security guarantees.

COMMENTS: In the Gastein Convention of August 1865, Austria and Prussia disposed of the Duchies.[53] Without prejudice to the rights of either Power, Schleswig was assigned to the King of Prussia, Holstein to the Emperor of Austria, for purposes of administration. This provision was very ambiguous, however, and disputes about the precise juridical status of the Duchies and the meaning of the dispositive terms of the Convention were a major formal clause of the Austro-Prussian War. Prussia was authorized to build a canal across Holstein, and Lauenburg was annexed to Prussia. There were other provisions relating to customs, railroads, telegraph lines, and the rights of the parties to use the harbor of Kiel. After the Austro-Prussian War, the Duchies were annexed in their entirety by Prussia.

WAR OF THE PACIFIC (1879–1883) Peru and Bolivia vs. Chile

WAR AIMS: Chile wanted to continue to exploit nitrate deposits in the Antofagasta province of Bolivia and intended to defend its investments there. Bolivia feared Chile's intentions and sought to defend its territory. Bolivia also wanted to put an end to Chile's economic aggrandizement at the former's expense. Peru wanted to deprive Chilean miners and industrialists of the privilege of exploiting nitrates in Tarapacá, Tacna, and Arica provinces and thus secure revenues from them for the Peruvian treasury.

OUTCOME: The allies were thoroughly defeated by Chile's army and navy. Bolivia was deprived of access to the Pacific. Peru was occupied for a time and lost territory to Chile.

WAR-ORIENTED STATES: United States, Argentina, and to a lesser extent France, Britain, Italy, and Germany (because of the damages sustained by their nationals in the war) were war-oriented.

FACTORS FOR PEACE: Peru and Bolivia were defeated. Chile secured her objectives by military means.

ALLIANCES: In 1873, Peru and Bolivia concluded a secret defensive and offensive alliance, directed principally at Chile, whom they expected to refuse to accede to their demands for rights to areas being exploited by Chileans. The impact of the defeats suffered at the hands of Chile effectively dissolved the alliance.[54] After early 1881, and the fall of Lima, Bolivia was not in a position to assist Peru—and indeed had not effectively assisted Peru before that time! The allies concluded separate instruments of settlement with their adversary.

53 *Ibid.,* Vol. 18, pp. 2–6.
54 Galdames, Luis, *A History of Chile,* trans. by Cox, I. J. (Chapel Hill: University of North Carolina Press, 1941), pp. 324 f.

THE SETTLEMENT: PRELIMINARIES: In mid-1880, Chile occupied Tacna, Arica, Tarapacá and Antofagasta. England offered to mediate the dispute. Chile accepted, Peru refused. The U.S. then offered to mediate, and the parties accepted. The Conference of Arica failed, as the allies refused to accede to Chile's demands for the formal cession of Tarapacá and Antofagasta. The cease-fire arranged prior to the conference ended, and hostilities were resumed. In 1881, the U.S. entertained thoughts of intervention, and Peru's leaders believed the U.S. would intervene. This did not come about, however; and after about 2 years of guerilla warfare and a change of government, Peru decided to accept Chile's peace terms.[55] The war against Bolivia continued until the truce of 1884. As Bolivia's leaders could not bring themselves to recognize formally the loss of territories, they refused to negotiate a peace treaty until a later time. Bolivia did agree to a truce in December, 1883, another in April, 1884, and a definitive truce in November, 1884.

POLITICAL SETTLEMENT: PERU AND CHILE: Separate protocols were negotiated for ending the occupation regime, although Chile had the right to remain in Peru during the peace negotiations (up to the time of the exchange of ratifications) in areas she deemed necessary for her security.

The Treaty of Ancón, 20 October 1883, re-established peace and ceded Tarapacá to Chile in perpetuity.[56] Tacna and Arica were to remain in the possession of Chile for 10 years, subject to her laws. After the expiration of this term, a plebiscite was to determine which of the two parties was to secure permanent sovereignty over the provinces. The state obtaining them would pay 10 million pesos to the other party. A special protocol would detail plebiscite procedures.

Several articles dealt with the apportionment of proceeds from the seizure and sale of guano; another with sharing guano deposits on Lobos Island; and still another provision established procedures for composing differences over allocation of the guano.

Commercial relations between the parties were to be restored on a prewar basis. Peru recognized the legality of the judicial and administrative acts of Chile during the occupation. Indemnities for Chilean citizens who had suffered injury to their persons and property during the war would be considered by an arbitral tribunal. (Chile had promised Britain, France, and Italy to secure an indemnity for their citizens.)

SETTLEMENT BETWEEN CHILE AND BOLIVIA: The agreement of 4 April 1884 was termed a *truce,* which it was; but it also had important political consequences. The state of war was declared to be at an end, although either party could renew hostilities after giving one year's notice. The

---

55 *Ibid.,* pp. 333–4.

56 Martens, *Nouveau Recueil de Traités,* 2° Série, Vol. 10 (Göttingen: Librairie de Dieterich, 1885–6), pp. 191 f.

parties agreed to negotiate a peace treaty.[57] (They never did so, although Bolivia formally ceded Antofagasta to Chile in perpetuity in 1904.)

Chile was given the right to govern occupied areas (as defined by Chilean law). In this indirect way, Chile gained sovereignty over Antofagasta, the former Bolivian province between the Andes and the Pacific, depriving Bolivia of access to the sea. If there were difficulties over the extent of the areas ceded, a commission of engineers named by the parties was to settle the dispute.

Goods seized by Chile in Bolivia were to be returned to their rightful owners, or an indemnity must be paid. An arbitral tribunal was established to settle questions of restitution of property damaged or seized during the war.

Commercial relations between the signatories were restored. Chilean goods were to be free of all customs duties in Bolivia, with the same privilege extended to Bolivian goods in Chile. A protocol was to be negotiated to implement this provision. Goods destined for Bolivia and sent through Chilean ports, including the port of Antofagasta, were to be free of all special charges and would be treated on a most favored nation basis. Customs on goods coming through Arica were to be apportioned.

COMMENTS: The settlements were incomplete and inadequate, many "elements of settlement" being omitted. Indeed, the dispute over Tacna and Arica lasted until 1929 and troubled the relations of the three states until that time.

THE BOER WAR (SOUTH AFRICAN WAR) (1899–1902)
Great Britain vs. South African Republic and the Orange Free State

WAR AIMS: Britain sought the consolidation of her Empire, retrieval of her prestige, and the preservation of the rights of the predominantly British "Uitlanders" in the Boer republics. The Republics fought to defend their independence.

OUTCOME: The Republics were defeated at a very high cost to the British. They became colonies in the British Empire.

WAR-ORIENTED STATES: Germany and France (and the United States, in a minimal way) were war-oriented.

FACTORS FOR PEACE: The Boers were defeated. Their leaders decided that the guerilla war they had been fighting since 1900 could not preserve their independence and would result only in further devastation.

ALLIANCES: In their treaty of alliance of March, 1897, the Boer Republics agreed to defend each other with all available force if the independence of one of them were threatened.[58] They would consult promptly in the event of a threat or attack and would negotiate a protocol respect-

57 *Ibid.*, pp. 610–14.
58 *Ibid.*, Vol. 25, pp. 327–9.

ing the rights and duties of officers and citizens of the republic that gave such assistance. The treaty also looked toward the formation of a federative union, and the Boer governments agreed to formulate proposals for such and for a Council of Delegates of the two parties. Needless to say, the alliance was a close one, as both states' aims were wholly compatible.

THE SETTLEMENT: PRELIMINARIES: After a military success in standard set-to battles, the British annexed the Orange Free State in May, 1900: It became the Orange River Colony. The South African Republic was annexed in September and became known as the Transvaal. Both colonies were governed under martial law for the duration of the war, and laws were promulgated by the decree of a military governor.[59]

When it appeared that many of the Boer leaders were willing to negotiate an end to the guerilla war, a meeting of the delegates of the Boer commandos was called to meet in Vereeniging, with the permission of the British Commander. After long debate, the Boers agreed to accept the British terms.

MILITARY SETTLEMENT: By the Peace of Vereeniging, 31 May 1902, the Boer commandos agreed to lay down their arms and recognize Queen Victoria as their lawful sovereign.[60] The manner of their surrender was to be arranged by the British Commander. Burghers in the field or prisoners of war outside the colonies were to be permitted to return after they had sworn allegiance to the Empress.

POLITICAL SETTLEMENT: The effect of the acquiescence of the Boers in the Peace of Vereeniging was their loss of independence and their acceptance of colonial status for the Transvaal and the Orange River Colony and the right of the British to determine their political future.

No civil or criminal proceeding was to be brought against persons because of their actions during the war, except for certain acts contrary to the usages of war. Personal liberties and property of colonists were recognized by Britain. The Dutch language would be used in law courts and taught in schools where the parents of students desired it. Rifles could be licensed to persons requiring them. Franchise for the natives was not to be decided until after the introduction of self-government.

Military administration was to be succeeded by civil government at the earliest possible date, and representative institutions were to be introduced. Special commissioners would be appointed in each district of the colonies to assist in the restoration of property and in the supply of staples. Britain would provide a loan of 3 million pounds for the colonies for reconstruction and make loans to individuals. No special tax to meet the costs of the war was to be imposed.

COMMENTS: The Transvaal achieved full self-government in 1906; the

---

59 *Ibid.,* Vol. 32, pp. 136 f.

60 Roloff, Gustav (ed.), *Das Staatsarchiv,* Vol. 67 (Leipzig: Duncker & Humblot, 1903), pp. 131 f.

Orange River Colony, in 1907. In 1909, these colonies joined Natal and the Cape Colony in the Union of South Africa.

THE BOXER REBELLION (1900–1901)
China vs. Austria-Hungary, Belgium, France,
Great Britain, Italy, Germany, Japan,
Netherlands, Russia, Spain and the United States

WAR AIMS: China's aims were defense and retribution against foreigners for practices incompatible with Chinese sovereignty. The allies' aims were to protect their legations and to obtain guarantees for their commercial and diplomatic dealings with China.

OUTCOME: Peking was occupied by the allies. The Imperial Court fled and acquiesced in the allied peace terms. The war did not extend throughout China because the viceroys of south and central China refused to obey the Imperial decrees and maintained order in their provinces.

FACTORS FOR PEACE: The allies defeated the Boxers and the Chinese forces in Chihli. The war-party of the Imperial Court, lacking the support of other elites, recognized that further resistance would be senseless. The allies' aims were limited and appeared moderate to some Chinese elites.

ALLIANCES: The alliance was *ad hoc,* based upon informal agreements among the allies' ambassadors in China, in consultation with their respective governments. The U.S. would have refused a formal alliance in any case. There was agreement on the need to relieve the legations at Peking and on the necessity of extracting from China an indemnity and promises against the recurrence of the use of force against diplomats or merchants. Nonetheless, the major powers were each intent upon securing their own interests in China. In short, the alliance was not expected to last, and did not last, beyond the settlement.

THE SETTLEMENT: PRELIMINARIES: China exchanged letters with the U.S., Russia, and Japan in a vain effort to secure a peace acceptable to the Court. During this period, Russia was concerned with establishing favorable post-rebellion relations with China and sought to ingratiate herself with the Court. When China did agree to send plenipotentiaries to negotiate (after a dispute over whether negotiations should be in Peking or Tientsin), the allies challenged their competence; only when this question was cleared up, did negotiations begin. The Powers submitted a Joint Note to China in December, 1900; and China accepted its terms in January, 1901.[61] It is worth pointing out that the diplomatic

61 The documents discussed are collected in Clements, P. H., *The Boxer Rebellion* (New York: Columbia University Press, 1915). See also Tan, C. C., *The Boxer Catastrophe* (New York: Columbia University Press, 1955), pp. 215 f.

activity in the fall and winter of 1900–1901 was largely among the allies, who sought to arrive at a common position and seek common terms. China began to implement some of the provisions of the Joint Note; and on 7 September 1901, all the parties signed the Peace Protocol.

MILITARY SETTLEMENT: China agreed not to import arms and munitions. She was to recognize the right of the allies to station guards at their legations. The Taku forts were to be demolished, and the allies were given the right to occupy specified points on the China coast. Allied troops were to be evacuated from Peking by 17 September; from Chihli, by 22 September.

POLITICAL SETTLEMENT: The Chinese recognized that the legation area in Peking was exclusively for the use of the powers; no Chinese might reside there.

Treaties on navigation and commerce between the signatories were to be revised, and a conservancy board was established for the Yellow River. The Tsung-li Yamen (the Imperial Bureau of Foreign Affairs) was to be reorganized on lines indicated by the Powers; and Court ceremonial was modified to eliminate practices not compatible with Western notions of the relations of sovereign states.

As a guarantee against the revival of the Boxers or similar movements, China agreed to impose the death penalty for membership in any antiforeign society, and to hold her officials strictly accountable for antiforeign troubles.

The penalty provisions of the Protocol were extensive. China was to pay an indemnity of 450 million Taels (about $345 million) over a period of 39 years, at 4% interest. Provisions for servicing the debt were included with the stipulation that security for the indemnity would be the Imperial Maritime Customs, native customs, and the salt gabelle. The current tariff on imports was to be raised 5%. China was also required to send an emissary to the German Emperor to convey China's regrets for the assassination of the German Minister, Baron von Kettler, and to Japan, to express regrets for the murder of the Chancellor of the Japanese legation. Monuments were to be erected for these diplomats, and expiatory monuments were to be erected in cemeteries desecrated by Chinese citizens. Imperial edicts condemning certain officials to death, exile, and suicide were required—and had in fact been issued by the date of the Protocol. Other officials were rehabilitated. Civil Service examinations were suspended for 5 years in cities where foreigners had been murdered or had been subjected to cruel treatment. There were no provisions for the adjustment of disputes.

COMMENTS: As is evident, the penalties imposed upon China were extraordinary, even for a state that had acquiesced in its defeat (at least in battles around the capital). No attempt was made to transform China into a protectorate or colony. Indeed such a move would have demonstrated how truly incompatible were the Allies' war aims.

The preceding summaries provide examples of both formal and informal alliances. We saw, on the one hand, the formal alliances of the Second Anglo-Dutch and Crimean Wars, based upon rather detailed treaties of alliance; on the other hand, we saw the informal alliances of Austria and Prussia in the War over Schleswig-Holstein and the alliance against China in the Boxer Rebellion, both based upon *ad hoc* military agreements, and the Austro-Russian alliance against the Ottoman Empire in the war of 1787–1792, resting upon the private interview and correspondence of the Emperors.[62] We have also seen instances of offensive and defensive alliances: the offensive alliance of England and Münster in the Second Anglo-Dutch War; the defensive alliances of the Crimean War and of the Boer Republics in the Boer War; and the offensive and defensive alliance of Peru and Bolivia in the War of the Pacific.[63] In the latter war, neither ally was able to help the other to any great extent in the face of defeat. The alliance lacked utility for its partners—and this was also true of the Anglo-Spanish alliance in the Last War of the Habsburg-Valois Rivalry.[64]

62 Most of the coalitions of states involved in the wars summarized in Chapter 5 (complex internal wars) and Chapter 9 (multilateral wars) were based upon formal treaties of alliance. The following informal alliances are exceptions: Austria and Saxony, and Russia and the pro-Russian Poles, in the War of the Polish Succession (*infra,* pp. 214–7) ; the alliance of Russia with Roumania, Serbia, and Montenegro in the Russo-Turkish War of 1877–8; and the Russo-Turkish alliance during the First War of Mehemet Ali against the Sultan (until formalized by the Treaty of Unkiar-Iskelessi) .

63 Among others discussed in Chapters 5 and 9, the Anglo-Dutch alliance of 1578, formed during the Dutch Revolt (*infra,* pp. 208–14) , was a defensive alliance, as was the Anglo-Turkish alliance of the Russo-Turkish War of 1877–8 (pp. 228–33). During the War for American Independence (pp. 217–22) , the Franco-Spanish alliance of 1779 was offensive in nature. Offensive-defensive alliances include the Great Power coalition of 1840, formed during the Second War of Mehemet Ali (pp. 226–8) ; the French alliance with Spain and Sardinia (1734) in the War of the Polish Succession (pp. 214–7); and the French partnership with Britain and the United Provinces (1595) during the Dutch Revolt (pp. 208–14) . The Franco-American Alliance (1778) in the War for American Independence (pp. 217–22) was also an offensive-defensive alliance. Other examples fitting this classification can be found in the multilateral wars discussed in Chapter 9.

64 The Anglo-Dutch alliance of 1585, during the Dutch Revolt (*infra,* pp. 208–14) , was not a very useful one for the rebels, and indeed it could be regarded as dysfunctional: The Dutch were pleased to have the English troops

Incompatibility of war aims of the coalition partners will lower the efficiency or utility of an alliance, and often results in dissolution or in a separate peace. Examples in the preceding summaries were the alliance of France and the Pope in the Habsburg War, of England and Münster in the Anglo-Dutch War, and of Austria and Russia during their war against the Turks. The alliance of the United Provinces and France barely survived the Anglo-Dutch War, and the allies became enemies within a year of the settlement. Prussia and Austria, allied against Denmark in 1864, were at war by 1866.[65] We have also seen examples of the isolation of an "enemy" by alliance formation: England in the Anglo-Dutch War and Russia in the Crimean War were effectively isolated, in the latter case by an alliance network of nonbelligerents as well as belligerents.[66]

The selected wars also exemplified some of the aspects of external war settlement discussed earlier. But, because of the greater number of states involved in the complex external war and because certain of the states were obligated to cooperate with allies, there were some noteworthy distinctive characteristics of the settlements we have summarized. One formal treaty of peace might be obligatory for all belligerents (as in the Crimean War or the Boxer Rebellion), or there might be separate treaties for different belligerent pairs (as in the Habsburg-Valois War,

---

withdraw. The French alliance with the Polish Dzikow Confederacy (1735) in the War of the Polish Succession had no military utility. Other nonutilitarian alliances can be found in the multiplicity of alliance relationships that characterized the multilateral wars discussed in Chapter 9.

65 In wars analyzed subsequently, we find additional examples of one or more allies deserting wartime coalitions as a result of incompatibilities in war aims. Because of a quarrel over the disposition of Mantua, Spain and Sardina refused to cooperate with their French ally in the War of the Spanish Succession infra, pp. 357–66). The Dutch deserted their alliance in the Franco-Dutch War of 1672–9 (pp. 340–7), and Austria left the Second Grand Alliance in the War of the Spanish Succession (pp. 357–66). In the War of the Austrian Succession (pp. 366–74), Portugal and Savoy deserted France in 1703 and eventually went to war against her. The Grand Alliance of the European War of 1683–1700 dissolved in increments: first Savoy left, then Britain and Holland, then Spain, and finally the Emperor. And war-aim incompatibilities between Prussia and Britain in the Seven Years' War in effect dissolved their alliance.

66 Toward the end of the Napoleonic Wars (infra, pp. 392–405), France was isolated. The Grand Alliance of the European War of 1683–1700 (pp. 347–57) accomplished the same goal. In the Seven Years' War (pp. 374–9), a coalition of continental European powers, coupled with Britain's disagreements with and lack of understanding of Frederick's policies, resulted in the isolation of Prussia.

the Anglo-Dutch War, or the Russo-Turkish War of 1787) .[67] The settlement might be definitive and final; or it might be left incomplete, with further negotiations necessary either between belligerents (Bolivia and Chile after the War of the Pacific) or between allies (Austria and Prussia after the war against Denmark over Schleswig-Holstein). We saw preliminary mediatory conferences of belligerents and war-oriented states (e.g., the unsuccessful Conference of Vienna in 1855) [68] and peace conferences to settle all issues after there had been agreement on preliminaries (e.g., the Congress of Paris of 1856, which had important consequences for European public law as well as for world politics) .[69] Because this kind of war does involve more than two parties, the interest of war-oriented states is heightened, and it is often in their interest to mediate, to support a party as a non-belligerent ally, or eventually to become an active belligerent.

As in the case of simple external wars, the effects of defeat (and more generally, the relative bargaining strengths of the belligerents) determine the character of the settlement.[70] The nearly complete defeat of the

67 See Table 9–1 (p. 339) for the structure of particular multilateral war settlements. In the War of the Polish Succession (*infra*, pp. 214–7) the Definitive Treaty of Peace of Vienna was a multilateral peace treaty, as were the Treaty of Berlin, settling the Russo-Turkish War of 1877–8 (pp. 228–33) and the peace settlement of the Greek Revolt (pp. 222–5) arranged by the Great Powers. In the last two settlements, Russia and the Ottoman Empire concluded separate, bilateral treaties of peace. In the Dutch Revolt (pp. 204–14) and the War for American Independence (pp. 217–22), the belligerents also achieved a settlement through bilateral treaties of peace.

68 There were preliminary mediatory conferences during the Chaco War (*supra*, pp. 76–9), the Hungarian Rebellion of 1703–11 (*supra*, pp. 104–5), and the Greek Revolt (*infra*, pp. 222–5). There were unsuccessful preliminary conferences at Cologne, during the Franco-Dutch War of 1672–9 (*infra*, pp. 340–7), at Gertruydenberg (1710) in the War of the Spanish Succession (*infra*, pp. 357–66), and at Breda (1746–7) in the War of the Austrian Succession (*infra*, pp. 366–74). During the latter war, at Liège (1747–8), France and Britain succeeded in reaching agreement to hold a general peace congress at Aix-la-Chapelle. A mediatory conference during the Greek Revolt enabled the Great Powers to arrive at an arrangement they intended to impose upon the belligerents if Turkey refused to acquiesce. A similar scheme, a conference for mediation and for the imposition of a settlement, was adopted by the Powers during the Second War of Mehemet Ali against the Sultan (pp. 226–8). See also the discussion of conferences of war-oriented states in Chapter 7.

69 Such were the Vienna Conference, finally settling the War of the Polish Succession (*infra*, pp. 214–17), and the Congress of Vienna, providing a complete settlement for the Wars of France against Europe (pp. 392–405).

70 See note 64 in Chapter 2, and notes 28 to 30 in Chapter 3.

Boers led to the annexation of the Boer Republics by Britain. The unchallengable superiority of Chile in the War of the Pacific resulted in the complete satisfaction of that state's war aims, viz., ths acquisition of the maritime provinces of Peru and Bolivia. In the Habsburg-Valois War, the loss of Calais to French arms produced in England an ardent sentiment for peace and, ultimately, recognition of the "temporary" loss. The "losing" states of Denmark in the Schleswig-Holstein War and China in the Boxer Rebellion acquiesced in the demands of the victors after a series of defeats, with the prospect of further defeats if hostilities continued. But in the Crimean War, Russia remained a formidable foe, although she sustained defeats. This fact, coupled with the limited war aims of her adversaries, resulted in the balanced peace settlement of Paris. In the Habsburg War, both Spain and France, and in the Second Anglo-Dutch War, both Holland and Britain, were financially and psychologically exhausted. The settlements reflected the military stalemate.

The Crimean War also illustrated a "complete" settlement, the various problems that had arisen before and during the war being thoroughly aired and fairly resolved at the Congress of Paris.[71] While the Treaties of Câteau-Cambrésis, ending the Habsburg War, were not complete (since elements of a settlement were omitted), they were "adequate" in the circumstances and preserved peace between France and Spain for about 35 years. The settlements of the Schleswig-Holstein War and the War of the Pacific were incomplete and, as it turned out, inadequate, failing as they did to normalize the relations of the allies and the belligerents and leading to further conflict.

71 See note 65, and also notes 67 to 71 in Chapter 2.

The Settlement of
Complex Internal Wars

CHAPTER 5

Classification

For the purpose of simplifying our discussion, we distinguish three types of complex internal war:

1. The state-faction internal war, in which a single state is allied with one of the factions and the other faction is allied with no states or factions.

2. The alliance-faction internal war, in which one of the factions is allied with a coalition of states and the other faction is allied with no other states or factions.

3. The internal-external war, in which each faction is allied with a single state and each of the states so connected to a belligerent faction is at war with the other.[1]

General Outcome and Modes of Settlement

The State-Faction Internal War

In this kind of war, state A is allied with a faction x who is waging war against faction y (see Figure 5–1).[2]

1 For a discussion of internal wars in which the states allied to the factions are not at war with each other (proxy internal wars), see Chapter 7. In this chapter, we deal largely with internal wars involving two opposing factions; but there may exist a multiplicity of warring factions (see the Greek and Laotian Civil War summaries). The analyses offered here are still generally applicable in such a situation, but we must then also appraise the effects of multiple inter-faction relations upon the peacemaking process.

2 State A is actively belligerent and is regarded as an enemy by faction y. In addition to combat troops, the state may supply faction x with technicians and

We consider, in turn, four possible outcomes of the war: defeat of the nonallied faction y; defeat of the faction x to which state A is allied; the disengagement of state A; and a stalemated war. In each case, we shall consider the impact of outcomes such as these upon the possible modes of settlement of the war. Later, for the other types of complex internal wars, our discussion will follow the same general pattern of analysis.

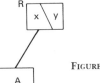

FIGURE 5-1.   General   form   of   the state–faction internal war.

1. Defeat of the nonallied faction. Faction y may be defeated, in which case faction x, the ally of state A, will have won the war. The reader will recall that we have posited two basic aims of belligerents in internal wars: control of the apparatus of the state and independence. In the hypothetical case under consideration, a victory by faction x will mean either that x assumes full control of the apparatus of state R or that faction x becomes independent of the authorities of state R and establishes a wholly new state, X.[3]

We must, of course, determine first whether state A is allied to the insurgents or to the incumbents. If y were an insurgent faction, we would have a war in which state A was allied to the incumbent's, x. In a war for control of the state apparatus, the defeat of the insurgents, y, means that the incumbents, x, retain control of state R. In effect, what in our hypothesis was a case of state-faction alliance is, in legal theory, a state-

---

service personnel, weapons and ammunition, and various forms of financial support. However, state A might limit its support merely to recognizing a state of belligerency within R or recognizing x as the legitimate government of R. It might provide propaganda support for the allied faction or other forms of support short of active involvement. When state A is not a belligerent, we call it a war-oriented actor (see Chapters 6 and 7).

In this discussion we employ conventional letters for the states and factions as follows: State A is the state-ally; x, the incumbent faction; state R, the state within which the internal war is being waged; and faction y, the insurgent faction. In the case of wars for independence, the succession states are designated by the capital letters X or Y, depending upon whether faction x or y controls the new state.

3 If x were merely seeking autonomy rather than complete independence, a victory for x would mean that the faction's leaders would assume some measure of control over a limited portion of state R.

state alliance. At the end of the war, with the defeat of the insurgents, there is a *de facto* state-state alliance.[4] (See Fig. 5–2.)

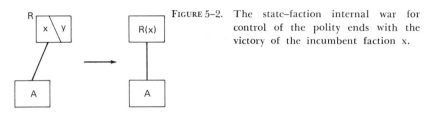

FIGURE 5–2. The state–faction internal war for control of the polity ends with the victory of the incumbent faction x.

If the war is a war for independence and faction y is insurgent, its defeat means (as before) that faction x remains the legal government of state R. Success in the war couples the original *de jure* character of the government of R by faction x with a *de facto* character. State A, during the war, will be legally allied to state R because, as an ally, it recognizes that faction x is the *de jure* government of state R. In functional terms, however, it will be allied with faction x, which at the war's end becomes, functionally, a state-ally of state A.[5]

Let us suppose, however, that state A is allied with the insurgents (faction y). In a successful war for control of the state apparatus, faction y ousts faction x and becomes the legal and *de facto* government of state R. The war thus transforms the alliance A-y from a state-faction to a state-state alliance.[6] If faction y is fighting for its independence, defeat of faction x will mean that a new state, Y, is created out of the body politic of state R, originally governed by faction x[7] (see Fig. 5–3).

4 See the Wars of Mehemet Ali (pp. 225–8) and the War of the Polish Succession (pp. 214–7). These examples are properly *alliance-faction* wars. They nonetheless serve as models for the outcomes discussed here. The study of internal war settlements at this level of analysis is a very complex subject, and I prefer to start with simple cases: hence, my classification of internal wars and the organization of this chapter. The discussion is in the nature of a series of scenarios, supported in many instances by historical examples.

5 There are no examples in my sample of wars for independence in which the insurgents were unsuccessful against incumbents allied to one or more states. Perhaps the nearest example is the Armenian Revolt (see the First World War, pp. 405–28).

6 See the War of the Polish Succession (pp. 214–7) and the Peninsular War (in Spain) during the Wars for French Hegemony in Europe (392–405).

7 See the Dutch Revolt (pp. 208–14), the War for American Independence (pp. 217–22), the Greek Revolt (pp. 222–5), the Russo-Turkish War of 1877–8 (pp. 228–33), and the First World War (pp. 405–28), in which the Allies could have been said to be allied with the factions that became the Habsburg successor states.

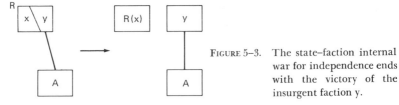

FIGURE 5–3. The state–faction internal war for independence ends with the victory of the insurgent faction y.

State A, as an ally of faction y during the war (and presumably for a time after the war) is in opposition to state R with its government, faction x. In fact, the government of state R (that is, faction x) would probably meet the A-y alliance with a declaration of war against state A, since A's support of faction y could be regarded by faction x as an attempt to subvert the state and would therefore be a belligerent act. At the war's end, state R would continue in existence; and its role in the peace settlement will be important.[8]

During the fighting, in the war for control of the state apparatus (A allied to the insurgents y, who are successful against faction x, the incumbents) the war would have the character of an external war if faction x, as the government of state R, were to declare war on state A—which it would probably do. However, with the defeat of faction x, state R, which is legally in a state of war with state A, would be taken over by faction y (an ally of state A). Hence state R and state A could remain allied after the defeat of the incumbents.

Let us return to the situation where state A is allied with incumbent faction x. The complete defeat of faction y (insurgents) obviates the need for peace talks, whether the war was for control of the polity or for the independence of faction y. Disposition of persons affiliated with the defeated insurgent faction would probably be regarded as a matter of state R's internal politics; and attempts by state A to influence the course of postwar events within state R would probably be unacceptable to R and could be regarded as an illegal interference in R's domestic affairs. Such interference could, of course, result in the dissolution of the A-x ($= A$-R) alliance. But whatever the outcome, the point is that there will be no peace conference and no peace settlement as these terms are usually understood. Any discussions that followed at the end of the war would have the character of intra-alliance (A-R) discussions, not formal peace talks, although the discussions and official policies adopted to remedy the effects of the war could be considered as a peace settlement.

8 For simplicity, I prefer not to subsume this case (i.e., A–Y successful in winning independence from faction x of state R) under the category of state–faction internal war, because it has the character of an external war. Rather, we will regard this as a special instance of the internal-external war. The wars listed in note 7 are internal-external wars. In their internal aspects, they illustrate how a state-faction or alliance-faction internal war ends.

With state A allied to insurgents (y) in a war for control of state R, there would also be no formal peace negotiations after the defeat of the incumbents (x). Faction y and the government of state A might have to take steps to regularize their relations as, by helping the insurgents, A would not be on friendly terms with R. But these steps would not have the character of peace negotiations, although states A and R might eventually have to settle a number of issues that had arisen during the hostilities. In a war for independence, A's alliance with the insurgents y would probably provoke state R (governed by faction x) to declare war on state A. This war would also have the character of an external war; and with the success of the insurgents and the declaration of independence of state Y, the peace settlement would require agreement between three parties: A and Y on the one hand and state R (x) on the other.[9]

2. Defeat of the allied faction. Let us suppose that state A is allied with incumbent faction x, and that x is defeated in the war. In a war for political control of state R, the insurgent faction y would take over the apparatus of state R; and the policy with respect to members of faction x and, generally, the internal consequences of the war would be a matter of R's domestic politics (see Fig. 5–4).[10]

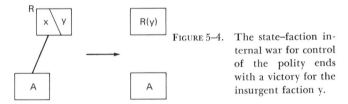

Figure 5–4. The state–faction internal war for control of the polity ends with a victory for the insurgent faction y.

There would probably be no peace conference between states A and R. But the outbreak of hostilities between them is at least conceivable. After all, state A's policies, based upon its support for the incumbents, will have been frustrated; and the insurgent faction's attitude toward state A would be one of profound distrust because of that support. If the parties managed to avoid war, we would expect that state A would refuse to recognize the new government of state R in the immediate postwar period. Recognition might eventually be accorded, but the relations between A and R would come to have the character of relations between independent states in time of peace.

If we assume that A is allied with the incumbent faction x, but the war is a war for independence, success of the insurgents y means that a new state, Y, will be established. The alliance between state A and state R (governed by the incumbent faction x) might or might not outlast the

9 We can subsume this case under the internal-external type wars.
10 See the War of the Polish Succession (pp. 214–7).

defeat and the peace conference. Certainly A and R will continue to exist as states. There will indeed be peace negotiations, primarily to ratify the fact of state Y's juridical existence, and state A will undoubtedly take part in these talks (see Fig. 5–5) .[11]

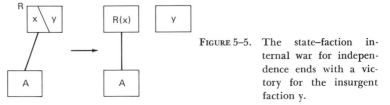

FIGURE 5–5. The state–faction internal war for independence ends with a victory for the insurgent faction y.

The settlement of the war would proceed according to the scheme for the settlement of simple internal wars outlined in Chapter 3. The presence of state A's representatives at the peace talks might serve to strengthen state R's bargaining position relative to the newly independent state Y. Whatever aim state A had in becoming involved in the internal war on the side of the incumbent faction—whether to preserve the status quo or to maintain or achieve dominance by frustrating the insurgent's bid for an independence that could create too independent a state Y in a region A dominated or sought to dominate, or whether A sought to achieve some ideological objective such as the defeat of an ideologically alien insurgent faction y—whatever the aim of A, it would have been frustrated by the victory of the insurgents and the resultant independence of state Y. At the peace talks, A's representatives might attempt to recoup some of the military losses of its ally, R (and perhaps recoup its own losses as well), by limiting the gains of state Y. State A might thus support state R in an effort to condition the juridical independence of state Y in the hope that at some future time the limitations upon its sovereignty will serve as the pretext for controlling the state, when either state A or R is in a stronger power position vis-à-vis state Y. Granting complete or limited independence to state Y, R (supported by A) might seek to limit the area or resources acquired by Y or to obtain special privileges for their nationals doing business within the territory soon to be put under the jurisdiction of state Y. Whether these efforts succeed or fail depends upon the extent of faction y's military victory against faction x (state R), and hence, the relative strength of Y's bargaining position. It also depends upon the extent to which the policy makers of R (and A) hope to achieve a normal and peaceful relationship with state Y in the near future and whether state R is subjected to political pressures from within or from without (that is, from other war-

11 See the First World War (pp. 000–00): Germany, Turkey and Bulgaria were allied with the losing "incumbant faction," Austria-Hungary.

oriented states, including its ally, state A). The policies of state A could evolve during the course of the war or the peace negotiations to a point where A and R might come to oppose each other over a common policy concerning state Y. If this opposition became intense, the alliance would dissolve, and state R would be left alone to negotiate with the representatives of state Y. State A might even support Y, thereby winning concessions from state Y or state R. Or, opposed to the complete independence of Y, A might withdraw from the peace talks and, in an extreme case, declare war on state Y.

If state A were allied to the insurgents y, and the incumbent faction x defeated them in a war for either independence or control of the state, the incumbent government would probably regard the support of insurgents by state A as an act of war and declare war on A. With the defeat of state A's ally (faction y), A and state R (governed by faction x) must settle the conflict between themselves. This would have the character of a settlement of an external war. In the absence of a state of war between A and R, the defeat of the insurgents means the end of the war.[12] There would be no peace conference in the usual sense, although states A and R might eventually have to normalize their relations strained by the roles each played in the internal war.[13]

3. Disengagement of the allied state A. If state A disengaged from the war, the outcome would ultimately be determined by the relative capabilities, strategies, and determination of the two factions. The war would assume the character of a simple internal war, and its settlement would assume the character of a settlement for the simple internal war discussed earlier (see Fig. 5–6).[14]

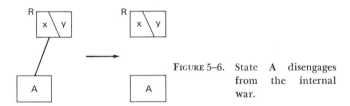

FIGURE 5–6. State A disengages from the internal war.

State A could disengage either abruptly or over an extended period of time. In the latter case, it would gradually limit its involvement by reducing incrementally all forms of support for the faction or by elimi-

12 See the Allied intervention in Russia in 1918–22 during and after the First World War (pp. 405–28).

13 There indeed was a peace settlement for the Danish intervention in Germany during the Thirty Years' War (pp. 379–92).

14 Germany disengaged from the "Whites" in the Finnish Civil War; and the Allies disengaged from the White Russian factions during the Russian Civil War (see the First World War, pp. 405–28).

nating first one and then another form of support. In any event, complete disengagement before the end of hostilities would mean that the two factions between themselves settle the political fate of the other and of their state *R*. It will end in the defeat of one or the other or the political survival of *both;* and it will therefore require both to negotiate their future relations.

State *A* might, however, become involved in a war with the incumbent faction in a formal way, that is, state *R* might put itself formally in a state of war with state *A*. If the incumbent faction survived as the lawful authority of state *R*, the leaders of state *A*, in disengaging from the war, would probably want to reach an agreement with the leaders of state *R* respecting the terms of the disengagement, an eventual cease-fire and, if need be, a political settlement. In other words, *A* and *R* would have to hold peace talks and reach a peace settlement.[15] Without other allies involved, this settlement will have the character of a peace settlement of a simple external war.

In our hypothetical case, state *A* disengages; the insurgents *y* are left to fight on alone against the incumbents *x*. In general terms, the reason for *A*'s disengaging will be either its inability to fulfill its original war aims or, if still confident of its ability to fulfill them, it can do so only at unacceptable costs (as in the case where faction *y*'s armed forces had dealt *A*'s forces a series of defeats). Disengagement will thus be an effort on the part of *A*'s leaders to get out of the war as graciously as possible with as many gains as the situation permits.

Assuming *A* and *R* (faction *x*) are at war, the peace settlement between them would comprise the usual elements of an *external war* settlement.[16] The circumstances surrounding the ongoing internal war will have an effect upon the negotiations: Although there will presumably be a cease-fire between the forces of *A* and *R*, there will be none between the forces of faction *y* and state *R* (faction *x*). The relative strengths of the bargaining positions of the two former belligerents will of course be an important factor in determining what each party can obtain from the other. It is well to note that even though state *A* may want to disengage after a military defeat, the fact that *R* is still involved in hostilities might weaken *R*'s bargaining position. State *R* might, in fact, be willing to accommodate *A*'s disengagement without extracting a price for it.

Had state *A*'s policy of assisting the insurgents been successful, we would expect the peace settlement to reflect the sort of war aims that had originally motivated *A*'s policymakers. In disengaging, however, these policymakers are settling for something less. Indeed, state *R* may seek to incorporate guarantees in the peace treaty to secure it against state *A*'s interventionist policies that led to its support of the insurgents.

15 See the Dutch Revolt (pp. 208–14) and the settlement of the intervention of Denmark in the Thirty Years' War (pp. 379–92).
16 Chapter 2.

We can relate state A's *reasons* for becoming involved in the internal war to the war aims of belligerents in external wars. Disengagement by A occurs when these reasons (or hopes or expectations) are not, or cannot be, satisfied. The content of the settlement between A and R will reflect, to some extent, A's policymakers' original reasons for assisting the insurgents (compare Table 5–1 to Fig. 2–1 in Chapter 2).

TABLE 5–1. Reasons for intervention on the side of the insurgents.

Aim of state A	Reasons for assisting insurgents y against R (x)
dominance	State A might hope to weaken R and make it a less effective obstacle to its ambitions by replacing one government by another or by helping the insurgents to achieve independence thereby having two weaker succession states instead of one relatively strong state. Moreover, if successful, the new succession state would probably be an ally of state A.
ideological	The insurgents might have the same, or at least a similar, ideology as state A; or state R's ideology might be antagonistic to A's.
status quo	A state interested in the status quo is not apt to provide aid for insurgents, which are ordinarily the epitome of opposition to the status quo. If state R were itself a *revisionist* state, a status quo state (A) could take the initiative and seek to frustrate R's policies by supporting the insurgents.
consolidation of the state	There might be co-nationals of state A living in the territory of state R. If these co-nationals rebelled, A might support them hoping, if successful, to acquire the territory on which they lived and jurisdiction over them.
retributive	As a way of punishing state R, A might provide assistance to insurgents within R.
opportunistic	A's policymakers might seek to obtain some value from state R by taking advantage of the instability attendant upon the existence of an internal war in R. Presumably, A would not do this unless the insurgents were winning, or were expected to win.

4. The war stalemated. In a stalemated internal war, the factions will probably decide to negotiate a cease-fire and a political *modus vivendi*. If the state-ally (A) of one of the factions (x) has become a formal belligerent, representatives of that state will take part in the peace negotiations, provided that the state had not disengaged from the war before the decision to negotiate was made by the leaders of the factions. If state A has not been a formal belligerent, its policymakers might seek and obtain

(or the leaders of the allied faction might obtain for it) an invitation to the peace conference. Absence from the peace conference or failure to take an active part in the settlement process with the supported faction would constitute, in effect, disengagement by state A. For our discussion, we assume that A does play an active role in the peacemaking processes.[17]

In the preceding section, we noted the reasons for a state's giving assistance to an insurgent faction, relating them to the categories of war aims we had introduced earlier in discussing external wars (Table 5–1). To complete the preliminaries of our analysis, we briefly note in Table 5–2 the reasons impelling a state's policymakers to lend assistance to an incumbent faction.

The support the state gave the incumbent faction during the war and, subsequently, its policies at the peace talks will reflect its policymakers' efforts to realize, in concrete terms, their original reasons for providing aid to the incumbents. Indeed, whether it had aided the incumbents or the insurgents, state A would strive to achieve its war aims and thereby justify its reasons for intervening. It would do this either through negotiations tending toward peace or through devices designed to interfere with peacemaking. The factions will, in a general way, negotiate to settle the internal war (in the ways described in Chapter 3), but the presence of an active ally will affect the character of the negotiations and the final settlement. The settlement will still comprise the essential elements of any internal war settlement:[18] a cease-fire; disposition of the armed forces of all the parties, including terms to secure those forces against possible resumption of hostilities; and a definition of the status of the insurgents and of the future political relations of the insurgents to the incumbents. Should this definition of the status and relations assume the form of a partition of state R or the secession of the insurgents (and the establishment of a new state), then the settlement will include provisions delineating the boundaries of the territories assigned to each faction; terms defining the attribution of nationality or a definition of places of residence of the persons affected by the war; and still other provisions for security guarantees, normalization of relations, and the adjustment of disputes. State A's representatives will be in a position to influence the negotiations and thus the content of these provisions.

The state (A) allied to the faction will seek to maximize its gains at the peace conference, and it will try to achieve its war aims as they stand at the time the conference begins. The state will, in addition, support the

17 The Korean War (pp. 233–6) and the Laotian Civil War (pp. 236–40) were stalemated. One could argue that the War for American Independence (pp. 217–22) ended in a stalemate, even though the British had suffered local defeats. The external war conflicts of the War of the Polish Succession (pp. 214–7) were stalemated certainly.

18 See Table 3–1 in Chapter 3.

TABLE 5–2. Reasons for intervention on the side of the incumbents.

War aim of state A	Reasons for assisting the incumbents x
dominance	State A might want to preserve a friendly, accommodating government in control of state R against insurgents that might be less accommodating, or even hostile; or A might prefer to preserve the integrity of R (which had been an ally of state A) against insurgents who want to secede, thereby reducing the resources (and more generally) the capabilities of A's ally, R.
status quo	States interested in maintaining the status quo might or might not give aid to incumbents. If they do, it will probably be because they view any insurgency as a threat to the status quo, particularly if promoted from without by other states, in the name of a revisionist ideology. The reasons could, in any event, be similar to those of a state striving for dominance.
idological	To preserve the authority of a government or the integrity of state R, having an identical or at least sympathetic ideology to that of state A, policymakers of A might decide to support R's regime against ideologically hostile insurgents.
consolidation of the state	If there were co-nationals of A in a minority in state R, A would not assist the incumbents if the co-nationals were in revolt. If there were no nationals, A would not become involved (unless it had other aims) .
retribution	Incursions of insurgents across state A's frontier or losses incurred by state A or its nationals in state R due to insurgent policies and combat operations could prompt A's policymakers to aid the incumbents as a means of punishing the insurgents.
opportunity	While it might be unlikely that a state would become involved in an internal war for opportunity values, as it probably could not obtain them at low cost, the incumbents might in fact promise tangible benefits for A's assistance.

claims and policies of the faction to which it was allied, endeavoring to obtain the best possible terms of a settlement for the faction. Whether or not these two principal negotiating aims can be fulfilled depends upon the bargaining strength of the state-faction combination. The substantive discussions will dwell upon those matters relating to the war aims of the parties: in the case of the factions, primarily issues of control of the polity or independence; in the case of the state, the issues based upon one or more of the variety of war aims and reasons for intervening adumbrated above.

In the military settlement phase, the parties must not only agree upon the terms of a cease-fire and troop dispositons of the armed forces of the factions, but also upon terms affecting the armed forces of the allied state. Shall the state A's troops remain in the state R? If they are to remain, what should be the terms and conditions of their presence? If the troops are to withdraw, how and when should this be accomplished? In the political phase of the settlement, the parties will have to agree upon the terms for the future relations between the intervening state A and the government of state R, whatever form that government might assume. If the war had resulted in the independence of a wholly new state, the peace treaty will probably provide for A's recognition of the sovereignty of the new state and outline the basis for future political relations between them.[19] Terms normalizing the relations between the ally and the parent state would also be included. Should the factions demilitarize areas of the state or otherwise establish guarantees for the continued security of the factions thereby hoping to restore mutual trust and confidence, both factions could have an interest in getting state A to agree to respect such terms. State A, moreover, might be especially interested in the provisions relating to persons affected by the war, particularly if the nationals of A were in this class. Thus, if nationals of state A lived in state R (and the successor state) or if nationals of A did business in state R, A's policy-makers would certainly want to mitigate the effects of the war upon these nationals and, if possible, obtain minimal guarantees for the protection of their persons and their property. They might also seek additional commercial, or even political, privileges that would enable state A's leaders to influence the domestic political affairs of either state R or the successor state.

The Alliance-Faction Internal War

In an alliance-faction internal war, a coalition of several states is allied with one of the factions against the other faction (see Fig. 5–7).

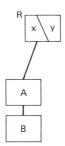

FIGURE 5–7.   General form of the alliance-faction internal war.

19 See Table 3–3 in Chapter 3.

Our analysis of the state-faction internal war is generally applicable to the alliance-faction war, with the one significant difference. Because one of the factions is allied to a coalition of states, not only must we be concerned with the effects of the faction-state alliance upon the course of the peace negotiations, we must also consider the intra-alliance relations of all the allied states with each other and with the faction and examine the effects on peacemaking of those relations. Thus, we must reckon with possible intra-alliance differences resulting from incompatible war aims.[20] These differences could produce serious disagreements among the allies and between the allies and the faction, leading even to the realignment of some states with the opposing faction. If the allies were allied to successful insurgents in a war for independence, they would probably have become involved formally in a war with the parent state (the incumbent faction). In the peace negotiations the impact of coordinated alliance policies (or discord within the alliance) will have to be assessed with respect to the elements of the settlement of both the internal war between the factions and the external war between the coalition and the parent state (see Fig. 5–8).[21]

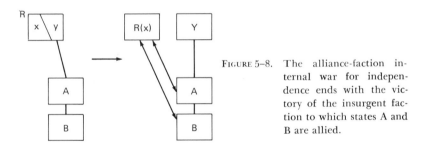

FIGURE 5–8. The alliance-faction internal war for independence ends with the victory of the insurgent faction to which states A and B are allied.

If the coalition were allied with the defeated faction (y), the loss might cause the dissolution of the alliance, with or without realignment of the states. Of course, there might be other factors promoting alliance cohesiveness even in the face of defeat in the internal war (including the involvement of the coalition in a wider external war). In any event, the relations between the alliance partners will have an effect upon the peace settlement. As we noted earlier, alliance with insurgents in a war for control of the polity or for independence often means formal war with the incumbent government. The peace settlement would then assume the character of a settlement of a complex external war.

20 Even in the state-faction internal war, we must compare the war aims of the state with those of the faction and look for incompatibilities (see Appendix II).

21 Examples are the Dutch Revolt (pp. 208–14), the War for American Independence (pp. 217–22), and the First World War (pp. 405–28).

Should the alliance disengage from the war, the factions will continue the war until there is a military resolution or until the faction leaders finally decide to talk peace. But, with coalition rather than single-state involvement, another possibility looms. Some, but not all, allied states might disengage. If all but one state disengage, we have a state-faction internal war; if one or more states disengage and realign to support the other faction, we have another form of internal war, the internal-external war discussed below. Finally, even with the disengagement of some states, a plurality of states might remain in the alliance, and the analyst would still be dealing with the alliance-faction internal war. However, the fact that *some* allies have disengaged can affect the course of peace talks. It may strengthen the bargaining position of the nonallied faction because of weakness revealed in a dissolving coalition. On the other hand, the allies remaining in the coalition could be shocked into making greater efforts to accommodate the policies of each other. The effects certainly cannot be predicted, but the analyst should be aware that there may indeed be some effects.

In the event that none of the allies disengaged, and the war ended in a stalemate, then all parties would probably be present at the peace talks, both factions and all the state allies of one of the factions.[22] As in the case of complex external wars, we would have to assess the possible effects of incompatible war aims upon intra-alliance relations and upon the peace settlement. We recall from our discussion earlier in the chapter that war aims are related to the reasons for the coalition's becoming involved in the internal war; and the war aims are an expression of those reasons (Tables 5–1 and 5–2). Peace negotiations will reflect the participants' efforts to achieve their war aims and to rationalize their reason for intervening.

The Internal-External War

In the internal-external war, each belligerent faction has at least one state-ally; and these states are at war with each other (see Fig. 5–9).

This kind of complex internal war can also be regarded as the prototype

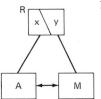

FIGURE 5–9. General form of the internal–external war.

22 True for the Korean War (pp. 233–6) and the Laotian Civil War (pp. 236–40).

of a war in which the incumbent government of a state (R) declares war on the intervening state (A), because the latter has intervened to provide assistance for the insurgents (see Fig. 5–10).

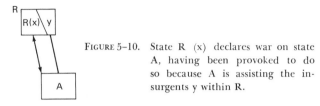

FIGURE 5–10.   State R (x) declares war on state A, having been provoked to do so because A is assisting the insurgents y within R.

An internal-external war might result from an internal war that had become internationalized by the intervention of foreign states. Or, an external war might become complicated by becoming coupled to an internal war which, until the coupling, had been wholly independent of the conflict between the states. But whatever way the war had come to assume its form as an internal-external war, peace negotiations would have to reverse the process; in a word, the conflict must be *de-escalated*.

There are several conceivable modes of settlement or resolution of the conflict.

1. *All parties* could agree to negotiate an end to hostilities: The factions $(x$ and $y)$ negotiate to settle the internal war; the state-allies of the factions $(A$ and $M)$ negotiate to settle the external war between themselves.[23] The peace talks would probably take place at the same time, and perhaps even around the same table. This would probably occur where the issues of the wars are interrelated.

2. One of the states (state A) might defeat the other state (M). State A would then be in a position to impose a peace settlement upon the defeated state; or it might still have to negotiate terms with the policy-makers of M.[24] In either case, state A would probably be in a strong enough bargaining position to cause M to disengage from the internal war. The war would then continue with state A allied with one of the factions (in what we have called a state-faction internal war).

3. Either of the states could disengage from the internal war.[25] The policymakers of the disengaging state might conclude that support for the faction was too much of a burden if the external war were costly. The external war would continue, and at some future time it too would end, by negotiation or by the imposition of a settlement. We should under-

---

23 The War of the Polish Succession (pp. 214–7) is an example, as are the Korean (pp. 233–6) and Laotian Civil Wars (pp. 236–40).

24 The termination of the Danish intervention in Germany during the Thirty Years' War (pp. 379–92) is an example.

25 See the Dutch Revolt (pp. 208–14).

stand that as the disengaging state has been involved in the internal war, the settlement processes for either the internal or the external war could be complicated by the interjection of issues pertaining to the other war. If this possibility were anticipated, the parties might decide to negotiate a settlement of both wars at one conference, should the wars end at about the same time. Even if the wars ended at different times, the parties might postpone settlement of the war that ended first until after there had been a cessation of hostilities in the other war. Even with the disengagement of one of the state allies, the internal war would probably continue with the other state remaining engaged. The conflict then assumes the form of the state-faction internal war.

4. Both states might disengage.[26] This would occur most probably by mutual agreement of the state belligerents as a step toward their negotiating an end to the external war. After effective disengagement, the factions in the internal war would continue hostilities until one of them had won a victory or until the war had reached a stalemated condition prompting the faction leaders to negotiate a settlement of the internal war. In the case of disengagement by either or both states, either faction might attempt to prevent the settlement of the external war, thereby hoping to re-involve their former ally in their internal war. Settlement of the external war might become more difficult under these circumstances.

5. The factions could agree to negotiate an end to the internal war, even though the states cannot (or do not) agree to end the connected external war.[27] This outcome is likely where the faction leaders perceive that the internal war is stalemated and continuing hostilities would neither produce substantial rewards nor exceed the costs to them of the internal conflict. The state allies might attempt to prevent the factions achieving a settlement, particularly where the state affected by the internal war (state R) had some strategic value for military operations in the external war. Settlement of the internal war under these conditions would be very difficult, or impossible. State R might even be occupied by one or both state belligerents.

If the factions were able to negotiate an end to the internal war without untoward results for the independence of their state, the faction leaders would have to isolate their military and political problems from

26 The Dutch Revolt (pp. 208–14) is an analogue of this. A more exact example is the Yemeni Civil War (1962–1969+), in which Egypt (the ally of the Yemen Republic) and Saudi Arabia (the ally of the Yemeni Royalists) both disengaged.

27 The Peace of Prague (1635) pacified the Holy Roman Empire for a time but left the external wars unsettled. And the Peace of Westphalia (1648) settled the wars internal to the Empire and most related external wars but left France and Spain at war with each other (see the Thirty Years' War, pp. 379–92).

those of the external war. As neither faction has been destroyed and the agreement of both is essential to a viable settlement, each will have to provide some guarantees to the other that its alliance with one of the belligerent states will not be reactivated for the purpose of waging the internal war. Thus, as a precondition of a settlement, the factions might require each other to withdraw from their alliances with the belligerent states. If the faction leaders have decided to accept a coalition government solution, withdrawal will probably be necessary in order to preserve the coalition in its early, tenuous days. But if state R were partitioned, then the administrations of the faction zones might retain their ties to the belligerent states, giving the states the opportunity to exploit the differences still subsisting between the factions after the settlement. The terms of peace for the internal war might have to include provisions guaranteeing that neither faction will permit its ally to intervene or otherwise involve state R in the external war or to use the alliance with the state belligerents to gain an advantage over the other faction within state R. It is quite possible that as the internal and external wars were once coupled, the cease-fire and settlement of the internal war will be unstable or metastable as long as the external war continues. With the settlement of the external war, issues directly affecting the earlier internal war settlement might have to be reopened and the settlement revised in the light of subsequent military and political developments relating to the course of the external war.

6. One of the factions might defeat the other faction, but the external war continue. If the internal war has been a war for control of the polity, the faction winning control of state R might remain allied to the state and at war with the other state (see Fig. 5–11). Or it could cease hostilities against the other state (M), although this would probably cause the dissolution of the alliance $(A–R)$, unless the state-ally (A) were sympathetic to state R's need for peace, in which case the alliance would remain intact during negotiations between the successful faction (R) and the opponent state (M). However, state M might not be receptive to peace feelers and might in fact carry on active hostilities against R, compelling the latter to remain an active belligerent. In any event, a final settlement of all issues would have to await the settlement of the war between the states A and M.

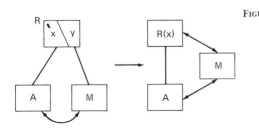

FIGURE 5–11. The internal–external war, with the factions waging a war for control of polity, results in a victory for faction x. The external war, A–R v M, continues, and the alliance A–x remains in being.

In a war for independence, were the incumbents to win, the situation would be similar to that discussed in the preceding paragraph: State R could remain in the alliance and at war, or it might try to arrange a settlement with the opposing states, Y and M, or either Y or M (see Fig. 5–12).

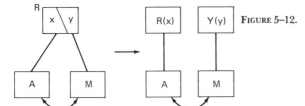

FIGURE 5–12. The internal–external war, with the factions waging a war for independence, results in a victory for the insurgent faction y, and recognition by R (x) of the new state Y. The external war, A v M, continues.

When insurgents win a war for independence, the result will almost surely be the establishment of a new state. At the time of the defeat of the incumbents (assuming that we can pinpoint a particular time), we will have this situation: One state (A) will be allied to the incumbent government of the parent state (R); the other state (M) will be allied with the newly independent successor state (Y). If R accepted the fact of its defeat, it would recognize the independence of Y and probably make peace with Y. Certainly, an adequate settlement requires resolution of all the issues arising out of the war and the new status of Y's independence, and therefore requires peace and the parent state's recognition of the separation of Y from R. States A and M might or might not remain at war. The faction leaders must determine their relations with the state belligerents of the external war (i.e., their ally and the state at war with their ally). In order to envisage what might ensue, we must consider the options open to the parent state and to the successor state.

THE PARENT STATE: The policymakers of the parent state (R) could decide to preserve the wartime alliance $(A–R)$ and continue hostilities against M. Certainly, if the parent state had interests other than the suppression of the rebellion, it would be able to fulfill its war aims relative to the other state only if it remained an active member of the wartime alliance. A clearcut defeat at the hands of the insurgents y might be enough of a shock to prompt the parent state's policymakers to seek a negotiated peace with both the successor state Y and state M. This could result in the dissolution of the alliance. But such may be the cost of the peace the parent state needs. After a cease-fire has been arranged (if indeed it can be arranged), the parent state R and state M must decide whether to negotiate a complete settlement of the war between them, or postpone that settlement until the external war (between A and M) has been resolved. It is quite possible that many of the issues could not be settled until all the parties to the internal-external war had agreed jointly to settle their differences.

THE SUCCESSOR STATE: The successor state Y has the same choices as the parent state R: It might remain at war with the adversary A of their ally M or it might negotiate peace with M. Unlike the parent state, however, the insurgents (in our hypothetical case) have won. The alliance may have brought success to the insurgents, who have succeeded in establishing a new state independent of R. This would prompt them to remain in the alliance ($Y–M$); and in fact, M might exert considerable pressure upon the policymakers of state Y to do so. There may indeed be an agreement between the insurgents and M, requiring either (but particularly the insurgents, who have achieved their aim) to refrain from making a separate peace until state A, the enemy of state M, has been defeated. But successor states, being newly established, have many internal problems that could constrain their policymakers to avoid external situations likely to prevent their solution. Hence, there will be a considerable incentive to settle the war with state A; and there will be pressures upon the insurgents to regularize their relations with the parent state as quickly as possible. Remaining at war with the ally (A) of the parent state (R) might delay the recognition by R of the independence of the successor state.

Termination and settlement of the internal-external war: The internal-external war can end in a variety of ways, as we have seen. However, it could be argued that it will rarely end with both the states A and M and the factions x and y of state R negotiating a settlement at the same peace conference.[28] One faction may believe it has a military advantage and refuse to negotiate even though the other faction and the states wish to negotiate. Or the factions, wearied of the war and convinced that they are stalemated, may be willing to work out a compromise political settlement for state R. The state allies, on the other hand, may not want peace, and they may even actively prevent the factions from negotiating. As the fortunes of one or another of the parties to the internal-external war rise and fall, so will their motivation for accepting a peace settlement. Time is an important element: At a given time, one belligerent may be ready to negotiate, another may not; at a later time the situation could be reversed. Moreover, the sheer length of the war could de-ideologize the war issues as a result of heavy casualties or economic costs, and the parties could agree to a cease-fire and a military settlement, but perhaps not a political settlement. If the latter were achieved at all, it would only be after the lapse of more time, when all the belligerents had agreed that they must at least attempt negotiations.

However unusual it may be to find examples of an internal-external

---

28 But see the examples in note 23 above. The settlements of the Korean (pp. 233–6) and Laotian (pp. 236–40) Wars provide the basis for the following discussion, as does the settlement of the Franco-Vietminh War in 1954 (see Randle, R. F., *op. cit.*) .

war terminated by a single peace conference attended by all the factions and the belligerent states, we will assume for discussion that we have just such a situation. Our comments about this sort of war will also be applicable, in certain circumstances, to the state-faction and alliance-faction internal wars.

In negotiating a settlement of an internal-external war, the states could seek a settlement of the simple external war questions; and the factions, a settlement for the simple internal war questions. Indeed, this will happen for certain issues. Thus the models for the settlement of simple wars we have described earlier will serve us once again—but only if we recognize their limitations. In the first place, some issues of the *external war* will also concern the factions of state R, and some of the belligerent states will be greatly interested in the issues of the *internal war*. In the second place, if the war has not naturally produced an interaction or interrelation of issues of the external and internal wars, the parties may deliberately interrelate them during the preliminaries to peace talks and during the conference. The leaders of a faction may conclude that by connecting a war aim or a policy to one of the states' aims or policies, it will have a better chance of achieving success; or the state, as a way of supporting its allied faction, may attach conditions to acceptance of peace proposals from the other state, conditions pertaining to the issues of the internal war, satisfaction of which would benefit the faction. However interrelated, the parties must at least attempt to solve the problems in which both the states and the factions have an interest. They may do so by the procedural device of distinguishing the external and internal aspects of the particular issue, allowing only the factions to settle the latter. This approach will be feasible only to the extent that the state-allies of the factions are willing to accept the fiction that certain issues are internal. Correspondingly, the factions could dispute the classification of other issues as external. If the parties were unable to accept some fictional device for threading their way toward a settlement of the internally-externally related issues, then those issues would not be resolved. Hostilities may not continue; and a kind of settlement could be reached. But it could not be a complete solution, nor would the political situation in the states affected by the settlement be very stable or conducive to friendly relations.

In the peace-feeler stage of the peacemaking process, the question, "Shall we negotiate or shall we continue waging war?" is the key question for the policymakers. If several parties are engaged in the war, unlike the simple wars in which only one other belligerent party is involved, the variables to be assessed by the decision-makers multiply. In the internal-external war, the decision to move toward peace is made difficult by the existence of at least four parties and by the fact that the issues of the war are interrelated, often in a quite bewildering way. Hence, a party might decide to wait until something "breaks" in its favor and so continue fighting (if it could). And there may be very practical reasons for an actor's refusal to negotiate: The faction leaders might be afraid that the state-ally will "sell them out" at the peace conference, or the state belligerents might want assurances that the factions will comply with peace terms. Hence, preconditions to negotiations will be important; and they will have to be negotiated before the parties can even begin considering substantive war issues. In order to allay the fears of the faction, the state may have to provide the faction leaders with more or less formal guarantees that the state will not accept a settlement that jeopardizes the existence or viability of the faction.

In the internal-external war, the problem of compliance is a formidable one. How can all the parties be made legally responsible for fulfilling the final terms of an adequate peace settlement? In our voluntaristic international legal system, a state cannot usually be obligated to perform certain acts unless its authorities consent to be bound in a fashion prescribed by that state's constitution. Thus, one state cannot usually obligate another state; and if a faction has some formal juridical status, however fictional—a status that is regarded as the equivalent of sovereignty by some of the state belligerents—then the faction could not become legally obligated without its consent. That is true *a fortiori* of the incumbent faction; but it is also true of the insurgents that have secured recognition from other states.

The problem of rendering the terms of a settlement obligatory for all parties arises early when the actors, having decided to negotiate, meet to discuss the procedures of the peace conference. For then, the question of the status of the belligerents, whether faction or state, is important. Shall this faction or state be invited to the conference? If invited, should it be permitted to participate as the juridical equal of others? One state may not recognize the government of the other state; and it is probable that one of the states will not have recognized the opposing faction. What then? If there is to be a settlement at all, then all the active belligerents, whose absence would render any settlement illusory, must be present or represented by a party acceptable to the absentee as well as the inviting state. If the parties were simply unable to agree upon these preliminary questions of status, they might have to negotiate a plainly inadequate settlement. It is often possible to have all belligerents present at the peace talks; and ways may be found for one state to maintain its policy of nonrecognition of the adversary state. But the problem of the status of the factions is particularly difficult. Are their representatives to be invited? If not, who will represent them? What assurances do the negotiators have that the factions will abide by a settlement? If the factions are to be invited, what status will their delegations have at the peace conference? And (again) how will the factions be obligated? If the factions were to be refused invitations, their leaders might decide to continue (or resume) hostilities; and the internal war would not be settled. Of course, if the factions were themselves determined to have peace, then the internal war could be settled between them. But many issues of the internal-external war would be left unresolved unless the factions accepted representation by their state-allies at the inter-state talks.

Nevertheless, the question—the hard question—remains: How will all the parties become obligated to fulfill the terms of the peace? The problem, restated in abbreviated form, is this: State A cannot obligate state M (that is fairly settled law, and quite generally accepted); and state A cannot obligate faction y or even its ally, faction x, especially where faction x is the incumbent government of an established state $R(x)$ and y is the government of a successor state y.[29] A factor may refuse to accept the peace settlement; and if that faction is a viable entity, the settlement could not then be an adequate one. The parties should then attempt to provide each other with assurances that the peace terms will be respected.

a. In the simplest case imaginable, all the parties would agree to a peace treaty, then sign and ratify it.

b. The first option, even if it could be agreed upon as the optimal form for a settlement document, still might not provide the parties sufficient assurance that the internal problems in which the states are interested and the external problems in which the factions are interested would be settled—and the settlement respected. State A and state M may then conclude an agreement, *inter se*, that settled many of the external war questions; and they might additionally obligate themselves to perform certain acts (and refrain from performing certain other acts) relative to state R and the factions x and y. In effect, the state belligerents would agree to a guaranteed disengagement from the internal war.

c. To complete the settlement, the factions x and y would agree upon the terms of a peace within state R (and between $R(x)$ and Y). Of course, such an agreement might actually supplement the treaty between states A and $M;$ or it might stand alone in the event the representatives of A and M could not reach agreement. In order to provide further assurances for themselves and their state allies, the factions could also execute an agreement obligating themselves to follow certain policies relative to states A and M (and perhaps other states). In other words, as neither faction can assure the other that the policies and activities of

29 If faction y were unsuccessful in achieving control of the polity or winning independence or autonomy and if it continued to remain in existence as a political group in the postwar era, it would of course be obligated to respect the terms of the settlement that the incumbents, $R(x)$, negotiated—to the same extent that any group or citizen of R would be so obligated.

their state-ally will be conducive to peace and the security of state R, then each would agree to refrain from dealing with the state-ally in particular ways. The factions thus purchase mutual assurances at the cost of self-imposed limitations upon their freedom of action.

d. The parties might vest authority in a supranational or international organization to police the terms of the settlement. The peace treaty could provide for the parties' concluding agreements with such an organization, and indeed they might execute an agreement of this kind during the peace conference. In such an arrangement, the international organization could be given powers of varying breadth: supervision of troop withdrawals, perhaps; inspection of demilitarized areas, bases, and air fields; or control of elections in state R. Assigning such functions to an international organization could provide the parties the security guarantees they believed they needed and induce them to have confidence in a peace settlement. Of course, the agreements concluded with the executive of the organization must make interstate cooperation obligatory. And they might also contain clauses pursuant to which the states agreed to perform certain actions (to disarm, demilitarize, or reduce the size of their armed forces) and refrain from other actions (entering alliances with other states or factions, building new bases, manufacturing weapons, intervening in the domestic affairs of state R, and so on).

The fact that one or both of the factions could not be easily and firmly obligated to abide by the terms of the peace treaty would be a *formal* problem only, if the state-ally fully controlled the faction, that is, if the faction were the puppet of the state-ally. Although the fiction of the independence of the faction may be preserved during negotiations (and in the language used in the peace treaty), there might indeed be a tacit understanding among the belligerents that one state-ally will see to it that the faction shall accept and keep the peace. In our state system, this might be as good as any written agreement which, in situations of crisis deemed to threaten the security of a signatory, could be broken.

As not all parties could be obligated, and the settlement may be incomplete or inadequate, the belligerents might decide that their only recourse is to enter a collective defense pact directed against possible aggression by the enemy state or faction. This will hardly eliminate tensions following the war; and it might prompt the other side to form its own collective defense organization. The result would be two hostile alliances facing each other, perhaps preparing for war. And a new war might easily occur, as domestic instability in state R could catalyze the war between the hostile alliances. Yet, during the peace negotiations, the belligerents may feel they have no alternative but to form a defense pact when it becomes apparent that the settlement will be incomplete because of the existence of nonobligated parties. It is conceivable that the pact would serve as a deterrent, in spite of the fact that it will not reduce tensions. The combination of a peace treaty and a defense pact could constrain the parties of the other side to conduct their foreign policy so as to avoid a violation of the treaty and avoid provoking the members of the defense pact and thereby precipitating a new war. The deterrent effect of a defense pact could, of course, compensate for the inadequacy of a settlement in providing security guarantees to certain of the parties. But it is, after all, something extrinsic to the settlement. It is a confession of its inadequacies and does not bode well for the future relations between the belligerents. While the recalcitrance of a faction or the refusal of a state to permit a faction to be represented at the peace conference might prevent a settlement, it need not necessarily do so, if the issues of the war have been de-ideologized or devalued below the thresholds for settlement. Then, however incomplete, however tenuous or temporary, the willing parties will at least agree to a cease-fire, and perhaps eventually a minimal political settlement.

Another procedural question likely to impede peacemaking (in addition to the status of the actors and the effects of the existence of nonobligated parties) is the question of the agenda.[30] Because of the interrelatedness of external and internal war issues, the problem of the content and order of the agenda may assume an especially refractory aspect. What questions shall be discussed by all the belligerents? What questions are of a domestic political nature, and which of these shall be discussed only by the factions? What questions do the states wish to reserve to themselves alone for decision? What matters do the parties want excluded completely from any consideration at the conference? Given agreement upon the issues to be discussed, and their categorization as external or internal, in what order shall they be discussed? These questions are crucial; at the very least they will appear so to the parties, for reasons we have already mentioned but would do well to mention again. There are some matters that the parties would not want broached at the peace talks.[31] They may feel that to do so would only embarrass them or result in attempts to undermine control of their polities or call into question principles that have formed the basis for their war aims and foreign policy. Secondly, as the issues of an internal-external war are usually interconnected in a complex fashion, resolution of one question is often a condition for the resolution of another; and placing one issue higher on the agenda than another might prejudice the negotiating position of some parties. In other words, the negotiators are apt to find that when they reach items further down on the agenda, they have been concluded (or estopped) by agreements reached in earlier discussions. Like the other procedural wrangles attendant upon negotiating a settle-

30 See Table 2–1 in Chapter 2 and Table 3–1 in Chapter 3.
31 Great Britain would not countenance the discussion of British "rights" on the high seas at the Congress of Vienna (see the Napoleonic Wars, pp. 392–405).

ment of a complex internal war, an agenda controversy can delay and even prevent peace talks. Resolution, if it can be effected, could come about in several ways: the parties might agree that there will be no agenda or that any issue may be raised at any time. Or they might stipulate that any matter settled earlier in the conference could be reconsidered later if it were connected in some way with a later agenda item. Finally, the parties might, after long argument, agree upon an agenda, the agreement being facilitated by events on the battlefield and in the capitals of the belligerents.

Having more or less disposed of procedural issues, the delegates to the peace conference can now turn to the substantive problems of the military and political settlement. The cease-fire and technical matters related to it should pose no special problems (special, that is, to the internal-external war). We have already discussed the cessation of hostilities for the simple external and internal wars and for the complex external war; and that earlier discussion is generally applicable to the internal-external war.[32] During the war between states A and M and within state R between factions x and y, there might have been conventional set-piece warfare between regular armies and guerrilla operations by irregulars. For a complete settlement, the cease-fire must, of course, be adhered to by all forces, and the agreement must be enforceable against all parties. We may find, however, that troops of either state (A or M) are on the territory of state $R;$ that troops of the factions have been fighting in either or both of the states. The negotiators must determine whether these troops are to be withdrawn. A very great number of permutations of possible deployments of forces at the war's end can be envisaged; and hence it is impossible to generalize about the provisions for the post-armistice disposition of troops. However, in the internal-external war in which all have agreed to bargain with each other at a single conference (rather than the case where some parties continue to wage war and others disengage and conclude a separate peace), we can safely assume that the states have pretty nearly equal bargaining power. Then, state A would obtain state M's agreement to withdraw its troops from $A;$ state M would secure an equivalent promise from state $A;$ both states would surely secure the agreement of the leaders of the factions to withdraw their forces from territories of A and M. It is also reasonable to conclude that the troops of the latter will also be withdrawn ultimately from state R. (Chances are that the factions will want to have all foreign troops withdrawn from their territory.)[33]

32 See the discussion, as well as Table 2–2 in Chapter 2 and Table 3–1 in Chapter 3.

33 In a stalemated war for control of the polity, one faction (x) might want to have contingents of troops from their state-ally (A) remain. It would almost certainly want the troops of the adversary state (M) withdrawn. But in order

For a discussion of the difficulties that might arise in connection with the demobilization and disarmament of the troops of the factions, the reader should consult Chapter 3, dealing with the settlement of simple internal wars. In the complex internal war, where neither faction had defeated the other, the problems would be similar, to the extent that the matter of foreign troops is disentangled from internal security questions. This is not to say that states A and M will not be able to influence interfaction negotiations concerning the military settlement. They will. But there will be a set of core problems that only the factions can resolve, however much the overall settlement for state R is influenced by states A and M.

In treating the territorial aspects of the settlement, the negotiators might find that the establishment of a special regime for state R is particularly attractive, if states A and M have actively intervened in R. They would promise formally to refrain from interfering in the domestic affairs of R.[34] They could agree to neutralize R and try to obtain the agreement of the factions to adhere to the neutralization provisions. Or they could create a special statute for the state that defined the principles of its foreign relations in its dealings with A, M, and others. Needless to say, the agreement of the factions to the special statute will be necessary; and while any terms infringing the sovereign prerogatives of state R would be resisted by the factions, it might indeed be the best possible solution in the circumstances if, for example, the peace conference has the task of establishing and recognizing the independence of a successor state (Y) and adumbrating the general nature of the relations of the parent and successor states. Special regimes of this sort (including the holding of plebiscites in any of the states involved in the war) limit the freedom of action of the actors. They will require the parties to forego certain privileges and policies. The real problem will arise if the policymakers of one of the states come to feel that they are foregoing too much relative to the other, thereby compromising their interests and security. Neutralization, like disarmament, is theoretically an attractive peacemaking solution. But historical evidence shows how difficult it is to maintain the neutral status of a state or territory.[35] Because of the competitive relations between states A and M after the war, the policymakers of either may be

---

to secure this withdrawal, faction x would probably have to acquiesce in M's (and faction y's) demand for the withdrawal of the troops of state A from the territory x controlled. In a war for independence in which the insurgents have been successful in obtaining the promise of the incumbents to grant them independence, there is usually no reason for foreign troops to remain in either the parent or successor states.

34 See the discussion, and Table 2–3 in Chapter 2.

35 Black, C. E. et al., *Neutralization and World Politics* (Princeton: Princeton University Press, 1968).

tempted clandestinely to support the government (or a faction) of state *R*. The latter might chafe under the restrictions of the statute of neutralization, especially if and when it comes to regard the statute as a means for preserving a *status quo* prejudicial to its interests. Then, the policymakers of *R* will want to rearm, increase the size of their armed forces, and obtain military aid from any state willing to provide it. But this is, in any case, a problem of the postwar period. The peace negotiators will of course try to anticipate how effective a special regime for *R* would be; and an estimate of complete ineffectiveness, or the opposition of some of the parties, might persuade them not to establish the regime. However, even with visible limitations, the only acceptable solution would be the one enabling the delegates to make peace: They might want peace (or at least a cease-fire) more than assurances that the solutions they adopted will have reasonable prospects of success.

Should the parties attempt to draft provisions dealing with the resumption of relations of the belligerents, legal questions of recognition could again arise. A state might refuse to accept the terms of a settlement of the internal war within state *R;* or it might refuse to recognize the independence of the successor state. In the face of such an attitude, the negotiators may have to omit terms dealing with the normalization of relations, leaving it to the states themselves individually to establish regular relations with each other in the postwar period, after sufficient time has passed to erase the memory of the war.

In the case of adjustment of disputes, the parties have the same options as belligerents in simple wars. The factions would want to outline procedures for the resolution of disputes between them. This will certainly be a matter with which the factions will want to deal between themselves; and they would undoubtedly regard any interference by states *A* or *M* as interference in the domestic affairs of state *R*.[36]

A future dispute between the factions could, of course, threaten the peace settlement. Would the character of the dispute as internal to state *R* prevent attempts by others (including *A* or *M*) to resolve the dispute? To answer this question, we would have to assess the power position of state *R*. As Modelski has written, there are no intrinsically internal questions, especially where the effects of a conflict are felt beyond the borders of a state.[37] A matter is internal only to the extent that the state (*R*) can get other states to recognize it as such. A state with great capabilities will more likely obtain the acquiescence of other states in its determination of internality than will a state with few capabilities (and a relatively low power position). Small states will find that other states

36 See the discussion, and Tables 2–5 and 2–7 in Chapter 2.
37 Modelski, George, *International Conference on the Settlement of the Laotian Question, 1961–62* (Canberra: Australian National University, 1962), pp. 21 f.

and international organizations will more readily intervene in disputes that in the case of great powers would be regarded as internal.

Summaries of Settlements of Some Complex Internal Wars[38]

In the summaries of complex internal wars that follow, we have only one example of the state-faction war, the First War of Mehemet Ali.[39] There are, however, several examples of alliance-faction wars and internal-external wars: In the former category fall the Dutch and Greek Revolts, the War for American Independence, the Russo-Turkish War of 1877–1878, and the Second War of Mehemet Ali;[40] and in the category of internal-external wars are the War of the Polish Succession, the Korean War, and the Laotian Civil War.[41] The latter very closely approximates what I have called the *proxy internal war,* a war whose structure is the same as the internal-external war, but in which the state-allies are not actively belligerent.[42] We will consider the settlement of proxy wars after considering the role of war-oriented actors in the peace-making process in the next two chapters.[43]

THE NETHERLANDS (DUTCH) REVOLT (1566–1609)
Dutch rebels, Britain (1585–1604), and France (1595–1598) vs. Spain

WAR AIMS: Initially, Dutch aims were merely the removal of Spanish troops and autonomy; but they soon included complete independence. Spain's aim was the maintenance of control over the Netherlands and, as against England, dominance of the seas, preservation of Catholic orthodoxy, and settling scores with the state that had been supporting the

38 As in the preceding chapters, the reader is referred to the Bibliography for additional documents and studies dealing with the summarized peace settlements.

39 But see the discussion of the First World War (*infra,* pp. 405–28): the Arab Uprising in the Hejaz and the German alliance with the "White" Finns in the Finnish Civil War also exemplify state-faction internal wars.

40 The Grisons Struggle of the Thirty Years' War (*infra,* pp. 379–92) and the Allied interventions in the Russian Civil War during and after the First World War (pp. 405–28) can also be regarded as alliance-faction internal wars.

41 The Seven Years' War (*infra,* pp. 374–9) and the Wars of the Spanish (pp. 357–66) and Austrian (pp. 366–74) Successions were multilateral wars that had characteristics of the internal-external war as we have defined it. In the Wars of France against Europe (pp. 392–405), the Peninsular War (1808–13) is also in that category.

42 In the Thirty Years' War (*infra,* pp. 379–92), Denmark, Sweden, and several German Protestant princes were France's proxies until the latter became a belligerent in 1635.

43 See Chapter 7.

rebels. Spain's aims, as against the French, were the preservation of a Catholic monarchy in France and the maintenance of security along the French border with the Netherlands. Britain's aim was the weakening of their Spanish competitor and then defense against the Armada; France's aim, defense of her frontiers against Spanish attacks.

OUTCOME: The rebels won *de facto* independence for the northern Dutch provinces of the Netherlands. The Walloon provinces remained part of the Spanish Empire. England destroyed the Armada and eventually made peace with Spain in 1604, after the death of Elizabeth I and after James I had become King. France and Spain made peace in 1598. Spain did not recognize, *de jure*, the independence of the United Provinces until 1648, in the Treaty of Münster (as part of the settlement of the Thirty Years' War) .[44]

FACTORS FOR PEACE: Philip II died in 1598 and with him, his ideal of Empire, but not before he had realized that the Netherlands ". . . had been a millstone around his neck and had dragged him from the height of power to the abyss of disaster."[45] The war had cost Spain dearly. Both Philip III and Archduke Albert of Austria, married to Isabella, daughter of Philip II, to whom her father had bequeathed the Netherlands, determined on a truce. To embark upon further attempts to reduce the northern provinces would have cost too much and might not have succeeded. Although a war party in the United Provinces, supported by the army, privateers, and war contractors, wanted the war against Spain to continue, general war weariness, the need to undertake reconstruction, and some pressure from Britain and France induced the rebels to agree to a truce. Indeed, the fact that James I had agreed to peace with Spain in 1604 was a sobering event for the Dutch and sped discussions for peace that were going on even at that early date.

France and Spain made peace in 1598, because Philip realized that it was fruitless to continue to dispute the succession of Henry of Navarre. Philip also wanted peace with France so he could once more attack the rebels. In France, there was war weariness (after 2 generations of civil wars) and unhappiness with the English alliance (Elizabeth, it appeared to Henry, refused to support France sufficiently) .

England and Spain made peace because they concluded that continuation of the war was not worth the costs: Spain could not hope to defeat England; and the parties' expeditions and counterexpeditions, while spectacular, were expensive and futile.

WAR-ORIENTED STATES: Holy Roman Empire.

---

44 See pp. 379–92. In that complex (multilateral) war, Spain and the United Provinces again went to war with each other in 1621.

45 Vlekke, B. H. M., *Evolution of the Dutch Nation* (New York: Roy Publishers, 1945) , p. 161.

ALLIANCES: 1. Alliances internal to the Netherlands:[46] The Alliance of Nobles (1566) was a loose association of Dutch noblemen, the purpose of which was the prevention of religious persecution. All the provinces of the Low Countries united against Spain under the terms of the Pacification of Ghent (8 November 1576). Spanish troops were to be expelled, and matters of general interest were to be settled by a meeting of the States General after peace had been restored. The Union of Utrecht (23 January 1579) was more of a constitutional settlement than an alliance, and it stipulated that the provinces were to act as a single state in dealing with other states. The Union's purpose was to resist Spain. Freedom of conscience and provincial autonomy in matters of religion were guaranteed. The Union, however, included only the northern Dutch provinces, thereafter known as the United Provinces of the Netherlands (and comprising Holland, Zeeland, Utrecht, Guelderland, Friesland, Groningen, and Overijssel). Like many confederations, the Union had no truly strong central authority. In times of crisis, it lacked adequate cohesiveness, and its policies were often inefficiently implemented. In July, 1581, the United Provinces issued a declaration that Philip was no longer their sovereign, and they thenceforth regarded themselves as independent.

2. External alliances: A mutual defense alliance between Britain and the States General was formed in January 1578. The alliance of August 1585 was the more important, however, because pursuant to its terms, England sent troops to the Netherlands under the Earl of Leicester, who also became Governor-General of the Dutch.[47] The defensive treaty of alliance was paid for, in other words, by the Dutch surrender of part of their sovereignty to the English. Leicester's force did not substantially help the United Provinces, and the Governor-General's policies caused a constitutional crisis in Holland. In 1588, full sovereignty was restored to the Council of State after Leicester left. The alliance remained in being, although England, confronted with the threat of the Armada, could not provide further active assistance to the Dutch.

After the French declaration of war on Spain in 1595, France joined Britain and the United Provinces in an offensive and defensive alliance (May and October, 1596).[48] The Dutch benefited from recognition by both Britain and France and from the fact that Spain was diverted from concentrating on the rebellion. But the allies did not coordinate their operations, and English aid to France was meager.

In 1603, after the Peace of Vervins, France and Britain concluded a secret treaty of alliance guaranteeing the independence of the Low Coun-

46 Geyl, Pieter, *The Revolt of the Netherlands* (New York: Barnes & Noble, 1958), pp. 85 f., 149 f., 169 f., 184 f.

47 Great Britain, *A General Collection of Treatys,* 2nd ed. (London: Knapton *et al.,* 1732), Vol. 2, pp. 81–2, 83. See also pp. 89 f., 92 f.

48 *Ibid.,* pp. 97–102, 103–19, 120–7.

tries. Each promised to defend the other with a specified amount of aid if either were attacked by Spain.[49] This alliance was supplemented by another in January, 1608, between France and the United Provinces.[50] Defensive in nature, it never had to be put into operation; but its existence probably did contribute to the forces impelling Spain to make peace.

THE SETTLEMENT:

1. FRANCE AND SPAIN[51] MILITARY SETTLEMENT: In the military provisions of the Peace of Vervins, letters of marque were annulled, and Spanish troops were to evacuate Brittany and other areas with the aid of the French King, who would be reimbursed for his expenses by Spain. The latter would also provide hostages as a surety for the restitution of all territories to the French. A cease-fire was to be proclaimed as of the date of the signature of the Treaty (2 May 1598). Prisoners of war and other interned persons were to be free without ransom. There was also to be a cease-fire for two months with the English and Dutch in order to allow them to send delegates to Vervins to negotiate a peace settlement. This did not take place, however, and Spain's war against these states continued.

POLITICAL SETTLEMENT: Peace between the parties was proclaimed. The Treaties of Cateau-Cambrésis were confirmed and incorporated by reference in the Peace Treaty.[52] The parties were to avoid all hostile acts and punish their subjects who violated the Treaty's terms.

For purposes of territorial exchange, the status quo of 1559 was adopted. Thus, Spain agreed to return Calais, Picardy, Ardres, Monthulin, Dourlans, and Blavet to France, without damage or alternation and according to the procedures specified. (The Spaniards could remove their artillery and equipment, however.) Flanders and Artois were to retain the privileges accorded their inhabitants by the French. With the permission of the Pope, commissioners of the parties would arrange the division of specified lands into dioceses. If the Spanish King gave the provinces of the Low Countries to the Infanta Isabella (as he did later in 1598), they would nonetheless be understood to come within the terms of this Treaty.

The subjects of either party could travel freely (with their goods) in the realm of the other. Subjects of the one party who had been detained or otherwise prevented from leaving the domains of the other were to be permitted to leave; and all persons were vested with the same rights to

49 *Ibid.*, pp. 128–31.
50 Bernard, Jacques, *Recueil des Traitez* (Amsterdam: Henry et la Veuve de T. Boom, 1700), Vol. 3, pp. 39–41. This was supplemented by a Treaty of Guarantee, signed on 17 June 1609, *ibid.*, pp. 52–3.
51 *Ibid.*, Vol. 2, pp. 616–23; Vol. 3, pp. 828–9.
52 See pp. 157–60.

property they had had in 1588. Judgments and sentences occasioned by the war against the subjects of either party were nullified. Other provisions defining the rights and liberties of persons affected by the war were included in the Treaty.

The only other terms of significance were those that sought to bring an end to the war between France and the Duke of Savoy, with mediation by Pope Clement VIII. A cease-fire was agreed upon, but the agreement was tenuous; and a final settlement was not reached until January, 1601 (in the Peace of Lyons) .[53]

2. ENGLAND AND SPAIN[54] MILITARY SETTLEMENT: By the Treaty of London of 19 August 1604, it was agreed that prisoners of war were to be released, letters of marque annulled, and the British were to prevent their soldiers from supplying arms to the Dutch and other enemies of Spain.

POLITICAL SETTLEMENT: The Treaty called for the abolition of all seizures and spoils occurring since April 1603 and proclaimed oblivion for all past offenses. It established perpetual peace and confederacy between the parties (which also included the Archduke of Austria). Nor would the parties aid rebels or traitors, attack the other for any cause, or consent to a treaty prejudicial to the interests of the other. They were also to renounce all alliances incompatible with the terms of the Treaty. (Most of these provisions were not carried out.) There was explicit recognition that the treaty of alliance between Britain and the United Provinces was to remain in force. Pursuant to its terms, Britain held Flushing, Brill, and other islands. Spain recognized this holding as legitimate. But Britain would give up these holdings when the Archduke proposed just terms for peace to the States General, and they turned them down.

Mercantile and commercial clauses were extensive. They were based generally on the concept of free trade, although Britain was not to be permitted to carry Dutch goods from Holland and Zeeland into Spain, or from Spain to other than British lands. The British also promised not to use Dutch ships in their trade until after the end of hostilities between the Dutch and Spanish.

British subjects would not be molested in Spain on account of their religion. Prewar concessions or privileges held by subjects of either party against the other were revived. If war were again to break out between the parties, their subjects were to be allowed 6 months to transport their merchandise out of each other's realms.

Britain agreed to mediate the war between the Archduke and the United Provinces.

53 Bernard, *op. cit.,* Vol. 3, pp. 1–4.
54 *A General Collection of Treatys, op. cit.,* Vol. 2, pp. 131–46.

COMMENT: In 1608, James I concluded a Treaty with the Dutch to guarantee the terms of the anticipated Treaty of Peace between the Archduke and the United Provinces.[55] Pursuant to its terms, Britain promised to assist the latter to obtain a secure peace. Both the Dutch and the English engaged themselves to defend the other against attack. In 1609 (after the Twelve Year Truce), France concluded a similar treaty with the Dutch.

3. SETTLEMENT OF THE DUTCH REVOLT: PRELIMINARIES.[56] The Archduke loosed a peace feeler in 1606. But the Dutch refused to negotiate if the Archduke (or Spain) continued to claim sovereignty over the United Provinces. Albert then indicated his willingness to negotiate with the Dutch ". . . in the capacity of, and as taking them for, free lands, provinces, and towns, against which they [Albert and Isabella] claim nothing." With this admission, an armistice was signed in April, 1607. Spain's hesitancy delayed the start of negotiations, which began in February, 1608. While the parties agreed on a separation based upon the principle of *uti possidetis,* the talks collapsed over the demand of the Dutch to have their right to trade with the Indies recognized (September, 1609). France and England pressed the parties to accept a permanent truce, if a peace settlement could not be negotiated. Maurice of Nassau, placing himself at the head of the war party, demanded absolute recognition of Dutch sovereignty and warned that a compromise truce was full of dangers. By the end of 1608, however, the war party accepted the need for a truce. Talks opened in Antwerp, and the Twelve Year Truce was signed at Anvers on 9 April 1609.[57]

MILITARY SETTLEMENT: The 12-year truce was to come into effect one year from the signing of its terms. (The delay was due to anticipated communications difficulties.) There was to be restitution for all seizures after the effective date of the cease-fire. No new forts were to be constructed during the period of the truce. The ships of war of the parties were prohibited from entering each other's ports without permission. Letters of marque were annulled.

POLITICAL SETTLEMENT: The Archduke declared, in the name of the King of Spain, that he would be content to deal with the States General of the United Provinces ". . . as he would deal with a free, independent state." Trade with the Indies was not specifically prohibited; and although both parties were to take steps to open their waterways, to render them navigable and to suppress piracy, the Dutch were not explicitly required to open the Scheldt to Antwerp (and they retained most of the estuaries).

55 *Ibid.,* pp. 157–61. The United Provinces were thus guaranteed by both France and England. See note 18.
56 Geyl, *op. cit.,* pp. 240 ff.
57 Bernard, *op. cit.,* pp. 43–7.

Free movement of citizens and free trade were to be permitted (the latter on a most-favored-nation basis). Persons whose goods were seized during the war could, in certain cases, obtain restitution without recourse to litigation. Persons who had fled were to be permitted to return to the country of their origin. In a secret article, the Spanish King agreed not to obstruct Dutch commerce in countries that permitted it.

The liberties of Dutch subjects in Spain were to be the same as those granted to British subjects in the Treaty of London (1604). Thus, the Dutch could not be molested on account of their religious beliefs. And in an appended Declaration, the French King promised to take steps to prevent an "innovation" by the Dutch in matters concerning the Catholic religion in areas of Brabant secured for the United Provinces.

COMMENTS: In the Peace of Münster (1648), the King of Spain recognized that ". . . the Lords States-General of the United Provinces, and the respective Provinces thereof . . . are free and sovereign states . . . unto which . . . he the Lord King makes no pretension, nor shall his heirs and successors for themselves, either now or hereafter, evermore make any pretension thereunto."[58]

WAR OF THE POLISH SUCCESSION (1733–1735)
Pro-Russian Polish faction, Russia, Saxony, and Austria vs.
Poles supporting Prince Leszczynski, France, Spain, and Sardinia

WAR AIMS: The Diet of Poland had elected Leszczynski King on 12 September 1733. A polish faction plotted to prevent Leszczynski becoming King, and its leaders invited the Russians to intervene to prevent execution of the Diet's decision. Augustus III of Saxony was offered as a candidate for the Polish Crown. Austria supported him in return for Saxony's promise to accept the Pragmatic Sanction, this agreement insuring the succession and integrity of the Habsburgs against probable claims of the Wettins of Saxony. (In essence, Austria wanted to consolidate their state through a consolidation of the rights of succession of the Habsburgs.) Saxony coveted the Crown of Poland. Russia coveted Polish lands and influence in Polish affairs.

France supported Leszczynski, in part because the Prince's daughter had been chosen as Louis' XV consort and in part because France sought to preserve a balance of power in Europe against Russia and Austria. Spain and Sardinia joined France in an alliance, being induced to do so by promises of gain.

OUTCOME: The proclamation of Augustus III as King of Poland on 5 October 1733 brought a French declaration of war against the Empire (but not against Russia). The war was actually fought in Italy and on the Rhine—not in Poland! A settlement was negotiated eventually (and

58 Article 1 of the Münster Treaty between Spain and the United Provinces: Parry, Clive, *The Consolidated Treaty Series*, Vol. 1 (Dobbs Ferry: Oceana, 1969), p. 72. See pp. 379–92.

a complex settlement it was), confirming Augustus King of Poland. Leszczynski became Duke of Bar and Lorraine. France and Saxony guaranteed the Pragmatic Sanction. (France was willing to do this because, on the death of Leszczynski, the duchies were to revert to his daughter, the wife of the King of France.) In Italy, Austria, Spain and Sardinia traded territory.

FACTORS FOR PEACE: On the part of the Great Powers, the principal factor for peace was the probable achievement of their war aims through negotiations and compromise and the apparent futility of pursuing those aims by further fighting. Poland gained nothing; and the desires of her nobles were of no importance in the decision to make peace.

WAR-ORIENTED STATES: Britain and Prussia.

ALLIANCES: Between the Russians and the Pro-Russian Poles, there was probably the most informal of understandings, and none whatever between those Poles and the Austrian Emperor. Austria had exchanged a promise with Saxony to support the candidacy to the Polish Crown of Augustus III in return for a Saxon guarantee of the Pragmatic Sanction. The French alliance with Spain and Sardinia of 1734 was an offensive and defensive alliance, and under its terms coalition armies were put in the field. By late 1734, however, the alliance was in difficulty because both France's allies wanted Mantua; and France's Minister, Fleury, refused to promise it to either. Their cooperation thereafter diminished. France entered a purely formal alliance with the Dzikow Confederacy (pro-Leszczynski Poles) in September, 1735.

THE SETTLEMENT: PRELIMINARIES: Peace negotiations began in 1735, and the Preliminaries of Peace were signed on 3 October 1735.[59] But such was the complexity of the war that negotiations toward a definitive peace continued intermittently for 3 more years, while a number of conditions precedent to a final settlement occurred or were arranged.

MILITARY SETTLEMENT: A standstill cease-fire came into effect on the date of the signature of the Preliminaries. Further negotiations took place; and as the implementation of military-related activities was closely tied to the performance of political acts, we take up the steps toward a definitive peace in chronological order.

POLITICAL SETTLEMENT: The Preliminaries of Peace stipulated that Leszczynski would retain the title of King of Poland and Grand Duke of Lithuania even after his abdication. He would be given the Duchy of Bar, as then held by the Duke of Lorraine, with the reversion of the Duchy to the French King. Augustus III was to be recognized as the King of Poland and Grand Duke of Lithuania by all states that took part in the pacification. Tuscany would be given to the House of Lorraine; and the Powers would guarantee the succession of Tuscany to that House,

59 Rousset de Missy, Jean, *Recueil Historiques d'Actes*, Vol. 13 (The Hague: Pierre Gosse, 1740), pp. 428–32.

whereupon Spanish troops were to withdraw and Imperial troops would be free to enter Tuscany. The privileges and rights of Poland were re-established, including the free election of the King.

The Emperor was to retain all his prewar lands and was also ceded Parma and Piacenza. The Spanish Bourbon, Don Carlos, was to take over the Kingdom of the Two Sicilies, with title of King (but in secundogeni-ture). The Powers were to recognize this arrangement. France was to guarantee the Pragmatic Sanction. Commissioners would be appointed to fix the boundaries of Alsace and the Low Countries.

Austria, France, Spain, and Sardinia signed the Preliminaries. It was agreed that the Tzarina and King Augustus would be invited to send delegates to the peace congress, that the Emperor would obtain the consent of the Diet of the Holy Roman Empire to the peace, and that other maritime powers would be invited also.

The formal acts of Leszczynski's abdication, the ascension of Augustus to the throne of Poland, and the recognition by Russia and France of the arrangement and of Augustus as King took place in 1736. Augustus also formally accepted the arrangement. In 1736, a series of bilateral declara-tions of peace was published, together with documents implementing the territorial exchanges envisaged by the Preliminaries and formal accep-tances of those arrangements.[60] The Pacification Diet of Poland (June–July 1736) reconciled the Polish Estates to Augustus.

Two Conventions (at Vienna) were also concluded, one on 11 April 1736, another on 28 August 1736.[61] These were essentially military conventions providing for the withdrawal of troops from former combat theaters and from territories ceded to different sovereigns. They pre-scribed how and when troop withdrawals would take place, required guarantees against seizures and damage to property, and commanded the military leaders to work out the details of their execution. The Conven-tions were complicated in the sense that the performance of one act by one party was often conditioned upon the performance of another act by another party. The procedures were logical, however, and methodical. Some acts could not be performed with safety in the quasi-anarchic European state system of the time, without the prior performance of another act by a former adversary. For example, the Emperor had to obtain the consent of the Empire to the Preliminaries of Peace. When this consent had been obtained, France would withdraw from areas she had captured from the Imperial armies; and when the Emperor secured these territories and others in Italy and the succession in Tuscany was guaranteed to the House of Lorraine by the Powers, the Duchy of Lor-raine was to be handed over to persons commissioned by Prince Leszczyn-ski. (I should point out that the cession of Tuscany to the House of

60 *Ibid.,* pp. 454 f.
61 *Ibid.,* pp. 432–41, 441–52.

Lorraine, in effect, constituted a cession to the Empire, as Duke Francis of Lorraine was the husband of Maria Theresa, later Empress of the Holy Roman Empire.)

The Definitive Treaty of Peace of Vienna was signed on 18 November 1738.[62] The peace of 1735 was made "perpetual." An amnesty was promulgated, and all causes of the war were declared to be forgotten. The Preliminaries of Peace, the Conventions of 1736, and the various formal acts of pacification of the Powers were incorporated in the Treaty. The Emperor and France explicitly expressed their approval of the dispositions and bound themselves and their heirs to observe them in perpetuity. Russia, Sardinia, Spain, and the new King of the Two Sicilies (Don Carlos) acceded to the Treaty and accepted the territorial dispositions. France accepted the Pragmatic Sanction. The boundary commission (with Austrian and French delegates) was to meet within 6 weeks at Freibourg and Lille to begin their job of fixing the boundaries of Alsace, Baden, and the Low Countries. Forts constructed on the Rhine during the war were to be demolished.

Prisoners of war were to be freed, and there was to be restitution to the subjects of the parties for injuries caused by hostilities. There were also some vague guarantees of the rights of subjects in the transferred territories.

Specified treaties were declared to be in force. The provisions for the apportionment of war costs (and other financial terms) of the Conventions of 1736 were incorporated in the Treaty. Free commerce was reestablished.

The Emperor and the French King agreed to guarantee the peace, and the other Powers that acceded to the Treaty did the same by their accessions. A commission was established at Nancy to resolve disputes connected with the arranged disposition of the Duchy of Lorraine.

COMMENTS: This was an external kind of internal war. One Polish faction had done little but elect a King; another faction invited the intervention of Russia. After that, the war and the peace became the concern of the Great Powers.

THE WAR FOR AMERICAN INDEPENDENCE (1775–1783)
Britain vs. The Thirteen Colonies, France (after 1778), Spain
(after 1779), and the United Provinces (after 1780)

WAR AIMS: The American colonies wanted independence. Britain wanted to maintain the integrity of her Empire and her commerce, first in the face of the colonists' rebellion, later against France and Spain. The Dutch sought to maintain and improve their commercial position. Hence, her merchants traded with the colonists, and her government decided to join the League of Armed Neutrality sponsored by the Russian Tzarina. This conduct was regarded as hostile, and Britain

62 *Ibid.,* pp. 421 ff.

declared war on the Netherlands in 1780 to maintain her supremacy on the seas. The Dutch fought a mainly defensive war (and their commerce suffered greatly). France aided the colonists and then became an active belligerent in order to reduce Britain's commercial power and to bring about at least a partial dissolution of the British Empire. Spain wanted Gibraltar.

OUTCOME: Britain recognized the independence of the United States and, despite her weaknesses, was able to secure fairly balanced and moderate treaties of peace from each of the belligerents.

FACTORS FOR PEACE: In Britain, Parliament was split on the advisability of continuing the war, the opposition also resenting the efforts of King George III to increase his powers over Parliament. By 1781, it was clear that only by a major and expensive military effort could the rebellion be suppressed. The colonists won their independence and were willing to negotiate the other terms of the grant of independence from Britain. The Dutch had sustained heavy losses. France was willing to negotiate because she had seen the British sustain the loss of some of her North American colonies; but now she did not want the new United States to be too strong in North America. Spain had failed to secure Gibraltar but would probably obtain some territory in America; hence, she was willing to negotiate a settlement.

WAR-ORIENTED STATES: Russia and the Holy Roman Empire.

ALLIANCES: 1. The Treaty of Alliance between France and the United States was signed on 6 February 1778 at Paris, along with a Treaty of Commerce.[63] The purpose of the former was to bind the allies to secure the independence of the U.S. If war between France and Britain broke out, the parties agreed to make common cause and assist each other as circumstances permitted. They also promised not to make a separate peace and agreed not to lay down their arms until the independence of the U.S. had been formally or tacitly recognized by Britain. Other states were to be invited to participate in the alliance. If the U.S. were to defeat Britain in the "northern parts of America" (i.e., Canada), France would look with favor on a confederation of those parts with the U.S. It was agreed that if the French should attack islands in the Gulf of Mexico and if this attack were successful, the islands were to go to France. Neither party would entertain claims against the other after the war for aid rendered during the war. This obviously favored the U.S., which had been receiving generous French aid since 1776.

2. By the terms of the Convention of Aranjuez (1779), France and Spain formed an offensive alliance against Britain. Spain promised to attack British possessions; France agreed to help Spain capture Gibraltar

63 Jenkinson, Charles, *A Collection of all the Treaties of Peace . . . between Great Britain and other Powers* (London: J. Debrett, 1785), pp. 254–9 and 242–54.

and promised not to make peace until this had been accomplished. In effect, this clause tied the U.S. to Spain's goal, as the U.S. was obligated not to make peace until France consented. During the war, France and Spain cooperated only in the campaign to seize Gibraltar—and that enterprise failed. In the summer of 1780, Spain and Britain actually engaged in negotiations for a peace settlement, but they did not succeed.

The Netherlands acceded to the alliance of the U.S. and France when Britain declared war on her. As in the case of Spain, the Dutch did not provide France with effective assistance against her enemy.

3. The League of Armed Neutrality was formed by Catherine II of Russia, who was indebted for the idea to Vergennes and the Danish statesman Bernstorff. Denmark, Sweden, and The Netherlands joined; Prussia, the Empire, Portugal, and the Two Sicilies later acceded. The League was a nuisance to Britain, although it never posed a serious threat to her security or trade. According to the principles of the League, neutral ships were permitted by right to navigate between ports of the belligerents. Property of belligerent subjects on neutral vessels could not be seized, except for contraband (defined narrowly as arms and munitions). To be legal, a blockade had to be effective. These principles finally became part of the "public law" of Europe in the settlement of the Crimean War.[64]

THE SETTLEMENT: PRELIMINARIES: During the war, offers of mediation by Catherine II and Emperor Joseph II were refused by Britain, as was the proffered mediation of Spain. The latter refusal led Spain's war party to persuade King Charles II to conclude the alliance of Aranjuez with France. After the events of 1781, the British decided to negotiate peace. Talks began in Paris and London in April, 1782. Britain was able to play on the differences in war aims of her opponents. She concluded a Preliminary Treaty of Peace with the U.S. on 30 November 1782;[65] not until 20 January 1783 were separate Preliminary Treaties concluded with Spain and France.[66] Spain's efforts to secure Gibraltar nearly caused the collapse of the negotiations. The separate Definitive Treaties of Peace were signed on 3 September 1783 with Spain, France, and the U.S. The Preliminary Treaty with the Netherlands was not signed until 2 September 1783; the Definitive Treaty, on 20 May 1784.[67]

64 See pp. 165–9.
65 Martens, *Recueil de Traités* (Göttingen: Librarie de Dieterich, 1818), Vol. 3, pp. 497–502.
66 *Ibid.*, pp. 503–9, 510–14.
67 The Definitive Treaty between Britain and France appears in Jenkinson, *op. cit.*, pp. 334–54; Britain and Spain: *ibid.*, pp. 375–92; Britain and the U.S.: *ibid.*, pp. 410–19; Britain and the Netherlands: *ibid.*, pp. 420–6. The Preliminary Treaty between Britain and the Netherlands can be found in Martens, *Recueil de Traités, op. cit.*, Vol. 3, pp. 514–8.

MILITARY SETTLEMENT: The cease-fire between Britain and the U.S. was declared effective from the date of signature of the Preliminary Treaty (30 November 1783). All prisoners were to be freed; and Britain agreed to withdraw all her forces from the territories of the U.S., whose bounds were described in the Treaty. It was stipulated that if, before the Articles of the Peace arrived in North America, additional territory were conquered, it would be restored without compensation to the original possessor.

In the Treaties with France and Spain, notification of a cease-fire was to be dispatched to all commanders in the field and on the high seas. Passports were to be issued to vessels to spread the news. Prisoners were not to be repatriated until after ratification of the Definitive Treaties (except in the case of the Netherlands, in which prisoners were to be released within 6 weeks after the ratification of the Preliminary Treaty).

POLITICAL SETTLEMENT: Many of the terms of the Preliminary Treaties were included in the treaties embodying the final settlements.

1. Anglo-American settlement: Britain acknowledged the independence of the 13 colonies, and the King relinquished all claim to them. The boundary was described in some detail—although not in enough detail to prevent future boundary disputes. Citizens of the U.S. were given the "right" to fish on the Grand Bank, other banks of Newfoundland, and in the Gulf of St. Lawrence, and the "liberty" to fish, but not to dry or cure, along the coast of Newfoundland. Rights to dry and cure were given for other coasts of British Dominions in North America as long as they were unsettled, but when they became settled, the rights were to be extinguished. Britain was given the right freely to navigate the Mississippi along its entire length.

Creditors of either party were to suffer no impediment in recovering *bona fide* debts. Congress was to recommend to the states the restitution of estates and property of "real British subjects" and persons who had fought against the U.S. And Congress would also recommend revision of the laws of the states in the interests of reconciliation and justice. These provisions caused difficulty during the negotiations. Considering the relationship between Congress and the states, they were too loosely drawn; and the problems they were designed to resolve were often not solved, which led to several serious and bitter postwar disputes.

A general amnesty was declared. But there were no provisions for guarantees or for penalties. Lord Shelburne anticipated that a commercial treaty would soon be negotiated, defining more clearly the future basis of relations between the states. Hence, there were no terms for adjustment of disputes or the normalization of relations.

2. Franco-British settlement: A "Christian, universal, and perpetual peace" was proclaimed between the parties, who promised to avoid all hostile acts and hold in oblivion all past acts of war.

Britain was to retain Newfoundland and cede the islands of St. Pierre and Miquelon to France, evacuating them within 3 months. Fishing areas were apportioned between them. Britain ceded the islands of St. Lucia and Tobago to France; France, the islands of Grenada, St. Vincents, Nevis, St. Christopher, and Monserrat to Britain. The parties in possession were to evacuate within 3 months. The inhabitants were not to be molested because of their religion and were to be permitted to leave the islands with their movable property within 18 months of the exchange of ratifications. Other provisions of the Treaty disposed of territories of the parties in Africa and India; and a boundary commission was to be appointed to fix the boundaries of their possessions in those lands. Britain promised to take measures to protect French trade in India.

Prisoners were to be exchanged after they had given security for their debts.

Specified treaties were declared to be in force. If within 4 months the allies of France had not acceded to the peace, or had not reached a separate accord, France would not give them aid that could be used against any British possessions. Within 2 years, a new commercial treaty was to be negotiated. Judgments rendered by courts during the occupation regimes of either party were confirmed. Prewar seizures and prizes would be disposed of according to the laws of the parties.

COMMENTS: France did not secure the large gains and revenues in India that Vergennes had hoped for. Britain emerged from an unhappy war with relatively good terms; for one reason, because the allies were separated by skillful British diplomacy, and for another, because with the weighty domestic and international problems confronting France and Spain, Britain was not negotiating entirely from a position of weakness.

3. Anglo-Spanish settlement: The provisions of the Anglo-Spanish Treaty were almost identical to the Anglo-French Treaty. The provisions concerning the disposition of territories were, of course, different. Spain was given Minorca and East Florida; Britain, the Bahamas, and her citizens gained the right to cut wood in a specified area of Central America. Commissioners were to be appointed to fix the boundary of this wood-cutting area. British citizens in Central America were permitted to reside in the area thus defined, but in that area only. The rights of the inhabitants in the transferred territories were guaranteed. Spain did not get Gibraltar.

4. Anglo-Dutch settlement: All conquered territories were to be restored. The Netherlands would not obstruct the navigation of English vessels in the "Eastern Seas." Commissioners were to be named to resolve disputes between the Dutch West-Africa Company and the English Africa Company. There was a minor exchange of territories in India. Procedures for the evacuation of occupied territory and the release of prisoners, as

well as guarantees for inhabitants, were similar to those of the French Treaty.

GREEK WAR FOR INDEPENDENCE (1821–1830)

Greek rebels and Russia (after 1828) vs. Turkey (Britain and France were not formally belligerent; but since they did manage to destroy the Turkish-Egyptian fleet at Navarino, it is proper to regard them as *de facto* belligerents on the side of the Greeks).

WAR AIMS: The Greek rebels wanted independence. The Turks sought to preserve the integrity of the Ottoman Empire. Russia wanted territory and sought further to weaken the Ottoman Empire and win the favor of the Greeks. Britain and France were moved to action not only by philhellenic public opinion, but also because their commerce in the Levant had been adversely affected and they wanted control over an unstable situation that could only accrue to the benefit of Russia.

OUTCOME: The Greeks won their independence, which was recognized by France, Britain, Russia, and the Sultan. A settlement was worked out under the auspices of the Great Powers.

FACTORS FOR PEACE: Turkey's navy had been virtually destroyed and her treasury almost exhausted. The Russians had won victories (at unexpectedly high costs to themselves) ; and Britain and France were pressing the Porte to settle the war in order to preserve the integrity of the Ottoman Empire.

WAR-ORIENTED STATES: Austria, Bavaria, and Prussia.

ALLIANCES: The Treaty of London, 6 July 1827, created an *ad hoc* alliance of Britain, France, and Russia.[68] The allies agreed to offer mediation to the Greeks and the Turks and demanded an immediate armistice as a preliminary to negotiations. The basis of the settlement would be the Greeks' recognition of the Sultan as their suzerain and the payment of an annual tribute to him. In secret articles, the allies further agreed that if the Sultan refused mediation, they would establish commercial relations with the Greeks and use force if necessary to pacify the Levant. Meetings of the Powers' ambassadors continued in London. In September, the Greek Provisional Government accepted the armistice proposals, but the Turks refused it. The Allies then instituted a blockade of the Ottoman Empire, with a warning to the British and French admirals to avoid hostilities (as their governments wanted to remain on reasonably good terms with the Sultan) ! After the Russian declaration of November 1828) placing the Morea under their protection.[69] An attack

68 Martens, *Nouveau Recueil de Traités* (Göttingen: Librairie de Dieterich, 1829), Vol. 7, pp. 283–90. See also Vol. 12, pp. 1 ff.
69 *Ibid.*, Vol. 9, pp. 53–4.

against the Morea was to be treated as an attack upon their dominions. They expressed the hope that the Porte would cooperate.

In October, 1826, much to the dismay of the Greek rebels, Turkey and Russia achieved a reconciliation with the conclusion of the Convention of Akkerman.[70] By its terms, Turkey had promised to withdraw her troops from the Danubian Principalities and had guaranteed freedom of navigation in the Straits. For the weakened Empire, beset with domestic troubles, the Convention had been a confession of weakness. It had also been the means to avoid war with Russia. The Powers knew that, Russia knew it, and so did the Porte. When the Sultan repudiated the Convention in 1828, Russia declared war on Turkey.

THE SETTLEMENT: PRELIMINARIES: The Minsterial Conference of London, seeking mediation of the internal war, lasted for five years. Subsequently, a supplementary conference of ambassadors was convened nearer to the site of hostilities. As the Russian armies advanced through the Principalities the Porte agreed to negotiate a settlement with the Russians. We will take up, in order, first the Russo-Turkish settlement and then the settlement for Greece.

1. THE RUSSO-TURKISH SETTLEMENT: The Treaty of Adrianople of 14 September 1829 (including a separate treaty respecting Moldavia and Wallachia) embodied the terms of the peace settlement between Russia and Turkey.[71]

MILITARY SETTLEMENT: Orders for a cease-fire were to be sent to all commanders. Prisoners of war were to be freed without ransom. When the territorial exchange provisions of the treaty were executed by Turkey, Russian troops were to evacuate all Turkish territories. Turkey was to build no forts in the Principalities.

POLITICAL SETTLEMENT: Moldavia and Wallachia were to remain tributary to the Sultan but were to be internally autonomous: the Porte must not interfere in their internal affairs nor permit Muslim subjects to reside on the left bank of the Danube. The Principalities were also to be free of duties and other impositions for 2 years, in view of the suffering experienced by the inhabitants during the war. The Hospodars (governors) would be elected from among the peoples of the Principalities (i.e., they were no longer to be Greek Phanariots). Russia guaranteed the settlement of Moldavia and Wallachia.

Serbian autonomy was confirmed although Serbia was to pay tribute to the Porte. Certain districts were added to Serbia. Russia gained some territory along the Pruth and the Danube and in Asia.

There were a number of provisions that protected the rights of Russian merchants in the Ottoman Empire. An amnesty for all persons was pro-

70 *Ibid.*, Vol. 6, pp. 1053–65.
71 *Ibid.*, Vol. 8, pp. 143–51, 152–5.

claimed, and the right of persons to leave with their movable property (and sell their fixed property) was recognized for a period of 18 months. Liberties of commerce and of culture for the inhabitants of the Principalities were recognized by Turkey.

Prior treaties were confirmed. The Sultan also bound himself to observe the Treaty of London (1827) and thereby obligated Turkey to respect the settlement of the Greek civil war arranged by the Allies.

Turkey was to pay an indemnity and $1\frac{1}{2}$ million Dutch ducats for damages sustained by Russian subjects during the War of 1806!

2. THE GREEK SETTLEMENT: PRELIMINARY PEACE TALKS: Through the remainder of 1829 and into 1830, discussions among the Powers continued (over Greek boundaries and Greek sovereignty). In February, 1830, the Allies sanctioned the Peace of Adrianople.[72] Britain's Prime Minister (Wellington), however, was having second thoughts about Greek independence. Meanwhile, the French (with British support) induced Egyptian troops to withdraw from the Morea. Allied occupation of East Rumelia seemed to insure that Greece would have some territory north of the Isthmus. By a series of Protocols, often too late for the events of the civil war, a boundary was set, running from Arta to Volos (26 September 1831).

MILITARY SETTLEMENT: Turkish troop evacuations were handled by the commanders in the field, and informally. The Allies were to remain in occupation of Greece until a force of 3500 Bavarian troops was sent to relieve them. Turkish troops, occupying certain areas, including Athens, were induced to depart by the promise of an indemnity and by the fact that the Sultan's Viceroy of Egypt (Mehemet Ali) was even then rebelling against the Sultan and was advancing into Syria and Asia Minor.

POLITICAL SETTLEMENT: The Convention of 7 May 1832, signed by France, Britain, Russia, and Bavaria, established Greece as an independent monarchy under the protection of the Great Powers.[73] The Sultan acquiesced in the settlement in July. The King of Bavaria accepted the Greek throne for his son, Otto. A Regency Council was to rule Greece until Otto's majority (1835). The Allies declared that they would announce their support for Otto to the Greek nation and attempt to secure recognition of the settlement from other states. The thrones of Bavaria and Greece were not to be united.

The Powers also granted a loan to Greece. Turkey was impliedly promised a small indemnity for the loss of territory. The territorial limits of Greece were those of the Protocol of 26 September 1831; hence, the northern boundary ran from the Gulf of Volos to the Ambraciote Gulf.

72 Hertslet, Edward, *A Complete Collection of the Treaties and Conventions . . . between Great Britain and Foreign Powers* (London: Butterworths, 1871), Vol. 12, p. 513.

73 *Ibid.,* Vol. 4, pp. 313–8; Martens, *op. cit.,* Vol. 10, pp. 550–70.

COMMENTS: The Greek rebels were torn by internal dissension that amounted to civil war on at least three occasions: from 1823 to 1824, again in late 1824, and finally in 1832, this last requiring French troops to restore order while a political settlement was being achieved. Whenever the Turkish adversary relaxed his pressure on the Morea, the Greeks fell to quarreling with each other. When the threat to them became real, they united. And after independence was achieved, the struggle for Greek liberties against Bavarian autocracy continued.

FIRST WAR OF MEHEMET ALI AGAINST THE SULTAN (1831–1832)
Ottoman Empire and Russia vs. Mehemet Ali, Viceroy of Egypt

WAR AIMS: Ali at first desired to add Syria to his *pashalik* (Egypt), and after early successes, he aspired to acquire lands in Asia Minor. The Sultan declared Ali a rebel and sought to suppress the rebellion and preserve the integrity of the Empire. Russia took advantage of the internal disorder to secure whatever advantages she could.

OUTCOME: A Russian fleet anchored at Constantinople, and Russian troops landed on the shores of the Bosporus. This induced Ali and the Sultan to negotiate a settlement favorable to Ali. The Russians, to the alarm of the Powers, negotiated a treaty of peace and alliance with Turkey.

FACTORS FOR PEACE: For the factions in the Empire, it was Russian intervention that sobered them up to the need for peace. Russia had never really become involved in the conflict; her forces simply engaged in an effective display of force.

WAR-ORIENTED STATES: France, Britain, and Austria.

ALLIANCE: The alliance between Russia and the Sultan was one of convenience and required by Turkey in the emergency of 1832, in the face of Ali's successes. There was probably an informal and perhaps secret agreement that foreshadowed the Treaty of Unkiar-Iskelessi, although that is not certain.

THE SETTLEMENT: With France as the mediator, the settlement between Ali (whom France regarded as a protegé) and the Sultan was accomplished through an exchange of letters, personal negotiations, and a firman that proclaimed the settlement to the Empire. The firman of 5 May 1833, to which Ali consented, gave the departments of Syria, Adana, Tarsus, and the districts of Jerusalem and Nauplia to him for his administration and confirmed his rule in Crete and in Egypt.[74] To Ali's son Ibrahim, the Sultan gave the title of Sheikh of Mecca and Djedda. There was to be a general amnesty. The Sultan was also to give Ali his "Imperial benevolence"; and Ali and Ibrahim were to keep the peace,

---

74 de Testa, Ignaz, *Recueil des Traités de la Porte Ottomane* (Paris: Amyot, 1865), Vol. 2, p. 378. See pp. 354 ff. for other documents relating to the settlement.

pray for the Sultan, and proclaim his sovereignty throughout their departments.

By the terms of the Treaty of Unkiar-Iskelessi of 8 July 1833, Russia and Turkey agreed to consult with each other on all matters that affected their peace, security, and tranquillity, to prepare themselves for mutual aid, and to furnish such aid as was necessary.[75] Russia explicitly promised to provide land and sea forces, as did Turkey; and while the obligation to furnish aid appeared mutual, a secret article provided that as a Russian demand for aid might embarrass Turkey, Russia would not make such a demand. In consideration of Russia's forbearing to exercise this right, Turkey promised to close the Dardanelles and not permit any warships to enter under any pretexts.

The alliance was to last 8 years. Specified treaties were to remain in force.

COMMENTS: The Powers were displeased with this Treaty, and France dispatched a note to Russia (October 1833) declaring that if Russia were to intervene in the Ottoman Empire, France would be free to adopt whatever policies the circumstances seemed to require, just as if the Treaty did not exist. Russia replied that the Treaty was purely defensive, and she intended, in any case, to ignore the French note. The whole affair left everyone dissatisfied (except the Russians), and within 6 years a new crisis erupted.

SECOND WAR OF MEHEMET ALI AGAINST THE SULTAN (1839–1841)
Ali vs. Ottoman Empire, Britain, Austria, Prussia, and Russia

WAR AIMS: Unhappy with the internal settlement of 1833, the Sultan renewed the war against Ali to settle old scores and to ensure more centralized control of the Empire. Ali sought to defend himself; and having done so very successfully, he then embarked upon an offensive war to aggrandize himself and his son. The Powers (except France, who favored Ali) wanted to stop the Pasha. But Britain also wanted to preserve the integrity of the Ottoman Empire, particularly against the Russians, and aimed to nullify the Treaty of Unkiar-Iskelessi. The Tzar hoped to divide France from Britain and to isolate what he still regarded as "revolutionary France"; and hence he agreed to joint action against Ali. (Britain feared that France and Russia, by espousing the side of their respective allies, would effectively partition the Empire between them.) Austria and Prussia also wanted to maintain the balance of power in the Near East and feared Russian intentions in Turkey.

OUTCOME: The Powers compelled Ali to accept a settlement by a show of force. In Syria, naval and land forces were deployed. War between France and England was narrowly averted.

75 Martens, *op. cit.,* Vol. 11, pp. 655–61.

ALLIANCES: A Conference of Ambassadors of the Great Powers opened in Vienna in 1839. The Powers dispatched a letter to the Porte on 27 July, informing the Sultan of their intention to intervene.[76] A series of talks was held in London in the fall. The end result was the Quadruple Treaty of London for the Pacification of the Levant, signed on 15 July 1840, by Austria, Britain, Prussia, and Turkey.[77] According to its terms, the signatories were to submit an "arrangement" to Ali; and if he refused to accept it, they would concert moves to put it into effect by force. If Ali moved on Constantinople, the Powers agreed to defend the capital and the Straits. A reserve Protocol declared that because the distances involved were so great the Powers would begin to make preparations for interdicting Ali's supplies between Egypt and Syria and for sending troops to Turkey.

The arrangement required Ali to evacuate Arabia, Candia, Adana, and other areas outside Egypt and Acre and Syria within 10 days. The Sultan would recognize the right of Ali and his heirs to administer Egypt in perpetuity and the right of Ali to administer Acre and Syria during his lifetime. If within 10 days Ali had not withdrawn his troops, the offer respecting Acre and Syria would be withdrawn. If within another period of 10 days, Ali had not accepted the arrangement, the Sultan would withdraw all offers and would be free to do whatever his interests dictated. The Sultan agreed also to close the Straits to all foreign warships, and the four Powers agreed to respect this "law."

Ali did not accept the arrangement, and the Powers concerted their deployment of forces on and off the coast of Syria in December, 1840.

MILITARY SETTLEMENT: The firmans of 23 May 1841, accepted by Ali in June, contained the terms for the settlement of the internal war.[78] Ali was required to withdraw his troops from all departments outside Egypt. He was permitted to have an army of 18,000 men, whose numbers could be increased in time of war, according to the advice of the Sultan. Each year, Ali was to send 400 troops to Constantinople for the service of the Sultan. Egypt's forces were to have the same insignia and flags as the Ottoman armies. Ali could appoint officers to ranks up to Colonel; but above that rank, the Sultan's permission was required. Egypt could build no warships without authorization from the Sultan.

POLITICAL SETTLEMENT: Egypt was confirmed to Ali and his heirs for purposes of administration. The Imperial reforming decree affecting the rights of persons, their goods, and their honor was to be executed in Egypt, together with other laws of the Empire. Taxes were to be collected

---

76 de Testa, *op. cit.,* Vol. 2, pp. 417 f.

77 Martens, *Nouveau Recueil Général de Traités* (Göttingen: Librairie de Dieterich, 1843), Vol. 1, pp. 156 ff.

78 Noradounghian, Gabriel, *Recueil d'actes Internationaux de l'Empire Ottoman* (Paris: Librairie Cotillon, 1900), Vol. 2, pp. 335–8.

in the name of the Sultan. Ali was to pay the Sultan an annual tribute and agreed to conform to the Sultan's regulations in the minting of money.

On 13 July 1841, a Convention on the Straits was concluded at London and signed by Austria, Britain, Prussia, Russia, and Turkey.[79] France was invited to accede, and did so. The Convention embodied the rule of the Quadruple Treaty: Turkey would permit no foreign warships in the Straits as long as Turkey was at peace, except for light warships in the service of friendly legations. Turkey would bring the Convention to the attention of all states with whom she had friendly relations and invite such states to accede.

RUSSO-TURKISH WAR OF 1877–1878

Empire vs. Montenegro, Roumanian rebels,

Serbian rebels, Bulgarian rebels, and Russia

WAR AIMS: The Sultan sought to preserve the integrity of the Empire and defend it against Russian encroachments. He sought also to end Russian intervention in the Balkans. Russia wanted Turkish territory and influence among the Slavs of Southeastern Europe. The Serbs, Bulgarians, and Roumanians wanted complete independence (a transformation of their status as subjects of their Turkish suzerain). Montenegro was *de facto* independent but not *de jure* independent, and the Turkish Army occupied a portion of Montenegrin territory throughout the war. Her leaders wanted complete independence.

OUTCOME: Serbia, Montenegro, and Roumania achieved independence. Bulgaria became an autonomous principality, tributary to the Sultan. Russia made some small territorial gains. The diplomatic intervention of the Great Powers induced Russia to renegotiate the Peace Treaty of San Stefano (3 March 1878) at the Congress of Berlin (June–July 1878) and to accept the settlement of the Treaty of Berlin (13 July 1878) which, *inter alia,* reduced the size of "San Stefano" Bulgaria and created another autonomous principality, Eastern Rumelia, tributary to the Sultan.

FACTORS FOR PEACE: The Turkish armies were defeated in the Balkans, and the Sultan feared the Russians would capture Constantinople. The Russians were willing to achieve their goals by negotiations rather than fighting, however. The rebel national groups essentially achieved their aims, viz., Turkish recognition of their independence.

WAR-ORIENTED STATES: Britain, France, Germany, Italy, Austria-Hungary, and Greece.

ALLIANCES: 1. In April 1878, Russia and Roumania concluded a convention according to which Roumania permitted Russia to move her troops into Roumania in order to move against Turkey. This conven-

79 Martens, *Nouveau Recueil Général, op. cit.,* Vol. 2, pp. 128–30.

tion occasioned the Turkish declaration of war against Russia on 24 April and was followed by the Roumanian declaration of independence in May and a declaration of war. Montenegro had been at war with Turkey since 1876. Serbia declared war against Turkey in December, 1877.[80] The alliance functioned through *ad hoc* military agreements. Russia's allies provided substantial support for her offensives. Without the allies, it is questionable whether Russia would have penetrated Turkish defenses.

2. On the eve of the Congress of Berlin, Britain and Austria concluded a working arrangement respecting their policies at the Congress; and Britain and Turkey signed an alliance agreement on 4 June 1878.[81] In it, Britain undertook to defend Turkey by force of arms if Russia retained Ardahan, Batum, and Kars and if she made any attempt to take possession of additional Turkish territory. The Sultan promised to introduce reforms for the protection of the Christian subjects of Turkey and transferred the island of Cyprus to Britain for occupation and administration, in order that Britain might better fulfill the terms of the alliance. An Annex to the agreement defined the conditions of the British occupation of Cyprus.

THE SETTLEMENT: First Phase: the Peace of San Stefano.

PRELIMINARIES: At the end of January, 1878, the Turks asked for terms. Russia required the Turks to accept a number of conditions before agreeing to an armistice.[82] The terms included recognition of the independence of Roumania, Serbia, and Montenegro, with a rectification of their frontiers; creation of an autonomous Bulgaria, with a Christian governor, tributary to the Porte, the boundaries of the new Bulgaria being coextensive with areas containing Bulgarian-speaking peoples; compensation to Russia for losses and costs of the war; safeguarding of the rights of Russia in the Straits; and guarantees for autonomous administrations in Bosnia and Herzegovina. The Sultan accepted the terms.

MILITARY SETTLEMENT: The Convention of Adrianople, 31 January 1878, established a cease-fire for the duration of peace negotiations.[83] Restitution was to be given for any violations of the terms of the Convention. Russia, Serbia, Roumania, and Turkey were bound by its terms; and Russia agreed to recommend a cessation of hostilities to the King of Montenegro. A demarcation line between the forces of the belligerents was specified, with a neutral zone on each side of it. Boundary commis-

---

80 For documents relating to efforts to settle the earlier war between Serbia and Turkey, which ended in February, 1877, see Martens, *ibid.*, 2° Série, Vol. 3, pp. 32 f., 85–168, 171–6. The Russo-Roumanian Convention of 1878 is on pp. 182–8.

81 *Ibid.*, pp. 272–5.

82 *Ibid.*, pp. 237–41.

83 *Ibid.*, pp. 241–4.

sions for Montenegro and Novi-Bazar were established (with a Russian delegate on each). Withdrawal times and routes were also specified. Turkey was to raise her blockade of ports on the Black Sea. Provisions were also contained in the Convention for the care of the wounded and for the protection of public and private property. Forts on the Danube and in the new states were to be razed.

POLITICAL SETTLEMENT: The Preliminary Peace Treaty of San Stefano, 3 March 1878:[84] The frontier between Turkey and Russia was described; Russia acquired the Dodrudja and, in Asia, took Ardahan, Kars, and Batum. Russian troops were to evacuate Armenia, which was restored to the Porte's control. The Bosporus and the Dardanelles were declared open in war and peace to the merchant ships of neutral states arriving and leaving Russian ports. Within 3 months of the conclusion of the Definitive Treaty, Russian troops were to be evacuated from the European provinces of Turkey (except Bulgaria) through ports on the Black Sea and the Sea of Marmora. In Asia, Russian troops would be evacuated through Trebizond within 6 months. Administration of occupied territories was to remain the same until Russian troops were evacuated. (It should be emphasized that none of these steps were to be taken until a definitive treaty was signed. The Treaty of San Stefano was a preliminary treaty.) The parties were also to begin to exchange prisoners of war after ratification of the definitive treaty.

Turkey recognized the independence of Montenegro, Serbia, and Roumania, and the autonomous but tributary status of Bulgaria. For each state, there were extensive provisions detailing frontiers: Montenegro was trebled in size, Serbia also gained territory, and Bulgaria was a quite extensive state with Black Sea and Aegean ports and frontage on the Danube. For each state, there were also provisions protecting the rights of persons to travel and trade. Russia was given the right to assist the boundary commissions or arbitrate disputes between the new states and Turkey. The internal administration of Bulgaria was the subject of several clauses, and Russia was given the right to supervise Bulgaria's internal affairs for two years. Bulgaria was also to have a national militia and a Christian Prince elected by the people. The Bulgarian tribute to the Porte was to be fixed by an agreement between Turkey, Russia, and others. Disposition or alienation of property was also provided for; and Turkey's limited rights in Bulgaria were described and guaranteed.

Bosnia and Herzegovina, under Christian governors, were declared autonomous principalities the administration of which could be modified by Russia, Turkey, and Austria.

The rights of subjects of all the parties to expatriate themselves, to move, to dispose of their property, to travel, and to trade were guaran-

84 *Ibid.,* pp. 246–56.

teed. There was also to be an amnesty for all persons. The treaties of commerce of the prewar period were declared in force.

The losses of Russia were placed at 1.4 billion roubles. As part payment of the indemnity, Russia would take the provinces of Ardahan, Batum, Bayazid, and Kars. These territories being valued at only 1.1 billion roubles, Turkey was to arrange a mode of payment of the balance to Russia.

THE SETTLEMENT: The Second Phase: the Congress of Berlin and after.

PRELIMINARIES: In February, 1878, Britain sent a fleet to Constantinople to remind the Russians that British interests in the Ottoman Empire must be served. Greece, Roumania, and Serbia also objected to the San Stefano settlement, particularly the size of the new Bulgaria. The Powers generally felt that Bulgaria would be a Russian client state. Count Andrassy of Austria urged that the Treaty of San Stefano be renegotiated at a congress of the Great Powers. Russia acquiesced because of these pressures and the threat of war with Britain and Austria. Berlin was chosen as the site of the congress because it appeared that Germany was disinterested, that Bismarck was a genuine "honest broker."

POLITICAL SETTLEMENT: The Treaty of Berlin embodied a definitive political settlement for the Balkans.[85] Yet, it was still preliminary in that it did not restore peace between Russia and Turkey. That was not accomplished until 27 January 1879, in the Treaty of Constantinople.

Only the northern third of the "San Stefano" Bulgaria remained. The new Bulgaria was bounded by Serbia, the Danube, the Black Sea, and the new province of Eastern Rumelia on the south. Macedonia was returned to Turkish rule. The independence of Serbia, Montenegro, and Roumania was again confirmed; and all gained some territory. Both Bulgaria and Rumelia were to have Christian governments and remain tributary to the Porte. For all the Balkan states, the Treaty specified the new frontiers and established Bulgarian and Roumanian boundary commissions composed of delegates of the signatories. The new states were also enjoined to respect the religious and cultural rights of their citizens. Bosnia and Herzegovina were to be occupied and administered by Austria-Hungary. Turkey would continue to administer the Sanjak of Novi-Bazar, although Austria had the right to maintain roads and a garrison in the old vilayet of Bosnia. The settlements could hardly be termed felicitous, however. Roumania did not obtain Bessarabia with its many Roumanian inhabitants; nor did Greece obtain Crete or Epirus. (In 1881, after negotiations with Turkey, mediated by the Powers, Greece did get Thessaly.) Austria now controlled the fate of Serbs in Bosnia and Herzegovina, which frustrated Serbia's ambitions in the Balkans.

85 Protocols of the Congress of Berlin appear in *ibid.*, pp. 276–448. The Treaty is on pp. 449–66.

With respect to Bulgaria, an Imperial Russian Commission was authorized to direct a provisional administration until the organic law was adopted. The consuls of the Powers would assist in this temporary administration, which was to last no longer than 9 months from ratification of the Treaty. An Assembly of Notables was to be convened immediately at Tirnovo to formulate the organic law. When this was accomplished a Prince of Bulgaria would be elected by the Bulgarian people and confirmed by the Porte. Then Bulgaria would become fully autonomous. The tribute payable to the Porte was to be determined by the Powers. There was to be no Turkish army in Bulgaria, and forts were to be demolished. Treaties in force between Turkey and the Powers applied to Bulgaria and could not be changed without their consent. Privileges of foreign merchants and travelers were to be recognized and protected. Muslims who left Bulgaria were permitted to have their fixed property protected and administered by third parties.

In the case of Eastern Rumelia, Turkey would provide forces for defense and construct forts on its frontiers, although a local militia was to maintain internal order. The governor was to be appointed by the Sultan with the consent of the Powers. A European Commission would elaborate a constitution, which would be proclaimed by the Sultan. A Great Power Commission (with Turkey's participation) would administer the finances of the province-state. All treaties in force between Turkey and the Powers were also in force in Rumelia. Occupation of the state (and Bulgaria) by Russian troops was limited to 9 months.

The Montenegro terms of the Treaty related mainly to territorial adjustments and dealt with the evacuation of troops and the movement of civilians (Muslims who might want to leave Montenegro and Montenegrins in Turkey). A portion of the Turkish public debt was to be assessed against Montenegro in proportion to the territory she had acquired. Montenegro was to obtain Antivari on the Adriatic and free navigation on the Bojana River, on the banks of which no forts were to be constructed except to protect Scutari. The waters around Antivari were prohibited to the warships of all nations, and forts in the vicinity were to be demolished. Austria was given the authority to provide maritime and sanitary police and the right to build a railroad.

In the case of Serbia, all prewar treaties were to remain in force until renegotiated. Serbia and Austria would directly negotiate a project for the construction of a railroad in Serbian territories. Serbian subjects in Turkey were to be protected by international law until an agreement could be reached. Evacuations of Turkish forces from Serbia (and Serb forces from Turkey) were to be completed within 15 days after ratification of the Treaty.

With respect to Roumania, it was agreed that the question of fishing rights in the Black Sea was to be submitted to the European Commission of the Danube for arbitration. The rights of Roumanian subjects in Turkey were guaranteed. The regime of the Danube was modified in some detail (Roumania, moreover, was to be a member of this Commission). Russia also obtained Bessarabia from Roumania.

In Asia, the terms of the San Stefano Treaty were generally duplicated. Turkey also promised religious liberty for all her subjects and undertook to care for the needs of the Armenians and provide them with security against the Kurds and Circassians. In these matters, the Porte was to report regularly to the Powers. There was to be no change in the status of the Holy Places.

In the Treaty of Peace of Constantinople (January, 1879), Turkey and Russia recognized the settlement of Berlin and agreed upon the size of the indemnity payable to Russia and other amounts payable to Russian citizens.[86] Turkish subjects who remained in areas ceded to Russia for more than 3 years were to become Russian subjects. An amnesty was declared. There were no additional treaties of peace with the states of the Balkans.

COMMENTS: C. J. H. Hayes commented that the Berlin settlement flouted the nationality principle and "drove the Balkan peoples mad. . . . Whatever satisfaction is afforded by the reflection that at any rate the Congress of Berlin preserved peace among the great powers in a time of severe crisis, must be qualified by the further reflection that the Ottoman Empire was made to pay—and to pay dearly—for the peace. Altogether, to maintain a 'balance of power' between 'hostile' Russia and 'friendly' Austria and Britain, the empire was shorn of more than half of its European area and population and left in a desperate condition."[87]

KOREAN WAR (1950–1953)

Democratic Republic of Korea (North Korea) and China vs. Republic of Korea (South Korea) and United Nations Command (United States, Britain, Australia, Belgium, Canada, Colombia, Ethiopia, Greece, Luxembourg, Netherlands, New Zealand, Philippines, Thailand, and Turkey)

WAR AIMS: North Korea sought the unification of Korea. South Korea (ROK) first fought to defend itself. When, with the help of U.N. forces, the North Korean forces were driven from the South in the fall of 1950, Seoul's aims escalated to the unification of Korea by force. China's aim was defensive, namely, to insure that U.S. forces or bases were not established north of the 38th parallel. The United States sought to preserve the balance of power in East Asia, her policymakers assuming that a victory for North Korea would create a communist threat to Japan. The

86 *Ibid.*, pp. 468–70.
87 Hayes, C. J. H., *A Generation of Materialism, 1871–1900* (New York: Harper & Row, 1941), p. 34.

U.S. and the other U.N. members that sent units, mainly small, to Korea were also interested in supporting the principle of collective security.

OUTCOME: As U.S.–ROK forces drove to the Yalu River, China intervened and drove the allies back across the 38th parallel. After a U.N. advance in the late winter and spring of 1951, the CPR launched additional assaults. The U.N. defense line held, however, and the Chinese not only suffered very heavy casualties, but were slowly pushed back to a line that ran athwart the 38th parallel. There, the fighting continued until the cease-fire in July, 1953.

FACTORS FOR PEACE: For the Communist forces, the costs of the war were high; and China's leaders wanted to embark upon reconstruction at home. In the U.S., discontent was rife. It is not impossible that the threats by the Eisenhower Administration to bomb China in the event her leaders insisted on continuing the war had some effect in persuading them to liquidate their commitment to North Korea.

WAR-ORIENTED STATES: Soviet Union, Japan, Britain, and the NATO allies of the U.S.

ALLIANCES: We know virtually nothing of the North Korean–China alliance or of the Soviet–North Korean alliance. Both China and the Soviets supported the claims and aspirations of the North Koreans. After the Chinese had intervened, they assumed almost complete control of combat operations. Of the problems to which this gave rise, we know little.

The agreements between South Korea, the U.N., and the states contributing to the war were of an *ad hoc* military nature[88] until late in the war, when the U.S. and the ROK negotiated a mutual defense treaty, which came into force in 1954.[89]

THE SETTLEMENT: PRELIMINARIES: There was a unilateral cease-fire on the part of the ROK and the U.N. Command in late 1951, after the preliminary talks to arrange a cease-fire at Kaesong had opened and had subsequently moved to Panmunjom. The unilateral truce did not induce the Communist forces to agree to proposals for a permanent cease-fire, and a war of attrition continued together with negotiations from 1951 to the signing of the Armistice Agreement in July, 1953. These negotiations had their interesting aspects even though they were protracted and often fruitless.

The true preliminary negotiations came after the failure of the Chinese offensives of early 1951 with "feeler" remarks by Soviet spokesmen and Trygve Lie's statement that the U.S. had the right to conclude a

88 See Goodrich, L. M., *Korea: A Study of U.S. Policy in the United Nations* (New York: Council on Foreign Relations, 1956), pp. 102 ff.

89 Curl, P. V., *Documents on American Foreign Relations: 1953* (New York: Harper, 1954), pp. 312–3.

cease-fire without further action by the U.N. The U.N. Commander broadcast an invitation to talks, which the enemy accepted, proposing to meet on a vessel in Wonsan harbor. The U.N. Command countered with the suggestion that the meetings be held at Kaesong in the no-man's land between the forces of the adversaries. This was accepted.

MILITARY SETTLEMENT: The belligerents signed the Armistice Agreement on 27 July 1953.[90] A demarcation line, at the line of contact of the belligerents, was adopted. Each side was to withdraw 2 kms. from this line. Subsequent provisions provided for civil administration in this zone. No hostile acts were to be committed in it, and no one was permitted to cross the demarcation line without the permission of the military commanders of the parties.

The cease-fire was to take effect within 12 hours of the signing of the Agreement, withdrawals within 72 hours. And within 10 days, the troops of the adversaries were to withdraw to rear areas.

The parties were to cease reinforcing and resupplying their armies in Korea, although replacement of damaged or worn-out weapons was authorized, as was the rotation of military personnel (35,000 per month) through designated ports.

A Military Armistice Commission (MAC) composed of representatives of the U.N. Command and the Communist forces was established to supervise implementation of the truce and to settle problems and alleged violations as they arose. A Neutral Nations Supervisory Commission (NNSC), with representatives of Sweden, Switzerland, Poland, and Czechoslovakia, was also established, primarily to supervise rotation of personnel and replacement of war matériel. Both the MAC and the NNSC were to have mobile inspection teams to assist them in their functions.

The military commanders agreed that within three months of the truce they would recommend that a political conference be scheduled to discuss the withdrawal of forces from Korea and the peaceful settlement of the Korean question.

Prisoner of war provisions were detailed. This problem had taken up a great deal of the negotiators' time and had deadlocked the conference. The U.N. Command refused to force repatriation of prisoners who refused to be repatriated. The Communist Command demanded repatriation of all prisoners, irrespective of their personal desires. The compromise reached was closer to the position of the U.N. Command. Within 60 days all prisoners of war and civilian internees were to be repatriated if

90 Great Britain, Foreign Office, *Special Report of the Unified Command on the Korean Armistice Agreement,* Command Doc. No. 8938 (London: Her Majesty's Stationery Office, 1953), pp. 14–33. For other documents supplementary to the settlement, see Folliot, Denise, *Documents on International Affairs, 1953* (London: Oxford University Press, 1956), pp. 357 ff.

they so desired. All others were to be released to a Neutral Nations Repatriation Commission (staffed by the member-states of the NNSC and joined by Indian representatives) which would also take over POW installations. For a period of time, visitation rights were granted to the parties for their nationals in the compounds. After the visitation period ended, those men who had not asked to be repatriated were to become civilians (within 180 days). In January, 1954, when the time for final disposition came, 14,000 Chinese and 7,500 Koreans elected to remain in South Korea (or to move to Taiwan). The NNRL was dissolved in February, 1954.

Finally, civilians who had lived north (or south) of the demarcation line on 24 June 1950 were to be permitted to move south (or north) of that line if they desired. Another committee was established to facilitate civilian movement.

POLITICAL SETTLEMENT:[91] In early August, 1953, the 16 states that had participated in the war under the aegis of the U.N. issued a guarantee of the integrity of the ROK and promised to come to its aid if it were again attacked from the North. In late August, the U.N. General Assembly approved the Armistice Agreement; and after much debate over who might participate in a political conference, decided that all states that had contributed forces could do so—and that the Soviet Union might participate "if the other side desires it." Meetings to plan for the political conference lasted from October through December, but they were broken off by the U.S. In February, 1954, the Big Four agreed at Berlin to take up the matter of Korea at the Geneva Conference in April, 1954. That conference remained deadlocked over the question of elections within Korea and was declared at an end by the U.N. allies. To date, there has been no political settlement of the Korean question.

LAOTIAN CIVIL WAR (1955–1962)

Centrist faction of Souvanna Phouma and United States (to 1960) vs. Pathet Lao, Democratic Republic of Vietnam (DRVN), China, and U.S.S.R. (1960–61) vs. Right-wing faction of Boun Oum (from 1960) and the U.S. (1960–61)

WAR AIMS: Each of the factions wanted to govern Laos. The DRVN favored the faction that would cooperate with its designs against the Republic of Vietnam, and DRVN leaders may also have had pan-Indochinese aspirations (i.e., they may have wanted eventually to incorporate Laos in an Indochinese state led by the DRVN). The U.S. sought to prevent the victory of the Pathet Lao, which would have made the defense of South Vietnam, Cambodia, and Thailand more difficult. China and the Soviet Union provided no combat troops, although Chinese

---

91 Rees, David, *Korea: The Limited War* (New York: St. Martens Press, 1964), pp. 435 ff. Randle, R. F., *Geneva, 1954: The Settlement of the Indochinese War* (Princeton: Princeton University Press, 1969), pp. 21–2, 157–68.

technicians and maintenance personnel were reported to be in Laos. China wanted to help the insurgent Pathet Lao, probably because their victory would have caused a decline in U.S. prestige in Asia, prevented the establishment of American bases in Laos, and offered the prospect of eliminating U.S. influence in Southeast Asia. The Soviets probably had similar reasons for helping the Pathet Lao; but they were by 1960 in competition with Peking for influence among the Communist parties of Asia and did not want to be outdone by China in supporting the left-wing Laotian insurgents. However, Souvanna Phouma was wholly acceptable to Moscow.

OUTCOME: The war seemed to have prospects of escalating further, which neither the Soviets, nor the Americans, nor most Asians desired. There was a composition and settlement (of sorts) reached by the factions, and an agreement neutralizing Laos was reached in July, 1962.

WAR-ORIENTED ACTORS: Britain and France; the regional states of Cambodia, the RVN, Thailand, Burma and India; and the states that had served on the International Supervisory Commission (ISC) for Laos: Canada, Poland, and India. These states together with the belligerent factions and the supporting powers (China, the U.S., and the Soviet Union) attended the Geneva Conference on the Settlement of the Laotian Question, 1961–1962. Also interested in the outcome of the war and negotiations were Australia, New Zealand, Indonesia, and the U.N.

FACTORS FOR PEACE: There was the fear on the part of the powers that the war would escalate. The near military collapse of the Boun Oum faction and the finding of a suitable modus vivendi, and possibly the hope that the arrangement would permit further gains for each in the postwar period, induced the factions to move toward peace. There was also the feeling among the powers that the settlement was acceptable and would enable each to pursue its goals afterwards.

ALLIANCES: Laos had SEATO "protection" by the SEATO Protocol (September, 1954) and had been given U.S. aid after 1955.[92] When the U.S. (although we should perhaps say the Department of Defense) became disenchanted with Souvanna Phouma and found a faction more to its liking after the Boun Oum-Phoumi Nosavan coup (1960), arrangements for aid to the latter were worked out on an informal, *ad hoc* basis. We know little of the content of the "alliance" between the Pathet Lao and the DRVN; but DRVN troops moved freely into and out of Pathet Lao-held areas after 1955 and often participated in attacks against Government points. Chances are that the arrangements among the Pathet Lao, China, the Soviet Union, and the DRVN were of an informal kind. Between 1955 and 1960 the Pathet Lao was in competition and conflict

---

92 Curl, P. V., *Documents on American Foreign Relations, 1954* (New York: Harper & Row, 1955), pp. 319–22.

with the Royal Laotian Government (Souvanna Phouma). After the attacks by the Boun Oum faction, the Pathet Lao and Souvanna allied to resist the right-wing faction.

THE SETTLEMENT: PRELIMINARIES:[93] In an exchange of messages in December, 1960, Britain and the Soviet Union (as Co-Chairman of the Geneva Conference on Indochina of 1954) called for a reactivation of the ISC for Laos and a reconvening of the Conference. In January, 1961, Cambodia proposed a 14-nation peace conference of 6 Western, 4 Communist, and 3 non-aligned states and Laos. China, the DRVN, and the Soviet Union had earlier called for a peace conference, but this was the first time that an acceptable distribution of invitees had been proposed. The U.S. demanded a cease-fire before it was willing to agree to the Cambodian proposals. When this was forthcoming, the ISC was reconvened (in part, to supervise the cease-fire in Laos): and the conference began in May, 1961. The opening was delayed by allegations that the cease-fire was not effective and by a dispute over the representation of the Laotian factions.

Negotiations proceeded on and off from May, 1961, until July, 1962. It was eventually agreed that a "political settlement" of the questions raised by the war, and over which the war had been fought, was an "internal" matter that had to be resolved by the factions themselves. This agreement, in principle, was made in June, 1961, and proclaimed in a document called the Zurich Communiqué.[94] Applying those principles, however, created problems that prevented an agreement among the factions and delayed the settlement for over a year. In July, 1962, a delegation of the Government of National Unity of Laos finally attended the Geneva Conference. Before that time, Boun Oum was not represented. (After June, 1961, the Pathet Lao and the Royal Laotian Government were both represented.) The Zurich communiqué called for internal and external policies that were later accepted by the factions and incorporated in the settlement documents. On 9 July 1962, the Royal Government indicated that there was agreement among the factions on an eight-point program: 1. application of the Five Principles of Peaceful Coexistence. 2. Insuring respect for the sovereignty and territorial integrity of Laos. 3. Refraining from the use of force in dealing with other countries and not interfering in their internal affairs. 4. Refusal to participate in any military alliance or to accept the protection of SEATO. 5. Prohibiting foreign interference in Laos. 6. Bringing about the withdrawal of foreign troops. 7. Accepting only unconditioned foreign aid. 8. Respecting all treaties, including those soon to be concluded among the

---

93 Modelski, *op. cit.*, pp. 6 f.

94 Great Britain, Foreign Office, *International Conference on the Settlement of the Laotian Question,* Laos No. 1 (1962), Command Doc. No. 1828 (London: Her Majesty's Stationery Office, 1962), pp. 13–5.

Powers at Geneva. The factions also agreed upon the composition of a coalition Government of National Unity, composed of representatives of the three factions, each holding specified portfolios in the coalition.[95]

The Conference produced two documents: a Declaration on the Neutrality of Laos, signed by Burma, Cambodia, China, the DRVN, France, India, Poland, the RVN, Thailand, the U.S.S.R., Britain, and the U.S.[96] and a Protocol to the Declaration of Neutrality, signed by Laos and the conference states.[97]

MILITARY SETTLEMENT: The signatories, noting the Laotian Statements of 9 July 1962, promised not to introduce troops or other military personnel into Laos or to seek Laos' adherence to any military alliance. They further promised to refrain from establishing bases in Laos and to respect the Laotian Government's wish not to recognize the protection of SEATO. The Protocol provided, in somewhat more detail, for the withdrawal of foreign forces from Laos under the supervision of a reactivated ISC. Emplacement of ISC inspection teams was to be made in consultation with the Laotian Government, as was the specification of withdrawal routes. Introduction of war matériel, except such as might be necessary for the defense of Laos, was prohibited. Within 30 days, prisoners, both civilian and military, were to be released. French installations in Laos were to be turned over to the Royal Government, and French troops were also to withdraw, except for training cadres the Laotians might want to remain behind. Continued supervision of the 1961 cease-fire was assigned to the ISC in conjunction with the Laotian Government. The ISC was to report to the Co-Chairman and generally see to it that the terms of the Declaration and Protocol were carried out. Laos would provide the ISC with transportation and communications facilities. The signatories agreed to bear the operating costs of the ISC according to a prescribed formula.

POLITICAL SETTLEMENT: The signatories agreed to respect the sovereignty, independence, neutrality, unity, and territorial integrity of Laos. They agreed to refrain from committing a series of acts, including the resort to force, that might impair the peace of Laos, and from using Laotian territory to interfere in the internal affairs of other states. The parties would appeal to other (nonsignatory) states to recognize the Declaration and Protocol. In the event of a violation, they would consult with the Laotian Government in order to consider measures to insure observance of their agreements.

COMMENTS: Owing to continued instability in the area, many terms of the Declaration were rendered meaningless by the activity of the DRVN and the U.S. in Laos and by the intensification of the war in Vietnam.

95 *Ibid.*, pp. 9–10.
96 *Ibid.*, pp. 15–8.
97 *Ibid.*, pp. 19–24.

Within a year, the coalition government had collapsed and the Pathet Lao representatives withdrew to the North to the Pathet Lao-held areas, which had never been effectively integrated into the areas under the exclusive jurisdiction of the Government.

Our examples have illustrated the several different modes of settlement of complex internal wars. In the Dutch revolt, the rebels' allies (England and France) disengaged and made peace with Spain; some years later, the factions reached a settlement. Russia made peace with Turkey about a year before the settlement of the Greek Revolt began to take shape under the auspices of the Great Powers (of which Russia was a very interested member). In the War of the Polish Succession, on the other hand, the belligerents attempted to achieve an overall settlement of the war issues for all parties, although the Polish factions played almost no part in this process. Indeed, the war had basically the form of a complex external war, one that was occasioned by the question of the succession to the Polish Crown, in which the Poles had what to us seems curiously little to say. The military settlement of the Korean War also encompassed all the actively belligerent states and factions, as did the settlement of the Russo-Turkish War.[98] We had no examples in this chapter of wars in which the factions made peace, but the state-allies remained at war.[99]

98 In the Thirty Years' War (infra, pp. 379–92), the parties were so numerous and the issues so intermingled that an over-all peace settlement was the only way adequately to end the war. The Peace of Prague (1635) was a settlement for the war internal to the Empire, but it left the intervenor powers unsatisfied; and hence, the war continued. The settlement of 1621, after the collapse of the Bohemian-Palatinate rebel forces, was a much less satisfactory arrangement, prompting the interventions in Germany that so prolonged the war. In the War of the Spanish Succession (pp. 357–66), Cologne and Bavaria, states of the Empire, remained in their alliance with France and at war with the Emperor, even after the settlement of Utrecht. The Peace of Rastadt did resolve many of the internal and external war issues and could also be regarded as an over-all settlement.

99 The Peace of Prague, referred to in the preceding note, is such an example, however temporary it was. In the War of the Austrian Succession (infra, pp. 366–74), the internal aspects of the war were resolved by 1745, after which the conflict was a pure external war that was settled in the multilateral peace congress at Aix-la-Chapelle. In the War of the Three Henries (1585–98), the last of the Huguenot Wars, a war that merged into the history of the Dutch Revolt when hostilities between Spain and France broke out in 1595, Spain allied with Guise and the Catholic League in order to insure the Bourbon Succession and eliminate heresy in France. After the death of Henry III in 1589, there were several claimants to the throne; but the central conflict of the internal war was between Henry of Navarre (later, Henry IV) and the Catholic League, supported by Spain. After Henry declared war on Spain in 1595, he secured the Pope's absolution and united France against the foreign

The Wars of Mehemet Ali and the Laotian Civil War showed how peace agreements first made between the warring factions were followed up by actions and agreements on the part of the state-allies or war-oriented states to complete what might properly be called the settlement of a complex internal war. In the Laotian War, the follow-up agreement was a guarantee of the neutrality of Laos by a number of war-oriented states, including the state-allies of the Laotian faction, the DRVN, China, and the U.S. In the First War of Mehemet Ali, after the firman proclaiming the basis for peace within the Ottoman Empire, Russia (the ally of the incumbent faction) reached a formal understanding with the Sultan. In the Second War, Austria, Britain, and Prussia undid this bilateral understanding, substituting for it a multilateral one—after the factions had made peace.[100]

The Dutch, Greek, and American Revolts and the internal wars of the Balkan peoples in the Russo-Turkish War were fought by the insurgents in order to achieve independence. The factions in the Laotian, Korean, and Mehemet Ali Wars fought for control of the polity. In all our examples of wars for independence, the insurgents succeeded; in the wars for control, they failed. While this result was entirely fortuitous (in terms of my selection of the wars for consideration), it does to some extent demonstrate that if the incumbents cannot completely suppress the insurgents in a war for control of the polity or if the insurgents succeed in a war for independence, negotiations for a settlement will ultimately be necessary. (As we have seen, whenever the rebels fail and are destroyed as an effective political force, there need be no settlement.) The examples also support the general proposition that, irrespective of the insurgent aims in an internal war, support from a state-ally substantially improves the faction's capacity to survive and its chances of success.[101]

---

enemy. By late 1595, he had worked out agreements of pacification with Mayenne and most of the League nobles. Thus, with the exception of Brittany, the factions had resolved their conflict and made peace before the settlement of the external war.

100 We should perhaps note here that, although the peacemakers at the Paris Peace Conference (1919 and after) sought to achieve an over-all settlement of the First World War and its *sequelae* (*infra,* pp. 405–28) they were unable to do so because none of the Russian factions attended the Conference; and indeed, the situation in Russia was so confused that the Allies did not know what leaders to invite or whether any peace agreement would be binding if the faction of the invitees were to lose. In the Seven Years' War (pp. 374–9), for various reasons, the external war (Britain and Portugal vs. France and Spain) was settled by the Peace of Paris (1763). The internal war (internal to the Holy Roman Empire) was settled through separate negotiations at Hubertusberg two weeks later.

101 These statements are further confirmed by the events and outcome of the multilateral wars discussed in Chapter 9.

In the wars for independence summarized here, the leaders of the "new" states of the Balkans (Bulgaria, Roumania, and Serbia) were dissatisfied with the Treaty of Berlin; and in the future, they would seek to nullify or avoid its terms. The Greek rebels were caught up in a civil war among themselves when their independence was finally assured; and their first years of autonomy were hardly happy ones. Thus, in these examples, even though the insurgents had won their independence, they assumed a revisionist attitude toward the settlements, hoping to achieve something more in the postwar period.

In several of the wars in the sample, the insurgent faction itself was divided or had split into two or more political entities. In the Laotian Civil War, there were three more-or-less rival factions (including the incumbent government of Souvanna Phouma). In the Greek Revolt, there were two and sometimes three Greek factions, fighting with each other at times but allied against the incumbent Turkish regime. Religious differences between Roman Catholics and Calvinists, coupled with the successful Spanish military occupation of the Walloon provinces, split the rebels of the Netherlands. Moreover, each province of the United Provinces was internally autonomous and could be considered a division of the rebel faction. Similarly, in the War for American Independence, each of the thirteen colonies was an autonomous state, although the colonies had united in their rebellion against the Crown. Externally, they were regarded as one faction, and the Congress was regarded as both symbolically and functionally the embodiment of the Colonies' unity. In the Russo-Turkish War, Serbia, Bulgaria, and Rumania, tributary to the Porte who was their suzerain, in effect constituted separate factions, cooperating (not quarreling) with their allies Russia and Montenegro in order to obtain Turkish recognition of their independence. In this case, the "factions" of the "insurgent faction" were not rivals.

In situations where one of the factions divides into competing, perhaps warring, groups, the internal war becomes still more complex, often bewilderingly so.[102] This is partly the result of the sheer proliferation of the parties and partly of the fact that intrafaction contests can prevent agreement on the terms of peace and impel the parties to continue or resume hostilities. In considering the bargaining situation at the peace conference and the possible content of a settlement, we must be aware that individual groups within a faction might form alliances with independent states (discussed in Chapter 4).[103] The alliances of the

---

102 See, for example, the complex alliance arrays of German princes in the Thirty Years' War (*infra*, pp. 379–92), or the number of factions in the Russian Civil War (pp. 405–28).

103 Although the Wars of the Spanish (*infra*, pp. 357–66) and Austrian (pp. 366–74) Successions and the Seven Years' War (pp. 374–9) were, in part, wars internal to the Holy Roman Empire—a rather moribund political entity

seven Dutch provinces during the Revolt of the Netherlands were "international alliances" *in micro:* They were formal constitutional arrangements between sovereign entities, whose tempestuous relations repeatedly affected the course and conduct of the war, the decision to make peace, and the content of the Twelve Years' Truce. In the Laotian War, the Pathet Lao and the Royal Laotian Government were adversaries until the appearance in 1960 of the Boun Oum faction, which succeeded in capturing Vientiane. After that event, Souvanna Phouma and the Pathet Lao cooperated in an *ad hoc* alliance of convenience.

Thus, we see the possibility that "internal alliances," i.e., alliances of several factions (or several divisions of factions) will affect, often decisively, the course of an internal war and its settlement.[104] And in the complex internal war, these *internal* alliances will add yet another dimension to an analysis of a peace settlement, the structure of which will have already been shaped and perhaps determined by the character of the state-faction alliances. Thus, in the Dutch, Greek, and American Revolts, the *external* alliances sustained the plural rebel factions and strengthened their bargaining position during peace negotiations. In the Dutch Revolt, the fact that the rebels' state-allies (France and Britain) had made peace with the incumbent (Spain) was an important factor in inducing the Dutch leaders to move toward peace. In these same wars, the relations between the plurality of insurgent factions (whether the Dutch provinces, the states of the new United States, or the two or three Greek insurgent groups) very greatly determined the peace policy of the rebel factions.

---

in the eighteenth century—the analyst can treat the factions of the Empire as independent states for at least one good reason: because they acted as such. Prussia, for example, was constrained very little by the fact that she was a state within the Empire and her King an Elector thereof. Alliances between factions were formed during these wars and during the Thirty Years' War (pp. 379–92), in the settlement of which the Emperor recognized the right of the German states to engage in foreign relations and form alliances as if they were sovereign states.

104 One of the major questions of the Congresses of Westphalia (*infra,* pp. 354–5) was that of "Imperial Affairs," particularly the rights and prerogatives of the German states. Resolution of these matters had to be made a part of the final settlement. In the First World War (pp. 405–28), the Allies had encouraged and supported, in various ways, the nationalities of the multinational Habsburg and Ottoman Empires. The settlement of the war had to address itself to the claims for independence of these groups.

War-Oriented Actors in the Political Environment of War

CHAPTER 6

The Interests of War-Oriented Actors

War-oriented actors are nonbelligerent states and organizations interested in the course and outcome of a war. They often attempt to influence the belligerents during hostilities and subsequent peace negotiations. As defined earlier, there are several kinds of war-oriented actor: the nonbelligerent ally; the great power; states located within the same region as the belligerents (particularly states sharing a common frontier with either belligerent); and international or regional organizations of states whose aims are the preservation of peace, the mediation of disputes, or the economic development of member states.

War orientation means that the actor's policies are framed with reference to the war. The war-oriented state might be primarily interested in supporting one of the belligerents, hoping to fulfill its goals—whatever they may be—through the eventual success of the supported party. This is the case with the nonbelligerent ally: Its support for the belligerent ally could result in victory and therefore in gains for the nonbelligerent. On the other hand, the war-oriented state might pursue policies designed to serve its interests, and its interests alone, without regard to the aims, policies, or survival of either belligerent. This sort of war-oriented actor might seek to keep the war going. Or it could attempt to mediate or favor one side and then the other.[1] Very few generalizations can be made at

---

1 During the Greek Revolt (pp. 222–5), Great Britain and France were war-oriented toward the crisis in the Levant and interested in maintaining a balance

this level of analysis. However, it can probably be safely asserted that the war-oriented international or regional organization will attempt to mediate or otherwise promote a peace settlement. The great power or the regional state may favor one of the belligerents and support peace moves only when the supported state desires them. But either type of war-oriented actor may also pursue a completely independent policy, using its influence either to prolong the war or to end it, depending upon the exigencies of its national interests at the time.

The policies of the war-oriented actor toward the war are conditioned by the following:

1. Its "war" aims.

2. The character of the relationship between the belligerents and the war-oriented actor.

3. The war situation, and consequently the bargaining strength of the belligerents relative to each other and to the war-oriented actors.

The goals of a war-oriented actor, whether for itself alone or for itself through the agency of one of the belligerents, can be classified in the same way as the war aims of the belligerents—hence we also call them the *war aims* of the war-oriented actor. They include dominance, maintenance of the status quo, consolidation of the state, ideological aims, and the acquisition of retributive or opportunity values. In the case of the parties engaged in hostilities, war aims are, of course, achieved by waging war. For the war-oriented actor, however, the war aims (of whatever kind or combination) are achieved by remaining at peace and by maintaining an active interest in the course of the war and the peace negotiations. Such interests in the war may give rise to antagonisms (even to "cold war") between war-oriented actors and may eventually lead to hostilities. Just as incompatible war aims can lead to the disruption of an alliance, incompatibility between the war aims of the belligerents and the war-oriented actors can have a number of important effects, including the

---

of power against an inexorably expansive Russia. They sought also to prevent the partitioning of the Ottoman Empire. These policies their policymakers pursued for the interests of their states alone. But in the face of the obduracy of the Porte and domestic opinion in favor of the Greek insurgents, British and French policies increasingly came to favor the rebels. Thus, the war aims of these states were to be achieved through the support of one faction. In the Last War of the Habsburg-Valois Rivalry (pp. 157–60), Venice was war-oriented; she supported neither party, and her diplomacy was directed toward the goal of preserving her independence over against the rival great powers, France and Spain. And in the Second War over Schleswig-Holstein (pp. 169–71), Russia, Britain, and France supported none of the belligerents but rather pursued policies that would accrue to their benefit. On the other hand, in the Korean War (pp. 233–6), the Soviet Union sought to further its interests by the support of a faction, as did the various allies of the Laotian factions in the Laotian Civil War (pp. 236–40).

dissolution of the alliance between non-belligerents and their belligerent allies or conflict between war-oriented actors themselves. Thus, if war-oriented actors are implicated in a war, we must describe (or isolate) both the war aims of the belligerent and the war aims of the war-oriented actor for itself alone or indirectly for itself through its supported belligerent, determine whether the aims of these parties are incompatible, and then weigh the consequences of incompatibility, if any.[2]

The second factor affecting the policy of the war-oriented actor is the character of the relationship between the relevant parties. Here again it is important to note the type of war-oriented actor: The identity of the actor structures the relationship with the belligerent in certain ways. A *state-great power* relationship or a *faction-great power* relationship will be different from the *state-organization* or *faction-organization* relationship. We must inquire into the relative power positions of the parties in these relationships, the capabilties of each and the influence of each on the policies of the other. The relationship of influence or control must be examined in two ways: First, how much influence does one party have over the other? Or, if one party chose to exert *maximum influence* upon the other party, how much influence could it bring to bear? Second, how much influence does one party *choose* to exert on the other party? The question is important, as an actor often chooses not to exert its maximum capacity to influence.

The policy of the war-oriented actor depends upon both the character of the war and the world political environment of the war. Thus, we ask, Is the party supported by the war-oriented state winning or losing? Is the war stalemated? Are hostilities spreading? Is the war threatening to deny values to the war-oriented actor: values in resources, territory, or influence with other actors? In addition to the issues immediately related to the war then being waged, there is also the political context of the war; and by *political context,* I mean factors both internal and external to the polity of the war-oriented actor (see Figs. 1–1 and 1–5). Thus, domestic political forces might be operative to change the war-oriented policies of the actor, or the constraints of coalition cooperation and policymaking might impinge upon the war-oriented policies of that actor. Other events in the larger context of the whole world arena could be relevant to the war and to the war-oriented actors' relationships with the belligerents or their orientation toward the war. We are at too general a level of analysis, however; and we must first examine the successive types of war-oriented actor and their war aims. Afterwards, we may perhaps make some helpful generalizations about war-oriented actors in the peace-making process.

2 See the discussion in Chapter 4 and in Appendix II.

Great Powers

A great power will not necessarily be a war-oriented actor. But if it were, it would likely be an important one. History has shown this to be so; and it has shown as well that great powers turn out to be war-oriented actors frequently enough to warrant separate consideration in an essay of this sort.[3] In the case of the external war, the war-oriented great power will at least be interested in the war and will frame or modify its policies in order to take advantage of the situation created by it. Thus, policy-makers of a dominant great power, or one seeking to become dominant, might regard the war as helping them achieve their goals.[4] The belligerents (A and B, for example) might have been rivals of the great power. Their involvement in war could enable the great power, G, to pursue policies that in time of peace would have been frustrated or otherwise obstructed by either A or B. In other words, the war between A and B could prevent either state from resisting G's drive for dominance. Even after the war has ended, the belligerents could be in a weakened condition. Anticipating this, the great power may attempt to prolong the war and otherwise interfere with peace talks, thus hoping to create optimum conditions for its policy of dominance at the war's end.[5] Even if A and B were relatively small states, G might nonetheless be interested in the war because of commercial advantages from the sale of weapons or foodstuffs,[6] or because of the added influence gained by G in the region of the

3 In 32 out of the 38 wars summarized in the preceding chapters great powers were war-oriented actors.
4 True of the Ottoman Empire in the Last War of the Habsburg-Valois Rivalry (pp. 157–60), of Germany in the Russo-Finnish War of 1939–40 (pp. 79–81), of France and Sweden in the Thirty Years' War (pp. 379–92) in the years before they became belligerents, and of France (and perhaps Britain) during the Dutch Revolt (pp. 208–14).
5 After the Peace of Prague in 1635 (in the Thirty Years' War: pp. 379–92), France went to war to achieve the aims she had theretofore sought by peaceful means. This action prolonged the war. After the Peace of San Stefano, in the Russo-Turkish War of 1877–8 (pp. 228–33), Austria and Britain indicated that they would interfere with the implementation of the Peace, and perhaps join in the war, unless Russia agreed to convene a general European Congress to revise it.
6 During Denmark's wars in the sixteenth century, Sweden (when a non-belligerent) gathered the commercial advantages in the Baltic resulting from the preoccuption of her rival. On the other hand, we also have situations where commercial losses cause great powers to be war-oriented and pursue active policies relative to the belligerents: for example, Russia in the War for American Independence (pp. 217–22), Britain and the United Provinces during the European War of 1683–1700 (pp. 347–57), and the Dutch (as well as Spain and Portugal) in the Seven Years' War (pp. 374–9).

war, should the neighbors of the belligerents fear that the war might encourage the intervention of a rival of G. The great power striving for dominance would then welcome the opportunity to involve itself in the region, gaining influence against rivals.

In an internal war between factions x and y in state R, the great power seeking dominance might be interested in either protracting or terminating the war, depending upon its relationship with state R and other interested states. Thus, if R were a rival of G, we might expect that G would welcome a war internal to R, as the result would be the weakening of a rival, or at least its preoccupation with domestic rather than external problems.[7] However, if R has had friendly relations with G, and has in fact supported G's policies against a rival third state, G would not welcome the internal war because it could lose the support of a friendly state.[8]

The great power might be interested in maintaining the status quo, and it would therefore be opposed to an external war that would have the probable result of upsetting the status quo. In that case, the great power will then seek to mediate the dispute, or prompt other states or international organizations to mediate.[9] But it is also conceivable that a great power would want the war to continue if it had the effect of preoccupying other states (including the belligerents) that were intent upon changing the status quo.[10] The war aim of consolidating the state is hardly one compatible with maintenance of the status quo; and if a war between two other states, A and B, enabled G to consolidate, then G would use whatever means it could (short of war) to take advantage of the war situation to acquire territory.[11] The same could also be said of

---

7 France welcomed the internal war in the Holy Roman Empire in 1618 and afterwards (in the Thirty Years' War: pp. 379–92), as well as the Hungarian Revolt of 1703–11 (pp. 104–5): They weakened her Habsburg rival.

8 This motivated American and British policymakers in the Struggle for Tunisian Independence (pp. 111–2). Both states were interested in the stability of France and in their NATO alliance and did not want to alienate the Arab states.

  The reader should note that G's support for either the insurgent or incumbent faction, support that could be construed as a *de facto* alliance of G and the faction (or indeed the actual formation of such an alliance) would convert G into a "nonbelligerent ally," according to our system of classification. We consider the nonbelligerent ally in the next section. Actual involvement of the great power on the side of one of the factions converts the internal war into one of the complex variants discussed in the preceding chapter.

9 This was true of the United States in the Chaco War (pp. 76–9) and in the War of the Pacific (pp. 171–3), of Austria and Prussia in the Crimean War (pp. 165–9), and of Britain and France in the Greek Revolt (pp. 222–5).

10 This could be said to have been true of United States policy during the Indochina War of 1946–54 and in the Laotian Civil War (pp. 236–40).

11 See the cases of Russia in the Greek Revolt (pp. 222–5), Prussia and Austria

any opportunity values sought by G. If the values, including territory for consolidation, could only be secured by a prolongation of the war between A and B, G would promote prolongation until the value was secured. If peace were necessary for the retention of the acquired value, then G would probably assume the role of a peacemaker.[12] If G's policymakers sought retribution, they would very likely declare war on the provoking state, or at the very least support another state currently at war with the latter.[13] In either case, G could not then be subsumed under our category of a war-oriented state seeking to fulfill its national interests for itself alone: in the first case (G declaring war), G would become an active belligerent and hence could not remain a merely war-oriented state; in the second case (G providing aid to a belligerent), G would be war-oriented but seek to achieve its war aims indirectly through the agency of the supported state. In the same way, the great power bent upon fulfilling ideological goals could probably not refrain from supporting a state having an identical or compatible ideology in a war against an ideologically antagonistic state. G could therefore fulfill its goals only by supporting the belligerent state or by becoming a belligerent.[14]

The great power interested in maintaining the status quo might be deeply disturbed by an internal war. The insurgent faction is, after all, seeking to overturn the status quo within the affected state; and this

---

in the Russo-Turkish War of 1768–74 (pp. 61–2), and Sweden in the Thirty Years' War (pp. 379–92) in the years before her direct involvement.

12 Prussia, when not a belligerent in the War of the Austrian Succession (pp. 366–74), sought peace for others in order to retain the territory Frederick had acquired by the success of his arms. Austria, in the Crimean War (pp. 165–9), used a policy of threats and proposals for mediation to achieve her aims of increased influence in the Balkans. Britain sought to prolong the Dutch Revolt (pp. 208–14), as it weakened her Spanish rival.

13 Spain and several German Princes went to war against France in 1688, during the European War of 1683–1700, after a period of anxious and resentful tolerance of French activity in the Spanish Netherlands and the Rhineland. Their war was a retributive war. The U.S. was motivated by retributive aims in going to war against Germany in the First World War (pp. 405–28) and against Britain in the War of 1812 (pp. 63–4).

14 Instances are: Imperial support for Spain in the Dutch Revolt (pp. 208–14), Holy League support for Austria against Turkey in the European War of 1683–1700 (pp. 347–57), and U.S. support for the Allies in the First World War (pp. 405–28). This illustrates the distinction I have made between the war-oriented actor attempting to fulfill its aims for itself alone and the same actor supporting one of the belligerents in order to attain its objectives through the latter by some means short of war. In the second case, support for the war aims of the belligerent is, of course, regarded by the war-oriented actor's policymakers as the way to fulfill whatever goals they have posited for their state.

could have implications beyond that state's borders, implying that some transnational ideology is efficacious in bringing about the overthrow of existing regimes. The great power might not want to become more actively involved in the internal war, but it could seek to mediate the dispute, hoping thereby to end a war that can only be prejudicial to its rather conservative interests. To the extent that the internal war occupied the attention of other, perhaps rival, powers and allowed the great power a freer hand to pursue goals of achieving some opportunity or ideological values, G would be interested in a protracted war until those values had been achieved, after which it could remain aloof or even become an active peacemaker, particularly where peace was essential for the retention of the value secured during the period of the internal war.[15]

In the last chapter, we considered the reasons why a third state might involve itself in an internal war. Similar reasons might also motivate the policymakers of the war-oriented great power, whose policymakers could decide that their state's interests could be served by supporting the war aims of one of the belligerents. This support need not involve the power in the war or in a formal alliance with the supported belligerent. However, it is not difficult to see that, in some cases, the relationship between the great power and the belligerent may actually become a *de facto* alliance. We will assume here that such a transformation does not take place.[16] In the external war between A and B, where A is seeking dominance, G will not likely support A's aims, as A and G would undoubtedly be competitors. If A were seeking regional dominance only and if its enhanced power position in that region were compatible with G's goals, cooperation would be possible, and A's war effort could be supported by G. In the event of rivalry, G would be much more likely to support B against A.[17] What we are saying, in effect, is that a great

15 Spain's support for the French Catholic faction (the Catholic League) in the Huguenot Wars of the sixteenth century (pp. 101–3), China's support for the Vietminh in the Indochina War of 1946–54, for the DRVN in the Vietnam War (1965+), and for the Pathet Lao in the Laotian Civil War (pp. 236–40); England's support for the Dutch rebels in the Dutch Revolt (pp. 208–14); and Sweden's support for the Protestant German Princes in the Thirty Years' War (pp. 379–92) all fall within the category of great powers assisting a co-ideological faction. Apart from the ideological aims of U.S. policies in Southeast Asia in the 1950s and 1960s, successive Administrations sought to curb China, regarding her as a state at least seeking regional dominance.

16 Where such a transformation does take place, we have the case of the non-belligerent ally as a war-oriented actor, considered in the next section of this chapter.

17 True of France in her support of Denmark and Sweden in the Thirty Years' War (pp. 379–92), of Germany in the Boer War (pp. 173–5), and of Turkey in the Last War of the Habsburg-Valois Rivalry (pp. 157–60).

power would find it difficult to countenance any drive for dominance by another state. Thus, if the aim of one of the belligerents, state A, is its own defense or maintenance of the status quo against an expanding state B, the great power will support A in an effort to frustrate B. And in the case where the great power was interested in the maintenance of the status quo, its policymakers may determine that the best way to achieve this end would be to support the belligerent with the same aim. Analogously, the great power would support the incumbent faction in an internal war. Hindering the success of insurgents might be necessary for the maintenance of the status quo.

If the great power and one of the belligerents have the same or a similar ideology and the external war can be viewed as a means for enhancing the attractiveness or efficacy of the ideology, the great power will support that belligerent. State A, embarking upon its own consolidation or seeking some opportunity value, could obtain the support of the great power, if the power's goals of dominance, promotion of its ideology, or the acquisition of a separate and different opportunity value could also be effected by means of the war of A vs. B, without G becoming involved in hostilities. In fact, the great power's policymakers might very rationally try to calculate which of the two belligerents could obtain the desired value for them and then support that state. We could say the same thing about a war of retribution by A against B: The war might offer G the opportunity for gain through the success of one of the belligerents; hence, G would support that belligerent. In a war for retribution, G might support the initiator of the attack to achieve its ideological aims, to become dominant, or to secure an opportunity value; but it might as easily support the attacked (or provoking) state for the same reasons. But if G sought to maintain the status quo, it would side with that state (whether provocateur or punisher) whose policies would have the effect of preserving the status quo. In certain situations, after all, it would have been the provoking state that had sought to secure gains at the expense of another state's values. The provocation offered could be regarded by G as one undermining the status quo; and its support for the attacking (punishing) state would continue so long as the latter did not, in turn, seek to make too many gains at the expense of the status quo. On the other hand, G may support the provoking state when (and if) it concludes that the provocation was justified, also in the interests of preserving the status quo.

If state A were waging war against B in order to consolidate its territories or its peoples, G's orientation toward the war would be a function of its own goals and the way it anticipated that these goals could be satisfied through its support of one of the belligerents. G's objectives of dominance or attaining some ideological or opportunity value might be realized by supporting state A at state B's expense, particularly if B were a rival of G. If G were a status quo power, it is difficult to see how its policymakers could support a state bent upon self-consolidation, as such a goal would of necessity change the status quo. G could of course support B, at whose expense A was seeking self-consolidation, in order to maintain the relative power positions of all states in a given region. If B shared G's ideology, we could expect the latter to support B against the expansive policies of A; and we would reach the same conclusion if G's policymakers feared that A's consolidation would enhance the position of A as a rival of G for dominance.

As with alliances, we must investigate the compatibility of the war aims of the related parties, in this case the war-oriented great power and the belligerents. We do this because the consequences of conflict in interactor relationships during peacemaking will have interesting and important consequences. A disparity in war aims between allies of a wartime coalition and war-oriented actors could prolong the war and change the direction of the peace negotiations. The war-oriented great power interested in promoting its own policies without reference to the interests of either belligerent might very well discover that its war aims conflict with those of the belligerents. The great power would continue to pursue its goals, of course; and this could result either in the prolongation of the war or its termination (by the mediation or intervention of the great power).[18] In the case of the power whose policies required it to support one of the belligerents, incompatibility of war aims between them could result in the power's reducing or cutting off its support;[19] and in the face of conflict over war aims, the great power might even offer its support to the other belligerent.[20] There is a third case we must not ignore: conflict between war-oriented great powers or between them and other war-oriented actors.[21] Analysis of such a situation can of course become quite complex. Incompatibilities in the war aims of several war-oriented actors could lead to sudden internationalization of the war. Or more gradually,

18 The aims of Britain and France in the Wars of Mehemet Ali (pp. 225–8) were incompatible, as were those of Sweden and France in the Thirty Years' War (pp. 379–92) before they became belligerents.

19 See the cases of Britain's support for Prussia in the Seven Years' War (pp. 374–9), Britain's and France's aid to the rebels in the Dutch Revolt (pp. 208–14), and England's support for the Palatinate in the Thirty Years' War (pp. 379–92).

20 The British realigned twice, when nonbelligerent, in the Franco-Dutch War of 1672–9 (pp. 340–7); and the United States turned its support away from Souvanna Phouma to Phoumi Nosavan in the Laotian Civil War (pp. 236–40).

21 Consider generally the period leading up to the Second World War, including the policies and aims of the powers during the Russo-Finnish War (pp. 79–81).

conflict arising out of the perceived incompatible war aims would lead to increased support from the war-oriented states, perhaps some escalation of the conflict with the introduction of new weapons or additional troops, and finally war.[22]

A Program of Analysis

The procedure for comparison of war aims is given in the fourth chapter and in Appendix II. We need not repeat that procedure in detail here. But we should be explicit about a program of analysis when war-oriented actors are involved, because some elements of novelty and increased complexity will be present. Such a program of analysis is given below.

1. Identify the great power's war aims.

2. Is G supporting one of the belligerents (let us say, state A) in order to achieve its war aims? (If not, see paragraph 3 below.)

a. Are the war aims of G and A incompatible? If so, what are the results of incompatibility?

The great power is supporting A because it is in its interests to do so. If the aims of G and A were visibly incompatible at the beginning of the war, G would never have supported A, and indeed might have supported the adversary B. If, during the course of the war, the war aims of G and A became incompatible (because either state formulated new aims, or incompatibilities were newly perceived, or the military or relevant political situation had caused a revision in either state's war aims), then G would probably refuse to continue supporting state A. In an alliance, the utility of preserving the interstate relationship may be such as to prevent war-aim incompatibilities from disrupting the alliance. But, in the case of war-oriented states, there exists only the most tenuous relationship, based solely on the national interests of the parties, interests that dictate that the great power should not formalize its relationship with the belligerent to any greater extent. (If there were such an impetus, G and A could, of course, form an alliance.) Thus apart from the inertia of policymakers, there would be nothing to prevent the incompatibilities of the war aims of G and A from resulting in a decision by G's policymakers to refrain from supporting A. Unless the support of the belligerent would provide G with positive benefits (expressed in terms of fulfillment of G's war aims), there would be no reason to continue the relationship, whatever its character. Given this incompatibility, G could follow one of three courses:

22 In any analysis of the relative incompatibility of war aims, we must remind ourselves that the great-power war-oriented state, like any ally in a wartime coalition, might itself have several inconsistent and mutually incompatible war aims.

i. It might decide to support the adversary, *B*. *G*'s leaders would adopt this course of action only if *B*'s war aims at the time of the break with *A* were compatible, that is, if *B*'s war aims would conceivably serve to promote the fulfillment of *G*'s war aims.

ii. *G* might become a non-war-oriented state. This could happen if overwhelming domestic problems or foreign policy problems unrelated to the war between *A* and *B* confronted *G*'s policymakers at the time of *G*'s disagreement with *A*. But it could also occur if *G*'s leaders calculated that the costs of pursuing the war aims were too high and concluded that the general policy goals of *G* could be better achieved by means other than adopting policies oriented toward the particular war, *A* vs. *B*.

iii. *G* could remain a war-oriented state, seeking to influence the course of the war and subsequent peace negotiations, without giving support to either belligerent.

b. Are the war aims of *G* and *A* compatible? If they are, then *G*'s policymakers might adopt one of a number of policies:

i. When and if *A* and *G* have realized their goals, *G* might seek peace through mediation and negotiations. The great power might follow this course if state *A* were losing the war and *G* hoped to salvage whatever values it had obtained up to that time.

ii. *G* might escalate the war, that is, increase its support for *A*, thus intensifying the war. *G* might even intervene and assume the role of an active belligerent. The great power's policymakers would follow this course if state *A* were losing the war and if peace negotiations would not yield the desired pay-off for *G* through the satisfaction of its own goals. In escalating or intervening, *G*'s leaders would obviously have to take into account the reactions of other war-oriented actors or belligerents, as these could alter the strategic equations sufficiently to bring other actors into the war—with unpredictable consequences. It is also conceivable that *G* would escalate in order to bring the war to a quick end, even if the supported state *A* were winning or otherwise in a strong military position.

iii. The great power might seek to prolong the war by pressing the supported belligerent to continue hostilities. This situation could arise if the belligerent had attained, or very nearly attained, its objectives or its decision-makers had concluded that a continuation of the war would not be worthwhile *and* if at the same time, *G*'s aims had not been achieved. Here, the policymakers of the great power hope to obtain their goals through the proxy of the supported belligerent, by pressing the latter to continue the war until *G*'s aims are realized. We would have a classic case of war aim incompatibility should *A* satisfy its goals while *G* has not (or vice versa) ; and in the event of incompatibility, the results discussed in subparagraph a would ensue.

3. Is *G*, as a great power, merely interested in the course and outcome of the war—merely interested, as opposed to interested sufficiently to

support one of the belligerents? Will *G,* in other words, pursue war-oriented policies for itself alone?

The war-oriented great power will be interested in insuring that the war does not take a course prejudicial to its policies and war aims. When one of the belligerent's war aims positively serve those of *G,* the power will assist that belligerent. When the war aims of one of the belligerents (*B,* for example) is positively antagonistic to *G*'s aims, the latter would want to see to it that *B* did not completely achieve its objectives, if this could be done. If state *B* were winning, *G* might attempt to prolong the war. *G* might even intervene against *B*; and in that eventuality, it might coordinate its military operations with state *A.* If the antagonistic state *B* were losing the war, or were otherwise in an unfavorable bargaining position, *G* might seek to promote peace talks between the belligerents. It is possible that the war aims of both the belligerents will be antagonistic to those of the great power; and in the context of the world political situation, *G* might have to accept the lesser of two evils and, while opposing the most antagonistic state (short of intervention and war), acquiesce at least temporarily in the gains of the least antagonistic state. Thus, the great power's choices are escalation and intervention, prolongation of the war by various diplomatic devices, or the encouragement of peace negotiations. In an effort to influence the course of the war, *G* might also decide to support one of the belligerents.[23] The course adopted by the policymakers of the power will depend upon an assessment of costs and benefits.

4. Finally, the analyst must identify all the great powers interested in the course and outcome of the war, determine the war aims of each, and attempt to compare these aims with the view toward assessing the probable war policies of each. In effect, the analyst must examine the variety of ways in which all the war-oriented great powers might interact with each other in respect to the ongoing hostilities. This is somewhat like an investigation into the incompatibilities of war aims; but the results of war aim incompatibility *for allies* are identifiable in the weakening or dissolution of a coalition. The results of different, even antagonistic, aims *among war-oriented great powers* are not readily identifiable at this level of analysis.

A Multiplicity of War-Oriented Great Powers

Let us review briefly the ways in which a great power might be oriented toward a war and the implications of our classification for a *multiplicity* of great powers. Support of great power *G* for belligerent *A* implies that *G*'s policymakers believed that assisting *A* in the war could bring positive benefits to their state, whatever its goals. It means that *A,* because of its involvement in a war with *B,* could provide benefits for *G.*

23 This situation has been discussed in paragraph 2.

Conversely, it implies that the nonsupported state B, in the fulfillment of its war aims, would cause G to sustain some costs (unspecified for the present). In another situation, the great power might be interested in the war for itself alone, with no intention or motive for assisting one of the belligerents. This is so because, as it will probably turn out, the war of A vs. B might in itself deny values to the great power, that is, either A or B or both, in implementing their war or peace policies, might cost G values it would prefer not to forego.

If there are *several war-oriented great powers,* their policymakers will formulate policies relative to the war, and relative to each other, with the design of maximizing benefits and minimizing costs. This is more than a truism in the context of this discussion. If rival great powers sympathize with and eventually support the belligerents in an external war, they do so because the war aims of the belligerents are identical, similar, or at least compatible with their war aims and because (as we have said) assisting a belligerent could offer the supporting powers positive benefits. The war between A and B then is a concrete expression of the rivalry between the war-oriented great powers.[24] We could, somewhat simplistically, describe the relations between great powers as falling on a spectrum of increasing conflict, with cooperation at one end of the spectrum and conflict in the form of war between the powers at the other end. In the case of war-oriented great powers and the simple external war btween A and B, the powers (G_1 and G_2) would intervene on the side of the supported belligerents and find themselves at war with each other. At the other end of the spectrum, G_1 and G_2 would cooperate, resolving their differences in order to foster peace negotiations between the belligerents. The reader can envisage a number of intermediate conditions of impure cooperation or conflict.

Let us assume that in the war of A vs. B, G_1 assists state A; and G_2 is interested in neither belligerent. G_2's policymakers do not want the war to force them to sustain costs that might put their state in an unfavorable position relative to G_1, to A, or to B. In a case of pure cooperation, G_1 and G_2 might promote peace talks, provide increased assistance to A (originally supported by G_1 only), or actively intervene jointly on the side of state A. If the policymakers of G_2 had decided to cooperate with G_1 to further their aims, then cooperation might take many forms, peaceful or hostile, toward B. In the case of pure conflict, G_1 would be at war with G_2. G_1 might be allied to its supported state, or it might not. G_2, however, would probably not ally with state B; but the situation is indeterminate at this level of analysis. We can be a bit more descriptive about still another set of relationships: where the war-oriented great power supported neither belligerent. In a situation of pure cooperation,

24 True of the rivalries of Spain and France in the Thirty Years' War (pp. 379–92).

G_1 and G_2 could promote peace negotiations, or agree to support either belligerent—whichever at the time seemed to be in a position to fulfill the joint interests of the powers. They might even agree to refrain from following a policy that could be regarded as war-oriented: they may, in short, become non-war-oriented states.[25] In a situation of pure conflict, we would have two independent wars in progress: A vs. B, and G_1 vs. G^2.

Nonbelligerent Allies

The nonbelligerent ally has an interest in the war, in part, because of its alliance with one of the belligerents. The former's freedom of action is somewhat limited, however, owing to the exigencies of coalition action. Unlike the great power war-oriented state, the nonbelligerent ally is interested in the course and outcome of the war for the belligerent ally (one particular state). As long as the nonbelligerent ally remains in the alliance with the belligerent partner, it will be constrained to support that partner, however minimally, against the adversary.

As in the case of alliances of belligerent states, war-aim incompatibility is an important variable. Incompatibility of the aims of a nonbelligerent ally (N) and the belligerent ally (A) could have the same results for the prosecution of the war and the negotiation of the peace as the incompatibility of war aims among partners in a wartime coalition. The alliance might dissolve; and N would end its support for A.[26] In an extreme case, realignment might take place, N allying with the adversary B, and perhaps even declaring war on A (see Fig. 4–2 in Chapter 4).[27] Short of realignment, A's position relative to B could be considerably weakened, militarily and politically, because of war-aim incompatibilities and the consequent reduction in N's assistance to A. The course and outcome of the war could then be altered in ways prejudicial to A. In cases in which this is a probable consequence, N might be able to exert considerable leverage on A by merely threatening to cut off aid; and in spite of glaring incompatibilities in war aims, A might then have to pay the costs of the alliance with N in the terms demanded by N.[28] A situation such as this

25 We have a number of examples of war-oriented great powers promoting peace: in the Greek Revolt (pp. 222–5) and the Crimean War (pp. 165–9), in the Russo-Turkish War of 1877–8 (pp. 228–33), in the Second War over Schleswig-Holstein (pp. 169–71), and in the Russo-Polish War (pp. 73–6).

26 An example is the ending of American support for the Centrist Faction in the Laotian Civil War (pp. 236–40).

27 See the case of Great Britain in the Franco-Dutch War of 1672–9 (pp. 340–7) in which, after she had made peace in 1674, she switched from an alliance with France to an alliance with the United Provinces.

28 Note the demands made and secured by Britain from the Dutch in the Dutch Revolt (pp. 208–14). Some of France's NATO allies pressed her to make peace in Indochina, Algeria, and Tunisia (pp. 111–2) because they believed

emphasizes the importance of the character of the relationship, in capabilities terms, between the belligerent and the war-oriented actor.

We might inquire whether a prewar alliance between N and A would survive the commencement of hostilities between A and B, without N's becoming actively involved. What sort of alliance is it that does not require the allies to assist each other, even to the point of declaring war, against a common enemy? That question is a fair one for collective defense alliances, of course. But there are many other types of alliances that do not require all the partners to declare war when one of them becomes involved in hostilities.[29] In some cases, however, state A might dissolve the alliance immediately after the war had begun, irrespective of war-aim compatibility, should N refuse to become a cobelligerent. But again, A's expectations might not have extended to N's direct involvement, either because of the terms of the alliance compact or because N's diplomats had persuaded A's policymakers of the inadvisability or inability of N to become a cobelligerent. Or perhaps A's position is so weak relative to either N or the adversary, B, that A will acquiesce in N's remaining nonbelligerent in exchange for whatever help N can furnish. If the alliance has been created during the war, presumably this question would not arise: N and A need only maintain compatibility in their war aims. If the war aims of the nonbelligerent ally and the belligerent were compatible (and as long as they were compatible), the ally would provide the belligerent with the support agreed to be necessary by the policymakers of each: It might be aid in money or in goods, weapons or technicians; it might simply be diplomatic support for A's policies.

N might, in time, become actively involved in hostilities. This could come about for several reasons:

1. State A might be losing the war, and N might be willing to accept neither the consequences of A's defeat nor further losses for A, including any losses that would put A in a weak bargaining position at the peace talks. Presumably, losses would prevent the ally, N, from fulfilling its war aims or reduce the efficacy of the alliance between N and A.[30]

2. Whether or not state A were losing the war, N might want to pursue its aims more directly than by remaining merely a war-oriented state. N's

---

she was frittering away her resources and also causing the loss of the good will of "Third World" states, thereby contributing to the frustration of the worldwide goals of the Western Alliance. Russia sought (unsuccessfully) to mediate the War of 1812 (pp. 63–4) because she believed Britain's resources were needed on the continent (see the Napoleonic Wars: pp. 392–405).

29 True of the Austro-Turkish alliance of the Crimean War (pp. 165–9) and the defensive alliance of Russia with Britain, Saxony, and Austria in the War of the Austrian Succession (pp. 366–74).

30 This was, in part, the motive behind China's intervention in the Korean War (pp. 233–6) and United States intervention in Vietnam in 1965.

decision-makers might feel that they could guarantee realization of their war aims only by declaring war upon A's adversary.[31]

3. State A might want to make peace with state B, but peace at that time might not be in N's interests. N could declare war on B and force A to remain at war. At the least, this declaration of war might destroy the chances for success of any peace moves by either A or B.[32]

4. A second war-oriented state might intervene on the side of the adversary B. In order to maintain a balance of power between the belligerents, where N's interests (including N's alliance) are implicated, N would declare war on B and the other intervening state.[33]

Even if the war aims of N and A are compatible, they are usually not wholly identical—and this means that there will be a variety of ways for either party to achieve its goals. The belligerent state A chose the path of war; the nonbelligerent ally has remained on the sidelines supporting its ally. For N to refuse assistance would probably mean the dissolution of the alliance, and N might want to preserve the relationship even with the unwanted war. Why should this be so? To answer this question adequately, we would have to inquire into the reasons-for-being of the alliance; but we might hypothesize that A could provide N with some valuable resource or equally vital commercial or communications arrangements. Or A might fit into an integral defense system with N.[34] (A and N might have common fortifications, for example.) Or the alliance might be based upon the concept of collective defense against a *nonbelligerent third state*. N would then be loath to see the disruption of the coalition as long as the threat from the third state existed. And even though state A was preoccupied with the war against B, the alliance might yet have a deterrent or defense value for N.[35] If the value of the alliance were very great for N, then the appearance of incompatibilities in the war aims of A and N would not produce a disruption in the alliance or a suspension of N's aid to A. The threshold of dissolution

31 Britain in the Dutch Revolt (pp. 208–14) pursued a more and more actively belligerent policy toward Spain until the two countries were in formal conflict.

32 For a time in 1954, a group of American policymakers believed that France wanted peace in Indochina at any price, and they recommended intervention to forestall this "surrendér." See my study, *Geneva 1954, op. cit.*

33 Consider the course of the Laotian Civil War (pp. 236–40) and the Korean War (pp. 233–6).

34 Britain's acquisition of sovereign rights in the Netherlands after 1585 (in the Dutch Revolt: pp. 208–14) permitted her to integrate that country into her defense schemes. After 1954, Laos was "shielded" by a SEATO guarantee and incorporated into an American conceived defense zone in Southeast Asia.

35 Britain's alliance with Holland in the Franco-Dutch War of 1672–9 (pp. 340–7) was of this sort and was aimed to deter France.

would have been raised because of external political constraints, to wit, the competition or threat of conflict between state N and states other than those involved in the war, A vs. B. But should external conditions change, should the conflict between N and others be resolved and the possible threats to N from these sources diminish, then the alliance between A and N could dissolve. Certainly, if N's policymakers disapproved of the war in the first place and assisted A only because of the value of the alliance for N's own interests (independent of the war), then a change in the external conditions could remove the constraint that forced N to tolerate A's involvement in a war N did not want. Then, we may expect that either N would dissolve the alliance or cease supporting state A.

Regional and Border War-Oriented States

The great power, because of its capabilities, usually has some modicum of choice whether it will assume the role of a war-oriented state. The regional or border war-oriented state has much less flexibility, primarily because of its location. It is most difficult for a state, located in the region of an ongoing war, to avoid being interested in the conduct of military operations near its borders. Proximity, indeed, not only results in interest in the course of a war and its outcome; it also brings with it the threat of involvement in hostilities. Military operations could spill over onto the territory of the regional state and make war unavoidable. Certainly the regional or border state will also have war aims (policy goals with reference to the war in its region). Very often, that policy is a response to the question, How do we remain neutral?

In our consideration of the war-oriented great power, we distinguished orientation toward the war generally from orientation toward a particular participant in the war. In either case, the great power seeks to fulfill its war aims in its own national interests. We could make a similar distinction for the regional war-oriented state, that is, we could consider the reasons for its orientation toward the war or the reasons for its orientation toward (and support for) one of the belligerents.

The regional state interested in obtaining dominance in the region or maintaining dominance already achieved could conceivably welcome the war between two states in the region if it resulted in the weakening of the two belligerents and in their inability to resist the policies of the dominant war-oriented state, either during or after the war.[36] On the other hand, if the war could conceivably prompt the intervention of a great power or a rival regional state, the war-oriented regional state might seek to promote peace negotiations between the belligerents, on the assump-

36 Spain in the Huguenot Wars (pp. 101–3) and the United States in the Cuban Revolt (pp. 107–8).

tion that a continuation of the war could only work against its policies of dominance by bringing in challenger states.[37]

The regional state interested in maintaining the status quo for its own defense (or for the preservation of its power position relative to other states) would tend to be concerned with the possibility of military operations extending to its territories, the seizure of its goods and vessels, or a blockade or other interference with its trade.[38] Such a state would, of course, be primarily concerned with maintaining the integrity and security of its territory and the preservation of the safety and property of its citizens. Its policymakers would probably attempt to mediate the dispute or to get other states or organizations to do so. Presumably, they would also take self-defense measures in the event the war came to threaten their territories or citizens.

The regional state with ideological aims would be interested in the outcome of a war in which its ideology played an important role. To the extent that the ideology might have been falsified by the war between A and B, the regional state (R) might be expected to favor a prolongation of the war. If the ideology were verified, R would probably favor the settlement of the war. Naturally, if R's ideological aims were coupled with another aim (dominance or consolidation, for example), its war policies might then be considerably different. The policymakers of R, seeking to consolidate their polity, could conceivably use a war between A and B to obtain the territories to which it laid claim within either state.[39] The instability generated in the region by the war might also help R obtain territory from states other than the belligerents.

In a war of retribution or for opportunity values, the preoccupation of the belligerents and other border states with the war might enable R to exploit the situation and obtain the values sought by its policymakers.[40] R might act more or less cautiously in seeking those values, to the extent that it wanted to avoid war. After all, if A had provoked R, the latter might seek to remove the provocation and might be able to do so more

37 This motive explains, in part, India's policy of conciliation in the Indochina War of 1946–54, the policies of Egypt during the Struggle for Tunisian Independence (pp. 111–2), and those of Saxony and Brandenburg in the Thirty Years' War (pp. 379–92) during the times when these Electorates were at peace.

38 This was Cambodia's concern during the wars in Indochina after 1954, when she became independent. It was also the profound concern of the Netherlands, Switzerland, and other neutral European states during the First World War (pp. 405–28).

39 This was an aim of the German Confederation in the Second War over Schleswig-Holstein (pp. 169–71).

40 True of Prussia in the Austro-Russian War against Turkey of 1787–92 (pp. 163–5), which sought a piece of Poland; and Sweden in the Seven Years' War (pp. 374–9), which hoped for Pomeranian territory.

effectively and successfully because of A's war with B. But A could not be expected to accept a loss to R of values of a magnitude great enough to threaten its vital interests or impair its ability to wage war against B. Only in the event that A were very seriously weakened, and perhaps defeated, would her policymakers acquiesce in R's actions to punish A (or to gain opportunity values). Otherwise, A would declare war on R. But this might be the consequence R had hoped to avoid.

The regional war-oriented state might sympathize with the belligerent whose war aims were similar and compatible with the war aims of R. Let us first consider the aims of the parties to an external war, A vs. B. If the belligerent, state A, were dominant or seeking dominance, R might be willing to defer to A's aims or acquiesce in A's demands. State R might have to assist A in some way, a payment perhaps to remain neutral and unscathed by the war. This payment or tribute could take the form of resources or money; or R might be required to permit A to use its territories for troop training or deployment. Thus, as long as R was willing to defer to A—and it might be willing, if A's dominance had given or would give R security—no conflict would arise between the neighbors. But, if R balked at A's demands or the regional distribution of power changed (i.e., if A lost capabilities relative to R or to other states as a result of the war), R might be faced with the possibility of war with A. Or at the very least, A (the dominant power) would impose sanctions upon R. The position of the regional war-oriented state, in these circumstances, could be improved by two devices in addition to the weakening or defeat of state A in the war: R might join a collective defense alliance with other regional states, or with at least one great power or R might secure a guarantee of its security from one or more great powers or from a collective security organization. In either case, R's efforts to preserve its integrity and security interests through cooperation with other states might deter A from taking steps against R prejudicial to the latter's interests. It is, in fact, open to any war-oriented regional state favoring the status quo to adopt the familiar policy of allying with others (or securing a credible guarantee from other states or organizations) to achieve a measure of security in the face of a regional war. Alliances and guarantees could give the feeling of security that proximity to the war denied.

If one of the belligerents favored the status quo, R would probably sympathize with or support that state, if R also wanted to preserve the status quo.[41] But should R's policymakers want to remain neutral, they

41 In the Last War of the Habsburg-Valois Rivalry (pp. 157–60), Venice wanted to preserve the status quo, as did Norway and Sweden in the Russo-Finnish War (pp. 79–81). Muscovy and Poland were concerned with Sweden's policies in Germany in the Thirty Years' War (pp. 379–92), as the outcome of the war there could affect their interests and capacity to maintain the status quo and the integrity of their territories.

could not support A to the point where they would provoke B and thereby elicit a declaration of war. Similarly, where A's ideology is identical or similar to state R's ideology, R will sympathize with A and perhaps provide some support, unless to do so would involve it in the hostilities it sought to avoid. Where one of the belligerents is seeking consolidation, the regional war-oriented state might provide support if A's acquisition of territories could weaken or otherwise work to the detriment of a rival of R in the region. Naturally, R would not welcome the possibility of loss of its own territories to either belligerent. If A is seeking retribution or an opportunity value, R would assist A if it could do so without costs, if A's success hindered B and B was a rival of R or otherwise threatened R's security.

The regional war-oriented state interested in maintaining the status quo would probably favor the incumbent faction in the case of an internal war, because insurgency is intrinsically aimed at upsetting the status quo.[42] There would be all the more reason for the regional state to want an end to an internal war should the instability in the region invite the intervention of other states.[43] As in the case of an external war, the internal war could also spill over the borders onto the regional state's territories. Were the policymakers of R to share the ideology of either faction, then we might expect R to assist the faction with a similar or a compatible ideology.[44] And if R's policymakers were bent upon attaining dominance, they might support whatever faction would cooperate with them in fostering their policies. The regional state interested in regional dominance would want to avoid giving a great power cause to intervene in that region (whether in an internal or an external war). Such intervention could result in a confrontation or war and thereby the frustration of R's limited regional aims. Once again, this emphasizes the need for the analyst to consider the policies and war aims of war-oriented states in the context of the state system at the time.[45]

---

42 Hence, the Imperial support for Spain in the Dutch Revolt (pp. 208–14) or the support for the Centrist Faction in the Laotian Civil War (pp. 236–40) by Cambodia and Thailand.

43 Indonesia, Burma and India anticipated that the instability generated by internal war in Southeast Asia would invite the intervention of the powers in the Indochina War of 1946–54, the Laotian Civil War (pp. 236–40), and the Vietnam War.

44 Thus, the Netherlands supported the insurgents in the English Revolution of 1688–9 (pp. 103–4), and the Arab states supported the Tunisian Nationalists in the Struggle for Tunisian Independence (pp. 111–2), for ideological motives.

45 We have interesting situations in which one group of belligerents in one war are war-oriented with respect to a second, wholly separate war: the belligerents of the Great Northern War of 1700–21 (Sweden vs. Russia, Denmark, and Poland-Saxony) vis-à-vis the War of the Spanish Succession (pp. 357–66); the

International Organizations as War-Oriented Actors

There are, as we have seen, several different types of international organizations, some with multiple functions. We need only consider how these organizations could conceivably be oriented toward a particular war: how, in other words, would the organization function relative to the situation created by the war, and to the peace negotiations and the peace settlement?[46] Collective security organizations may be regional or world-wide in scope. Their purpose, generally, is to prevent wars, to act collectively against an aggressor, and to assist in the settlement of wars. The functional international organization is another type, but not nearly so important for our purposes as the collective security organization. As the term *functional* implies, such an organization serves a particular technical purpose, concerned for example with health, aviation, war relief, or economic development. We will be concerned with functional organizations only to the extent that they play a role in the peacemaking process —or prior to the peace negotiations, if they have in some way affected the course of the war appreciably. While this is unlikely, we should not discount it entirely.

Contemporary international organizations like the League of Nations or the United Nations are quite complex and have many purposes. In our analysis, we treat the multiple-purpose, war-oriented organization as if it were composed of more than one simple organization, each with a single purpose. More often than not, we will be most interested in the collective security aspects of the international organization—in short-hand terminology, the simple collective security agency of the international organization. In theory, all collective security organizations will react toward war in a similar fashion: The aggressor will be identified and ordered to desist; if it fails to heed the command of the organization, the organization's member states will then apply sanctions designed to halt the war or at least to contain it. This is usually accomplished by the members' joint agreement respecting the nature of the sanctions that are to be imposed upon the aggressor, whether economic, diplomatic, or military.

---

anti-Habsburg powers in the latter war vis-à-vis the Hungarian Rebellion of 1703–11 (pp. 104–5) ; and in the European War of 1683–1700 (pp. 347–57) , the states that were belligerent in the Western Theater were war-oriented with respect to the war in the East (and vice versa) .

46 The discussion in this section is based, in part, upon F. P. Walters, *A History of the League of Nations,* 2 Vols. (London: Oxford University Press, 1952) , and Alan James, *The Politics of Peace-keeping* (New York: Praeger, 1969). It is also based upon a study of the settlements of several of the wars summarized in the preceding chapters and noted below.

In the case of an external war,[47] we may presume that the war-prevention functions of the international organization have either failed (otherwise the war would not have started) or simply not been utilized by the state actors (because the belligerents were not members of the organization or because the organization was disinterested). In attempting to assess the general policy of the organization relative to this external war, we may make a rather basic simplifying assumption: the organization will not purposely attempt to prolong the war. It may indeed be (or become) completely disinterested, in which case it is not a war-oriented actor. Some of its members may want the war protracted; other members may successfully prevent the organization from dealing with the war and its related problems. But as a collective security organization, it will, insofar as it deals in any way with the external war, seek to conciliate, mediate, or adjudicate the issues that make up the war aims of the belligerents; or it will persuade other states to do the same.

We can isolate two factors of importance that affect the actions and policy of the international organization (which should be kept in mind for the following discussion):

1. The identity and policies of the states that control the organization. These may be the great powers in some executive council of the organization; or it may be a bloc of allied or cooperative states.

2. The character of the functioning of the organization, determined by its constitution and the bureaucratic relationships that arise among its civil servants and agencies. We must ask, What is the character of the organizational sovereignty that has gelled over the course of the life of the organization?

In analyzing the relationship of the belligerents in an external war to the war-oriented international organization, we must ask ourselves what sort of response the organization would make to each of the war aims of the state actors. A collective security organization is status-quo oriented, at least to the extent that it does not favor war as the means to effect change in the relations of states. Naturally, it would be possible for an organization controlled by conservative states to follow policies designed to preserve the status quo against all change. In this case, the organiza-

47 The collective security organization is most frequently concerned with external war. Internal wars are more often than not regarded as falling within the category of domestic affairs of the affected state and not therefore a question over which the organization can take cognizance without interfering in the affairs of a sovereign state. Of course, this is not always true: There have been instances of a collective security organization's acting upon problems stemming from an internal war, as in the Indonesian War for independence, the Congo wars of the 1960s and the Korean War. See also Miller, Linda, *World Order and Local Disorder: The United Nations and Internal Conflicts* (Princeton: Princeton University Press, 1967).

tion would certainly pursue policies more favorable to the belligerent whose aim was also maintenance of the status quo. Yet, it is possible to imagine a collective security organization whose constitution would recognize the need for peaceful change, the practices and policies of which would permit rather radical shifts in the power position of states, short of war. Whether peaceful change did take place would depend upon whether or not the great powers and other interested states permitted *peaceful* change, even apart from the acquiescence of the collective security organization. Unless the latter is strong enough to compel states, or influential enough in the circumstances to persuade them, to permit the change, the policies of the organization and the interested states will diverge. Then change cannot take place peacefully.

The collective security organization would almost certainly condemn the war fought to obtain retributive or opportunity values. Spokesmen for the organization would insist that these values be obtained by peaceful means, or not at all. Some diplomats might look with sympathy upon the plight of the state that has been subjected to a series of provocations. But while some organizational action, including sanctions, might be taken against the provocateur, the organization could not permit a breach of the rule specifying no war except in self-defense, and preferably in a coalition with member states of the organization cooperating against an identified aggressor. Naturally, if the provoking state could be said to have committed a belligerent act, then a retributive war could also be regarded as self-defense.[48] The war-oriented international organization would not be opposed to a dominant great power, merely because it was dominant. It is only when that power seeks to aggrandize itself by waging war that the organization would seek to limit its goals. But the ability to wage war is a major element in the power position of any state (some would say that it is the primary element). A war-making capability permits the state to threaten—and threats very often persuade, or at least influence, smaller states. Threats also deter larger states. Without the occasional use of force, threats are not credible. A state bent upon dominance could not afford not to be believed. A state therefore builds up its war-making capabilities, and uses them on occasion. It is this occasion that would meet with the condemnation of the collective security organization, and the state seeking paramountcy would then feel the constraints of membership in such an organization. Faced with a determined coalition, the latter might change its policy for the time being and agree to

48 It would be a status quo defensive war. We ought also to remember that war aims do change in the course of hostilities; and a war for self-defense, started in response to a provocation that was clearly a belligerent act, might become a war waged by the belligerents for aims other than self-defense. When it does, the collective security organization will be apt to take a less sympathetic view of the state whose aims had become extended or enlarged.

negotiate peace.[49] If they could, the policymakers of a dominant power would attempt to prevent effective action by the organization during the debates in the assemblies or committees of the organization or by informal or extra-organizational diplomacy designed to prevent the formation of an effective war-making coalition.

Because the consolidation of a state requires the acquisition of territories, which is difficult to accomplish without war, we would expect a state bent upon consolidation to wage war. In doing so, it would expose itself to the sanctions of a collective security organization.[50] This would confront the organization with a classic dilemma: to prevent war, yet allow change (here, the consolidation of the state). However, peaceful change would meet with resistance from status-quo states; and given this resistance, it could appear to the revisionist state that war is the only means to satisfy its justifiable aspirations. The organization might find itself unable to decide whether it ought to prevent war and maintain order, certainly a pre-eminent principle-of-being of the collective security organization, or to support the claims of the consolidating state in order to prevent a future war, or to give effect to the perhaps universal principle (national self-determination, for example) underlying the claim of the consolidating state.

In the case of ideologies in conflict, proselytization of an ideology does not necessarily lead to war; but if an ideological war were to occur, the organization would probably sanction the state that took the first clearly identifiable belligerent act. But as this is difficult to determine, and usually gives rise to controversy, the organization might be unable to do more than attempt mediation.

A war involving a nonmember state might nonetheless interest the organization. Such a war could, of course, threaten the peace or stability of a region or the world.[51] We could distinguish two kinds of external war in this respect: a war between two nonmembers of the organization and one between a member and a nonmember. In the latter case, we can be certain that the collective security organization will be war-oriented and adopt positive policies toward the war and the peace negotiations. In the case of an external war between two nonmember states, it is easier to envisage a situation where the organization will not be interested in the war, if, for example, the nonmembers are small states or if the war is confined to a region remote from the interests of the great powers or the

49 Consider the case of Paraguay in the Chaco War (pp. 76–9).

50 The Korean War (pp. 233–6) and the Laotian Civil War (pp. 236–40) are cases in point.

51 The United States, not a member of the League, was an important actor in the Chaco War (pp. 76–9). China was a belligerent in the Korean War (pp. 233–6) and a war-oriented state in the Laotian Civil War (pp. 236–40), and in neither case was she a member of the United Nations.

members of the organization. In either case, the problem for the organization is the same: it would not have jurisdiction over a dispute involving a nonmember state, and would have no authority (however limited even in the case of member states) to require compliance with its mandates. It could not legally require the nonmember to account to the organization, to provide information, to permit mediation, or to accept as valid any resolutions, hortatory or mandatory. This is not to say that the organization could not influence the course of the war. To the extent that the member states were united against a nonmember or were in a position to impose effective sanctions, the nonmember could be deterred or would at least alter its policies to avoid the costs of those sanctions and ultimately the costs of a war with a coalition of the organization's member states. On balance, however, the war-oriented international organization would be a less important factor in a war involving a nonmember. Even in the case of external wars between *member states,* the collective security organization has been a less than effective means for the prevention of war in the existing state system.

The war-oriented collective security organization could be controlled by a particular bloc of states. In these circumstances, it would become an instrument for the achievement of the purposes of the controlling states.[52] Thus, the controlled organization might actually favor one of the belligerents, playing the role of a nonbelligerent ally under color of the legal authority of the organization's constitution. It might countenance certain forms of force by a favored state, without treating the situation as a state of war. It might regard an internal war with international ramifications as the purely domestic affair of the favored states.[53] At the very least, the controlling bloc of states could prevent the organization from following an effective policy toward the belligerents, whether that be a policy of sanctions, mediation, or merely of airing the issues. At the other extreme, the organization could become an active belligerent on the side of the favored party. It would, in other words, transform itself into a wartime coalition, organizing sanctions and military forces against the nonfavored state. There will, of course be a point at which the international organization, controlled by a bloc of states, would be faced with the departure of the nonfavored states (and others). It would then cease to exist as a real collective security agency. Short of resignation, the noncontrolling states could refuse to comply with resolutions passed by

52 The Chinese and Soviets regarded U.N. intervention in the Korean War (pp. 233–6) as dictated by the United States and fully under its control.

53 On the problem of internal wars and international organizations, see Linda Miller, *op. cit.,* and the wars cited in note 50. See also the Struggle for Tunisian Independence (pp. 111–2) and the Indochina War of 1946–54 (Randle, *op. cit.*). Consider also the "non-role" of the United Nations in the Vietnam War since 1965.

the bloc-controlled organization. It could refuse to pay dues or to contribute services and personnel. Where the controlling bloc did not want to move or could not move the expulsion of the recalcitrant members, their maneuvers might be effective in modifying organization policy. We note also that where the control is being contested—if other member states do not acquiesce in that control, and the issue of who controls is unsettled—the war-oriented policies of the organization would be apt to vacillate, reflecting the uncertain internal political situation within the organization.

There is one kind of control that should be mentioned separately, owing to its importance, and that is control by the great powers. These states usually occupy a unique place in the collective security organization. Indeed, their joining the organization is often conditioned upon conceding to them an increased measure of control over organization policy—either a veto or a form of voting weighted in their favor. The great powers can obtain this important concession because their power position is such that collective security measures without them would be illusory in matters affecting their interests. Even with a great power veto, states usually find they have room for implementing their own policies within the organization. Thus the great power may find it necessary to alter its policies in order to win the favor of the member states; or the smaller states may at least prevent the great power from using the organization as an instrument of its policy, one that would respond supinely to its demands.[54]

54 One should not ignore the peacemaking roles of forms of international organizations other than the U.N. (or the League of Nations) or supranational organizations (such as the OAS, OAU, and the like) : for example, the quasi-institutionalized conferences of war-oriented states convened to deal with the problems of a particular war (see Chapter 7) or special purpose commissions established to supervise or implement cease-fires and peace settlements (the Control Commissions for the Indochinese states after the 1954 and 1962 settlements or the Neutral Nations Supervisory Commission of the Korean War: pp. 233–6) .

War-Oriented Actors
and Peacemaking

The "Presence" of the War-Oriented Actor in the Peacemaking Process

The war-oriented actor can most directly affect peacemaking by actually being present at the peace talks. In the Geneva Conference on the Laotian Question (1961–62), the great powers and regional war-oriented states were present to defend their interests. In the Anglo-French War against China (1856–60), Russia and the United States were able to obtain by diplomatic means and by their timely and opportune presence at the peace talks almost the same concessions from China that the British and French had fought to secure. And in the Crimean War, Prussia and Austria played a major role in the peacemaking process by their presence at both the Conference of Vienna (1855) and the Congress of Paris (1856).

The war-oriented state may not be present at the peace talks, however. It may fail to secure an invitation from the belligerents; or its leaders may choose to remain aloof from the talks, perhaps to preserve anonymity or to obtain the distance that would enable its policymakers to disassociate themselves from the peace settlement. At the conference, of course, the war-oriented actor could further its aims directly through negotiations with the belligerents and other war-oriented actors. If absent from the conference, the actor would have to find other means to realize its aims.[1]

1 Indeed, a great power might demand revision of a settlement concluded in its absence. At the end of the Russo-Turkish War of 1877–78, the war-oriented great powers prevailed upon Russia to agree to revision by a general European congress of the preliminary peace of San Stefano (see pp. 228–33).

The diplomacy of peacemaking is of course a broader area of activity than *conference diplomacy* alone. It includes the efforts of war-oriented actors not present at the peace talks to achieve their war aims through ordinary diplomatic means, through the foreign offices of the belligerents and other war-oriented actors. Temporarily narrowing our focus to conference diplomacy, however, we note that absent war-oriented actors can realize their aims *at the conference* by being represented by a reliable and effective agent—a state present at the peace talks, willing to assume the task of supporting the policies of the absent principal. A nonbelligerent ally, for example, could rely upon a belligerent ally as its agent. China and the Democratic Republic of Vietnam represented the interests of the absent Pathet Lao and Khmer Issarak at the Geneva Conference of 1954 that ended the Franco-Vietminh War. In the negotiations for an armistice and peace in the Franco-Prussian War, Bavaria, Baden, Würtemberg, and Hesse were represented by Prussia, and after 18 January 1871 by the German Empire. It is of course true that these four states had become part of the Empire; but their hybrid juridical status even then entailed appreciable autonomy for them. While they probably could not have obtained an invitation to the peace conference, they saw to it that their interests were promoted by the Imperial negotiators. And we should also note that in the large conferences at the end of most multilateral wars, smaller states often manage to secure representation at the meetings of the great-power directors where the important decisions of the peace conference are made. The agent does not always serve the principal as effectively as the latter would like. Presence at the talks is then preferable. At the Conferences of Nijmegen (1678–79) and Ryswick (1697), the Emperor represented the Estates and Princes of the Holy Roman Empire. As the proceedings at these conferences showed, the Imperial delegates were not averse to making decisions prejudicial to the German princes when Habsburg interests could be promoted thereby.

In specific policy terms, how can the absent war-oriented actor influence peacemaking? It can do so at the conference through its agent-state by having the agent:

1. support the principal's war aims by submitting and advocating proposals formulated by the principal.

2. consult the absent actor in the formulation of its own proposals for settlement and pursue essentially its own policies, but with the additional purpose of serving the principal's aims as well. In the settlement of the Second War over Schleswig-Holstein, Austria consulted with representatives of the German Confederation, submitted their proposals, and modified her own with the view toward securing the support and sympathy of the German states against her Prussian rival. Austria also espoused the claims to the Duchies of the "absent" Prince Frederick of Augustenburg. In the peace of Rastadt (1713–14) between Austria and France, a part of the settlement of the War of the Spanish Succession,

the Imperial Delegation was the "agent" of the Princes and States of Germany. Although the Emperor, representing the Empire as well as Austria, had been empowered by the Diet to negotiate a settlement, he was also required to obtain the Diet's approval for a definitive treaty of peace, and his representatives had to negotiate with this fact in mind. Such a treaty was signed at Baden in Ergau in September, 1714, after the Diet had debated and then approved the Rastadt Treaty.

The war-oriented actor (as principal) can supplement its agent's efforts by:

1. publicly expressing its support for the agent's policies and settlement proposals, as the Soviet Union repeatedly declared its support for Chinese and North Korean proposals for an armistice during the Korean War.

2. using conventional and traditonal diplomatic channels to achieve its aims (and perhaps also the agent's aims).

3. offering to ally formally with the agent.

4. threatening to use force or actually intervening militarily in the war. In the War of the Bavarian Succession (Prussia vs. Austria: 1777–79), Catherine of Russia mobilized an army and threatened to intervene on the side of Prussia if the belligerents did not accept her mediation.

Even if the war-oriented actor has secured neither an invitation to the conference nor an agent to respresent its interests there, it may still influence the course of the negotiations by these four supplementary methods, particularly if the actor is a great power whose policies with respect to the war cannot be ignored by the conferees. The war-oriented actor could also convene a separate conference of war-oriented actors to consider matters arising out of hostilities. (We discuss such conferences later in this chapter.)

It should be emphasized that we have been considering the possible ways a war-oriented actor could affect peace negotiations. Whether and to what extent it would affect them depends upon the power position of the actor (a great power, for example, will usually be able to influence the conference to a greater degree than a small regional state). It also depends upon the intent of the policymakers of the war-oriented actor, who might choose to press the negotiating parties on some questions, but not on others.

Promotion or Prevention of Peace Negotiations

War-oriented actors may adopt a wide variety of policies toward peace negotiations. For the sake of simplicity, we treat these policies as having one of two consequences: promoting a peace settlement or preventing or retarding a settlement. Whether or not the policies of the war-oriented actor do, in fact, foster or prevent a settlement depends upon a number of variables, not the least of which are the policies of the belligerents, who could have decided to opt for peace or continue the war.[2] Admittedly, even this is a simplifying assumption, for policies of belligerents are complex and difficult to identify. Granted also that the categorizations of "wanting peace" or "wanting to continue the war" ignore the reasons why policymakers of the belligerents have made either of these decisions; nevertheless, it will be useful operationally to make the assumption and proceed as follows: In the first case, consider how a *war-oriented actor* can promote or prevent peace *when the belligerents want peace;* and in the second case, consider how the *war-oriented actors* can promote or prevent peace *when the belligerents want to continue the war.* We should remember that all belligerents must agree to (or acquiesce in) a peace settlement; otherwise the war will continue for *some* parties at least. Hence, our first hypothetical case (if the belligerents want peace) implies that both sides in the hostilities want to bring the war to an end. If, as often happens, only one of the belligerents wants peace, the policies of the war-oriented actor either supporting or opposing the belligerent state will have an important bearing upon developments. We will subsume that eventuality under the second hypothetical case, that is, a situation where the belligerents (or one of them) want to continue the war.[3]

2 By "opt for peace," I mean to include decisions made to begin negotiations, whether or not the policymakers believe that peace can be achieved.
3 Needless to say, the following discussion is in the nature of a scenario. My sample of peace settlements was not large enough to permit me to support incontrovertibly every assertion I make in this section. Having said this, I urge the reader to refer to the wars summarized in the preceding chapters and in Chapter 9, for examples of war-oriented actors promoting or preventing peace:

To promote peace: a. Mediation was employed by the United States and regional South American states in the Chaco War (pp. 76–9) and the War of the Pacific (pp. 171–3) ; Sweden and the U.S. in the Russo-Finnish War (pp. 79–81) ; the United States in the Cuban Revolt of 1869–78 (pp. 107–8) ; France, Britain, and Russia in the Second War over Schleswig-Holstein (pp. 169–71) ; Austria in the Crimean War (pp. 165–9) ; Russia and the Empire in the War for American Independence (pp. 217–22) ; Denmark, Venice and the Pope in the Thirty Years' War (pp. 379–92) ; Sweden in the Franco-Dutch War of 1672–9 (pp. 340–7) ; and Venice and Sweden in the European War of 1683–1700 (pp. 347–57) .

b. Arbitration was employed by the mediators of the Chaco War (pp. 76–9) .

c. A detailed plan for peace was offered to the Porte by Austria, Britain, France, and Prussia in the Greek Revolt (pp. 222–5) .

d. An express threat of war was made against Spain by the United States in the Cuban Revolt (pp. 107–8) ; against Turkey by the powers in the Greek

1. The belligerents decide to negotiate a peace settlement.

During the phase preliminary to the actual peace negotiations, the war-oriented actor can *promote* peace by acting as a conduit for peace feelers, by proposing compromises in the belligerents' demands for preconditions and procedures for negotiations, or by acting to neutralize the policies of other actors intent upon prolonging the war. The war-oriented great power or nonbelligerent ally that is actively supporting one of the belligerents might press the latter to take the initiative in proposing peace talks. It might formulate such proposals and then go on to determine how the feelers or memoranda containing preconditions or negotiating procedures should reach the adversary. A war-oriented great power, regional state, or international organization that is not too closely identified or associated with *one* of the belligerents could press both sides to moderate their preconditions to formal peace talks. They may also seek to lessen the intensity of the conflict by persuading or compelling other war-oriented actors to de-escalate; and they may offer solutions to sub-

---

Revolt (pp. 222–5); against France and Spain by Russia in the War of the Austrian Succession (pp. 366–74).

e. A stance implying that the actor might go to war was used by Austria and Prussia against Russia in the Russo-Turkish War of 1768–74 (pp. 61–2); Britain and France against Russia in the Russo-Finnish War (pp. 79–81); Britain, France, and Russia against Austria and Prussia in the Second War over Schleswig-Holstein (pp. 169–71); the United States against Chile in the War of the Pacific (pp. 171–3); and Austria against France (in 1813) in the last year of the French Wars for Hegemony in Europe (pp. 392–405).

f. An alliance with one of the belligerents guaranteeing territory in dispute was formed by Austria with Turkey in the Crimean War (pp. 165–9).

g. Sanctions were imposed by the League of Nations against Paraguay in the Chaco War (pp. 76–9) and Russia in the Russo-Finnish War (pp. 79–81). In the former case, the League imposed an arms embargo; in the latter, expulsion from the organization.

To prevent peace, a number of states have offered aid and encouragement to a party: Spain's aid to the Catholic League in the Huguenot Wars (pp. 101–3); the support given to the Hungarian insurgents in the Hungarian Rebellion of 1703–11 (pp. 104–5) by the anti-Habsburg powers involved in the War of the Spanish Succession (pp. 357–66); and British and French aid to the Dutch rebels in the Dutch Revolt (pp. 208–14). These powers later made peace with Spain and then encouraged the rebels to do likewise. To induce Spain to move toward peace, they guaranteed the Low Countries and France joined in a defensive alliance with the Dutch.

French diplomacy throughout the Thirty Years' War (pp. 379–92) could be viewed as one continuous effort to prevent any peace settlement for the Empire that would result in the increase in Imperial (Habsburg) power. Finally, we mention that in the Russo-Turkish War of 1877–8 (pp. 228–33) Britain and Austria used a show of force to prevent implementation of the Treaty of San Stefano.

sidiary issues involving third-party actors, hoping thereby to induce them to agree to a resolution of the conflict (or at least to refrain from impeding the progress of the belligerents moving toward peace talks).

In order to *prevent* negotiations, the war-oriented actor may intervene in the war; short of intervention, it could bring intolerable pressure to bear upon one of the belligerents, threatening to cut off military aid or technical assistance, propagandizing or appealing to bellicose internal political groups, or interfering with the channels of communication between the hostile parties during the critical preliminary negotiating phase. The actor could create doubts about the sincerity or good faith of either of the belligerent's proposals for peace talks by emphasizing ambiguities or omissions in the texts of the feelers, slights to the prestige of one party inherent in the procedures for talks suggested by the other party, or simply by fabricating and publicizing scenarios of ruin or defeat for the belligerents if either should accept the other's feelers. The mistrust engendered by war will make it easy for a war-oriented actor to aggravate the relations of the adversaries, if it is disposed to do so. While such tactics will not always succeed, delicate situations particularly susceptible to this type of disruption will arise as the belligerents move slowly toward a resolution of their conflict.

It is unlikely that a war-oriented *collective security organization* would engage in peace-preventive tactics of the sort described or deliberately seek to prolong a war. Nevertheless, it could do so: first, if the organization were controlled by a bloc of states interested in prolonging the war; or second, if it inadvertently adopted procedures the unintended effect of which were to exacerbate relations between the belligerents. Thus, the organization might make public, through debate, the fact of secret preliminary contacts between belligerents, and this could result in their discontinuance. The imposition of collective sanctions against one of the states might aggravate a situation: if ineffectual, the sanctions could make the policymakers of that state less willing to make peace. Should the organization discuss an ongoing *internal war,* the state affected may absent itself from the debate or even leave the organization, if it regards the war as an internal question with which the organization had no competence to deal.

The cease-fire is a central element of any peace settlement; and it is recognized as such by all parties. Hence, war-oriented actors that wish to *promote* a settlement will undoubtedly call upon the belligerents to end their war in at least a "stand-still" cease-fire. They may supplement their urgings by offering to supervise the battle zones after the fighting had stopped, perhaps proposing to interpose their own troops between the forces of the belligerents. They might offer food and other essentials to the belligerents as an inducement to end the war and then undertake to solve the human problems caused by it.

If a third-party state has intervened in the war, the war-oriented actor might impose sanctions upon it, forcing it to withdraw to simplify implementation of the cease-fire to some extent. The actors could also take the initiative in scheduling a peace conference. The very fact that this initiative has been taken by an interested but nonbelligerent party could conceivably make it easier for the belligerents themselves to agree to attend; and it may even provide them with a pretext for agreeing to a preconference cease-fire. As in the preliminary phase of negotiations, the war-oriented actor (the great power, regional state, or nonbelligerent ally) could also bring pressure to bear upon their favored or supported belligerent (threatening abandonment or punishment) in order to induce or compel it to agree to a cease-fire.

The war-oriented actor might be opposed to a cease-fire generally or to a cease-fire on a particular front or at a particular time. Its opposition might arise from calculations that its own security would be threatened or its political or economic interests prejudiced were one of the belligerents to be relieved of the burden of active hostilities. Whatever the reason, the war-oriented actor could hinder the moves of the belligerents toward a cease-fire. It could use its influence to prevent the cease-fire; and it could employ threats or force to achieve this aim. If its acquiescence were necessary in order for the belligerents themselves to feel secure after the armistice, it could withhold that acquiescence and even threaten to follow policies that would place one or both belligerents in a less secure position. In the implementation of the cease-fire, the cooperation of a regional state or a great power might be necessary. Withholding such cooperation could persuade the belligerents to continue the war.

A war-oriented actor can help or hinder the military administration of combat areas depending upon whether the policies of the administrator are compatible or incompatible with its war aims. If a military occupation regime, for example, were to become more or less permanent and if the occupying state was (or could become) a competitor of the war-oriented state, the war-oriented state would oppose plans for the occupation. If, moreover, the actor had opposed a cease-fire, then it might take rather drastic steps to prevent a peace-with-occupation agreement. Similarly, if the demilitarization or neutralization plans of either belligerent adversely affected the balance of power or created a breach in the actor's defense system, then it would oppose the peace settlement. If the disaffected actor did not succeed in preventing negotiations or a settlement, it might, in the postwar years, seek to undermine the settlement; and even if it did not intervene to prolong the war, the instability of the peace could lead to a new war within a short time.

Conversely, the war-oriented actor could promote the military administration provisions of the peace settlement by indicating its willingness to supply staples to the administrative authority, to oversee the administration and act as a kind of ombudsman and judicial reviewer. It could assist in a demilitarization scheme, if such were agreed upon, by promising not to sell arms to the states whose territories had been demilitarized. During the negotiations, the actor could make its intentions known in this regard; and, as in the preliminary phase, the war-oriented actor might measurably assist agreement simply by offering solutions that the belligerents themselves did not or could not propose.

The extent to which all or several of the elements of a political settlement were incorporated in the settlement of a particular war depends upon the extent to which the war had become de-ideologized and devalued by the belligerents. In other words, it depends upon how complete a peace settlement the belligerents actually want. Certain elements of a settlement are likely to be neglected where the issues of the war remained ideologized.

In the case of any element of the political phase of the settlement, the war-oriented actor could *promote* a peaceful settlement by offering solutions and compromises, tempering the immoderate demands of either belligerent, and generally acting as the conciliator. It could *prevent* peace by propagandizing issues, by planting seeds of distrust, or by increasing the instability of a particular region by intervening militarily, economically, or diplomatically. With respect to the territorial element, the actor might promote peace by offering to recognize or respect a particular compromise arrangement, perhaps by guaranteeing the new political status assigned to disputed territories. Where the belligerents are unable to agree upon the disposition of territory, the actor might propose a trade-off of values, some territory against other values (resources, guarantees of security, or economic advantage) . And where the war-oriented actor has not been too closely identified with either of the belligerents, it could support one of them in its demands for a particular disposition of territory, thereby inducing the other to make concessions. The nonbelligerent ally, the great power or regional state that had been tied in at least a *de facto* alliance to either of the hostile states, could *promote* peace by threatening to intervene. In some cases, this could also persuade a recalcitrant belligerent to make concessions.

The actor could interfere with a resolution of the territorial question. It could persuade the parties that the disposition of areas proposed by one or the other would threaten their long-term security. It could declare that it would not recognize or respect—and certainly not guarantee—a territorial settlement. A declaration of this sort might result in a loss of confidence in a particular peace plan. It could induce either belligerent to become more intransigent or induce third-party states to intervene on the assumption that nonrecognition by the war-oriented actors was an invitation to upset a particular settlement. And where a weaker state's leaders felt impelled to acquiesce in the territorial demands of the other, the actor could proclaim its support for the former, improving that state's capacity to resist. Yet, however laudable such support, it would tend to put off a settlement rather than facilitate one in the immediate future.

In the matter of persons affected by the war, the war-oriented actor could *promote* peace by offering aid to the belligerents in order to care for refugees, displaced persons, and prisoners. It could also provide transport or offer the use of transportation facilities on its own territories for the movement of persons. A functional international organization could be employed for these purposes. If none existed, the actor might propose to establish one, with other interested states. Where one did exist, the directors of the organization could intervene on their own initiative or on request of another war-oriented actor. The belligerents would have to consent to the activities of such an organization on their territories; but the actors might use what influence they had to induce the belligerents to accept the services of the functional organization. The state actor could also urge its own businessmen (and their nationals generally) to resume business relations with nationals of the belligerents, if the war had interrupted them.

In order to undermine a prospective agreement over "persons," the war-oriented actor might adopt restrictive economic measures, vitiating the reasons for either belligerent's accepting the agreement. The actor could also appeal to the national sentiments of the leaders and peoples of either belligerent against a proposed solution affecting their nationals.

The war-oriented actor could *promote* peace by enhancing the security of the belligerents and of other interested states. This it could do by a variety of means tailored to the context of the war. The actor could provide one belligerent with a guarantee of its security by agreeing to come to its aid if it were attacked by any state or faction. But in some situations, this would lead to the intervention of other states or to the other belligerent becoming or remaining refractory and unwilling to compromise. A guarantee to both belligerents, perhaps in the context of a collective security or collective defense organization, would be a better solution. The actor might also agree to refrain from selling arms and munitions to the belligerents or from establishing military bases on the territories of either belligerent. It is conceivable that in some situations, the formation of a *collective defense* organization between actor and belligerent would aggravate tensions; and, in that event, the actor could promote peace by agreeing not to enter such an organization with either belligerent. It might also do so by recognizing the neutral or demilitarized status of all or part of the formerly hostile states.

The war-oriented actor could *prevent* a settlement by encouraging one of the belligerents to continue fighting or by resisting the adversary's proposals at the peace talks, describing the proposals as a threat to their state's security. It might do some sabre-rattling of its own; and its threats might increase the uncertainty surrounding the issues under consideration at the conference, exacerbate the sense of insecurity felt by the belligerents, and thereby prevent compromise.

The resumption of relations between the belligerents and adjustment of their disputes are less essential to the *immediate* task of peacemaking. The war-oriented actor disposed to prevent peace is probably less able to interfere effectively during negotiations in respect to these elements of the settlement. Naturally, they are necessary for a complete settlement and for long-term stability in the region of the conflict. Yet, the normalization of relations between the former enemies and their agreement to submit future disputes to mediation would probably *not* affect the vital interests of the war-oriented state nor prevent the realization of its war aims. Nonetheless, its policymakers might want to create or maintain a condition of instability in the region of the war; and they could accomplish this goal by interfering in the affairs of either belligerent, by creating mistrust, and by belying the capacity of one of them to conduct its foreign affairs independently.

The war-oriented actor could *promote* peace in these problem areas by issuing a declaration of nonintervention or by proposing that future relations of the former enemy states and the adjustment of their disputes should take place within the context of an appropriate international organization. There, hopefully, greater objectivity would be achieved. The pressure to settle disputes would be greater, and the opportunity to accept mediation without loss of prestige would be offered to the belligerents.

If the peacemaking process in an internal war has reached the political settlement phase, it will of course have been made clear that the incumbent faction has not succeeded in destroying the insurgents. The war-oriented actor may *promote* peace, as in the case of an external war, by helping the factions find acceptable solutions. The war-oriented actor could perhaps persuade the insurgents to accept an autonomous status short of independence. Thus, the actor might press the incumbents to guarantee minimal political and civil rights to the rebels. In the war for control of the polity, the actor might help to define the status of the insurgents in a coalition with the incumbents. Or the actor might promote peace simply by refraining from interfering in the peace talks or by accepting the war and peace negotiations as the domestic concern of a sovereign state. The settlement of the war could also be promoted by an agreement among all the war-oriented states to respect a settlement or to treat the state of the factions as neutral or demilitarized or as the subject of a special economic or political regime.

A settlement could be *prevented* by the intervention of the war-oriented actor on the side of a weaker incumbent faction, steeling it to resume or continue hostilities rather than accept a compromise peace.

Thus, with additional economic and military aid, the incumbents, having at first acquiesced in the necessity of recognizing the rebels, would be able to continue the fight with renewed hope of suppressing them.

2. In the alternative hypothetical case, the belligerents (or one of them) do not want to negotiate and prefer to continue the war.

As in the preceding section, we note that the war-oriented actor can either promote or prevent a peace settlement. We need not consider the trivial situation when a belligerent's policymakers want to continue the war and the war-oriented actor acts to *prevent* a settlement. The war would not end. However, we do consider the other, more important question: How does a war-oriented actor promote peace when a belligerent wants to continue the war? It is usually done by exerting pressure upon either or both belligerents: for example, by withholding shipments of armaments, by threatening to suspend (or actually suspending) subsidies or economic aid, by curtailing trade and reducing investments in the business enterprises of the belligerents, or, as a last resort, by using force to separate the hostile parties. In the latter case, a credible threat of force is sometimes sufficient. The nonbelligerent ally or the great power or regional state in the position of a *de facto* ally of one of the belligerents could dissolve the alliance, with consequent material and morale costs to the belligerent ally. But these methods are not subtle; and war-oriented actors can often promote peace through diplomacy that keeps threats and the use of sanctions visibly in the background.

In the phase preliminary to negotiations, the actor could assume the role of the initiator of an exchange of proposals for negotiations. The actor could also suggest procedures by means of which representatives of the belligerents might discuss matters incident to the hostilities with the intention of reducing their scale and scope. Talks designed to de-escalate the war might conceivably be transformed into peace talks with the passage of time and the prodding of the war-oriented actor. But the belligerents might be unwilling to accept the war-oriented actor as a mediator if either believed that the actor had war aims incompatible with its own. In this situation, the actor could call upon another state or organization to proffer its good offices for promoting peace. Of course, there are no reasons why an objective international organization should not be an effective mediator—an *objective organization* being one not controlled by a bloc of states having aims antagonistic to either of the belligerents.

The war-oriented actor could propose procedures for prospective talks between the recalcitrant belligerents, and it could propose devices that would enable them to accept a cease-fire. However, we must recognize certain limiting factors operating to frustrate the actor's attempts to promote peace. Not being involved in hostilities, its proposals are more apt to be discounted or even repudiated by the belligerents. Most actors, however interested in a war, would be reluctant to become active belligerents; hence, they might not be able to make credible threats to compel the belligerents to negotiate. Moreover, there is no assurance that outright intervention would succeed in bringing the warring states or factions to the bargaining table. Even if successful, the actor could probably not get them to negotiate early; and the longer the armed intervention of war-oriented states lasted, the greater the costs to them. This prospect would tend to persuade the actor-state not to become actively involved in the war. As a consequence, the belligerents would conclude that the actor's threats were not credible; and the actor would then have failed to promote peace by threats. Thus, there is no overcoming the real obstacle to peace: the belligerents' emotional commitment to their war aims. And thus there is an essential need for devaluation and de-ideologization of the war to the point where the belligerents' policymakers can enter exploratory talks. The war-oriented actor could perhaps do much to educate the belligerents: it could show them there was indeed a rationale for a cease-fire, and a less costly means of reaching their goals; and it could show them possible alternative solutions to their disputes. But whether the belligerents will accept the solutions is another question; and it is the calculations of their policymakers respecting the gains they anticipate from a continuation of the war that are important. In an intensely ideologized war, the leaders of the belligerent states do not always rationally calculate gains and costs (and if they have done so, public opinion often prevents them from adopting a strategy that aims at less than maximum gains). Then, irrespective of the value of the rational solutions proffered by the war-oriented actors, the adversaries would not (or could not) accept them.

Given agreement among the belligerents on a cease-fire, the path to an adequate peace settlement would by no means be open, especially where the antagonists were reluctant to compromise on any matters unrelated to the maintenance of a precarious truce. And indeed there is no guarantee that the truce will continue to be observed or that it will be no more than a breathing period before the resumption of hostilities, if the belligerents will not or cannot discuss the questions of a more complete military and political settlement. The war-oriented actor could help to bring this about by mediation and conciliation—provided of course that the policymakers and the elites of the belligerent states could be made to see the desirability of further negotiations. If the armistice were tenuous, the war-oriented actors might first try to persuade the belligerents to adopt methods of maintaining the cease-fire and adjusting disputes over alleged violations. The organizational actor (or war-oriented states, in certain cases) could dispatch supervisory personnel and should institutionalize mechanisms for handling the complaints of the adversaries. To promote further negotiations, the actor could adopt one or more of the policies suggested earlier: proposing solutions and compromises, pressing the former belligerent state to accept proffered solutions even to the point of threatening economic or military sanctions, or offering to aid the less intransigent party and thereby forcing the other to compromise rather than suffer a relative decline in its capabilities. The actor could also offer one or both of the adversaries a guarantee of security, if it were the insecurity felt by them that was preventing a settlement. Or the actor could offer either party compensations in resources, trade, or even territorial values if the fear of an adverse change in power position had made one of the parties reluctant to compromise.

War Aims of the War-Oriented Actor and the Elements of a Settlement

We have seen that the war-oriented actor can influence the course of peace negotiations by being present at the peace talks or through the representation of an effective agent state; and the actor can either promote or prevent a settlement. But the precise character of the peace policies adopted by the actor will depend upon its war aims; and in the context of negotiations, those policies will have to be related to the elements of a projected military and political settlement.[4] Refer to

4 The discussion and analysis in this section is in the nature of a scenario. We have even fewer examples here than in the last section of the peacemaking role of war-oriented actors. The remedy for this defect is, of course, continued study and an enlargement of the size of our sample of wars and peace settlements. We ought to be aware that, because of the nonbelligerent status of war-oriented actors and their consequent "distance" from the settlement, there will be fewer cases where the actor's aims are translated into provisions of a peace treaty. At this time, however, we can make some rather good guesses respecting the probable policies of war-oriented actors. And this I have attempted to do in this section. As we would expect, where a war is terminated through multilateral talks, the actors' proposals (an expression of their war aims) form the basis—or at least an important part of the basis—of the settlement. This was true of the Congress of Berlin ending the Russo-Turkish War of 1877–8 (pp. 228–33); the Conferences of London convened to pacify the Levant during the Greek Revolt (pp. 222–5) and the Second War of Mehemet Ali (pp. 226–8); the Congresses of Vienna (1855) and Paris (1856) to settle the Crimean War (pp. 165–9); the Geneva Conferences of Laos (the Laotian Civil War: pp. 236–40) and on Indochina and Korea (the Korean War: pp. 233–6; Randle, *op. cit.*); and finally, the great peace congresses of Vienna and Versailles, among others considered in Chapter 9, ending respectively the Napoleonic Wars (pp. 392–405) and the First World War (pp. 405–28).

Also of interest, in that the war-oriented actor played an important role in negotiations, and indeed suggested substantive terms for a settlement, are the cases of the United States and regional South American states in the Chaco War (pp. 76–9); Dutch and British mediation at the Carlowitz conference

Figure 2–1, which shows schematically the factors that affect the translation of a belligerent's war aims into elements of a political settlement. Thus, we consider, for each type of war-oriented actor, the relationship between its war aims and the elements of a settlement of an external and internal war.

The Great Power and the Regional State

For the purpose of relating war aims to the elements of a settlement, we treat the great power and the regional state together. However, we distinguish between external and internal wars, as the elements of the settlement for each differ somewhat; and hence, the policies of the war-oriented actor also differ.

External War. The interest in a settlement evinced by a great power or regional state seeking to gain dominance will depend upon the relationship of the belligerents to the former and to other third-party states. If either or both belligerents in the war of A vs. B are rivals of the war-oriented actor (state W), the latter will probably pursue policies that could result in the weakening of its rival; and this might include protracting the war. During peace negotiations, state W will want a territorial settlement that will place its rival in a weakened power position and unable to resist W's drive for dominance. W's policymakers will seek to extract guarantees of security from the rival so that the latter would not only be unable to frustrate W's designs but also be incapable of threatening W and deflecting that state's policymakers from the pursuit of their goals. If either A or B is a *de facto* ally of W, guarantees might be easier to obtain, as the belligerent state will be in a position to act as the agent of W, coordinate its peace proposals with the dominant partner, and demand the guarantees W demands. If W's belligerent ally were in a weak bargaining position or had been defeated, W might still be able to cut the losses of its ally (and itself) by proclaiming its support for the ally and threatening and attempting to deter the stronger state. The great power actor would of course be better able to do this than a regional state with limited capabilities.

It is conceivable that both A and B might be friendly toward W (and willing to acquiesce in W's aim of dominance). Very probably, W will then play a mediatory role in the peace negotiations or at least seek to influence the belligerents, persuading them to arrive at a settlement that

---

and Sweden at the Ryswick conference in the European War of 1683–1700 (pp. 347–57); the Soviet Union during the Korean War and afterwards (pp. 233–6); the League of Nations in the Greco-Bulgarian Crisis of 1925; and the United Nations in the War for Indonesian Independence, the West Irian Crisis (1962), the Congo Civil War (1960–64), the War for the Independence of Cyprus (1954–59), and the Cyprus Crisis of 1963–4.

would eliminate the frictions between them. The war could, after all, hamper and distract W from its goal of paramountcy. In such a case, W would want a minimal exchange of territory or an equitable trade-off of territories for other values. W would want A and B to normalize their relations, although not to the extent of combining their capabilities in order to hinder W's aims; and W would probably want A and B to provide each other (and W) with some security guarantees.

The policies adopted by the war-oriented state will also be a function of the reactions of third-party states, both to the war and to the peace talks. Indeed, if a third-party war-oriented state were involved—not involved as a belligerent, but supporting either A or B—W's response would depend upon whether the third party could be regarded as a rival. If a rival, W would take a much more intense interest in the peace talks, treating the state that had *not* been aided by the third party as a *de facto* ally. W would be concerned to see to it that the settlement did not accrue to the benefit of a rival. The means adopted to this end could result in a deadlocked conference (or slower progress in negotiations, because of the interference of W and the third party). It could also result in the resumption or continuation of hostilities or in war between W and the third party.

If the aim of the war-oriented state were the maintenance of the status quo, its leaders would want the settlement to produce as little change in the prewar power positions of the belligerents as possible. State W might support the status quo aim for itself alone, preferring to maintain a balance of power in the region; or it might pursue that goal to help a *de facto* belligerent ally, the defeat of which would upset the status quo. W would thus want minimal territorial exchange, denial to either belligerent of access to the political processes of the other (where such access did not exist before the war), normalization of relations, provisions for the adjustment of future disputes between A and B, and mechanisms for security guarantees—all of which would tend to preserve the status quo. Again, if a third-party war-oriented state were to become involved, particularly a revisionist state, the status-quo actor would take a greater interest in the peace negotiations and would be concerned to see to it that the belligerents produce a more firmly guaranteed settlement, one designed to preserve the status quo against the third party.

The war-oriented state having an ideological war aim would be intensely interested in the outcome of peace negotiations between A and B, if either or both were his co-ideologues *or* if either or both had official ideologies antagonistic to W's. In the event that A and W have similar or identical ideologies, W will, of course, press for a settlement favorable to A and favorable to the validation and success of its own ideology. The ideological state would be most interested in the territorial and guarantees elements of the settlement and the provisions concerning persons

affected by the war. Certainly, the acquisition of territory by the belligerent co-ideologue state would tend to promote the ideology, as would
favorable provisions for ideologically sympathetic persons in the adversary state. If *A* and *B* have the same ideology as *W*, then *W* would
undoubtedly try to assume the role of mediator, especially if a third-party
state with an antagonistic ideology could profit from the war. Moreover,
it would hardly be proper to have states of the same ideologies quarreling
with each other, as ideologues often claim that their ideologies transcend
interstate power political conflicts of the traditional variety. Such conflicts can only weaken the attraction of the ideology for peoples of other
states and might indeed lead to heterodoxy and dissent among peoples
within the ideological states themselves or even to internal war between
ideologically antagonistic factions.

A war-oriented state seeking its own consolidation must achieve its goal
at the expense of the belligerents, state *A* or state *B* (or both), or at the
expense of a third-party state. In the former case (at *A*'s or *B*'s expense),
W's interest in the settlement would extend to insuring the weakness of
the state from whom the territory was or will be obtained and some
guarantee that the latter could not, in the near future, put itself in a
position to recover the lost territory. This could be accomplished at the
peace talks, in part, by supporting the belligerent (let us say, *B*) that is
the adversary of the state (*A*) losing territory to *W*, the object being so to
lessen the capabilities of *A* relative to *B* that *A* will, in the future, be
preoccupied with the threat from *B* and will not be capable, and might
even be unwilling, to reclaim territories from *W* (or to resist *W*'s demands for territories). In the case of consolidation at the expense of a
third-party state, *W*'s object would be to weaken the state from which it
had acquired territory. If the third-party state could increase its capabilities as a consequence of the victory of state *B*, then *W* must support state
A, and seek to place *A* in a better bargaining position at the negotiations,
with the policy of cutting *A*'s losses (and cutting *B*'s gains and, ultimately, the third-party state's gains).

If *W*'s goals were retributive, we must ask: retributive *against whom?*
If against state *B*, then *A* is the belligerent agent-state that will punish *B*,
assuming that *W* does not want to become involved in the hostilities and
could otherwise permit *A* to punish *B* and also obtain the guarantees that
would eliminate the possibility of future provocations. The war-oriented
state would probably be interested in the penalty provisions of the settlement of a retributive war, as *A*'s securing a penalty would inure to *W*'s
benefit. *W* might, however, want retribution against a third-party state
without the interference of *A* or *B*. The war-oriented state could secure
retribution if *A* and *B* were too preoccupied with their war or were
weakened by it. *W*'s interest in the settlement would reach those elements that could result in the reduction of the capabilities of either of

the states $(A$ or $B)$ most apt to assist the third-party state in avenging the punishment by W or eliminating the settlement W imposed upon the third-party state. The same reasoning would apply if W were to seek retribution against the third state during the peace talks between A and B, or if W were to become bogged down in a war with the third state: The rule is to preoccupy the potential rival or deterring state and seek to reduce that state's capabilities so far that it could not deny the retributive value to the punishing state nor prevent it from removing the provocation by obtaining security guarantees.

A very similar rule applies in the case of a war-oriented state seeking to obtain an opportunity value. W's interest in the settlement of the external war between A and B, if W seeks an opportunity value from B, requires the strengthening of A's bargaining position so that W indirectly benefits from A's gains (or minimal losses) and thus obtains or retains the opportunity value. If W is seeking the value from a third-party state, W will have no interest in the war unless it is to insure (to the extent that it can do so) that neither A nor B will have the capacity or desire to take the value away.

Internal War. The war-oriented actor might be interested in an internal war because of the war's impact upon the relations of states in the region or because the support given to one of the factions by others impels the actor to be interested in the war. The actor may actually support one of the factions or at least sympathize with it. At the peace talks, such support or sympathy would find expression in the actor's peace plans and proposals favorable to the supported faction—to the extent that the war aims of the supported faction and the war-oriented actor are compatible.

In the internal war, an actor's policies must be tailored to the situation, taking into account whether insurgents are to be supported as against the incumbents (or vice versa) ; whether the insurgents have been successful, partially successful, or have failed; and whether the internal war is a war for independence or a war for control of the polity.

In a war for independence, the supporter of the successful insurgent faction will undoubtedly seek to maximize the territory of the new state and include in the peace treaty provisions favorable to the new state's nationals, for example, nondiscrimination in business enterprises; access to markets, waterways, and other transportation routes; use of fisheries; a most favored nations clause in commercial treaties; or nationalities clauses guaranteeing the civil rights of those persons in the parent state who will seek to change their nationality to that of the successor state. The war-oriented actor could also be expected to propose inclusion of security guarantees for the successor state. In this, the war-oriented actor might urge the new state to join a collective security and perhaps also a collective defense organization. It might itself guarantee the new state through a mutual defense pact and provide it with military and technical aid, or it could promote the security of the successor state by facilitating normalization of the latter's relations with the parent state and other states in the region. In the case where the war-oriented state had supported the unsuccessful incumbents, it is conceivable that it would even then want relations between the parent and successor state to be normalized and any future disputes between the two mediated. However, the supporting state could help the parent state resist the maximum territorial demands of the new state and reduce the other values sought by the latter.

If the incumbents have been successful, the war-oriented state might act to moderate the internal policies of the victors to prevent excessive repression.[5] The state that has supported the insurgents will probably find that it will have little influence upon the incumbents if the insurgents are defeated; the supporter of the incumbents will have some influence, perhaps enough to persuade the incumbents to grant some measure of autonomy to the defeated rebels. This, however, is an internal matter about which the affected states' leaders (the incumbents) are usually extremely sensitive. Rebellion is not welcomed by incumbent regimes; and pressures from an ally or a friendly war-oriented state might only result in strained relations between them, with no appreciable change in the regime's policies toward the insurgents.

The policies of the war-oriented state toward the factions in the peace negotiations ending a war for independence will depend upon its war aims, just as in the case of an external war. In analyzing the settlement policies of the power and regional state, we must relate the war aims of these actors to the specific reasons their policymakers had for favoring either the insurgents or the incumbents (assuming that one of the factions is favored). We perform an analysis similar to that in Chapter 5 where we related the war aims of the belligerent state to the reasons for its involving itself actively in the war on behalf of the insurgents or incumbents to which it was allied.[6] Supporting the incumbents in the war for independence, the actor would seek to minimize the amount of territory granted the new state of the successful insurgents and minimize other advantages connected with the settlement (rights of nationals of the new state, guarantees of security, and the like). In the event the incumbents were successful, the status quo actor would probably refrain from interfering in the postwar internal policies of the incumbents, unless the war had so enhanced the power position of their state that the shift in itself sig-

---

5 This presumably would not be a war ending in negotiations, but rather one in which the insurgents would simply stop fighting after their defeat.

6 We saw there how unlikely it would be for a status quo great power or a regional state to support insurgents in an internal war.

nificantly altered the status quo. In that case, the actor might try to influence the domestic policies of the incumbents or adopt positive policies toward other regional states in order to maintain a local balance of power.

The actor seeking dominance could support either faction in a war for independence, depending upon which is acquiescent in the dominant state's goals. The ideological actor would probably support the faction having a compatible or identical ideology. The content of the peace plans of the war-oriented great power or regional state, whether ideologically motivated or seeking dominance, would also depend on the extent of success or failure of the favored faction and therefore on the probable consequences of the war's outcome in costs or benefits for the war-oriented state.

In the internal war for control of the polity, the war-oriented state could play a significant part through its influence for a compromise peace. If either the insurgents or the incumbents win outright, the actor must probably confine its policies to normalizing relations disrupted by the war. In a condition of stalemate, however, the war-oriented actor might be able to induce de-escalation, the decoupling of state allies, and eventual settlement. This it could do by the usual means of proposing solutions, pressuring the parties to accept proffered peace plans, even threatening to impose sanctions upon them, and offering to guarantee the settlement reached by the parties. The actor's war aims might call for a complete settlement and the return of peace and stability to the state affected by the internal war. On the other hand, the actor might seek only minimal agreement between the factions in order to exploit instability and unsettled conditions for its own benefit. Whatever the aims of the war-oriented actor, we must again emphasize the limitations upon its ability to influence the course of the internal war for control and the course of the negotiations for its settlement. But having said this, we must recognize that *if* the factions in a war for control are willing to negotiate at all, they must have concluded that a military resolution of the war is not presently possible. Thus, they *might* (emphasis upon *might*) seek all the support they could get to reinforce their bargaining positions relative to each other. Yet, the situation also invites the war-oriented state, so disposed, to hinder the peacemaking process: substantial support from the latter is apt to induce the faction leaders to become intransigent and less willing to compromise.

The status quo state is likely to support a settlement resulting in a minimal change in the internal conditions of the state affected by the war. Hence, it would tend to favor partition rather than an easily subvertible coalition government and some minimal political status for the insurgents rather than partition. The same could also be said of the actor that has favored the incumbents. Conversely, the war-oriented great power or regional state that has supported the insurgents would hope to see the gains of the latter maximized: a position of control (or potential control) for the insurgents in a coalition government or partition with administrative authority for them over wide areas of the state. Those actors that genuinely wanted a viable settlement or those whose war aims could be satisfied by a composition between the factions would prefer to see additional guarantees: demilitarization or disarmament, prohibitions on alliance formation, and equal political and civil rights for the members of both factions. Such an actor would prefer to see the factions normalize their political relations as quickly as possible after the cease-fire. A guarantee of the settlement of the war for control of the polity by the war-oriented great power or regional state would be most unusual, although several such actors might agree among themselves to refrain from disturbing the settlement and from intervening in the internal affairs of the state formerly affected by the internal war.

The Nonbelligerent Ally

A nonbelligerent ally may be either a great power or a regional state. We note that alliances rest upon the mutual interests and common policies of the coalition partners. The great power has interests in many areas; hence, it could be an ally of a state in almost any region of the world. Regional states ally in fulfillment of some regional goal, whether functional (economic development or promotion of trade, for example) or for the collective defense of their region. The nonregional state (that is not a great power) is unlikely to have common goals with other states in regions far removed from it. Thus, we would probably not find these states allied; and we would be unlikely to find a "non-great" power in a region distant from the scene of hostilities as the nonbelligerent ally of one of the belligerents.[7] What we have said is of course true for wartime alliances where it is the mutual interests expressed in the war aims of the partners that provides the cement of the coalition. But there are alliances based upon reasons other than the partners' war aims in a particular war. Thus, for example, states *A* and *N* might be allied for the purpose of promoting their security interests in Asia, *A* being a European great power, *N* an Asian state of medium capabilities. State *A* might be at war with state *B,* another European power. If *B* has no interests in Asia, *N* would probably remain neutral, with *A*'s acquiescence, the alliance

---

7 Autonomous states of an empire (or the independent states within entities like the Commonwealth or the French Union) could be the exception to this generalization: The interests of the component states as members of the empire might make them war-oriented regardless of their geographical distance from the war. And it is conceivable that any state would be war-oriented if its nationals resident abroad were adversely affected by the war (note the War of the Pacific: pp. 171–3) .

remaining viable. Thus, the NATO allies of the United States were nonbelligerent allies with respect to the Vietnam War, but the alliance remained substantially intact.

What has been said in the chapters on alliances in external wars is relevant as a supplement to the discussion earlier in this chapter of the peace policies and war aims of the great power or regional state in the peacemaking process. We should note once again that the nonbelligerent ally's policies and power position in regions of the world other than the region of the war might have to be revised in light of the actual or prospective peace settlement. In other words, even though an alliance might serve purposes unrelated to the issues of the war, including the purposes of the nonbelligerent great power in another part of the world, a peace settlement might indeed affect those other purposes—in altering the balance of power in the region of the war and thereby altering the global balance of power or by inducing one of the former belligerents to turn to another region for compensating values in lieu of the values it did not obtain in the settlement. The settlement might also bring stability (or instability) to the region of the war and to the states formerly involved; and either of these eventualities might be unwelcome at the time to the nonbelligerent ally.[8]

There may be a difference of opinion among allies with respect to how much each has sacrificed in the war effort; and this difference could be especially deep among belligerent and nonbelligerent allies. The situation would not be very much ameliorated were the nonbelligerent ally to declare war just prior to the opening of peace talks. The involved allies would feel that the nonbelligerent could have done more, that the latter should not be entitled to a significant share of the values derived from a peace settlement, whether war spoils (territory, resources, or currency) or intangibles, such as access to policymaking in defeated states, favorable trade agreements, or guarantees of security. The nonbelligerent ally could come to feel that its allies did not understand the reasons for its staying out of the war; and it might demand that the alliance provide it with greater influence in the peacemaking process, even though it had

8 An active belligerent, necessarily being present at the peace talks, would be an ideal agent of the nonbelligerent ally, as the two states are allied. The alliance presumably would have a value for them, either for purposes unrelated to the war (in which case, the partners may want to preserve the alliance in spite of the war in order to achieve or retain the values provided by the alliance) or for benefits derived during the war. Even where the values obtained by the coalition partners are neither related to war aims nor productive, the sheer inertia of the allies in their ordered relationships to each other could prevent dissolution of the alliance. In any event, if the alliance were viable, the nonbelligerent ally would probably be represented by the belligerent ally at the peace talks.

not been an active belligerent. But whatever divergence there may be in war aims—and an ally's remaining a nonbelligerent indeed implies a difference in war aims—the divergence will only be exacerbated by the noninvolvement of the nonbelligerent ally. Its policymakers may conclude that they might better have achieved their aims outside the alliance. Failing to secure an adequate presence at the peace talks or faced with a settlement that would adversely affect its interests, the nonbelligerent ally would almost certainly withdraw from the alliance. It might, of course, merely threaten to leave and thereby win some influence in the council of the alliance or at the peace negotiations; or it might attempt to modify the prospective peace agreement to a form more acceptable to itself. The threat to leave the alliance could also be coupled with a threat to assist the adversary. If the possibility of a realignment existed, the belligerent allies might acquiesce in the nonbelligerent ally's proposals for peace. Whether or not the alliance remained viable, the nonbelligerent ally would very likely remain a war-oriented state.

The relations among nonbelligerent and belligerent allies will not necessarily be conflictual. The former might indeed value the alliance highly enough to acquiesce in having minimal influence. Its policymakers simply might not want the dissolution of a valued alliance to result from disagreements relating to a war in which it had been a nonbelligerent. After all, if its war aims had been important enough, the nonbelligerent ally would have joined in the hostilities to achieve its goals by fighting for them—and perhaps also to persuade its coalition partners that it was willing to make sacrifices for the benefit of the belligerent allies collectively. The nonbelligerent ally might, moreover, perform a positive function in mediating incompatibilities in the war aims of its belligerent partners. Provided that it assumed an undemanding role in the peace negotiations, accepting the consequences of its nonbelligerency in its minimal influence in obtaining substantial modification of the elements of the settlement, the nonbelligerent ally would be regarded as a disinterested party by the belligerent allies. In this situation, it would be an ideal mediator of alliance disputes.

International Organizations:

External Wars. The neutral and disinterested international organization could play an important role in the settlement of an external war, and this is true of both collective security *and* functional organizations. In principle, the war aim of such organizations is to end hostilities or, if that is impossible, to lessen the human and material costs of the war and to prevent escalation. These ends can be achieved in the phase preliminary to negotiations by the use of suitable representatives as mediators, by furnishing formulas for peace feelers and prompting either belligerent to initiate them, by airing the views of the belligerents and war-oriented states, and generally by acting as the agent for proposing compromises in war aims. In the military settlement phase, the organization might assist in the implementation and supervision of the armistice and provide military administrators for territories in the battle zones (or oversee the administrators of the belligerents). It might also provide a military force to keep the belligerents apart, reducing substantially the potential for renewed violence after the cease-fire.[9] A functional organization could also furnish relief for war-ravaged areas, distributing food, clothing, and medicine, operating communication networks, and providing transportation until the authorities of the state having jurisdiction over the war zones could assume responsibility for these tasks. The belligerents must, of course, consent to whatever operations the functional organization undertook; and this will usually also be the case for the collective security organization, although the latter could conceivably decide to force its operations upon the belligerents, which could result in attacks on the organization's forces and administrators. If the organization is willing to use force against the belligerents, it has the choice of actually using force or merely threatening its use in order to keep a precarious peace. The threat of economic sanctions might be efficacious in the right circumstances. Here, however, we move into the area of *peace-keeping methods*.[10] In the context of our analysis, peace-keeping plays a part in the over-all peacemaking process, as it is necessary to keep the peace after a

9 Bloomfield, L. P., *et al.*, *International Military Forces* (Boston: Little, Brown & Co., 1964). See pp. 105–171 (essays by Herbert Nicholas, B. E. Urquhart, E. H. Bowman & J. E. Fanning) for a discussion of the functions of U.N. forces in the Suez and Congo crises. Bowett, D. W., *United Nations Forces: A Legal Study* (New York: Praeger, 1965).

10 James, Alan, *The Politics of Peace-Keeping* (New York: Praeger, 1969); Burns, A. L. & Heathcote, Nina, *Peace-Keeping by U.N. Forces from Suez to the Congo* (New York: Praeger, 1963); Bloomfield, L. P., "Peacekeeping and Peacemaking," *Foreign Affairs,* Vol. 44, No. 4 (July, 1966); Cox, A. M., *Prospects for Peacekeeping* (Washington, D.C.: Brookings, 1967); Frydenberg, Per (ed.), *Peace-Keeping: Experience and Evaluation* (Oslo: Norwegian Institute of International Affairs, 1964); Frye, W. R., *A United Nations Peace Force* (New York: Oceana, 1957); Young, Oran R., *Trends in International Peacekeeping* (Princeton: Center of International Studies, 1966); Young, Oran R., *The Intermediaries* (Princeton: Princeton University Press, 1967); Wainhouse, David W., *et al.*, *International Peace Observation* (Baltimore: Johns Hopkins, 1966); Rosner, Gabriella, *The United Nations Emergency Force* (New York: Columbia University Press, 1963); Stegenga, J. A., *The United Nations Force in Cyprus* (Columbus: Ohio State University Press, 1968); Holmes, J. W., "The Political and Philosophical Aspects of U.N. Security Forces," *International Journal,* Vol. 19, No. 3 (Summer, 1964), pp. 292–307.

cessation of hostilities so that the belligerents can move into substantive peace negotiations.

The international organization may very well be interested in every element of the political settlement. In respect to a territory, the international organization might establish rules for a plebiscite and supervise the voting: it could formulate the statute of a free territory and administer it; it could assume a supervisory role in the transitional phases of an occupation regime when it was being established and when the occupying state relinquished its authority; it could become a quasi-permanent administrative authority in its own right of the territories of either or both belligerents; and it could arbitrate or mediate territorial disputes over boundaries or the uses to which lands or transportation arteries are put.

The functional organization could provide transport for refugees and prisoners of war to places of their origin, and relief for devastated areas. The collective security organization could supplement the security guarantees exchanged by the belligerents. Whether these supplementary guarantees are of value depends upon the viability of the organization, whether it has (or can muster) the forces necessary to fulfill a guarantee, and whether it has in the past demonstrated a willingness to carry out its security functions objectively and effectively. Probably no organizational guarantee would be effective against a great power belligerent unless other great powers had determined to act collectively against it in the context of the organization.

The great power could of course prevent collective action of the organization whose constitution required unanimity among the powers. In the case of medium-range powers or small states, an organization's guarantee, backed by the great powers, could be effective. Yet, if these states were war-oriented, they would undoubtedly be reluctant to permit the organization to frustrate their war aims by its intervention. They would resist by legal and extra-legal means. History supports the belief (perhaps, the prejudice) that an organizational guarantee is minimally credible. But, while the formal guarantee will not have much weight in the peace negotiations (or in the postwar years), the collective security and functional organizations could attempt to create the conditions of stability that would be the functional equivalent of a guarantee. Either form of organization could do this by promoting mediation and by normalizing the relations between the former belligerents.

The international organization could provide the forum through which the former belligerents reestablished commercial and diplomatic intercourse and removed the adverse legal effects of their past war. The organization could assist these efforts by establishing institutional mechanisms for extending the benefits of multinational trade, aid, and economic agreements to the belligerents. And cooperation among them in the operations of a functional organization could facilitate normalization of relations. The common enemy uniting the hostile parties would be their mutual needs, or any dangers that threatened them. Finally, an acceptable international organization might be invited by the belligerents to mediate the conflicts of interests or war aims that are the reasons for the war. The organization's representatives could also obtain the agreement of the parties to mediate their future disputes in order to prevent resumption of hostilities. In fact, if the organization were successful in bringing the belligerents together at the peace talks, it would not be unusual for it to assume continuing duties in the postwar years, supplementing whatever mediation provisions are contained within the peace treaty. Usually, the belligerents must consent to the mediatory role of the organization. But if the war had become devalued to the extent necessary to allow the policymakers of the belligerents to entertain proposals for the adjustment of their disputes, then we would expect them to give the already involved organization the mandate to continue its mediation in the future. The organization could institutionalize its role of postwar mediator by establishing an agency for that purpose—composed of international civil servants or representatives of states acceptable to the belligerents, who might incorporate in the peace treaty an agreement to refer disputes to the agency thus established. We may expect that most states will want to retain as flexible a posture as possible relative to their disputes with each other. Thus, they might be reluctant to commit themselves to future mediation, except in the most general and ambiguous terms. It would be the supplementary task of the organization to persuade the former belligerents to undertake to commit themselves to mediation in fairly definite terms.

The international organization dominated by a bloc of states will be a less effective peacemaker to the extent that the bloc is prejudiced for or against one of the belligerents. The latter would then regard every peace proposal as suspect. The belligerents' official attitudes to the policies of the *bloc-dominated* organization would be analogous to their attitudes toward rival war-oriented *states,* and their reactions could be similar. Nonetheless, the involvement of a bloc-dominated international organization in an external war might change the character of the response of the belligerents. They might be compelled to adopt the fiction that a single, theoretically objective organization was dealing with the problems of the war; and as long as they were members, they would have to respond, in a formal way, according to the terms of their obligations pursuant to the constitution of the organization—no matter who controlled it. But the reality of bloc-domination could not be ignored, whatever the fictions, whatever the formal language of the policymakers of the belligerents. They will frame their policies with reference to the acts and policies of the bloc that dominated the organization, principally to controller-states, not to the controlled international organization. Their policies, in short, will be designed only to *appear* to be commensurate with their obligations to the organization.

Internal War: Since the Second World War, we have seen several scores of states achieve independence. The United Nations has been war-oriented toward the wars for independence because of the importance the concept of national self-determination has assumed (and because this principle was incorporated in the U.N. Charter). Nevertheless, the role of the U.N. has been minimal. It was effectively excluded from playing even a minor role in the wars for independence of Algeria or Indochina, although its role in the settlement of the Indonesian war was substantial.

In the war for control of the polity, the U.N. has been even less significant. First, the theory of a rebellion for control of a state (the whole state) does not ordinarily rest upon any principle as universally attractive as national self-determination; second, the internal war is usually regarded as a matter of the domestic affairs of the state affected, and the U.N.'s competence does not extend to the domestic affairs of its member states; and third, the member state has status in the organization, while rebels do not. The U.N. member can influence the content of the organization's agenda and move to exclude from debate matters relating to the internal war (unless a third-party state has intervened in the war, in which case the organization might be invited to take action against the intervenor). In cases of internal wars for control, we see that incumbents generally win; insurgents win occasionally; and stalemated outcome is rare.[11] If the incumbents win, there are no negotiations. In this event, the organization could at most appeal to the victors to follow a policy of reconciliation, as any other approach to the war by the organization would be regarded as an officious interference in the state's domestic affairs. If the insurgents win, the organization will be faced with the often difficult problem of determining the status of the state-member, particularly if other members refused to recognize the new government or to establish normal diplomatic and commercial relations with it. As in the preceding case, there will be no negotiations, and the organization must usually rest content with hortatory appeals.

Should the internal war end in a stalemate, the organization could conceivably play the mediator. History does give us a few recent examples of this.[12] There should be no reason for the domestic jurisdiction exclusion to prevent any action. The stalemated factions could probably use

11 Modelski, George, "International Settlement of Internal Wars," in J. N. Rosenau, *International Aspects of Civil Strife* (Princeton: Princeton University Press, 1964). For a discussion of the legal and political problems of intervention in internal wars, see Falk, R. A. (ed.), *The International Law of Civil War* (Baltimore: Johns Hopkins, 1971).

12 James, Alan, *op. cit.*, Chapter 3.

the good offices of a mediator, and it should not matter whether that service is proffered by a disinterested state or an international organization, provided that the peacemaker is approved by both factions. In fact, there would be ample room for the international organization to play a creative role, for example, by guaranteeing the settlement eventually reached by the factions. The existence of a guarantee could in itself deter either faction from using force to achieve its goals.

The *functional* organization could also assume a useful role. As in the external war, it could provide technical assistance to either faction to return the economy and society of the state more quickly to a condition of stability. If the solution adopted by the factions were partition, then an organization could supervise the implementation of the division of the state into the two (or several) administrative divisions and, in the future, promote the unification of the state through elections. It is well to realize that tasks such as these constitute intervention in the domestic affairs of the state affected by the war; as such, they would undoubtedly be resisted or resented by at least some of the elites of that state. If the international organization were to be permitted to assume the function of an *internal war peacemaker,* it must not be dominated by any bloc of states, particularly those in any way interested in the internal war; and it must conduct its operations in the most prudent and disinterested way possible. Any act that could be construed by either faction as biased or indiscreet could result in the end of the organization's mandate to promote the peace.

The war-oriented international organization can assume (and since the Second World War, has assumed) a more flexible role in wars for independence. If the insurgent faction were successful in achieving independence—perhaps with the help of the international organization—then the organization could help the new state establish relations with member states and with the parent state as well. It could do this by inviting the new state to join the international organization; it would create thereby a situation in which the member states would have to deal with the new state in the context of the organization's operations and problems. Of course, any state bent upon ignoring the new state would still be able to do so, but it would be a bit more awkward to maintain such a stance with the new state occupying a seat in the councils of the organization. By joining a collective security organization, the new state would also secure a guarantee of its existence and its territorial integrity. While this guarantee might be of little value relative to the great power, it could have a significant deterrent effect upon smaller states. By establishing itself as a going concern in the context of the international organization, the new state would gradually become an acceptable member of the state system, and its seizure or invasion less admissible. There are many instances in history of states refusing to come to the aid of a new state that has been attacked by another, stronger state. But international organizations have at least created a sense of the injustice of such an attack—and the moral approbrium may in itself constitute a sufficient deterrent to the prospective attacker. Perhaps one day the international organization's collective security function might become effective enough to guarantee the existence of the new state until its capabilities reached a more adequate level for defense and it became a viable polity having internal coherence and stability.

Conferences of War-Oriented States

It may be in the interests of war-oriented states to establish or improve their channels of communication during hostilities. To this end, they may agree to confer, formally or informally, and to exchange information and proposals concerning the external or internal war in which they have some interest. Such a conference might meet very irregularly and for a short period of time or regularly and for so long a period of time that it becomes institutionalized and a permanent characteristic of the diplomacy of the participating states. The conference becomes, in effect, an organization of war-oriented states, a cooperative enterprise with purposes formulated by the partcipants, the most important being the prevention of the escalation of the war and the involvement of the war-oriented states. International organizations of the twentieth century are of course the most highly evolved form of the war-oriented state conference.[13] The League of Nations and the United Nations and such regional organizations as the Organization of American States and the Organization of African Unity have been forums for the discussion of problems connected with a number of wars in which their member states have become involved. They have also been the source of conflict-limiting schemes and proposals for peace. In this capacity, the League functioned successfully in the Greco-Bulgarian War (1925) and unsuccessfully in the Ethiopian War (1935–38) and the Japanese intervention in Manchuria (1931+). The U.N. played a unique and important part in the settlement of the War for Indonesian Independence (1945–49), the Arab War against Israel in 1948, the Suez War of 1956, the Congo Civil War (1960–62), and the Cyprus Civil War (1963–64).

In any conference of war-oriented states, the initiating parties must decide where and when they will meet, what other states will be invited to attend, and the procedures to be followed at the meetings. All participating states will demand, and no doubt obtain, the right to be regarded as sovereign equals, although differences in power position will influence decisions—the stronger states perhaps exerting a veto on collective deci-

13 As independent and functioning organizations, they have been war-oriented actors too, as we have seen.

sions. Questions of substance discussed by the conference and the course
of action determined by its participants are likely to be of the following
sort:

1. The states agree not to intervene in the war with their armed forces.
This agreement might be carefully hedged to protect the war-oriented
states against many hypothetical eventualities. It might be precise or
ambiguous, published or kept secret. The reason-for-being of the London
Conference of Ambassadors, called to deal with the First Balkan War
(1912–13), was the at least tacit agreement of the great powers not to
intervene in the Balkans. The settlement reached under the auspices of
the Conference failed; but the fact that the powers had met and exchanged their views and proposals and made clear their policies had the
salutary effect of preventing the unilateral intervention of either Austria
or Russia. During the Spanish Civil War (1936–39), the European
powers signed a nonintervention agreement and established a Non-Intervention Committee. While the agreement was soon violated by Germany,
Italy, and the Soviet Union, and the Committee's proceedings took on an
air of futility, many interesting schemes for insuring strict nonintervention were discussed. The Four Power Conferences on the Middle East
were convened to determine whether the tenuous cease-fire after the Six
Day War of 1967 could be transformed into a more permanent settlement. It represented a temporary commitment on the part of the Soviet
Union, the United States, France, and Great Britain not to exacerbate
the Arab-Israeli conflict by military intervention nor escalate it into a
war involving themselves.

2. Unable to agree not to intervene, the conference might establish
rules for intervention and inform each other how and when each will
intervene, usually upon the occurrence of a contingency that directly
affects the vital interests of one or more of the participating states. Thus,
state G might warn the others that if another third-party state sent troops
against state A, G would supply aircraft to A or perhaps troops. The
conference might decide that it is permissible to give the belligerents
economic or technical assistance, but no armaments; or they might agree to
provide arms, specified as to type, quality, and number, with the view to
maintaining a balance of armaments among the belligerents. In the 1827
Treaty of London and in subsequent agreements made during the Conference of Ambassadors in London, France, Britain, and Russia agreed
upon the terms of their intervention in the Greek Revolt. And again in
respect to the Arab-Israeli conflict after 1967, the Soviet Union and the
United States conferring independently of the eventually moribund Four
Power Conferences agreed upon the limits of their aid to their protegés in
the hope that with this understanding they would avoid a conflict with
each other.

3. The participating war-oriented states might also formulate policies

concerning other war-oriented states that are not taking part in the conference, either because they have not been invited to participate or because they have refused to do so. As the war or peace policies of such states would affect the course of the war and peace negotiations in important ways, the conference states would perhaps want to agree upon a common stance relative to the nonattending state: they might seek reduction of that state's influence upon the belligerents curbing its involvement in the hostilities, or conducting diplomacy through the usual channels with that state so as to modify its war aims and policies. In the Second War of Mehemet Ali against the Sultan (1839–41), the Ambassadorial Conferences of Vienna and London determined the form of a settlement acceptable to the participants (Britain, Austria, and Russia) and submitted the "arrangement" to the Sultan and Mehemet Ali. France had refused to take part in the Conferences; and the other powers had to formulate plans with reference to the possible and probable responses of this nonparticipating power.

4. The conferring states might also attempt to reach an understanding relative to the general region of the war, agreeing upon the need to refrain from exploiting regional instability created by the war in order to maintain a local balance of power or agreeing to alter their commercial, cultural, or aid policies in the region.

5. If the war-oriented states were so disposed, they might take a collective part in the peacemaking process. Presumably, being war-oriented, they would indeed be interested in influencing the peace talks and in determining the structure and content of the peace settlement; but they could more or less agree to coordinate their policies toward the peace negotiations, either because they believed that collective action was intrinsically desirable or perhaps because they believed that collective action would more likely be effective in influencing the negotiators. The latter motivation, resting on each state's self-interest, was controlling in the collective pacifications of the Levant in the nineteenth century. With the advent of the League of Nations, there has been more verbal support for collective action for peace, although the policymakers of each participating state are no doubt as conscious of reasons of state as their diplomatic ancestors.

6. The war-oriented conference states might jointly propose settlement terms; or they might confer, agree to disagree, and then each submit its own peace proposals to the belligerents. This process of conferring and proposing solutions could continue through the late stages of the war and throughout the peace talks. The persistent efforts of the American states to conciliate the disputes underlying the Chaco War illustrate how conferences of war-oriented states can be intimately involved in peacemaking. During the Second War over Schleswig-Holstein (1864), the Conference of London signally failed to persuade the belligerents to accept the

variety of peace proposals made by the participants. Nonetheless, what was significant (at least for our purposes) was the recognition by the belligerents of the right of the Conference powers to involve themselves in the settlement process.

The effect of the conference of war-oriented states upon the belligerents might be substantial or nil, depending upon the intensity of ideologization of the war and the ability of the war-oriented states to influence the belligerents—which in turn depends upon the credibility of the threats, express or implied, accompanying the proposals made by the conference, upon the war-weariness of the belligerents, and upon the policies of other nonparticipating war-oriented states. In extraordinary circumstances, several or all of the war-oriented states might agree to *impose* a proposal or solution upon intransigent belligerents, as in the Greek Revolt or the Second War of Mehemet Ali. This would probably entail the use of force. In certain situations, the mere threat of force will suffice, if the prospective move by determined war-oriented states is credible. In 1913, during the First Balkan War, the Conference of Ambassadors agreed to send several ships to blockade Scutari and force the Montenegrins to withdraw. This did not succeed. A naval squadron alone could not have forced evacuation, and in the circumstances the threats of the Western European powers were not credible: They had repeatedly aired their fears of a general war and their desire to avoid the use of force. On the other hand, the Austrian threats were credible; and when the Montenegrin king realized that Austria-Hungary would intervene, he ordered evacuation. We would expect—as would belligerents—that war-oriented states would be reluctant to impose a solution unless they could feel assured that costs would be minimal and the intervention would succeed within a reasonable time. Naturally, their policymakers must feel that their vital interest will be prejudiced by a continuation of the war and that intervention will not adversely affect their power positions relative to other states and to each other. As it would be unusual for intervention to be this "antiseptic" or to have *predictable* and *minimal* consequences, imposition of peace proposals upon belligerents is a rare and unusual course of action. The interventions of Austria, Russia, and France (1820–22) after the revolutions in Italy and Spain were operations designed to apply counter-revolutionary theories of government, to restore monarchs to their thrones, and to maintain in Europe regimes acceptable to the intervenors. The military operations were short-lived, succeeded, and gave rise to surprisingly few international repercussions. This was one of the rare occasions when intervention had minimal costs for the intervening war-oriented states. Naturally, the conference states might agree to employ rigorous methods short of force, individually or collectively, to induce the belligerents to make peace or to accept some compromise proposal designed to get negotiations moving.

The conference of mediating war-oriented states may eventuate from the de-escalation of a complex war in which these states are belligerents. (There are indeed instances of an *individual state* assuming the role of mediator after a period of active belligerency: e.g., Britain and Sweden in the Franco-Dutch War, 1672–79.) Mediating conferences would also have the character of a rule-making conference, in which the participating states attempted to formulate rules for further or additional de-escalation and for preventing their reinvolvement in the war. This might be more difficult to do than in the case of the conference of states that had never been involved in hostilities. The memories of the war will die hard, and many of the issues will continue to be intensely ideologized. However, given the commitment to de-escalation, based upon an undoubtedly difficult decision to decouple from the war, the war-oriented states could conceivably achieve a working arrangement at the conference that would result in the formulation of sound peace proposals. We have examples of conferences of former belligerents in the Thirty Years' War and the European War of 1683–1700 in which various German states called conferences to discuss ways of limiting damage to their lands and pacifying the Empire.

After hostilities have ceased and a peace settlement is achieved, the war-oriented participants at the conference have a choice of options. They may dissolve the conference and rely upon the traditional channels of diplomacy to conduct their foreign relations; or they may agree to continue their meetings in the postwar years. They might prefer the latter course if they had concluded that the terms of the peace treaty needed their supervision, concurrence, or coordinated action. Or they might wish simply to preserve a reasonably successful forum for coordinating their policies generally. In the absence of a formally constituted international organization or an organization competent to deal with the war, such a course would be an attractive one.

The conference of the war-oriented states could collapse well before the end of the war or *before* the belligerents had reached a settlement. Termination of the conference need not necessarily lead to armed conflict among the former conference states or to actual intervention in the ongoing war. But it does, of course, represent a worsening of relations and reduced cooperation among them and an end of the joint effort to influence the belligerents and prevent escalation—all of which (even short of war) would probably affect the peacemaking process adversely. Why should the conference be forced to dissolve? For reasons similar to those for the dissolution of an ordinary alliance: incompatibility of war aims (i.e., goals or policies) of the partners or an inability to achieve the objects of those aims within the context of the conference. The war-oriented state might come to regard the conference as a means for unduly hampering the achievement of its aims. Its policymakers would then prefer the greater flexibility that nonparticipation offers: If one of the conference states declares war on one of the belligerents (or otherwise intervened) or if a third-party state does so, the reason-for-being of the conference has disappeared, and the remaining states might end the unsuccessful conference and pursue completely independent policies.[14] Finally, states other than war-oriented actors or other nonparticipating war-oriented states might present the conferring states with problems unrelated to the war in areas of the world far removed from the region of the war. These problems could induce a participating state to restrict its activities in the region of the war, withdraw from the conference, and perhaps even become non-war-oriented.

Proxy Internal Wars and Their Settlement

In the fifth chapter, we discussed the nature and settlement of complex internal-external wars: those internal wars in which third-party states support and ally themselves with the belligerent factions and in which the states are also at war with each other (see Fig. 7–1). We turn now to

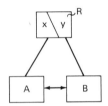

FIGURE 7–1. Schematic structure of the complex internal–external war. States A and B are at war with each other, as are factions x and y.

consider the proxy internal war in which the states involved are not belligerents but are rather one of the kinds of war-oriented states treated in this and the preceding chapter. The prototype structure of the proxy internal war is shown in Fig. 7–2.

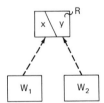

FIGURE 7–2. The prototype proxy internal war. The war-oriented states w_1 and w_2 are not at war, but are merely "oriented" toward the belligerent factions.

In Figure 7–2, the war-oriented states, W_1 and W_2, can be assumed to be either great powers or regional states that favor and support the factions, or they may be nonbelligerent allies of the factions: W_1 allied to faction

14 Of course, the states that have not intervened in the war could still agree to continue their collective efforts to prevent escalation, even in the face of hostile policies and acts on the part of a former conference associate.

x, W_2 to faction y. The proxy internal war will usually be a war for control of the polity. In a war for independence, the incumbents would probably regard support for the insurgents by an outside state as a belligerent act warranting a declaration of war and thus resulting in what we have called an internal-external war. Where hostilities between the war-oriented state and the incumbents do not occur, we may subsume the internal war for independence under our category of proxy wars. Before the entry of France into the War for American Independence in 1778, that war could be regarded as a proxy war. Vergennes' policy of aiding the rebellious colonies was motivated by his desire to fragment the British Empire and thereby improve France's power position relative to her traditional enemy. Not until enough French policymakers had become convinced that the colonists could win and that French interests would be better served by more overt participation was the Franco-American alliance formed. In June, 1778, the proxy war became an internal-external war.

Why should a war-oriented state support a faction? In the case of a nonbelligerent ally, the answer is obvious: As long as the alliance lasts, the partners will undoubtedly coordinate their policies. As for the great power or regional war-oriented state, there may be a variety of reasons. The reader might refer again to the tables in Chapter 5, describing the rationale for third-party state intervention.[15]

The fact that a multiplicity of war-oriented states were involved in the internal war as nonbelligerent opponents adds another dimension to the problem. The competition between such states induces them to support the opposing factions in order to accomplish their policy aims relative to each other. In other words, W_1 and W_2 place themselves in a position of potential conflict with each other by supporting factions x and y. They hope to realize their war aims—if we may call them that—through the agency of the belligerent factions, without engaging in combat themselves. Support for either faction might enable the war-oriented state to test the resolve of a rival state to resist whatever policies the former is pursuing; and these policies could pertain to areas remote from the scene of the internal war. For if one state (W_1) demonstrates an intention to parry another state (W_2) in the nonbelligerent confrontation of a proxy internal war, W_2 might be forced to reassess its strategy in other regions of the world, taking into account W_1's determination and willingness to resist. The proxy war could also enable the war-oriented states to test new weapons or provide combat experience for a select group of its soldiers or technicians.

15 The lists in Chapter 5 are meant only to be heuristic. Other reasons could probably be adduced were we to make a more detailed historical study of complex internal wars.

Incompatibility between the war aims of the faction and the war-oriented state could result in the reduction or withdrawal of support by the state. Moreover, incompatibility between the aims of W_1 and W_2 relative to each other may also be crucial. Can these aims be achieved without war between W_1 and W_2? If not, then the proxy war will escalate into an internal-external war. If they can be realized short of war, W_1 and W_2 would provide the factions with the support necessary to enable either to serve the interests of the war-oriented states by means of the *internal war*. That aid would continue for as long, and just so long, as those interests were served. It is conceivable that the policymakers of the competitor war-oriented states would conclude that their aims could be achieved by means other than support for the factions, which after all does carry with it the risk of war between their states. That determination might have been prompted by either external or internal political developments, a better understanding of the competitor's war aims, or by a realization that support for the factions was too costly. Having made this latter determination, the policymakers of W_1 and W_2 could disengage from the internal war and let the factions themselves resolve their differences by force of arms or by negotiations. Thus, the course of the proxy war and the possibilities for its settlement depend to a great extent upon the character of the relations between the war-oriented supporters of the warring factions. Yet, the relations between the supporting states, while competitive, are not as embittered as they might be were the states actually at war. The values sought by their policymakers and elites are not as intensely ideologized as they would be in the internal-external war. Given the fact of nonbelligerency and the additional fact that few (if any) lives have been lost in a war with the rival war-oriented state, the peacemaking process ought to be only slightly more complicated than in the case of the simple internal war.

The proxy internal war could evolve in several ways:

1. Either or both war-oriented states might decouple or disengage. Examples are the Yemen Civil War (1962–69) and the Greek Civil War (1946–49). Disengagement could indicate a loss of interest in the war, with the state becoming non-war-oriented. This state of affairs naturally implies that there is a complete break with the supported faction; and no further aid would be provided. The states (W_1 and W_2) could disengage as a result of a mutual agreement arrived at through negotiations similar in nature to peace negotiations, the parties either compromising on the issues that were the grounds of their rivalry in order to avoid a possible war or reducing the costs of their competition incurred by their support—perhaps expensive support—for the belligerent factions. In the Yemen Civil War, the U.A.R. supported the Republican faction; Saudi Arabia the Royalists. Disengagement was brought about by mutual agreement of the rival states with Sudanese mediation. The U.A.R. agreed

to remove Egyptian troops from Yemen; Saudi Arabia promised to stop aid to the Royalists. This was accomplished, but the internal war continued through 1969. Of course, decoupling could also result from a host of domestic and world political pressures upon the war-oriented states' policymakers. Britain and the United States supported the Greek government during the Civil War of 1946–49. The Soviet Union and Yugoslavia aided the Greek Communists. The incumbents were eventually successful, in part because, after defecting from the Soviet Bloc, Yugoslavia closed the Greek frontier and prevented supplies from reaching the Communists.

2. Either faction might defeat the other. The war-oriented state that has sustained high costs because of the loss of the war by its supported faction would acquiesce in the outcome, resorting to only diplomatic means to minimize the consequences of defeat. The Spanish Civil War (1936–39) foreshadowed the Second World War in that the Soviet Union, supporting the Republicans, was a rival of Germany and Italy, which provided extensive aid to the Nationalists. When the latter had defeated the Republican incumbents, the Soviet Union took no action except to denounce French and British recognition of Nationalist Spain.

3. The factions could agree to negotiate a settlement—and may in fact resolve their conflict through such negotiations. The war-oriented states would then be in the same position as identical states in the simple internal war, although the degree of participation might be greater. Because of their support for the factions during the war the states might be able to secure an invitation to the peace talks and actively promote their own interests. In the Cyprus Civil War (1963–64), Greece and Turkey supported their respective Cypriot "nationals." The U.N. mediated a settlement between the factions while the U.S., Britain, and other interested states, together with the U.N., brought about a cooling off of the antagonisms between Greece and Turkey. These two states reached an informal *modus vivendi* with respect to internal Cyprus politics. During the extremely complex Congo Civil War (1960–62), the antagonists of the Cold War and the proponents of differing schemes for African political order collided indirectly through their Congolese proxies. A U.N. force checkmated the Lumumbists and eventually forced Tshombe, head of the secessionist Katanga regime, to negotiate a renunciation of his declaration of independence. The central government, by a combination of negotiations and the use of force, ended the secession of Orientale province. The United Nations was the principal forum of the often bitter conflict between the war-oriented states while a settlement was being reached in the Congo. And during the settlement of the Laotian Civil War (1955–62) (which I have classified earlier as an internal-external war, but which could also be looked upon as a proxy internal war), the three Laotian factions negotiated in Zürich while the war-oriented states,

including those that had played a rather active belligerent role, met in Geneva to attempt a settlement. Although the Geneva powers had first adumbrated the general form of the peace settlement, no final agreement was reached until the factions had composed their differences.

4. The war-oriented states could go to war with each other, transforming the proxy war into an internal-external war. This might occur during the course of the proxy war, as the rivalry between the states intensifies, and the policymakers decide to escalate the conflict as a means of achieving their goals. As we have noted, the War for American Independence was a proxy war for a time, until France went to war with Britain in 1778. And until the U.S. escalation of the Vietnam conflict in 1965 (or if you prefer, the DRVN escalation after 1962), the Vietnam War was a proxy war: the incumbent RVN regime vs. the insurgents who after 1960 called themselves the NLF of South Vietnam. The U.S. supported the former, the DRVN the latter; both sides were temporarily content to pursue their goals by support for their belligerent proxies. A war-oriented actor might also object to its supported faction's agreeing to a settlement and might then become more actively involved in the internal war, intending so to complicate the situation that further peace moves would be impossible. It could do this by committing troops to the internal war. The rival war-oriented state would probably not countenance such active intervention and would either declare war or send troops of its own to engage the forces of the rival state. In either case, we have an escalation of the proxy war, with real war between the war-oriented states. This kind of escalation occurred during the Laotian Civil War when, after the Kong Le coup, the government of Souvanna Phouma made an accommodation with the Pathet Lao in 1960, an accommodation unacceptable to the United States government. The latter supplied arms and other aid to the right-wing Boun Oum-Phoumi Nosavan faction in southern Laos. After Phoumi Nosavan marched north and captured Vientiane, the Soviet Union increased its involvement in Laos, as did the DRVN (which had in any case been interfering in Laotian affairs since the early Fifties).

A negotiated settlement, as we understand it, would occur by the first mode (disengagement by the war-oriented states) or by the third mode (where the factions reached a settlement). It would very rarely occur by the second (one faction defeating the other), as the victorious faction would undoubtedly destroy the defeated faction as a political force in the affected state.

Multilateral Wars
and Their Settlement

CHAPTER 8

Form and Analysis of Multilateral Wars

Many actors are involved in a multilateral war. Because of this multiplicity of parties, the war is almost invariably extended geographically over wide areas. There is no one form of multilateral war. Sometimes states alone are involved; in other cases, states and factions. Sometimes the actors are arrayed in alliances against each other; at other times, some of the actors are in alliances, while others are not. However, it would be most unusual to find a multilateral war in which there were no alliances.

In the war depicted schematically in Figure 8–1, two alliances (circled by dotted lines) —one consisting of states A, C, and E and the other of states D, F, and H—are at war with each other (indicated by arrow 1). Independently of the interalliance war, states A and B are also at war (arrow 2) ; and state G is at war with the alliance DFH (arrow 3) but is not formally allied to ACE. State R is a regional state; states N_1, N_2, and N_3 are nonbelligerent allies and, as such, are all war-oriented.

Figure 8–2 illustrates another form of the multilateral war. Alliance PRT is at war with alliance QS (arrow 1). State N_0 is a nonbelligerent ally of QS. There are, moreover, two internal wars complicating the situation: in state R, between factions x and y; and in state S, between factions u and v. State O has come to the assistance of faction y. Faction x, the incumbent government of state R, has declared war on state O (arrow 2). State P has also provided aid (in a *de facto* alliance) for the insurgents, u, of state S, in order to help its own war effort against QS.

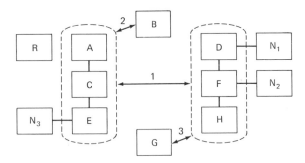

FIGURE 8–1.   One form of a multilateral war between states.

Multilateral wars can be analyzed in several ways. Indeed a more complete appreciation of the character of the war and the peace settlement could be attained by examining the multilateral war from more than one perspective. In a first method of analysis, according to belligerent group, we reduce the structure of the multilateral war to a number of simple and complex external and internal wars. We do this because a multilateral war can degenerate into a series of simpler wars (see Figure 8–4) ; and because, in any event, such an analysis can better enable us to perceive possible modes of settlement in even the most complex situations. Thus, the multilateral war among the states diagrammed in Figure 8–1 can be reduced as follows: alliance *ACE* vs. alliance *DFH* (a complex external war) ; state *A* vs. state *B* (a simple external war) ; and state *G* vs. alliance *DFH* (a complex external war) . Finally, we consider the roles of the war-oriented states: *R*, a regional state, and states N_1, N_2, and N_3, the nonbelligerent allies. We note that *G* is at war with the alliance *DFH*, but is not allied with *ACE;* that *B* is at war with alliance *ACE* but is not allied with *DFH*. This is not to say that *G* and alliance *ACE,* and state *B* and alliance *DFH*, will not have some common interest in defeating their adversaries. They are simply not allied formally. In Figure 8–1, the states are arrayed (*G* with *ACE* on the left, *B* with *DFH* on the right) to suggest that during the course of the war the states might be functionally allied with the alliances because of the structure of the multilateral war. A functional alliance is not a *de facto* alliance; and it is certainly not a formal, *de jure* alliance. It is an analytical fiction in which the analyst is permitted to indulge because states (*G* on the one hand and the alliance *ACE* on the other) are independently pursuing similar (although perhaps not wholly compatible) war aims against a *common adversary* (alliance *DFH*) . One other point of interest: in the simple external war of *A* vs. *B,* the states *C* and *E* are, in effect, nonbelligerent allies of *A* and may be treated as such, at least, in one mode (of several possible modes) of analysis.

The multilateral war diagrammed in Figure 8–2 (a war between states

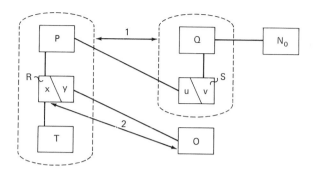

FIGURE 8–2.   One form of a multilateral war between states
and factions.

and factions) could be reduced in a similar fashion. Alliance PRT is in a
state of war with alliance QS, where state R is led by incumbent faction x
and state S by incumbent faction v. (This is a complex external war.)
The only war-oriented state is the nonbelligerent ally, N_0, of state Q;
and its relation to Q and the wars in which Q is involved must be
separately considered. Using a simplifying device, we could isolate the
simple internal wars: incumbents x vs. insurgents y in state R and incumbents v vs. insurgents u in state S. But, because of the alliance ties of
the factions with other states, the wars are not simple, but rather complex
internal wars. They may be reduced as follows: state R (faction x) vs.
state O (a simple external war) or faction x of state R allied with states P
and T vs. insurgent faction Y (a complex internal war). We note that P
and T are belligerent allies of R (x) against the insurgents Y. The states
are *nonbelligerent allies* of R (x) as against state O, provided that whatever aid P and T supply to R (x) has not resulted in hostilities with O.
Finally, state Q is allied with the incumbents of state S against insurgent
faction u, in turn allied to PRT. This is also a complex internal war.

Analysis of the multilateral war according to belligerent groups is not
the only mode of analysis, however. We could also reduce the war's
complexity by treating it according to regions of hostilities or theaters of
operations.[1] Thus, wars between states in one region or on one front
would be considered separately from wars between states in another
region. We might even introduce another simplification by subsequently
analyzing the actors according to belligerent groups *in a region*. In addi-

---

1 All the wars in our sample in Chapter 9 have been analyzed at least according
to belligerent group. For analysis according to theater, see the European War
of 1683–1700 (pp. 347–57), the Wars for French Hegemony in Europe (pp.
392–405), and the First World War (pp. 405–28). The latter two wars and the
Thirty Years' War (pp. 379–92) can also be treated as a series of discrete wars
each having an independent settlement.

tion to the factor of space, time also provides a factor around which we might hinge our analysis.[2] If one state makes peace before the other belligerents, there is one actor less in the multilateral war, and the war then becomes somewhat less complex. Similarly, the dissolution of alliances, the decoupling of states from internal wars, and their consequent deescalation could also simplify the multilateral war. We would therefore have to be apprised of the changing structure of the war over time.[3]

We could also categorize each state or faction in the multilateral war according to the war aims of the belligerents. The war aims of each actor would perhaps have to be made more concrete by specifying the *particular objectives* of the belligerents. But the purpose of such an analytical exercise must be to achieve simplification. In this, it is like the preceding suggested modes of analysis. It is unlike them, however, in that we do not first attempt to reduce the multilateral war to a number of separate simple and complex external and internal wars. To illustrate, let us suppose that we have the following states involved or interested in a war.

actor		*war aims*
alliance ACE	A:	seeking dominance
		ideological
	C:	consolidation (at state B's expense)
		ideological
	E:	ideological
		retributive (against B)
state F		ideological (counter ACE)
state G		status quo: maintenance of position
alliance of BD	B:	status quo: defense (against ACE)
	D:	status quo: maintenance of position
war-oriented states HIJ	H:	status quo: maintenance of position
	I:	ideological (counter ACE)
	J:	ideological
		status quo: maintenance of position

It appears that the moving, revisionist states are A, C, and E in alliance led by state A seeking dominance. They evidently share a common or

2 See the Thirty Years' War (pp. 379–92) and the Napoleonic Wars (pp. 392–405).

3 The war might become more complex as other states become involved in an escalating war. But, in the late stages and during the peacemaking phase, this would be less likely to happen. While we must be aware of the structural changes in war over time, analysis of the multilateral war according to region or according to belligerent group will usually be more useful and efficacious than one according to time.

quite similar ideology. The status quo states, resisting the hegemonic policies of the *ACE* alliance, include the alliance of *B* and *D,* and state *F* and state *G.* The war-oriented states, *H* and *I,* are more closely oriented toward the war aims of *BD* than to the aims of *ACE.* The war-oriented state *J* has the same ideology as *ACE,* but prefers to see the status quo maintained. We may diagram the multilateral war as shown in Figure 8–3:

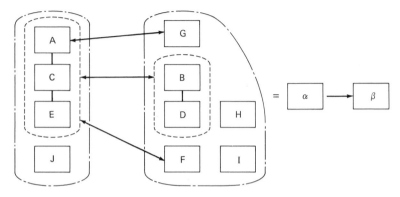

FIGURE 8–3. A form of a multilateral war in which the belligerents and war-oriented states are grouped according to common interests and war aims.

In order to simplify the war, we treat all the states favoring the status quo as a single bloc of states, α; the revisionist states as a single bloc β. Included within these blocs are the war-oriented states, which, while not actively belligerent, will very likely seek to influence the peace negotiations and hence may be considered as part of the blocs indicated. Thus, in a somewhat procrustean fashion, we have "reduced" our multilateral war to a simple external war. As a first approximation, we might treat the settlement of that war as equivalent to the settlement of a simple external war.[4]

Treatment of a multilateral war in this way by an analyst *decision-maker* could have several important results. The victorious bloc of states (comprising alliances or completely autonomous states) could impose a single peace treaty upon the defeated bloc: Both blocs would regard the treaty as embodying the settlement *for all parties.* Subsidiary or peripheral problems could be resolved in supplementary treaties, but it would be the treaty negotiated between the blocs (regarded as a simplifying mechanism for the complicated multilateral war) that would constitute

4 See the First World War. The Franco-Dutch War of 1672–79 (pp. 340–7) and the European War of 1683–1700 (pp. 347–57) could be regarded as wars of great coalitions against France.

the central agreement of peace. Were this procedure adopted (or rather, this perspective—for it is more of a way of looking at the war than it is a procedure of analysis), the great powers might tend to slight the lesser powers, leaving the resolution of the questions about which the latter are most concerned to supplementary treaties—perhaps spending little of the peace conference's time and effort to deal with them, with a resulting unrealistic or inadequate settlement. The small states must sign the principal treaty and receive comparatively few values, in effect being told by the great powers and the states that agree with them that this is the way the great powers want their war settled. This raises the vital question, How shall a war be analyzed? How shall it be categorized, and how treated by the analyst?[5] Indeed, analysts might come up with very different answers, particularly analysts from different belligerent states— and these differences might prevent early negotiations and settlement.

Other formal matters in the peacemaking process could be affected by the *analyst decision-makers'* treating the multilateral war as if it were a war between two major blocs. Procedural questions that arise during the preliminary phase could be resolved for or against many of the actors: such questions as what actors will be invited to the peace talks; what privileges they will have; when and how they will be permitted to introduce proposals and resolutions; and how they will vote. Smaller states could be procedurally (and substantively) prejudiced by having to accept the bloc approach of the great powers, as if they belonged to one or the other of two fictitious blocs. Naturally, the state—whether small or large—could adopt a number of techniques to slow or prevent a settlement until its demands were met or at least until its interests in modified formal procedures were adopted (that is, until the conference came to create exceptions in its procedural paradigm of the multilateral war— exceptions in favor of the state or faction that did not quite fit into the paradigm of the war between two blocs). In the military and political phases also, questions of substance could arise from a simplification of the multilateral war in analytical terms. Should, for example, there be one simultaneous cease-fire for all belligerents on all fronts, or should some of the states in the bloc be permitted to conclude separate cease-fires? Must all the belligerents and war-oriented states arrive at the settlement of their political disputes at one peace conference between the rival blocs, or could there be several peace conferences (and perhaps several independent treaties of peace)? We shall consider answers to these questions later in the chapter.

In proposing these various methods of reducing the multilateral war to a less complex form, we must ask ourselves what it is we are losing in the approximations we make. We can meet this problem by asking how the multilateral war differs in character from simple and complex external

5 See Appendix I.

and internal wars, the nature and settlement of which have already been discussed. Certainly, there are the differences mentioned at the beginning of this chapter: the relatively great numbers of belligerent and war-oriented actors involved and the consequent wide geographical extension of hostilities. (The war is fought in many regions and often on many fronts.) Geographical extension is rather important. It is not unlikely that in a multilateral war all or most of the great powers would be involved as active belligerents. The question arises, where will the fighting be done? Naturally, the powers will want to avoid, if at all possible, military operations on their own territories. This means that the great powers will seek to do their fighting on the territories of small states. But even with fairly complete control of military operations by the powers—even if the leaders of the powers did not deliberately plan operations upon the territories of smaller states—the multilateral war would tend to spill over, sometimes in an uncontrolled fashion.[6] And not only will the armed forces of the many belligerents be forced to carry the war to neutral soil, but blockades, interruption of commerce, and detention of persons will have wide and prejudicial economic and political effects for a number of nonbelligerent states. Thus, we can say that in a multilateral war, there will be many war-oriented states; and there will be a variety of pressures upon these states to become active belligerents. The war-oriented state will not remain neutral if its trade and its economy are threatened with irreparable destruction, or especially if belligerent acts were committed on its territories. And this is all too likely to happen in the multilateral war.[7]

Apart from the adverse effects of a multilateral war upon most neutrals, the war could offer more advantages to the state that was seeking opportunity values, simply because the great number of actors involved and the correspondingly greater number of issues in dispute present opportunities for leaders of states seeking gains at low costs.

The multilateral war will result in more permanent damage to certain regions than the simple or complex wars, where the damage can be absorbed in a relatively short time by the states of the region, as the wars are localized and the area of damage limited—at least geographically. In the multilateral war, however, there are fewer states that have not been adversely affected by the war, and the amortization of damages and costs of war and the recovery of peoples takes a much longer time. There may then be no sizable, wealthy bloc of states that could absorb the costs of the war in a short time.

6 We could say that the greater the number of interacting autonomous states, the greater will be the probability of unforeseen consequences following from the decisions of their policymakers.
7 The Thirty Years' War, the Napoleonic Wars, and the First and Second World Wars were extensively internationalized.

Another reason for the analytical complexities of the multilateral war—related to the greater number of belligerent actors—is the correspondingly greater number of war aims "seeking satisfaction," as it were. In the complex war, an alliance can often be treated as a single actor, the war aims of the coalition partners being treated as identical.[8] Only if the partners are at odds over the achievement of their aims will this simplification result in analytical difficulties. In the multilateral war, on the other hand, we are confronted with difficulties of this sort at the outset, for we have a variety of kinds of state relationships involved: states within alliances, states fighting independently of the alliances, and states having different enemies.[9] Of course, each of these parties has war aims; and the analyst will be hard put to find a pattern of distribution of aims suitable for classifying and analyzing the peace settlement process. With states more closely associated with some states and not others, we will find it difficult to make generalizations about war aims except that the latter may overlap for some states but not for others. The situation will be further complicated by the multiplication and transformation of war aims during the course of the war. We could analogize this to the *three-body problem* in mechanics: The greater the number of units to analyze, the greater the number of possible permutations of the variables, and the more inadequate an analysis will be. The analyst simply cannot hope to approach a comprehensive solution. So, in a multilateral war, the great number of actors gives rise to a greater number of parameters of state-to-state or state-to-faction relations. The possibilities for advantage or disadvantage increase during the course of the war, and hence a belligerent is more apt either to add other war aims to its original war aims or to change its aims. Thus, not only do war-oriented actors see opportunities and then become actively belligerent, but the belligerents themselves see opportunities created by the large number of actor-to-actor war policy options. Hence, all actors (belligerent and war-oriented), because of complex cross-pressures, would probably modify their policies and thereby transform or add to their war aims.

For each of the elements of the settlement, the multilateral war presents more problems and even new problems. Because the war is extended in space and involves the *territories* of both the belligerents and those states to which the war had extended, the territorial settlement must include provisions for the resolution of diverse sorts of questions. Historical territorial claims, questions of territory for defense, demilitarization, disposition of areas into special categories (free territories or plebiscite areas), and even the creation of new states—all will have to be negotiated. The sheer magnitude of the territorial adjustments required is apt to strike the peacemakers as overwhelming.

8 This is a simplification, of course. It can be done only if the war aims of the allies are compatible.

9 Instances are the European War of 1683–1700 and the First World War.

The problem of displaced persons and refugees will also be magnified in the multilateral war; and there will also be questions of nationality and legal rights of the many persons who have resided in areas subject to a change in jurisdiction during and after the war. Feeding and housing large numbers of people in devastated areas will pose special problems. Questions of status of contracts, insurance, business relations, judgments, and property rights of individuals and corporations might be so numerous and diverse that the peacemakers may have to establish a permanent agency for systematically dealing with them. With respect to guarantees of security, the extended nature of the multilateral war again is a primary factor. The great powers will of course seek to obtain a level of at least sufficient security in all areas of the world in which they have interests. The smaller states will also want security, near their borders surely, but in the immediate geographical region as well. The security problems of all parties involved in the war will very probably be interconnected. The security of *A* depends upon the policies of *B* and *C;* but those policies depend, in turn, upon their achieving a measure of security against *A* and other belligerents *D* and *E,* at some distance from *A's* borders; but *D* and *E* cannot make concessions to *B* and *C* unless they in turn obtain guarantees from *F*—and so on. Thus, *A* cannot obtain guarantees unless all (or most) of the other belligerents also obtain guarantees. The policymakers of state *A* will undoubtedly know this and will be sure to insist on a comprehensive security scheme. The guarantees element, therefore, is likely to prove a very thorny negotiating issue.

There are no special problems with respect to the resumption-of-relations element other than the fact that many more states must normalize their diplomatic and commercial relations than in the simple or complex war; because of the numbers of actors involved, this adjustment might take some time. We could surmise that the greater time it takes the states to resume relations after a cease-fire, the greater chance there will be that some hostile act will occur, exacerbating relations and leading even to a resumption of hostilities rather than to a normalization of relations.

Any effort to provide for the adjustment of disputes in the treaties of peace will probably have to rely upon multilateral schemes. If left to the states themselves to work out after the settlement, procedures for mediation are apt to be long in coming and might not be adopted. The comprehensive settlement of the multilateral war would require *multilateral* adjustment of future disputes.

Multilateral War: A System-Transforming War

The multilateral war transforms the state system.[10] The power positions of all the parties, whether actively belligerent or merely war-

10 I thank John R. Romagna for suggesting the expression *system-transforming wars* and for discussing this concept with me.

oriented, change during the course of the war. The peace settlement itself restructures the system in fundamental ways. The war aims of the belligerents, particularly the great powers, could be said to have required for their satisfaction a restratification of the system. As the system was structured before the war, the values sought by the prospective belligerents seemed unobtainable short of the restructuring that only war seemed able to bring about. When war seems to be necessary to a substantial segment of the elites of the great powers, the state system is then in a condition that might be called *pathological*. Whether or not the catastrophe of a multilateral war can be avoided and the war aims sought by the revisionist states satisfied depends upon the variety of peace-keeping initiatives that might be taken by states or international organizations.

The multilateral war could destroy existing states and empires and create new states.[11] Countries upon whose territories the war had been fought suffer loss of resources, businesses, and the lives of their peoples; they consequently decline sharply in relative power position. The victorious belligerent or war-oriented state that has been able to profit from the increased demand for certain commodities and armaments will improve its power positions relative to the rest of the states in the system, and certainly relative to the defeated states. In the multilateral war, it will, in fact, be difficult not to experience a change in power position, just as it will be difficult to remain neutral when the effects of the war are felt over wide areas. Most states in the system sustain either positive or negative changes in their capabilities. Thus, the relative power positions of the nonbelligerent actors will change along with those of the belligerents.[12]

The multilateral war is so extensive that most statesmen will frame their policies with reference to the ongoing multilateral conflict. This means that the states cannot be other than war-oriented. And war-

11 The First World War saw the end of the Ottoman, Habsburg, German and Russian Empires; the French Wars for Hegemony in Europe (pp. 392–405), saw the end of the Holy Roman Empire and the Napoleonic Empire. France lost virtually her entire colonial empire in North America in the Seven Years' War (pp. 374–9). The Third Reich was destroyed in the Second World War.
12 The decline of Spain from a great power, evident at Cateau-Cambrésis (Last War of the Habsburg-Valois Rivalry: pp. 157–60) and catalyzed by the Dutch Revolt (pp. 208–14), was sealed with the Peace of Westphalia, ending the Thirty Years' War (pp. 379–92). Prussia was recognized as a new great power through the acquisition of Silesia in the War of the Austrian Succession (pp. 366–74). The First and Second World Wars vastly increased the power position of the United States. Japan's rank as a power was recognized by virtue of her performance in the Russo-Japanese War (1904–5) and her participation in the First World War (pp. 405–28). The Soviet Union became a more important world power as a result of the Second World War.

oriented states that have changed their relative power positions—and most are bound so to change—will want to participate in the peace negotiations or, short of participation, to be heard. The settlement of the war will have to be comprehensive, and the conferences organized to permit consideration of the proposals of all interested states. This will present a considerable number of problems. Realizing that the settlement may solidify or even improve the favorable balance of power created by the war, some states will be determined to preserve their gains and other states to reduce their losses, knowing that the peace settlement of the multilateral war can undo some losses—that diplomacy might accomplish, in part, what armies have failed to accomplish. Moreover, the settlement could lay the basis, in a *new constitution for the state system,* for a long-term secular trend toward improved power positions for some. The defeated or adversely affected states might thus insure themselves important future gains. But to do so, they will want to take an active part in the peace conferences. Thus, at the end of a multilateral war, we see not only greater numbers of belligerents and war-oriented states playing a role in the peacemaking process, but also a greater number of war-oriented states demanding a voice in the prospective settlement.

Changes in the capabilities or power positions of the state-components of the state system is not the only significant alteration caused by multilateral war. Of equal importance is the change of the perceptual structures and expectations of the elites of almost all states (and factions). The war will transmute the image the leaders of a particular state have of their own state's position and role in world affairs. It may, for example, convince them that they are no longer a great power; their policies for peace then would be modest, perhaps more modest than their real capabilities permitted. Or another state's leaders, by virtue of the performance of their armies and their territorial and resource acquisitions, could come to believe that it was a great power. Their subsequent political behavior would then be dictated by the image they have of themselves and of their state. The perceptions the elites have of *other* states' power positions and possible roles in the world will also be transmuted in the multilateral war. As a result of defeats, the great power might no longer be treated as such by other states—or at least might be treated with much less deference, even as a great power. Hence, the policymakers of the latter are apt to find that their threats are no longer as credible as they were in the prewar era. Client states might then look to others for favors or security guarantees or render deference to other states. A cognitive restructuring of images might be more drastic than changes in the capabilities of the actors. A slight decrease in power position of a great power, coupled with a change in the image its elites have of themselves—in this case, an image of reduced effectiveness—would result in other states' treating the great power very differently. Their image of the great power would now be that of a perhaps dramatically weakened, and much less credible, state. In sum, the multilateral war will have the effect of transmuting the image-structure of the states in the system, changing the images the states have of themselves and of their allies and adversaries.

The elites will tend to perceive the multilateral war as a *world war*. In planning for peace, they are apt to be reluctant to settle for anything less than a total solution, one in which the adversary is defeated, even obliterated. Thus, if there is still a hope of such a victory, there will be some hesitancy in moving toward a compromise peace. Hope of a total solution is undoubtedly a result of intense ideologization of the issues, but it is also a consequence of the *interconnectedness* of the war aims of the many belligerents and war-oriented states in the war. The elites see the total solution as the *simplest solution*.

Perception of the war as a world war will have an important bearing upon the peace plans of the elites. As they may understand that a comprehensive settlement of the war is necessary, they might tend to favor grandiose solutions of the manifold problems created by the war; they may tend to ignore the potential for modest, piecemeal, or discrete solutions, in favor of an overarching plan for a new world that might be impossible to implement. It will, of course, be difficult to achieve a realistic resolution of the conflict, rather than one that attempts to impress a form of order incongruent with the structure of the state system the war has engendered. It is difficult also because the peace settlement is a creative work: The peacemakers should know that their constitution cannot freeze the power positions of all states, and it would be wrong to do so even if possible. They should know that what they do will provide the framework for the peaceful or conflictual interrelations of states for many years. They may therefore be tempted to experiment with utopias —constitutions that ask impossible things of statesmen and states of every size. An unrealistic, incongruent, and utopian settlement will remain largely unimplemented. It could lead to disillusion, conflict, and war.

Termination of the Multilateral War

How does the multilateral war end? One could assume that it will end as either simple or complex wars end: victory for either of the belligerents or differing degrees of stalemate. But it is not quite that simple. A stalemate affecting all the parties is very unlikely.[13] One or more of the

---

13 I am not saying this is bound to happen. I am merely saying that a stalemate affecting all the actors is most unlikely, because after a time, whether because of depleted resources or loss of élan, some actors will decide to negotiate and make peace. When this occurs, the multilateral war will have moved in the direction of greater structural simplicity. As the summaries in the next chapter reveal, most multilateral wars do not end with the complete defeat of

belligerents will usually decide to make peace with particular adversaries. The war will de-internationalize, fewer actors will remain belligerents, and eventually the war will reduce itself to complex or simple wars or a series of such wars fought independently on different fronts. The multi-lateral war that ends as a multilateral war will usually end with the victory of one of the major groupings of belligerent actors. Owing to the diversity of the states and factions within each of the groupings, and the diversity of their war aims, *victory* will probably mean different things to each actor.[14] Some states could realize their war aims completely; others might be quite dissatisfied with the values they had obtained during the war or after the peace settlement. Thus, the termination of the multi-lateral war often leaves many questions unresolved—and these often lead to conflict in the postwar era.

The pattern of evolution toward settlement of the multilateral war is illustrated schematically in Figure 8–4.

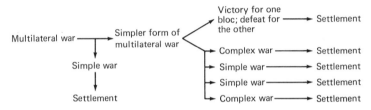

FIGURE 8–4.   Possible structural evolution of a multilateral war.

The figure adumbrates the magnitude of the task confronting the analyst peacemakers, who must either resolve the questions of the entire multi-lateral war in *one* comprehensive settlement or attempt a piecemeal settlement—that is, try to resolve the issues between some of the actors separately from the approximately simultaneous resolution of the issues for other actors. This suggests two basic modalities for peace talks: a single peace conference with all the belligerents and most, if not all, war-oriented actors, on the one hand; and on the other, separate peace conferences among different groups (or even adversary pairs) of belliger-ents. In the piecemeal mode, peace talks could be held contemporane-ously or sequentially. The latter would be preferable if the resolution of one set of questions among some of the belligerents is prerequisite to the

---

either belligerent bloc. It could be argued that, in such situations, the states that remained belligerent to the very end were stalemated in the sense that they were not able to achieve the complete satisfaction of their war aims.

14 The term *victory* could be taken to mean that one state (or group of states) was in a stronger bargaining position than its (or their) adversary. We should not necessarily construe victory to mean what it has meant in the two World Wars of this century; namely, the complete defeat of an adversary and the imposition of peace terms upon it.

resolution of another set of problems. It is evident that the single peace conference for all parties will be a big operation, and perhaps a cumbersome one. It will have to be organized and run just as if it were an international institution—and indeed it might become such, what with the importance of the issues considered and the numbers of states and factions affected by its decisions.[15]

If the multilateral war had naturally reduced itself to a series of simple or complex wars, then each could be settled according to the modes and procedures described in the preceding chapters. The war might even be so reduced by "artificial" means: by the peacemaking efforts of an international organization or a disinterested state. Such a state is almost certainly going to be war-oriented; but it might be "disinterested" in respect to some of the belligerents and therefore acceptable to them as their mediator.[16] These peacemakers would settle some phase or segment of the multilateral war, each such segment being regarded as a simple or complex war. Over the course of time, the entire war might be settled in this fashion: a piecemeal settlement extended over a long period of time during which hostilities could very well continue. However, in the piecemeal settlement, there is always the possibility that some problems will not be solved because they are interstitial. Such problems arise from the interconnectedness of the many states' war aims and can probably be resolved only if all the states that have an interest in the outcome are consulted and consent to their resolution. But this might, in effect, require the convening of a conference of all the belligerents; it might require the peacemakers to face the task of attempting an over-all solution of the war. Then, a single peace conference would have to be convened. In any event, the peacemakers should at least apprise themselves of the existence of interstitial problems and attempt their resolution.

Comprehensive Settlement by a Single Conference

Let us suppose that the great power belligerents have agreed to an armistice and a single peace conference for the settlement of the war. Let us suppose further that other belligerents and the most important war-oriented states have acquiesced in this decision.[17] Whether the war has

15 For a summary of multilateral wars concluded by both single and separate conferences, see Table 9–1 in Chapter 9.

16 Even belligerents can act as mediators for theaters or issues in which they are disinterested. The mediatory roles of Sweden in the Franco-Dutch War of 1672–79 (pp. 340–7) and of Britain and Holland in the European War of 1683–1700 (pp. 347–57) are cases in point.

17 There may be no explicit decision by all the belligerents to terminate their war by a single or by separate peace conferences. It may just happen one way

ended (or will end) with victory for some of the states or whether it has ended in stalemate, the men who plan the conference will have to decide how they will respond to the at least partial restructuring of the state system. Presumably the conference ought to reflect the new structure in terms of the status of the convening states, their right to be heard, to present proposals, and to vote. Thus the question, "Who ought to be invited?" will assume great importance; and indeed an even more vital question will arise: How shall the small states and the middle-range powers be integrated in the peace conference organization and in the postwar state system?[18]

Organizing a single conference for the settlement of the multilateral war will require great skill; and in the most preliminary planning phase, the question of the role of all participating states is bound to arise. The great powers will undoubtedly insist on being "directors" of the conference, the more so if they have sustained heavy losses in the war. Directorship entails a predominating voice in the formulation of peace plans and in the ultimate settlement, with a veto over proposals the directors' policymakers regard as unfavorable. Each great power will want to follow the rule, "no settlement without my consent"; collectively they will almost certainly insist on "no settlement without our consent." The smaller states, on the other hand, will be jealous of their sovereign equality and will seek to increase their influence in the circles of the mighty. Their leaders will always have to balance insistence on being heard against the possibility of being ignored. Naturally, the smaller states could create many problems for the great powers, not the least of which would be continuing hostilities, and that might be singularly unwelcome to the powers, causing embarrassment and perhaps heightening tension among them.

The problem of the relative role and power position of each state will arise with respect to the organization of the formal plenary sessions of the conference (at which, incidentally, very little business is likely to be conducted and very few decisions made, simply because they are too unwieldy a forum). But the problem will also arise in other forms. How will restricted sessions be organized? What states will be represented on

---

or the other, depending upon whether some parties move to make a separate (early) peace; whether alliances remain intact or dissolve; and whether the great powers involved can decide upon procedures which others can be forced or induced to follow. The Congress of Vienna (Napoleonic Wars: pp. 392–405), the Peace Conference of Paris (First World War: pp. 405–28), and the Münster-Osnabrück Conferences could be regarded as examples of a comprehensive settlement by a single conference.

18 The small states were not assimilated to the decision-making mechanisms of the Congress of Vienna, for example, much less so than in the Congresses of Westphalia or the Paris Peace Conference of 1919.

the technical or functional committees and commissions? And if certain states are to be excluded from particular forums (whether or not they acquiesce in the exclusion), there is still the matter of access to the decision-making center so that peace proposals can obtain an audience among the limited number of participants in the principal councils of peacemaking and on the committees. The smaller states cannot rely entirely on the plenary sessions or on the informal milieu—the parties, soirées, corridor meetings, and the like. They will be most disgruntled if they do not have a state (preferably a great power) agent to represent them at the decision-making center.

Disagreement and dissatisfaction arising from effective exclusion from conference forums will probably result in an incomplete settlement.[19] The excluded states might disassociate themselves from particular terms of the settlement; they might refuse to sign or ratify the peace treaty; they might withdraw from the conference and attempt to conclude a separate peace; or failing all these, resume hostilities. An incomplete settlement is usually an inadequate settlement, and an inadequate settlement is hardly conducive to peace and stability in the postwar world.[20] There may, in fact, be no *postwar* world, as the war could continue, even reinvolving those states that were satisfied with the terms of the settlement and those states most reluctant to precipitate a breach of the armistice. There is, of course, the possibility that the great powers and a sufficient number of other states will make a positive decision to go ahead with the conference and a subsequent settlement in spite of the existence of one or more recalcitrant states.[21] The sum total of the capabilities of the states moving toward peace might be sufficient to deter the others and prevent them from breaching the peace eventually established.

Another issue likely to cause disagreement is the agenda.[22] We have already mentioned the importance of agenda questions in connection with the settlement of simple and complex external wars; and we have seen how the discussion of some issues was limited and the resolution of

19 The Imperial Delegation was excluded by Austria at Ryswick (European War of 1683–1700; pp. 347–57); and, in effect, the small states of Europe were excluded from the "directorates" of the Congress of Vienna and the Paris Peace Conference of 1919.

20 For a discussion of inadequate settlements, see Chapter 12.

21 For instances of recalcitrant parties, see the cases of the Pope at the conclusion of the Congresses of Westphalia; Spain at the Congress of Vienna; and Turkey at the end of the First World War. In the War of the Spanish Succession, Austria and the Empire were unhappy enough with the trends at Utrecht to withdraw, continue hostilities for a time, and then make peace at Rastadt.

22 On questions of agenda, conference procedures, and representation, see the subsections entitled "preliminaries" in the settlements analyzed in Chapter 9.

others predetermined by control over the agenda formulation process. Dissatisfaction with an agenda, if it precludes raising matters vital to the national interests of some states, coupled with dissatisfaction arising from the organization of the conference, which may have the effect of denying them access and influence over important committees, will contribute to the incompleteness and inadequacy of the ultimate settlement—not only for the dissatisfied states, but also over all. The peace conference must attempt to solve every major question that has arisen out of the war—and by *major question,* I mean those considered vital by all the belligerents and at least the most important war-oriented states. To the extent that the conference is unable to do this (or is hindered by a dominating group of states), the settlement will be inadequate. Unresolved questions regarded by dissatisfied states as in their interests would all too likely trouble the peacemakers in the postwar era; and they are apt to find that they will have to resolve the issues again, after some future war that need not have taken place had the questions been aired at the peace conference following upon the multilateral war.[23] This is not to say that domestic or world political pressures might not prevent the directorate from resolving the problems that are of such vital concern to the smaller or weak states. Indeed they may. But it is to say that the directorate should at least give the appearance of doing justice to all states, granting the weaker states some measure of representation or including their proposals on the conference agenda in some form, however limited. Justice will not appear to have been done if the small state is denied access to the decision-making center, if its business is excluded from the agenda and its proposals ignored.

While the single peace conference is functioning, it may take on the appearance of an international organization. Its task might be limited to restoring peace; but that task is intrinsically a broad one in the case of a multilateral war. We need only recall the organization of the Congress of Vienna or the much more complicated organizations of the Versailles

---

23 We have a number of cases of important unresolved questions in the settlements analyzed in Chapter 9. In the Peace of Westphalia, the issues dividing France and Spain were left unresolved: Their war continued until 1659. The disposition of Rhineland territories was unclear, and matters of Imperial justice were left unsettled, as was the Jülich-Cleves Succession at the end of the Congresses of Münster and Osnabrück. The Ryswick Clause (European War of 1683–1700: pp. 347–57) was productive of disputes in Germany, as it appeared to allow religious innovation in violation of the Treaty of Münster. In the War of the Spanish Succession (pp. 357–66), Spain refused to negotiate peace with Austria. They went to war again from 1718–20. The 1919 Peace Conference of Paris could not resolve questions relating to Russia, in part because the participants could not decide which Russian faction to invite. Reparation was another question that was left unsettled in 1919.

Peace Conference and the Congresses of Westphalia. The Versailles Conference had the task of policing the armistice, supervising the disarmament and partial occupation of Germany, establishing boundaries for new states and collapsed empires, formulating a constitution for a new world organization, recognizing governments, and negotiating a peace settlement commensurate with the revolutionary changes that had occurred since the outbreak of the war. To accomplish this, the conference was organized into a welter of specialized or functional commissions (Labor, War Guilt, Submarine Cables, etc.), Territorial Committees (Teschen, Czech, Belgian and Danish, etc.), and Ad Hoc Committees (Rhineland, Reparation, Colonies, Financial Clauses, etc.); and at the center were the Plenary Conference with no real power and the Council of Ten (subsequently the Council of Four) that constituted the directorate of the conference. Finally, there was a General Secretariat, providing services and some continunity to this ongoing peacemaking phenomenon, which can be described as an experiment in international organization of a very special kind.

The decision-making center might comprise all states that are to participate in the conference, or it might simply consist of a directorate of the most important states that had fought in the multilateral war, probably the great powers, and possibly some middle-range states. The great powers might decide to admit one or more small states to the directorate on an *ad hoc* basis to take part in decisions affecting them or perhaps merely to give the appearance of wider representation. Whether such "guests" of the great powers will have equal voting rights is another question. Participation of the smaller states would have to be negotiated before or during the early phases of the peace conference.

There are a variety of ways of organizing the great-power directorate, but all are related to the manner in which these states decide to resolve the complex issues of the war. Thus, the powers could decide to handle all problems within the directorate itself. Where the problems are complex and highly technical, however, they will find that they must delegate some investigatory powers and perhaps even decision-making authority to functional commissions. The composition and mandate of the commissions will be matters of concern to the powers; and their delegates will certainly serve on them, possibly along with representatives of other concerned and smaller states. It is unlikely that the great powers will abdicate their veto over decisions of the specialized committees, which could engage in fact-finding and then submit recommendations to the directorate for final action by the great powers. Thus, all committees would be accountable to the decision-making center.

The other major mode of organization is, as we have mentioned, equal representation for all belligerents on the principal conference decision-making body. As it will probably be more difficult for such a body to resolve all the technical questions that are bound to arise, there will thus be more logic in the delegation of authority to committees. Although the center might retain final authority, the committees could be entrusted with substantial decision-making powers, particularly if they were composed of all the belligerent states affected by (or interested in) the resolution of a particular issue. After a decision, other war-oriented states could be given the right to appeal to the plenum of the conference.

Other possible modes of conference organization might combine the two just discussed: for some questions, the plenum would make the decisions; for others, the great power directorate. Initially, the participating states might opt for an organization that reflects their intention of resolving the war issues on a piecemeal basis. The separate groups of states' delegates would then set up separate peace conferences, each with its own decision-making center. But each conference may still be required to account to a plenum or directorate of a conference of all belligerents. This mode is to be distinguished, however slightly, from the purely piecemeal mode of settling a multilateral war in which the separate conferences are autonomous and the delegations are accountable directly to their foreign offices without the intermediary of an over-all conference.

The organization of the conference will, of course, be very much affected by the outcome of the war. In the event of a stalemated multilateral war, all the great powers would probably make up the directorate; all the belligerents—and perhaps the war-oriented states as well—would be represented on the conference plenum. If some states are clearly the victors, they have the choice of excluding the losers from a conference directorate or plenum. They may even prevent the defeated states and factions from meeting collectively prior to receiving the terms of the peace settlement. Yet, if the defeated are to be permitted to lead an autonomous postwar existence, then it will be wiser to assimilate them to the peace conference processes, with or without limitations upon their competence to propose solutions or to vote. Naturally, wiser counsels might not prevail if the legacy of bitterness is great, as it is apt to be after a multilateral war.

Piecemeal Settlement by Separate Conferences

One question to arise during the later stages of the war will be whether to adopt a piecemeal approach toward the peace settlement and hold separate peace conferences.[24] Having determined upon a piecemeal settlement, the belligerents must then decide what principles to follow in fixing the composition of the several peace conferences—whether to

24 See note 17. Examples of piecemeal settlement include the Franco-Dutch War of 1672–9 (pp. 340–7), the Wars of the Spanish (pp. 357–66) and Austrian (pp. 366–74) Successions, and the Seven Years' War (pp. 374–9).

invite states belonging to belligerent groups or whether to establish a separate conference for each major issue (war aim) of the war. In the case of the war diagrammed in Figure 8–1, we could envisage conferences between states A and B, between alliance ACE and alliance DFH, with war-oriented states N_1, N_2, N_3, R, and B also in attendance; and a conference between state G and alliance DFH, with the nonbelligerent allies N_1 and N_2 also present. A classification of the state-actors according to their major interests in the outcome of the war or peace settlement could yield a different set of possible conferences. If we suppose that the alliances ACE and DFH originally declared war and remain at war because of their competition in two regions of the world; that this competition has also brought B into war against A and G against DFH (where B and G are in the same region), then the following conferences would be possible: with respect to the issues related to the first region, ACE and DFH; with respect to the second region, alliance ACE, alliance DFH, states B and G. If the coalition partners have different levels of interest in each of the regions, the constitution of the separate conferences might conceivably be different, the allies with the greatest interest in the outcome assuming the key negotiating roles, the other allies acting more like nonbelligerent allies.

However many conferences are scheduled, the decision-making structure of each must be determined; it will assume some variation of the two major modes discussed in the preceding section: with the great powers controlling all decisions in a conference directorate *or* with all states having equal authority. But another question arises: how will the separate conferences be related to each other? If conferences are sequentially scheduled, each conference could base its decisions and proposals on those of the preceding conferences; and the issues resolved at the earlier conferences would undoubtedly be binding upon the successive conferences, at least to the extent of common subject matter. If a succeeding conference were permitted to reopen issues, peace negotiations would be prolonged. Whatever coordination is required for sequential conferences will have to be provided by the foreign offices of the belligerents. In the case of simultaneous conferences, the question of their interrelation is of a different sort, but as (if not more) important, especially if the peacemakers have made an effort to deal with the interstitial problems arising from the interconnectedness or overlapping nature of the war aims of the states. Such coordination can also be effected through the foreign offices of the participating states, through liaison committees established especially for the purpose of facilitating communication between conferences, or finally, through the directorate or secretariat of the conferences.[25]

25 Coordination between the Münster and Osnabrück Congresses (the Thirty Years' War: pp. 379–92) was effected by each of the major actors having delegates, observers, or spies at both.

Liaison committees could be mandated to deal with all problems mutually affecting two or more conferences. But they might also be *ad hoc*— that is, established to deal with a problem that had more or less recently arisen, one discovered to be of concern to the two conferences. Hence a mixed committee of representatives of the two conferences would be set up specifically to deal with it.

Preliminaries to Negotiations and the Military Phase of the Settlement

We might reasonably expect that alliances in a multilateral war would coordinate their military operations by establishing a joint coalition staff committee, war council, or even a joint command. In the late stages of the war, this instrumentality—let us call it the *joint staff committee*— would undoubtedly be assigned important tasks having a bearing upon future or ongoing negotiations between the belligerents.[26] Not only would such a committee have the duty to prosecute the war in its late stages, it would arrange for the surrender of the forces of the adversaries (or of their forces to the adversaries), assuming that the war, as a multilateral war, did not end in a stalemate. If victorious, it would advise the policymakers of the desirable conditions of an armistice and propose provisions for its implementation and the disposition of all troops, both their own and the enemies'. The joint committee could also be assigned command responsibility for carrying out the terms of the cease-fire agreement, with authority to employ military sanctions against intransigent parties.

It is possible that the belligerents will want to establish an armistice supervisory commission of nonbelligerents; but in the multilateral war, this relinquishing of control would probably be regarded as too great a sacrifice (or a risk) after the burdensome costs of war, especially when the great powers anticipate some benefits in the form of guarantees of security and the acquisition of resources or territory, benefits that might be more easily secured by direct and complete control over the armistice through a joint staff committee. The situation at the end of the stalemated multilateral war might be such as to suggest that control of the cease-fire by a commission of "disinterested" nonbelligerents would be more desirable. In that event, the great powers might grant some measure of authority to such a body, retaining ultimate control through their own joint staff committee; or, in order to promote the settlement of a stale-

26 There was some coordination among the Chaumont Allies at the end of the Napoleonic Wars and among military commanders in Prague and Nürnberg after the Thirty Years' War (pp. 379–92). The Allied Supreme War Council at the end of the First World War is the most interesting example in our sample because of the sophistication of the organizational techniques employed.

mated war, they might try to reach agreement with their adversaries upon the competences and composition of a more neutral supervisory body that possessed sole authority over the implementation of the terms of the cease-fire agreement.

Moving to peace in the multilateral war will be more difficult procedurally than in the complex war.[27] The form, content, and mode of transmission of the peace feeler, or a reply to one, could be worked out among allies, within whatever alliance consultative body existed. But means for coordinating policy among allied and non-allied states in the multilateral war will usually be lacking; and it would be hard to create. Moreover, as the number of belligerent actors is great, there will be a higher probability that some states would not want to begin negotiations, while others would be desperate to do so. Some states would have their war aims nearly achieved; others might anticipate success after several months more of fighting. Uneven progress toward success or failure in the satisfaction of war aims would hinder cooperative action in moving toward negotiations.[28]

An international organization could function as the channel for the communication of peace feelers. This raises the question of the role such an organization might play in the entire peacemaking process for the multilateral war. The collective security organization could very well have been discredited (as was the League of Nations) for having failed to prevent the outbreak of the war or its escalation. In that event, its role, if any, in peace negotiations would be small. An organization that had been deemed a failure could hardly be expected to influence the policymakers of the belligerents or persuade them to utilize the agencies of the organization for important tasks in planning for peace or in implementing the peace settlement. The functional organization, on the other hand, would still have its functions to perform during the war and afterwards. It could be regarded as a failure only if it had not fulfilled its *functional tasks*. This is not to say that the belligerents will not want a collective security or functional organization to play a role in the postwar world, for they undoubtedly will; but it is to say that they will probably not want to rely upon prewar organizations to assume duties relating to the peace settlement, as the older organizations could be deemed to have failed to prevent the war.

The multilateral war, being multiregional, will undoubtedly be fought in more than one theater. Thus, when confronted with the question of when there shall be a cease-fire, the peace negotiators will also have to

27 Once again, the reader may refer to the preliminaries of the wars analyzed in Chapter 9.

28 True in the cases of the Franco-Dutch War of 1672–9, the European War of 1683–1700, the War of the Austrian Succession, Seven Years' War and the Napoleonic Wars.

consider in what theaters there should be cease-fires and how the cease-fires at the various fronts are to be coordinated.[29] A truce on one front might antagonize other parties fighting on other fronts and exacerbate relations to such an extent that a settlement would be made more difficult to realize. Some of the belligerents might feel that parties that had agreed upon an armistice were attempting to close out one theater of operations in order to concentrate their forces in other theaters. This is a matter that will be of great concern for allies, as separate truces could give rise to antagonisms within the alliances. But the multilateral war will complicate matters because of the different kinds of belligerents involved: some members of the alliances are nonbelligerent allies with respect to some of the adversaries. Here, too, questions of how the armistice is to be implemented could result in refractory disputes among allies or among states that had at least agreed upon the desirability of talking about a cease-fire (or even "talking about talking").

If the multilateral war were settled piecemeal, then the armistices for each segment could be separately arranged and would come into effect at different times. If an over-all settlement were projected, the belligerents must agree whether to have a simultaneous cessation of hostilities on all fronts or to schedule or permit separate cease-fires. Simultaneous cease-fires will be desirable if the defeated adversaries were in one cohesive coalition, the surrender of which could be more efficaciously arranged *in toto*, or if separate surrenders might give rise to the suspicion among the victor states that any one of them seeking the first cease-fire wanted to achieve a strategic advantage over the others. A single over-all cease-fire also has the attraction of simplicity: there is one common cease-fire for all belligerents on all fronts. Further elements of the military and political settlements can then be negotiated without being influenced by combat operations; and restoration and normalization of relations between all states—both belligerents and war-oriented states—can more quickly be put in train. But many factors will militate against the single armistice. If the defeated adversaries are separated by great distances,[30] or if they have not been, or are no longer, conjoined by an effective alliance, piecemeal cease-fires might be necessary. If the victorious alliance were in disarray, each state or bloc of states within the coalition might independently conclude armistices with the defeated states, whenever the latter could be persuaded or compelled to submit. In the stalemated multilateral war, the single cease-fire would seem to be the best approach. There are, after all, no victors, no defeated states; and a simple, definitive ending of hostilities would seem to be in the interests of all belligerents. Yet, conflicts of interests among allies and quasi-allies,

29 Important in the First World War and in the War of the Spanish Succession.
30 See the phased cease-fires for navies in the Wars of the Spanish and Austrian Successions and the Seven Years' War.

domestic pressures to continue or to stop the fighting, and military exigencies (preventing battlefield losses, for example, or moving troops to another front to forestall an offensive, feeding and equipping troops, or preventing domestic unrest by the use of troops that would otherwise be needed for external combat) —all would work against the single armistice, constraining the stalemated belligerents to accept or to propose separate cease-fires. There might also be positive reasons for compelling them to adopt this course. The stalemated multilateral war could be perceived by the policymakers of the belligerents as so complicated that they may decide to resolve what issues they can, when they can. Thus, they might welcome the opportunity to conclude any cease-fire possible in the circumstances; or, still looking to an overall settlement of the war, the key policymakers (those of the great powers, for example) might agree to negotiate an armistice on the most important fighting fronts and begin their talks for a complete settlement, allowing the belligerent states of lesser importance to continue the fighting if they chose (or tolerating, with minimal costs, combat between their own forces on fronts of lesser importance).

In arranging for an armistice on a single front (in a simple or complex external war, let us say), the negotiators will naturally be concerned for the security of their respective forces. They will not agree to a truce if it will have the effect of putting one of the belligerents in an advantageous military position vis-à-vis the other.[31] Where separate cease-fires are to be arranged for the settlement of a multilateral war, we must consider an additional factor: the possibility that, having negotiated a cease-fire on one front, a state (so disposed) could conceivably move its troops and armaments to another active front. Other belligerents would want to prevent this, because it would undoubtedly place one or more of them at a disadvantage. Moreover, the full benefits of a separate cease-fire on one front would not accrue to the states concerned, as the war would probably be intensified on other fronts and the military balance of power would certainly have been altered. A great power determined to move its troops from one front to another could probably not be prevented from doing so by other than coercive means; and even in the case of a small state, prevention of interior troop movements might be neither possible nor desirable under the circumstances. The peace negotiators could,

31 For an effort to gain some security through agreement on the disposition of troops, see the Treaty of Vigevano of 1696 (European War of 1683–1700: pp. 347–57) that neutralized Savoy; the agreement of the signatories, Great Britain and the United Provinces, to give no aid to the enemies of either (the Franco-Dutch War of 1672–9: pp. 340–7); the prohibitions relating to Catalonia and Portugal in the cease-fire agreement at the end of the War of the Spanish Succession; and the allowance of the continuation of the siege of Maastricht in the War of the Austrian Succession.

however, seek to reach an agreement that would make such movements illegal, which might deter them. Of course, it is the threat of force or disadvantage behind this sort of agreement that would do the deterring. A "disadvantage" might be condemnation by friendly states, pressures from domestic interest groups that are demanding a de-escalation of the war, or a widening of the war on the still active front—a widening that would cause the moving state to incur unacceptable costs in men and armaments. Assuming that the belligerents can agree upon provisions for preventing the movement of troops, we would expect them to require the troops on the armistice front to remain within assembly areas close to the line of contact until demobilization. They would probably also require them to demobilize within a relatively short time or be reassigned to noncombat operations, and to leave their weapons and armaments at collection points near the cease-fire line. While this all sounds a bit utopian, we should remember that given the right conditions (if, for example, the belligerents want peace enough or fear for their military operations on other fronts against other states), such an agreement might indeed be possible.

The Political Settlement: A Constitution for the State System

With an increase in the complexity of a war (as the number of involved actors increases), peacemakers become ever more pressed to make the peace settlement something more than rules for the resolution of the conflict between former belligerents. In the simple external war, the belligerents are intent upon resolving their particular dispute; and their peace treaty creates the law for their future dealings, at least with respect to the subject matter of the conflict. The peacemakers are not impelled to provide rules for the policies of war-oriented actors (if there are such); and indeed, to attempt to regulate third-state political action would probably be regarded as officious. It would, in any case be ineffectual. But in the multilateral war, the peacemakers do more. They establish a new world order; they create a constitution for the state system. Since the war has been widely internationalized, a compact among the belligerents and war-oriented states will, of necessity, affect all states. For, short of opting out of relations with the belligerents, the non-war-oriented actor has no choice but to accept the new basis for interstate relations, and to adjust its policies to the new order.

The erection of a new order follows from the intention of the peace-makers (and the policymakers and elites or peoples whom they represent) to provide a systematic, revised basis for interstate relations and to avoid the catastrophe of another multilateral war. Even apart from the intentions of the negotiators, the new constitution will arise, in many cases, from the peace settlement itself. In the resolution of the multiplicity of issues of the war, particularly the interstitial or interconnected issues which require the concurrence of many parties, and in negotiating the detailed matters that comprise the elements of the peace settlement, which are themselves interrelated, the peacemakers will be obliged to work toward a comprehensive settlement—one that will function to modify and order the relations of all the actors in the state system.

After the First and Second World Wars, statesmen of the world formulated charters for peacekeeping organizations whose purpose was to provide a modicum of security for their members and prevent war. These charters were indeed new constitutions for the state system; but they were only one part—although a very important part—of those constitutions. The *peace treaties* also adumbrated a constitution for the state system, as did the many understandings of the peacemakers, both written and unwritten, that made up the peace settlement. Thus, a *constitution* consists of the peace treaties, any charters of regional and worldwide organizations of states, and the informal agreements that establish the rules for interstate relations in the postwar era consented to by the states that accept a peace settlement.

The two most important elements of the peace settlement of the multilateral war are the territorial and security guarantees elements. The two are obviously related. Since the state is a territorially based political entity, territorial readjustments after the war modify the character of the system, shifting resources to some states and taking them away from others. The territorial settlement, in a word, restratifies the state system on a new basis. Security guarantees are designed to preserve the new configuration of states and interstate relations. Over time, the guarantees often acquire an acceptability, a kind of legitimacy, that further strengthens the constitution of the system. Guarantees are not necessarily intended to preserve the status quo, to prevent all change—although history shows that this has been their usual effect, because it seems to be what the status quo great powers at the time have wanted.[32] Of course, provisions for peaceful change, for future modification of the peace settlement's terms, could be formulated. They would provide a safety valve, effective in keeping the peace in the years after the war, when weakened or developing states have so improved their postwar power positions that they can eventually aspire to a reordering or restructuring that would take into account their new power positions. War is, of course, one way to force such recognition, at very great costs to all. A peace settlement that allowed for change and for future restructuring of

32 Noteworthy efforts to preserve the status quo are the prohibitions against religious innovations in the Empire made a part of the Peace of Westphalia; the settlement of the claims to the restored Rhinelands (the Reunions) after the peace of Ryswick (European War of 1683–1700); and the Holy Alliance at the end of the Napoleonic Wars.

the system might be hard to achieve, as statesmen after a multilateral war are most concerned with the immediate and pressing problems of the past war. But it would make for a better and a more complete settlement if there were recognition of the need for flexibility, if the security guarantees element was not designed to freeze the status quo, and if the settlement included terms for the adjustment of future disputes and the resumption of relations on an ameliorative basis.

The peace settlement could be regarded as the formal arrangement that determined the nature of the *disputes* of the postwar period, the frequency and intensity of those disputes, and, in part, whether or not they will lead to war. The settlement in no way makes war inevitable; but the probability of war can be decreased if the peacemakers try to anticipate the kinds of disputes the mutilateral war *settlement* might engender—and then establish the procedures and institutional means for preventing and resolving them.

The really difficult aspect of the settlement of the multilateral war is the resolution of the interstitial or interconnected political questions that are an expression of the conflicts between the belligerents and the war-oriented actors. As we defined it earlier, an interconnected problem is one in which each element is so closely connected to the remaining elements that the solution of one in effect requires the solution of all.[33] Thus, for example, the security of state A depends, in part, upon the territory awarded it. But that award is conditioned upon giving territorial compensations to states B and C at the expense of D; this in turn will pose a threat to D's security, since D will be weaker relative to at least states A, B, and C. Further dependencies could be envisaged, with other actors interested in territorial compensations and security guarantees, and the satisfaction of each actor's claims dependent upon the satisfaction of some of the claims of the others.

At the peace conference the negotiators often find that they can resolve the relatively simple questions—ones in which few states are interested. But the interconnected political questions are often a log jam to further progress. They may cause a breakup of the conference. They could require a revision of negotiating procedure, with the convening of piecemeal conferences to solve the problems that can only be solved by a limited number of states. But even the simplest issues are often dependent upon the interconnected questions; and not until these are resolved will the others also be resolved. Thus, having reached the interconnected questions, the conferees are apt to become stalemated. There will be no evidence of progress until the interconnected questions are disentangled and solutions for the problems, as they affect the separate actors, are found.

33 The question of the disposition of Poland and Saxony at the Congress of Vienna is an example of such an interconnected problem.

What then permits the resolution of an interstitial or interconnected question?

1. A decision to resolve all issues against the parties in a weaker bargaining position could vastly simplify matters.[34] Weaker parties include the states or factions defeated in the war or the smaller or medium-range states that are weaker relative to the great powers. Where the victorious or stronger actors can ignore the claims of others, the number of actors that have to be taken into account in framing a settlement of a particular issue is reduced. The price might be very high, however, because the ignored parties will be converted into opponents of the settlement. Thus, in fact, it is probably the least desirable way to simplify compromise and resolution of the interconnected question.

2. Some of the parties might seek some composition of the issues among themselves, as among alliance partners, and then use their compromise solution as a starting point for bargaining with other parties.[35] States that have reached such a solution do not ignore the weaker states. They simply attempt to resolve questions among themselves in a smaller forum and arrive at a solution they can all live with.

3. Some of the parties might threaten war or actually renew hostilities against the parties they regard as intransigent.[36] The threat might emanate from one actor or group of actors and be directed against the old (and former) adversaries; or there might actually be a realignment of parties during the negotiations, with a new bloc of states, sharing some common interest in a particular kind of settlement, threatening both former allies and enemies. This again is not an entirely happy solution, because it risks war; and if it succeeded, the states or factions that gave in would become embittered and might refuse to respect the terms of the settlement in the postwar period.

4. The negotiators might reach agreement by a trade-off of values, a process similar to the practice of territorial compensations.[37] As a price for agreeing to a compromise, some of the parties could be given territory, resources (or future rights to resources or income from them), guarantees of security by the offer of a collective defense pact or membership in a collective security organization, pecuniary compensation, bene-

---

34 This was done against many German princes in the Thirty Years' War, against Saxony and Spain in the Napoleonic Wars, against a recalcitrant Austria in the War of the Austrian Succession, and against Germany and the Central Powers in the First World War.

35 See the Napoleonic Wars and the First World War.

36 An alliance of Britain, Austria, and France threatened to go to war against Prussia and Russia over the Poland-Saxony question at the Congress of Vienna.

37 This was a characteristic of the bargaining at the end of all the wars treated in Chapter 9.

fits in trade or favorable commercial arrangements, or a promise of technical assistance. They might be given ideological values such as rights to the practice of religion or recognition of one state's right to protect such practice in another state, or even promised an agreement to promote certain ideological principles, singly or collectively (as in the Holy Alliance for example). Often, prestige counts for a great deal in the compromise: and a hesitant party might be persuaded to make concessions by means that increase that party's prestige, through recognition and by the promise of equal treatment as an accepted member of the "club" of states, or by admission to the conference directorate, or to an international organization. Promise of assistance or support for a state or faction with respect to matters unrelated to the issues of the multilateral war is another possible trade-off value, as is a promise to refrain from the exercise of a right that one party possesses.

5. The conferees might decide not to decide, hoping that the cease-fire and settlement will keep the peace, that with the passage of time, deideologization (or devaluation) of the issues will occur.[38] In effect, this passive "solution" relies upon the evolution of the state system to bring about the changes that solve the interconnected problem the negotiators are unable to solve or transforms surrounding conditions so that it is no longer necessary to solve the problem. Unfortunately, an unsolved problem can lead to a resumption of hostilities. Still, this kind of "muddling through" is one approach to complexity. Fatigued or exasperated after long negotiations, the conferees might settle what they can and leave the remainder unsettled. And this device might work, for the state system will change during the postwar period: New states are established, new alliances are formed, and new ideologies replace, modify, or supplement old ideologies. International organizations, through the accretion of competences, modify the behavior of states. Natural catastrophes or technological progress and economic development alter the relative power positions of states. Finally, war might break out between states or factions over issues wholly unrelated to the war aims of the belligerents formerly involved in the multilateral war. This is obviously not a desirable way for change to come about within the state system; but the point is that if war were to occur between some of the actors, the consequences of that war might be such as to resolve the question the negotiators at the peace conference had been unable to resolve. For the war would certainly change the power positions of the belligerents; and thus, some actors might be eliminated from contention over the issues of the interconnected question. Those issues might themselves become partially resolved by the war or at least become less important to resolve.

38 Questions relating to the 1609 judgment against Donauwörth, the Reichshofrat, and Imperial justice were put off by the Westphalian conferees until the next session of the Reichstag.

6. Finally, the conference policymakers might decide to refer the question to an appropriate international organization—perhaps to an agency of the organization they themselves have just established, or to an *ad hoc* commission given the mandate to attempt a solution of the interconnected question.[39] This is, of course, another decision not to decide; and it too relies upon the passage of time and a hoped-for de-ideologization. But, with the reference of the question to a specially constituted agency, there is at least some promise of responsible and responsive consideration of the claims of the unsatisfied states or factions most vitally interested in the question. Even apart from offering solutions to the interconnected question (after the settlement has been reached and in the postwar era), the *ad hoc* agency could have the additional value of promoting de-ideologization of the question. Technically, the interconnected question will be as difficult for the agency to solve as it was for the conference, at least in the early postwar period. Thus, the agency will have to employ one or more of the techniques listed above in order to deal successfully with its assigned question.

39 At Westphalia, the matter of the Duchy of Lorraine was to be referred to arbitrators or to await the settlement of the Franco-Spanish War. It was understood that many of the questions unsettled at the time the Paris Peace Conference of 1919 adjourned were to be considered by the Conference of Ambassadors and by the League of Nations.

Multilateral
War Settlements
in Modern History

Because of the complexity of the multilateral wars summarized in this chapter, we depart somewhat from the pattern of analysis followed in earlier chapters. The role of alliances in the peacemaking process, for example, could be examined only briefly in the wars of the first group (the Franco-Dutch War of 1672–1679, the European War of 1683–1700, the Wars of the Spanish and Austrian Successions, and the Seven Years' War) and hardly considered at all in the extremely complex wars of the second group (the Thirty Years' War, the Wars of France against Europe, and the First World War). Naturally, this omission does not mean that alliance relations were not significant during the wars or the peace talks. Space could not be allotted, moreover, to a discussion of the war aims of *every* belligerent, as so very many were involved in the wars. In the second group, only the war aims of the great powers are described; and in the first group, if the war aims of the minor parties and small states are mentioned at all, it is in the briefest terms.

The peace conferences that ended the multilateral wars here considered were often highly formalized affairs. But again, because of space limitations, we could dwell neither upon the organization of each conference nor upon the attendant political problems and consequences of whatever organization the parties adopted—just as we have had to give short shrift to the often interesting negotiations that were an integral part of the peacemaking process of all the wars analyzed in this book. However, the consequences of the multilateral wars were on the whole more widely written about, both by the participants and by historians, than were settlements of simple and complex wars; and thus the analyst of peacemaking interested in pursuing an investigation of multilateral war settlements will be able to uncover and collect materials from which he may learn about the bargains and agreements the parties made (or failed to make) as they moved toward peace.[1]

In the period from which the wars were selected for consideration (1500–1971), there have fortunately been comparatively few multilateral wars. In addition to the eight summarized here, there are only two such wars whose settlements we have not examined: the Great Northern War (1700–1721) and the Second World War (1939–1945).[2] These wars were of immense importance, of course; and their settlements are highly instructive. But for the purposes of this study, a sample of eight multilateral wars was deemed sufficient.

The wars in the first group are analyzed according to the ways in which the major actors were involved in them, with an indication of dates when each of the parties became belligerent or made a separate peace. The analyses of the settlements—including the first brief summaries, *Patterns of settlement,* added to clarify the often complex disposition of belligerents at the war's end—for the most part follow a form dictated by this approach. For example, the European War of 1683–1700 had two principal combat theaters: the Eastern, in which the Ottoman Empire was

---

1 Where possible, I have supplied references to such works in the bibliography or the notes to the summaries that follow.

2 As we noted in Chapter 1 (Table 1–1 and footnote 1), it is often difficult to distinguish a multilateral from a complex external war. In view of this fact, some readers might wish to argue that the modern era has seen more than ten multilateral wars. Having surveyed the period, 1500 to 1970 however, it is my judgment that there were indeed no more than ten such wars; that only two wars come close to being multilateral: the War of the Holy League (1511–14: France vs. the Pope, Venice, Spain, England, the Emperor, and the Swiss Cantons); and the War of the North (1654–61: Sweden vs. Denmark, Poland, Prussia, and Russia). Because the structure of these wars is really quite simple, I prefer to regard them as complex external wars. Moreover, their outcome and settlement were not as significant as even the simplest of the multilateral wars, the Seven Years' War (pp. 374–9). This latter point is not meant to deny that settlements of complex external wars cannot be of tremendous historical significance: witness the Peace of Augsburg ending the German Religious War of 1552–5 or the Peace of Cateau-Cambrésis (1559) ending the Wars of the Habsburg-Valois Rivalry (pp. 157–60). (Although I have not done so, it is possible to regard the entire series of Habsburg-Valois Wars from 1494–1559 as a single multilateral war. But since this series was punctuated by a number of periods of peace—more indeed than either the Thirty Years' War or the Napoleonic Wars—I prefer to regard the wars as discrete. This does not detract from the fact that the Peace of Cateau-Cambrésis was designed to resolve, and did resolve in great part, the issues that underlay this dynastic conflict.)

involved, and the Western. In the description of that war, we distinguish between these theaters and then analyze the settlement according to the belligerent actors in each. In the second group, the complexity of the wars made it necessary to adopt several different approaches for a better understanding of their settlements. Thus, each war was first analyzed by identifying the *major* actors, usually the great powers. In the case of the Thirty Years' War and the Napoleonic Wars, it was also possible to regard the single multilateral wars as made up of a series of discrete, independent, and less complex wars. And a better understanding of the Thirty Years' War is obtained by treating it as having passed through several phases: first as a war internal to the Holy Roman Empire and then as three internal-external wars in succession, with the interventions respectively of Denmark, Sweden, and France. The First World War was analyzed according to the major actors and theaters of operations, with separate mention of the wars that grew out of the central European war and its settlement.

Apart from the departures of some allies and apart from separate earlier peace settlements (or preliminary settlements that turned out to be of a temporary nature only), the multilateral wars examined here ended as indicated in Table 9–1. Comparison of the settlement summaries with Table 9–1 will serve to clarify the ways multilateral wars have ended and the probable modes in which future multilateral wars might end—should man survive them.

TABLE 9–1.   Settlements of Some Multilateral Wars.

War	Site of Peace Talks	Dates of Talks	Form of Peace Treaties
Group I Franco-Dutch War	Nijmegen	1678–79	series of bilateral treaties of peace
European War 1683–1700	Ryswick	1697	bilateral treaties
	Carlowitz	1699	bilateral treaty between the Ottoman and Holy Roman Empires
	Constantinople	1700	bilateral treaty between Ottoman and Russian Empires
War of the Spanish Succession	Utrecht	1713–15	bilateral treaties

TABLE 9–1.   (continued)

War	Site of Peace Talks	Dates of Talks	Form of Peace Treaties
	Rastadt	1714	bilateral treaty between France and the Holy Roman Empire
War of the Austrian Succession	Aix-la-Chapelle	1748	multilateral treaty
Seven Years' War	St. Petersburg	1762	bilateral treaty between Russia and Prussia
	Hamburg	1762	bilateral treaty between Sweden and Prussia
	Paris	1763	multilateral treaty
	Hubertusberg	1763	bilateral treaties between Saxony and Prussia, and Prussia and Austria (the latter comprehending the states of the Empire)
Group II Thirty Years' War	Westphalia (Münster and Osnabrück)	1645–48	two multilateral treaties and a bilateral treaty between Spain and Holland
Napoleonic Wars	Paris	1814; 1815	bilateral treaties between France and each Ally
	Vienna	1814–15	multilateral treaty
First World War	Paris	1919–23	multilateral treaties between the Allies and each defeated state

Wars of the First Group

FRANCO-DUTCH WAR OF 1672–1679

STRUCTURE OF THE WAR: This was a war between France and her allies and the United Provinces and their allies. In 1672, the war took the form of France, Britain, Sweden, Cologne, and Münster vs. Holland. In 1673,

Cologne and Münster left the war. But, by the end of that war, a coalition had formed against Louis XIV. It consisted of the Emperor (Austria), Spain, and Lorraine, who were later joined by the Palatinate, Mainz, Brunswick, Brandenburg, Denmark, and even France's former ally, Münster (1675). Britain made peace in 1674.

PATTERN OF SETTLEMENT: 1. Articles of Peace were signed on 15 September 1673 between the Dutch on the one hand and the Archbishop of Cologne and the Bishop of Münster on the other.[3] The Dutch-Münster Treaty of Peace was signed on 22 April 1674; the Dutch-Cologne Treaty on 11 May 1674.[4]

2. Britain and the Dutch made peace by the Treaty of Westminster, 19 February 1674.

3. Apart from these early settlements, the primary war (France vs. Spain, Holland, and the Emperor) continued until 1678. The Peace of Nijmegen comprised a series of treaties of differing dates, illustrating a piecemeal settlement of multilateral war.

France and the United Provinces made peace in August, 1678, and also concluded a treaty of commerce and navigation. Spain made peace with France in September. A Franco-Austrian treaty was signed in February, 1679. The Dukes of Brunswick concluded their accord at Zell with both France and Sweden in February.[5] Then, in March, 1679 (at Nijmegen), the Bishop of Münster made peace with France and Sweden in separate treaties of peace.

In that same month, France and Sweden on one side and Denmark and Brandenburg on the other negotiated a cease-fire agreement at Nijmegen. At St. Germain-en-Laye in September, 1679, Brandenburg signed a single peace treaty with both France and Sweden. Denmark made peace with France at Fontainebleau and with Sweden at Lund (both in September, 1679).

Finally, Sweden and Holland reached a settlement agreement and signed a peace treaty in October, 1679, at Nijmegen.

WAR AIMS: Louis XIV sought the territorial aggrandizement of France at the expense of the Empire and in the Spanish Netherlands. He also wanted French commercial superiority over the Dutch. He was, moreover, a candidate for the Imperial Crown. Charles II of England wanted to achieve naval and commercial supremacy over the Dutch. He was induced to ally with France by a subsidy from Louis XIV, which he thought would make him independent of Parliament. Sweden, Münster, Cologne, and even Brandenburg were in the pay of the French monarch.

3 Bernard, Jacques, *Recueil des Traitez et d'autres Actes Publics* (Amsterdam: Henri et la Veuve de T. Boom, 1700), Vol. 4, pp. 325–6.

4 *Ibid.*, pp. 332–4, 334–5.

5 Garden, Guillaume le Comte de, *Histoire Générale des Traités de Paix* (Paris: Amyot, 1848–87), Vol. 2, pp. 116–7.

The Swedish regency wanted to maintain control of the Baltic and guarantee the security of Pomerania. Cologne and Münster wanted subsidies and any other values that could be achieved through an alliance with a great and increasingly dominant power like France. By 1674, Spain and Austria had become convinced that the ambitions of Louis XIV threatened the integrity of their dominions, their dynastic security, and the European balance of power (calling his policies a threat to the "peace of Christendom"). The lesser German princes allied with the Emperor because they believed it was necessary to maintain the status quo in the face of the threat from France. Denmark sought profit at the expense of Sweden and France, when it appeared that they were becoming isolated and would not win.

FACTORS FOR PEACE: Even before 1678, it became clear to the French that they could not achieve their aim of dictating terms to Holland. They had, moreover, a coalition of Europe against them; they were weary of war and were concerned with rebellion at home and the threat of English intervention on the side of the Dutch. In the United Provinces, there was also disunity at home and war weariness. Preliminary negotiations, by the French, revealed that the Dutch could be wooed away from their allies by territorial and commercial concessions. The fact that the Dutch were about to make peace with Louis XIV and that the French king was willing to work out a compromise settlement induced the Spanish to agree to peace. The Emperor was concerned about the gains the Elector of Brandenburg had made (and would make, if hostilities continued) and deserted him to sign a treaty of peace with the French. Standing by its Swedish ally, France was able to compel the Elector and Denmark to agree to a not unfavorable peace settlement with Sweden (and with France).

England left the war in 1674 because of Parliamentary restiveness and because Charles II lost confidence in his ally's ability to secure the values Louis had promised him. A change in the domestic situation did enable Charles to sign an agreement with Louis in 1676, in which both promised to refrain from concluding any treaty of peace or alliance without the consent of the other. But once again, increasingly pacific and pro-Dutch public and parliamentary opinion forced Charles away from France until he concluded the Anglo-Dutch alliance of 1678.

WAR-ORIENTED STATES: Sweden was a rather reluctant and ineffectually active ally of France. Despite this alliance, some of the belligerents accepted Sweden's ultimately abortive mediation efforts in 1673 and again in 1678. (Thus, we see that even one of the belligerents can be a mediator for *some* issues in dispute for *some* of the belligerents.) England was also a war-oriented state when she was not a belligerent after 1674. At Nijmegen, the British mediated the Franco-Dutch negotiations, after having signed a treaty of mutual and reciprocal guarantees with the

United Provinces. Poland and the Ottoman Empire were peripherally war-oriented.

ALLIANCES: The belligerents on either side were joined by a series of bilateral and sometimes multilateral alliance agreements, some offensive and others defensive.[6] The most important coalitions were the Franco-Swedish of April, 1672, a defensive alliance directed against the Dutch, and the Alliance of the Hague, 30 August 1673, an offensive alliance against France between Spain, the Emperor, and Holland.[7] Brandenburg, Brunswick, Lorraine, Denmark, Münster, Osnabrück, and Newburg acceded to this latter treaty. The shifting structure of the war was mirrored in the patterns of alliances, in their formation and in their dissolution. Toward the end, the Dutch moved to make peace, irrespective of the interests and desires of their allies. The Emperor, moreover, deserted Brandenburg. France stood by Sweden, however. Thus, France was not confronted by a united and viable coalition during the talks at Nijmegen.

SETTLEMENT: PRELIMINARIES: Sweden offered its good offices for mediation in 1673, and a congress of the powers (France, Britain, the United Provinces, the Emperor, Spain, Brandenburg, and Sweden) then met in Cologne. The negotiations were getting nowhere when the Congress was suddenly dissolved after the arrest, in violation of international law, of a minister of Cologne by troops of an Imperial regiment. After exchanges of notes and proposals in 1675, Nijmegen was agreed upon as an acceptable site for a peace congress. The belligerents seemed in no hurry to begin the talks, however. France's delegates did not arrive until June, 1676; Spain and Austria delayed, still hoping for battlefield gains that would put them in a stronger bargaining position. The congress opened on 3 March 1677, but still negotiations made little progress. Britain and the Dutch achieved a rapprochement, concluded an alliance, and agreed upon terms for the general peace. Louis XIV continued to entertain pretensions wholly unacceptable to his adversaries, who vowed to continue talks only until 10 August 1678. Fully expecting no results, they agreed to resume the war after that date. Louis held out until the very last minute and then dramatically offered to sign a compromise peace treaty.

SUMMARY OF SETTLEMENTS: 1. *Britain and Holland:* Peace was secured by the terms of the Treaty of Westminster, 19 February *1674,* a date on which a cease-fire was also to take effect.[8] Periods of grace were set for seizures of ships on the seas at great distances from London, after which

6 On the alliances of this war, see Garden, *ibid.,* Vol. 2, pp. 83 ff. See also Bernard, *op. cit.,* pp. 746 f., 365 f.

7 Garden, *op. cit.,* Vol. 2, pp. 95–7.

8 *A General Collection of Treatys of Peace and Commerce* (London: Knapton, 1732), 2d Ed., Vol. 3, pp. 275–81.

complete restitution was to be made. There was to be a restoration of all territories (a return, in other words, to the *status quo ante*). The Dutch agreed to honor the British flag in defined areas of the high seas. The Treaty of Breda (1667) and the 1668 navigation treaty were renewed. Rules for trade to the East Indies were to be examined by commissioners appointed by the parties. If the Commissioners could not make a decision, Spain was to arbitrate. Finally, the Dutch were to make an indemnity payment to the British. In a secret article, the parties agreed to give no aid to the enemies of either.

On 10 January 1678, after William III had arranged to marry Princess Mary, a niece of Charles II, the United Provinces and Britain signed the agreement of alliance, which also contained preferred terms for peace. The signatories agreed to defend each other and to concert moves against France in the event Louis refused to accept their terms for peace.[9]

2. *France and the United Provinces:* The Treaty of Peace between the French and the Dutch was signed at Nijmegen on 10 August 1678.[10] Not only was peace proclaimed, but the parties also agreed to help each other and not to consent to any treaty that might cause injury to either. In the war between France and Austria that was even then being waged, the Dutch promised to remain neutral and to respect the engagements Spain was to make with France, particularly those concerning Spain's neutrality. The parties also agreed to a peace based upon the principle of *uti possidetis,* except that Maastricht and environs were to be restored to Holland. Conditions for the evacuation of occupied territories were delineated. The practice of Roman Catholicism was to be conserved in territories retained by the Dutch.

There was to be restitution to named nobles; and it was declared that any persons whose goods had been confiscated for reasons of the war should recover them without recourse to law. Catholics in Maastricht were to enjoy their property rights and benefices. The exaction by France of contributions in Maastricht was to continue for three months after the exchange of ratifications. France agreed to restore to the Prince of Orange his lands and goods in France, Franche-Comté, Charleroi, and Flanders.

Comprehended in the Treaty were Britain, Sweden, the Duke of Holstein, the Bishop of Strassburg, and Prince William of Furstenburg; also comprehended, if they willed it, were Portugal, Venice, Savoy, Switzerland, Bavaria, and Brunswick-Hanover.

A Treaty of Commerce signed on the same day as the Peace Treaty established commerce on the prewar basis.[11] The property of private citizens was no longer liable to seizure for the public debts of their sovereigns. Duties imposed upon the subjects of one party were to be the

9 *Ibid.,* pp. 317–23. See also *ibid.,* Vol. 1, pp. 177 ff.
10 *Ibid.,* Vol. 1, pp. 193–201.
11 *Ibid.,* pp. 202–18.

same as those imposed by the sovereign of the other party upon his own subjects. Also included were rather detailed provisions regulating trade with the enemies of either party. It was agreed that all goods on enemy vessels could be seized, as well as contraband from neutral vessels. Consuls were to be exchanged.

3. *Spain and France:* Although William of Orange (and others) sought to prevent a settlement between Spain and France, peace was secured by means of the Treaty signed at Nijmegen on 17 September 1678, a cease-fire having already been put into effect on 19 August.[12] Franche-Comté, Artois, and areas of Cambrésis, Hainaut, and Flanders were ceded to France; the latter ceded Limburg, Ghent, Charleroi, Coutrai, Oudenard, and other towns to Spain. Commissioners were to be appointed to supervise the transfers and liquidate all debts. The judgments rendered by French courts in lands held under the terms of the Treaty of Aix-la-Chapelle (1668), but now returned to Spain, were to be enforced. There were extensive provisions for the protection of persons affected by the territorial transfers and restitution of property. Specified treaties were declared to be in effect. Finally, Spain promised to remain neutral and to refuse aid to the enemies of France.

4. *France, the Emperor (Austria), and the Empire:* In the Treaty of Peace, signed on 5 February 1679, a cease-fire was proclaimed.[13] The Peace of Westphalia was to serve as the basis for peace. France renounced the right to garrison Philipsburg. The Emperor gave up Freibourg and agreed to permit the French to use a road from Breisach to Freibourg. France agreed to restore the Duke of Lorraine to his lands on condition (*inter alia*) that Nancy and Longwy be retained by France. (The Duke refused to accept these conditions, and his domains were therefore never restored to him. They remained subject to French sovereignty.) The subjects of all transferred territories were to enjoy their prewar rights and property.

The Emperor was to use his good offices to end the war between France and his allies (Denmark, Brandenburg, Münster, and Brunswick). If his terms for peace were not accepted, he would no longer aid the latter in any way. While the war in the north continued, France was to have the right to garrison specified towns. Britain was comprehended in the Treaty.

5. *Sweden, the Emperor and the Empire:* The Peace Treaty of these powers was also signed on 5 February 1679.[14] The Peace of Westphalia was reaffirmed, and the Emperor agreed to use his good offices to end the war between Sweden and the Emperor's war-time allies. (Articles and

12 *Ibid.,* pp. 218–33.
13 *Ibid.,* pp. 234–45.
14 Du Mont, Jean, *Corps Universel Diplomatique du Droit des Gens* (Amsterdam: Brunel, 1731), Vol. 7, Part I, pp. 389–91.

Conditions on the Suspension of Arms were signed on 31 March 1679, by representatives of France, Sweden, Denmark, and Brandenburg.) [15]

6. *Münster:* At Nijmegen, Sweden came to terms with the Bishop of Münster on 26 March 1679; France on 29 March.[16] Sweden obtained portions of the Duchies of Bremen and Verden and agreed to a cash payment to the Bishop. To France, the Bishop promised his neutrality and adherence to the terms of peace concluded with the Emperor the month before. Both parties agreed to withdraw their troops from the territories of the other. France guaranteed Münster and also made a cash payment to the Bishop. France retained the right to send troops across Münster in time of need.

7. *Brunswick:* The Dukes of Brunswick made peace with France and Sweden at Zell on 5 February 1679.[17] Brunswick ceded Bremen to Sweden, and France made a cash payment to the Dukes.

8. *Brandenburg:* At St. Germain-en-Laye, France and Sweden concluded their Treaty of Peace with the Elector of Brandenburg.[18] In spite of victories against Sweden, Brandenburg was isolated in 1679; and as France stood with Sweden, the Elector was compelled to return Western Pomerania (with Stettin and Stralsund) to the latter. The limits of this retrocession were defined; and the rights of its inhabitants guaranteed. French troops were to evacuate Brandenburg's territories after the exchange of ratifications. Brandenburg agreed not to assist Denmark if the latter remained at war with France. France made a cash payment to the Elector.

9. *Denmark:* France and Denmark signed a peace Treaty at Fontainebleau on 2 September 1679.[19] Denmark agreed to restore her conquests in Scania and the Baltic to Sweden, accepting a small cash payment in return.

On 26 September, Sweden and Denmark made peace at Lund.[20] Territories were to be restored to the prewar status quo. Schedules for evacuation were provided. A commission was constituted to fix the boundaries between the signatories. Prior treaties were declared to be in force. In 1680, Sweden would send commissioners to meet with Danish and French commissioners to discuss navigation and commerce in the Sound. Otherwise, commerce was to be returned to a prewar basis. A general amnesty

15 Bernard, *op. cit.,* Vol. 4, p. 429.

16 *Ibid.,* pp. 426–9, 424–6.

17 Garden, *op. cit.,* Vol. 2, pp. 116–7.

18 Bernard, *op. cit.,* Vol. 4, pp. 433–7. The Treaty was dated 29 June 1679. See also Ward, A. W., *et al.* (eds.), *The Cambridge Modern History* (New York: Macmillan, 1934) , Vol. 5, p. 652.

19 Bernard, *op. cit.,* Vol. 4, pp. 440–4. *The Cambridge Modern History, op. cit.,* Vol. 5, pp. 45, 571.

20 Bernard, *op. cit.,* Vol. 4, pp. 444–50.

also extended to persons who had served the enemies of their sovereigns; and there was to be a restitution of all property and goods seized during the war, although the revenues or fruits of this property need not be restored. Neither party was to enter an alliance to the prejudice of the other.

10. *Sweden and the United Provinces:* A Treaty of Peace and a Treaty of Commerce were signed by these powers on 12 October 1679 at Nijmegen.[21]

SIGNIFICANCE OF THE SETTLEMENT: Louis XIV had failed in his bid for hegemony in Europe, but French influence was felt everywhere at Nijmegen and the other peace conferences. French diplomacy had very effectively limited the ability of the anti-French coalition to secure a settlement that could be firmly relied upon to deter Louis' ambitions. What was more, Europe knew that France had the ability to try again to achieve supremacy in the near future. Perhaps the powers had learned that only a coalition could prevent this. In any event, the Peace of Nijmegen did not have the same importance as the Peace of Westphalia or the later settlements of Utrecht (1713) or Vienna (1814). Europe was too soon involved in yet another multilateral war and the settlements did not (and could not) take on an aura of permanence; and also the participants did not look upon the settlements in the way the Westphalia peacemakers looked upon theirs—as definitive and a permanent constitution for Europe. Moreover, the arbiter of Europe himself, Louis XIV, did not accept the Peace of Nijmegen as anything more than a temporary and provisional arrangement. It offered him a period of recovery until he could once more attempt to transform Europe into a French Imperium.

THE EUROPEAN WAR OF 1683–1700 (including THE WAR OF THE HOLY LEAGUE and THE WAR OF THE LEAGUE OF AUGSBURG)

STRUCTURE OF THE WAR: Turkey declared war on Austria in 1683. Louis XIV's efforts to acquire territories (Reunions) along the Rhine and his imperial ambitions prompted him to send an invasion army northward into the Spanish Netherlands. Spain then declared war on France. The Emperor supported Spain (and, of course, opposed France); but he wanted to avoid a two-front war (in the East and in the West) and did not become an active belligerent on the side of Spain. After victories in the Spanish Netherlands and in Catalonia, Louis offered severe truce terms to Spain from a position of commanding military strength. Spain and the Emperor accepted these terms at Regensburg (Ratisbon), agreeing to a twenty-year truce.[22] Although the Emperor had impliedly accepted the Reunions by agreeing to the terms of the truce, he regarded

21 *Ibid.,* pp. 453–6. See also Du Mont, *op. cit.,* Vol. 7, Part I, pp. 432 f.
22 Garden, *op. cit.,* Vol. 2, pp. 123–7.

the agreement as provisional, one that would permit him to concentrate on the Turkish threat first.

In March, 1684, a coalition was formed against the Turk. The Holy League, as it was called, included Poland, Venice, the Papacy, and the Empire. While men from all over Europe joined in this crusade, the assistance offered by Brandenburg, Bavaria, and Saxony was especially important, the latter two Electorates having joined the Emperor in formal alliances. Russia also supported the Pope and became an active belligerent somewhat later. Hanover aided Venice.

War in the West broke out again in 1688 with France's invasion of the Palatinate. By that year, a great coalition against Louis XIV had taken shape. The League of Augsburg (the German princes included Brandenburg, Hanover, and Hesse-Cassel) had been joined by Austria and Spain in 1686 (although Spain did not become an active belligerent immediately). After the war had begun, the United Provinces and Britain (after her Glorious Revolution) acceded to the League in 1689. Sweden and Savoy joined in 1690. As in the Franco-Dutch War, Louis found most of Europe arrayed against him.

PATTERN OF SETTLEMENT: 1. The only defector from the Grand Alliance was the Duke of Savoy, induced to leave the coalition by Louis XIV's skillful diplomacy. Savoy made peace with France at Turin in August, 1696. Two months later, the cease-fire treaty of Vigevano was negotiated among Savoy, Spain, and the Emperor. This agreement brought about the evacuation of foreign troops from Savoy.

2. While Louis' separate negotiations with the coalition partners and the desertion of Savoy caused disarray in the Grand Alliance, the major states in the western war together negotiated a peace settlement at Ryswick. They did sign separate treaties—a practice in accord with the egocentric policies of the states. France and Britain signed a peace treaty on 20 September 1697 at Ryswick, as did France and Spain. On the same day, France and Holland made peace and also concluded a twenty-year commercial treaty. The treaty between France and Austria (and the Empire) was signed on 30 October 1697.

3. The eastern war between the Empire and Turkey was wound up by the Treaty of Peace of Carlowitz, 26 January 1699. On the same day, Poland signed a separate peace treaty with Turkey. Polish and Imperial ambassadors also negotiated an Instrument of Peace *for* Venice, subsequently accepted by the Signory (7 February 1699).

4. Russia and the Ottoman Empire signed their peace treaty at Constantinople on 13 June 1700.

WAR AIMS: Both Turkey and France dreamed of erecting empires at opposite ends of Europe; and in both cases, the territorial acquisitions were to be at the Holy Roman Empire's expense. In addition to the Rhenish Reunions, Louis also sought territory in northern Italy, the

Spanish Netherlands, Africa, and America. The members of the Grand Alliance therefore fought essentially defensive wars and sought to maintain a balance of power. As against the Turks, the members of the Holy League were also motivated by Christian ideology, just as Kara Mustafa's imperial aims were conditioned by Muslim ideology. Protestant opinion in Europe was, moreover, outraged by Louis' revocation of the Edict of Nantes and his persecution of the Huguenots. Spain sought retribution for the imposed peace of Regensburg. The United Provinces wanted to maintain their commercial and colonial position against French incursions. England's colonial possessions were also pawns in the competition for empire between France and England. The German states wanted security guarantees and retribution against the French for the conduct of their armies east of the Rhine.

FACTORS FOR PEACE: The Duke of Savoy believed his allies were secretly negotiating peace with France and were prepared to compromise his interests. As Louis XIV was willing to make peace on terms favorable to the Duke, the latter left the Alliance and made peace.

Both France and Austria had realized by the early 1790s that the war would probably not result in a clearcut victory for either side. Louis was prompted to take the initiative in moving toward peace because of the war costs and poor harvests and, more importantly, because the prospect of dividing the allies could be pursued, and indeed was pursued, with skill and advantage. The German princes also desired peace; and the Emperor had difficulty in moderating that desire. The allies made peace on the basis of the terms France offered, because negotiations offered the prospect of greater net gains than a continuation of the war and because the allies did not (and could not) trust each other to cooperate in war or in the peace talks.

In the East, the Turk had been beaten, and the allies knew they could obtain their goals through negotiations. The Emperor did not want further to exploit by force Ottoman weakness at this time because he, like Louis XIV, was very much aware that the question of the Spanish Succession must soon arise; and he wanted to be relieved of the burden of a War in the East in order to be prepared for a new war in the West.

WAR-ORIENTED STATES: In the first (Franco-Spanish) phase of the war, from 1683–1684, the Empire was a war-oriented state of a very peculiar sort. Implicated in the dispute between the active belligerents, the Emperor succeeded in avoiding hostilities; but he signed the Truce of Regensburg and obligated himself to its terms. At this stage, most of the German princes were interested in the outcome of the war. For the remainder of the war, with its eastern and western theaters, the states involved in the East were often war-oriented with respect to the war in the West (and vice versa). Events in the two theaters also affected moves toward peace. Thus, in 1687 and again in 1688 the Turks, after suffering a number of defeats, asked the Emperor for terms. Negotiations got nowhere; and after France invaded the Palatinate in 1688, Turkey demanded too favorable conditions, and the Emperor broke off talks. The Turkish leaders had assumed that Austria's reluctance to be involved in a two-front war would induce the Emperor to conclude a more generous peace.

ALLIANCES: The network of alliances was quite complex in detail; simple, if we take a macroscopic view, and remember that in the West, France fought the Grand Alliance.[23] In the East, it was the Ottoman Empire against the Holy League and its supporters. It is interesting to review the structure of the alliance system in the Western war, a not untypical example of alliance networks in a multilateral war:

1. An alliance between Sweden and Holland was formed in 1681; its purpose was to preserve the settlements of Westphalia and Nijmegen. The Emperor and Spain acceded in 1682. The alliance was renewed in 1686. Sweden and Austria concluded a separate treaty of alliance and cooperation in 1682.

2. The Circles of the Upper Rhine and Franconia allied with the Emperor in 1682; the Circles of Bavaria and Franconia with him in 1683. In both cases, the alliances were established to prepare a defense against France.

3. Sweden and Brandenburg made a secret agreement in 1687 to maintain the settlements of Westphalia, Nijmegen, and St. Germain. The year before, Brandenburg and the Emperor had concluded an agreement for keeping the peace of the Empire.

4. In 1686, Spain and Sweden entered the defensive League of Augsburg, which also included the Emperor (for himself and for Austria), the Elector of Bavaria (for himself and for the Circle of Bavaria), and the Circles of Franconia, Saxony, and the Upper Rhine.

5. Britain and the United Provinces concluded a Treaty of Friendship and Alliance in 1689.[24]

6. The Grand Alliance began to form in early 1689. By the Treaty of Vienna of 12 May, Holland and the Emperor agreed to act in concert against France and her allies, to coordinate their military operations, and to consult with each other about problems of peacemaking.[25] Included was a provision for settling disputes between the signatories. Britain entered this alliance in December, 1689; Spain in June, 1690. Other accessions included the Elector of Mainz, the Circles of Franconia and Swabia, the Electors of Brandenburg and Saxony, the Bishop of Münster, the Palatinate Electors, the Dukes of Brunswick, the Electors of Bavaria and Cologne, and the Duke of Lorraine. The alliance was renewed in 1695.

23 *Ibid.*, pp. 128 ff.
24 *A General Collection of Treatys* . . . , *op. cit.*, Vol. 1, pp. 287–90.
25 *Ibid.*, pp. 275–80. See also Garden, *op. cit.*, Vol. 2, pp. 139–40.

7. Spain and the Duke of Savoy negotiated and signed a defensive treaty of alliance and partition on 3 June 1690. Savoy and the Emperor signed a similar treaty the next day. In October, 1690, Britain and Holland concluded a treaty with Savoy which admitted the Duke into the Grand Alliance, the maritime states agreeing to pay Savoy a subsidy and acquiescing in the territorial arrangements of the Savoy treaties with Spain and the Emperor.[26]

These formidable alliances were broken by Louis XIV's late-war diplomacy. Savoy deserted (1696), then England and Holland, then Spain. The Emperor did not want to continue the war alone; so he made peace. The German princes were too small, too weak, and too divided to resist the diplomacy of the great powers during the peace talks.

THE SETTLEMENTS: PRELIMINARIES: As early as 1690, Sweden had offered its good offices to mediate the war issues; but this was refused by the allies (although France did accept). Charles XI continued to attempt mediation, but to no avail. In 1693, Louis XIV issued a proposal for peace through his ambassador to Sweden, the Count d'Avaux, but this too failed to win the interest of the allies. Equally unsuccessful were meetings that same year in Switzerland, between France and the Emperor, mediated by a Venetian nobleman. France and Holland also undertook ultimately abortive negotiations in 1694 at Liège; again in 1695 at Utrecht. In 1696, Charles XI once again used his good offices to foster an exchange of notes among France, Austria, and the United Provinces. France declared that it desired no change in the settlements of Westphalia and Nijmegen. But when the allies asked for a more precise statement from Louis XIV's representative (again, Count d'Avaux), they were refused, and no further progress was made. Louis did succeed in detaching the Duke of Savoy from the Grand Alliance in 1696 by a combination of promises of gain and threats of utter destruction.

SUMMARIES OF SETTLEMENTS: 1. *France and Savoy:* The Treaty of Turin was signed on 29 August 1696.[27] By its terms, Savoy renounced treaties of alliance with the Emperor and promised to obtain a declaration of the neutrality of Italy from all powers concerned. If this could not be obtained, Savoy would then unite in an offensive and defensive alliance with France, attack Milan, and declare war on all those that opposed the alliance. The city and citadel of Pignerol were restored to Savoy, but its fort was to be razed and the Duke must not undertake to rebuild it. France was also to return Nice, Villafranca, and other conquered territories to Savoy. She would make restitution for damages only after German and Spanish troops had been evacuated from Savoian territories. France agreed not to make peace with either Spain or the Empire without comprehending Savoy in the settlement. The Treaties of Münster, Pyrenees, and Nijmegen were declared to be in force. Savoy was guaran-

26 *A General Collection* . . . , *op. cit.*, Vol. 3, pp. 334–44.
27 *Ibid.*, Vol. 1, pp. 290–9.

teed protection by France, but (commensurate with its neutral status) Savoy's army was limited. The commercial *status quo ante* was restored. There were, finally, provisions dealing with ambassadorial protocol, the restitution of benefices, and an amnesty.

By the Treaty of Vigevano, 7 October 1696, between Savoy, Spain, and the Empire, the latter two powers agreed to suspend all hostilities in Italy and withdraw their troops provided that France surrendered Pignerol and two other towns to Savoy and that a cash payment was made to the Emperor to cover the expenses for troop withdrawal (a payment to be made by Tuscany, Mantua, Modena, and Genoa, which Savoy was to collect).[28] Hostages were exchanged to guarantee performance. And Savoy agreed to declare war on France if the latter did not restore Pignerol.

Discussions between France, the Emperor, and Holland continued intermittently through 1696 and 1697. Meanwhile Louis XIV's offer to recognize the Protestant succession in England and concede commercial advantages to the maritime powers induced them to undertake peace negotiations with France at Ryswick in May, 1697. Swedish mediation substantially eased the preliminary as well as the principal negotiations. The Emperor reluctantly sent delegates to this conference. He had concluded that he could benefit neither by a continuation of the war nor by a separate peace. The Empire also sent a deputation, the role of which was limited by the Emperor's diplomacy. He even refused to permit its members to attend meetings with the French. The negotiations were difficult and complex. France and Britain had reached agreement by July, but the signature of their treaty was delayed until the Emperor and France reached an accord in September.

2. *France and England:* These powers signed their Treaty of Peace at Ryswick on 20 September 1697.[29] Louis acknowledged William III King of England, recognized the Protestant succession, and agreed to refuse aid to any rebels against England's monarchs. With the peace, commerce was established on a prewar basis, and the subjects of the parties were to enjoy all the liberties, privileges, and immunities of prior treaties. As respected the territorial settlement, it was agreed that there should be a return to the *status quo ante,* with a restoration of lands within 6 months of ratification. Commissioners were to be appointed to consider the claims of both parties to the Hudson's Bay territory. Britain would, however, restore lands in Canada taken from France during the war. The Governor was also to be liberated, and commissioners were to determine the value of the property confiscated by the English and award damages

28 *Ibid.,* pp. 300–2.
29 *Ibid.,* pp. 302–8.

to France. The Prince of Orange was to be restored to all his lands by the French (pursuant to terms of the Treaty of Nijmegen). The Treaties of Turin (1696) and St. Germain-en-Laye (1679) were confirmed. Letters of marque were annulled, and all ships seized on the high seas after specified dates were to be restored. Violators of the Treaty would be punished. In the event war broke out between the parties, the subjects of one power were to be allowed 6 months to leave the lands of the other with their goods. By a secret article, Britain promised not to aid the Emperor in the event he refused to accept French terms before 1 November 1697.

3. *France and the United Provinces:* Holland and France signed a Treaty of Peace and a separate Treaty of Commerce at Ryswick on 20 September.[30] The terms were quite similar in many respects to the English Treaty, including a Dutch promise not to aid the Emperor after 1 November. Lands, honors, and goods seized during the war were to be returned to the rightful owners. Both parties agreed to return to the *status quo ante* and restore conquered territories. Pondichery was to be returned to the French East India Company; Holland would return Bergen-op-Zoom to the Count d'Auvergne. Each party, moreover, renounced its claims and pretensions against the other. The Treaties of Turin and St. Germain were also confirmed. In the Treaty of Commerce, the parties agreed to place themselves on a prewar commercial basis. Private persons were not to be imprisoned for the public debts of their sovereign. The citizens of France were to be treated like the citizens of Holland when traveling or doing business in the United Provinces, and similar rights were extended to Dutch citizens in France. The tariffs of 1667 were to be observed until new ones could be negotiated within 3 months. It was agreed that "free ships" meant "free goods," except for contraband, and were therefore not subject to seizure. No consuls were to be exchanged, but Dutch agents could reside where the court normally resided.

4. *France and Spain:* Peace, amnesty, and oblivion of all past offenses and a cessation of hostilities became effective on the date of the signature of the Treaty of Peace between France and Spain, also signed at Ryswick on 20 September.[31] The parties agreed to restore all territories seized during the war, and France in particular promised to return to Spain the Reunions of the Spanish Netherlands, a list of which was appended to the Treaty. Spain was very much the gainer by these terms, for France restored Catalonia (with Barcelona), Luxembourg, Charleroi, and Mons with their fortresses undamaged, Ath, Courtrai, and the Reunions of Lux, Namur, Brabant, Flanders, and Hainault, among others (except for 83

30 *Ibid.,* pp. 309–17, 317–32.
31 *Ibid.,* pp. 333–47.

specified villages). In the event the parties disagreed over the extent of territorial restitutions, they were to submit the disputes to the United Provinces for arbitration.

The subjects of either party in occupied territories were to be restored to their prewar rights, honors and benefices, including the right to alienate property and to emigrate with their goods. There was to be free movement of persons between the lands of either party. French withdrawals were to be expeditious: they were to begin *after* ratification; and the French could take with them their artillery and provisions, aided if necessary by the governors of the provinces through which they moved. Revenues from areas in the hands of the French were to be retained by them until the lands were restored to Spain. Contributions would cease only after ratification. Judgments of the courts of the possessing state, before or during the war, were declared to be valid, although all persons were to have the right of judicial review.

The Treaties of Turin and Nijmegen were confirmed. Dinant was to be ceded by France to the Bishop of Liège and the Ponza Islands in the Mediterranean by Spain to the Duke of Parma. The secret article attached was similar in content to those of the English and Dutch Treaties.

5. *France, the Emperor, and the Empire:* The Treaty of Peace between France, the Emperor, and the princes of the Empire was signed at Ryswick on 30 October 1697.[32] An armistice was declared effective from that date. The Treaties of Westphalia and Nijmegen were declared to be the basis of the pacification. France agreed to return specified lands to the Emperor, but not Alsace or Strassbourg. The retroceded lands, moreover, were taken subject to the clause that the transferee would effect no change in the religious status of the transferred lands. (During the course of the war, the Edict of Nantes had been revoked, and Roman Catholicism had been introduced into the lands occupied by France. This was, incidentally, a change in the religious status quo established and forbidden by the Treaty of Münster.) Article 4 of the Treaty of Ryswick provided that neither the Emperor nor the princes—especially the Protestant princes—of the Empire could effect an innovation with respect to the practice of Catholicism in the lands returned to them. This question was to become the subject of bitter controversy in the Diet of the Empire.

Particular articles required restitutions for the Electors of Triers, Brandenburg, and Palatine and the Dukes of Würtemberg and Lorraine (who reacquired Lorraine except for Saarlouis and Longwy). French troops were to have the right of traversing Lorraine to the frontier of France after giving notice to the Duke and promising to do no injury to his lands or his subjects. Thus, France in effect withdrew from

32 *Ibid.*, pp. 360–386. For a discussion and summary of the Peace of Ryswick, see Garden, *op. cit.*, Vol. 2, pp. 111 f., 159 f., 164 f.

the right bank of the Rhine and restored Freibourg, Breisac, and Philipsburg, agreeing also to demolish the fortresses on the left bank. The parties agreed to the free navigation of the Rhine.

The Treaty included the usual provisions guaranteeing the rights of their subjects to emigrate from the transferred territories, promising restitution to them for confiscated goods and real property. The benefices awarded by France to eligible recipients and the judgments of the courts of the lands occupied by France were valid and must be recognized by the Empire. Commerce was to be re-established on a pre-war basis. The customs of 1670 were adopted; but it was understood that a new commercial treaty would be negotiated soon after ratification.

No new claims would be raised against the restored lands by any of the parties. If nonsignatories had claims, they were to be examined in a convenient place. The Treaties of Turin, Westphalia, and Nijmegen were confirmed. It was agreed that it was permissible to enter into alliances to strengthen the peace. Sweden, as a mediator, and all the electors, princes, and states of the Empire, and Switzerland were comprehended within the terms of the Treaty, which was signed by France, the Emperor, and 17 "members" of the Empire. The Protestant states refused to sign, even though Louis threatened to resume hostilities against them. When the Diet voted for ratification of the Treaty on 26 November 1697, it formally declared that the Catholics would never make use of the Ryswick clause (Article 4) to the prejudice of the Protestants or contrary to the tenor of the terms of the Treaties of Westphalia. The quarrel in the Diet was renewed when the Emperor ratified the Treaty on 12 December, but made no mention of the declaration of the Diet in favor of the Protestants.

6. *The Ottoman and Holy Roman Empires:* Austria was in an exceptionally strong bargaining position, as her armies (and the contingents of the other states of the Holy League) occupied the territories they intended to retain. Mediated by William III and the Dutch, the Treaties of Carlowitz, signed on 26 January 1699, ended the war in the East. The Treaty between the Empires provided for a cease-fire that was to continue for 25 years.[33] Hungary, Transylvania, and Siebenburgen, except the Banat of Temesvar, were transferred to Austria. A boundary commission was to meet on and after 22 May to fix the boundaries of these cessions (and of Croatia). Turkey was to raze her forts on the Theiss and Morava Rivers; and demilitarized zones were established for those areas

---

33 *A General Collection* . . . , *op. cit.,* Vol. 4, pp. 290–301. At this time, the Ottoman Empire would negotiate only a *cease-fire* with its Christian adversaries, not a *peace treaty.* The Empire refused to conclude any peace arrangement with the "infidel." I thank Prof. Jacob C. Hurewitz of Columbia University for calling my attention to this fact.

as well as the Dan and the Save. Austrian garrisons were to withdraw from Bosnia.

Hungarians that had emigrated from Turkish lands to Austria during the war were to be given security and freedom, but might be resettled away from the new frontiers. No more subjects of the Porte were to be permitted to emigrate to Austria, however; and if they did so, they were to be returned to Turkey. There was to be free trade between the parties. Ambassadors were to be exchanged who were to work out the details of trade arrangements. Generally, trade was to be conducted on a most-favored-nation basis. One article stipulated that ambassadors must be given immunities commensurate with the public law of Europe; another, that monks and priests were entitled to practice Roman Catholicism in the Ottoman Empire on the same basis as that granted by previous Sultans. Prior treaties were declared to be in force.

7. *Poland and the Ottoman Empire:* In this settlement, embodied in the second of the Peace Treaties of Carlowitz, Poland agreed to evacuate Moldavia; and Turkey agreed to cede Podolia and part of the Ukraine to Poland.[34] The Tartars would be removed from Moldavia. The Polish Ambassador to Turkey was to be allowed to make representations on behalf of Catholics in Turkey. In other respects, the Treaty was similar, in its standard clauses, to the Austrian Treaty.

8. *Venice and the Ottoman Empire:* The Instrument of Peace for Venice and Turkey was signed at Carlowitz on 26 January, after being negotiated by the Imperial and Polish Ambassadors "in hopes that it will be accepted by Venice." It was accepted on 7 February.[35] The Morea and parts of Dalmatia (the boundary of which was to be fixed by a commission) were to remain in the possession of Venice. Mainland Greece and the islands of the Archipelago and Ragusa were to remain under Turkish sovereignty. The Gulf of Corinth was open for the use of either party; and both were to attempt to rid the Gulf of pirates. The Porte agreed to levy no excessive contributions or taxes on Venetian subjects in the transferred territories. The frontiers of the parties were to be demilitarized. Prewar trade treaties were confirmed; and with respect to slaves and religion, the latest prewar customs were to be observed. A cease-fire was to be effective at varying times after signature of the Instrument, depending on the distances of the theaters of war from the conference site.

9. *Russia and Turkey:* At Carlowitz, Russia and Turkey agreed to a cease-fire for 2 years, Azov to remain in the possession of the Russians. On 13 June 1700, they concluded at Constantinople a second agreement.[36]

34 *Ibid.,* pp. 302–8.

35 *Ibid.,* pp. 309–22.

36 Noradounghian, Gabriel, *Recueil d'Actes Internationaux de l'Empire Ottoman* (Paris: Librairie Cotillon, 1897), Vol. 1, pp. 197–203.

By its terms, the parties agreed to continue the cease-fire and to renew it in the future. Territories around the Dnieper River were to be restored to Turkey and the fortresses on the river razed. The Porte was prohibited from constructing forts in the retroceded territories. Azov was to remain in the possession of Russia (but Russia did not obtain access to the Black Sea). A demilitarized zone was also established around Perekop. Peoples living in the transferred territories were not to be molested in the enjoyment of their rights or their trade. The subjects of Russia were to refrain from excesses against the inhabitants of Taman, the Crimea, and such areas. Cossack pirates were to be punished. Prisoners of war were to be released, except for Muslims, whom the Porte might detain. Agents of the Czar would be permitted to move freely throughout the Ottoman Empire to expedite the release of prisoners.

A treaty of commerce was to be negotiated, and future disputes were to be settled amicably. If Russia sent an agent to Constantinople, he was to have the same privileges and immunities as representatives of other powers. Russian pilgrims to the Holy Places were to be permitted to travel without hindrance and without paying special taxes. Finally, an ambassador was to be designated by the Czar to complete the work of pacification.

SIGNIFICANCE OF THE SETTLEMENT: Once again the balance of power in Europe had been maintained against the ambitious Louis XIV whose France was the single strongest power in Europe. After the Revolution of 1688, England joined Austria as a counterbalance against France. Not since Elizabeth I had England played such an important role on the continent; and she would continue to play an increasingly decisive role there, as well as on the seas and in the colonies.

WAR OF THE SPANISH SUCCESSION (1701-1714)

STRUCTURE OF THE WAR: In this war, the alliance of Britain, the United Provinces, and Austria, joined by a number of German states (including Brandenburg-Prussia), was pitted against an alliance of France, Spain, and Portugal, joined by Bavaria, Cologne, and Savoy. Both Portugal and Savoy deserted their French ally and adhered to the English alliance in 1703. Bavaria capitulated to Anglo-German forces in 1704.

PATTERN OF SETTLEMENT: Separate treaties of peace were signed by the belligerents. The Emperor refused to participate in the negotiations at Utrecht. He made peace with France at Rastadt, for himself (for Austria) and for the Empire, on 6 March 1714. A treaty of peace was never concluded between Spain and the Empire.

The Peace of Utrecht included the following: (a) The Anglo-French Treaty of Peace, 11 April 1713 (about one year before the Emperor made peace); (b) The French-Dutch Treaties of Peace and Commerce of 11 April 1713; (c) The peace treaty between France and Portugal of 13

April; (d) The treaty between France and Brandenburg-Prussia of 11 April; (e) The peace treaty between France and Savoy, also of 11 April; (f) The Anglo-Spanish Treaty of Peace of 13 July 1713; (g) The Treaty of Peace between Spain and Savoy, one month later (13 August 1713); (h) The treaty between Spain and the Dutch, 26 June 1714; and (i) The treaty between Spain and Portugal, 6 February 1715.

WAR AIMS: Louis XIV's aim was the aggrandizement of France and his dynasty by the acquisiton of Spanish lands and the Spanish throne for his grandson, Philip of Anjou. Leopold I of Austria wanted the throne for his son, Archduke Charles.

Neither Britain nor Holland would permit French occupation of the Spanish Netherlands or such a change in the balance of power as the Bourbon possession of both the French and the Spanish crowns implied. The maritime powers also sought an amelioration of Spanish commercial policies which, under French influence, operated to the prejudice of their trade. Portugal was at first allied with the French and Spanish, almost under duress. By 1703, it appeared that Britain and Austria were firmly resolved to make war on France and that the British could aid Portugal by sea. This was enough to persuade the Portuguese to desert France, whose supremacy no longer seemed inevitable. Portugal then joined England after obtaining security guarantees from her.

Savoy's policies were dictated almost purely by calculations of what states could provide the opportunity values the Duke wanted: hence, his shift from the Franco-Spanish alliance to the potentially more successful English-Dutch-Austrian alliance in 1703. In the Empire, the German princes, except Cologne and Bavaria, cooperated with the Emperor because they feared the French and welcomed Anglo-Dutch subsidies.

FACTORS FOR PEACE: By 1708, after a series of stunning victories by the allies, France was ready to negotiate peace, Louis having given up his dream of French hegemony in Europe. The Spanish Succession question had not been resolved, however, and the war continued for more than four years until a solution acceptable to most of the powers was found. This solution was regarded as acceptable by a new Tory government in England and by the allies on *both sides* (but not Austria), who were weary of war and convinced that there was no way out of the military stalemate, except by negotiations and compromise. Both England and the United Provinces were to receive desirable commercial and colonial gains by the terms of peace Louis indicated he was willing to accept; and the principle of the separation of the French and Spanish thrones was to be written into the public law of Europe. The Emperor made peace because, without allies, he could not hope to put a Habsburg prince on the Spanish throne. Spain too was willing to make peace provided the allies recognized Philip of Anjou (Philip V) as King of Spain; and by 1713, all except Austria were so willing.

WAR-ORIENTED STATES: In the Italian theater, Venice and the Pope were interested in the course of the war. Turkey was also war-oriented. The Hungarian Revolt created a situation that Louis exploited, and it constituted an important distraction for Austria. But the most important series of events that bore upon the War of the Spanish Succession was the Great Northern War of Sweden against a coalition of Russia, Denmark, and Poland (and the Elector of Saxony, who was also King of Poland). The two major wars were wholly separate; but their participants were very much interested in developments of the war in which they were not involved. Britain was tied to Sweden by an alliance that in 1700 brought English ships into the Baltic and enabled Sweden's Charles XII to force terms on Denmark. (Britain was also allied with Denmark by the Treaty of Odenall of 20 January 1701, an alliance that obligated the Danes to close their ports to warships if war broke out on the continent!) After defeating Poland-Saxony and imposing peace terms on the Elector in 1707 at Altranstädt, Charles XII was asked by both Britain and France to intervene on their side in the central European war. He did not do so, but instead turned to deal with Russia, the last state in the coalition against him. After the defeat of the Swedish army at Pultava in 1709, Britain and Holland assiduously and successfully moved to isolate the Northern War, for Hanover and Brandenburg-Prussia had been planning to intervene in the north in order to share the spoils of the disintegrating Swedish Empire. Britain wanted to be assured that the military efforts of Brandenburg and Hanover would be concentrated against the French, where they were needed (at least from the point of view of the maritime powers). The Great Northern War ended after the War of the Spanish Succession, with the Treaties of Stockholm (1719), Frederiksborg (1720), and Nystad (1721).

ALLIANCES: There were several significant alliances.[37] 1. The Second Grand Alliance was based upon the treaty among England, Holland, and the Emperor of 7 September 1701.[38] In that agreement, the allies promised, in vague terms, to secure an "equitable and reasonable satisfaction to his Imperial Majesty for his pretension to the Spanish Succession" and to provide sufficient security for the dominions and commerce of the maritime powers. No peace was to be made without these goals being achieved, nor without a guarantee against the reunification of the French and Spanish thrones. Specifically, the Dutch were to be assured a Barrier in the Spanish Netherlands for their security; Austria was to acquire Milan, Tuscany, and the Spanish Netherlands, together with Naples and Sicily. Prussia joined this alliance in December, 1701. The German

37 Garden, *op. cit.*, Vol. 2, pp. 232 ff.

38 *A General Collection* . . . , *op. cit.*, Vol. 1, pp. 415–21. See also *ibid.*, Vol. 4, pp. 330–3, and Garden, *op. cit.*, Vol. 2, pp. 243 f.

princes, having instituted some organized defensive measures in 1700, formally acceded to the Grand Alliance on 22 March 1702. Included were the Circles of the Rhine, Franconia, Swabia, and Austria. The Electorate of Trier and the Circle of Westphalia acceded a few months later; and Savoy acceded in 1703. Sweden also joined the Alliance in 1703 but was to take an active part only after she had made peace with Russia and Poland. In all cases, commitment to the alliance required the provisioning and deployment of troops or ships. Subsidies from England were sometimes arranged; and in some cases, promises of territories were given. (In the case of the Elector of Brandenburg, the Emperor agreed to recognize the former as the King of Prussia.)

2. The agreements of the allies with Portugal were also significant. There were two treaties, the commercial treaty between Britain and Portugal of 27 December 1703;[39] and the treaty of offensive and defensive alliance of 16 May 1703 among the Emperor, Britain, Holland, and Portugal.[40] Not only was Portugal drawn away from her alliance with France and her ports put at the disposal of the British navy, but the allies obligated themselves not to make peace so long as any French prince ruled Spain. This ambitious undertaking quite possibly prolonged the war.

Because of fundamental disagreements between the Emperor and his allies—disagreements that Louis XIV assiduously cultivated—Charles VI made peace with France separately at Rastadt; with the others, at Utrecht. Indeed, Austria felt that England had betrayed her by agreeing to negotiate on terms that did not acknowledge Habsburg rights to the Spanish Crown. However, this disarray in the alliance did not substantially prejudice England's interests, nor those of the allies relative to France. If anything, the allies had to be more concerned about their English ally's extensive acquisitions!

THE SETTLEMENT: PRELIMINARIES: Exploratory peace talks between representatives of France and Holland were held as early as 1705 and again in 1706. Talks in March, 1709, were secret, but both Britain and Austria learned of them and did all they could to cause them to fail, because they felt the time was not right: Their governments still hoped to fulfill their war aims completely. In May, 1709, the four powers sent their representatives to The Hague, where Prince Eugene and Marlborough submitted a draft agreement in 40 articles to the French. After some concessions, Louis XIV declared that he could not accept them: He refused to contemplate the use of force to remove his grandson from the throne of Spain or even to attempt to induce him to abdicate by peaceful means before the ratification of the peace treaty. Negotiations ended and the

39 *A General Collection* . . . , *op. cit.*, Vol. 4, pp. 334–5.
40 Almon, John, *A Collection of all Treaties of Peace, Alliance and Commerce* (London: Almon, 1772) , Vol. 2, pp. 331–42.

war continued, although not without further exchanges of proposals for a compromise. Britain and Holland concluded the First Barrier Treaty on 29 October 1709.[41] By its terms the United Provinces guaranteed the English succession in the House of Hanover; and Britain promised to help the Dutch secure 19 fortified places in the Spanish Netherlands as a "Barrier" against French aggression.

French overtures in late 1709 and early 1710 led to yet another preliminary peace conference, at Gertruydenberg, from March through July, 1710. But this too failed to achieve any signal results, and hostilities continued.

In 1711, the Whig ministry in Britain was replaced by the Tories, who wanted peace. Emperor Joseph I died, to be succeeded by Archduke Charles, the Habsburg claimant of the Spanish throne. The Tories were not about to wage war to enlarge the Austrian Habsburg realm by the addition of Spain. Preliminary negotiations continued throughout 1711. The talks of Utrecht between the Allies and France began in January, 1712. When the conference first met, there was no armistice. From 1711 on, strains began to appear in the coalition, and Austria came to perceive the settlements in very different terms than did her maritime allies.

SUMMARIES OF THE SETTLEMENTS: A Treaty for the Suspension of Arms was signed on 19 August 1712 between France and Britain.[42] This was subsequently extended 4 months. The armistice was to begin on 22 August and run to 22 December. Spain agreed to lift the blockade of Gibraltar. All ships seized as prizes after specified dates were to be restored. Britain agreed not to permit her vessels to be used to transport arms or men to Portugal or Catalonia, although it was permissible to return Portuguese soldiers in Catalonia to Portugal, or German soldiers in Catalonia to Italy. France and Portugal accepted a four-month cease-fire on 7 November 1712. The Treaty for the evacuation of Catalonia was signed on 14 March 1713 and finally implemented in the autumn of that year.[43]

In the Second Barrier Treaty between Britain and the United Provinces (29 January 1713), the signatories formulated a scheme for the cession of the Spanish Netherlands to Austria, with whom Britain would use its good offices to persuade the Emperor to permit the Dutch to fortify designated areas.[44]

1. *France and Britain:* The settlement between these states was contained in the Treaty of Peace of Utrecht (11 April 1713) and in the Treaty of Navigation and Commerce concluded the month before.[45]

41 *A General Collection* . . . , *op. cit.,* Vol. 2, pp. 479–91.

42 *Ibid.,* pp. 553–5.

43 Garden, *op. cit.,* Vol. 2, pp. 303–4.

44 *A General Collection* . . . , *op. cit.,* Vol. 3, pp. 364–73.

45 *Ibid.,* pp. 398–439. The Treaty of Commerce is on pp. 440–70.

France accepted the English succession in the House of Hanover and promised to give no aid to any who opposed this succession. Letters of marque were declared void. The stipulations with respect to prizes in the Armistice Agreement were to remain in force. Violations were not to be an occasion for the renewal of hostilities, but violators would be punished. If war did break out, the subjects of one party living or trading in the other's domains were to have 6 months to leave with their movable property. Free commerce was restored with the 1664 tariffs adopted as a base. The most-favored-nation principle was also adopted as the basis for trade between the parties. A commission was to be established in London to determine tariffs for specific commodities.

The Crowns of Spain and France were forever to remain separate. Philip V renounced his claims to the Crown of France, and the Dukes of Berry and Orleans renounced their claims to the Crown of Spain. The forts at Dunkirk were to be razed and the harbor filled within 5 months. (This offered English commerce some protection against privateers.) France ceded to Britain the Hudson's Bay territories, St. Christopher, Nova Scotia, and the City of Port Royal; and France recognized British sovereignty in Newfoundland. Britain granted French subjects the right to emigrate from the ceded Canadian territories and also gave them liberty to catch and dry fish in specified seas and areas around Newfoundland. French fishermen were to be excluded from Nova Scotia. Commissions were established to fix the boundary between French and British possessions in Canada and assess the amount of damages to be awarded the English Hudson's Bay Company (for damages sustained at the hands of France during peacetime). Cape Breton Island was acknowledged to belong to France; it could be fortified. In territories transferred to Britain, Roman Catholicism was to be conserved to the extent that English law allowed. French subjects in North America would not molest the Indians; and Indians friendly to the English living in French Canada were to be permitted to trade and travel freely.

France promised that in the treaty ultimately concluded with the Emperor, as respected matters of religion, the Peace of Westphalia was to be observed. Britain guaranteed the peace treaties between France and Portugal and between France and Savoy. The Hanse towns, Sweden, Tuscany, Genoa, and Parma were comprehended in the Peace Treaty.

2. *France and Portugal:* By the Peace Treaty of 13 April 1713, the sovereigns of France and Portugal made peace.[46] France renounced all claims to lands in Northern South America and in the region of the Amazon and renounced the right to navigate the Amazon. Other standard provisions were incorporated in the Treaty.

3. *France and Brandenburg-Prussia:* In the Peace Treaty of 11 April,

46 Garden, *op. cit.,* Vol. 2, pp. 309–10.

France confirmed the Treaties of Westphalia respecting the religious and civil governance of the Empire and transferred territories in Upper Guelders and Neufchatel to Austria (with the permission of the King of Spain), which would then transfer them to Prussia.[47] France recognized the Elector as King of Prussia, and Prussia renounced all claims to the Principality of Orange and the Franche-Comté.

4. *France and Savoy:* France recognized the Duke of Savoy as the King of Sicily and agreed that the succession of the Spanish Crown should reside in the male line of the Duke in the event Philip V died without heirs.[48] Specified treaties were declared to be in force. France ceded Nice and Savoy to the Duke; a later treaty (1760) established the frontier on the summit of the Alps. The earlier cessions of Montferrat and the lands between the Po und Tanaro Rivers were confirmed to the Duke. The Treaty of Peace, like the Prussian Treaty, was signed at Utrecht on 11 April 1713.

5. *France and the United Provinces:* The settlement between these belligerents was incorporated in two treaties, one of peace and another of commerce, both signed on 11 April 1713.[49] France agreed to cede the Spanish Netherlands to the Dutch; and after Barrier security arrangements had been made, the Dutch were to transfer the lands to Austria. France would secure Bavaria's renunciation to the Low Countries. (During the War, France had induced Spain to award the Netherlands to Bavaria.) As in the English Treaty, the renunciations of Philip V of Spain (and others) were declared to be public laws of Europe. Finally, France agreed to accord Holland the same commercial privileges as the latter had held under the Treaty of Münster. Nor would France seek to obtain greater commercial advantages over the Dutch either in Spain or in the Indies than she had held in the reign of Charles II.

6. *Britain and Spain:* The Treaty of Peace signed on 13 July 1713 between Spain and Great Britain was one of the two principal instruments of the Utrecht settlement (the other being the Anglo-French treaty considered earlier).[50] Spain adhered to the law that separated the Crowns of Spain and France, recognized the Hanoverian succession, and promised to aid no one who opposed it. The usual declarations of eternal friendship were incorporated in the Treaty, along with the terms promulgating amnesty and release of prisoners. All earlier treaties of commerce were confirmed. Trade with the Spanish West Indies was to be on the same basis as that of the reign of Charles II; and Spain agreed not to give France the right to trade with Spanish colonies in America. Most-

47 *Ibid.,* pp. 310–14. See also Du Mont, *op. cit.,* Vol. 8, pp. 356 f.
48 Garden, *op. cit.,* Vol. 2, pp. 314–6; Du Mont, *op. cit.,* Vol. 8, pp. 362 f.
49 Garden, *op. cit.,* Vol. 2, pp. 317–9.
50 *A General Collection . . . , op. cit.,* Vol. 3, pp. 470–92.

favored-nation treatment was to be accorded the subjects of the signatories in respect of duties and other impositions on trade. Spain gave Britain the exclusive right to introduce Negro slaves into Spanish America for 30 years and also leased the British trading company lands on the River Plata.

Spain ceded Minorca and Gibraltar to Britain. There was to be no communication between Gibraltar and the contiguous Spanish territory, although the British could buy provisions in Spain. The practice of Roman Catholicism was conserved. No Jews or Moors were to be permitted to live in Gibraltar. Trade with the Moors was allowed, but no Moorish warships were to be admitted to the fortress harbor. If Britain were to sell Gibraltar, Spain was to have the right to buy it.

Spain granted full amnesty to the Catalonians and promised to restore all privileges and property to them. She ceded Sicily to the Duke of Savoy; but in default of male heirs, it would revert to the Spanish Crown. Britain guaranteed this settlement and agreed to prevent the alienation of Sicily to any other state. Spanish subjects in Sicily and Sicilian subjects in Spain were to remain unmolested in the full enjoyment of their rights.

All earlier treaties of peace and commerce were in force. In the event of a breach of the Treaty, the violators would be punished, but war would not be declared. In the event of war, subjects of either party were to have 6 months to leave the lands of the other with their goods. Comprehended within the terms of the Treaty were Sweden, Tuscany, Parma, Genoa, Danzig and Venice. By a separate article, Britain guaranteed the territorial integrity of Spain.

7. *Spain and Savoy:* The principal feature of interest in the Spanish-Savoian treaty of peace, signed on 13 August 1713, was the settlement for Sicily just referred to.[51] The Duke was crowned King of Sicily in November. (Neither the Pope nor the Emperor recognized him, however.) Spain also confirmed the earlier cession by Austria of Montferrat and Milan to Savoy.

8. *Spain and the United Provinces:* The Treaty of Peace, signed on 26 June, was primarily a commercial treaty.[52] Spain granted the Dutch most-favored-nation treatment except for the English monopoly in the slave trade with Spanish America. The Treaty of Münster was renewed; and the law respecting the separation of the thrones of France and Spain was affirmed.

9. *Austria, The Empire, and France:* Dissatisfied with the Utrecht settlement in that Habsburg claims in Spain were passed over by the maritime powers (and unhappy because Alsace had not been ceded to Austria), Emperor Charles VI continued the war. He ordered his repre-

51 Garden, *op. cit.,* Vol. 2, pp. 324–6.
52 *Ibid.,* pp. 340–3.

sentative to leave Utrecht and refused to associate himself with the terms of the pacification. Suffering setbacks in the fall of 1713, however, he then became willing to negotiate. France, in a state of economic exhaustion, agreed to meet secretly with Austria at Rastadt. The conference began on 26 November, was interrupted for a time while the delegates reported back to their sovereigns, but it resumed in February, 1714. The important Preliminary Treaty of Rastadt was signed on 6 March 1714.[53] France and Austria were parties to it. The Solemn (i.e., Definitive) Treaty of Peace was signed at Baden in Ergau on 27 September 1714 by the same parties.[54] By the later date, the Austrian plenipotentiary had the authorization of the Diet to sign on behalf of the Estates and Princes of the Empire.

An armistice was to become effective from the date of the signature of the Rastadt Treaty. With its ratification, contributions were to cease, and the release of prisoners was to begin. Within 15 days of ratification, the parties would begin to evacuate their troops from the Netherlands, Cologne, and Bavaria. As respected commerce, the *status quo ante* was to be restored.

The Treaties of Westphalia, Nijmegen, and Ryswick were confirmed. In general terms, the territorial settlement restored the right bank of the Rhine to the Empire, the left bank being retained by France. Freibourg and the Breisgau forts were to be returned to the Empire, in the condition they were in when occupied, within 30 days of ratification of the Definitive Treaty. The Rhine was open to the free use of the parties, but the forts along the Rhine were to be razed at France's expense. France, moreover, gave up the Spanish Netherlands to the United Provinces, which had consented to their eventual transfer to Austria. The benefices granted by France to the Netherlands during the war were to be conserved. Provisions to protect the civil liberties of the inhabitants of the Netherlands were also incorporated, including an amnesty, a guarantee of rights to hold property, to travel, and to trade, and a promise of restitution for goods confiscated during the war.

Other areas to be restored to the Emperor were described. The Archbishop of Cologne and Maximilian Emmanuel of Bavaria were to be restored to their Estates, titles, and honors. Both of them were to renounce all claims and pretensions against the Habsburgs and swear obedience to the Emperor. In time of peace, Bonn was not to be garrisoned. France consented to the elevation of the House of Brunswick-Lüneburg to the electoral dignity in Hanover.

Territorial guarantees were exchanged. The parties agreed to respect the neutrality of Italy, and the claims of the Italian princes were to be

53 *A General Collection* . . . , *op. cit.,* Vol. 4, pp. 338–57.
54 *Ibid.,* pp. 358–77.

referred to conferences for composition. Finally, the Rastadt Treaty recognized that the Emperor must obtain confirmation of the Peace from the Diet.

The Definitive Treaty of Baden for the most part confirmed the arrangements made in the Rastadt Treaty. All restorations prescribed therein were to be made within 30 days of the exchange of ratifications of the Baden Treaty. The Diet of the Empire empowered the Austrian delegate both to sign the Treaty and to promise ratification on its part. The claims of Habsburg princes in Italy were not to delay implementation of the settlement; but an attempt to settle them was to be made later.

10. *Spain and Portugal:* A settlement between Spain and Portugal was formally achieved with the signing of the Treaty of Peace on 6 February 1715.[55] There were small territorial gains for Portugal on the River Plata. Spain was to be awarded damages for the seizure of her vessels.

11. *Spain and Austria:* Austria refused to negotiate a peace settlement with Philip V.

SIGNIFICANCE OF THE SETTLEMENT: The settlement was an application of the principle of equilibrium. Separation of the French and Spanish Crowns was acknowledged as a public law of Europe. Britain's refusal to continue the war on behalf of the Austrian Habsburg's aspirations in Spain was a tacit admission that the joinder of the Austrian and Spanish thrones—as in the reign of Charles V—was equally unacceptable. Whether in Europe or in the colonies, among the great powers or the small, through compensations and acknowledgments of kingly dignity the balance of power in the state system had been maintained.

THE WAR OF THE AUSTRIAN SUCCESSION (1740–1748)

STRUCTURE OF THE WAR: The war between Britain and Spain, which broke out in 1739 (known as The War of Jenkin's Ear), merged into the general European conflict that started with the Prussian invasion of Austria's province of Silesia. Bavaria and France became embroiled on the side of Prussia. Frederick II (later "The Great") deserted his French ally twice, briefly in 1741 and again in 1742, each time making peace with Austria. Meanwhile, Sardinia had allied with Austria; and after a period of neutrality, England (and Hanover) did the same. By 1743, the English were in a *de facto* state of war with France, as were the Dutch. Spain allied with France in 1743.

In 1745 Saxony, which was allied with France and Bavaria from 1741–1742, declared war on Prussia, which had again become involved in hostilities on the side of France. Allied to Prussia were the Palatinate and Hesse. The Republic of Genoa agreed to permit French and Spanish troops to cross her territories and thus also became a belligerent. But by

55 Garden, *op. cit.,* Vol. 2, pp. 343–45.

the end of 1745, both Saxony and Bavaria left the war. Prussia and Austria also came to terms. By the beginning of 1746, the structure of the war was: France, Spain, and Genoa vs. Britain, Austria, Sardinia, and the United Provinces. In late 1746, Genoa made peace with Austria.

PATTERN OF SETTLEMENT: Prussia reached agreement on a preliminary cease-fire with Austria in October, 1741 (the Convention of Kleinschnellendorf). Frederick went to war again, however; and the success of his arms impelled Maria Theresa to agree to the cession of Silesia to Prussia in the Preliminaries of Peace of Breslau (11 June 1742), subsequently confirmed in the Definitive Treaty of Peace of Berlin (28 July 1742).[56] But Frederick went to war against Austria once again. This episode was terminated by the Peace of Dresden (25 December 1745). Bavaria and Austria made peace at Füssen on 22 April 1745. Saxony and Prussia signed a peace treaty, also at Dresden, on 25 December 1745. Britain and Prussia were never formally at war. The two parties signed proposed articles of peace (the Convention of Hanover) on 26 August 1745.[57] These terms were rejected by Austria at the time, but they may be regarded as having established *de facto* peace between Britain and Prussia after their *de facto* war. Genoa made peace with Austria in late 1746; but her people rose in rebellion against the Austrian occupation force. The siege of Genoa continued until 1748.

The settlement of the war was brought about through negotiations at Aix-la-Chapelle. The Definitive Treaty of Peace of Aix-la-Chapelle was signed on 18 October 1748 by Britain, France, and Holland, the three principal belligerents. The following acceded to the Peace: Spain, Sardinia, the Duke of Modena, the Republic of Genoa, and Austria. Unlike the form of the settlements of the preceding three multilateral wars we have considered, the War of the Austrian Succession was brought to a formal end by a *single* multilateral peace treaty, rather than by a series of bilateral treaties.

WAR AIMS: Mercantile interests and, specifically, the elaboration of a commercial empire prompted Britain to declare war on Spain in 1739. With respect to her colonies, Spain fought a war to preserve the status quo and to defend her colonies and her trade.

Prussia's King Frederick sought territories and resources. Relative to Prussia, Austria fought to maintain the integrity of the realms of the House of Austria. Frederick's attack had been occasioned by the death of the Emperor Charles VI, offering what the Prussian King regarded as a

56 Rousset de Missy, Jean, *Recueil Historiques d'Actes* . . . (Amsterdam: Meynerd Uytwerf, 1745), Vol. 18, pp. 27–33, 33–45. A brief discussion of the Kleinschnellendorf Convention can be found in Garden, *op. cit.*, Vol. 3, pp. 262–4.

57 Wenck, F. A. W., *Codex Iuris Gentium* (Leipzig, Weidmann, 1788), Vol. 2, pp. 191–203. See Garden, *op. cit.*, Vol. 3, pp. 345–7.

favorable moment for aggrandizement. This Emperor Charles had drafted the Pragmatic Sanction in 1713, which bequeathed all Habsburg dominions to his daughter, Maria Theresa. The Emperor had spent much time and money securing the assent of relatives, Estates of the Empire, and foreign powers to the Sanction so that the Succession in Austria would not be questioned or result in the dissolution of the Habsburg Empire. However, after Prussia's invasion of Silesia, France allied itself with Prussia and with Bavaria, supporting the pretensions of Charles Albert of Bavaria to the Imperial Crown. This decision was motivated by the hope for gain and retribution against France's traditional Austrian enemy.

Britain became involved in hostilities against the French because her policymakers sought gains in the French colonies in America and India, the defense of Hanover (of which George II was Elector), and containment of France on the continent.

Sardinia's Charles Emmanuel alternately wished to secure his dominions against attack and to ally himself with the coalition that could promise him opportunity gains from a successful war. Dutch policy was comparatively weak and vacillating. The support they did give to the Anglo-Austrian alliance was ineffectual, based upon both fear of the French and more specifically, the desire to secure the Austrian Netherlands from attack by France. But the Dutch burghers did not want to become involved in a war that would damage their trade and banking relations with the rest of Europe. Both Spain and France were interested in Italy because they sought strategic advantages over Austria and additional client states or dominions. Genoa fought to defend its lands against the Austrians.

FACTORS FOR PEACE: Prussia was in a state of economic and moral exhaustion; yet Frederick did obtain Austrian recognition of Prussian sovereignty over Silesia. Having achieved this major aim, he was willing to make the concessions necessary for Austria's acceptance of the loss of territory. As for Austria, her armies had been dealt a series of defeats at Frederick's hands; and British threatened to cut off subsidies if Austria did not make peace with Prussia. Besides, France had refused to accept Maria Theresa's peace proposals. The war with France would continue; hence for Austria, peace with Prussia was necessary. Moreover, Austria's policymakers decided for peace because other powers were willing to accept the Pragmatic Sanction and agreed to recognize Maria Theresa's husband, Francis Stephen, as Emperor. (He had been elected Emperor on 4 October 1745.)

Both France and Holland were in a state of economic exhaustion. These powers and Britain realized that a compromise peace based upon reciprocal compensations was possible. French naval losses had been high, French foreign trade ruined. Even in Britain, there was fear of bankruptcy. Spain made peace because France did so.

WAR-ORIENTED STATES: When the belligerents were not actively involved in hostilities, they were war-oriented: for example, Prussia after the Peace of Breslau in 1762 and again after the Peace of Dresden in 1745; Bavaria after the Peace of Füssen; and Britain before 1744 (and in respect to the central conflict between Prussia and France against Austria). Holland was *de facto* belligerent after 1743. (Its policies often seemed to be those of a nonbelligerent ally, however.) The principalities and republics of Italy, other than Sardinia and Genoa, were also war-oriented in respect to the war in the Italian theater; but they were able to influence the policies of the principals in a minimal way only. Turkey was also interested in the war, if for no other reason than because her traditional enemy in Europe, Austria, was engaged. Russia and Sweden, themselves at war with each other from 1741 to 1743, were peripherally interested in the European war, Russia more so than Sweden because it appeared for a time (1747–1748) that she would be asked to supply mercenaries to the maritime powers. Russia was tied to Britain, Saxony, and Austria by defensive alliance.

ALLIANCES: There were at least twenty coalition agreements among the belligerents and war-oriented states.[58] The pattern of alliances here, as in so many other complex or multilateral wars, reflected the changing structure of the conflict. (An analysis of that pattern, which we will not undertake here, would also tell us something of the evolution of the power positions of the parties.)

In the first phase of the war (from 1740 to the Peace of Breslau), the Anglo-Austrian-Hanoverian association was based upon two agreements: the treaty of defensive alliance and subsidy between Britain and Hanover of June, 1741, and the Austro-Sardinian treaty of defensive alliance of February, 1742. The Franco-Prussian tie was based upon the Treaty of Nymphenburg of May, 1741, between France and Bavaria, to which both Prussia and Saxony acceded. This alliance remained intact into the second phase of the war (from 1742 until the Peace of Dresden in December, 1745), but with important changes: Spain acceded to the alliance by means of the Treaty of Fontainebleau (with offensive as well as defensive terms);[59] Saxony deserted the alliance and switched sides; Bavaria made peace in April, 1745. In the spring and summer of 1744, Prussia, Charles VII (the Holy Roman Emperor), and France gave each other guarantees for their dominions, agreed to settle their disputes by mediation and adjudication, and allocated responsibilities for combat operations.

On the other side, the allies (Britain, Sardinia, and Austria) regularized their coalition in the Treaty of Worms, 13 September 1743, according to which guarantees were exchanged and specific offensive tasks were assigned to each signatory.[60]

58 See Garden, *ibid.,* Vol. 3, pp. 255 ff.
59 *Ibid.,* pp. 297–300.
60 Almon, *op. cit.,* Vol. 2, pp. 53–68.

In the third phase (1745–1748), the states continued to conclude new and supplementary treaties of alliance.[61] During the preliminary and principal negotiations for peace, the coalitions were not strong and were subject to the weakening effects of the usual jealousies of its members.

France was able to play off Austria against Britain; and Sardinia was opportunistically independent. The ties between Britain and Holland and between France and Spain were somewhat closer because in each case one partner (Spain and Holland) was weak and dependent on its ally for support in securing gains at the peace talks. Apart from their desire to follow sound power political principles in attempting to split allies, French and British policymakers understood that only between themselves could the issues of colonial empire be resolved.

SUMMARIES OF SETTLEMENTS: 1. *Bavaria and Austria:* When Charles II died in January, 1745, his son Maximilian II of Bavaria, realizing that he had no good grounds for reviving his father's claims to the Imperial Crown, made peace with Austria by the Treaty of Füssen, 22 April 1745.[62] Maria Theresa renounced all claims for damages against Bavaria and promised to restore the Elector to all his territories. She also agreed to levy no further contributions in Bavaria and to withdraw her troops promptly. Maximilian renounced all claims against the House of Habsburg and promised to support the candidacy of Maria Theresa's husband Francis Stephen, the Grand Duke of Tuscany, to the Imperial throne. When the latter was elected Emperor on 13 September 1745, Franco-Prussian plans for influence in the Empire through their control of a "puppet" Emperor had thus failed utterly.

2. *Prussia and Austria:* After a series of brilliant victories over Imperial forces, Frederick agreed to the rather moderate Treaty of Peace of Dresden, signed on 25 December. A permanent cessation of hostilities was to commence on 28 December in Silesia, Glatz, and Bohemia.[63] Imperial troops were to be withdrawn from all territories recognized to be Prussian under the terms of the Treaty of Breslau, which was acknowledged by the Empress as the basis of this settlement. By the terms of the Breslau Treaty, Austria had ceded Upper and Lower Silesia, except the Principality of Teschen and the village of Troppau, to Prussia in perpetuity. Prussia agreed to conserve the status quo respecting the Roman Catholic Religion in these territories and was to assume payment of the public debts hypothecated to English merchants. In the Dresden Treaty, the parties renounced all claims for war damages, Prussia additionally renouncing all claims against the Empire or Austria. There were the usual provisions for the restitution of property seized during the war, the

61 Garden, *op. cit.,* Vol. 3, pp. 319 ff.

62 *Ibid.,* pp. 324–5.

63 Rousset, *op. cit.,* Vol. 19, pp. 432–41. The Treaty between Prussia and Poland-Saxony appears in *ibid.,* pp. 423–31.

release of prisoners, and an amnesty for persons irrespective of their opinions. Free commerce was to be restored. The King of Prussia, in his capacity as the Elector of Brandenburg, acknowledged Francis I (Francis Stephen) as Emperor. The parties also exchanged territorial guarantees. Restitution was to be made to the Elector Palatine. Poland, Hesse-Cassel and Great Britain (whose King was the Elector of Brunswick-Lüneburg) was comprehended in the Dresden Treaty.

Since the Breslau and Berlin Treaties (1742) were confirmed, and indeed served as the basis for the Peace of Dresden, we must mention some noteworthy terms of the earlier agreements. The Empress renounced all rights to the Crown of Bohemia and agreed to secure a formal act of renunciation from the Estates of Bohemia. The amnesty was extended to subjects of one party who had served the other, and these were to have their prewar rights and liberties restored to them. Property and goods of individuals confiscated during the war were to be returned, provided the owner rendered submission to the sovereign within whose lands the property was situated.

Thus Frederick withdrew from the war for the third and last time; and he deserted his ally, France, once again. While he secured Silesia, by agreeing to acknowledge Francis I as Emperor, he formally gave up the Franco-Prussian scheme for interfering in the affairs of the Empire. The Diet of the Empire finally came around to guaranteeing the Dresden Treaty in 1751.

3. *Prussia and Poland-Saxony:* The Peace of Dresden also included a Treaty of Peace between Prussia and Poland-Saxony, signed on 25 December, the suspension of hostilities being effective from the date of signature. Saxony with Leipzig was given a guarantee by Frederick. The former was to pay Prussia an indemnity; but the latter would cease all impositions and contributions and evacuate Prussian troops from the territories of the Elector by specified times. Poland ceded a small parcel of territory on the Oder to Prussia; and Prussia granted the Elector-King the right to pass through Silesia into Poland. Trade abuses were to be eliminated. Prussian investors in Saxony were guaranteed reimbursement. The Protestant religion was to be conserved in Saxony according to the terms of the Peace of Westphalia. The Queen of Poland (the daughter of the late Emperor, Joseph I) renounced all rights given to her under the Pragmatic Sanction with respect to Silesia and territories ceded to Prussia by the Treaty of Breslau.

Britain guaranteed the cession of Silesia and Glatz, and promised to secure the guarantees from the Dutch and the princes of the Empire (finally given in 1751).

4. THE PRINCIPAL SETTLEMENT: PRELIMINARIES: The United Provinces entered talks with France as early as 1745 and invited Austria to participate in a peace congress. As Austria rebuffed these proposals, the peace

moves achieved no result. Secret negotiations between France, the Dutch, and Britain were undertaken at Breda in September, 1746. The English prolonged the talks, to the irritation of the French, and proposed that representatives of Austria and Sardinia be admitted—which France refused to permit. The conference collapsed in the spring of 1747, and France then formally declared war on the United Provinces. (Before 1747, France was in only a *de facto* state of war with Holland.)

At the beginning of 1748, a Russian army had moved across Poland, prepared to intervene in the war pursuant to the terms of a subsidy treaty signed by Austria and Russia in June, 1747.[64] The appearance of this army and the dangerous position of the Dutch as a result of the French seizure of Bergen-op-Zoom induced new peace feelers. Representatives of France and Britain met at Liège and agreed to call a general congress. Ministers of the powers began to arrive in Aix-la-Chapelle in March, 1748. The congress opened in April, but hostilities continued. Britain, France, and the United Provinces signed Preliminaries of Peace on 30 April,[65] and they agreed to order cessation of hostilities within 6 weeks—with the exception of the French siege of Maastricht, which was to continue. By a secret article, the signatories obligated themselves to execute the provisions of the Preliminaries even though no other powers consented to its terms. However, if the others persisted in refusing to accede, the signatories would deny them the benefits of the Treaty. Protesting the projected settlement terms for the Two Sicilies, the Austrian delegate finally acceded on 31 May and agreed to a cease-fire to run from August until December. Sardinia, Modena, Spain, and Genoa also acceded by June. The Preliminaries (and supplementary accords) required the parties to restore all conquests made during the war. Since the Russian auxiliaries had continued their movement into Franconia, France, somewhat troubled by this advance, promised to withdraw from the Low Countries a force equal to the size of the Russian force, if Britain would request the latter to return to Russia. This was done, and a Definitive Treaty was then discussed and finally signed on 18 October 1748.[66]

SUMMARY OF SETTLEMENT: Peace and amity were proclaimed, along with an oblivion for all past offenses and the restoration of all persons to their prewar property, dignities, and benefices. Specific treaties were declared to be in force. Prisoners and hostages were to be returned without ransom, after they had given sureties for their debts. Ships seized after the expiraton of the terms set in the Preliminaries were to be

64 Garden, *op. cit.,* Vol. 3, pp. 354–60.
65 Rousset, *op. cit.,* Vol. 20, pp. 158–66.
66 See *ibid.,* pp. 147–348, for the documents of the Congress. An English translation of the Treaty of Aix-la-Chapelle appears in Jenkinson, Charles, *A Collection of all the Treaties of Peace, etc. . . . .* (London: Debrett, 1785), pp. 370–409.

restored. As prescribed by the earlier agreement, Austria was to cede Parma, Piacenza, and Guastalla to Don Philip, second son of Philip V of Spain, and the Ticino frontier to Sardinia. Within 6 weeks of the exchange of ratifications, troop withdrawals from occupied areas were to be effected and specified forts rebuilt. (Artillery and stores were to be left undamaged.) Within 15 days, the commanders of the forces of the parties would meet in Brussels to work out the details for implementing withdrawals and methods of restitution. Prescribed also was the content of the official acts of cession and renunciation to be promulgated by Austria and Sardinia for an Italian settlement. It was agreed that Genoa and Modena would take possession of their prewar territories within 6 weeks of ratification. It was recognized that restitution of lands in the Americas might take longer than 6 weeks; hence, Britain was to furnish two hostages to France as sureties for the restoration of Cape Breton, Isle Royale, and the West Indies. The Anglo-Spanish Asiento (slave trade) Treaty of 26 March 1713 was renewed. (This was a gain for the British.) The Treaty of the Quadruple Alliance (1718) was confirmed, and the signatories thus formally recognized and guaranteed the English succession in the House of Hanover. The Pragmatic Sanction was also confirmed. Silesia and Glatz were guaranteed to Prussia. (The legal effect of this provision was unclear. Prussia was, after all, not a party to this Treaty, nor did Frederick seem willing to accept obligations under it, which seemed necessary if he were to enjoy the guarantee.) The parties also exchanged security guarantees and agreed to adjust their problems amicably. Britain, France, and the United Provinces signed the Definitive Treaty. Austria, Spain, Sardinia, Modena, and Genoa acceded. Additional conventions concluded in 1748 and 1749 set forth the details for prisoner exchange, evacuations, contributions, and restitutions.[67] The commercial Treaty of Madrid (5 October 1750) between Spain and England and the Tri-Partite Treaty of Alliance and Guarantee (for the Italian settlement, concluded in 1752) between Austria, Sardinia, and Spain supplemented the Peace of Aix-la-Chapelle.

SIGNIFICANCE OF THE SETTLEMENT: The problem of the Austrian succession was solved both by the death of Charles II (Charles Albert of Bavaria), who had been a creature of France, and through the acknowledgment and recognition by the signatories of the Dresden and Aix-la-Chapelle Treaties of the Habsburg Emperor, Francis I. Austria emerged from the war still a great power. The settlement was based upon a return to the *status quo ante,* with the major exception of Frederick's gain of the wealthy province of Silesia. The acquisition ensured that Prussia would be a great power and that Austria would have an effective rival in Germany. France could, moreover, feel secure as long as Austria and Prussia

67 Wenck, *op. cit.,* Vol. 2, pp. 428–31.

were rivals, the Dutch remained weakened, and the coalition suffered from the independent attitudes of its members. But for all the conflict in the colonies during the war, there had been few territorial changes. And Anglo-French competition was to lead to more strategically decisive changes with the settlement of the Seven Years' War in 1763. Thus, despite British victories in America, France remained in a strong enough position after 1748 to challenge Britain's drive for a colonial and commerical empire. The settlement also ushered in an era of peace in Italy: Problems of domestic consolidation of both Bourbon monarchies in Sardinia and Sicily minimized competition between the two main ruling houses; and with Austria preoccupied with Prussia, the traditional Habsburg-Bourbon rivalry was not likely to be resumed for a time.

THE SEVEN YEARS' WAR (1756–1763)

STRUCTURE OF THE WAR: Prussia, Britain, and Hanover (joined by Portugal after 1762) were at war with a coalition of France, Russia, Austria, and the Empire (and some 30 German states) , Saxony, Sweden, and Spain (after 1762) . Saxony was occupied by Prussia in 1756 and was out of the war thereafter. Both Russia and Sweden made peace with Prussia in 1762. Brunswick and Hesse were also belligerent allies of Britain.

PATTERN OF SETTLEMENT: By the Treaty of Peace of St. Petersburg, 5 May 1762, Czar Peter III made peace with Prussia. Sweden and Prussia signed the Peace Treaty of Hamburg, 22 May 1762. Britain, France and Spain signed the Definitive Treaty of Peace of Paris on 2 February 1763, and Portugal acceded to this Treaty on the same day. On 15 February 1763, the Treaty of Peace between Prussia and Austria (and the Empire) was concluded at Hubertusberg. In a separate treaty, signed the same day, Prussia made peace with the Elector of Saxony (who was also the King of Poland) .

WAR AIMS: The coalition against Prussia that Kaunitz had shaped was to serve, once the war had begun, to avenge Austria for the loss of Silesia in the wars of 1740–1745 and to render Prussia forever incapable of threatening the paramountcy of Austria in Germany or in Europe. Not having received the security assurances from Austria he had requested, Frederick struck first, at Saxony. We may presume he did this to defend Prussia, since he did believe that the anti-Prussian Coalition would soon move against him. But he also intended to hold the wealthy Electorate in pawn until he obtained Austrian guarantees—or was forced out. The attack on Saxony brought the other states of the Coalition and Prussia's British ally into the war. Both France and Britain competed for supremacy of the seas and dominance in North America, India, and the West Indies. Russia sought territorial acquisitions. Sweden was subsidized by France, but her leaders also hoped to secure Pomerania from Prussia. The German princes were subsidized by the Emperor, and probably also feared Prussia. Spain became involved because she had long nursed colonial and commercial grievances against Britain, and France promised to cooperate toward acquiring lands and fisheries for Spain in America and toward re-establishing Spanish trading rights. The Portuguese fought to defend their state against a Spanish invasion. Their part in the war was limited to their own defense and to providing port facilities for the British navy.

FACTORS FOR PEACE: Russia's contributions to the coalition were never great, because Empress Elizabeth was reluctant to expend too many men and resources on behalf of Austria. When Elizabeth died in January, 1762, she was succeeded by Peter III (the Duke of Holstein-Gottorp), an ardent admirer of Frederick and one who distrusted the Austrians. He made peace with Prussia within four months.

Sweden left the war because of her economic difficulties and the war weariness of her people.

The British decision to negotiate peace was made because George III wished to be rid of Pitt and involvement in a continental war: Peace offered the king an opportunity to break the Whig oligarchy. Although France had been defeated on the seas and in the colonies, her negotiators were able to extract concessions from rather incompetent British diplomats, particularly Lord Bute, who seemed to want to be a peacemaker at high costs to his country. The British thus alienated their Prussian ally, who rejected British offers of mediation (and this led to separate peace talks at Hubertusburg). Austria had been deserted by her allies—including France, whose leaders had become more concerned about the colonial than continental aspects of the war. Lastly, Spain was impelled to make peace because her ally, France, refused to continue the war to secure better terms for Charles III; and Spain could not wage war alone.

WAR-ORIENTED STATES: Russia and Sweden remained interested in the outcome of the war after they had made peace in 1762. Spain and Portugal were war-oriented *before* they became belligerents in 1762. The Dutch, with whose trade the English continually interfered, very nearly came into the war on the side of France. Both Denmark and the United Provinces were closely interested in the war owing to its effects on their commerce. Denmark was also war-oriented because (among other reasons) Czar Peter III intended to make war on her. He did not do so, for he was assassinated in June, 1762, to be succeeded by his wife Catherine (the Great) who decided to eschew all wars for the present, new or old.

ALLIANCES: The alliance between Britain and Prussia was based upon the Treaty of Westminster of January, 1756 (a defensive alliance) and the Treaty of London of April, 1758, a subsidy treaty in which Prussia agreed to use her forces for the "common cause."[68] The latter agreement was renewed each year until 1760. By then, the relations between the

68 Garden, *op. cit.,* Vol. 4, p. 58.

allies had begun to deteriorate so that by the end of the war, the alliance could be said to have dissolved. Frederick negotiated his peace settlement separately from Britain, even refusing the offer of British mediation.

The Treaty of Versailles (actually two conventions) was signed on 1 May 1756, and was the basis for the great coalition against Prussia and Britain.[69] Originally between France and Austria, Russia acceded later in the year. Initially an agreement of neutrality and defensive alliance in the ongoing Franco-British war, it became by mid-1757 the basis for the Austro-French and Austro-Russian defensive and offensive alliance against Prussia. By supplementary agreements, the preceding bilateral alliances were converted into a multilateral alliance to which Sweden eventually acceded. Spain also joined by the terms of the Family Compact of August, 1761, between the monarchs of France and Spain, who promised to give their protection to all Bourbon princes.[70] They guaranteed each other's dominions; and France promised not to make peace until Spain's claims against Britain were satisfied. The Versailles coalition was unwieldy and never succeeded in defeating Frederick decisively. Sweden and Russia left the alliance and the war in 1762. As in the War of the Austrian Succession, the peace negotiations that had the widest implications took place between Britain and France—at Paris.

The alliance between Sweden, Russia, and Denmark of March, 1760, was also noteworthy. The signatories attempted to prevent the effects of the European war from being felt in the Baltic and prohibited the entry of vessels of war into that sea.

THE SETTLEMENT: PRELIMINARIES: French peace feelers in the summer of 1761 led the British to undertake preliminary peace talks to determine whether there was enough common ground for compromise. These talks collapsed. France then concluded the Family Compact with Spain in August, and Spain entered the war in January, 1762. By the early summer, both Sweden and Russia had made peace, and Spain had suffered humiliating defeats in Portugal and in her colonies. France again initiated peace moves, which were avidly taken up by Lord Bute and his ministerial colleagues. These eventuated in the Preliminary Articles of Peace, signed at Fontainebleau, 3 November 1762. Austria and Prussia subsequently opened negotiations at Hubertusburg.

SUMMARIES OF SETTLEMENTS: 1. *Prussia and Russia:* The Treaty of Peace of St. Petersburg (5 May 1762) restored peace and promulgated a general amnesty.[71] Neither party was to take part in the continuing war or make any commitments contrary to the interests of the other. The

---

69 For a discussion of the alliances of the Seven Years' War, see Garden, *ibid.,* pp. 18 ff.

70 *Ibid.,* pp. 74–81.

71 Martens, G. F., *Recueil de Traités* (Göttingen: Librairie de Dieterich, 1817), 2nd ed., Vol. 1, pp. 30–7.

cease-fire of 16 March was made permanent. Russia was to lend her good offices to promote peace between Sweden and Prussia; and both parties promised to promote continental peace, albeit in rather vague terms. Within two months of the signature of the Treaty, Russia agreed to return all territories that had been occupied by Russian troops during the war. Thus, because of Peter III's admiration for Frederick, Prussia was not only saved from invasion but reacquired Pomerania and East Prussia as well. A separate article provided regulations for Russian troops of occupation as they withdrew. Frederick made a separate commitment to assist the Czar in a projected war against Denmark.

2. *Prussia and Sweden:* In the Treaty of Hamburg, 22 May 1762, the cease-fire of Ribnitz of 7 April was confirmed.[72] The Treaty of Stockholm of 1720 was to be the basis for peace. Swedish forces would therefore evacuate all lands occupied during the war. Free commerce was re-established, and trade through the port of Stettin was placed on its 1761 basis. Sweden promised to take no part in the Prussian war against Austria and to preserve a strict neutrality. Sweden was also to continue as a guarantor of the Peace of Westphalia. Prisoners were to be freed and contributions cease.

3. *Britain, France, and Spain:* A cease-fire was to begin on the date of the signature of the Preliminary Articles: 3 November 1762.[73] Prisoner exchange would begin after the ratification of the Definitive Treaty (signed at Paris on 2 February 1763).[74] Ships taken as prizes after the lapse of a specified number of grace days were to be restored with all damages repaired. The grace period varied in length with distance from home waters in order to allow notice of the peace to reach distant warships and privateers.

France renounced claim to Nova Scotia, Canada, the Grenadines, St. Vincent, Dominico, Tobago, Senegal, and her conquests in the East Indies. France also promised to restore all territories (together with fortresses and artillery) belonging to Hanover, Hesse, and Brunswick. After ratification of the Preliminaries, she would also evacuate (but not restore) Prussian territories. Both Britain and France were to remove their troops from Westphalia, Saxony, and the Rhineland, with the permission of Maria Theresa. Britain guaranteed the rights of Roman Catholics in all areas ceded by France; she further guaranteed the rights of all French subjects to sell their property to British subjects and emigrate within 18 months. Frenchmen were also to have the "liberty" of fishing and drying on the coasts of Newfoundland and in defined areas of the Gulf of St. Lawrence. Britain ceded St. Pierre and Miquelon to France; but these islands were not to be fortified. Free navigation on the

72 *Ibid.,* pp. 37–42.
73 Almon, *op. cit.,* Vol. 2, pp. 261–71.
74 *Ibid.,* pp. 272–96.

Mississippi was guaranteed. Britain also transferred Guadeloupe, Martinique, and Gorée to France. In the Preliminaries of Peace, and in greater detail in the Definitive Treaty, Britain and France agreed on an exchange of lands in India. It has been said that in spite of its overwhelming superiority over France in the colonial areas, Britain allowed France to retain some colonies in order to secure France's assent to a more favorable settlement for Prussia, specifically to the retention of Prussia's western possessions.[75]

In respect of the Spanish settlement, Minorca was secured to Britain. Spain ceded all her American territories east of the Mississippi (i.e., the Floridas) to the latter and renounced all fishing rights in the vicinity of Newfoundland. Spanish ships seized as prizes were to be submitted to the jurisdiction of British admiralty courts and disposed of according to the rules of international law. Britain agreed to raze her forts in Honduras within four months of the ratification of the Definitive Treaty. Spain agreed not to molest English woodcutters in Honduras, however. Britain was to return Cuba to Spain. Portugal was included within the terms of the Articles, and France and Spain promised to suspend hostilities against Portugal and restore all occupied lands. Portugal acceded to the Definitive Treaty, which incorporated most of the terms of the Preliminaries. It provided further that New Orleans was to remain subject to French sovereignty. Treaties still in force were specified. (The commercial treaties between England and Spain were revived under this provision.) The Elector of Brunswick-Lüneburg was included in the Treaty and guaranteed by it.

4. *Prussia and the Empire:* The Treaty of Peace between Prussia and Austria was signed at Hubertusburg on 15 February 1763.[76] A suspension of hostilities was to be effective from this date. Contributions were to cease, and prisoners were to be freed without ransom. The parties renounced all subsistence claims for the prisoners they had detained; and they established a commission to facilitate prisoner repatriation. The Emperor renounced all claims against Prussia and to territories ceded to Prussia by the terms of the Treaties of Breslau and Berlin. Prussia thus would retain Silesia. Within 21 days of the exchange of ratifications, Imperial forces were to evacuate Prussian territory, restoring all forts to the condition they were in when occupied. Prussia guaranteed the rights of Silesian Roman Catholics to public worship and to the ownership of property. Specified treaties were declared to be in force, and the parties promised to negotiate a commercial treaty. Both exchanged security guarantees: The Emperor guaranteed all Prussia; the latter guaranteed all Imperial lands *in Germany.* Saxony and the Estates and princes of the

75 Lindsay, J. O. (ed.), *The New Cambridge Modern History* (Cambridge: Cambridge University Press, 1957), Vol. 7, p. 484.
76 Martens, *op. cit.,* Vol. 1, pp. 136–45.

Empire were comprehended. In a secret article, Prussia agreed to support the candidacy of Archduke Joseph for the King of the Romans. On 20 March, the parties stipulated that a number of other states were comprehended in the terms of the Peace: for Austria, they were France, Sweden, Poland (as the Elector of Saxony), and the princes of the Empire; for Prussia, they included Britain, the Elector of Brunswich-Lüneburg, and the Landgrave of Hesse-Cassel. Both parties agreed to include Russia.

5. *Prussia and Poland:* The peace treaty between Prussia and Poland was signed at Hubertusburg on 15 February.[77] The cease-fire of 11 April was made permanent. Both parties renounced all claims for damages. This was particularly favorable to Prussia, as the latter had subjected Saxony to heavy contributions during the war. Prussia was to begin evacuation of Saxony and its dependencies after signature and to complete its withdrawal within 3 weeks after the exchange of ratifications. Austria would also begin evacuations at the same time. Technical provisions regulated the routes for withdrawal, supply of the armies, and encampments. Leipzig, Torgau, and Wittenberg were to be restored to Saxony, together with their forts in the condition they were in when occupied. Prussia was to deliver up all prisoners and hostages, unless they preferred to remain in the service of Prussia. The Peace of Dresden was renewed. Commissioners were to be appointed to regulate commerce on an equitable basis. The Elector of Saxony was given the right of passage through Silesia to Poland. The parties also exchanged guarantees. Financial provisions to protect creditors of Saxony were also incorporated in the Treaty.

SIGNIFICANCE OF THE SETTLEMENTS: France was excluded from the North American continent (except for New Orleans), but she retained commercially valuable possessions in the West Indies, Africa, and India. In spite of the defeats she had suffered at Britain's hands, France would thus remain a great power. Britain's command of the high seas was established beyond doubt, and her colonists in North America were now more secure than ever before. Prussia and Austria would remain rivals on the continent, but Frederick's acquisition of Silesia was recognized. Prussia was a great power, although it had lost one ninth of its population in the war and was nearly bankrupt. One could quite fairly conclude that a balance of power in Europe had been preserved by the war and the terms of the settlement.

Wars of the Second Group

THE THIRTY YEARS' WAR (1618–1648)

STRUCTURE OF THE WAR: A. General structure (a first approximation): France, Sweden, Denmark, United Provinces, and the German Protestant

77 *Ibid.*, pp. 146–66.

Princes vs. the German Catholic Princes, the Holy Roman Emperor (Austrian Habsburgs), and Spain.

B. Structure of the central war according to its phases:

1. War internal to the Holy Roman Empire (The Bohemian and Palatinate War), 1618–1625: Bohemian nobles, the Elector of the Palatinate (Frederick V), the Estates of Moravia, Lusatia, and Upper Austria, and Transylvania (1620) vs. Emperor Ferdinand II, Bavaria, Saxony, and the Catholic League (German princes).

2. The Danish intervention, 1625–1630: Denmark (subsidized by France), the Estates of Lower Saxony (subsidized by England), and Transylvania (1626) vs. Austria (i.e., the Emperor), Bavaria, and the Catholic League.

3. The Swedish intervention, 1630–1635 Sweden (allied with, and subsidized by, nonbelligerent France), Pomerania, Brandenburg (1631–34), Saxony (1631–34), and the Estates (or Circles) of Upper and Lower Rhine, Franconia, and Swabia vs. Austria, Bavaria, and the Catholic League.

4. The French intervention, 1635–48: France, Sweden, United Provinces, Hesse-Cassel (from 1636), Savoy, Portuguese insurgents (from 1640), Catalonian insurgents (from 1640), and Weimar (from 1639) vs. Austria, Spain, Bavaria, the Catholic League, and Saxony and Brandenburg (both occupied by Sweden in 1635; signed truces in 1641).

C. The multilateral war as a series of less complex wars:[78]

1. The Bohemian-Palatine War (see B.1.).

2. The Grisons Struggle, 1620–22, was an internl war between Habsburg and anti-Habsburg factions. Austrian-Spanish forces intervened and imposed a settlement, dividing the Grisons Confederation and placing it under military administration, thus giving Spain control of the Alpine passes.

3. Spanish-Dutch War, 1621–48. After the expiration of the Twelve Year Truce, Spain renewed the war against the United Provinces. As the war continued, its antagonists and its issues became more and more intertwined with the parties and issues of the central European war.

4. The Danish War (see B.2.).

5. The Swedish-Polish War, 1621–29. This war was ended by the Truce of Altmark (25 September 1629), mediated by France. Poland ceded Livonia and the right to administer Prussian customs to Gustavus Adolphus. Poland thus lost access to the Baltic, and Sweden was free to intervene in Germany against the Habsburgs.

6. The War of the Mantuan Succession, 1627–31: Spain, Austria and Savoy (1627–29) vs. France and Savoy (1629–31). The war was ended by

78 Steinberg, S. H., *The Thirty Years' War and the Conflict for European Hegemony* (New York: Norton, 1966), pp. 30 f.

the Treaty of Cherasco (19 June 1631). France was allowed to occupy the Grisons, and the French Duke Charles of Never-Gonzaga received Mantua and Montferrat. In spite of the victories he had won during the war, the Emperor had to accept this hard peace settlement because of Swedish intervention in Germany. In a separate treaty, France ceded part of Montferrat to Savoy in exchange for Pignerol, with its fortress that gave France easy access to northern Italy.

7. The Swedish War (see B.3.).

8. The War of Smolensk, 1632–35: Sweden and Russia (until 1634) vs. Poland. Russia and Poland concluded their Peace Treaty of Polyanovka in June, 1634; and Sweden and Poland agreed to the 20-year Truce of Stuhmsdorf in 1635.

9. The Franco-Spanish War, 1635–59: This war was very much a part of the central war (see B.4.), but it lasted well beyond the Peace of Westphalia until its termination in 1659 by the Treaty of the Pyrenees.

10. The Swedish-Danish War, 1643–45. Sweden was aided by Hamburg and the Dutch. Denmark was decisively beaten and signed the Treaty of Brömsebro (25 August 1645), in which she ceded substantial territories to Sweden.

PATTERN OF SETTLEMENT: Apart from the settlements of the minor wars already noted (C.2., 5., 6., 8., and 10.), the settlements for the central multilateral war can be regarded as of two kinds:

A. Settlements that turned out to be termporary because of subsequent events and decisions:

1. This category comprises the settlements imposed by the Emperor early in the war after the defeat of the insurgents in the Bohemian-Palatine War (B.1., C.1), including the "settlements" in 1621 and after, comprising the Catholicization of Bohemia, execution or proscription of many nobles, and the seizure of their property; the award of the Electoral dignity of the Palatinate to Bavaria and the partitioning of the Palatinate between Spain and several German Princes in 1623; and after victories against the Danes, the proclamation of the Edict of Restitution (6 March 1629), restoring to the Roman Catholic Church all properties taken over by Protestants since the Transaction of Passau (1552), reintroducing Catholic prelates into secularized seats in Germany and authorizing the expulsion of dissenting subjects.

2. Also in the "temporary" category was the settlement negotiated with the Danes (B.2. above) after the victories of Imperial forces against them, in the Treaty of Lübeck (22 May 1629), according to which Denmark agreed to refrain from interfering in Imperial affairs in exchange for the restoration of Danish territories.

3. Finally, there was the important settlement concluded between the Emperor and Saxony known as the Peace of Prague (30 May 1635). It was subsequently adhered to by most of the Estates, thus becoming a

"Law of the Empire."[79] The Peace substantially increased the political, judicial, and administrative powers of the Emperor within the Empire. It failed to bring about a general peace because it neither included nor satisfied the anti-Habsburg powers, France, Sweden, and the United Provinces.

B. Permanent settlements:

1. The Peace of Westphalia (a pan-European settlement) included the Treaty of Peace between Spain and the United Provinces at Münster, 30 January 1648; the Treaty of Münster, 24 October 1648, between France, the Emperor, and the Electors, Princes, and States of the Empire; and the Treaty of Osnabrück, 24 October 1648, between Sweden, the Emperor, and the Electors, Princes, and States of the Empire.

2. The Peace of the Pyrenees, 7 November 1659, between Spain and France.

WAR AIMS OF THE MAJOR ACTORS: Emperor Ferdinand II sought to consolidate Habsburg control of the Empire and centralize Imperial power in the Germanies, converting the Empire into a more integrated state. He sought also to undermine Protestantism in the Crown Lands of Austria (and in the Empire, generally), in order to promote the unity of the Church. Finally, he assisted the Spanish Habsburgs because of the family tie and because he sympathized with Spain's anti-French and Anti-Dutch policies.

Spain's Philip III and Philip IV wanted to reconquer the rebellious Dutch "provinces." They also sought to consolidate Spanish power in Italy, to contain France by surrounding her with Habsburg territories, and to secure influence within France, as in the period before Henry IV—in short, to maintain (or reattain) the imperial power position the Habsburgs had held under Charles V (or Spain had held under Philip II).

France and Sweden fought for the "restitution of German liberties." This can be interpreted to mean that they opposed the Habsburg attempt to transform the Empire into a centralized state. If the Emperor could be compelled to recognize the sovereign rights of the German princes, the balance of power among them in Germany would provide France and Sweden with a modicum of security; and it would constitute a guarantee against Austria, which was seeking hegemony in central Europe. Sweden sought to achieve political and commercial dominance in the Baltic against Denmark, Poland, and certain German princes. France wanted to end the Spanish threat to her existence once and for all; and she strived

79 *Ibid.*, pp. 67–9. Garden, *op. cit.*, Vol. 1, pp. 52 f. We should perhaps emphasize that although the Peace of Prague and other preliminary settlements were temporary, they were settlements nonetheless: they provide data on the character of the peacemaking process. This is true as well for the preliminary settlements of the First World War and the Wars of France against Europe.

to secure territory and resources that would ensure her security and provide her with opportunities for consolidation and future expansion.

The Dutch fought to preserve their *de facto* independence (and thereby remain a commercial power of the first order).

King Christian of Denmark was probably as little motivated by religious principles as Gustavus Adolphus. He intervened in Germany in 1625 in order to obtain territories in northern Germany, firm up Danish control of the entrance to the Baltic, and establish Danish dominance in the north over Sweden.

Of the German Princes, Bavaria's Maximilian I played the most important role in the war. He sought to promote Catholicism in the Empire through the Catholic League, which he had organized, and through his support of the Emperor. But he too had more mundane aims, to wit, securing territory and the Electoral dignity.

The Protestant Estates and Princes wanted the restoration, recognition, and expansion of their political and religious rights in the Empire, including implementation of the Peace of Augsburg (1555) and admission of Calvinists to the benefits of that Peace. Many Princes, particularly the Electors of Saxony and Brandenburg, sought more material opportunity values whenever they believed they could get them.

FACTORS FOR PEACE: By 1640, all the belligerents had sustained heavy losses, and war weariness was widespread. If their treasuries were not near bankruptcy, their peoples were restive under the weight of war taxes. Among their policymakers, many wanted peace and worked diligently for it. Ultimately, as in any negotiated settlement, it was the willingness to compromise that permitted the final settlements to be made. And this willingness stemmed from different pressures and circumstances within the polities of the belligerents.

In the case of the Habsburgs, the accession of Ferdinand III was an important factor for peace: he was more pragmatic than his father, and less committed to the latter's religious ideals. Moreover, he could obtain compensations from within Germany for the compromises he might have to make to France or Sweden. In Sweden after 1644, Christina, who took control of the reigns of government from the aristocracy, had made up her mind to seek peace. Both Sweden and France could look for gains from Germany, also.

In the United Provinces, growing fear of French policies induced the burghers to agree to peace with Spain. Spain's willingness to recognize Dutch independence *de jure* was of course the primary factor for peace. And Spain acquiesced in this because after the overthrow of Olivarez (1643) her leaders wanted peace with the Dutch in order to concentrate Spain's limited resources against the French.

Most of the German princes sought peace—and needed peace. In the final settlement, many lost territory, honors, and revenues; but their overall power position was such that they had little bargaining strength —and certainly no unity. The religious settlement did accrue to the benefit of many of them, however. Their willingness to acquiesce in losses (as shown during negotiations for the Peace of Prague in 1635) arose from their expectations that with the support of Sweden and France, their sovereign rights would be recognized by the Emperor and their religious rights respected, even over the opposition of the Pope.

By 1659, France and Spain were ready to make peace with each other. Spain had been deserted by her allies and was confronted by another alliance which, if its partners became belligerent, might force additional losses upon her. Both parties, moreover, could obtain gains from the Duke of Lorraine, Spain's former ally.

WAR-ORIENTED ACTORS: When the belligerents were not involved in hostilities, they were usually war-oriented. And if belligerent in one theater (either formally or functionally belligerent), they might be nonbelligerent but war-oriented in *another* theater. (This is true of most multilateral wars.) Thus, Sweden waged war in central and northern Europe; but with respect to hostilities in Italy, she was merely a war-oriented state—as were Spain and France in relation to the wars in eastern Europe.

There were several war-oriented actors that were never belligerent:

1. *Great Britain:* James I and Charles I were pro-Spanish and anti-Austrian. James I furnished some money to the Protestant princes in the Palatine War. He abhorred rebellion, however, even though his son-in-law, Frederick V of the Palatinate, had been elected King of Bohemia by the rebellious Estates; and he refused to intervene even though Puritan opinion at home wanted him to aid the Protestant cause. Britain's foreign policies vacillated as the internal political situation became increasingly embittered and as the era of the Great Rebellion approached.

2. *The Papacy:* Pope Urban VIII (1623–44) was anti-Habsburg and pro-French. He preferred France (and Bavaria) to promote the Catholic Reformation in Europe, not the Habsburgs.

3. *Muscovy:* The Protestants hoped for the Russians to create a diversion in the east during the Bohemian War, but this did not materialize. From 1628–33, Sweden received some important staples from Moscow. After the War of Smolensk, Muscovy remained war-oriented but very much on the periphery of affairs.

4. *The Ottoman Empire:* Turkey itself was minimally war-oriented, although the Princes of Transylvania (Gabriel Bethlen and George Rakoczy) on at least two occasions waged aggressive wars against Austria, wars that had few consequences for the central conflict, however.

5. *Poland:* When not at war with Sweden, Poland was peripherally war-oriented.

6. *Italy:* The Grand Duke of Tuscany was pro-Spanish and subsidized the Emperor. In the War of the Mantuan Succession, Venice was a non-

belligerent ally of France, and she was anti-Habsburg. But her diplomats were mediators at Susa in 1629 (between France and Britain) and again at Münster. The other Italian states were war-oriented but played very minor roles during the war and at the peace congresses.

THE SETTLEMENT: PRELIMINARIES: The Pope invited the Catholic princes to send delegates to Cologne in 1636 to see whether some basis for peace negotiations could not be found. Both the Emperor and the King of Spain sent envoys, but France refused, regarding the proposed congress as a means to divide her from her Protestant allies, who would never have attended such a meeting in any case. In 1640, the Emperor convened a Diet in Ratisbon for the purpose of settling the war within the Empire. When the Protestants realized that the Emperor's terms were not much different from the terms of the Peace of Prague (and thus, the amnesty would not include the Estates of Bohemia or the nobles of the Palatinate), they refused to accede to the Emperor's proposals. Preliminary negotiations continued in Cologne and Lübeck. By 1641, it was clear that a peace conference was to be held, but in *two* towns. First, Cologne and Hamburg were proposed and turned down. Then, Catholic Münster and Protestant Osnabrück were accepted officially in the Preliminary Treaty of Hamburg (25 December 1641), the negotiations for which had been mediated by the King of Denmark. The congress cities were declared to be neutral territory, and safe-conduct passes were to be given to the delegates of the participants. At Münster, the Pope and Venice would mediate; at Osnabrück, Christian IV of Denmark was the mediator. The Congress (the assemblies at the two cities were in theory one Congress) was to open on 25 March 1642. France ratified the Hamburg Treaty in February, 1642, still hoping to mobilize the lesser German Princes against the Electors. The Emperor temporized: he did not ratify the Treaty until July, 1642. Spain finally ratified it in early 1643. And the new date for the opening of the Congress was set for 11 July 1643. The question of the representation of the Estates and Princes of the Empire at the Congress was resolved finally in 1645 (by the Emperor): All who were entitled to vote in the Diet were invited to the Congress. This decision required—or led to—a unique form of organization of the delegates of the Empire and its States at the Congress. At Münster *and* at Osnabrück, there was a College of Electors, a College of Princes, and a College of Cities (6 colleges in all). Before the Emperor could bind the Electors (for example), he had to secure the consent of the Colleges of Electors at both Münster and Osnabrück and then the consent of the three Colleges at either Münster or Osnabrück—depending upon whether the subject matter related to the French-oriented negotiations at Münster or the Swedish-oriented negotiations at Osnabrück.[80]

80 Garden, *ibid.,* pp. 80–7, provides a table showing the composition of the peace congresses.

The Emperor also conceded to demands for a general amnesty without exceptions. A consequence of the decision to admit the states of Germany to the Congress was their recognition as "fully qualified representatives of the Empire and as independent members of the society of European states."[81]

The remainder of 1643 and all of 1644 was taken up with problems relating to the organization, protocol, and procedures of the Congress. Only in mid-1645 did the conferences begin—and then not officially. Discussions simply took on a more formal aspect, particularly with the presentation of Sweden's terms on 1 June 1645. During negotiations, hostilities continued.

A. *Spanish-Dutch War:* Treaty of Münster, 30 January 1648.[82]

MILITARY SETTLEMENT: All hostile acts were to cease with the publication of the peace treaty. Because of the distances involved between the metropoles of the parties and their colonies, a schedule of effective dates of the cease-fires was provided. After these dates, restitutions would be made for all seizures; letters of marque would no longer be issued; and prisoners of war were to be freed without ransom. Spain agreed to demolish identified forts; and both parties agreed to construct no new forts in the Low Countries. They also promised to obtain confirmation of the neutrality of the United Provinces from the Emperor and Empire. (After ratification, the Dutch were to confirm their neutrality to the Emperor).

POLITICAL SETTLEMENT: Spain recognized the complete independence and sovereignty of the United Provinces. Each party was to retain the lands possessed by it at the time of the signature of the Treaty, both in Europe and in the colonies. (Thus, the Dutch retained areas in Brabant, Flanders, and Limburg.) Spain retained rights to navigate within the East Indies but could not extend those rights; and Dutch citizens were forbidden to trade with the Spanish lands in the East Indies. In the West Indies, the subjects of either party were prohibited from trading with the subjects of the other. These restrictions contrasted with the terms for trade relations in Europe, where the Treaty required free commerce between lands and free movement of persons.

The parties agreed to cooperate to free their sea lanes of pirates and render rivers and seas navigable. The United Provinces were allowed to close the Schheldt Estuary and identified canals. (This led to the rise of Amsterdam in commercial importance and the economic decline of Antwerp.)

Agreements in force were listed; and several articles established regulations for the imposition of tolls on an equitable basis and guaranteed the rights of merchants, seamen, and consuls.

81 Steinberg, *op. cit.,* p. 78.
82 Parry, Clive (ed.), *The Consolidated Treaty Series* (Dobbs Ferry: Oceana, 1969), Vol. 1, pp. 1 ff. See also Garden, *op. cit.,* Vol. 1, pp. 165 f.

The subjects of either party were permitted to conduct the exercise of their religions "modestly" in the lands of the other party. Spain agreed to extend to Dutch citizens the same rights to free conscience she had extended to the British. All persons who had left either Spain or Holland during the war were to enjoy the benefits of the Treaty and could return to the place of their former domicile in security.

There were extensive provisions of general and specific restitution of property. Judges of the parties were commanded to aid in the process of making restitutions.

B. *The settlement of the central war:* Treaties of Osnabrück and Münster, 24 October 1648.[83]

MILITARY SETTLEMENT: A cease-fire was to take effect after the signature of the Treaties of Peace. The Emperor was to order execution of an armistice throughout the Empire. Prisoners would be released according to terms of agreements made by the commanders of the armies of the principals, who were also to prescribe procedures for implementing the cease-fires (Art. 16, Osnabrück; Arts. 104, 105, 110, Münster). Meetings between commanders began in Prague in late 1648 and continued at Nürnberg into 1650. A Military Convention respecting evacuation of troops was signed by Sweden and the Empire in October, 1649, and a Supplementary Agreement in July, 1650. Similarly, France and the Empire signed Military Conventions for implementing the military terms of the settlements in January and October, 1649.[84] The Münster Treaty provided for the renewal of the Imperial Circles in order to maintain the public peace. (Art. 125).

POLITICAL SETTLEMENT: The principals to the Osnabrück Treaty were Sweden, the Emperor, and the Empire; to the Münster Treaty, France, the Emperor, and the Empire. The substance of the Treaties and the negotiations leading to them can be subsumed under the following headings:[85]

1. Imperial affairs.
   a. amnesty.
   b. rights and prerogatives of the states.
   c. grievances (material and spiritual).
   d. re-establishment of commerce.
2. Satisfaction of the Crowns of France and Sweden.
3. Guarantees of the peace.
4. Implementation.

83 The Treaty of Osnabrück appears in Parry, *op. cit.,* Vol. 1, pp. 119 ff. See also Koch, C. G. de, *Histoire Abrégé des Traités de Paix* (Basle: Chez J. Decker, 1796–7), Vol. I, pp. 119 f.; and Du Mont, *op. cit.,* Vol. 6, Part I, p. 469. The Treaty of Münster appears in Parry, Vol. 1, pp. 271 ff.

84 These supplementary agreements are collected in Parry, Vol. 1, pp. 383 f., 389 f., 397 f.; 463 f.; Vol. 2, pp. 1 ff., 211 f.

85 Garden, *op. cit.,* Vol. 1, p. 147.

A perpetual peace was declared to subsist between the signatories and their allies. The amnesty was to apply to all states and nobles. (Arts. 1 & 2, O & M).[86] Spain was comprehended in the Osnabrück Treaty, but excluded from the terms of the Münster Treaty, because France had not made peace with Spain. Moreover, by Art. 3 of Münster, the parties were obligated to refrain from assisting the enemies of any one of them; and by this provision, the Emperor was forbidden to aid Spain. The general amnesty was supported by the declarations that restitutions would be made to reestablish prewar property and religious rights (Art. 3 of O; Arts. 6, 7 of M). The provisions of the Treaties spelled out in great detail the specific restitutions that were to be made. Among the most important were the creation of an eighth Elector for the Count Palatine of the Rhine and the retention by the House of Bavaria of the Electoral dignity awarded to it by Ferdinand II; restoration of the Lower Palatinate to the Count Palatine and retention of the Upper Palatine by Bavaria; amnesty and restitution for the subjects of the Emperor in Austria; and amnesty for the adherents of Sweden in the Empire. (See Arts. 4, 49–52 of O; Arts. 10–26; 28–34, 40–45 and 90 of M.)

In the Osnabrück Treaty, the Emperor gave satisfaction to Sweden through the cession of Pomerania (except lands reserved for Brandenburg), Rügen, Bremen, Werden and Wismar, the territory at the mouths of the Oder, Weser and Elbe, and the right to send delegates to the Imperial Diet (Art. 10 of O). Satisfaction was also given to Brandenburg, through the cession of a portion of Pomerania, Magdeburg, Halberstadt, Minden, and Werden (Arts. 11 and 14 of O); and to Cassell and Mecklenberg-Schwerin by means of small compensations in revenues or lands (Arts. 12, 13 and 15 of O). The Treaty of Münster also provided for satisfaction of Hesse-Cassell (Arts. 50–62). Satisfaction was also provided for the Swedish Army in the form of a cash payment of 5 million Reichsdollars, as a precondition of their disbanding and withdrawing from Germany. The payment was to be made in three installments by the Circles of the Empire, although the Austrian and Bavarian Circles were exempted. (Art. 16, sec. 6 of O). In part, this served as monetary compensation for the Protestant exiles of Austria and Bohemia, who were forced to remain outside the Habsburg Crown Lands because the amnesty did not extend to these Protestants and the religious settlement of the Osnabrück Treaty did not apply to Habsburg Crown lands; hence, they could not practice their religion in their former homeland.

In the Münster Treaty, satisfaction was given to France, Mantua, and Savoy, with France taking the lion's share. She acquired the cities of Metz, Toul, and Verdun, and part of Alsatia with the fortress of Breisach

---

86 In this summary, I shall use the letter O to mean the Treaty of Osnabrück;
    M, the Treaty of Münster.

and Philipsburg, which gave France easy access to Germany in the event of a future war. In addition, the Emperor ceded all Imperial rights in the "landgraviate of Alsace" to France. The ambiguity and vagueness of this clause led to future disputes. (Later, Louis XIV would argue that he was entitled to all of Alsatia.) France was required to return the rest of Breisgau to the Emperor, along with the Black Forest region and Seckingen (with the cities of Strassburg and Hanau). Arrangements were made for the apportionment of the public debts of the ceded territories. The French King also promised to preserve the Catholic religion as maintained by Austria and to abolish all religious innovations made during the war. Fortresses on the right bank of the Rhine were to be demolished; and free commerce on the Rhine was to be preserved. (See Arts. 71–89, 92–94 of M.) Pursuant to the terms of the Treaty of Cherasco (6 April 1631), guaranteed by France and Austria (Arts. 97–8 of M), the Duke of Mantua was to receive a cash payment; and Savoy was to acquire Montferrat (except Pignerol, which was ceded to France).

Basle and the Swiss Cantons were declared to possess "quasi full Liberty and Exemption from the Empire, and so no way subject to the Tribunals of the said Empire. . . ." (Art. 6 of O; see Art. 63 of M.) This declaration relieved France of fears for her security from that quarter and enabled the Swiss to remain neutral in the postwar period (and it also avoided the encirclement of Basle by French forts).

As Lorraine was implicated in the Franco-Spanish quarrel, the Münster Treaty required the principals to refer the controversy over that Duchy to arbitrators or wait upon a settlement of the war between France and Spain. (Art. 5 of M.) The Emperor and Empire consented vaguely to the settlement of the war for Dutch Independence between Spain and the United Provinces. (Art. 4 of M.)

The Electors, Princes, States, and Free Towns of the Empire were restored to their "ancient rights." They were permitted to enter into alliances with each other and with foreign powers, as if they were completely sovereign, provided that the alliances were not directed against the Emperor. They retained the right to meet in the Diet and vote taxes, to declare war, and to ratify peace settlements (theretofore prerogatives solely of the Emperor). They were authorized (as before) to re-establish the Circles and elect the King of the Romans. (Arts. 8, 17 of O; Arts. 64–70, 117 of M.)

All burdens on commerce were to be removed and completely free trade was re-established. The rights of the Electors and Princes of the Empire to the use of the interior rivers were also to be restored. (Art. 9 of O; Arts. 67–69 of M.) All contracts, debts, and obligations of any kind extorted by violent means during the war were abolished. Sentences and judgments rendered during the war were to be reviewed to determine whether they comported with the spirit of the Treaties. As necessary, they were to be voided, modified, or confirmed. (Art. 4, Secs. 44–48 or O; Arts. 37–41 of M.)

The religious settlement was contained in the Treaty of Osnabrück, Articles 5 and 7 (which were incorporated by reference in the Treaty of Münster). The Pacification of Passau (1552) and the Peace of Augsburg (1555) were confirmed, and the anti-Protestant Edict of Restitution (1629) was abrogated. All Electors, Princes, and States of the Empire were to be treated on the basis of complete equality, whether Catholic or Lutheran. Restitution for religious grievances, particularly as this affected the clergy, was to take place on the basis of the rights the aggrieved parties had on 1 January 1624. (The Protestants had for some time demanded 1618 as the "standard year"; the Catholics, 1630). Thus, monasteries, churches, foundations, colleges, and hospitals, and the rents and revenues derived from them, were to be restored to the 1624 possessors. The persons to whom goods and revenues were to be restored were to hold them peaceably until the religious controversies were finally resolved. If they were not resolved (and they were not, of course), then the holders were not to be troubled by lawsuits or duress, and the religious provisions of the Treaty were to become a perpetual law (Art. 5 of O). If an ecclesiastical officer changed his religion, he forfeited his right to his benefice and its income. But any officer removed from office for religious reasons after 1624 was to be returned to that office.

Calvinists were declared to be beneficiaries of the Passau and Augsburg settlements. The signatories recognized that the Protestants formed two parties, Lutherans and Calvinists. These parties agreed that if a prince went over to the religion of the other party, it was permissible for him to bring new preachers to his court without prejudice to the religious rights of his subjects. If a community wanted to change its (Protestant) religion, the prince could allow this—again without prejudice to the rights of others. (Art. 7 of O.)

No new laws were to be passed to "wound the conscience or hurt the cause" of either Protestants or Catholics. Catholic subjects residing in a Lutheran state (and viceversa), who had no right in 1624 to practice their religion, were to have that right in the future. They would be permitted to practice their religion *privately* (and in their neighborhoods) and allowed to send their children to foreign schools. They had no right to public worship, however. Persons in Catholic states who had held the right in 1624 to practice Lutheranism retained that right in the future. But the general rule, *cujus regio ejus religio,* still held. If a Prince wanted to keep religious dissidents in his lands, he had to accord them tolerance. He could, however, order them to leave; and the dissident himself was free to leave—without his goods and without hindrance—if he so desired.

Excepted from all these provisions were the Habsburg Crown lands.

Catholicism was the only legitimate religion there; no liberty to practice either of the Protestant religions was recognized, and dissidents were not free to emigrate lawfully.

The institutions of the Empire were to be reformed with equal representation between Catholics and Protestants. Religious disputes were to be settled by an amicable composition between Catholic and Protestant groups—not by a majority vote. And any disputes—religious or otherwise—among the signatories of the Treaties were to be negotiated or submitted to judicial process. Recourse to force was prohibited. (Art. 17 of O; Arts. 114, 115 of M.) Magistrates of the Empire, moreover, were to forbid attacks on the Peace of Westphalia and of Passau and Augsburg. All the parties promised to defend and protect the settlement and to punish violators. Several questions were left unresolved for the Imperial Diet to consider at its next sitting: dissolving the judgment against Donauwörth (1608); the Cleves-Jülich succession, rights of the Reichshofrat, and the general question of "Imperial justice."

After signature, the Emperor was to publish edicts requiring implementation of the Treaties' terms. If any Prince failed to appoint commissioners to execute the terms of the restitutions, the Emperor could make the appointments himself. (Art. 16 of O; Arts. 105–107 of M.) In the immediate postwar period, the parties negotiated several supplementary agreements concerning procedures for making restitutions, the most important of which were the Recès of 26 June 1650 between Sweden and the Empire and the Recès of 2 July 1650 between France and the Empire.[87] Both were designed to expedite and carry to completion the restitutions.

The Treaties were declared to be the fundamental and supreme law of the Empire. (Art. 17 of O; Art. 110 of M.) Venice was comprehended in the Münster Treaty, which ended with the declaration that the terms thereof should not prejudice the rights of France's allies, the Dukes of Savoy and Modena, in the war in which they were engaged in Italy against Spain. The Osnabrück Treaty comprehended, among others, France, England, Poland, Portugal, Denmark, Muscovy, and Spain. The Emperor appended a declaration in which he refused to recognize any other King of Portugal than Philip IV of Spain.

C. *The settlement between France and Spain:* (The Peace of the Pyrenees, 7 November 1659). We bring this summary to a close by noting briefly that this settlement provided for the marriage between Louis XIV and Philip IV's daughter (a marriage that would one day lead to the devolution of the Spanish throne upon the House of Bourbon). The Pyreneean divide was made the border between France and Spain. The latter ceded territories in the Spanish Netherlands to France (Artois,

87 Parry, *op. cit.,* Vol. 2, pp. 89 f., 203 f.

Gravelines, Montmedy) and renounced all claim to Alsace. The Duke of
Lorraine was required to cede lands to France also and to raze the fortifications at Nancy. France restored the Franche-Comté to Spain, defected
from the alliance with Portugal and Catalonia, and made restitution to
Condé (a leader of the Fronde). Thus was the reduction of Spain to a
lesser power consummated.

COMMENTS: The Peace of Westphalia ended a melancholy chapter in
Western history. It formalized the abandonment of the ideal of a united
Christendom and went far to establish a secular European state system.
The religious issues were never resolved. The interim solution became
the permanent solution. And this was not entirely inadequate, because
religion counted for less in European politics after 1648. The Peace of
Westphalia determined the nature of international relations afterward
and the character of the future quarrels between the states of Europe.

In a very specific sense, moreover, the settlement provided a new
constitution for the Empire. It created, in effect, an international state
system *in micro* in Germany. It gave many of the attributes of sovereignty
to the Princes, but it also prevented the Empire from being an effective
modern state. It was explicitly illegal for the House of Austria, or for any
German Prince bent upon centralization, to infringe the ancient rights
and prerogatives of other Princes and states. Coupled with this constitutional incapacity to become what France was even then becoming was the
Empire's decline in power position. It had lost the Alsace to France and
Hither Pomerania to Sweden, and the mouths of its great rivers were in
foreign hands. War losses, internal migrations during the wars, and a
stagnant economy were further evidence of its decline. Germany's neighbors, particularly France, were not standing still, of course. Indeed,
French influence on the Rhine was especially forbidding. If the outbreak
of the war, and its course, demonstrated how unintended consequences
follow from great policy decisions, the peace settlement did also. Germany was to remain constitutionally medieval for as long as the Empire
lasted.

THE WARS OF FRANCE AGAINST EUROPE (including
THE EXTERNAL WARS OF THE FRENCH REVOLUTION
and THE NAPOLEONIC WARS) 1792–1815

STRUCTURE OF WAR: A. General structure according to the usual involvement of the Great Powers: France vs. Great Britain, Russia, Austria,
and Prussia.

B. Structure of the central and related wars:

1. *The First Coalition* (1792–97): France vs. Austria, Prussia (made
peace in 1795), Sardinia (made peace in 1796), Britain (from 1793;
remained at war after 1796), United Provinces (from 1793 until conquered in 1795), Naples (from 1793–1796), Spain (from 1793 to 1795),

Portugal (from 1793; remained at war after 1796), the Papacy (made peace in 1796), and the Italian and German States.

2. *Egyptian Expedition* (1798–1801): France vs. Britain and the Ottoman Empire.

3. *War in Central Europe and Italy* (1798–99): France vs. Switzerland (conquered in 1798), the Papacy (conquered in 1798), Piedmont-Sardinia (conquered in 1798), and Naples (conquered in 1799).

4. *The Second Coalition* (1798–1802): France and the Batavian Republic (United Provinces) vs. Britain, Russia (until 1799), Austria (to 1801), Portugal (to 1801), Spain (to 1800), Naples (to 1801), and Turkey (effectively at peace after 1801). (Note: Napoleon negotiated a modus vivendi in the form of a Concordat with Pius VII in 1801.)

5. *The Third Coalition* (1803–1807): France, Switzerland, Baden, Bavaria, and Würtemberg vs. Britain (remained at war after 1807), Austria (until 1805), Russia, and Prussia (an effective member of the coalition for only a month in 1805; also at war for one month in the fall of 1806). (Note: The French Empire was proclaimed in 1804; the Holy Roman Empire was ended in 1806; and Napoleon established the Confederation of the Rhine in 1806, which thereafter was his pawn. Russia, in alliance with France, was formally at war with Great Britain from 1807–12, but Russia's contribution to the French war effort was nil, and did not prevent the former's realignment with Britain in 1812.)

6. Franco-Austrian War of 1809: French Empire vs. Austria.

7. Russo-Turkish War (1806–12).

8. Russo-Swedish War of 1808.

9. Peninsular War (1807–13): French Empire and Spain (Joseph Bonaparte on the throne after 1808) vs. Portugal, Britain (after 1808), Spanish rebels (after 1808), and Russia (after 1812).

10. Russian Campaign (1812): French Empire and Prussia (made peace with Russia in late 1812, then an alliance in 1813) vs. Russia and Britain (a nonbelligerent ally in this theater, but subsidizing Russia).

11. *The Fourth Coalition* (1812–14): French Empire and Denmark (treated by Britain as an enemy since 1807; a *de facto* ally of France after seizure of the Danish fleet in that year) vs. Britain, Russia, Prussia, Austria, Portugal, Spanish rebels, and Sweden (ally of France in 1810, but entered war against her in 1813).

12. *Napoleon's Hundred Days* (1815): France vs. Britain, Prussia, Russia, Austria, United Provinces, Portugal, Denmark, Sardinia, Switzerland, Bavaria, Baden, Saxony, Würtemberg, and other German princes and towns.

PATTERN OF SETTLEMENTS: The wars preceding the War of the Fourth Coalition were usually ended by means of bilateral treaties of peace. Because there were ten such wars (according to our classification) and several, and often many, states were involved in each war, the quantity of peace treaties and truce agreements is simply too great to consider here. They are of course important to an understanding of the course of the war and the transformation of the war aims of the major actors; and they do offer us insights into the peace settlement process, confirming some of the generalizations made in preceding chapters. However, in view of the overarching settlement reached at the Congress of Vienna, these pre-1814 peace settlements appear for the most part (although not entirely) to be temporary, modified by the final settlements for Europe and for France.

A. The settlement for France:

1. By the Treaty of Fontainebleau, 11 April 1814, Napoleon abdicated; and in the First Peace of Paris, 30 May 1814, hostilities ended. A Franco-Spanish Treaty of Peace was signed on 20 July 1814.

2. After Napoleon's Hundred Days, the Second Peace of Paris, 20 November 1815, restored peace. An Anglo-Austrian Convention (2 August 1815) made Napoleon a prisoner in Britain's custody.

B. Settlement for Denmark: Treaties of Peace were concluded between Denmark, and

1. Sweden, at Kiel, 14 January 1814 (Sweden acquiring Norway from Denmark).[88]

2. Britain, at Kiel, 14 January.[89]

3. Russia, at Hanover, 8 February.[90]

4. Prussia, at Berlin, 25 August 1814 (wherein Denmark having acquired Swedish Pomerania and Rügen from Sweden ceded these to Prussia).[91]

5. Spain, at London, 14 August 1814.[92]

C. The general settlement: A pan-European settlement was reached during the Congress of Vienna (September, 1814–June, 1815); and the Final Act of the Congress, 9 June 1815, embodied that settlement. Additional conventions and protocols after the date of the Final Act both implemented and completed the arrangements made at Vienna.

D. Russia had made peace with Turkey at Bucharest, 28 May 1812, and, *inter alia*, secured Bessarabia.[93]

WAR AIMS OF THE MAJOR ACTORS: France's original declaration of war against Austria and Prussia in 1792 was supported by Royalists and Revolutionaries alike. Both groups believed that a foreign war would aid

---

88 Martens, G. F., *Nouveau Recueil de Traités* (Göttingen: Librairie de Dieterich, 1817), Vol. 1, pp. 666–77, hereinafter cited as "Martens (N.R.)." A cease-fire agreement had been concluded at Rendsburg on 15 December 1813 between Denmark and the Allies: *ibid.*, pp. 657–8.

89 *Ibid.*, pp. 678–80.

90 *Ibid.*, pp. 681–3.

91 *Ibid.*, Vol. 2, pp. 65–7. See also pp. 332–5.

92 *Ibid.*, Vol. 3, pp. 306–8.

93 *Ibid.*, pp. 397–405.

their respective causes. Very soon, particularly after the elimination of the King and his supporters, the war became for France a means to spread revolution to the rest of Europe. Even when revolutionary ardor, at least in its original form, was much less intense after 1794, France's policymakers, and especially Bonaparte after Brumaire, still sought to establish a new order in Europe, a French Empire that would bring French culture and rationalized, modern forms of government to the benighted.

Austria and Prussia sought opportunity values through intermeddling in France and through their support of the *émigrés*. They and the other partners of the First Coalition were shocked by the execution of Louis XVI; and their aim became the destruction of the regime that had committed regicide. But even as early as 1793 or 1794, the motive that was to become increasingly dominant was in evidence, namely, the preservation of a balance of power in Europe over against a France bent upon the achievement of hegemony. Yet having said this, we must realize that the goal of equilibrium was often little understood. When the powers were offered gains, when they could hope to cut their losses, they deserted the anti-French coalitions on several occasions.

The British fought to preserve the integrity of their Empire and to overcome the effects of Napoleon's Continental System. Eventually, Russia also had to reject that system because her economy was being adversely affected. And of course, during the Campaign of 1812, Russia fought a defensive war for her survival.

In the last stage of the war (the Fourth Coalition), the powers finally came to understand the need for cooperating in order to defeat Napoleon —but even then, he very nearly divided them once again by offering them short-term opportunity values. During the Congress of Vienna, the general goals of the great powers were fairly much in accord, directed to achieving an equilibrium in Europe, preventing a resurgence of France, and re-establishing legitimate governments in the states of Europe.

FACTORS FOR PEACE: The way was open for a final and definitive peace settlement with the capitulation of the French and Napoleon's agreement to abdicate. Whatever the goals of the powers and their small state allies, it appeared that they could be secured at a congress by means of negotiations. The French, moreover, had no reason to continue the war, even though the allied armies had not occupied France completely and had not destroyed her armies utterly: it appeared that a France ruled by a Bourbon would be able to come through a negotiated settlement rather well.

WAR-ORIENTED STATES: During periods when former or future belligerents were nonbelligerent, they were war-oriented (unless they ceased to exist because absorbed into the French Empire). The United States was also war-oriented and was eventually involved in a war with Britain from

1812–1814. Persia was at war with Russia during the first decade of the nineteenth century but was only peripherally interested in the European wars. The Russo-Persian War ended in 1813.

SETTLEMENT OF THE CENTRAL WAR: PRELIMINARIES: In the Treaties of Kalisch (28 February 1813) [94] and Breslau (19 March 1813), [95] and subsequent supplementary agreements, Prussia and Russia agreed to ally against France and to drive her from Germany. [96] This was the beginning of yet another coalition against the French (the Fourth). Napoleon accepted Austria's tender of her good offices and signed the Armistice of Pleiswitz in early June, 1813. [97] He did this because Austria was mobilizing her troops, pressures within the French Empire were mounting for attempts to end the seemingly interminable wars, and Napoleon thought he could once again divide Prussia and Russia by separate negotiations. The Pleiswitz Truce was extended until about mid-August. Meanwhile, Austria, Russia, and Prussia had agreed to present proposals to the French, refusal of which was to bring Austria into the war. Napoleon refused; and Metternich spun out the negotiations at Dresden and Prague, as the Austrian army readied itself. By October, Britain and Bavaria had joined the coalition, all the allies having bound themselves not to make a separate peace. By February, 1814, Allied armies invaded France. And in February and March, the protagonists met once again to discuss terms of peace at Chatillon and Troyes. The six weeks of talks conducted while the war continued led to no results acceptable to the Allies. They firmed up their relationship by the Treaties of Chaumont of 1 March 1814, the constitutional documents of the Grand Alliance, and prepared to march on Paris. [98] (Württemberg agreed to an armistice with Austria and Prussia in November, 1813, and joined the Alliance against France. Bavaria, Baden, and Hesse broke with France's Confederation of the Rhine. Naples, renouncing claims to Sicily and disavowing Joachim Bonaparte as King of Sicily, formed a bilateral alliance with Austria in

94 *Ibid.,* pp. 234–44.

95 *Ibid.,* Vol. 1, pp. 564–6.

96 The Coalition was firmed up by the Treaties of Reichenbach (14 June 1813) between Britain and Prussia, *ibid.,* pp. 571–3, and Britain and Russia (15 June 1813), *ibid.,* pp. 568–71, 573–81. It was further strengthened by the bilateral Treaties of Töplitz (Austria and Russia, Prussia and Russia, and Prussia and Austria; 9 September 1813): *ibid.,* pp. 596–609; by the Anglo-Austrian Treaty of 3 October 1813: *ibid.,* pp. 607–9; by the Treaty of Ried (Austria and Bavaria of 8 October 1813) : *ibid.,* pp. 610–4; and others. See *ibid.,* pp. 643–654, 660–6; Vol. 4, pp. 96–110.

97 *Ibid.,* Vol. 1, pp. 582–8. Inter-Allied agreements for the disposition of Allied forces in Germany appear in *ibid.,* pp. 615–42.

98 *Ibid.,* pp. 683–8. Britain and Spain (under Ferdinand VII) concluded a Treaty of Friendship and Alliance on 5 July 1814 (*ibid.,* Vol. 4, pp. 118–25) .

January, 1814. Naples and Britain concluded a cease-fire agreement in February.)

Paris capitulated on 31 March. On 6 April, the French Senate promulgated a new constitution, which required the restoration of the brother of the late king. By 12 April, Napoleon had been persuaded to ratify the Treaty of Fontainebleau which brought about his abdication.[99] On the same day, a cease-fire agreement was concluded between Allied and French commanders.[100]

The first settlement with France: The armistice of 12 April 1814 established a demarcation line between the forces of the contending armies in northern and central France. The Convention of 23 April made the duration of the cease-fire indefinite.[101] The Allies agreed to evacuate French territory, and France agreed to withdraw all her forces from occupied areas by specified dates. Provision was made for release of prisoners, restitution of prizes, and lifting of the blockade. Transfer of territory to French magistrates was to be accomplished when legitimate authority had been reestablished in France. Additional military conventions in April and May spelled out details for a truce and for the evacuations of French forces from Italy, care of the wounded, subsistance of forces, and plans of march.[102] In Italy, the cease-fire had become effective on 16 April; in Genoa, on 18 April; in other "departments beyond the Alps," on 27 April.[103]

In the Treaty of Fontainebleau, Napoleon had renounced for himself and for his heirs all right to the Crown of France and the Empire. He was to be given the Island of Elba as a separate, independent principality, with an income and a contingent of guards. He was required to restore certain sums to the French treasury.

In the bilateral treaties of Paris, 30 May 1814 (the First Peace of Paris), peace was formally restored between the Allies and France.[104] The frontiers of France were defined, and they were in general the frontiers of 1 January 1792. Boundary commissions were established to mark and run the new boundaries. Britain agreed to restore the French colonies of 1792, except Tobago, St. Lucia, and a few others. Sweden was to return Guadeloupe; Portugal was to return French Guiana. Malta was

---

99 *Ibid.,* Vol. 1, pp. 695–703.
100 *Ibid.,* pp. 703–5.
101 *Ibid.,* pp. 706–13.
102 *Ibid.,* pp. 713–6.
103 *Ibid.,* pp. 716–20; Vol. 3, pp. 303–4; Vol. 5, pp. 34–7.
104 *Recueil de Traités et Conventions entre la France et les Puissances Alliées* (Paris: Rondonneau et Decle, 1815), pp. 6 ff. A secret article describing the boundaries of The Netherlands appears in Martens, G. F., *Nouveau Supplémens au Recueil de Traités* (Göttingen: Librarie de Dieterich, 1839), Vol. 1, p. 329.

recognized as belonging to Great Britain. Subject to regulation by a Congress that the powers agreed to hold in Vienna within 2 months, the parties acknowledged the sovereignty of the House of Orange in The Netherlands, the independence of Switzerland, free navigation on the Rhine, and a new federation of the German states.

There was to be an amnesty for persons of all political persuasions. Britain agreed to extend trading rights on a most-favored-nation basis to French subjects in India and fishing rights on the basis of the 1792 agreements to Frenchmen in the Western Hemisphere. In lands that had changed their sovereigns, inhabitants were to be permitted to have 6 months to dispose of their possessions and leave. France was to pay individuals all sums due on contracts for supplies and requisitions.

The Allies renounced all claims against France for advances made to her during the war, and France reciprocated. The powers agreed to name commissioners to arrange an amicable settlement of public and private claims.

The signatories exchanged guarantees of the settlement terms.[105]

France and Spain signed a separate peace treaty on 20 July. Duplicating the Treaties of 30 May, it also provided for a mixed commission to resolve disputes over money claims, for a restoration of commerce on the basis of 1792 treaties, and for mutual restitutions of confiscated properties.[106]

The final settlement with France: The Congress of Vienna had not yet wound up its work when Napoleon returned to France. Immediately, the powers declared him an outlaw, reconfirmed the First Peace of Paris, and committed the Grand Alliance to prevent permanently any future efforts on the part of Napoleon to seize power in France or to create trouble for Europe.[107] In May, the Austrian and Neapolitan commanders concluded an armistice agreement for Naples.[108] The Battle of Waterloo (18 June 1815) was the end of Napoleon's schemes. In July, pursuant to an armistice agreement, the French armies were required to evacuate Paris within 3 days and take up positions behind the Loire.[109] And in August, Napoleon was formally recognized as a prisoner of Great Britain.[110] From July to November, the Allies discussed the terms of the second

105 The Great Power signatories of the Treaty of Chaumont agreed to maintain their forces in the field until a definitive peace was concluded (Convention of 29 June 1814: Martens (N.R.), *op. cit.*, Vol. 2, pp. 40–1.)

106 *Ibid.*, pp. 42–3.

107 *Ibid.*, pp. 107–8. A Treaty of Alliance was signed on 25 March 1814: *ibid.*, pp. 109–49. Britain concluded a number of subsidy treaties with the allies from May to August: *ibid.*, pp. 186–213.

108 *Ibid.*, pp. 279–82.

109 *Ibid.*, pp. 567–9.

110 *Ibid.*, pp. 579–81.

settlement with the French; but this time there was less willingness to be lenient, and the Allies (particularly Prussia) were intent upon imposing a rather more harsh peace upon France.

The bilateral treaties of the Peace of Paris (The Second Peace of Paris) were signed on 20 November 1815.[111] The French frontiers were to be those of 1790; and France was required to pay an indemnity of 700 million Francs. Allied forces were to be deployed on the frontiers of France for five years. (The details of the occupation regime were contained in a separate convention.) Provisions of the First Peace of Paris were incorporated by reference, as were those of the Final Act of the Congress of Vienna. The parties also concluded other conventions governing payment of the indemnity and liquidation of claims against France.[112]

The Treaties of Paris were guaranteed by the Great Powers, who renewed their alliance in a series of accords executed on 20 November 1815 (the Treaties of the Quadruple Alliance).[113] They agreed to maintain the settlement the French King had accepted on that very day, to take steps to preserve the tranquillity of Europe, and if attacked by France, to go to war against her, each of them providing 60,000 troops. They promised to renew these arrangements in the future, particularly after the occupation of France had ended.

The settlement for Europe: The Final Act of the Congress was initialled on 9 June 1815 by Austria, France, Great Britain, Portugal, Prussia, Russia, and Sweden (but with reservations by the latter).[114] Disputing the Italian settlement, the required cession of Olivenca to Portugal, and the right of the great powers to make decisions for the lesser states of Europe (including herself), Spain refused to sign. The small states were invited to adhere to the Act and eventually did so, with

111 *Recueil de Traités . . . entre la France . . . , op. cit.,* pp. 35 ff.

112 *Ibid.,* pp. 47 ff. The text of the Treaties of Peace of the Second Peace of Paris also appear in Martens (N.R.), *op. cit.,* Vol. 2, pp. 656–65. See pp. 666–707, 650–55 for the supplementary conventions.

113 *Ibid.,* pp. 708–12.

114 Great Britain, *General Treaty of Congress, Signed at Vienna, June 9, 1815* (London: T. R. Harrison, 1847). Space does not permit us to discuss the organization or diplomacy of the Congress of Vienna. So serious had the dispute among the Great Powers over Poland and Saxony become by January, 1815, that Austria, Britain, and France entered into a secret defensive alliance directed against Prussia and Russia. See Martens, *Nouveau Supplémens . . . , op. cit.,* Vol. 1, pp. 368–74. The alliance had a sobering effect upon the latter Powers, and a compromise settlement was eventually reached. Volume 1 of the Martens, *Nouveau Supplémens . . . , ibid.,* contains important correspondence and protocols relating to the negotiations at the Congress: p. 330 ff.; and see Martens (N.R.), Vol. 2, pp. 249–58.

the exception of the Holy See and the Ottoman Empire. Formal signing took place on 19 June (except for Spain; and for Russia, who signed on 26 June).

1. The public law of Europe: The powers declared that they would strive to eliminate trade in Negro slaves by all means as promptly as possible and attempt to get other states to adhere to their declaration, which was dated 8 February 1815 and incorporated by reference in the Final Act of 9 June.[115] The Declaration had been signed by Austria, Britain, France, Portugal, Prussia, Russia, Spain, and Sweden.

The powers also agreed upon rules for the precedence and rank of diplomatic agents,[116] and upon the need for a law for international rivers.[117] Thus, states crossed by international rivers agreed to regulate commerce and navigation by common consent and, in any event, to respect rights of free trade on those rivers. Within 6 months of the end of the Congress, a commission was to meet to formulate regulations for the rivers, including uniform duties, police powers, tow paths, and particular regulations for identified rivers (Rhine, Neckar, Main, Moselle, Meuse, and Scheldt). (Arts. 108–117.)

2. Germany (Arts. 43–64): A German Confederation was established by the Princes and Free Towns of Germany, and by Austria, Prussia, Denmark, and the Netherlands, its declared object being the security of Germany and the independence of the confederated states. All state members of the confederation had equal political rights and each was declared to be a sovereign state. A Diet was established to conduct the affairs of the Confederation. Austria was to furnish the presiding officer. A scheme of ordinary voting for general business and weighted voting for constitutional matters was also adopted. The first task of the Diet was to draft the fundamental laws of the Confederation and "organic institutions for external, military and internal relations." The members, the leading states being Austria, Prussia, Bavaria, Saxony, Hanover, Württemberg, and Baden, exchanged guarantees and promised to come to the aid of any member that had been attacked. They also promised not to make war on each other; and, if disputes arose between them, to submit them to the Diet or to a judicial body for resolution.

Territorial adjustments were also made within Germany (Arts. 43–51). The Federative Constitution of Germany of 8 June 1815 was incorporated in the Final Act by reference.[118]

3. Prussia and Hanover (Arts. 23–42, 118/6): Prussia secured the port of Danzig, parts of the Duchy of Magdeburg, Essen, Halberstadt, Cleves,

115 *Ibid.*, pp. 412–14.
116 *Ibid.*, pp. 429–30.
117 *Ibid.*, pp. 414–29.
118 *Ibid.*, pp. 335–60.

Neufchatel, Ravensburg, Erfurt, Minden, Mark, and Westphalia (among others) and ceded to Britain (for Hanover), East Friesland, Goslar, Hildesheim, and part of Lingen. Britain was to cede part of the Duchy of Lauenburg to Prussia, which was then to cede it to Denmark. The Boundaries of Prussia were delineated; and it was agreed that a boundary commission would be established to run the boundary between Hanover and Prussia. The King of England was acknowledged to be the King of Hanover (no longer an Electorate, but now a Kingdom). The territories of the Electorate of Brunswick-Lüneburg were also awarded to Hanover.

Hanover was to keep the Ems River navigable and permit Prussian subjects to trade through the port of Emden. Provision was also made for uniform tolls, warehousing, military roads, and inspection of goods, these being part of the Prussian-Hanoverian agreement of 29 May 1815, incorporated in the Final Act by reference.[119]

4. Saxony (Arts. 15–22): Saxony lost about two thirds of her territory to Prussia, the cession being guaranteed by Austria, Russia, Britain, and France. The inhabitants of the ceded territories were to be allowed to emigrate and remove their property without hindrance or fines. Prussia promised to care for all its subjects on "liberal principles." In the lands of both Prussia and Saxony, all communities and religious establishments were to retain their privileges, properties, and rents; and no one was to be persecuted for acts committed after the war had begun. The peace treaty between the two parties, dated 18 May, was incorporated by reference in the Final Act (Art. 118–4).[120]

5. Poland (Arts. 1–14, 118/1 to 118/3): A Free Territory of Cracow, the boundaries of which were described, was established under the protection of Russia, Austria, and Prussia, who also recognized its neutrality. An Annex to the Final Act provided a basic law for the Free Territory; and the treaties between Russia and Prussia (3 May) concerning the relations of these states to that Territory were incorporated by reference.[121]

The bulk of the Grand Duchy of Warsaw was ceded to Russia, the Czar promising to give it a distinct administration and provide for the "internal improvement he thinks desirable." Prussia acquired that part of the Duchy known as the Grand Duchy of Posen. The Polish subjects of Austria, Prussia, and Russia were promised representation and national institutions "the governments think proper." Russia was to cede Tarnopol in Eastern Galicia to Austria.

With respect to Poland, the parties to the Final Act, including of course the states most directly concerned, proclaimed a general amnesty

119 *Ibid.*, pp. 300–7.
120 *Ibid.*, pp. 258–75. See also pp. 602–5.
121 *Ibid.*, pp. 213–23, 223–37, 238–49.

and agreed to prosecute no one for any civil or military incidents that had occurred in Poland during the war. There was also to be free navigation of the rivers of Poland and free trade through its ports.

6. The Netherlands (Arts. 65–73, 118/10): The Netherlands was declared to be a Kingdom under the Prince of Orange-Nassau. Its boundaries were described. In addition to the original United Provinces, the postwar Netherlands was also to include the Walloon (Belgic) provinces of the former Austrian Netherlands and the Duchy of Luxemburg (which was also a part of the German Confederation). The order of succession in the House of Nassau was set forth, and a small territorial adjustment was made with Prussia. An Annex guaranteeing the religious, cultural, and commercial rights of the Walloons was attached; and the four treaties of 31 May between The Netherlands, Britain, France, Russia, and Prussia defining the limits of the Kingdom were incorporated by reference in the Final Act.[122]

7. Switzerland (Arts. 74–84, 118/11): The integrity and independence of the 19 confederated cantons of Switzerland was recognized.[123] Valais, Geneva, and Neufchatel were constituted three new cantons; and Basle was to be incorporated in the Berne Canton. Sardinia ceded part of Savoy to Geneva. Both Sardinia and France agreed to allow the use of roads across their lands connecting Geneva with other cantons. A financial settlement among the cantons was also provided for. Swiss neutrality was recognized by the powers in November, 1815.[124]

8. Sardinia and Italy (Arts. 85–104, 118/12 to 118/14): Liguria with Genoa were united to Sardinia; and an Annex was attached defining the basis of the union, including the protection of the rights of the citizens of Genoa.[125] Also incorporated in the Final Act were the five agreements of the powers with Sardinia of 20 May, defining the limits of Sardinia (now including Savoy, Nice, and Piedmont as well as Liguria), and recognizing the acquisition of Genoa.[126] The King of Sardinia recognized that northern Savoy formed part of the "neutrality of Switzerland," guaranteed by the powers. If hostilities occurred in or near Switzerland, Sardinian forces were to withdraw and refrain from intervening. They were to be permitted to retire through Switzerland.

The powers recognized Austrian territories in Italy (Lombardy, Venetia, and Dalmatia), and the bounds thereof were defined. There was to

122 *Ibid.*, pp. 301–6, 316–31, 23–37, 37–40, 643, 590–602.

123 The convention forming the Helvetic Confederacy appears in *ibid.*, Vol. 1, pp. 659–60, and Vol. 2, pp. 67–75. For the Acts of the Congress concerning Switzerland, see *ibid.*, Vol. 2, pp. 149–66. See also *ibid.*, Vol. 4, pp. 161–86, 190–213.

124 *Ibid.*, Vol. 2, pp. 714–6; Vol. 4, pp. 186–8.

125 *Ibid.*, Vol. 2, pp. 167–72; Vol. 4, pp. 214–24.

126 *Ibid.*, Vol. 2, pp. 283–94, 84–90.

be free navigation of the Po, and the riverine states were to name commissioners to regulate the use of the river. A Bourbon, Ferdinand IV, was recognized as King of the newly consolidated Two Sicilies (Naples and Sicily). A territorial settlement for the Holy See was provided. Empress Maria Louisa (wife of Napoleon) acquired Lucca (with reversion to the Grand Duke of Tuscany, who also happened to be Archduke Ferdinand of Austria) and Parma, Piacenza, and Guastalla (with reversion to be determined by the Great Powers and Spain). Tuscany and Modena were awarded to the House of Habsburg-Lorraine.

9. Portugal (Arts. 105–107): Portugal agreed to restore French Guiana to France, and the powers promised to use all amicable means to restore to Portugal the province of Olivenca, then possessed by Spain.[127]

10. Great Britain: Several of Britain's wartime territorial acquisitions were confirmed to her: Ceylon and Cape Colony (from the Netherlands); islands in the West Indies (from the Netherlands and Spain); Malta; and Helgoland (from Denmark). The Dutch were compensated by Britain's assuming half of Holland's debt to Russia and by an additional cash payment. The Netherlands retained the Dutch East Indies. Britain was also made "protector" of the Ionian Isles.[128]

Even before the Congress began, Castlereagh secured the consent of Russia, Prussia, and Austria to the exclusion from the agenda of questions relating to "British Maritime Rights." This automatically ensured British supremacy on the high seas. It also ensured that the subject would not even be discussed (let alone challenged) at the Congress.

11. The Holy Alliance: In a separate agreement of 26 September 1815, Russia, Austria, and Prussia formed an alliance that was, in part, a guarantee of the Vienna settlement.[129] Britain's leaders, distrusting the nebulous purposes of the Holy Alliance, refused to join. The three monarchs agreed to remain united, regarding each other as "compatriots" and fathers of the subjects and soldiers of each. They were to direct their policies in the spirit of fraternity in order to protect religion, peace and justice; and they held themselves available to provide aid to each other in the event one of them were in need, as if they belonged to a single Christian nation (with each of the monarchs a delegate of God, governing three branches of the same family). Each would strengthen himself in the "principles of Jesus Christ." Acceding to the Treaty were the Netherlands, Württemberg, Switzerland, and the Hanseatic towns of Hamburg, Lübeck, and Bremen.

Although the powers guaranteed the settlement with France (in the

127 Britain concluded a Treaty with Portugal (on 22 January 1815, *ibid.*, pp. 91–100), the terms of which provided for the abolition of trade in slaves for compensation to Portugal for ships seized by the British during the war.

128 *Ibid.*, pp. 637–42.

129 *Ibid.*, pp. 630–2.

sense that they would concert their actions if France were to renew her aggression), there was no general guarantee of the Vienna settlement. Disparate ambitions among the great powers were too clearly in evidence when the Congress had got down to serious bargaining. It is possible that even with the competition among the powers, some sort of general guarantee could have been drafted. But British parliamentary opinion was opposed to a guarantee that would have the effect of legitimizing Russian acquisitions in Eastern Europe and providing some pretext, however small, for Russian expansion in the Levant. In the Treaties of the Quadruple Alliance (20 November 1815), Castereagh did succeed in incorporating an article providing for regular meetings of the Allies in the future. This slim provision was the procedural basis for the Concert of Europe afterward.[130]

COMMENTS: One aim of the powers was to contain France; this was accomplished through the Quadruple Alliance and the territorial settlement embodied in the Final Act. Thus, an enlarged Sardinia, Prussia, The Netherlands, and an internationally guaranteed Switzerland surrounded the country that had "disturbed the peace of Europe" for almost a quarter of a century. England in Hanover could back up Prussia; Austria in Italy could reinforce Sardinia. The settlement was guided by two other principles. The first, and by far the most important, was the principle of *equilibrium* or balance of power; and the second was the principle of *legitimacy*. Equilibrium was achieved (or was thought to have been achieved) through a series of reciprocal territorial concessions. It was also to be seen in the main peacemaking decisions: the Bourbon restoration, the moderation of the First Peace and even the Second Peace of Paris, and in the Quadruple Alliance, particularly in the provision that looked toward a functioning Concert of Europe. "The period 1814–15 is indeed one of the best examples of Europe's classical balance of power in operation. Uncounted documents of the period utilise its terminology, acts of all description were justified in equilibrist terms, plans of all and sundry commonly embodied its concepts and aims."[131]

The principle of legitimacy underlay the Bourbon restoration and the Holy Alliance. But as C. K. Webster observed, it was not followed with any consistency: "[A] large number of potentates, dispossessed by the French Revolution, never regained their sovereignty, and their protests at Vienna were unavailing. The Congress, in fact, found it necessary to accept the *faits accomplis* of the Napoleonic regime; and this meant the suppression of a number of small states, republics as well as monarchies— on the whole to the great good of Europe."[132]

130 Additional documents relating to the settlement can be found in *ibid.*, Vols. 2–4, and in Martens, *Nouveau Supplémens . . . op. cit.*, Vol. 1, *passim.*
131 *The New Cambridge Modern History, op. cit.*, Vol. 9, p. 665.
132 Webster, C. K., *The Congress of Vienna* (London: Bell, 1945), p. 147.

Ignored, even discouraged, were the principles of self-government and national self-determination (the *principle of nationality* as it probably would have been called at this early date) .

THE FIRST WORLD WAR (1914–1919+)

STRUCTURE OF THE WAR: A. General structure of the European War: France, Russia, Britain, Italy, and the United States vs. Germany, Austria-Hungary, and the Ottoman Empire.

B. Detailed structure of the European War: France, Great Britain, Belgium (occupied in 1914), Russia (left war in 1917), Montenegro (occupied in 1914), Serbia (conquered in 1915), Italy (at war with Austria-Hungary from 1915; with Germany, from 1916), Portugal (from 1916; *de facto* belligerent from 1914), Roumania (from 1916; conquered by the Central Powers in 1916; made peace in 1918; but re-entered war in 1918), Greece (from 1917), and the United States (from 1917; not at war with the Ottoman Empire or with Bulgaria)

vs.

Germany, Austria-Hungary, Ottoman Empire, and Bulgaria (from 1915). [Note: In 1917 Brazil, Cuba, Guatemala, Haiti, Honduras, Nicaragua, Panama, and Costa Rica declared war on Germany. Bolivia, Ecuador, Peru, Dominican Republic, and Uruguay merely broke off diplomatic relations. None of these states were truly active belligerents. Albania was occupied and partitioned by Italy and Greece (1914), occupied by Austria (1915), and then liberated by Italy, Serbia, and France (1918).]

C. War in East Asia and the Pacific: Japan and China (from 1917) vs. Germany (Note: Japan and China were antagonists, not allies; but they remained nonbelligerent with respect to each other.)

D. Wars internal to the Ottoman Empire:

1. Arab uprising (1916–18) : Arabs of the Hejaz and Britain vs. Ottoman Empire.

2. Armenian Revolt (1915–19+) : Armenians and Russia (from 1916) vs. Ottoman Empire.

3. War in the Maghreb (1914–19+) : Senussi and Arab allies vs. Italy (in Libya, 1914–19+), France (in Algeria and Tunisia, 1915–16), Britain (in Egypt, 1915–16).

E. Wars arising from conditions created by the central European War and its settlement:

1. Greco-Turkish War (1920–23).

2. Uprisings in Germany: In 1918, sailors and workers rebelled against the government of the Kaiser, being responsible, in part, for his abdication. In January, 1919, the Sparticist Uprising was crushed by the Social Democratic Provisional Government. In 1920, disaffected army officers and soldiers revolted against the Weimar Republic. This revolt, known as the Kapp Putsch, was also crushed.

3. Hungarian War (1918–19): Hungary vs. Roumania. The war continued with increased intensity during the Bolshevik regime of Bela Kun (March–August, 1919), with France, Britain, Italy, and the United States following a policy of containment of Hungary and urging the Roumanians toward moderation.

4. Russian Revolution (1917 +): In the March Revolution, the Czar was forced to abdicate; in the October Revolution, the Bolsheviks secured control of the government of Russia.

5. Russian Civil Wars (1918–22): Bolsheviks vs. a number of mostly noncooperating, distinct anti-Bolshevik ("white") factions (including the factions led by Denikin in the Don Valley and the Caucasus, Kolchak in Siberia, Wrangel in the Crimea, Yudenich in Estonia, Petliura in Bessarabia, and the Cossacks in the Urals). The Allies intervened in the Civil War (1918–22): Britain, the United States, and France in Murmansk-Archangel (1918–19); France on the northern coast of the Black Sea (1918–19); Britain in Central Asia and the Transcaucasus (1918–19); Japan (1918–22), the United States (1918–20), and Britain (1918–19) in Siberia; and the Czech Legion (1918–19), fighting against the Germans in the Ukraine in early 1918 and thence to the Urals and across Siberia to Vladivostok, fighting against Bolshevik units.

6. Finnish Civil War (1918–20): "White" Finns and Germany (until November, 1918) vs. "Red" Finns and U.S.S.R. The "White" Finns defeated the "Reds" and eliminated them by terror techniques. Until 1920, the Finns remained in a state of technical civil war against the Soviet Union.

7. Russo-Polish War (1920–21) [133]

8. Vilna dispute (1919–23): Poland vs. Soviet Union. Subsequent to the peace treaty between the U.S.S.R. and Lithuania (12 July 1920) and the cession of Vilna to Lithuania, the war took the form: Poland vs. Lithuania.

F. Theaters of combat: Western Europe (France, Belgium, and Luxemburg); Eastern Europe (Russia, Austria-Hungary, and Roumania); Northeastern Italy; The Balkans and northern Greece; Mesopotamia; Egypt and the Maghreb; The Hejaz, Jordan, Palestine, and Syria; Armenia; German Africa (Togoland, Cameroons, German Southwest Africa, and German East Africa); Persia; and The Pacific and East Asia.

PATTERN OF SETTLEMENTS:

A. The principal settlements: Treaties of peace were imposed upon the defeated Central Powers by the Allies.

1. Germany: The Treaty of Versailles, 28 June 1919. The United States did not ratify this Treaty and signed a separate peace treaty at Berlin on 25 August 1921.

---

133 See the summary in Chapter 2 at pp. 73–6.

2. Austria (the Habsburg Empire having disintegrated) : The Treaty of St. Germain-en-Laye, 10 September 1919.

3. Bulgaria: The Treaty of Neuilly, 27 November 1919.

4. Hungary: The Treaty of Trianon, 4 June 1920.

5. Ottoman Empire: The Treaty of Sèvres, 10 August 1920. This Treaty was never implemented, because of the successful resistance of the Kemalist Turks. Its terms were superceded by the Treaty of Lausanne, signed 24 July 1923 by the powers (but not the U.S.) and by representatives of the Angora Assembly (which proclaimed Turkey a Republic in October, 1923).

B. Settlements relating to the Soviet Union:[134] The great-power directors of the Paris Peace Conference could not decide how best to solve the problems created by the Bolshevik Revolution, although they were in agreement on not moving to recognize the new Soviet regime. Apart from the rather important act of abrogating the Treaty of Brest-Litovsk (and the Treaty of Bucharest), there was no Conference solution to the Russian problem and hence no Conference settlement. The states were left to deal with the Soviet Union and related East European questions apart from the formal peacemaking apparatus of the Paris Conference. Thus, the settlements between the U.S.S.R. and other states came about through various *ad hoc* agreements, reached after 1919:

1. Within the Soviet Union: The Bolsheviks secured and maintained their control of central Russian territory, defeating all the important "White" factions by 1921. The interventions of the powers in Russia were reversed, and their troops removed: France, Britain, and the United States by 1920, Japan by 1922. In none of these cases was there a settlement, as we have used that term. After 1921, the new government of the "Russian Empire" gradually consolidated and extended its control.

2. The Baltic area: The Soviet Union recognized the independence of the Baltic states that had formerly been a part of the Russian Empire: Estonia, in the Treaty of Tartu, February, 1920;[135] Lithuania, in the Treaty of Moscow, July, 1920;[136] Latvia: in the Treaty of Riga, August, 1920;[137] and Finland: by the Treaty of Dorpat, October, 1920.[138] Poland and the Soviet Union concluded the Peace Treaty of Riga in March, 1921. A technical state of war between Poland and Lithuania lasted until

134 Thompson, J. M., *Russia, Bolshevism, and the Versailles Peace* (Princeton: Princeton University Press, 1966) ; Stein, B. E., *Die Russische Frage auf der pariser Friedenskonferenz, 1919–1920* (Leipzig: Kohler und Amelang, 1953).

135 Shapiro, Leonard (ed.), *Soviet Treaty Series* (Washington, D.C.: Georgetown University Press, 1950), Vol. 1, pp. 34–40.

136 *Ibid.*, pp. 50–4.

137 *Ibid.*, pp. 54–8.

138 *Ibid.*, pp. 69–75.

peace negotiations were arranged by the League of Nations in 1927.[139] (For all practical purposes the Polish-Lithuanian War over Vilna ended in 1923 with the occupation of the city by a Polish force.)

3. Germany: The Treaty of Brest-Litovsk of March, 1918, was imposed by Germany upon the Soviet Union.[140] The Treaty, which embodied a rather draconic settlement, was formally an agreement between "Russia" and the Central Powers. It was supplemented by the Treaty of Berlin and a Financial Agreement, signed at Berlin in August, 1918.[141] The Central Powers had earlier concluded a separate peace Treaty with the Ukraine (February, 1918) on much more favorable terms, which converted the Ukraine into a client state of Germany. During armistice and peace negotiations, in the absence of Soviet representatives (but certainly with the approval of the Bolshevik government), the Allies required Germany and the other Central Powers to abrogate the Treaties of Brest-Litovsk and Berlin; in short, to undo legally and in fact, the settlements imposed upon the Russians. It was not until April, 1922, at Rapallo, that the Soviet Union and Germany concluded an agreement normalizing their relations:[142] they renounced all war claims against each other and re-established diplomatic relations. Prior to the Rapallo Treaty, the two states had concluded a number of technical military conventions and agreements respecting repatriation of prisoners and interned civilians.

4. The Allies: France recognized the Soviet Union *de jure* in 1924, as did Britain, Italy, and Greece.[143] Britain however had concluded a trade agreement with the Soviets as early as March, 1921;[144] and this constituted *de facto* recognition. Italy's postwar relations with the Russians were also based on a political and economic agreement that predated *de jure* recognition, namely, the Preliminary Agreement of Rome, December, 1921.[145] Japan also reached a preliminary accord with the Soviets in April, 1920, but their relations were not truly normalized until the Con-

---

139 Walters, F. P., *A History of the League of Nations* (London: Oxford University Press, 1952), Vol. 1, pp. 399–400.

140 Shapiro, *op. cit.*, pp. 1–2, 4–22.

141 *Ibid.*, pp. 23–5, 25–7, 27 f. A more complete collection of the Brest-Litovsk documents can be found in *Texts of the Russian "Peace"* (Washington, D.C.: U.S. Dept. of State, 1918). Germany's Peace Treaty with the Ukraine appears in Speidel, *Der Friede im Osten* (Heilbronn: Schell'scher Verlag, 1918), pp. 1 f.; and an English translation appears in Wheeler-Bennett, J. W., *Brest-Litovsk: The Forgotten Peace* (New York: St. Martin's Press, 1966), pp. 392–402. The Treaty of Bucharest (between Roumania and the Central Powers), signed on 7 May 1918, is in Speidel, pp. 76 ff.

142 Shapiro, *op. cit.*, pp. 168–9. See also pp. 198–9.

143 *Ibid.*, pp. 282, 226, 232, 234.

144 *Ibid.*, pp. 102–4.

145 *Ibid.*, pp. 158–9.

vention of Peking, 20 January 1925.[146] A settlement and formal re-establishment of relations between China and the Soviet Union was arranged in 1924.[147] The United States did not recognize the Soviet Union until November, 1933.[148]

5. Eastern Europe: A Provisional Agreement on Future Relations was signed in December, 1921, between Austria and the USSR; *de jure* recognition was extended in 1924.[149] Czechoslovakia and the Soviet Union concluded a Treaty of Friendship and Commerce in June, 1922, at Prague. But *de jure* recognition was not extended until 1934.[150] Yugoslavia did not even enter into diplomatic relations with the Soviets. Relations with Bulgaria, Hungary, and Roumania were almost nonexistent, although Roumania negotiated with the Soviets on the question of the status of Bessarabia, which continued to prevent better relations between the two states. The three finally recognized the Soviet Union in 1934.[151]

6. Turkey: Relations between Russia and Turkey were regularized by a series of treaties of friendship dating from March, 1921. A Treaty of Commerce and Navigation was concluded in 1927.[152] Part of Armenia became the Soviet Socialist Republic of Armenia in December, 1920; and Turkey recognized the status of the SSRA in the Treaty of Kars, October, 1921.[153] The southern portion of Armenia was absorbed into Turkey. Thus, there was not even the shadow of a settlement between the Kemalists and the Armenians (or between the Soviets and the Armenians).

C. The new states: The war led to the collapse of the Habsburg, Russian, and Ottoman Empires, and thence to the establishment of a number of wholly independent states and quasi-colonies (known as *mandates*). The succession states of the Habsburg Empire were Czechoslovakia, Yugoslavia, and Hungary; and although the latter had occupied a very special local status in the Habsburg Empire before the War, it was treated by the Allies as an enemy. The succession states of the Russian Empire (discussed above) were Poland, Finland, Estonia, Latvia, and Lithuania; those of the Ottoman Empire were the Hejaz (with the autonomous sheikhdoms of the Arabian peninsula) and the mandated territories of Palestine, Transjordan, Iraq, Syria, and Lebanon.

D. The Paris Peace Conference also created the League of Nations, the Covenant of which, together with the major peace treaties, provided a constitution for the postwar state system.

146 *Ibid.*, pp. 44, 283–5.
147 *Ibid.*, pp. 242–4.
148 *Ibid.*, Vol. 2, pp. 82–6.
149 *Ibid.*, Vol. 1, pp. 147–50, 234.
150 *Ibid.*, pp. 173–4; Vol. 2, p. 106.
151 *Ibid.*, Vol. 2, pp. 108, 94, 106.
152 *Ibid.*, Vol. 1, pp. 100–2, 136–7, 160–1, 313, 326–9.
153 *Ibid.*, pp. 136–7.

GREAT POWER WAR AIMS: The Habsburgs sought to preserve the integrity of their realm and finally to crush Serbian resistance and rebellion. Even in the late stages of the war, when Austria-Hungary had sustained severe losses, pressures to move for peace could be attributed to the goal of saving the Empire. Germany's war aims are still a matter of controversy. Early in the war, defense was an aim: for if Germany did not support Austria, she might be without allies afterward. But German policymakers, reasoning in that way, also sought more. Some would say the Germans wanted hegemony in Europe; others, that they wanted to become at least one, or perhaps the only, leading power in Europe. As the war progressed, conservative German policymakers still fought for a Greater Germany, for a peace with compensations, and even annexations.

France, Britain, and Russia wanted to maintain a balance of power in Europe and to prevent any significant change in the power position of Germany. Preservation of the integrity of the alliance system of the Allies was also a goal. France wanted retribution against a traditional enemy, particularly as the costs of war mounted. Her leaders wanted firm guarantees against any future threat from Germany. Britain fought also to remove the effects of German aggression against Belgium, which also posed a threat to the security of the home island. She also wanted to maintain her superiority on the high seas over against an increasingly competitive German navy and merchant marine. The United States entered the war because her leaders wanted to prevent the domination of Europe by Germany and because there were more commercial ties with (and more sympathy for) the Allied cause. The war became more and more ideologically flavored after 1916. With the departure from the war of Czarist Russia and the entry of the United States, national self-determination and ridding the world of German "militarism" became the Allies' very effective slogans, and indeed a part of the substance of their war aims. Many Allied policymakers became convinced they were working for the good of all mankind.

Japan and Italy sought territorial and other opportunity gains, although the ideological enthusiasm of the Allies did affect public opinion in Italy. Czarist Russia also fought for the promotion of her own (and Pan-Slav) interests in the Balkans.

FACTORS FOR PEACE: The Allies (except Russia) had in prospect, in the fall of 1918, the probability of achieving their war aims after the Central Powers had accepted their terms for armistices—terms that, when implemented, would prevent resumption of hostilities by their enemies. Russia, under the Bolsheviks, left the war in 1917 because her leaders needed peace to consolidate their control and to recoup devastating war losses. Austria-Hungary made peace because her armies and her Empire were disintegrating; and apart from the obvious futility of continuing the fight, it was thought that peace might yet permit the Habsburgs to salvage their lands on a new juridical and political basis. Germany's acceptance of armistice terms stemmed from the realization of her leaders that the homeland could be invaded, that victory was not possible, that their armies and the homefront were not "reliable," and were indeed afflicted by a profound war weariness. They also believed that a peace based upon Wilson's Fourteen Points was acceptable.

WAR-ORIENTED ACTORS: The Netherlands, Switzerland, Sweden, Norway, Denmark, and Spain were regional war-oriented states. Most of the other independent states of ths world felt the impact of the war. And, as in the preceding multilateral wars, whenever the belligerents were not involved in the hostilities, they were war-oriented.

THE SETTLEMENT: PRELIMINARIES: When Allied forces broke through the Salonika front, Bulgarian leaders decided they must ask for terms. They did so, and capitulated on 30 September 1918. At the end of October, Austria asked for an armistice: Her Empire was disintegrating along with her armies. The Austrian armistice was signed on 4 November. On 30 October, the Ottoman Empire also capitulated after an English-Arab force captured Damascus and Aleppo, and it became clear to the Porte that Allied forces could soon stage an attack against Constantinople from Macedonia. In France, the Allies penetrated the Hindenburg Line in early September, causing the German military leaders to press the Chancellor and Kaiser to ask for terms. On 4 October, Prince Max of Baden asked President Wilson for a peace based upon the Fourteen Points. Wilson consulted the Allies, who were induced to go along, in part, by the threat that the United States would sign a separate peace if they did not do so.[154] Meanwhile, additional letters dealing with the preconditions of an armistice were exchanged by the German and American governments. The Germans were led to believe that if they forced the abdication of the Kaiser, peace terms would be easier. Certainly, the Wilson correspondence implied that Germany must install a democratic government if a peace settlement was to be negotiated. The Allies, however, extracted further guarantees for their security: Germany must withdraw from all occupied territory and permit temporary occupation of the right bank of the Rhine. The Germans accepted these terms and signed the armistice on 11 November. Thus ended the hostilities that took at least 10 million lives and destroyed four empires.

The Fourteen Points were a part of the understandings of the parties before negotiations began. Several of the glosses upon them were not transmitted to the German policymakers.[155] They read as follows:

154 Temperley, H. W. V. (ed.), *A History of the Peace Conference of Paris* (London: Frowdy *et al.*, 1920–1924), Vol. 1, pp. 91–136, 236–357, 428 ff.; Rudin, H. R., *Armistice, 1918* (New Haven: Yale University Press, 1944); Mayer, A. J., *Politics and Diplomacy of Peacemaking* (New York: Knopf, 1967), pp. 53–116.

155 Czernin, Ferdinand, *Versailles, 1919* (New York: Capricorn, 1964), pp. 10–20.

Point	*Gloss*
1. Open covenants openly arrived at.	Confidential negotiations were not precluded, although they would not be binding.
2. Freedom of the seas (Britain's reservation respecting her right to retain her earlier discretionary practices was transmitted to the Germans.	Abolition of blockade was not intended.
3. Removal of economic barriers.	Protection of home industries would still be possible. There was to be a prohibition of discriminatory tariffs among members.
4. Reduction of national armaments.	The powers would accept this in principle only.
5. Impartial adjustment of all territorial claims, with strict observance of the principle of national self-determination.	German colonies were to be the property of the League. Only the colonial questions opened by the war were subject to this rule; hence, the British and French empires were exempt from the application of Point 5.
6. Evacuation of Russian territory. Russia's independent determination of her own development and policies was guaranteed.	
7. Restoration of full sovereignty to Belgium.	Belgium was to be indemnified for *all war costs*. (This and the gloss to Point 8 were transmitted to Germany.)
8. Freeing of French territory and the rectification of the "wrong" done by Prussia with respect to Alsace-Lorraine.	France was to be indemnified for actual damage done (but not all war costs).
9. Readjustment of Italian frontiers along lines of nationality.	Italy could have Trentino; but Germans north of the Brenner frontier were to have autonomy.
10. Autonomy accorded to the peoples of Austria-Hungary.	Complete independence was to be coupled with guarantees for racial and linguistic minorities.
11. Roumania, Serbia, and Montenegro were to be restored; and Serbia given access to the sea.	Bulgaria was to receive some territorial conpensations.
12. The Turkish frontiers of the Ottoman Empire were to be assured, as was	Britain and France would obtain mandates in the Middle East; Armenia was

autonomy of the peoples of the Empire and the opening of the Dardanelles to the commerce of all states under international guarantees.

to be independent; Greece would obtain Smyrna; Constantinople and the Straits were to be placed under international control.

13. Erection of an independent Polish state with access to the sea.

The questions of whether East Prussia was to be severed from Germany and whether Danzig was to be a free port were left open.

14. Establishment of a League of Nations.

THE SETTLEMENT: The peace conference opened in Paris on 12 January 1919. It would continue until mid-1920, although most of the delegations left after the signature of the German treaty in June, 1919. The organization of the conference is a fascinating subject, but it is a matter that cannot detain us because it is large enough for a separate study.[156] We could say the same thing about preconference and conference diplomacy, the bargaining between the principal powers, and the interrelation of domestic politics and world politics. The major areas of discussion at the conference were the League of Nations, French security, reparations from the defeated Central Powers, new states (including mandates), and questions relating to Italian territorial claims. With respect to the dispositions of territories, the conference frequently worked in the shadow of the secret treaties concluded earlier among the Allies: These were bargains made in the early years of the war when Britain, France, and Russia were willing to promise much in order to win allies in the desperate struggle then being fought.[157]

We shall find it most convenient to consider separately the settlements the Allies made with each of the Central Powers.

156 Marston, F. S., *The Peace Conference of 1919: Organization and Procedure* (New York: Oxford University Press, 1944); Hankey, Lord, *The Supreme Control of the Paris Peace Conference, 1919* (London: George Allen & Unwin, 1963); Caldis, C. G., *The Council of Four as a Joint Emergency Authority . . .* (Geneva: Graduate Institute of International Studies, 1953); Temperley, *op. cit.*, Vol. 1, Chapter VII. The Supreme War Council of the Allies evolved into the Supreme Council of the Paris Peace Conference, the principal decision-making center of that Conference. This entity, in turn, became the Ambassador's Conference in 1920, comprising the ambassadors of Britain, France, Italy, Japan, and the United States, who arrogated to themselves the competence to deal with matters arising out of the peace settlements, including reparations questions. In this role, the Conference supplemented, and often competed with, the Council of the League.

157 Temperley, *op. cit.*, Vol. 4, pp. 278–347; Vol. 6, pp. 1–22, 368–90, 602–16, 631–8.

Germany: The armistice between Germany and the Allies:[158]

A cease-fire on the land and in the air was to take place 6 hours after signature of the Armistice Agreement; on the sea, the cease-fire was to be effective immediately. The Germans were to evacuate Belgium, France, Luxemburg, and Alsace-Lorraine within 15 days. Troops found in those territories after the period of grace would be made prisoners. The German withdrawal from territories that formed part of Austria-Hungary, Roumania, Turkey, and Russia was to take place "as soon as the Allies shall think the moment suitable, having regard to the internal situation of these territories." Finally, the Germans were to evacuate the left bank of the Rhine, bridgeheads around Mainz, Coblentz and Cologne, and a 10-kilometer-wide zone along the right bank. The latter evacuations were to be accomplished within 31 days of the signing. Occupation forces were to move into the areas left by the Germans, including the bridgeheads (but not the neutral zone). Troop movement regulations were set forth in some detail in an Annex. Civil administration in the occupied areas of Germany was vested in local authorities under control of the Allied High Command.

Repatriation in Germany of interned civilians was to be completed within 15 days. Allied prisoners of war were also to be repatriated; but German prisoners were to be detained until the conclusion of the preliminaries of peace. Germany was to cease all requisitions in occupied territories. The Treaties of Brest-Litovsk and Bucharest were declared void. Requirements of a financial nature were imposed on the German government in order to guarantee payment of reparations by Germany in the postwar period.

The German armies were to surrender 5000 guns, 25,000 machine guns, 3000 mortars, and 1700 airplanes; and in order to give the Allies control over transportation, Germany was also to surrender 5000 locomotives, 150,000 wagons, and 5000 motor lorries. Annex 2 defined the extent of Allied control over transportation and communications. In the naval clauses, the Germans also agreed to surrender all their submarines, 10 battleships, 6 battle cruisers, 8 light cruisers, and 50 destroyers; and to disarm all other naval and river vessels and place them under the control of the Allies at designated ports. The Allies were also to be guaranteed access to the Baltic by the surrender of all forts by the Germans in and around the Cattegat and by the sweeping of all mine fields and the removal of obstructions. The Allied blockade of Germany was to continue, however, and German merchant ships at sea were still liable to capture. Germany was to notify neutral countries that all restrictions placed upon their trade with the Allies during the war were cancelled. Transfers of German ships to a neutral flag were prohibited.

158 Martens (N.R.), 3° Série, *op. cit.,* Vol. 11, pp. 172–82, 191–3, 209–14, 220. See also pp. 214–9, 221–38. Temperley, *op. cit.,* Vol. 1, pp. 459–80; Vol. 2, pp. 1–20, 255–344.

The Allies were given free access through Danzig and on the Vistula to areas occupied by Germany in the East in order to supply the people with staples and to maintain order. There were also specific provisions prohibiting the destruction or removal of ships, supplies, goods, and stores in areas that German forces were to evacuate. An International Armistice Commission, under the command of the Allies, was established in order to insure execution of the Armistice Agreement. The Armistice was to last 36 days. It was renewed on 13 December, on 16 January 1919 with amendments, and again on 16 February, for an indefinite period. In the last extension, the Germans were required to stop their fighting against the Poles in Posen and elsewhere and withdraw behind a specified line.

The Versailles Treaty, signed 28 June 1919:[159]

Military clauses: By 31 March 1920, at the latest, the German army was to be reduced to 10 divisions, not exceeding 100,000 men, of which no more than 4,000 were to be officers. The General Staff was to be dissolved. (Art. 160.) Paramilitary forces (for internal security) were to be reduced to their 1913 strength (Art. 161). Germany's armaments were to be held at a level specified in some detail in the Treaty (84,000 rifles, 792 heavy machine guns, 84 howitzers, and so on). Munitions were similarly limited, and all excess arms and munitions were to be surrendered to the Allies. Germany undertook to notify the Allies of the location of all plants manufacturing arms and munitions and to close down those the Allies required. Germany was also to disclose the location and nature of all fixed forts, with a description of their armaments. Importation of arms into Germany was prohibited, as was the manufacture of poison gases, the nature and mode of manufacture of which Germany was to disclose to the Allies (Arts. 164–172 and Tables 1–3 in Part V, Section I). A 50-kilometer-wide zone east of the Rhine was to be demilitarized at specified times (Arts. 42–44, 180). Universal compulsory military service was abolished: The German Army was to be based upon long-term enlistments. All mobilization measures were prohibited; and Germany was also forbidden to send military attachés or missions abroad and must prevent her nationals from serving in the armed forces of other countries. Military schools and the like were to be held to a minimum (Arts. 173–179).

The German Navy was to have no submarines; and its strength must not exceed 6 battleships, 6 light cruisers, 12 destroyers, and 12 torpedo boats, with a personnel strength of no more than 15,000 men of whom no more than 1500 were to be officers (Arts. 181–3). Enumerated warships and other ships in excess of the limit were to be surrendered to the Allies, along with all submarines and their docks and construction sites (Arts. 184–191). The Navy was to sweep the North Sea of mines (Art. 193).

159 Martens (N.R.), 3° Série, *op. cit.,* Vol. 11, pp. 323–677. See also pp. 677–85 and Temperley, *op. cit.,* Vol. 3, pp. 105–336. The Annexes appear on pp. 337–46.

Like the Army, the Navy was to be organized on the basis of long-term enlistments (Art. 194). Fortifications that could deny free access to the Baltic were to be razed, and this included the demilitarization of Heligoland (Arts. 115, 195–6).

Germany was to have no military or naval air forces. Within two months of signature, all air force personnel were to be demobilized (Arts. 198–9). Importation or manufacture of aircraft was forbidden, and surrender of specified materials was required (Arts. 201–2). However, the wording of the prohibitions did not deny to Germany the right to maintain a civil aviation force. Landing rights and overflights by Allied aircraft as well as aviation regulations were provided for in Articles 313–320. In respect of internal aviation, the Allies were to have most-favored-nation rights (Art. 318).

Ad hoc inter-Allied Commissions of Control were to oversee the implementation of the military clauses for Germany. The Commissions could establish their base of operations at the German capital and were to be permitted to move freely throughout Germany. Their operating expenses were to be borne by the Germans (Arts. 203–210). Repatriation of all prisoners of war and interned civilians was to be supervised by a commission with Allied and German representatives. The parties waived their claims for maintenance costs; but Germany was to bear the costs of repatriation and furnish the necessary transportation (Arts. 214–224).

POLITICAL CLAUSES: Articles 27–30 defined the borders of postwar Germany. East Prussia was severed from Germany proper. To France went the Alsace-Lorraine (Arts. 51–79 and Annex to Part 3, Section 5); to Belgium, Eupen-Malmedy (Art. 34) and Moresnet (Arts. 32–33). The Saar was placed under League trusteeship for 15 years (with title to the mines of the Saar vested in France) (Arts. 45–46 and Annex to Part 3, Section 4). At the end of the 15-year period, a plebiscite would be held to determine the political disposition of the Saar. Upper Silesia was to be divided between Germany and Poland on the basis of the results of a plebiscite (Art. 88 and Annex to Part 3, Section 8). Luxemburg was excluded from the Zollverein; and Germany promised to respect the Duchy's neutrality (Arts. 40–1). Germany also agreed to accept whatever regime the Allies, Belgium, and the Netherlands negotiated to replace the Treaties of 1839, establishing Belgium's prewar juridical status (Art. 31). She also agreed to respect the independence of Austria (Art. 80) and the new states of Czechoslovakia and Poland, and their boundaries as fixed by the Allies (Arts. 81–3, 87–8). She renounced title to Memel and a defined area including the city of Danzig (Arts. 99–100) and ceded to the Allies a part of the old Duchy of Schleswig, where a plebiscite was to be held to determine the wishes of the population respecting annexation by Denmark (Arts. 109–114). Germany also renounced sovereignty over her colonies in favor of the Allies (Arts. 118–127). She undertook to respect whatever arrangements the Allies had made, or might make, with

Turkey, Bulgaria, and Russia (Arts. 116–7, 155). She renounced all capitulations and extraterritorial rights and specified rights and privileges in China (Arts. 128f), Siam (Arts. 135f), Liberia (Arts. 138–40), Morocco (Arts. 141f), and Egypt (Arts. 147f), and recognized the French Protectorate over Morocco and the British Protectorate over Egypt. Japan was Germany's successor to special rights in the Shantung Peninsula of China (Arts. 156–8).

In the transfers of territories, the draftsmen of the Treaty invariably provided terms requisite to the accomplishment of the transfers. Included here were: nationality provisions (e.g., who retained their German nationality, who gained—or could gain—a new nationality);[160] regulations for resident German nationals;[161] waivers by Germany of claims for compensation for confiscated property or the internment of German nationals;[162] transmissions of archives and documents;[163] disposition of properties (what public property went to the new sovereign, for example);[164] and allocation of the public debt.[165] The provisions governing the plebiscites were often quite detailed, with procedures for voting, delimitation of areas subject to plebiscites, and administration vested in International commissions.[166] Boundary commissions were established for the Saar (Art. 48), Poland (Art. 87), and Danzig (Art. 101). Germany and Poland agreed to negotiate treaties regulating railroads and communications facilities across the Danzig corridor and Silesia (Arts. 89, 98). Detailed provisions for the government of the Saar and French ownership of the Saar coal mines (Chaps. 1, 2, Annex to Section 4, Part 3) and the status of Danzig were also included in the Treaty. Danzig was to be a free city under the protection of the League, with a constitution drawn up by representatives of the city in consultation with a League High Commissioner (Arts. 102–3). A treaty between Poland and Danzig (and the Allies) was to be negotiated in order to regulate the City's commercial relations with Poland (Art. 104).

160 In respect of the Alsace-Lorraine, see the Annex to Section 5, Part 3; for Belgium, see Arts. 36–38; for Czechoslovakia, see Arts. 84–85; Poland, Art. 91; Danzig, Art. 105; Schleswig, Arts. 112–113.

161 For the former German Colonies, see Art. 122; for Morocco, Art. 143; Egypt, Art. 149.

162 For Siam, see Art. 133; for China, Art. 137.

163 For the Alsace-Lorraine, see Art. 52; for Shantung, Art. 158.

164 For the Alsace-Lorraine, see Arts. 256, 56, 60 f.; for Upper Silesia, Art. 90; for Danzig, Art. 107; the former German Colonies, Art. 120; China, Arts. 130–131; Siam, Art. 136; Morocco, Art. 144; Egypt, Art. 153; Shantung, Art. 157.

165 For the Alsace-Lorraine, see Arts. 55, 77, 254–255, 257; for Czechoslovakia, Art. 86; Poland, Art. 92; Danzig, Art. 108; Schleswig, Art. 114; Egypt, Art. 151.

166 For Silesia, see Art. 88; for East Prussia, Arts. 95–97; Schleswig, Arts. 109–111; for the Saar, Chapter 3 of the Annex to Section 4, Part 3.

In Part 12 of the Treaty, Germany obligated herself to insure freedom of transit for all persons, goods, vessels, and mails originating with or traveling to any of the Allied powers across her territories (Arts. 321–30; 365–375 specifically concerned railroads). The Elbe, Oder, Niemen, and Danube were declared to be international rivers. Riparian states were given rather specific rights and duties respecting these rivers; and commissions for the Elbe, Oder, and Niemen were established to regulate the international river regimes (Arts. 331–45). The competence and duties of the older Danube, Rhine, and Moselle commissions were elaborated, somewhat to the prejudice of Germany's former rights (Arts. 346–62). In the ports of Hamburg and Stettin, Germany was required to lease free zones to Czechoslovakia (Arts. 363–64). The Kiel Canal was open to the vessels of all states at peace with Germany, on a footing of equality in respect of charges, inspection, disembarcation of passengers, and use of facilities (Arts. 380–86). Commerce and shipping between the Allies and Germany was to be re-established on a most-favored-nation basis, and in no case was Germany to discriminate against the commerce of the Allies (Arts. 264–275). If Germany engaged in international trade, she ". . . shall not . . . be deemed to have any rights, privileges or immunities of sovereignty" (Art. 281).

The rationale for the reparations Germany was required to pay was contained in Article 231:

"The Allied and Associated Governments affirm and Germany accepts the responsibility of Germany and her allies for causing all the loss and damage to which the Allies and Associated Governments and their nationals have been subjected as a consequence of the war imposed upon them by the aggression of Germany and her allies." Thus, Germany was required to reimburse Belgium for all sums borrowed by the government of the latter from the Allies (Art. 232), make restitution for all cash, securities, animals, documents, and objects taken during the war (Arts. 238–9, 245–47), and pay ". . . compensation for all damage done to the civilian population of the Allied and Associated Powers and to their property . . ." (Art. 232). A Reparations Commission was established to determine the amount of reparations Germany must pay, draw up a schedule of payments, and apply the principles of the Treaty in their deliberations (Arts. 233–244). Annexes spelled out in some detail the competence of the Reparations Commission and the classes of damages for which Germany must make reparation.[167] Finally, Germany agreed

---

167 The classes of damages included: personal injuries and death as a result of acts of war, cruelty, or mistreatment; pensions and compensation to members of the Allied armed forces (and the dependents of the members); costs of aid to prisoners of war; family allowances for persons mobilized during the war; and all damages to private property.

to replace losses to the merchant marine and fishing fleets of the Allies as a result of the war, to make delivery of specified amounts of coal, dyes, and drugs, and to renounce in favor of the Allies identified submarine cables (Annexes 3, 5–7 to Part 8, Section 1). Part 9 established priorities upon the German Treasury to insure payment of reparations and occupation costs. It also contained other financial provisions (Arts. 259–63).

The Allies expressed their intent to try William II for offenses against international morality and the sanctity of treaties (Art. 227). Germany recognized the right of the Allies to try persons for "acts in violation of the laws and customs of war" and agreed to turn over accused persons for trial (Arts. 228, 229–30).

The Covenant of the League of Nations, a quite complex collective security organization, was incorporated in Part I of the Treaty (together with a list of original members and states invited to accede).[168] An International Labor Organization, a functional international organization, was established in Part 13.

Apart from the terms already discussed, others provided a basis for the restoration of relations between the former belligerents. The list of treaties in force and those terminated was detailed (Arts. 282–295). These provisions also included a clause according to which the Allies could notify Germany of other bilateral treaties they wished to renew (Art. 289). Other terms related to the liquidation of debts of nationals of the belligerents (Art. 296 and Annex); private and industrial property (Arts. 297–298 and Annex, 306–311); and the status of judgments and contracts including contracts of insurance (Arts. 299–303 and Annex). A Mixed Arbitral Tribunal, with representatives of Germany and the Allies, was established to administer these provisions and determine the validity of private claims of nationals of any of the former belligerents (Arts. 304–5 and Annex).

Germany undertook to respect the treaties the Allies might make with her wartime allies (Art. 434). She also barred all claims against any of the Allies arising out of the war (Art. 439).

As a guarantee, German territory west of the Rhine was to be occupied by Allied troops for 15 years, with substantial evacuations every 5 years, subject however to the stipulation that if ". . . the guarantees against unprovoked aggression by Germany are not considered sufficient by the Allied and Associated Governments, the evacuation of the occupying troops may be delayed to the extent regarded as necessary for the purpose of obtaining the required guarantees" (Art. 429). If the Reparation Commission found that Germany had failed to fulfill its obligations respecting reparations, during or after the occupation, the Allies were to

168 Temperley, *op. cit.*, Vol. 2, pp. 21–39; Vol. 3, pp. 51–65, 111–23 (containing the Covenant); Vol. 6, pp. 426–538. Walters, *op. cit.*, pp. 15–80 and *passim*.

be permitted to reoccupy those areas (Art. 430). Germany bore the costs of the occupation (Art. 249). An agreement among France, Belgium, Britain, the United States, and Germany detailed the nature of the occupation regime and was incorporated as Annex 3 in the Peace Treaty. Apart from the security guarantees obtained by being a member of the League, France sought additional (and indeed more substantial) guarantees from Britain and the U.S. She secured these—or thought for a time she had—in the form of two bilateral treaties with her two allies. The treaties were also made a party of the Versailles Treaty (Annexes 1 and 2).[169] According to their terms, Britain and the U.S. would immediately come to the aid of France in the event Germany committed an unprovoked act of aggression against her. Britain ratified this treaty in November, 1919. The U.S. did not ratify it; and Britain declared herself relieved of her obligations because of the U.S. failure to ratify.

The Versailles Treaty was duly ratified by all the signatories except the United States. The senate having failed to give its consent to ratification, the U.S. moreover could not become a member of the League. On 25 August 1921, Germany and the U.S. concluded a short Treaty of Peace at Berlin, which incorporated by reference portions of the Versailles Treaty.[170]

Austria-Hungary

MILITARY SETTLEMENT:[171] The Allies signed an Armistice Protocol with Austria-Hungary on 3 November 1918, and from that date a cease-fire was in effect on land and on sea. The army of the then-disintegrating Empire was to be reduced immediately to 20 divisions that must withdraw to lines specified in the Protocol (essentially to within the prewar frontiers). The Allies would occupy ". . . such strategic points in Austria-Hungary at such times as they may deem necessary to enable them to conduct military operations or to maintain order" (Art. 4). Immediate repatriation, without reciprocity, of Allied prisoners was required, as was the surrender of all submarines and warships and the razing of fortifications. Other standard provisions were incorporated in the Protocol.

A separate Convention of 13 November regulated the conditions of the armistice as applied to Hungary.[172] Within 8 days, the Hungarian army was to evacuate to specified lines and then demobilize to a strength of not more than 8 divisions. The Allies were to have the right to occupy sites

---

169 Temperley, *op. cit.*, Vol. 3, pp. 337–40; Martens (N.R.), 3° Série, *op. cit.*, Vol. 16, pp. 3–5, 5–7.
170 *Ibid.*, Vol. 11, pp. 917–23. See also pp. 924–9.
171 *Ibid.*, Vol. 11, pp. 163–71; Temperley, *op. cit.*, Vol. 4, pp. 499–509.
172 Martens (N.R.), 3° Série, *op. cit.*, Vol. 11, pp. 183–5; Temperley, *op. cit.*, Vol. 4, pp. 509–11.

fixed by the Commander-in-Chief. Hungary was to place railroad em-
ployees and rolling stock, horses, ships, and military supplies, in specified
quantities, at the disposal of the Allies. Hungary must break off relations with Germany. And she must place postal services, transportation,
and communications facilities in the hands of the Allies, who were
enjoined, however, to refrain from interfering in the internal affairs of
Hungary.

The Treaty of Peace, signed at St. Germain-en-Laye on 10 September
1919, elaborated upon the basic demilitarization terms of the Armistice
Protocol.[173] The Austrian army was to be reduced to 30,000 effectives,
drawn from long-term enlistments. As in the German treaty, the armaments of this army were limited, military schools were regulated, the
importation of arms and munitions forbidden, and their manufacture
limited to one factory. Naval forces were also limited, and the air force
was abolished. Austrian military missions to other countries were prohibited. Inter-Allied Commissions of Control would supervise implementation of the terms of the military settlement. In other respects, the
St. Germain Treaty contained clauses almost identical to those of the
Versailles Treaty.

The military clauses of the *Treaty of Trianon,* signed on 4 June 1920,
were patterned after the Versailles Treaty and were also in almost all
respects similar to the Austrian treaty, except that the Hungarian army
was to have a strength of 35,000.[174]

POLITICAL SETTLEMENT: The Treaties of St. Germain and Trianon
formalized the breakup of the Habsburg Empire, applying the principle
of national self-determination, sometimes according to the desires of the
intermingled "nations" of Eastern Europe, sometimes according to the
exigencies of geography and the power political interests of the major
Allies, but never wholly logically—for it was impossible to apply that
principle logically in the Balkans and not create more problems than
could be solved. South Tyrol went to Italy; Croatia, Slovenia, Bosnia,
and Herzegovina joined Serbia (and later Montenegro) to form the new
Serb-Croat-Slovene State—the future Yugoslavia; Transylvania was ceded
to Roumania; and Slovakia to the new Czechoslovak State. Roumania
also gained the Banat, Bukovina, and Bessarabia (the latter from Russia). A plebiscite was to be held in the Klagenfurt area to determine
whether the inhabitants preferred to become nationals of Austria or
Yugoslavia. Hungary renounced right and title to Fiume and agreed to

173 The Treaty of Peace of St. Germain appears in Martens (N.R.), 3° Série,
   op. cit., Vol. 11, pp. 691–839. Temperley, *op. cit.,* Vol. 5, pp. 171–304 contains a useful table comparing the terms of the St. Germain and Trianon
   Treaties.
174 The text of the Treaty of Peace of Trianon appears in Martens (N.R.),
   3° Série, *op. cit.,* Vol. 12, pp. 423–565.

accept the disposition made of it by the Allies (who after bitter dispute left it to the diplomats of Italy and Yugoslavia to resolve, which they did in 1924 when Italy acquired most of the Istrian Peninsula).[175] The Burgenland was to be part of Austria, and rights to it were renounced by Hungary, although the latter was able to secure Sopron at a later date. Austrian independence was to be inalienable except as determined by the Council of the League. Her leaders were therefore to abstain from any act that might compromise that independence. Both Austria and Hungary acknowledged the obligatory force of the Peace Treaties of the Allies with Germany, Bulgaria, and Turkey, the annulment of the Treaties of Brest-Litovsk and Bucharest, and the settlements designed by the Allies for Belgium, Luxemburg, and Schleswig. They also agreed to recognize whatever settlements the Allies might reach with the government or governments of the former Russian Empire. The Allies reserved the rights of Russia to restitution and reparations. In respect of extra-European rights, Austria and Hungary renounced capitulations, special privileges, leases and extraterritorial rights in China, Siam, Egypt, and Morocco and recognized the Protectorates of Britain and France over the latter two states, respectively.

In their treaties, Austria and Hungary undertook to protect minorities within their borders. The peace treaties also included provisions for attributing nationality to persons within transferred territories or to others desiring to expatriate themselves (Austria, Arts. 70–82; Hungary, Arts. 61–66). Property of persons in the transferred territories was also protected (Austria, Arts. 263–275; Hungary, Arts. 246–259).

As in the case of Germany, both Austria and Hungary accepted responsibility for war losses incurred by the Allies and recognized the competence of the latter to try persons who were alleged to have violated the laws and customs of war. They also undertook to pay reparations in amounts determined by Reparation Commissions, according to procedures outlined in the Treaties. The definition of damages for which reparation must be made was as broadly drawn as that in the German Treaties. Restitution of sequestered objects, securities, animals, and other property was also to be made.

The financial provisions of the Treaties were particularly important because the Habsburg succession states were implicated in the arrangements. Thus, the public debts of Austria and Hungary were allocated between themselves and these states (A, Arts. 203–4; H, Arts. 186–7), and conversion of securities and currencies was to some extent permitted (A, Arts. 205–7; H, Arts. 188–190). Commerce was generally to be conducted

175 Curry, Muriel, *Italian Foreign Policy, 1918–1932* (London: Nicholson & Watson, 1932); Albrecht-Carrié, René, *Italy at the Paris Peace Conference* (New York: Columbia University Press, 1938); Lederer, I. J., *Yugoslavia at the Paris Peace Conference* (New Haven: Yale University Press, 1963).

on a most-favored-nation basis vis-à-vis the Allies. Poland and Czechoslovakia made a special undertaking to Hungary and Austria respecting the exportation of coal, foodstuffs, and other raw materials (A, Art. 224; H, Art. 207). Extensive provisions relative to debts and contracts were also incorporated in the Treaties.

The Covenant of the League of Nations was incoporated in the St. Germain and Trianon Treaties, as were the terms establishing the I.L.O. The Danube (from Ulm) and a portion of the Morava and Theiss Rivers were declared to be international rivers, subject to the special regimes defined by the Treaties and the public river law of Europe.

Mixed arbitral tribunals were to be formed to resolve problems and disputes that might arise under the economic and financial terms of the Treaties. In the event a dispute arose "between interested Powers with regard to the interpretation and application . . ." of provisions relating to ports, waterways, and railroads, the League was to resolve it.

Having failed to ratify either Treaty, the United States concluded modifications of them with Austria at Vienna (24 August 1921), and with Hungary at Budapest (29 August 1921). These instruments formally restored peace between these parties.[176]

Bulgaria

MILITARY SETTLEMENT:[177] The Armistice Convention with Bulgaria was signed on 29 September 1918. It was a simple document, requiring evacuation of Greece and Serbia. In Bulgaria, Bulgarian authorities would continue to govern, even in areas occupied by the Allies (but there, they would be under the control of Allied military authorities). The Bulgarian army was to be reduced to 3 divisions. Germany and Austria were to have 4 weeks to withdraw their troops from Bulgaria. The military clauses of the Peace Treaty of Neuilly-sur-Seine, signed on 27 November 1919, were contained in Part 4, their content almost duplicating those of the German and Austrian Treaties.[178] The maximum size of the Bulgarian army was 20,000 men, based solely upon long-term enlistments. A frontier guard of 3000 men was also permitted. Other limitations and prohibitions to insure the demilitarization of Bulgaria were similar to those for Germany. Bulgaria was permitted to have lightly-armed patrol craft for her coasts and the Danube.

POLITICAL SETTLEMENT: Bulgaria lost a slice of Dobrudja to Roumania and was cut off from the Aegean by the cession of the Thracian coast to Greece. She recognized the Serb-Croat-Slovene State, its borders and the

---

176 Martens (N.R.), 3° Série, *op. cit.*, Vol. 11, pp. 910–7; Vol. 12, pp. 566–70.

177 *Ibid.*, Vol. 11, pp. 126–7; Temperley, *op. cit.*, Vol. 4, pp. 511–3.

178 The text of the Treaty of Neuilly appears in Martens (N.R.), 3° Série, *op. cit.*, Vol. 12, pp. 323–423; Temperley, *op. cit.*, Vol. 5, pp. 305–58.

independence and integrity of Austria, Greece, Hungary, Poland, Roumania, and Czechoslovakia. She agreed to respect the rights of minorities
resident in Bulgaria and promised to implement a general amnesty. She
recognized the force of the peace treaties the Allies had concluded with
her former Central Power allies and undertook to recognize whatever
settlement the Allies might reach with the succession state or states of the
former Russian Empire. Bulgaria also recognized the French Protectorate
over Morocco and the British Protectorate over Egypt. Admitting that by
joining "in the war of aggression which Germany and Austria-Hungary
waged against the Allied and Associated Powers," she was responsible for
loss and damages suffered by them, Bulgaria agreed to pay reparations in
the amount of 2.25 billion gold francs. She also promised to restore
objects, animals, and securities taken from the states upon whose territories Bulgarian armies had been active. Reparation and restitution
procedures were similar to those contained in the Austrian and German
Treaties. The clauses relating to the restoration of commercial relations,
financial arrangements, contracts, debts, industrial property, and navigation were also patterned after the Austrian Treaty. The Covenant of
the League, the clauses establishing the I.L.O., and terms providing
procedures for the resolution of disputes arising out of the peace settlement and for its limited revision were also contained in the Treaty.

Turkey

MILITARY SETTLEMENT: An Armistice Convention was signed with
Turkey at Mudros on 30 October 1918.[179] Surrenders of garrisons
throughout the Empire were directed, and the Turkish army was ordered
demobilized to a strength necessary only for surveillance of the frontiers
and maintenance of internal order, the size of this army to be negotiated
at a future date. The Dardanelles and the Bosporus forts were to be
occupied by the Allies; and the straits were declared to be open. Prisoners
and interned Armenians were to be handed over to the Allies in Constantinople. The Allies had the right to occupy strategic points in
Turkey ". . . in the event of any situation arising which threatens the
security of the Allies" (Art. 7). They also reserved the right to occupy
Armenia if disorders arose there. Turkey was to withdraw her troops
from Persia and Trans-Caucasia. The Allies were to be given control over
Turkish railways and communications facilities. Finally, Turkey was
obligated to break off relations with Germany and Austria.

POLITICAL SETTLEMENT: As part of the settlement, the Allies had agreed
among themselves that Greece was to obtain Smyrna. The landing of
Greek troops there in May, 1919, precipitated a war between Greece and
Turkey and catalyzed a nationalist reaction in Turkey that eventually

179 Martens (N.R.), 3° Série, op. cit., Vol. 11, pp. 159–63; Temperley, op. cit.,
    Vol. 4, pp. 513–5.

led to the abolition of the Caliphate and a confrontation with Britain. The Allies occupied Constantinople in March, 1920, and induced the Porte to sign the Treaty of Sèvres on 10 August;[180] but this Treaty was never implemented (although many of its terms were incorporated in the Peace Treaty of Lausanne). France negotiated an agreement with the Kemalists in October, 1921.[181] By its terms, the signatories declared themselves to be at peace. France withdrew from Cilicia and retroceded part of Syria to Turkey. In April, 1922, Italy also made peace with Turkey in exchange for certain commercial advantages.[182] In September, French and Italian forces withdrew from the neutral zone on the Asian side of the Straits; British troops alone remained. Fortunately, Ataturk did not attack them, but rather concluded an armistice at Mudania on 11 October.[183] By its terms, demarcation lines between Greek and Allied forces on the one hand and Turkish forces on the other were established in Eastern Thrace and in Asia. Greek troops and civil servants were to withdraw within 15 days from all interior areas, their movement (and the withdrawals of Turkish units also) supervised by Inter-Allied forces. The latter were to withdraw within 30 days after the last Greek units had departed. Allied forces were permitted to remain within defined areas of the Constantinople and Gallipoli peninsulas until a peace treaty was signed.

The Treaty of Lausanne and its subsidiary conventions were signed on 24 July 1923 by Turkey, Great Britain (and the British Empire), France, Italy, Greece, Japan, Roumania, and the Serb-Croat-Slovene State;[184] and parts of the Financial and Economic sections were acceded to by Belgium and Portugal. (The United States had not been at war with Turkey and did not therefore sign any peace treaty with her.) Turkey renounced sovereignty over Egypt, Mesopotamia, Libya, Cyprus, Arabia, the Levant, and all territories other than the Anatolian Peninsula. She retained areas on both sides of the Straits, including Adrianople in Thrace, and Constantinople. Islands in the Aegean were ceded either to Greece or to Italy. The Allies agreed to the abolition of all capitulations and passed over their scheme for a separate Armenian state. Turkey agreed to a special regime for the Straits that guaranteed free transit for the ships of all nations in time of peace and established rules for transit during time of war. The Treaty, patterned after the Versailles Treaty,

---

180 Martens (N.R.), 3° Série, op. cit., Vol. 12, pp. 664–779; and see also pp. 779–809.
181 Ibid., pp. 826–32.
182 Gathorne-Hardy, G. M., A Short History of International Affairs (London: Oxford University Press, 1960), p. 121.
183 Martens (N.R.), 3° Série, op. cit., Vol. 13, pp. 336–8.
184 Ibid., Vol. 13, pp. 342–90. See also pp. 391 ff.

especially in the detailed regulations of its many subjects, included provisions for the protection of minorities in Turkey, the assumption of new nationalities for persons affected by territorial transfers, restitution of property seized during the war, payment of the Ottoman debt, establishment of mixed arbitral tribunals for the resolution of questions arising under the Treaty, and regulations governing communications and sanitation. With the ratification of the Treaty, Allied troops were withdrawn from Turkish territory. The negotiated character of the Lausanne Treaty (as opposed to the imposed Treaties of Versailles, Trianon, Neuilly and St. Germain) was clearly evident. Additional conventions respecting commerce, conditions of residence, business and jurisdiction, and the exchange of Greek and Turkish peoples were annexed to the Treaty— and were evidence of bargains among states intent upon establishing peace on a compromise basis.

New States: Poland, Czechoslovakia, and Yugoslavia signed treaties guaranteeing complete protection of the "life and liberty" of all inhabitants irrespective of their place of birth, nationality, language, race, or religion. (Because Roumania had so very many minority peoples within her borders, her policymakers also obligated their state in a similar way.) [185] Minorities were to have equal rights under law, and there was to be no discrimination in public employment or in the professions. The use of any language was to be permitted. In public schools in areas where minorities predominated, instruction was to be in the language of the minorities. The minorities' right to establish and control their own religious, social, and educational institutions was also recognized. Habitual residents of areas that made up the new states were declared to be nationals thereof, unless they desired to expatriate themselves. Another major section of these treaties dealt with regularization of diplomatic relations among the new states, the U.S., France, Japan, Italy, and Britain (and the Commonwealth). Hence, clauses relating to diplomatic representation, tariffs, navigation, communications, and transit were incorporated therein. In the Polish treaty, the Vistula was made an international River; in the Roumanian treaty, the Pruth was given that status. Czechoslovakia was required to give a special autonomous status to Ruthenia.

Several of the succession states of the Ottoman Empire and the colonies of Germany were not to have independence but were made mandates of the great powers. There were three types of mandates: *A* mandates, for states most advanced politically and economically (states almost ready for independence); *B* mandates, for states that appeared to the powers to require assistance and supervision (and which would attain independence eventually); and *C* mandates for entities that were to be adminis-

185 Temperley, *op. cit.,* Vol. 5, pp. 112–49, 432–70.

tered as part of the polity of the mandatory. Mandates were assigned as follows:

A Mandates: Lebanon and Syria to France; Iraq, Palestine, and Transjordan to Britain.

B Mandates: Togoland and the Cameroons to Britain and France; Tanganyika to Britain; Ruanda-Urundi to Belgium.

C Mandates: South West Africa to the Union of South Africa; The Marianas, Caroline, and Marshall Islands and the northeastern part of New Guinea to Australia; Western Samoa to the U.S.; and Nauru to Australia.

COMMENTS: Without doubt, the settlement of the First World War has been the most debated peace settlement in history. Assessments of it vary. Emotions are even yet kindled by questions of responsibility for the war, the adequacy of the settlement, the roles of the leading statesmen, and the soundness of the theories offered to justify the peace plans the negotiators proffered, as well as the inevitable compromises they made. That German elites were humiliated, there can be no doubt: they had anticipated a settlement in accordance with their own interpretation of the Fourteen Points. They had the settlement imposed upon them; they had been asked to admit their responsibility for the war, when they (quite rightly) believed that the Allies bore a share of the guilt; and they lost territory (including their colonies) to the Allies according to principles that were not applied equally to other states, most particularly France and Britain. If these penalties were to be justified by the fact that Germany lost the war, then the settlement could probably be criticized for not being stringent enough. As Palmer has written, the settlement was too lenient to destroy Germany, too severe to conciliate her.[186]

The functioning of the postwar state system in Europe and the security of its component states depended upon a strong France.[187] Yet, she was not strong enough to sustain the task. Moreover, France did not receive the security guarantees from Britain and the United States her policymakers deemed necessary as a part of the *quid pro quo* for the concessions they had made at the Paris Conference. (Clemenceau had relented in his demands against Germany because he was offered security treaties with the U.S. and Britain.) French policy toward Germany in the first decade after the war was stern. Indeed, it appeared to the Germans (and to some Englishmen and Americans) as vindictive and avaricious.

Given the economic state of the former Central Powers and of the whole of Europe—particularly when viewed in relation to the loans

186 Palmer, R. R., *A History of the Modern World*, 3rd Ed. (New York: Knopf, 1965), p. 702.

187 Seaman, L. C. B., *From Vienna to Versailles* (New York: Harper, 1963), p. 205.

made by the U.S. to her Allies—the reparations clauses of the treaties of peace were unrealistic, ultimately harmful to the international economic relations of Europe and the world, and contributed to the domestic financial instability of the Twenties.[188]

The Conference had created a host of new democracies in areas where democratic principles were alien to the peoples and elites. In their applying the principle of national self-determination, the conference decision-makers created new minorities to take the place of the old—although in all fairness we must recognize the nearly insurmountable task the diplomats faced in trying to create states from the remnants of the fallen empires. The peoples of the belligerents had been stirred by wartime propaganda, which played upon traditional animosities and created new hatreds even where they had not existed before. The memory of the war, the human and material losses, and the oftentime artificial antipathies that propaganda had aroused could be assuaged only by the passage of time. No settlement, however wise, could have done this alone. And it is in any case doubtful whether a human catastrophe like the First World War could ever be adequately settled. The League of Nations held out great hopes for preserving the peace; but even here there were portents of troubles. The defeated states were not members; and neither were the United States and the Soviet Union. Indeed, it boded ill that the latter two powers were not properly encompassed within the settlement and remained on the periphery. There were ambiguities and lacunae in the Covenant that could permit a state to resort to war legally. Moreover, the League could be fairly criticized as a device for preserving a status quo favoring Britain and France. Still, creative diplomacy and enlightened state policies could have cured whatever defects the League had, just as state egoism and hegemonic policies could destroy it.

In diplomatic history, the settlements produced by the Congress of Vienna, the Paris Peace Conference of 1919, and the Congresses of Westphalia, Nijmegen, Ryswick, Aix-la-Chapelle (1748), Utrecht and Rastadt represent more than just the termination of wars. They more or less reconstituted Europe: Nijmegen, Ryswick, Aix-la-Chapelle, and even Utrecht to a lesser extent than Westphalia, Vienna, and Paris (1919). Nonetheless, all ended wars that had transformed the state system in important ways. The latter three settlements (those of Group Two) were truly constitutions for the state systems of Europe and the world. The treaties of peace of the first group invariably incorporated references to the treaties of the principal preceding settlements, particularly the Peace

188 Keynes, J. M., *The Economic Consequences of the Peace* (New York: Harcourt, Brace, 1920) ; Burnett, P. M., *Reparations at the Paris Peace Conference from the Standpoint of the American Delegation* (New York: Columbia University Press, 1940) .

of Westphalia, the legal effects of which were to be felt for over a century and to whose authority lawyers and diplomats and even the clergy appealed when international disputes arose. The settlements of the Thirty Years' War, the Napoleonic Wars, and the First and Second World Wars—and to a somewhat lesser extent, the War of the Spanish Succession—were also constitutions in the usual sense of that word because they solidified relations among secular independent states, relations that had been rendered more fluid and more anarchic by system-transforming multilateral wars. They also established diplomatic and legal rules for international relations and determined the nature of future conflicts, not only among the former belligerents, but of other states in the state systems as well. They did of course fix the structure of the then-current system in terms of the territory and resources of the belligerents and war-oriented states and hence fixed their power positions and the images that policymaking elites held of their allies and competitors. The fact that the settlement of the First World War was followed by another major war within two decades and the fact that the settlement of the Second World War was stretched out over a period of more than two decades (and is even now still incomplete) do not in any way detract from the quality of these settlements as constitutions. They have furnished (and will continue to furnish) rules and principles for the governance of contemporary interstate relations.

Domestic Politics
and Peacemaking

In the first chapter, we noted that de-ideologization occurs if ideological or power political values are repudiated as a result of a change in either the government or the composition of the elites or if these values are put aside because others are now deemed more important. Ideological values may become less intensely held with the passage of time; and power political values may become outmoded or irrelevant, especially if the military situation worsens and the existence of the state is threatened. There is probably no generalized calculus enabling us to predict how and when de-ideologization will proceed far enough, when the important thresholds will be crossed, permitting negotiations and a settlement. But when the elites and decision-makers, and possibly the public in certain polities, hold intensely to the ideological and power political values over which the war is fought, peace will be impossible. The intensity of commitment to these values must diminish if a settlement is to be made, or even attempted.

Intensity of commitment to certain values is related to the will of the elites or the public to continue the war. We must, of course, appreciate the importance of possessing capabilities for waging war. After all, one object of war is to render the adversary incapable of fighting; his material incapacity will bring about the requisite devaluation, and his policy-makers will then decide to seek peace. But men have fought on long after a catastrophic reduction in their state's capabilities—if they had the *will* to do so. Hence, the central object of war must be to destroy the adversary's will to fight, in which case he will move to make peace even though he has sufficient war-making capabilities.

When we speak of de-ideologization or devaluation, we are at a macro-political level of analysis. If we are truly to understand the origins of peace, we must probe more deeply into the nature of the policymaking structure of the belligerents and investigate the domestic aspects of war termination. In doing so, we must be careful to distinguish three kinds of problems. The first is the particular character of the belligerents' domestic situation that permits or constrains the policymakers to bring the war to an end or prevents them from doing so. We deal with this situation in the first section, The Domestic Origins of Peace. The second problem of how the policymakers of a belligerent can influence the domestic political processes of their adversaries in order to demoralize them and weaken their bargaining positions is treated in the second section of this chapter, Transnational Pressures in the Domestic Peacemaking Process. Finally, there is the very broad subject of the relationship between domestic politics and the course and conduct of the war, the planning for peace, and peacemaking. In order to understand the nature of a war, it is necessary to inquire how various domestic groups or forces influence the decisions of the policymakers of belligerents and war-oriented actors. This should be done in all stages of the war: when the decision to go to war is made and when the war aims are adumbrated or revised, when strategy for the conduct of the war is formulated, and when policies relating to that strategy are implemented. Because these matters relate more to the origins of war and its conduct than to peacemaking and the structure of peace settlements, we will not deal with them in this essay. However, we do consider two other areas. Planning for peace, including the elaboration of possible and desirable structures of the postwar order and the means, both military and diplomatic, for realizing the designs, we deal with in the next chapter. In the last section of this chapter (Domestic Politics in the Negotiation of a Peace Settlement), we turn to the second area, the relationship between the peace settlement process and the groups and forces internal to the belligerent polity.

The Domestic Origins of Peace

The decision-makers of a belligerent actor are subject to a number of influences, both external and internal, that will, in various circumstances, move them to make peace or strengthen their resolve to continue to make war.[1] Externally, these influences derive, in part, from the war itself, its military and political impact, and the enemy's military operations and propaganda. External pressures also arise out of the relations with allies

1 This section of the chapter appeared in substantially its present form in *The Annals of the American Academy of Political and Social Science*, Vol. 392 (November, 1970), pp. 76–85, and was also entitled "The Domestic Origins of Peace." Permission to include this essay in the text of this chapter is gratefully acknowledged.

and certain war-oriented actors.[2] Internally, pressures upon decision-makers originate with the elites of a polity, the news media, the legislature (if any), and the public. But whether the decision-makers respond to such pressures is another matter entirely. That depends on the source, the intensity of the pressure, and other factors, including the personalities and the determination of the decision-makers, the structure and stability of the government (enabling the policymakers to resist, or compelling them to yield to the pressures), and the skill of the policymakers in neutralizing pressures—from any source.

The Public

Even in the democratic polity, public opinion establishes only broad limits to the exercise of authority by policy-makers. Hence, the latter usually enjoy wide discretion in formulating war and peace policies, discretion that can be broadened even further by manipulation of the news media (if that is possible), by patriotic appeals, or by techniques for dividing the opposition. Yet, having said this, we must recognize that public opinion is a force with which policy-makers must ultimately reckon, even in authoritarian or totalitarian polities. This is especially true when, in war, the public is called upon to make heavy material and personal sacrifices.

There are several situations that can lead a public to demand peace.

1. The sheer length of the war may be one, particularly where sacrifices in lives and material values have been great and where no end is in sight, or where the war has forced a lowering of the standard of living. In 1954, substantial segments of the French public came to demand an end to the protracted war in Indo-China against the Vietminh—and by 1958, an end to the Algerian war—both of which appeared to require years more of fighting without the promise of victory. By 1917, the Russian people were profoundly war-weary; army desertions were high, and the people enthusiastically supported any group that promised peace—Bolshevik, Menshevik, or Social Revolutionary. Disaffected Dutch public opinion pressed for a settlement of the Indonesian war in the late forties, a war that was having an adverse effect upon the Dutch economy.

Where other wars and domestic problems increase the level of tension within a polity, and the people attribute these difficulties to the war, there will be a demand for peace. The Disraeli government was brought down in the elections of 1880: Britain had experienced setbacks in the Afghan and Zulu wars, difficulty with the Irish and the Boers (eventuating in limited independence for the Transvaal), and a depression. And

2 Enough has been said, I think, about alliances (in Chapter 4) and war-oriented actors (in Chapters 6 and 7) to permit the reader to envision the sorts of external pressures that might move policymakers toward or away from peace.

racial, urban, and environmental problems in the United States in the sixties convinced many that the Vietnam war was to blame and that American disengagement was required.

2. Battlefield defeats may persuade the public that the war cannot be won or that it is simply too costly to continue. Included here are those defeats that are largely psychological—significant because of their impact upon public opinion, not because they have even locally resulted in the destruction of the military capabilities of the belligerent. The capture of Dien Bien Phu by the Vietminh in May, 1954, increased the demands for peace in Indo-China to shrill proportions in France.

3. Actual or threatened invasion of the territory of the belligerent may be enough to change opinion in favor of a peace that would prevent invasion and the losses inevitably associated with it. Or, where invasion has occurred, public opinion may favor a peace that would cut losses and prevent the country from being completely overrun. Allied bombing of Italian cities and the invasion of Sicily and Italy in the Second World War increased opposition to the continuation of the war; in 1943, this took the form of severe and extensive labor strikes.

4. A shift in the values of the majority or an influential minority of the people, leading them to believe that the war is illegal, immoral, or ineffective for achieving other values that are now deemed more important, can lead to a demand for peace. Italy again offers an example: The values and ideology of fascism seemed much less attractive and less valid to the Italian people in 1943 than they did in 1939. There were other, more important values to be preserved in 1943.

The Legislature

In polities in which the legislature is not entirely subservient to the will of the executive, the legislators' pressing for peace will very probably have some effect upon policymakers' war and peace policies. To the extent that the legislature is responsive to public opinion, the previously described situations that seem *to the people* to require peace or war will elicit a similar response from the legislators.

But to the list of war situations tending to shape public opinion, we add others in the case of the legislature. If, in the formulation of its war policies, the decision-makers have infringed upon any of the rights and prerogatives of the legislature—or seem to have done so, in the opinion of the legislators—there is sure to be opposition to those policies. Because the executive could be deemed to have violated the constitution, the legislature might not only oppose those policies specifically alleged to infringe upon its rights, it might come to oppose any war policies, including those within the executive's competence. The same results would follow if legislative leaders had determined that policies were being inefficiently or incompetently executed, with a wasteful expenditure of funds and lives. They could refuse their support and coöperation, hoping to have the executive and his advisers replaced.

The controversies between Parliament and the Stuart monarchs throughout the seventeenth century provide several illuminating examples of royal policies that Commons opposed because its members believed the king had infringed their prerogatives through arbitrary taxation and arrest, and later—during the Restoration—through mismanagement. The constitutional crises were often focused in Parliamentary opposition to wars or war policies of the Stuarts.

In recent United States history, the Korean war stimulated congressional resentment against the President, because Truman had sent troops to Korea without consulting Congress. Opposition, in part, took the form of support for the Bricker Amendment, a constitutional amendment that sought to limit the President's treaty-making powers. It ultimately failed to win Senate approval, because officials of the Eisenhower Administration showed themselves to be studiously solicitous of congressional opinion. In the more recent Vietnam war, many American legislators have felt that Johnson and Nixon have abused their "war powers" by committing troops to combat in Indo-China, and have infringed upon congressional prerogatives by failing to consult with legislative leaders or to ask for a declaration of war. The protracted character of both the Korean and Vietnam wars and the fact that neither offered the opportunity for a clear-cut victory were responsible, in part, for congressional exasperation.

The legislature is an institution; and in the democratic polity there are institutionalized means for the legislature to exert its influence more or less regularly upon the executive. Aside from elections and referenda, the public has no such formal means of access.

If the legislature wants peace, several means of pressing the policy-makers are available.

1. The legislature may threaten to withhold, or actually withhold, appropriations for war-related activities, military or otherwise. In the Second Anglo-Dutch War of 1664–1667, when lack of success humiliated the Commons, Parliament refused to vote liberal allowances for the war and established its right not only to vote supplies but also to audit accounts. And in the Third Anglo-Dutch War (1672–1674), realizing that the war was a design of Charles II to end Dutch independence and permit Catholic France to conquer Europe, Parliament withdrew England from the war. In 1864, the Prussian House of Representatives refused Bismarck funds for war with Denmark over Schleswig-Holstein because it regarded the war as antinational, part of a plan to hand the duchies over to the King of Denmark in order to avoid a popular form of government.

2. The legislature may also conduct public debate, carrying its opposi-

tion to the war policies of the executive directly to the elites or to the public, intending thereby to mobilize opinion against the war (and, if elections are at hand, some of the legislators may run for office against the incumbent decision-makers).

3. Whenever possible, the legislature can pass laws or resolutions that may hamper the executive in the implementation of his war policies; also, hearings can be scheduled with the same intention, and perhaps with the same effects. U.S. Senate hearings on Vietnam were scheduled for this purpose. The Reichstag passed the Erzberger Peace Resolution in July, 1917, although Chancellor Michaelis, to appease the Supreme Command, stated that he would be guided by his own interpretation of it. This deprived the resolution of the effect intended by the Socialists and center parties, who had been interested in a negotiated peace to end the First World War. In 1780, the House of Commons, resentful of the personal policies of George III, resolved that the influence of the crown in the conduct of the war against the American colonies was growing and that it ought to be diminished. Responding to Opposition demands for a negotiated peace, Lord North in December, 1781, agreed minimally that it would not be expedient to send more troops to North America.

4. In some polities, where the legislature is all-powerful, its members may vote "no confidence" in the executive, the ministers of which will then be compelled to resign. This constitutional power of the legislature will insure that the policymakers are responsive to its will; and the mere threat of a no-confidence vote will often be enough to modify official policy. (Hence Lord North's policy change, as noted.) With the resignation of the ministers, a new government can be formed, one that undoubtedly will adopt new war policies and move toward peace. In February, 1782, Commons adopted the Conway Resolution to end the war against the colonies; and Lord North asked the king for permission to resign—a permission ultimately given. The new Rockingham cabinet had as one of its principles independence for the American colonies. The French National Assembly in June, 1954, forced the resignation of Premier Laniel, in part because of his failure to end the war in Indo-China. They voted to install Pierre Mendès-France, who promised an "honorable settlement" within thirty days, or his resignation. He achieved a settlement.

In many polities, the legislature will be powerless to influence determined policymakers;[3] and even in democratic polities, in a wartime

3 Napoleon III had achieved some initial successes at great expense in an attempt to establish a Catholic and Latin Empire in Mexico in the early 1860s. Maximilian of Austria had been proclaimed Emperor of Mexico in 1863; but questions began to be raised in France about the wisdom of this "Great Idea" of the Emperor's. Thiers leading the Liberal Opposition in the Legislative Assembly (a body with few powers), denounced the Mexican adventure as

emergency, the executive may be able to ignore, prorogue, or dissolve an intransigent legislature. Charles I summoned the "Short Parliament" to vote taxes to support his war against the Scots. He dismissed the Parliament when it refused to do so; but he was forced to agree to the Peace of Ripon (1640) because of a lack of money. The techniques enumerated above thus remain significant for states where the legislatures play more than a decorative role.

Nonmilitary Elites

To the extent that the elites control the legislature through patronage or influence and mobilize the opinion of a majority of the general public, the legislature will itself be responsive to elite opinion. The discussion in the preceding sections is relevant here whenever the legislature does reflect elite attitudes, or whenever public opinion can be said to have been shaped by the elites. Situations likely to give rise to a desire for peace (or for a continuation of the war) on the part of the public will also be operative in the case of the elites—as members of the public.

But elites have special interests beyond their general interests as citizens of the state or as a faction at war. If the length of the war or the loss of resources threatens to deprive them of the values to which these particular interests attach, we may be sure that they will press the decision-makers to take measures to preserve those values—and if need be, to end the war in order to do so. Thus, for example, party leaders in a democratic polity will be especially sensitive to the opinion of their constituency; and if prolongation of the war is unpopular, the leaders will try to influence the decision-makers for an early end to the war, lest the war's unpopularity reduce their influence within the party or result in a falling away of the party's public support.

The split between the Independent and Conservative members of Parliament in 1648 (during the English Civil War) became focused on

---

wasteful, one that led to financial confusion at home and loss of prestige abroad. The Opposition tied the Mexican question (and others) to its demand for constitutional evolution toward guarantees of the "indispensable liberties" of the French people. Although Maximilian needed more French troops in 1865, Napoleon refused to send them because of the worsening European situation and because of threats from a United States that could now act more boldly abroad after the end of its Civil War.

Thus, the vocal Opposition in the Legislative Assembly had not been a major influence in Napoleon's decision; but it was a factor in the turmoil of domestic politics that very much disturbed the Emperor. In 1866, Napoleon decided to disengage gradually and to withdraw his troops from Mexico; and two months after the last French units departed, Maximilian was betrayed and executed (May, 1867).

the question of Parliamentary war policy. The Independents wanted to prosecute the war to a decisive conclusion; but the Conservatives, fearing the radicalism of the Independents and the possible costs to them if the Independents were to win a clearcut military victory, favored waging a defensive war; some even entered negotiations with the king to end hostilities. The Independents were able to prevail, and about one hundred Conservatives were excluded from Parliament in Pride's Purge. By 1708, Britain and its allies could be said to have won the War of the Spanish Succession against Louis XIV. But Whig demands upon the French king were excessive, and the war continued. The isolationist Tories opposed the Spanish policy of the Whigs, a policy that had led the Whigs to demand bases in France for future military action against Spain. Obtaining an election victory in 1710, after much intrigue (and the collapse of negotiations with the French once more—and again because of Whig demands), the Tories finally succeeded in opening peace negotiations.

Increasing domestic discontent was one of the reasons Napoleon III agreed to peace with Austria at Villafranca in 1859. While the Liberal Party supported the emperor's nationalities policies (thus encouraging Italian aspirations, among others), the Catholic Party's worst fears were confirmed when antipapal uprisings occurred in northern Italy. This party's opposition to a continuation of the war, together with the importunities of the empress and Count Walewski, French Minister of Foreign Affairs, persuaded Napoleon of the need for peace.

Business leaders and members of certain political and social groups will prefer—indeed, they often demand—peace overtures if the values for which they have associated or organized are threatened by a continuation of the war. This will be particularly true when invasion is imminent; but it will also be true where the social and economic impact of the war has been severe. Of course, demands for peace will not originate with these elites unless there has been a change in their value priorities: but they often become less ideologically dedicated to the war effort when their values are jeopardized. More than the public, whose interests tend to be general, amorphous, and frequently tied to non-material, ideological values (even in a late or costly phase of war), the elites, solicitous of the loss of their particular and concrete interests, could be impelled at an earlier time to compare the benefits of a longer war with the costs, in terms of the values in which they are interested—and conclude that peace is necessary.

News media owners and directors may serve the interests of one or another of the elite groups of which they are members or with whom they most closely identify. But they may also take a self-serving position, perhaps ideologically oriented, perhaps adopted for business reasons (exploiting war or peace sentiments in order to sell newspapers or air time). If the policy-makers have infringed the prerogatives of the media owners (by censorship or by harassing journalists), the media may then wage a campaign of blanket condemnation of war or peace policies, irrespective of their merit.

The efficacy of the news media lies in their ability to educate (or propagandize) the public and other elite groups. They can mobilize opposition or support; and in a democratic polity, the policymakers can ill afford to alienate all the media elites. In authoritarian or totalitarian polities, the news media are controlled by the incumbent regime, which can manipulate the content of the news to further the ends of its policies, whether for peace or for war. Controlled news can bring about de-ideologization, a lessening of the intensity with which the public and the elites hold to the values for which the war has been waged—just as it can stir up hatred of the enemy. In the First World War, government propaganda became an instrument of war; the news media misled the masses; and they were in part responsible for the length of the war, for the difficulty of peacemaking, and for the inadequacy of the peace settlements.[4]

Decision-Makers and Their Advisers

Division of opinion among the decision-makers and their advisers leads to ineffective and vacillating policies; and this is as true when the policy-makers ponder over whether they should move toward peace as it is at any other time. In June, 1940, the Reynaud cabinet was divided in the face of the rapid German advance through northern France. Ideological differences played a part. Some of the ministers had strong anti-Republican and anti-Marxist leanings and favored reaching a *modus vivendi* with Hitler. Others wanted to hold out as long as possible and make a stand in North Africa. Policy differences among the ministers went hand

4 We ought to include religious elites in our discussion of non-military elites. In some cases serving the interests of a transnational religion (e.g., Islam, Roman Catholicism), in others, the interests of a state church (e.g., Lutheranism, Anglicanism), religious elites have had, at various times, an important influence on policymakers' decisions for peace or for war. We distinguish two channels of influence for a transnational religion: 1. influence exerted by the head of the religion—for example, the successful mediation by Pope Nicholas V of the war between Venice and Milan in 1454 or the unsuccessful efforts of Pope Innocent X to prevent the Catholic princes from agreeing to the Peace of Westphalia (1648), ending the Thirty Years' War—and 2. the decentralized efforts of the subordinate or local clergy within a particular state. This is the equivalent of efforts by state churchmen to influence policymakers for peace. To the extent that religion, as an ideology, influences the war or peace policies of a belligerent, the religious elites will ordinarily have greater access to the decision-makers and perhaps also increased influence in shaping decisions.

in hand with an inability of French military leaders to agree upon a strategy to defend France. There seemed to be a paralysis of command. The cabinet finally voted to capitulate, Reynaud resigned, and Marshal Pétain formed a new government and requested an armistice.

In the late Fifties, successive French governments could neither prosecute the Algerian war in earnest nor negotiate a settlement. Such was the Constitution of the Fourth Republic that, with respect to an issue that divided the National Assembly and the cabinet (as the Algerian war had done), a premier could not remain in office long enough to follow a consistent plan or implement his own policies.

Strong Leadership. Strong and resolute leadership that avoids or prevents division of opinion among military leaders or civilian policymakers or deals forcefully with it when it does arise can have the opposite effect; and France again provides us with examples. President Charles de Gaulle, equipped with powers given him under the Constitution of the Fifth Republic, ended the Algerian war, initially allowing certain French Army commanders and the *colons* to be deceived about his intentions (they believed he would fight to retain Algeria), out-maneuvering them, and then neutralizing their opposition to Algerian independence. Clemenceau's leadership in the First World War stood not for peacemaking, but for a continuation of the war until it was won. He ruthlessly put down a mutiny of French troops in the spring of 1917, crushed labor strikes, arrested and prosecuted peace advocates, all in pursuing a policy against what he called "defeatism."

The strong personalities of Clemenceau and De Gaulle point up the importance for or against peace initiatives and peacemaking of the individual decision-maker's personality, his predilections, prejudices, and idiosyncrasies. A psychological study of belligerent leaders in any war would no doubt help explain why a decision to negotiate peace or continue the war had been made. An extreme example is that of Tsar Peter III: Such was his admiration for Frederick the Great that he saved Prussia from almost certain defeat at Russian hands in the Seven Years' War by making peace four months after his accession to the throne.

Where more than one policymaker is involved in a decision, personal conflicts between them can also play a vital part in a decision to move toward peace. But role differences are also important, and nowhere is this more evident than in the diverging perspectives and approach to the problems of a particular war, of military leaders on the one hand and civilian leaders on the other. Thus, while civilian leaders may begin to question the efficacy of war, we sometimes see military leaders pressing for a continuation of war because they believe that victory (or at least a limited success) is imminent or because they want an opportunity to vindicate the honor of the armed forces after a series of defeats or because the war has not provided sufficient glory for them. Louis Napoleon rejected an Austrian proposal for the settlement of the Crimean War in 1855 because he was afraid of the effects of a premature peace on the honor of the French Army. In the summer of 1945, Japanese military leaders feared the destruction of Japan, but yet they wanted to preserve their country's honor by fighting to the death. On the instructions of the Emperor, the Suzuki government sought ways to end the war; and while American armistice terms were eventually accepted, the Japanese peace-makers narrowly missed assassination by military extremists.

War can also serve the career goals of the officers of the armed forces and the reserves or improve their status in the polity. But we must be chary of too-easy generalizations. If a war were to threaten destruction of the army or the officer corps, it is conceivable that military advisers of the executive would come to favor peace initiatives. Thus, in September, 1918, Field Marshal Ludendorff notified the Kaiser and his chancellor, Prince Max of Baden, that it would be necessary to ask for an armistice. Although blaming civilian leaders and defeatism on the home front, he believed that a cease-fire was essential to preserve the integrity of the army and the officer corps.

The ministries of the polity's executive are usually organized along functional lines. The attitudes of the ministers and their staff or civil servants will to some extent be shaped by the effects of the war on the performance of their ministry's functions. Traditionally, the civilian directors of the military and the minister of war (if any) tend more to favor the views of the leaders of the armed forces than does the foreign minister; and internal functional ministries will tend to be concerned about the relative proportion of the budget allocated to war and to the domestic programs they supervise. A lengthy and costly war could per-suade the bureaucrats of the need for peace in order to allow continua-tion or expansion of the programs they administer.

In part because of human inertia, decision-makers often find it difficult to change their war policies and may even conclude that any change is indefensible. Embarking upon peace negotiations is a difficult enough decision; it requires a rethinking of war aims, extensive planning, and the formulation of goals of a possible peace settlement. Moreover, deci-sion-makers will often be loath to abandon policies they have origi-nated—because they are *their* policies, and abandonment is (or at least can be construed as) an admission of error or incompetence. Such an admission, because of the inferences the elites and the public draw from it, may have unpleasant consequences for the leaders, particularly in a war where costs have been high. The policymakers could be publicly condemned; they might lose their constituencies (popular or oligarchi-cal); and their political careers would probably be at an end. They might feel that history would hold them responsible for the war or for errors in judgment in the implementation of war policies. Anticipating these consequences, the policymakers may resist moves toward peace, hoping that the military situation will improve, that delay will allow time for diplomatic moves to succeed in obtaining foreign assistance or better conditions for peace negotiations, or that some untoward event will adversely affect the enemy's capacity to wage war.

Possible Misperceptions. Decision-makers can misperceive the war, the nature of the domestic and international environments, and the character of the allies and the adversary. Their image of the capabilities and intentions of the enemy could be that of an earlier stage of the war, if they have not adjusted to changed conditions with the passage of time. Cognitive dissonance may be at a low level—or be ignored; and this will be more likely to happen in a polity where news is controlled by the decision-makers, who come to believe in their own stereotypes of environmental conditions. A regime that has isolated itself from the public, that does not adequately monitor public or elite opinion, will not even have a valid image of its own domestic political situation. If the gap between image and reality grows too wide, rebellion and a *coup d'état* can occur; or the people may give up supporting the war effort, ministers of the executive resign, and the army refuse to fight.

The question of what is too wide a gap between image and reality depends upon the polity and the situation. Even in a democracy, with a free press and elites with access to the executive, misperceptions can occur. Certain cultural characteristics may be shared by all nationals, whether elites or decision-makers; and these may, to some extent, determine what in the environment is perceived and what is ignored. The culture may, in short, limit structurally the ability of its members to apprehend objective conditions—or at least certain kinds of conditions associated with the course and conduct of the war. Finally, whatever the nature of the polity and its cognitive limitations, even the smallest gap between image and reality can be fatal in certain situations—fatal either to the war effort or to the ability of the policymakers to survive politically within the polity.

Ideology also affects the way individuals perceive political and social action and can be responsible for misperceptions that prevent or discourage the policymakers from making moves toward a settlement of the war. The Protestant ideology of the members of the Long Parliament prevented an early settlement of the Civil War and the issues it raised. Hatred of foreigners and the attachment to the Chinese world view, which amounted to an ideology, coupled with the unique ideology of the Boxers, led to the so-called Boxer Rebellion, and so colored the outlook of the Empress Dowager and her advisers that they ignored peace feelers from commanders of the allied expeditionary force that was moving inexorably toward Peking. Only after the capital had been taken and the court had fled was a peace negotiated.

In certain circumstances ideology may promote peace: among belligerents of the same ideology, for example (particularly where ideological unity seems to be necessary because of threats from an antagonistic ideology). Thus, Cromwell was prompted to make peace with the Dutch in 1654 because he believed that all Protestant states should be united. Of course, too much cannot be made of the naturalness of peace between "co-ideological" states. Where policymakers deem political power factors more important than their ideology, *and they can control the people and the elites* (and perhaps rationalize decisions in ideological terms), they may make war on a state having the same official ideology. We find many examples of this during the wars—more or less religious wars—of the sixteenth and seventeenth centuries. Indeed, a policymaker so disposed might even ally his state to another with an antagonistic ideology, as Louis XIV, the Most Christian King of France, made an alliance with the Sultan of the Ottoman Empire against the Holy Roman Emperor.

Until the decision-makers themselves experience a shift in their value priorities—away from ideological values to either more modest or more pragmatic aims—they will refuse to make the decisions necessary for peace. The great ideologue, Lenin, was expeditiously pragmatic when it came to making peace with Germany in March, 1918. He did not let his ideology stand in the way of the hard peace of Brest-Litovsk, a peace that his regime needed to consolidate itself, a peace that Russian soldiers and Russian peasants demanded—but one that almost split the revolutionary leaders because it was, after all, a punitive peace with reactionaries and violated the principles of socialism.

Transnational Pressures in the Domestic Peacemaking Process

Public and elite opinion and the resolve of the military and civilian decision-makers can be influenced by activities largely under the control of the adversary. Domestic political forces within the polity of one belligerent (state A) can be manipulated by the adversary (B) in order to weaken A's determination or undermine its bargaining position. One obvious way would be for state B to inflict a decisive military defeat upon state A's armed forces. This method could be generalized to include all military operations by an adversary's forces designed deliberately to influence the domestic politics of state A so that policies more favorable to the attainment of B's war aims could be forced upon A's policymakers as they responded to the induced domestic forces. Of course, any defeat in the field will have some demoralizing effects upon the domestic situation of a belligerent. But there are military operations planned less to bring immediate tactical returns than to change elite or public opinion within the adversary's polity, bringing about a devaluation of war aims. The leaders of that belligerent, by virtue of the adversary's success, could find themselves in a position of having to cope with an unfavorable domestic political milieu, which would make the conduct of the war and the formulation of war policy more difficult and often embarrassing in view of the restrictions placed upon the leaders. In the French Indochina War, the Vietminh assault upon Dien Bien Phu was planned, in part, to secure a victory that would cause political disarray in Paris and strengthen the bargaining position of the communist delegations at the Geneva Conference on Indochina. The fall of the stronghold in May, 1954, was a severe psychological blow to the French, and increased the determination (and the numbers) of the parties bent on ending the war. Later, in 1968, in the Vietnam War, the Tet offensive produced a shock reaction within the United States and intensified demands for American withdrawal from Indochina. While the available evidence suggested that the Vietcong and the DRVN expected spontaneous uprisings in their favor to occur in the cities, there is no doubt that the attacks were also motivated by a desire to embarrass the Saigon government and strengthen the peace parties there and in Washington.

Included in the military techniques an adversary might employ to produce domestic pressures for peace or for concessions are the attack upon a state's cities (with the intention of demoralizing the inhabitants) ; surprise attacks on areas theretofore regarded as inaccessible or safe from the enemy's forces (again, the Tet offensive comes to mind, and the capture of English naval stations by the Dutch during negotiations to end the Anglo-Dutch War of 1664–1667) ; guerilla or partisan activities behind the lines of one belligerent; or inflicting an unanticipated defeat upon a unit of a state's elite forces. All these techniques presuppose that the adversary has the military capability to carry them out. Obviously, that is not always the case; lacking that capability, an adversary must employ other means if an attempt were to be made to influence the domestic politics of a state. We should also recognize that some of these military techniques might not succeed—and could backfire. The Prussian bombardment of Paris in the Franco-Prussian War was authorized by Bismarck to induce the French to surrender more quickly. It not only failed to bring this about, it aroused the indignation of the neutral states of Europe. And in the Second World War, the German bombing of London and the later Allied bombing of German cities actually stiffened the resolve of the inhabitants.

The adversary could also use certain diplomatic and political techniques to promote increased domestic pressures upon state A's policymakers. Peace feelers could be launched with the intention of persuading groups within the polity of the actor of the desire for peace on the part of the adversary's policymakers. (Certainly, Ho Chi Minh's peace feelers to the French in December, 1953, in the late stages of the French Indochina War were made with that purpose in mind.) If negotiations were actually to begin, the forum of the peace talks might be used for the same purpose: to point up the warlike proclivities of *A*'s policymakers. Proposals for resolution of the conflict, for mediation or arbitration by an international organization or by war-oriented states could cause disarray among *A*'s leaders and bring elite and public opinion to bear upon them. The 1632 peace plan of Gustavus Adolphus of Sweden during the Thirty Years' War was, in the opinion of some historians, designed primarily to create dissension among the German Princes of the Empire and win allies for the Swedish and Protestant cause against the Habsburgs. In any event, state *B*'s peace moves could indeed be accepted by various groups within state *A* as an opportunity to end a war they regarded as too costly, unjust, or protracted—or, on the other hand, could be rejected by other groups as insincere and capable of hindering the country's war effort. This very division of opinion could work to the benefit of the adversary.

A belligerent might attempt to catalyze civil war within the polity of an adversary, hoping thereby to strengthen its bargaining position through the domestic weakness of the latter. A modern example of this in the First World War was the German plan to weaken the Russian war effort and force the Czar to make a separate peace by acting in sympathy with rebel groups in the cities (and by returning Lenin to Russia in April, 1917). Another example is Spain's policy toward her enemy, France, at the end of the Thirty Years' War. While most of the states of Europe agreed to the Peace of Westphalia in 1648, the two powers remained at war. Spain stubbornly demanded the surrender to her of French conquests. She promoted dissension within France through a pro-Spanish party, and by appealing to those of the nobility and the middle classes who were tired of the war and angered by the prospect of increased taxes. (As Friedrich put it, the French crown ". . . in its bankrupt state had started to tax even those who were able to pay!") [5] The civil wars of the Fronde that ensued prevented the settlement of the Franco-Spanish War, because they distracted French arms and encouraged Spain to hope for a favorable outcome of the French internal strife. Mazarin and the Queen Regent eventually restored order (by 1653), but France and Spain did not make peace until 1659. The internal war in France had not, in the last analysis, served Spanish war aims; and the war's cost bankrupted Spain. [6]

Similarly divisive effects could be achieved if one state entered into negotiations with the allies of another state. Whether or not the talks were initiated with the genuine intention of reaching agreement upon a settlement, the fact that some allies were moving toward peace could

5 Friedrich, C. S., *The Age of the Baroque, 1610–1660* (New York: Harper, 1952), p. 237.

6 For a summary and analysis of the settlements of the Thirty Years' War, see pp. 379–92.

induce groups within the remaining actively belligerent states to press their policymakers to take more positive steps for peace. This is a special case of the dissolution and reversal of alliances discussed in Chapter 4.

Where there is strong sentiment for peace within a polity that is losing the war, the adversary (B) might offer to negotiate a reasonably generous peace provided that the peace forces replaced A's present leaders. This appeal for a *coup d'état* could, in some cases, weaken A's war efforts and, if successful, hasten a peace favorable to the adversary. Allied propaganda in the First World War promised a just peace for a "democratic Germany"; and during the negotiations leading to the armistice in the fall of 1918, Wilson's note to the Germans of 23 October established the precondition that led to the Kaiser's abdication.

> [The] President deems it his duty to say . . . that the nations of the world do not and can not trust the word of those who have hitherto been masters of German policy, and to point out once more that in concluding peace . . . the Government of the United States can not deal with any but veritable representatives of the German people who have been assured of a genuine constitutional standing as the real rulers of Germany.[7]

And in 1814, the realization that Britain and Austria favored a Bourbon restoration and would not make peace with Napoleon (or any Bonaparte) persuaded Marshal Marmont to place his corps at the disposal of the allied sovereigns and also induced Talleyrand and the Senate to call the brother of Louis XVI to the throne of France, in the name of the French people.

Even if the appeal for a change in government did not result in at least an attempted coup, state A's leaders might feel obliged to make concessions to the peace forces by moving toward peace.

One belligerent might also be able to persuade a collective security organization or a supranational authority, like the papacy for example, to condemn the other as an "aggressor," or to denounce the war as "unjust." Apart from the value of such a move in mobilizing the support of other states against the aggressor, it could also prompt groups within the denounced state to urge settlement in order to erase the stigma of the supranational authority's condemnation. However, League of Nations condemnation of the Japanese move into Manchuria and Italian aggression against Ethiopia in the Thirties failed either to deter those states or to arouse domestic opposition against their policymakers.

There is, finally, the use of propaganda as a means to exert pressure transnationally upon domestic public and elite opinion. Propaganda assumes many forms: radio broadcasts, leaflets, pamphlets, even moving pictures and literature. Effective propaganda can create difficulties for a

7 Dickinson, G. L., *Documents and Statements Relating to Peace Proposals and War Aims* (London: George Allen and Unwin, 1919), pp. 256–7.

state's leaders because, as a consequence of the news circulated by the adversary, they will have to contend with the opposition of an aroused, often articulate group of elites and with an increasingly hostile public opinion. There are, of course, some polities that are comparatively impermeable to the propaganda activities of an adversary. They achieve impermeability through censorship, jamming of radio broadcasts, punishing listeners of foreign broadcasts as the Germans punished listeners of British broadcasts in the Second World War (or by collecting private radios as did the Soviets shortly after the German invasion in 1941), and by restricting the movements of their citizens, particularly journalists and soldiers. Impermeability can also be achieved by counter-propaganda methods, such as circulating news by means of public loudspeakers, a technique employed by the Soviet Union in 1941 and more recently by the Communist Chinese, or by doctoring or slanting newspaper accounts of events. "Supervision" of newspapers antedates this century, of course: Metternich, for example, manipulated opinion within the Habsburg Empire during the Congress of Vienna through his control of the *Österreichische Beobachter;* and in the era before newspapers, the content of pamphlets was sometimes closely controlled by the authorities in order to promote their war aims. The pamphleteering of the antagonists, Spain and Portugal, during Philip's successful campaign to unify the Iberian peninsula in 1580 is a case in point: Philip's propagandists developed the theory of the Spanish king's hereditary rights to the Portuguese throne in their pamphlets; Ferdinand's propagandists, the disasters of Spanish rule in other countries—both efforts were supervised by the Kings' ministers.

Even in open polities, such measures are resorted to; and in a war for survival or in a war that is intensely ideologized the media elites and the policymakers often substantially distort news above and beyond the inevitable distortion present in any publication. Distortion occurs naturally where foreign news is collected from only one source: In the First World War, almost all the news of the war that appeared in American newspapers had been filtered through English censors, and most sources of news were controlled by the English. Since there was no German-American news service, the American perspective on the war was shaped largely by the English. The press in the American colonies was hard hit by the Stamp Act and the Townshend duties on paper; and the predominantly Whig publishers quickly came to regard themselves as the principal victims of British tyranny. They were loud in their demand for independence and propagandized "liberty" and justifications for rebellion. Undoubtedly, the publishers would have denied that they were propagandists; but the distortions in their reporting converted their papers into rather effective propagandistic instruments all the same.

Positive counter-propaganda techniques can also be used by officials to counteract the adversary's propaganda, in order to persuade the reader or listener to discount foreign news and rumor. Policymakers of even democratic polities have engaged in official propagandizing to mobilize their publics and neutralize enemy propaganda.[8] In the First World War, in fact, the information agencies of France and Britain that were organized (or those in being at the beginning of the war) were mainly concerned with home propaganda. They turned quickly to propagandizing neutrals, and shortly thereafter to their enemies.

Of particular interest to us are the effects of propaganda activities upon the peacemaking process. In the late stages of a war or during peace negotiations, the propaganda of either belligerent might be especially effective, for then the people and the armed forces are far more susceptible to appeals for peace. They are more likely to be war weary, disenchanted, or opposed to the war because of the losses they have sustained. In some cases, state B's propaganda could produce pressures for peace within state A that would compel A's policymakers either to make concessions favorable to B or to accept onerous peace terms. This was the intention of Bolshevik propaganda for peace in 1917; and although it did not succeed in ameliorating the terms of the Treaty of Brest-Litovsk, continued propaganda efforts afterwards promoted disaffection and the desire for peace within the Germany Army and considerably worried Allied policymakers as well. The millions of leaflets dropped behind German lines by the Allies in the summer of 1918 were designed to undermine the German Army's morale. The results are summed up briefly by Chambers:

> The German authorities made valiant efforts to neutralize this "poison raining down from God's clear sky." The warning and the imprecations in the German press and in army orders, and the offers of rewards for leaflets collected and threats of punishment for their concealment are all evidence of the efficacy of the Allied campaign. During the German retreat prisoners were constantly brought in with propaganda in their possession and confessed to its influence upon them.[9]

Propaganda is designed to promote the interests of each belligerent. It is self-serving. If hostile, it could hinder the peacemaking process, intensifying ideological conflicts (preventing de-ideologization), and persuading the parties that the other side had no real intention of reaching an adequate and binding settlement.

One party might demand that the other desist from its propaganda

8 Lasswell, H. D., *Propaganda Technique in the World War* (New York: Knopf, 1927). Smith, B. L., *et al.*, *Propaganda, Communication and Public Opinion* (Princeton: Princeton University Press, 1946) is an annotated bibliography of the subject.

9 Chambers, F. P., *The War Behind the War, 1914–1918* (London: Faber and Faber, 1939), p. 497.

activities as a precondition of its consent to negotiate a cease-fire and peace settlement. If the other party were to refuse, the war might continue; and if negotiations had actually begun, continued propagandizing could lead to a resumption of hostilities. Either states or factions, understanding the aggravating effects of propaganda, could reduce their activity just prior to or during peace talks; doing so could in fact be taken as a mutual token of good will or seriousness of intent in entering negotiations. Third-party mediators will undoubtedly try to persuade the belligerents of the importance of reducing their propaganda in order to produce conditions for an adequate settlement. Where neither belligerent is willing to forego propaganda directed against their adversary, and peace talks do continue, negotiations would take place against a more or less "cold war" background. Agreement upon some elements of the settlement, perhaps some rather vital parts, might be impossible to obtain. Where the military position of one on the beligerents is untenable, or where its defeat was complete and the victor imposed a settlement, the weaker party could probably not protract the peacemaking. After all, a defeated state will have to accept a peace, perhaps at any price, including the toleration of the victor's propaganda. But a propaganda campaign could have the effect of increasing the feeling of bitterness after the settlement. Resumption of normal postwar relations between the adversaries would not be a peace of reconciliation; and stability within the region of the war would be precarious. One need only recall the difficulties of peacemaking in 1919 and the subsequent instability of Eastern Europe deriving from the animosities between people aggravated by the propaganda of the First World War. The propaganda of the Entente Powers aimed to dissolve the Habsburg Empire and cultivated the nationalist sentiments of the peoples of the Balkans. It preached hatred of the Austrians, extolled the virtues of independence for each "nation," and exploited economic and cultural differences and even the racial prejudices of the peoples in the area. Within the victor states, public opinion was intensely anti-German and had been so inflamed by home propaganda that a punitive peace rather than a peace of reconciliation was imposed on Germany.

If propaganda designed for domestic consumption has too intensely ideologized the issues discussed at the peace conference, the other parties to the negotiations may fear that any agreement they reach would be a mere paper agreement, one that could not be implemented because of the condition of the public opinion of the state whose responsibility it is to implement them. If there were a basis for the suspicion that the policymakers do in fact control the media and are waging too intense an internal campaign against the adversaries and the possible terms of the settlement, the other parties could conclude that the policymakers are not genuinely interested in peace. They will be less disposed to compromise, and the peace talks will consequently be prolonged and the adequacy of the settlement impaired.

Domestic Politics in the Negotiation of a Peace Settlement

During negotiations for peace, domestic political groups can promote both cooperation among allies and compromise between adversaries through pressures upon policymakers and negotiators. They can also force the peacemakers into inflexible negotiating positions and cause the breakup of the peace conference. Thus, for the entire peacemaking process, we must be aware of the nature and intensity of domestic pressures upon the peacemakers in order to understand why they have followed a particular course of action.

Military Elites

Military elites are the repository of the honor of the country and of the armed forces: that is at least what military leaders believe. In the projected settlement, they will seek to lessen the impact of defeat and its implications for their country and their honor. If victorious, they will usually urge exploitation of the adversary to obtain maximum military advantage for their forces for a long time after the settlement. In the stalemate, they are apt to make the task of negotiating a compromise settlement very difficult for the policymakers because of their insistence upon merely military solutions. In polities where the military play an important role in policy formulation, their acquiescence is needed before any settlement can be accepted. And if the civilian policymakers were to agree to a settlement the military felt was dishonorable, they might attempt a *coup d'état,* which, if successful, would enable them to become the makers of peace policy. The Japanese staff officers who plotted the abortive coup against the Suzuki government in August, 1945, regarded the United States surrender terms as abhorrent. They believed that the Emperor was badly advised and that it would be better either to fight on for acceptable terms or to perish gloriously. They believed they must persuade the Emperor of his duty to Japan and his imperial ancestors or become themselves the Japanese policymakers.

The military elite's notion of an "acceptable" peace would very likely be more demanding than that of the civilians, so much so that either belligerent might have no other course but to continue combat until a military decision could be reached or until the military elites revised their concept of peace. In the Arrow War of 1860, a militaristic faction in the Chinese court wrecked peace talks by ordering an attack upon the Anglo-French negotiators, then traveling under a flag of truce. The faction wanted to continue resisting to prevent a settlement that would permit foreigners to trade in North China and conduct diplomacy directly with the court in Peking. The allies did resume hostilities; they captured the Chinese capital and obtained the terms the militarist faction sought to avoid. In 1920, Mustafa Kemal's coup was successful. He aroused first the army and then the Turkish people against the punitive Treaty of Sèvres, and against the Sultan who had consented to it. That Treaty purported to be a settlement of issues arising from Turkey's participation in the First World War on the side of the Central Powers. It awarded Smyrna to Greece and spheres of influence to France and Italy. After Kemal had forced the Greeks from Smyrna and Eastern Thrace, he won recognition of the independence and integrity of the "new" Turkey in the Treaty of Lausanne (1923).

Even in a polity where there is firm civilian control of the armed forces, military elites will invariably hold important advisory roles during the peace negotiations. Certainly, their technical advice will be required in the military phase of the settlement process; but even before, during preliminaries, we could expect the military to be concerned lest the civilian negotiators foreclose issues whose resolution they deem vital to the security of the state and the armed forces. It was, in part, such a concern that led the Prussian Chief of the General Staff, General Helmuth von Moltke, to contest Bismarck's advice and access to King William in the late stages of the Franco-Prussian war and to submit his own conceptions of the peace to the King. At one point, he dealt with a representative of the French government to discuss an armistice. Bismarck confronted the King with Moltke's tactics and succeeded in obtaining a directive ordering the General to give the Chancellor no further cause for complaint. It is interesting to note that the Prussian military wanted the Alsace-Lorraine; and even if Bismarck had not been disposed to give way on this point, he could not have prevailed, such was the strength of military (and elite) opinion on the question. During negotiations for a truce in January, 1971, Moltke told the Crown Prince that he wanted to fight "this nation of liars to the very end!" When the Prince asked about the political implications of such a policy, Moltke replied that he was ". . . concerned only with military matters."[10]

A policymaker determined to move toward peace can more easily ignore contrary military opinion in respect to *political* questions in the preliminary phase than during discussions of the cease-fire, deployment of troops, military administration, and demilitarization. On these matters, the military cannot be ignored; and it is here that they can more easily enlarge the areas of their advice, often encroaching upon purely political matters that might be only remotely connected to the military questions about which the military elites are (or claim to be) expert. In the political settlement phase, the advice of the military elites will undoubtedly be preferred when the negotiators deal with territorial and security questions. For here, the policymakers will be compelled to determine the

10 Howard, M. E., *The Franco-Prussian War* (London: Hart-Davis, 1962), p. 436.

probable consequences of settlement proposals for the security and prestige of the armed forces.

The possible role and effectiveness of military elites in the peace process depends upon a number of factors.

1. For example, how important are the military in the policymaking processes of the particular belligerent state or faction? What roles do the constitutions of these actors assign to the military elites in policymaking—if any? If their role is sufficiently important, we can, of course, treat the military as executive decision-makers; and indeed they might be *the* decision-makers, as in Cromwell's Protectorate, or more recently, in several states in the Middle East and Latin America.

2. Can the military become important extraconstitutionally; and if so, under what circumstances? If the military elites are denied legal access to the decision-making center, they could seize control of that center. In certain polities, the coup has become a not unusual form for the transfer of authority.

3. If the military elites played only advisory roles in policymaking, what positions do they hold, how important are these for peacemaking— or how important *can these positions be made* if filled by the skillful military politician or statesman? Do the military elites have access to the policymakers at least some of the time? The sheer availability of military opinion is certainly important; and so is the persuasiveness of the military advisor himself: one man might be able to convince the executive of the validity of his advice, another might not. Marshals Hindenburg and Ludendorff were so highly influential in their dealings with the Kaiser that one would not be too far wrong in saying that they controlled German foreign policy after 1916. In the First World War, General Robert Nivelle, who was named Commander-in-Chief of the French forces (replacing Joffre), was a very persuasive man. And Marshal Foch exercised immense influence at the Paris Peace Conference in 1919.

4. Can the military mobilize support from groups that are in a position to bring pressure to bear upon the policymakers? Other elites might support the military, which could compel the policymakers to accept their advice. Of course, they will very often meet with resistance from other elites within policymaking councils—from legislators perhaps, or from the news media; and we cannot forget that the military leaders might themselves disagree over policy and thereby reduce their own effectiveness.

5. Can the military advisors rely upon successes in the field or upon proved advice given in the past to persuade the executive of the soundness of their views? The past performance of the military elite will determine, to some extent, whether the policymakers will be willing to accept their counsel or give them key advisory roles. Success in this regard depends upon whether the armed forces had fought well or poorly, whether the

military leaders had commanded effectively, and whether the advice given by the leaders during the war had been shown to be prudent or imprudent, "right" or "wrong."

The Legislature, the Elites, and the Public

In polities where consent of the legislature is required for a peace settlement, legislative leaders can have a very great influence upon policymakers. They could determine the character of the peace plans, indirectly through pressures on the executive; directly, if appointed by the executive to take part in peace negotiations. Where the legislature will be called upon to pass treaty-implementing legislation, the policymakers might be constrained to consult closely with legislative leaders during peace talks. Legislative powers over trade regulations, appropriation bills, and powers of taxation could be used to present the resumption of relations between the former belligerents—and could hinder adequate implementation of the peace treaty's terms, thus causing a failure of the peace settlement. The most notable recent instance demonstrating the importance of the legislature in peacemaking is the American Senate's refusal to give its consent to the ratification of the Versailles Treaty. Had Wilson shown some willingness to compromise with anti-Treaty Senators and had he earlier appointed at least one of them to the American delegation to the Paris Peace Conference, it is probable that the débâcle of nonratification could have been avoided. In the settlement of the Thirty Years' War, an *ad hoc* quasi-legislature of the Holy Roman Empire was established when the Emperor invited representatives of the Estates to participate. *Collegia* of Electors and Princes sat at Münster and Osnabrück and greatly complicated the proceeding, as each decision for the Empire had to be approved by the *Collegia*.

During or just prior to peace talks, the mere threat to resort to devices to obstruct a particular kind of settlement might be enough to convince the policymakers to consult with legislative leaders and to accept their proposals for a settlement. Of course, the executive might have a compliant legislature, especially where the representatives belonged to the same party as the head of the government or where official policies have had wide popular appeal. But, even in the case of a refractory legislature, policymakers could take advantage of the division of opinion in that body to prevent its interference in the negotiations. Nevertheless, the legislative support that can be obtained often must be paid for in modified policies and by giving the legislators access to the peace planners. During negotiations to end the Seven Years' War, Lord Bute was able to stave off Pitt and outmaneuver or appease recalcitrant members of his own party by changing the composition of his cabinet. Bute's peace plans did incorporate *some* of Pitt's own proposals, however; and Bute, of course, took great pains not to antagonize his own party or the King. (This is not to say that he handled negotiations with the French ably or properly. He did not.) In a parliamentary form of government, like Great Britain's, the peacemakers are responsible to the cabinet, which must have the confidence of the parliament. The ministers must take care to preserve that confidence through justifications of their peace policies, by answering interpellations, or ultimately, by calling elections that might change the complexion of parliament in their favor.

As we have seen, the legislature will represent both popular and elite opinion. It might press for imposition of penalties upon the adversary or for the acquisition of territory in response to public demand for such. The Parliament elected in the "khaki elections" of December, 1918, reflected the anti-German sentiments of the English people, who demanded that Germany be made to pay heavily for the war. As to the size of reparations, discussions in the Council of Four revealed that ". . . (any) figure that would not frighten them [the Germans] would be below the figure with which he [Lloyd George] and M. Clemenceau could face their peoples in the present state of public opinion. . . ."[11] Legislative leaders might also ask the policymakers to include provisions in the peace treaty that would benefit certain groups or corporations variously affected by the war. Lord Shelburne's policy of reconciliation with the newly independent American colonies was motivated, in part, by his desire to benefit British commerce, just as Pitt's imperial policies in the Seven Years' War favored and were supported by the commercial classes, particularly London merchants. Shelburne was in a position to determine the content of the peace settlement; Pitt was not, since he was forced to resign before negotiations for peace had begun.

Regional interests will also be reflected in legislative efforts to influence the settlement process. The American delegation to the peace conference at Ghent in 1814 reflected sectional interests in the United States. The British accepted the principle of the *status quo ante bellum* with one exception: either the U.S. must relinquish fishing rights in Canadian waters *or* recognize the right of the British to navigate freely on the Mississippi. John Quincy Adams, from Massachusetts, opposed the former, as any good New Englander would have; Henry Clay, of Kentucky, no less vehemently opposed the latter. This difference led to a protracted squabble within the American delegation, which was only resolved when the British proposed that both problems be reserved for future discussions. As this example illustrates, intense debates among members of a particular state's delegation to peace talks can result when several interests or regions are represented and the values sought by each

11 Mowat, C. L. (ed.), *The New Cambridge Modern History,* Vol. 12 (Cambridge: Cambridge University Press, 1968), p. 218.

are incompatible. The conflicts of interest must be resolved if the delegation is to function properly.

Regional pressures upon the legislators will be particularly intense where portions of the state have been invaded or damaged or where the economy of these regions has suffered disproportionately relative to other areas. If state territory must be ceded (because of defeat), the inhabitants of that area and their representatives will undoubtedly clamour for alternative solutions or for measures to ameliorate the actual or threatened dislocations caused by the cession of territory.

In general, it is safe to say of public opinion that if war has been remote, with no damage to property within the state, there will be some (but not excessive) demand for peace, for an end to bloodshed, and for the benefits that would come with the lifting of wartime restrictions on consumption, commerce, and travel. Where war costs to the victor have been heavy, where the state has been invaded, and the people of the state or faction have suffered grievously and many lives been lost, the people (and their representatives) will press for a retributive peace. Such was true of the Italian people (among others) after the First World War. They strongly supported their leaders' demands for territories of the former Habsburg Empire as compensation for their war losses and for their contribution to the Entente war effort. Of course, even if no losses have been sustained, there will be a demand for compensations or for retribution if a public's expectations have been cultivated by propagandists. Propaganda had been so successful in Italy that after the Congress of Berlin in 1878, the Italian Foreign Minister was mobbed and subsequently thrown out of office because he returned without war spoils. (Italy had not even been a belligerent in the Russo-Turkish War that the congress of powers was convened to modify!)

Unfortunately, in terms of the potential success of the peace settlement as a basis for stability, the retributive element is the least important and most apt to cause future difficulties. The people and many (but certainly not all) members of the legislature will not usually concern themselves with the really important elements of the settlement (resumption of relations and adjustment of disputes) or with *technical* arrangements for security guarantees, territorial adjustments, and provisions for persons affected by the war, unless they (or their constituents) were directly affected by these provisions. Except in the matter of slave trade, Castlereagh had pretty much of a free hand at the Congress of Vienna, as public opinion and the Opposition were largely ignorant of continental affairs. However, when he tried to get cabinet consent to a treaty of guarantee, he failed because it was easily understood that such a treaty might lead to British involvement in a continental war, and opinion was opposed to any more foreign entanglements. This was a simple issue, upon which Castlereagh's opponents could focus.

Policymakers might propagandize a grand design for peace in an attempt to induce the public and the legislators to become interested in a complete and more adequate arrangement for peace.[12] Such was certainly the intention of the Fourteen Points and also of the Atlantic Charter (1941) and the United Nations Declaration (1942) of the Second World War. These concepts of peace were useful propaganda weapons, of course, but they were also undeniably sincere designs for what their proponents thought would be a better world. Another purpose, more political in nature, was the mobilization of internal opinion that could be used against parochial and vested interests that might press for self-serving peace terms, impairing the adequacy of the settlement.

Elites could influence policymakers by direct contact or indirectly through members of the legislature. Certain goals might better be secured by direct pressure upon the executives, assuming that the elites had access to them. Other goals can only be achieved through the legislature, particularly goals requiring the passage of enabling or regulatory legislation (those matters over which the legislature had constitutional control). The elites could use the legislative channel if its members owe a political debt to them or if the elites (news media elites, for example) mobilize public opinion for or against issues—and against legislators.

It is impossible to generalize about settlement questions that elites seek to have resolved in their favor. Some groups will be pragmatic, interested in those matters concerning the financial well-being of themselves or of their businesses. Others will be concerned for the honor of their country or for their own prestige or the prestige of the elites of their class; and still others will be interested in the proselytization of ideologies they have espoused, or in the pursuit of programs they believe will do justice to some or all the belligerents. We cannot really anticipate what elements of the settlement will prompt the elites to press their claims and what others will elicit a complete lack of interest. However, there have been those occasions when even the most *technical* questions, about which we would expect only the negotiators to be apprised, have been seized upon by the elites and proclaimed as vital to their programs. Thus, even highly technical, intricate questions can become intensely ideologized. Of course, what might impress one observer as an unusually technical problem might to another be an important matter affecting vital national interests. The United States negotiators at the Paris Peace Conference were startled by the complexities of Balkan politics and the exasperating debates over Teschen, the Banat, Klagenfurt, Fiume, and Eastern Galicia. To the leaders of the nations claiming the disputed territories, these matters were far from being technical.

We can summarize our discussion thus far, indicating schematically

12 On "designs for peace" (as peace plans), see Chapter 10.

how the analyst might undertake an inquiry into the problem of the impact of elite opinion upon peacemaking efforts.

1. Who are the elites, and what are their interests? Identification of the elites will also require a description of their reasons-for-being as groups or entities separate from other elites and the general public.

2. How are the interests of these elites related to the war aims of the state or faction and to the military and political elements of the prospective peace settlement?

3. How have the interests, and consequently the programs of action, of the elites been modified or otherwise influenced by the propaganda of the adversary or of their own policymakers or allies; by the character of the war—whether external or internal, simple, complex or multilateral; and by the fact that the war has been won, lost or stalemated?

4. How can the elite group make its influence felt? Do the elites have access to the policymakers; and if so, what is the character of that access? How can the policymakers be brought around to accept the program of the elites? Access to the policymakers must, after all, be coupled with an inclination on their part to accept the programs or proposals of the elites; and this inclination might be induced by threats to deprive the policymakers of political values, by the persuasiveness of the elite lobbyists, or by the promise of political rewards that elites are in a position to deliver.

What means are available to the executives to deny the elites access to them, or to avoid their proposals? In order to out-maneuver them, the policymakers could employ rewards and punishments, reliance upon other elites, and institutional devices or public opinion—if it could be mobilized.

Planning
for Peace

CHAPTER 11

Although there is apt to be a greater need (and greater impetus) to plan for the settlement of a multilateral war than for simple wars, policymakers of belligerents and war-oriented actors must make an effort to anticipate the end of even the simplist of wars, and adjust their domestic and foreign policies accordingly. They must formulate a plan for the preferred structure of the postwar world order (or for simple wars, the preferred character of local interstate relations). They must coordinate military operations with their peace plans in mind and arrive at a military strategy commensurate with their image of postwar interstate relations. They must also coordinate their policies with allies and decide upon the future of their wartime coalition. And they must adopt negotiating tactics and procedures designed to achieve their war aims and peace plans at the peace talks (insofar as these goals are achievable at this stage of the war). Finally, they will have to prepare the polity for peace. This includes estimating and allowing for the impact of the peace settlement upon domestic economic and social relations.

Simple external and internal wars will have minimal impact beyond the immediate belligerents, and although there may indeed be several war-oriented states interested in the outcome of the war, the settlement will be local, and the peace plans of the parties will be limited to problems the belligerents believe will arise in their own postwar relations. On the other hand, in wars that have become internationalized (complex and multilateral wars), the parties will be impelled to think in terms of world order, of the complex interrelation of many states, factions, and international organizations.

Statesmen who feel the need for considering and evaluating alternative structures of a world order do so in several ways:

1. Through discussions during the war with allies and friendly war-oriented states, discussions in which the peace plans of each of the parties are compared and tested against the standard of each party's national interests.

2. By concluding treaties with the closest allies whose war aims are most compatible with those of the moving party, the treaties predetermining certain features of a postwar world order for the signatories, and thereby for other states affected by such a predetermination.

3. Through a commission specifically established to study and weigh various policy alternatives and the possible forms of a world order, including requirements of each alternative form, its costs and consequences, its practicability and limitations.

Coordinated Peace Planning

Discussions with allies are invariably a feature of wartime coalition diplomacy. Coordination of military operations, agreement upon the strategic theory underlying the prosecution of the war, and resolution (if possible) of war aim incompatibilities are essential for the successful functioning of the coalition.[1] It is only natural then that allies should also come to consider the possible structure of postwar regional and world orders. When it appears that the allies will be victorious—when it is they who have the task of shaping the world into which they and their adversaries fit—the allies will undoubtedly be impelled to discuss peace planning collectively. States that are losing the war are under much less compulsion to do this since they may conclude that they would have little to say about future world order. Stalemated belligerents, on the other hand, will undoubtedly enter into discussion with their respective allies

---

1 During the Second World War, the Allies coordinated their military operations and strategic planning and, later, their peace planning to some extent. Feis, Herbert, *Churchill, Roosevelt, Stalin* (Princeton: Princeton University Press, 1957); Feis, Herbert, *Between War and Peace: The Potsdam Conference* (Princeton: Princeton University Press, 1960). Of course, whenever there are mechanisms for consultation among members of a coalition, there will be some discussion of plans for peace. Yet, *coordinated* peace planning during the Napoleonic Wars and the First World War was rudimentary compared to the joint planning of the Second World War. Nicolson, Harold, *The Congress of Vienna* (New York: Viking Press, 1961), pp. 119 f., 219 f.; Tillman, S. P., *Anglo-American Relations at the Paris Peace Conference* (Princeton: Princeton University Press, 1961); Trask, D. F., *The United States in the Supreme War Council: American War Aims and Interallied Strategy 1917–1918* (Middletown: Wesleyan University Press, 1961).

as they jockey for stronger negotiating positions at the forthcoming peace talks.

Procedural questions may arise during the course of the interallied peace planning, most of which could be easily resolved. Of course, there could be some delay over the question of the desirability of consulting specific war-oriented states, particularly if there were questions about their contribution to the war effort or their loyalty to the coalition, or if their war aims conflicted with any one of the allies. But by far the greatest proportion of the discussion will arise over the most important of substantive matters: the preferred form of the postwar order. In seeking to place itself in particular relationships with others, each state will want to secure gains realized in the war, reduce losses, obtain maximum security, and insure itself a viable future existence. It will, in short, continue to press for satisfaction of its war aims (perhaps changed or supplemented somewhat, now that peace is in view). Peace planning discussions could then be the scene of hard bargaining among the allies and their war-oriented associates. The outcome would vary. Conflicting images of regional or world order could be composed, of course; or they could lead to conflict between coalition partners. The continued need to prosecute the war might provide an incentive to compromise, however.

Predetermining Agreements

With the intention of guaranteeing the acquisition of certain values in the postwar period, to the extent possible, some of the allies might enter into treaties promising to support each other's claims.[2] These may be secret since to publish them could lead to early disagreements among the allies during the course of the war. Moreover, by keeping the treaties secret, the signatories might also hope to assure themselves of gains by preserving the integrity, and hence the effectiveness, of the alliance as the instrumentality for securing such gains by force of arms and later, during the peace talks, by the joint assertion of claims. Efforts to predetermine the postwar order, in however small a way, invariably affect nonsignatory states; and these parties could come to oppose the premises and consequences of the treaties if their interests were in any way compromised. If they were unified in their opposition (and they might not be if they needed the support of one of the signatories in support of their own claims), they might be able to vitiate the effects of the treaties during the coalition discussions of the peace plans or afterward at the peace talks. If not, the satisfaction of the signatories' claims would rankle the parties in

2 We see examples of such agreements in many of the wars analyzed in this study: among others, The War of the Spanish Succession, Chapter 9, pp. 357–66, and the First World War, pp. 405–28 (where the "Secret Treaties" profoundly affected the peacemaking process).

opposition; and to the extent that the settlement recognized such claims, it would be inadequate as to those parties. This could introduce a cause for discord in their postwar relations.

Planning Commissions

A state could establish a commission to reflect upon the postwar order, propose alternative peace plans, and study the problems and costs of each alternative.[3] The commission would be technical in the sense that it would have to be staffed by experts: It would include persons having knowledge of the areas affected by the war; it may also include economists, bankers, engineers, and lawyers. The executive decision-makers of the particular state would have to determine the composition of the commission, its budget, and therefore the size of its research staff. They might also decide to invite the allies to send commissioners, thereby assuring some measure of cooperation at this technical level. In fact, a joint allied commission of experts could provide the necessary technical information needed by allies in their political discussions at the ministerial or heads-of-state level. In addition to composition and budget, the decision-makers would have to delimit the competence of the commission and determine how its work product will be utilized. Thus, they must determine the relationship of the commission to other agencies of the government, to the military planners, to the peace negotiators, and to other interallied agencies of consultation. Decisions respecting these relationships are vital if the commission is to do more than produce reports that would merely be filed away for the use of curious scholars and if the technical expertise of the commissioners is to be used effectively by the policymakers and negotiators in their striving for a more complete and adequate peace settlement. Minimally, the commission must have its own executive or legislative *enabling act* providing general guidelines according to which it will function. But, to be truly effective, the commission must become a part of the domestic and interallied decision-making network.

It is conceivable that an existing international agency could provide the belligerents with the services of an acceptable technical peace planning commission. In fact, with the technical competence of functional organizations at its disposal, the agency might be able to provide a

3 A group or commission known as "The Inquiry" was formed in the United States to prepare for a peace settlement of the First World War. See Gelfand, L. E., *The Inquiry: American Preparations for Peace, 1917–1918* (New Haven: Yale University Press, 1963). The British also established a peace planning commission in the Foreign Office in the winter of 1916–1917 (*ibid.*, pp. 121–123), and the French formed a *Comité d'études* in early 1917 (*ibid.*, pp. 124 f.). These agencies did not coordinate their peace plans or negotiating strategies, although they did exchange information.

commission of unusual competence, one that could fulfill in desirable ways the peacemaking tasks assigned to it by the members. States would probably want rather complete control over peace plan formulation, however, and it is unlikely that they would rely solely upon an international commission. In other words, the states could accept the international commission as a supplement to their internal policymaking agencies.

Peace Plans

The greater the number of states or factions involved in a war, and the greater a war's extension and internationalization, the greater will be the felt need to *plan* for the peace. With increasing complexity, an increased number of actors will have been affected by the war, and postwar normalization of interstate (or faction-state) relations will be difficult and will have consequences for many parties. But, in the construction of images of interstate order before the settlement of the war, we must ask, for what kind of state are the peace planners doing the imagining? A great power has worldwide interests; and even if it were a belligerent in a simple external war, its policymakers would be apt to frame their peace plans with those worldwide interests in mind. They would tend to treat the simple external war and the projected settlement in the global setting of their state's relations with allies and adversaries. The small state, on the other hand, would have more limited interests. In the simple external war, it would be concerned with the local structure of interstate relations and with the regional balance of power. It might even limit its projections for peace to relations with a single adversary. However, in the multilateral war, the policymakers of the small state could be forced to broaden their peace planning horizons, because their own security and economic welfare would be tied to the resolution of a number of questions that concern areas well beyond their own immediate locality. The peace conference might find the small state's negotiators taking part—or at least attempting to take part—in discussions concerning regions geographically remote from their own, in technical questions that are the primary concern of other states. For the great power in a multilateral war, it would be absolutely essential for it to assume a thoroughly global perspective in its peace planning. It could not do otherwise, even though its policymakers might want to restrict their state's postwar involvement to certain areas of the world.

It is probable that in every state's projections of the shape of the postwar world, there will be a mixture of realism and idealism, of *realpolitik* and utopianism. The difficulty in determining the importance of each tendency, whether power political, idealistic, or some mixture of both, is complicated by the fact that statesmen are rarely candid about the policies they have adopted. Sometimes ideals are sincerely held; at other times, ideals are used to cloak the coldest realism. But the fact that statesmen feel they must appeal to ideals, even if insincerely proclaimed, does seem to show that they serve some purpose, not the least of which is the importance, not to say sacredness, of these ideals for elites and publics who are in a position to require the policymakers to justify themselves and their policies. We cannot stop to consider the psychological or socio-logical basis for the appeal of ideals. We only note that in the formula-tion of peace plans, in the earliest attempts to shape images of a regional or world order, policymakers' motivations are very complex. Their schemes for interstate order may be purely and simply utopian—al-though that is very unlikely. They may be based upon the most methodi-cal realpolitical calculations; they may be realistically based, but offered with a patina of idealism; or proponents may formulate a scheme they believe will benefit mankind, failing to recognize the self-serving quality of an ostensibly altruistic plan.[4]

The purely power political plan for peace will, of course, be directed to the security of the state and the satisfaction of important war aims by peaceful means.[5] But even the idealistic or utopian plan cannot ignore

---

4 An historical figure like Woodrow Wilson, who played such an important role in peacemaking, invites the thoughtful reader to inquire into the schemes for world order of a prominent leader whose motives are even yet controversial. Levin, N. J., Jr., *Woodrow Wilson and World Politics* (New York: Oxford University Press, 1968) ; Mayer, A. J., *Political Origins of the New Diplomacy, 1917–1918* (New Haven: Yale University Press, 1959), pp. 368 f. But others, Metternich or Castlereagh, for example, also challenge us to determine the balance of realism and idealism in plans for peace. Kissinger, H. A., *A World Restored* (New York: Grosset and Dunlap, 1964). Refer also to the section in Chapter 1 entitled "Values—Ideological and Power Political."

5 The term *security* is ambiguous and has been used in various ways by policy-makers. In examining a policy adopted to insure the security of a state, we should ask: how is the term being used? For what purposes is security required? The answers will be obvious when the survival of the state is in question; but frequently, survival itself seems to require (or is deemed to require) self-aggrandizing, even aggressive, policies in particular circumstances. *Security* might also refer to the operations of the state's nationals and businesses abroad—in guaranteed safety without interruption, for example. Thus, it be-comes necessary to pierce the veil of terminology used by the policymakers in the elaboration of their plans. Probably, we shall see them asking themselves how, in light of the current and future distribution of friendly and competitor states, they could realize their aim of achieving dominance, maintaining the status quo, or insuring the success of their ideology. The question will not be framed in such general terms, but will rather deal with specific states or specific regions. The term *security* could then be used by the policy-makers to indicate what guarantees would be necessary to enable their state to achieve the specific objectives they have decided upon—whether ideological, maintenance of the status quo, or dominance.

security: The plan of one who did would undoubtedly be discarded by the state's elites, as would the peace planner himself. To the end of achieving security, the policymakers must identify future enemies and friends and attempt to determine the intentions of their policymakers. They must assess the national capabilities or power of all actors and evaluate projections of power levels for each during the postwar period. They must then try to relate data on capabilities and intentions for each actor into one coherent plan for the peace settlement. The peace planners will no doubt have a preferred scheme for maximizing their security. They may anticipate that during the peace talks they may have to accept less than their initial demands, and indeed they should do so where they must bargain with allies or with competitors having at least some modicum of bargaining strength.

Amending the Clausewitz slogan, we could say that peace permits the achievement of a state's war aims by means other than use of force. Thus, in the framing of a peace plan, the policymakers will usually propose the settlement that would provide the setting most conducive to the continued, but peaceful, striving for the realization of those goals that were the objects of their war aims. If they were in a position of strength and their allies were cooperative, they could look for substantial and reasonably early success. If in a weak bargaining position, they would have to be patient, anticipating some returns for their efforts only after the lapse of a period of time. The difficulty in respect of so many of the generalizations in a study of this sort is "the exception," and there are exceptions here, of course. The war may have convinced the policymakers of the futility of seeking their war aims. They may, in fact, abandon them, and revise their value priorities. Nonetheless, evidence does show that leaders learn the lessons of history very slowly. Our generalization is therefore of more than passing interest. In postwar periods of peace, states do continue to compete for the values that were the objects of their war aims in the preceding war.

The peace plan will not be forged solely at the high altitudes of world politics. Domestic pressures will be extremely important. If, for example, a state's policymakers, concerned about the designs for regional dominance of an ally, were to determine on the basis of their state's security interests alone (excluding sentiment, moral arguments, or the desire to do justice) that a peace of reconciliation was necessary, their embittered elites or publics might force them to demand a vindictive peace. Public opinion might also prevent a democratic polity from cooperating with other states in the formation of a collective defense or collective security organization. And military elites in authoritarian or totalitarian polities could press their peace planners to demand territory and security guarantees that allies and adversaries alike regarded as excessive in the circumstances.

Because peace planners do not work solely for or among those who understand or accept the game of power politics, they often feel impelled to find principles (camouflaging principles, if you will) that are more acceptable. Indeed the war might have convinced them of the necessity and desirability of avoiding future wars, finding principles to promote cooperation among states, and adjusting disputes rather than permitting them to escalate into war. With these concerns in mind, the peace planners could try to institutionalize war prevention through collective security and functional international organizations. Or short of this, they could propose the establishment of a more or less formalized series of conferences among states to deal with future crises.[6] They might try to find some generally acceptable principles of regional or world order, recognition of which by the other interested states would provide a kind of community of interests, where adherence to common principles could constrain states to avoid conflict. Examples include such principles as *equilibrium and legitimacy* in the Napoleonic Wars, *making the world safe for democracy* or *national self-determination* at the end of the First World War, the *restitution of German liberty* during the Thirty Years' War, and *one world* or *the four freedoms* in the Second World War. While one might be hard put to find complete or even adequate application of these principles, they did at least mobilize elite and popular opinion in support of the war and the peace settlements.

A peace plan could be conceived on a grand or utopian scale. The state's policymakers might feel that empire was within their grasp after a war, particularly after a multilateral war. Fired by the desire to bring order and stability to the world, peace planners might hope to persuade others to accept their state's benign imperium.

World government has also been proposed as a suitable and desirable way of organizing the world of states. States would form a federation headed by a central government selected at regular intervals by the governments—and perhaps even the peoples—of all states. And, with the gradual advance of the technology of communications, it has been thought possible to create a genuine community of the world's peoples by appealing to what are supposed to be universally recognized principles of humanity. Thus, the interests of states would give way, after a period of education, to the interests of mankind. The presuppositions behind this form of world order are analogous to those of the natural law school of international law. The proponents thereof take the position that there are legal principles that peoples regard as binding upon all rational

6 Such conferences would be similar to those of war-oriented states discussed in Chapter 7. An example is the series of conferences held after 1815 by the great powers of Europe, which came to be known as the Concert of Europe, based upon Article 6 of the Final Act of the Congress of Vienna and the renewed Quadruple alliance.

beings, principles essential to harmony and cooperation against a refractory, even hostile cosmos, principles prerequisite to the survival of mankind and cultures threatened by increasingly efficient means for their destruction.

Peace plans may well be less all-encompassing than these, however; and in simple and complex wars they are indeed likely to be less grandiose. A great power might propose *spheres of influence* for itself and for other great powers. Like the world-empire solution, this scheme could be proposed for wholly self-serving ends, for example, the exploitation of states and peoples falling within the great power's area of administration. Yet, it could also be offered in the sincere belief (however incorrect in the circumstances) that control of a sphere by a great power would tend to preserve peace and enhance the prosperity of all peoples, the theory being that only great powers have the capability to administer a number of states and that a great power's responsible administration will reduce the anarchy in the relations of a multiplicity of separate states. The important decisions of international relations would then be made by a consortium of a relatively few great powers. It would probably be much easier to secure the agreement of half a dozen independent great powers than to secure a like agreement of thirty, or sixty, middle-range and small states. The state bent upon dominance might even prefer the sphere-of-influence plan for peace over the plan for empire; and if the putative imperial state could control the other great powers, it could afford to allow them to control their own spheres of influence, tacitly reserving the right to intervene anywhere if its vital interests should be threatened, or if events in any region were likely to undermine the established order.[7]

After a war, states might agree to form regional and functional organizations with limited membership, the most common form being the regional collective-defense organization. Such groupings of states (or alliances) have a long history, although not until the twentieth century have they rested upon a formal organizational apparatus.[8] Given a plurality of regional blocs of states, international relations becomes at least, in part, interbloc relations. Cooperation with allies in the formulation and execution of foreign policy will constitute a constraint, limiting the independence of individual states to some extent. Whether constraint of the collectivity will be a good thing or not is unpredictable. Bloc

7 See Liska, George, *Imperial America: The International Policies of Primacy* (Baltimore: Johns Hopkins Press, 1967); Liska, George, *War and Order: Reflections on Vietnam and History* (Baltimore: Johns Hopkins Press, 1968).

8 Hinsley, F. H., *Power and the Pursuit of Peace* (Cambridge: Cambridge University Press, 1967); Hodé, Jacques, *L'Idée de Fédération Internationale dans l'Histoire* (Paris: Editions de la Vie universitaire, 1921); Hemleben, S. J., *Plans for World Peace Through Six Centuries* (Chicago: University of Chicago Press, 1943).

coordination can as easily lead to a heightening of tensions as it can to the resolution of disputes. Great powers bent upon directing world political forces in their own interests, as an alternative to delimiting spheres of interest, usually attempt to control regional organizations and thereby achieve some measure of control over the small and middle-range member states. Of course, the policymakers of the latter eventually see through the schemes of the powers and try to coordinate collective efforts vis-à-vis the great power to enable their organization (or alliance) to act as the equivalent of a great power. If the smaller member states succeed in unifying themselves on foreign policy matters, the organization may indeed be a force to reckon with. Thus, in the 1960s, it was suggested that a truly unified Europe could come to be the competitor or balancer of the super-powers, the United States and the Soviet Union.

Human behavior, individual or collective, is always difficult to predict. In spite of this, peace planners often try to anticipate the probable nature of future disputes that are likely to give rise to war. If they were genuinely concerned to frame a plan for world or regional order, permitting statesmen to act positively to prevent future wars, they will tailor their conference or organizational modes of peacekeeping to the predicted character of the disputes. They might anticipate that one or more of the defeated adversaries (if such there were) will be the source of future tensions; and they could, perhaps unwisely, adopt collective defense measures against those states or restrict particular policy options open to them (through compulsory disarmament, for example, or trade embargoes, or some other disability upon their capacity to act autonomously in world affairs). The difficulty of predicting the form and sources of future disputes between states arises in part from the very inadequate understanding peace planners have of the probable nature of pressures for change that will build up in the postwar period. The settlement itself, as the law for interstate relations, will tend to favor the status quo; and even if provisions are wisely made for peaceful change, such arrangements will be intrinsically difficult to implement where status quo–oriented states regard it as in their interests to prevent change—or some form of it. We cannot get around the fact that at some point after the settlement, when the states that want change confront those that want to prevent it, both sides have to ask, How important is it to avoid war? The answer unfortunately might be that it isn't important at all. Nevertheless, the unevenly successful experiments in peacekeeping that men have tried have been directed to two ends: to persuade policymakers that it is indeed important in the circumstances to avoid war and that, if they were to conclude that war was beneficial or unavoidable, they would have to contend with some response from a collectivity—hopefully a community—of states.

Ideologies and Peace Plans

Ideologies often provide models of world order. While they may prescribe ideal or utopian images of interstate relations—starting with states as the basic units of their desired system—other sorts of ideologies often demand a radical restructuring of world political relations. The old order of states, being corrupt, must be discarded. Put another way, the *state* must be transcended. Communities of true believers must replace it; and peoples must come to accept the precepts of the ideology as their guide to social and political action. A war might very well have been fought over such an ideology, the success of which would have meant the unavoidable destruction of the status quo. If the ideological state were the victor, its peace plan would look toward the establishment of the ideology within the polities of the defeated states. If the ideological state were defeated, then the victors might plan to preside over the ideology's extirpation in the postwar era, as nearly as that could be accomplished. As we have seen, defeat could promote disenchantment with an ideology; victory, confidence in its principles. The success of the ideological state in one war will usually lead to the construction of a peace plan requiring the militant proselytization of the ideology to yet unaffected states and areas. Repeated successes lead to ever more ambitious peace plans, and these usually lead to more wars, until the spread of the ideology is stopped, either by defeat at the hands of adversary states or through loss of élan and confidence.

The techniques of peacekeeping and traditional diplomacy are sometime powerless to deal with a militant ideology. Passions are so intensely aroused that the threshold of de-ideologization often cannot be crossed, and peacemaking cannot progress. But more than that, the proponents of the ideology often scorn peacekeeping as unworthy and as the corrupt methods of an old order. They advocate violence, perhaps for the sake of violence or perhaps because it will more swiftly lead to the order they want. Or they rationalize violence because it is the necessary means to becoming "new men" or to creating "new communities" based upon human and communal relationships that will someday be devoid of conflict. Defeat of the ideological state or effective propaganda designed to bring about de-ideologization could allow peacemaking to proceed.

An ideology can be promoted or proselytized by direct confrontation; and an external war could result. But often, the ideological state will attempt to achieve its aims through subversion, by overturning the government of the opponent state, replacing it with an ideologically sympathetic faction. In other words, the ideologues promote internal war. It is possible that peace planners, recognizing the capability of this method for spreading an ideology, will want somehow to structure postwar relations in ways that will either promote or prevent internal wars for control of the polity. If the ideological state had not been defeated and its elites and leaders still had confidence in the efficacy of their ideology, they might incorporate schemes in their peace plan for promoting its spread. If the nonideological or counter-ideological states had been victorious or were in a strong bargaining position, they would undoubtedly want their peace plan to hold the ideology in check and foster de-ideologization. We could expect this sort of planning by the belligerents during the late stages of the complex internal or multilateral wars or by war-oriented actors after any internal war. The policymakers of the state actually affected by the internal war will indeed have a peace plan, the most vital one of all, namely, the continued existence and integrity of their state. In short, their peace plan would be the domestic plan for the postwar viability of the state after the disruptions of the internal war.

The following table adumbrates the ways in which peace planners might try to shape the postwar interrelations of states in the direction of either checking or promoting an ideology.

TABLE 11–1. General character of peace plans designed to affect the ideology.

Check the ideology	Promote the ideology
Issue a declaration that peace will be made only with a faction of the adversary state having a different ideology; that normalized relations in the postwar era require a faction of different ideology in control of the adversary states.	Make peace and normalize relations only with those states of identical or compatible ideologies.
Create institutions and procedures to deter or halt the intervention of an ideological actor in other states of different or antagonistic ideologies. (On the other hand, the states opposed to the ideology might favor a more aggressive strategy, incorporating loopholes in their provisions against intervention in order to enable them to support factions of different ideologies.)	Create situations and institutions that will permit easy intervention in other states where domestic conditions there indicate that the ideology might be successfully introduced.
Use propaganda and educational technique to catalyze de-ideologization, by showing the fallacies of the ideology or extolling other values (e.g., peace and domestic order, the benefits of "progress" or technology that the ideology allegedly denied the people of the ideological state).	Propagandize the ideology; extol its successes, play down its defeats and its internal inconsistencies.

TABLE 11–1.   (continued)

Check the ideology	Promote the ideology
Adopt power political policies designed to weaken the ideological "Mecca" state: do not resume normal relations; impose trade embargoes; create a collective defense pact aimed at the ideological state; take the territory or resources of the ideological state, if that is possible.	Strengthen the power position of the ideological state, and strengthen the ideology by purifying it and the ideological cadres.
Prevent external wars that will have the effect of spreading the ideology.	Plan for ideological external wars in circumstances, and with states, where they are likely to be won by the ideological state.

The Content of Peace Plans

It was suggested earlier that the content of a peace plan was related to three factors: the kind of state for which the peace planners formulated the plan (great power, middle-range or small state), whether that state was an active belligerent or merely war-oriented, and the type of war. We proceed to consider these relationships, very briefly and schematically, in the following tables.[9]

TABLE 11–2.   The peace plan of a great power as a function of the character of the war.

simple external war belligerent:	The plan will concern the future power positions of the great power and its adversary, and the possible nature of future relations with the adversary. It will be limited in scope *unless* (a) the war has in some way become related to other of the world-wide interests of the great power; (b) the power originally went to war in order to promote an already conceived, comprehensive plan for regional or world order; or (c) the war was regarded by the power's policymakers as one of a type they would like to avoid in the future. In any of these cases, the plan would then be of wider scope, commensurate with the breadth of the power's interests in other regions.

9 We assume that the war-oriented great power is war-oriented toward one faction in a simple internal war. If another state supports the other faction, we have, in effect, a proxy internal war.

The discussion subsumed under simple wars is also relevant to our consideration of the probable content of peace plans for actors in complex and multilateral wars.

By definition, a war-oriented state is an *intervenor-belligerent* in a complex internal war.

TABLE 11–2.   (*continued*)

war-oriented:	The plan will assess the prospective relations of the belligerents with each other, and their future power positions, as well as the great power's prospective relations with the belligerents. The plan will be limited in scope, unless any of the exceptions noted above holds, in which case, the plan would be substantially broader.
simple internal war belligerent:	If the power were afflicted with an internal war, the peace plan of either faction will tend mainly to be directed internally, to questions relating to the integrity and viability of the polity. This is certainly true of the incumbents. The insurgents will be concerned to achieve control, autonomy or independence. The plans of either faction might be broader if either were inclined toward some trans-national ideology, in which case each would plan to coordinate policies with co-ideological states or factions.
war-oriented:	We must ask why it was the great power had become interested in this internal war, for the answer to this question would very likely tell us a great deal about the peace plan. If the supported faction had been successful, the power's plan will continue to contain elements designed to promote its interests, originally its reasons for supporting the faction. If the non-supported faction had won, the power must find ways to cut its losses. In either case, the plan will address itself to the nature of future relations with either (or both) of the factions, and to the likelihood of internal disorder re-occurring. And since the reasons for assisting a faction may relate to the regional or world-wide interests of the great power, the plan must then also address itself to those interests, to the extent they have been affected by the internal war.
complex external war belligerent:	The plan must obviously encompass the relations within the alliance of which the power is a member (and this includes an estimate of the power positions and prospective policies of its partners). The great power must, therefore, take into account the peace plans of the allies; and it might even coordinate procedures for constructing a single alliance peace plan. The plan must deal with the adversary state's role in the world, and its relations with the allies and other states (and with the great power, of course). Thus, the plan will of necessity have to be more broadly conceived than in the case of the simple external war. The power might be constrained to modify its plan in the interests of alliance harmony (above and beyond the modifications inevitably required when negotiating with an adversary having some bargaining strength).

TABLE 11–2. (continued)

war-oriented:	As in the case of the simple internal war, the content of the plan will bear some relation to the reasons the power's policymakers had been interested in the course of the war, usually because of the effects a complex war will have upon its relations with other states. The plan is thus likely to be broadly conceived, reaching the many geographical and issue areas affected by the war.
complex internal war belligerent:	If the great power had been afflicted with an internal war, its plan must extend beyond domestic and interfaction relations, because of the active involvement of one or more other states. The future power positions and policies relative to the power of such states must also be anticipated.
war-oriented:	Where the great power has actively intervened in an internal war affecting another state, it will be interested in postwar relations between itself and the state (and in the interfaction relations, if any). The costs sustained in the war will impel the power to press its postwar plan for peace with vigor. That plan is apt to be quite broad for the alliance-faction war, for example. But that will also be true for the state-faction war, if the policies of other war-oriented actors had prompted the power to intervene originally.
multilateral war belligerent or war-oriented:	The peace plan will be of the broadest sort, co-extensive with the great power's multifarious worldwide interests. The plan might be as functionally comprehensive as it is broad in its security and territorial terms. As the power may expect to determine the structure of future interstate relations with other powers, its sense of responsibility might extend beyond its own interests to preventing wars and promoting harmonious relations.

TABLE 11–3. The peace plan of the small state as a function of the character of the war.

simple external war belligerent:	The plan will concern future relations with the single adversary, although it could be broader in scope if regional problems had been created by the war or a war-oriented actor, particularly a great power or international organization, existed and was in some way implicated in the war. In either case, the small state's plan would still have to be a modest one. Thus, the planners might try to anticipate contingencies in order to be prepared for them; but they could do little to shape the relations between *other states*.

TABLE 11-3.   (*continued*)

war-oriented:	The peace plan will probably be restricted to forming an image of postwar relations with the belligerents. As in the case where it is a belligerent itself, the state's policymakers could not hope to use their limited capabilities to press the realization of a more than modest plan. However, we should not underestimate the power of ideas: proposals offered by the small state's planners, in their state's interests, could be espoused by other greater states that have the means to implement them. It is often in the small state's interests to bridle the larger powers through collective security or functional organizations, and through devices to prevent wars that might result in their being overrun.
simple internal war belligerent:	The plan of one or the other faction will be directed to domestic problems within the polity.
war-oriented:	The reasons for a small state being war-oriented are usually more limited than those of a great power, and limited to regional matters. The peace plan will be correspondingly limited—to achieving the small state's war aims in the postwar period (if that is possible), and to establishing some basis for future relations with either or both factions. The interest of other states (as in the proxy war) could constrain the small state to plan for contingencies brought about by them, however.
complex external war belligerent:	The peace plan of the small state, like the great power, will have to take alliance relations into account as well as relations with the adversary. Because security will be vital for the small state, its policymakers might be intent upon preserving the alliance as a security guarantee in the postwar era. The alliance could also be a forum where the proposals of the small state would be given more serious consideration than in an international organization or at the peace talks. Without extended interests in other regions of the world, the planners of the small state will formulate a plan emphasizing relations with allies, and it will be only peripherally concerned with non-regional problems. As we noted before, the small state will be interested in any comprehensive schemes for its self-preservation and security, although like any state, it could have some modest hegemonial ambitions relative to other small states.
	The small state would be interested in problems that interested its allies, because such problems will ultimately affect *its* own relations with the allies, and very probably its own security. However, interest in such

TABLE 11-3 *(continued)*

	problems will not be as intense, nor will they seem to require as much time for consideration by allied policymakers.
war-oriented:	The peace plan will be restricted to the regional relations of the future and to the achievement of those goals that made the small state war-oriented.
complex internal war belligerent:	The active involvement of other states in an internal war within the small state will compel either incumbents or insurgents to plot their future relations with the intervenors. These reasons could have been either power political, ideological, or a mixture of both; and the peace plan of the small state must address itself to such issues and to the domestic problems of the polity after the war, problems that might have been compounded by the intervention of other states.
war-oriented: (the small state as an active belligerent-intervenor) :	A small state can not usually intervene in states distant from itself owing to its limited capabilities. It could intervene, however, in states in its region. The peace plan of such a state would reach regional problems created by the war and those questions that had provided a basis for its intervention.
multilateral war belligerent or war-oriented:	While the small state's plan would likely emphasize relations with regional states and allies, and the problems of its own future security, its policymakers might also more ambitiously propose far-reaching changes in the relations of all states in the hope of realizing security in an improved international environment. The war would have served as a reminder that widespread war inevitably forces war upon the small states of the world. As the small state's plan will have been offered by a state with relatively modest ambitions, the plan might be more acceptable to the directorate of great powers.

We could, of course, construct a similar table for middle-range states, but the two preceding tables will serve as patterns for the reader inclined to formulate another. In any case, the two extremes in capabilities are sufficient for our purposes. The plan of the middle-range state will have some of the characteristics of the great-power plan and some of the small-state plan.

Military Operations and Peace Plans

As a war nears its end, we are likely to find the policymakers and military leaders of the belligerent actors formulating their military plans with two objectives in mind: strengthening their negotiators' bargaining position at the peace talks and modifying military operations in order to realize their war aims in accordance with their own peace plan. The two objectives need not be related, for a local victory might enable a state or a faction to bargain more effectively but not necessarily help fulfill a peace plan. A state in a weak bargaining position might formulate an altogether modest plan based upon its anticipated imminent defeat. It would coordinate its military operations accordingly (retreat for the redeployment of troops, for example) without substantially improving its bargaining position. Yet, if the two objectives can be accomplished through the same military means (and they often can be), the state is most fortunate. An economy of lives and resources is then achieved by its armed forces as they move to implement the peace plan and, at the same time, improve the bargaining position of their peacemakers.

Coordination of military operations among allies and coordination of the peace planners' strategies with those of the executive decision-makers and military commanders are important. Indeed, the discovery that there must be coordination is in itself a significant accomplishment, a discovery not always made (and if made, not always implemented effectively). For the defeated or weak state, the advantages of this sort of preparation for peace are not quite so evident; but they do exist. If its policymakers were prepared to grapple with the consequences of defeat early on in the peacemaking process, the returns could be appreciable. In fact, proper coordination of military operations and peace plans could enable the defeated state to overcome the effects of defeat in a shorter time after the settlement: by confronting the victors with military *faits accomplis* that would cost too much to change; by persuading the victors of the benefits of its peace plan for some of the allies and thus dividing the victorious coalition; and generally, by adopting modest postwar (or late war) goals and pursuing them with singlemindedness and shrewdness.

With the view to fulfilling a peace plan, a state's military leaders might:

1. Move to occupy strategic points, such as river crossings, forts, cities, and ports or mountain redoubts, points that could give the occupying state control over regions for which its peace plan envisaged control.

2. Plan offensives or redirect offensives to seize resources or to secure territory for occupation or annexation in an attempt to improve their state's postwar power position relative to the adversary or allies.

3. Occupy areas that could be easily controlled after the cease-fire, with the intention of rationalizing a prospective truce line.

4. Seize territories or strategic points for bargaining purposes only (as opposed to seizure for their security value) so that they can be later exchanged for other values during negotiations or after the settlement.

5. Redeploy the armed forces to other theaters of combat or to areas

that have theretofore been quiescent, for use as a deterrent against adversaries or allies.

6. Plan for the security of the armed forces and occupied territories during the post-armistice period (and to this end, redeploy or demobilize troops, reorganize command structures, and standardize equipment, ordnance, and logistics procedures commensurate with the truce and peace settlement arranged).

7. Impose (or modify previously imposed) military government upon selected areas in order to improve control and guarantee delivery of resources from these areas or in order to implement policies that would succeed in persuading the inhabitants of the good intentions of the occupying state.

8. Begin constructing fortified zones to protect strategic areas.

9. Destroy weapons, aircraft, and naval vessels in order to prevent a victorious adversary from capturing or acquiring them under the terms of the demilitarization clauses of a truce agreement or peace treaty.

10. Where one's adversary had been defeated, make provision for receiving the surrender of its armed forces and prepare for assuming a supervisory role over those forces in the immediate post-armistice period.

Military success or defeat induces policymakers to change their war aims—to dispense with some aims and to adopt others. Of course, this process will continue during the late stages of the war until there is a permanent armistice. As we have seen, certain military operations will be carried out pursuant to a peace plan. These operations could acquire a momentum of their own, and their success or failure might be significant enough to induce a revision of the plan. When any significant military event changes the bargaining strength and power position of one of the belligerents, the peace planners must properly amend their original plan to take into consideration changed circumstances and the possibility that, because of them, the postwar world will be a rather different place than they had anticipated. Success or failure might have altered the policymaker's image of the postwar world, the structure of interstate relations, the efficacy of ideologies, and the prospects for war-preventing institutions. Another important instance of interaction between war aims and peace plans, on the one hand, and the course of the war on the other, is de-escalation; and it is to that process we now briefly turn.

De-escalation

We have seen that de-escalation occurs in complex and multilateral wars when a belligerent state decouples from a supported faction and agrees to a cease-fire or when an ally moves for a separate peace after leaving a wartime coalition. De-escalation can come about without structural simplification of the war, without one of the belligerents becoming nonbelligerent. It occurs when:

1. A belligerent reduces the intensity of fighting by deploying fewer units of its forces, by scheduling fewer attacks, by going over to the defense, or by reducing the amount of firepower used in an attack.

2. A belligerent closes out a theater of operations.

3. One of the parties agrees to refrain from using a particular class of weapons.

4. An alliance dissolves as a result of disagreements arising out of war-aim incompatibilities or the conduct of the war, and the disarray of the former allies prevents the massing of forces or firepower against the adversary.

A belligerent could move for a cease-fire with some or all of the adversaries. Of course, this is what we would expect of decision-makers who want peace. But de-escalation can also be used as a tactic of war: A belligerent could move for peace with *one* adversary only, hoping to lure that party away from an alliance. It might prefer to resolve the conflict with the least troublesome of the adversaries in order to concentrate its armed forces against other more formidable rivals. The use of de-escalation as a bargaining tool is seen where a state makes peace with some of the adversaries to achieve a propaganda victory, perhaps to win the favor of theretofore hostile (but nonbelligerent) war-oriented actors, to appease public or elite opinion at home, or to escape the condemnation of an international organization. The policymakers of one of the parties might calculate that since the end of the war was not in sight, in order to prepare for the "long haul," they ought to de-escalate, perhaps by making peace with some of the adversaries, perhaps merely by reducing the intensity of combat operations. War costs can thus be spread over a longer period of time.

De-escalation could also be used to signal an intention to decrease the level of fighting and to invite the adversary to do likewise, with the hope that all parties could move toward an armistice without *appearing* to betray a lack of resolve by the actual initiation of peace feelers. The signal could be directed to induce the belligerent's allies to come around to certain of the de-escalating state's policies, or to war-oriented actors, perhaps to persuade them that the time is propitious for mediation efforts, perhaps to threaten them with possible losses if the belligerent were to close out a theater of operations or leave the war. De-escalation can be taken to mean many things to the different parties interested in the outcome of a war; but if it is designed to carry a message to an adversary or an ally, the message must be clear enough to avoid misinterpretation. Before moving to de-escalate for signalling purposes, policymakers ought to weigh the likelihood and consequences of a misinterpretation.

A particular state's peace plan could require de-escalation to achieve some advantage over current or prospective competitors by making peace with some of the adversaries or to conserve the de-escalating state's capabilities so that it will be in a stronger position after the general settlement and thus be able to cope with anticipated rivals in the postwar era. Planned de-escalation might be intended to reduce operations on one front in order to concentrate forces on another. Or the de-escalating state might move to occupy as much territory as possible for exploitation or development after the war. All these de-escalatory schemes could be subsumed under the planning of military operations pursuant to a peace plan, to enable the belligerent to obtain a preferred ordering of its postwar world.

De-escalation affects peace planning. It naturally requires changes in the peace plan of the de-escalating belligerent—and perhaps also changes in its war aims and in its military strategy. Moreover, the peace planning of the other belligerents and war-oriented actors would probably have to be modified in important ways as a result of the de-escalation of another. Thus, where the de-escalating state decided to make a separate peace, the remaining belligerents would have to modify their strategy to take into account the fact that one party was leaving the war. This adjustment could be especially important for the partners in a wartime coalition, who must subsequently bear the costs of the war without one of their number. Indeed, the departure of one party could lead to a protracted war, costly for the deserted allies, who might decide to penalize the departing partner by imposing sanctions or (during the peace settlement) denying the de-escalating state values prospectively obtainable from the adversaries after the settlement. Moreover, policymakers of other states could come to question the reliability and credibility of the de-escalating state. The remaining belligerents could well inquire whether the latter should (or could) play a role in the postwar scheme they had designed. They might be impelled to make their plans for a peace without the active cooperation, perhaps even with the hostility, of the de-escalating state. Their interpretation of the significance of de-escalation, their reading of the "signal" from the departing state might tell the planners what the intentions of the policymakers of the former were, what plans they had for the postwar world, and whether these were compatible or incompatible with their own war aims and peace plans. Thus, they would have to shape a whole new image of the departing state's political character and its role after the settlement. Even in the case where the de-escalating state did not leave the war but merely reduced the level of fighting on one front, the meaning of these moves for the plans of other belligerents would have to be weighed by their policymakers.

Preparing the Polity for Peace

Conscription, co-option of industries to war purposes, and the propagandizing of war issues produce social and economic problems for belligerents, even in the simplest of wars. Peace planners must therefore anticipate the consequences for their polity of the process of demobilization and peacemaking. It is not a question of returning to the *status quo ante,* for that cannot usually be done, certainly not after a major war. It is a problem, frequently ignored—of easing the dislocating consequences of moves toward peace. Recent history has shown us that there are often some attempts to cope with the domestic consequences of peace, although these are desultory and inefficient. Only in the twentieth century, with the development of modern techniques of economic analysis and social and economic planning, has the preparation for peace become a possibility.[10]

Peace planning for the polity encompasses:

1. demobilization of the armed forces,
2. economic planning,
3. reconstruction,
4. propaganda (or re-education),
5. reorganization of the government.

In respect of demobilization, it must be decided how many men are to be demobilized (and consequently, how many are to be continued on active duty). This determination is derived from an estimate of security needs for the postwar period. A decision on the optimum size of the armed forces can, of course, be substantially affected by domestic pressures to demobilize quickly and completely. In any event, procedures must be established for discharging the men from active duty. Often the forces themselves must be reorganized as some units become depleted and other units eliminated. Weapons must be stockpiled, although small arms could conceivably be carried off by the men if the war ended in a chaotic fashion.

Economic planning for peace is a vast project, and we can do no more than adumbrate some of the problems here. First, the belligerent will have to deal with the economic impact of demobilization, the unemployment resulting from a flooding of the market with numbers of veterans

10 Leontief, W. W., and Hoffenberg, Marvin, "The Economic Effects of Disarmament," *Scientific American,* Vol. 204, No. 4, April, 1961, pp. 47–55; Melman, Seymour, *The Peace Race* (New York: George Braziller, 1962), pp. 80–99; Melman, Seymour (ed.), *Disarmament: Its Politics and Economics* (Boston: American Academy of Arts and Sciences, 1962), particularly the essays of Emile Benoit (pp. 134 f.) and R. C. Raymond (pp. 158 f.).

seeking jobs within a relatively short space of time.[11] Second, the conversion of industries producing armaments and war-related goods to consumer goods industries will have to be implemented, preferably with minimal unemployment, and without a depression. The prospective external instability of postwar interstate relations would, no doubt, induce policymakers to go slow on conversion so that their state will retain some warmaking potential for as long as there was a threat of war. Third, wartime controls such as rationing, price and wage controls, and credit restrictions would probably be removed. Fourth, welfare programs for veterans (grants, subsidies, and loans) or for persons and businesses that have borne the costs of the war, might also be adopted. (We should recognize that in a democratic polity, matters such as these will be controversial: there might well be intensive lobbying for government benefits.) Fifth, some provision must be made for paying off debts that have arisen from the funding of war costs and a concomitant minimization of the effects of debt liquidation upon the value of the currency. The belligerent may have borrowed from domestic financial sources or from allies. In either case, some mode of repayment of principal and interest must be negotiated with the creditor. Thus, a state in a weak bargaining position might be required to pay an indemnity in gold, currency or other resources. The peace planners must deal with the problem of how to make these payments with minimal damage to the economy (if that is possible—and it might not be, if the indemnity were punitive). They could, of course, attempt to devise schemes for avoiding payment.

Reconstruction is properly part of economic planning. In war-ravaged polities, costs of reconstruction will be very heavy. Until railroads, bridges, housing, and other elements of the economic infrastructure are repaired, many other postwar recovery programs, public or private, cannot be implemented. Priorities for reconstruction will undoubtedly have to be adopted. This process will not proceed solely from considerations of the proper or rational order for optimum economic recovery, but also from the pressures vested interest groups exert upon the policymakers and from the influence of certain foreign policy determinants: for example, whether threats from other states are serious and credible, whether reparations have been required, or whether there are costs to participating in a collective security organization.

It might be necessary for the policymakers to undertake a campaign to persuade elites or publics of the need for peace. Having made a decision

---

11 Sparrow, J. C., *History of Personnel Demobilization in the United States Army* (Washington, D.C.: U.S. Department of the Army, 1951); Samuelson, P. A., and Hagen, E. E., *After the War, 1918–1920: Military and Economic Demobilization of the United States and its Effect upon Employment and Income* (Washington, D.C.: U.S. Government National Resources Planning Board, 1943).

to negotiate a settlement, the leaders will want to maximize their bargaining flexibility and to convince their allies and adversaries that they have the support of their polity. If the elites or the public opposed peace negotiations (if, for example, the war issues have not become sufficiently de-ideologized), the leaders will be unable to achieve a compromise settlement. In short, domestic opinion will have to be prepared for peace. But more than that, it will have to be prepared for the particular kind of peace settlement the peace planners envisage, and eventually for the settlement the leaders obtain, including acquiescence in obligations imposed by the peace treaty. Propaganda must then extend to justifying the probable postwar role in regional or world affairs the belligerent will play—in particular, for the benefit of the attentive elites, who, because of their economic interests, patriotism, or ideology, might be affected by the peace plan and who might also be in a position to create political difficulties for the peacemakers. It is also likely that the policymakers will have to rationalize their domestic postwar economic and social policies for the same elites.

The war emergency could have demonstrated that the government and bureaucracy were incompetent or inefficient or that their policies were defective or deficient or could not be implemented at reasonable costs. There might be some feeling among the policymakers and elites that the war had caused the government to grow too large. In these cases, as part of postwar planning, the policymakers might undertake to reorganize the government and perhaps to amend the constitution, with the view to introducing desirable reforms necessary if the belligerent were in a weak bargaining position and the "victors" demanded political reforms. But any former belligerent might have to contemplate government reorganization to enable it to assume responsibilities for regional or world security or for participation in an alliance or an international organization.

Nonbelligerent war-oriented actors, no less than the active belligerents, will also undertake to prepare their polities for the peace. The economic impact of the war upon the great powers, regional states, and nonbelligerent allies could conceivably be as great, or greater, than that for some of the belligerents. Creditor states will want to negotiate acceptable schemes for the repayment of war loans to debtor states. Leaders of international organizations and alliances will have to attend to the probable consequences of postwar interstate relations upon the functioning of their organizations. They too might find that an administrative reorganization will be necessary, that steps must be taken to improve the financial condition of their organizations, particularly if they are to function in the new conditions of the postwar world.

The Failure
of Peace Settlements

An obvious consequence of the failure of a peace settlement is the resumption of hostilities. Whether we ought to go farther and regard as a failure a settlement followed by intense and bitter competition between the former belligerents or by any conflict short of war depends upon our standards for determining success or adequacy of a peace settlement. Inadequacy of a settlement is the most common cause of failure. But inadequacy does not inevitably lead to that result, for defects can be corrected by statesmen intent upon avoiding war and resolving conflict by peaceful means. Thus, some inadequate settlements need not fail, for failure can often be prevented.

In one sense, an inadequate settlement is unavoidable. Every settlement has some *intrinsic inadequacy*. Given the present state system, absolute security can never be achieved by any state; and an acceptable or sufficient level of security is not always (and perhaps not often) attainable. Any particular settlement fits into the matrix of interstate relations, which are conflictual and characterized by tension, the frequent occurrence of crises, and prevailing feelings of fear or insecurity among world elites. The settlement will inevitably be affected by the unstable or metastable character of this system and will therefore be intrinsically inadequate. Moreover, a settlement has ramifications beyond the immediate belligerent parties. Reciprocally, conflicts elsewhere in the system, whether in the form of war or tensions short of war, will affect states seeking to make peace. Even if nonbelligerents did not deliberately involve themselves in hostilities in any way, the conflictual character of interstate relations not only makes peacemaking more difficult for any particular war, however limited in geographical scope or in the means of force employed, however few in number the belligerents, it also renders the settlement inadequate. The more stable the international order at any one time, the less intrinsically inadequate will a settlement be.[1]

The intentions of the peace planners are, of course, quite important. If the parties had agreed upon a basis for the resumption and normalization of relations, for example, their intention to do so would not have been fulfilled were there no re-establishment of diplomatic relations or if the former belligerents were to continue to discriminate against each other in their commercial dealings. Thus, failure can result when at least one of the parties does not implement the terms its peace planners originally intended to make a part of the peace settlement, where intentions do not lead to performance. We say then that, in respect to the unfulfilled provisions, the settlement might have been inadequate. I use *might* advisedly, because events over which the parties had little or no control could have occurred to render the terms of the settlement nugatory or ineffectual. If this had happened, we could not fairly term the settlement provisions in question inadequate, unless the peacemakers could have anticipated the vitiating events and failed to take steps to prepare for them or prevent them, if they could.[2] There can be no doubt that supervening events can exert prodigious pressures upon the parties and make it appear to their policymakers that resumption of hostilities was neces-

---

1 Intrinsic inadequacy can be regarded as the probability that a settlement will be inadequate in the circumstances. It depends on the character of the war, the environment of the war, and the parties. The more complex a war, the less likely will it be that the peacemakers can isolate and resolve all the essential questions. Thus, settlements of multilateral wars will be more intrinsically inadequate than settlements of simple wars. If the environment of the war is unstable—if, for example, other independent wars are being waged in the region, if great powers are in conflict, if ideologies that catalyze internal wars are being proselytized, the settlement of a particular war will not only be made more difficult, but its intrinsic inadequacy will also be greater. Finally, we say that the probability of a settlement's success also depends upon the character of the parties: Are there any internal instabilities that might prevent a state's implementation of the settlement? Do domestic political groups exist that could sabotage the peace? What other foreign affairs problems do the parties have that could conceivably prompt a violation or avoidance of peace terms?

2 Nor could we call a settlement inadequate if war broke out between the parties years later, if the later war were "new" in terms of the war aims of the belligerents. We would be justified in describing the settlement of the earlier war as a failure if the issues involved in the later war were not different from those of the earlier or, if different, could reasonably have been anticipated and remedied in the first settlement.

sary. Yet, the actual declaration of war is an act that is fully within their control. If the leaders of both sides refused to declare war against each other, there would be no war between them. They could recognize the need to realize the aims of the peace settlement and try to avoid war by the peaceful adjustment of differences that might have arisen because of the occurrence of events they could not control. Naturally, if formerly hostile parties were forced into war (by an intervening great power, for example) we could hardly attribute this turn of events to an inadequate peace settlement.

If in establishing a standard to judge the adequacy of a settlement, we required the peacemakers to anticipate and prepare for occurrences that might undermine their agreement, we in effect raise a more general question with respect to our notion of inadequacy: namely, should we not hold the negotiators of a peace settlement to a standard higher than their intentions? Should we not use another test: What ought the peacemakers to have done? Clearly, in certain instances, they will have omitted to consider, or they will have refused to consider, a particular problem— they will not have intended to settle it. But perhaps they *ought* to have so intended. Our problem thus reduces to the question: What matters ought the parties resolve between themselves in order to achieve an adequate settlement? To answer this question with any kind of specificity, we must describe the sorts of inadequacies that do arise out of the work product of peacemakers.

Kinds of Inadequacies

1. Failure of peace negotiations: The failure of the belligerents to reach any agreement whatever, because of the collapse of the talks, is hardly the failure of a settlement, since no settlement had been reached. But if the parties have at least agreed upon a cease-fire, the collapse of talks could lead to renewed war, and this limited but important part of the military settlement would then have failed.

Peace talks fail when one of the parties breaches a cease-fire agreement, either by the resumption of hostilities or by a violation of the implementation provisions that places the party in a position to resume military operations with a greater advantage than he had before the cease-fire. They fail if there was no cease-fire and one of the belligerents secures a victory or sustains a defeat, perhaps from an attack in violation of a tacit understanding among the belligerents to maintain the status quo and the party adversely affected decides it cannot continue negotiations because of its less favorable bargaining position. And peace talks also fail when an actor does not fulfill the terms (or violates the terms) of a provisional or preliminary treaty of peace. If one of the negotiators concludes that the other is bargaining in bad faith or is intent upon deceiving the negotiators, he will undoubtedly break off the talks. Indeed, any bargaining behavior on the part of a state or faction that profoundly disappoints the expectations of the other could lead to this result.

If the peace terms of one belligerent are too demanding or differ substantially from the terms discussed during the preliminaries, the adversary may balk. Negotiations might then collapse or at least be hindered, as might also follow from disagreement over a point deemed essential by one of the negotiating parties, if further talks seemed useless to them. Indeed, it is conceivable that if one of the parties could be assured that hostilities would not be resumed, they would prefer an uneasy truce without peace talks, rather than a prolongation of acrimonious or technical negotiations that might be embarrassing for a government pressed by militant groups at home.

If one party uses the talks as a propaganda device and there are no "returns" for the other, they are not likely to be fruitful. Moreover, negotiations may be impeded by the intervention of a third party, a state not theretofore involved in peacemaking efforts, that might employ force or create diplomatic or economic difficulties for the parties to prevent a peace settlement. A belligerent ally that had refused to enter the peace talks could also play the role of a spoiler, intervening to prevent its allies and the adversary from continuing negotiations to achieve a settlement it regarded as undesirable in the circumstances. If the talks were being mediated by a third party, the use of indiscreet, perhaps even improper, means to secure agreement and resolution of the issues might call into question the neutral, disinterested status of the mediator and impel one of the parties to suspend the talks. The same result would ensue if the mediator were discovered to be prejudiced in favor of one of the belligerents.

If the talks were prolonged, the parties might become convinced that nothing could be achieved. Extrinsic events, not the least of which might be the progress of their armies or their negotiations with actual or prospective allies, would assume more decisive importance in determining the course of the war and the shape of a settlement. The parties would then need little to persuade them that continued negotiations were valueless. When during the course of the negotiations, one belligerent was in the position of having had all issues of interest to itself resolved, it could decide to leave the talks or recall its prestigious representatives or plenipotentiaries, leaving relatively low-ranking civil servants in attendance. The result would be the same if the negotiators and policymakers of one of the parties became impatient or bored or if the influence of antagonistic domestic political groups that believed nothing more could be accomplished at the talks had become very great. The effects of the departure of a participant will usually be adverse. And indeed, other states might be induced to leave. Discouraged by the departure of one party and the implications of that departure for the prospective adequacy of the settlement they may produce, other negotiators might be unable to avoid the complete collapse of the talks. Certainly, the "bargaining equations" will be changed by the departure of a state. If a state ceases to support its allies (or demand support from them, if needed), its allies may find their bargaining strength lessened (or multiplied). Accordingly, adversaries of the departing state could be helped or hindered to some extent by the shift in intra-alliance power positions at the conference.

As we have seen, a variety of domestic political events and pressures could induce a state's policymakers to continue a war. Such a decision could mean the end of peace talks if these had been in progress. But a coup, a peaceful change of government, or merely a change in the composition of a cabinet need not necessarily produce a decision to continue waging a war. But such changes could lead to failure where they engendered new peace policies, new negotiating techniques, or proposals of the sort described in the preceding paragraphs.

A dispute over peace terms among partners within an alliance could persuade some of them that peace talks can only work to their detriment. Their allies might appear to have established too intimate a negotiating relationship with the adversary; they might appear all too willing to compromise on issues vital to themselves and to the alliance. Whenever allies fail to support each other during negotiations for peace or fail to live up to standards any one member expects of others, the disappointed member could adopt a policy of interference with the progress of the talks, causing delay or simply leaving the discussions.

Peace talks do acquire a momentum of their own, however. They take on an independent existence in certain situations. Then, a discontented party will be less willing to bear the onus of breaking off the talks, since this could result in considerable propaganda gains for others. Yet when truly vital interests are affected, no state's policymakers will deny themselves the alternative of disrupting peace talks. If walking out were unacceptable, there are still a number of negotiating techniques they could use to frustrate the progress of the negotiations.

2. We continue now to enumerate other kinds of inadequacies a settlement may possess. The parties might agree to an armistice, *and no more,* which could end the war; but in the circumstances, it may not be an adequate settlement and may lead to fighting in the near future. An armistice agreement, after all, does not resolve the issues that had divided the belligerents. It is merely recognition by them of the fact that further fighting will lead to losses and is no longer an acceptable means for the satisfaction of their war aims. Only if the cease-fire represents a decision to forego the values implicit in the war aims will it have any permanence. A bare agreement to stop the fighting may or may not

enable the antagonists to live in peace afterward. Thus, we can say that an armistice agreement alone is an inadequate settlement if at least one of the belligerents retains its original war aims and intends to pursue realization of them by military means after the reconstruction, repair, and resupply that a peaceful respite offered; if both parties modify their war aims, but the war has created conditions calling for amelioration by the joint agreement of the former belligerents, and the failure to agree gives rise to conflicts; or if the belligerents change or foreswear their war aims, but the armistice agreement itself creates a situation that produces tension or conflict between the parties.

3. The cease-fire agreement itself might be defective in a technical sense: the cease-fire line might be badly drawn or assembly zones designated in indefensible areas, exposing certain units to the enemy and generating a sense of insecurity. There might have been a failure to include provisions for the security of forces during regroupment and withdrawal, or ambiguously drafted provisions that lead to disagreements over, for example, the dates for a truce or for withdrawals, or the identity of units to be redeployed. Other technical defects could arise if the agreement was carelessly drafted.

4. The existence of *non-obligated parties* is another kind of inadequacy which arises if some of the belligerents have agreed to a cease-fire while others have not; or if all have agreed to the cease-fire, but some have not agreed on political or other military issues and therefore have refused to acquiesce in the settlement reached by the agreeing parties. States that were not present at the peace conference, but which ought to have been present (war-oriented states, for example), could become troublesome, nonobligated parties as their interests in the outcome of the war will not have been adequately dealt with if they have not been given a hearing at the conference. Not only might the war-oriented actor engage in actions prohibited to the obligated parties, they might also pursue policies designed specifically to destroy the settlement. This suggests that the principal belligerents ought to invite the war-oriented actors to participate in the peace talks or ensure that they are represented by an agent-state acceptable to the war-oriented actor's leaders. Moreover, the failure to anticipate the origination in the postwar era of new and interested parties could render the settlement inadequate. New states might be established; new factions might arise within a state formerly afflicted with an internal war; or states not theretofore war-oriented might become interested in the problems resolved or created by the settlement. All these will, of course, be nonobligated, because they were not in existence at the time of the truce or peace settlement.

In a democratic polity, the legislature may refuse to ratify a settlement the policymakers believed desirable; and if there were no ratification, the state would remain a nonobligated party. Such a state, under the principle that it is not bound to perform duties pursuant to a treaty to which it has not given its consent, would be in a position to take action in derogation of the settlement the other belligerents had reached. A non-obligated party could induce the others to resume the war in order to protect themselves. As a truce is a tenuous agreement, easily undone by any incident that causes suspicion or reawakens distrust or antipathy on the part of the policymakers, the nonobligated party is in a position to catalyze conflict.

5. The political settlement will be inadequate if the peace negotiators have not reached all the issues and leave unresolved some of the disputes that were the basis for the war. It will also be inadequate if some of the issues are left unresolved for some of the parties, who would undoubtedly regard the settlement as incomplete if at least one issue in which they are interested remains "live" and likely to prompt them to resolve it through self-help in the postwar period. The piecemeal settlement of a multi-lateral war, for example, might be too piecemeal. In other words, it might be fragmented, because the uncoordinated negotiation of issues at separate conferences had failed to resolve the complex (interstitial) questions.

6. The political settlement may contain provisions that actually in-duce one of the former belligerents to commit a belligerent act. Thus, a settlement that is excessively punitive or contains provisions that could be construed as committing some of the parties to joint action against a third, or insults the leaders, institutions, or ideology of a party could easily induce the latter to attempt to throw over the settlement at some point in the postwar era. In this sense, the settlement is dysfunctional: It is the occasion for experiences that produce extreme bitterness or con-vince the peacemakers or their peoples that it was wrong, strategically unsound, or costly to have negotiated in the first place and a mistake to have agreed to a settlement. The settlement may symbolize the defeat, exploitation, and insulting of a state, and it may thus provide the basis for a re-ideologization of the issues between the antagonists. It may come to be a domestically exploitable political issue that any of the political parties or figures can use to win support to achieve electoral success or to take the minds of the people off domestic hardship or the lack of success of their administration's program.

A settlement could be dysfunctional without necessarily leading to the outbreak of a new war (although that is certainly the worst of the conse-quences) if it prevents the normalization of relations between the bellig-erents and other actors; if it contributes significantly to tensions between states; if it prevents internal economic development or creates instability *within* any state (perhaps leading to revolution or *coup d'état*); or, finally, if it interferes with the functioning of an international organiza-tion, contributing to its inability to prevent or contain conflict.

7. While complete in its resolution of all outstanding disputes between the parties, the political terms of the settlement might be procedurally defective: They might omit provisions for the implementation of substantive terms; procedures might be incomplete or unrealistic in the conditions existing at the time implementation is required, or ambiguous and productive of disagreements.

8. The settlement might be tied to extrinsic questions, to performance of certain acts by a third party, for example, or to other agreements to be negotiated at some future time. If there were a possibility that the extrinsic acts would not be performed or the extrinsic questions left unresolved, the settlement will be incomplete or regarded as such by the parties that had hoped for the actualization of the contingencies upon which the peace agreement depended. Where the parties relied upon the mutual fulfillment of the obligations imposed by the settlement treaty, nonratification by one would cause great concern for the viability of the settlement.[3] Or where one belligerent had extracted an agreement from another at the cost of promising to conclude a defense pact with it, failure to do so would leave the disappointed party bound by the peace treaty, but determined to undo the order established by it to the extent that its security interests, without a defense pact, required. The former belligerents might agree upon a settlement which necessitated an act beyond their control to perform (or to have performed: an act of a third-party state, for example). Performance of this act could be a condition of their own implementation of the terms of the settlement. Whatever the expectations of the former belligerents, the nonperformance of an act by the third party could lead to nonperformance by the signatories; and the substantive aspects of the settlement would be incomplete to that extent. Such a settlement would be inadequate. Thus, peace negotiators should avoid, if possible, tying their performance to that of another or to some extrinsic event over which they have no control.

9. Changed conditions are often cited by a signatory of a treaty as providing justification for the nonperformance of obligations pursuant to its provisions. Whatever the legal merit of such a claim, it is often enough advanced. Peacemakers should appreciate that their own settlement document could itself become nullified or redundant were some of the parties eventually to claim that conditions at the time of the settlement had now changed, that it was permissible to ignore some of its provisions and to refuse to perform some of its terms. The peacemakers ought therefore to draft their settlement with changed conditions in mind. This

---

3 A treaty with a democratic polity is subject to the vagaries of its domestic politics. Thus, nonratification is always possible. But the ratification process is an unavoidable "extrinsic matter" in making peace with a democracy, which lends to the intrinsic inadequacy of the settlement.

is not a wholly unreasonable or unrealistic requirement. The peace planners of the belligerents must do more than resolve the issues of the past; they must also plan for the future as they formulate peace proposals. Indeed, they can hardly avoid doing so. In effect, they must project the probable character of the "changed conditions" with which they will have to deal. Hence, it is correct to say that a settlement would be inadequate if the negotiators did not agree upon acceptable responses to changed conditions that could be anticipated, or if they failed minimally to agree upon procedures for adjusting any possible disputes that might arise from the existence of an anticipatable changed condition. This preparation should include not only devices for mediation of the substance of a dispute, but also attempts to remedy the adverse effects of changed conditions on the peace settlement itself, in order to maintain the integrity and viability of the postwar order created by it.

10. The settlement might also be inadequate if the peace agreement were ambiguous in its essential terms, which could lead to future disputes over the original intent of the peacemakers. Ambiguity will arise if the draftsmen do not appreciate the significant differences in word meanings, connotations, or nuances in the several languages in which the treaty is drafted. On the other hand, the treaty may be drafted too hurriedly, or the draftsmen may be careless or inexperienced. But even where the treaty is written by the most competent draftsmen, ambiguities may arise. Recognizing this fact, the peace negotiators ought to include a provision for the interpretation of the treaty in the event of a disagreement over its meaning and the original intent of the parties, which could ameliorate some of the problems that arose from vague language. We should understand that if ambiguity affects an essential provision, it might not be curable by any means short of renegotiation.

11. Even if the negotiators have dealt with all the issues that had divided the parties and resolved them to their satisfaction, the settlement would still be inadequate if, in the circumstances at the time of the agreement or in the circumstances that could reasonably be anticipated, it did not or could not create the regional or world order contemplated by the policymakers of the parties. In short, the settlement might be unrealistic, too grandiosely conceived, or lacking in technical details to establish the means, institutional and otherwise, for a postwar order. The peacemakers might simply have expected too much of themselves and their peoples, who, anxious to return to private peacetime pursuits, might lose interest in implementing the provisions of a settlement they regarded as onerous, expensive, and unproductive. As time passes, the costs and the suffering of the war will be forgotten, as will the felt need for the revised order envisaged in the peace treaty. And if some of the issues of the past war remain intensely ideologized, there will be all the more reason for

the still antagonistic parties to neglect to support, by cooperative measures, the postwar order established by their treaty.

12. There are also inadequacies common to each element of the settlement.

a. Territory: As we have seen, a territorial settlement may take the form of an outright cession of territory, the creation of a new state or a free territory, or the establishment of a plebiscite area or an occupation or demilitarized zone. One of the parties may be given some form of access to or through the territory of another party or the right to acquire the resources from it. The settlement will be defective if, in the circumstances, the size of the territory affected by the settlement regime is too small to be functionally viable for the purposes for which the regime was created; or of a shape and size insufficient for its security, given regional or world tensions; or finally, if it is too large and appears to constitute a threat to the security of another state. The settlement will also be defective if the people inhabiting the territory are hostile to the regime imposed or violently resist its imposition. And if a territorial cession and the new boundaries resulting therefrom are unacceptable to public opinion in the transferee state as well as in the transferor state, the territorial settlement is not adequate. We should appreciate how very difficult it has been finally and equitably to resolve a territorial dispute in which the antagonists advance conflicting historical and cultural claims. In such a situation, even if the best solution in the circumstances were adopted, the settlement would possess an intrinsic inadequacy.

b. Persons: Because terms of the peace settlement relating to citizens and corporations are not ordinarily regarded by the decision-makers as having a direct bearing upon the continued existence of the state, inadequacy in this area may not cause the settlement to fail. More than likely, the inadequacy would lead to domestic problems in the polities of the signatories, which could have world political repercussions. Some possible defects are: technical faults in the nationalities provisions that result in statelessness or dual citizenship for many persons, or lead to involuntary expatriation and inadequate procedures for repatriating refugees and prisoners of war, or for feeding and sheltering persons in the combat theaters. The loss of property or citizenship, and even the loss of life, that could result from the failure of the peacemakers to confront and deal with the problems of the individual that the war has engendered will produce a legacy of bitterness. Normalization of relations between the former belligerents will of course be made more difficult. In the future, the memory of needless, post-armistice losses suffered at the hands of "incompetent" peacemakers could produce a major change in the domestic politics of the actor that would, in turn, cause a revision in its foreign political goals—perhaps toward more militantly retributive policies.

c. Guarantees of security: The settlement will be inadequate if key states, particularly great powers, had refused to agree to or respect a guarantee of security—or the language of the guarantee was ambiguous, allowing one of the guarantors to avoid honoring it. The ambiguity could create suspicion among other guarantors that a loophole or an escape clause exists, and they might be induced to act as if there were no guarantee at all. There may indeed be situations in which no guarantee could be wholly adequate—after internal wars, for example, where the threat of subversion remained. If the guarantee were conditioned, this might in itself constitute an escape clause, since a guarantor is apt to conclude that conditions cannot be satisfied—and they may be physically impossible to satisfy. If that were the case, the remedy would be renegotiation. But the postwar situation might not permit this, or one of the guarantors might regard it as undesirable. In any event, if one of the parties anticipates that a condition will become unfulfillable, it would be a deception to offer the condition as something that could be met in the future. If other parties are deceived, if they rely upon the conditioned guarantee as 80% reliable when it is only 10% reliable, their discovery of the true state of affairs will render the guarantee completely worthless as a deterrent to aggression, an arms race, or mobilization. The guarantee, moreover, might be improper or excessive in the circumstances, producing instability rather than stability in an area, creating feelings of insecurity rather than security among the publics and policymakers of the states affected by it. For example, one party to a settlement might secure the demobilization and disarming of the forces of an adversary to the extent that a neighbor of the latter will no longer be deterred from following an adventuristic policy in its region; or a guarantee might be the pretext for the intervention of a great power in the affairs of a particular state, an intervention that will increase tensions in an area and prompt other states to intervene as well. In either case, a simple collective guarantee might have sufficed. In drafting guarantee provisions, the peacemakers must be aware of the need for moderation and the efficacy of tailoring the guarantee, in precise terms, to anticipatable threats to the peace.

d. Resumption of relations: If a party to the settlement has been permanently relegated to an inferior political position, and if its capacity for entering into normal diplomatic relations with others, particularly great powers, has been permanently impaired, the settlement is inadequate. If it prevents recognition and the exchange of ambassadors or bars a state from becoming a member in international organizations or cooperative regional enterprises, the state will undoubtedly be converted into a bitter opponent of the settlement, determined to undertake a revision of it at the earliest opportunity. Moreover, if the terms for the normalization and resumption of relations between belligerents interfere with economic development, trade, or commercial relations, or with the fiscal or monetary policies of the parties, the political settlement is defective. For, if either party has grounds for believing that the other is seeking to place it in an inferior economic position, improved relations will be hindered rather than promoted. And if the settlement provisions have the effect of restricting the operations of a particular belligerent's business enterprises, the managers of these enterprises would press their states's policymakers to take remedial action, urging violation of the terms of the settlement, if need be. A settlement that antagonizes an important segment of an actor's elites would not be acceptable to them, and its implementation may be resisted whenever possible.

e. Adjustment of disputes: A settlement is also inadequate if provisions for the adjustment of future disputes between the parties are entirely omitted or left incomplete and if, in the circumstances, the peace planners can reasonably anticipate that disputes touching the essential terms of their settlement will arise.[4] Procedures are incomplete if gaps in them permit one of the parties to resort to force within too short a period of time after a dispute arises or if they are not sufficiently comprehensive to require the parties to move through one procedural channel after another during a "cooling-off" period. In other words, the procedures must be designed deliberately to protract the dispute if either party appears to be dissatisfied enough to resort to force. The parties should attempt to entangle themselves in a web of procedures for dispute settlement. This does not guarantee that a dispute will be settled peaceably, as a determined policymaker can always cut through the procedural Gordian Knot and resort to force. But such is the importance of form that policymakers will generally endeavor to adhere to forms, or at least appear to do so. If there were a state system with an authority structure that could compel states to comply with mandates to settle their disputes by prescribed peaceful means, a particular peace settlement would fit into a matrix of legal relationships: Parties to it would have recourse to the authority structure in the event a disagreement arose—much the same as in private law which protects a contractual relationship by public judicial or executive authority when a dispute threatens to prevent the fulfillment of its terms. In the case of peace treaty provisions for the peaceful settlement of a dispute, there could be adjudication for justiciable controversies and mediation or arbitration for the remainder. Sanctions to enforce such procedures would have to be made an element in the authority structure of the state system. Unfortunately, we have not

4 The parties might omit mediation terms, intending to rely upon the peace-keeping mechanisms of an existing international organization. This would avoid an inadequate settlement provided that all the parties were obligated to avail themselves of organizational mediation procedures and the organization itself was not dysfunctional as a peacekeeping entity.

as yet reached this utopia. Even within the polity of a single state, sanctioning authority often does not exist in the wake of an internal war. The parties to a peace settlement, if they provide for the adjustment of their future disputes at all, will likely rely upon devices for mediation and perhaps adjudication and, on rare occasions, arbitration. To guarantee compliance with the decision of a judicial body, the parties could agree beforehand to comply automatically (thus submitting to the compulsory jurisdiction of the judicial body). But even here, noncompliance could result if the security of the state were threatened.

f. Penalties: There will be situations at the end of a war where the elites of a polity and their policymakers will expect penalties (if they have lost the war, for example). As long as the harshness of the penalties does not exceed the expectations of the decision-makers of the defeated state, the penalties are likely to be accepted with minimal rancor. But should they be too onerous, should the defeated state's policymakers regard them as dishonorable, the entire settlement will be unacceptable to them. And there are good reasons for terming such a settlement inadequate, although some would argue further that the presence of any penalty provision renders a settlement inadequate. Without going quite that far, we can at least argue that penalty clauses must be realistic: They must not go beyond the ability of the defeated actor to perform; they should be fixed as to quantity and quality of resources or other identifiable objects or fixed as to the amount of money required in payment on fixed due dates. Unless in their wisdom a victor's policymakers decide to destroy the defeated state, the penalty imposed should permit the latter to continue to exist and develop economically. It is probably also wise to frame the penalty clauses in neutral, technical language, without attempting to assign guilt or responsibility for the war. The adequate settlement aims at securing the acceptance (or at least the acquiescence) of all the former belligerents and war-oriented parties, without giving insult, without providing grounds for revenge on the part of revisionist states, and without excessively stirring up emotions of the peoples of any of the affected parties (or promoting the goals of any anti-peace-settlement party within any state).

Failures Deriving from Causes Other than Inadequate Settlements

A settlement might fail if a state other than the former belligerents came to play an active, interventionary role in matters that were once the sole concern of the original belligerents, matters to which their war aims were directed or with which the settlement dealt and perhaps even resolved. Third-party involvement or intervention could take a number of forms, the effect of any one of which could bring about a renewal of hostilities between the former belligerents, or create a wholly new politi-

cal situation within the region with which the peace treaty was concerned
so that the settlement became irrelevent and redundant to the relations
of the parties to it. A third-party state might declare war on one of the
former belligerents or on another state in the region. In either case, the
new war could spill over onto the territories of the parties, who might be
impelled or induced to become involved in hostilities once again, either
against the third-party or against the former adversary. The war, of
course, creates a situation of tension and instability that could render the
peace settlement a nullity or an historical curiosity.[5] In a war between
two wholly different states, the new belligerents might simply refuse to
respect the territorial integrity or neutrality of the former belligerents or
the terms of their peace settlement.

A third-party state need not go so far as to initiate war in order to
undermine a peace settlement. That state's policies relative to one of the
former belligerents may be such as to cause the collapse of the peace. The
state could do this by playing upon mutual suspicions or fears or by
creating pretexts for war, by propagandizing to prevent de-ideologization, or by increasing the political, social, and economic instability
within the region of the former belligerents (or within the polity of the
state once afflicted with an internal war, in order to exacerbate relations
between the factions). And the third-party state need not act deliberately, with the premeditated intention of destroying the peace settlement.[6] Pursuit of goals that had had little to do with the original belligerents or their settlement could still have the effect of undermining it.
This is particularly true of a state like a great power the policies of which
often have quite dramatic ramifications for other states, even where none
was intended. If the peace settlement depended upon the political and
economic stability of the parties for its success or upon the preservation of
peace between other states in order to provide adequate regional security,
then certainly a war between other states or even a peaceful trade conflict
(a tariff war for example) or a "cold war" between ideologically antagonistic third-party states could cause the failure of the settlement.
Even an economic recession within an important power could have
repercussions abroad and create conditions of economic stability that
would not permit the settlement to work.

War, whether between third-party states or the former belligerents, is
not the only event that would produce a new situation rendering the

5 The nullified or outmoded settlement could retain value as a precedent for a
future peace among the belligerents of the new war.
6 Deliberate acts indicate that the peace settlement ran counter to the vital interests of the third-party state, so much so that its policymakers decided to
induce a renewal of the war by extraordinary methods, declaring war on one
of the former belligerents or on another third party in part to undo the consequences of the settlement, in part to achieve other aims.

settlement redundant. New ideologies might arise, new states or new factions might be established, and economic and technological development within states, including the original belligerents, might create conditions and unique interstate relations that supersede those envisaged in the settlement. Even the appearance of a new generation of decision-makers, perhaps backed by a new generation of elites, might result in the obsolescence of the settlement, particularly if they were activistic or adventuristic and impelled by new aspirations for the glory of their country. Rejecting the policies of their predecessors, terming them tired, uninspired, or reactionary, the novices could embark upon policies one effect of which would be the modification, perhaps the destruction, of the order established by the settlement. Such a course might be deliberate—adopted specifically to undermine the peace. However, the new leaders might also revise or revolutionize their foreign policy for other purposes, one of the effects of which, unintended or incidental, would be the destruction of the settlement regime.

This raises the question of the solidity of any settlement from its inception. We have often remarked that the issues of the war must become sufficiently de-ideologized for a settlement to become possible. In a given situation, an only partial settlement may be possible (merely a cease-fire, for example) because the thresholds for a more complete settlement have not been crossed. According to our definition of inadequacy, a partial settlement, while it might be the best obtainable under the circumstances, is not necessarily an adequate settlement. Even if the parties were able to draft a complete settlement, it might be a formal one only, masking serious ideological or value differences. Such a settlement would be a tenuous and fragile thing, easily undone by "new situations," one which new generations of elites might quite correctly characterize as hypocritical because it was nothing more than a paper agreement. An important consideration for the durability of any settlement is the way the policymakers and their future successors within the elites regard and perceive it. Looking at the settlement as adequate or tolerable, these policymakers might intend to make it last, and indeed try to do so. On the other hand, they may regard the settlement as temporary, a mere hiatus to be used for their advantage before embarking upon a course that might require the use of force. The settlement would then be treated as an expedient, permitting the state to make use of the period of peace in some way to foster the long-range designs of its policymakers.[7] Such a set-

7 In discussing postwar policy designs, we must inquire to what extent a former belligerent's war aims are retained in the postwar period, and whether these aims are compatible with the obligations assumed by that party pursuant to the terms of the peace settlement—or indeed, whether the aims are compatible with the very notion of peace itself. After all, a peace settlement is a conservative arrangement: It cannot avoid freezing the status quo that rests upon the post-hos-

tlement would not (and could not) be treated as a device for the per-
petuation of peace and the improvement of relations between the parties.
While they may indeed be anxious to avoid war if they can—at least until
they are prepared for it—implementation of the settlement terms would
not be carried out with a sense of responsibility or duty to the peoples of
the former belligerents or the region, but rather as strictly and solely
serving the interests of a particular state. I do not mean to imply that
egoism does not also move policymakers of states that take a peace settlement seriously, deeming it to require interstate cooperation and perhaps
even some small sacrifices in the interest of the community of states. It
often does. But then at least, *sacre egoismo* is tempered by altruistic, com-
munity-oriented sentiments, which may be enough to provide the basis
for international relations that could ameliorate whatever inadequacies
there were in the settlement.

Where, on the other hand, a state's policymakers approach a settlement
cynically, its shortcomings often become magnified. They look for loopholes in its terms. They might violate whatever terms they can with
impunity; and they may eventually risk sanctions or war by violating
essential provisions in order to achieve an important goal. A settlement
that is treated by one party as a mere expedient, to be used solely to
further its own national interests, will very likely fail because the party

---

tilities power positions of the belligerents. Policymakers whose war aims were,
or had become, defensive or maintenance of the status quo will usually support
a settlement or at least acquiesce in its terms. States whose policymakers sought
dominance, retribution, or consolidation are likely to press for a revision of
the settlement if these aims remain unsatisfied. The same is true where
ideologies played an important part in bringing about war or in preserving
the belligerents' will to fight (and where de-ideologization has not taken
place). Thus, some war aims, if retained as aims after the war, are incompatible
with the continuation of the terms of an unrevised settlement. Revision, however, can be attempted by many means, and not necessarily by force. Certainly,
when a revisionist state resorts to force, we call the settlement a failure. But
what if the revisionist party employs devices short of war to accomplish its
goals? It could, for example, seek to secure the general agreement of other
obligated parties to the proposition that because the settlement was inadequate
from the point of view of the revisionist state, it was inadequate for all, or if not
inadequate, then inequitable. Were the others to refuse modification, the moving party would have the choice of resorting to force or acquiescing once again
in the determination of its former adversaries. On the other hand, if the others
agreed to renegotiation, it would not necessarily be an admission by them that
the settlement was inadequate or even inequitable. They may believe simply
that it was the expedient thing to do. It would be wise, of course, to subject a
settlement to automatic, periodic review. Negotiations having the intent of re-
vising peace terms may prevent failure and may cure inadequacies that are discovered in the post-war period.

has not been inspired by a sense of responsibility and the will to make it work. Evidence of a will to ignore the terms of a peace settlement might also serve to prompt the other parties to take the same cavalier attitude: Attitudes of irresponsibility are contagious and induce reciprocally reinforcing policies and acts which increase the chances of failure, as each of the parties takes steps (indeed, rushes) to counter the policies of the others. These steps might themselves be in violation of the terms of the settlement or at least demonstrate a lack of faith in its durability and point up the parties' unwillingness to work cooperatively toward the regime contemplated by it. Certainly, any action deemed to prejudice the security of one of the states will prompt the others to take steps to protect themselves, irrespective of the terms of the settlement, irrespective of the destructive effects of those steps on the postwar order.

Remedies for a Failing Settlement

If a settlement has failed or is failing, the parties to it have the option of resorting to traditional diplomatic techniques, preventive diplomacy, and peacekeeping to avoid war and reduce tensions. They could undertake steps to preserve or promote their peaceful relations with the aid of an international organization; or, between themselves alone, they could attempt to negotiate away their differences—in either case, independently of and without reference to the peace settlement. They might wish to do this because they believed their problems were new ones, that the peace arrangement ought to be superseded because it was unsatisfactory, outmoded, or irrelevant. Of course, the parties do have other choices. Indeed, in the early postwar period, the settlement could probably not be totally ignored; and in any event, neither side might want to ignore it. The alternative remedies then are either to remove the settlement's inadequacies or (if they are able) to remove the supervenient cause extrinsic to the settlement that is bringing about the failure.

An inadequate settlement usually can be repaired. If the policymakers of the parties desire to do so, they would undertake to renegotiate the peace treaty, completing it where it is incomplete, resolving the problems they had left unresolved at the peace talks. Renegotiation could proceed through a special conference or through the foreign ministries of the parties. In lieu of renegotiation, the parties may simply try to arrive at an understanding as to which provisions they regarded as valid and binding, making a declaration to that effect. In short, the parties would try to salvage whatever parts of the settlement were workable, maintaining their obligated status with respect to those provisions and reformulating the remainder if they could reach a compromise with respect to them.

The other course would be for the parties to remove the extrinsic cause of failure, if they could do so; and if they could not, to take steps to ameliorate the unsettling or menacing situations that have arisen. Thus, if a third-party state has intervened in their affairs, they might attempt to eliminate the intervention or its more troublesome consequences. If a new war in their region has broken out, they might agree upon their responses to it or upon the nature and limits of their policies toward the new belligerents. They might also cooperate to abate the adverse political and economic effects of the war. They could try to stabilize their relations, much as any war-oriented states might do, in order to preserve the order established by their settlement; or they might try to diminish the effects of proselytizing ideologies by censorship or counter-propaganda techniques. They might even attempt to restructure in a rather radical way regional or global international relations in order to secure a sounder basis for peacekeeping and thereby insure that their own settlement will continue to keep the peace between them. For their own elites and publics, the policymakers of the parties must obtain acceptance of the terms and general order established by the settlement, perhaps even developing it into a symbol of peace or of the other values the elites of their polities hold dear. All these steps presume that the parties want to take them. However, this might not be the case: the issues of the past war might have remained intensely ideologized well into the postwar period, or the policymakers might regard the settlement as a device solely to facilitate achievement of their unabandoned war aims, and then dispense with it. The same negative factors might also be operative in inducing the parties to avoid remedying an inadequate settlement. If it were to them a mere paper agreement, providing no security, no material or spiritual values, it might not be worth correcting. Then, if they wanted to avoid conflict, they would have to take positive steps to keep the peace without reference to the terms of their earlier settlement.

Improved Settlements

It is true that men do not always keep their promises, and states do not always fulfill their treaty obligations. Apart from their transcendent obligatory force—if indeed they have such—promises and treaties do perform utilitarian functions. Of what use would a peace treaty be if the parties to it could not anticipate that the others would also carry out their obligations, at least to some extent? It is because men do keep their promises often enough that contracts and treaties are possible. Confronted with a valid, unambiguous, "airtight" clause in a duly ratified treaty, policymakers generally fulfill its terms; and it is the principle of *pacta sunt servanda* that more or less induces this compliance. However one expresses it, whether natural law commands performance, whether the utility of the principle demands for it that respect that will enable all states to relate to each other in regularized and predictable ways, policymakers are deterred from ignoring treaty terms. When the violation of a treaty becomes a necessity, however, when the obligated state's very existence is threatened, nothing will stand in the way of a breach. Yet even here, policymakers go out of their way to justify the breach by an appeal to other principles: changed conditions voiding the treaty (*rebus sic stantibus*), national self-determination, proletarian solidarity, or the command of Scripture. This appeal often masks the real motivating principle of reason of state. Naturally, this principle of necessity can also command the violation of a perfectly adequate, technically correct peace treaty.

There are many times, however, when policymakers find treaty evasion merely desirable. It is in this area that we can hope for improved peace settlements, without being entirely utopian. In anticipation of the time when policymakers might seek to find loopholes in their treaty of peace, both to avoid its terms and to appear not to commit a breach of a treaty obligation (and hence to act contrary to the principle of *pacta sunt servanda*), peace planners ought to insure ahead of time the legal integrity of their settlement by taking steps to secure the best possible peace treaty. When of this mind, they can be persuaded to choose their treaty draftsmen carefully and to enjoin them to produce a document clearly and precisely expressing the exact nature of the agreement between the parties. They must consciously avoid ambiguity in every passage unless, of course, ambiguity is a precondition of agreement. (A clear delineation of the obligations of each of the parties is not always possible. Ambiguous terms then mirror an ambiguous agreement—an incomplete and hence inadequate agreement. Until the parties can resolve the questions about which they have had only a partial meeting of the minds, the language of their draft—if indeed they bother to insert it into the treaty at all—is bound to be ambiguous.)

Timing might also be of the essence. While haste may be necessary in situations where there would otherwise be no settlement, a hastily drafted treaty is more likely to contain defects. On the other hand, delay could also have its undesirable consequences: One party might be persuaded that the other did not want agreement. Domestic and world political conditions could change, and the time would no longer be suitable for a settlement. The peacemakers thus must strike a balance between too little time spent on negotiations and drafting and too much time.

It will also be necessary for the policymakers of the belligerent states to recognize that planning for the peace negotiations (as well as peace planning for the postwar period) is essential. They or their peace planners must determine the limits imposed on their plans by the character of the war and the strength of their bargaining position. An assessment of the latter is often surprisingly difficult, as many statesmen labor under illusions while they are waging war. We could hope that they will find objective planners who will apprise them of a fair estimate of their state's power position, whatever the expectations of the public and its leaders. According to the postulate that the character of the war determines the character of the peace, the planners must analyze the structure of the war and assess the implications of that structure for peace negotiations and the settlement.[8] They ought then to consider the relationship between the structures of the war and possible settlements, on the one hand, and their postwar policy goals, on the other, and decide upon appropriate foreign and domestic policies. Thus, their analysis would not only answer the question, What peace settlements are possible? but also help to answer the question, What policies throughout the peacemaking period, and afterward, are possible? If necessary, the policymakers ought to embark upon an "education-for-peace" program, with at least two purposes in mind: first, to devalue (or de-ideologize) the issues of the war and hence to make peace domestically possible; second, to prepare the polity for the peace settlement the policymakers think likely to obtain after negotiations. In this way, domestic opposition to the peace and to the implementation of the settlement, could be minimized. All the thresholds of settlement could then be crossed by the negotiators.

The peacemakers must also be aware of the sorts of inadequacies that might be incorporated adventitiously in their settlement. Some of these were listed in the preceding section of this chapter. They should avoid them where agreement to do so can be obtained. The analyst should also ask, What is the best settlement *in the circumstances?* Dissatisfaction arises where what is best in the circumstances for one party is not also accepted as such by the other parties. With this in mind, the peacemakers ought perhaps to confront the question squarely: Can we move toward a settlement that is, in the circumstances, acceptable to all parties? If they cannot, they again ought to understand clearly in what respects their settlement is not acceptable. They would then have some basis from which to prepare for the anticipatable inadequacies referred to earlier. Conversely, they might try to determine what is clearly an inadequate settlement in the circumstances: for these pitfalls might be avoided even if the optimum solutions to problems could not be gained.[9]

8 Whether they follow the systematic program of analysis offered in this book is not important; but they ought to recognize that thought must be given to how the character or structure of the war determines the structure of its settlement and how the war might end. To this end, I think it desirable for scholars to continue to study peace settlements of the past and devise programs of analysis that could be genuinely helpful to policymakers and peace planners.

9 In the postwar period, it might even be possible for the parties to come to the conclusion that their peace settlement had become dysfunctional in preserving peace or in preventing the development of normal political and economic relations between them. Such a realization would be the first step in negotiations leading to the desirable supersession of the settlement.

Following Kant's principle that no one should do anything in war that will make reconciliation impossible, policymakers and peace planners ought to refrain from conducting their military operations in the late stages of the war in such a way as to render peacemaking more difficult. And their plans for peace ought not make war more probable. In order to accomplish this, however, the policymakers of the belligerents should have begun to think of the peace long before the war has ended. Acting on the principle that a multilateral war is more difficult to settle adequately than a complex war, and a complex war more difficult to settle than a simple war, they ought to direct their wartime diplomacy to containing hostilities and to preventing internationalization of the war. War-oriented states and international organizations ought to attempt this also, whether or not the belligerents act according to these precepts or invite the others so to act. It is perhaps fortunate that we have, or can at least hope for, organizations that will seek to contain war and will take steps to provide incentives for deterring internationalization of conflict and perhaps devise sanctions toward the same end. But as a war's termination occurs in the context of a variety of world political occurrences and as a peace treaty alone is not always the entire settlement (supplemented as it often is by informal understandings and separate treaties of guarantee or commerce), the peace planners must think of the entire world political environment. They ought to consider schemes of regional and world order that would provide the most adequate guarantees both for their state's security and for the execution of the terms of the peace treaty. In this regard, there is little basis for optimism, however—at least for the present—since even among theoreticians there is no agreement as to the nature of either an ideal world order or a plurality of regional interstate systems that do not within each of them contain the seeds of conflict between competing or ideologically disparate orders. And within the orders envisaged, instabilities generated by technological change, population growth, economic and political development, and proselytizing ideologies render illusory schemes for maintaining peace. The irony is that were these problems to be solved or controlled, there would probably be no more wars and therefore no more settlements; and hence, concern over the adequacy of peace settlements would be moot. But unless the problems are solved, we can expect every peace settlement to have some degree of intrinsic inadequacy which, given the weaknesses of men, will lead to more wars.

Epilogue

There are discernible patterns in the ways wars end. What I have called the structure of war (the numbers of belligerents and the way they are involved in the war) determines *possible* outcomes and modes of settlement. The *actual* outcome depends upon which party has won. More generally, it is a function of the military situation at the war's end. When there is a settlement (and there will be when neither party is totally destroyed), its form and content are functions of the extent to which the parties' bargaining strength permits the transformation of their war aims and peace plans into the terms of a settlement. The effectiveness of a party's bargaining power, in turn, depends not only upon its military power position but also upon the configuration of domestic political forces within its polity, the cohesiveness of the alliances to which it belongs, the power positions of its allies, the sorts of war-oriented actors that exist, and the aims of these actors and their ability to translate their war aims into policies that influence peacemaking. Other, even remote, events and actors in the state system occasionally mitigate or augment the effectiveness of a belligerent's policies. An appraisal of all these factors in a systematic analysis enables us to characterize the peacemaking process, to describe its meaning for the parties, and ultimately to estimate its historical significance. There is no way of telling for certain when (and whether) these factors will influence peace negotiations or determine the content of a peace settlement; hence, we have the rather detailed analysis of the preceding chapters relating to the conditions under which they can become determinants, and the consequences when they have become such. To this end, the discussion of the book identifies the most important variables and shows their interrelationships to enable the student better to understand the termination of past wars and even to help the analyst-policymaker adumbrate settlements for ongoing wars.

Just as it is inadmissible to expect to learn enough about peacemaking by limiting one's studies to wars since 1945, it is not sufficient to take a partial view of the settlement process. Analytical breadth, as well as historical depth, are necessary. The settlement process is a whole, and it must be studied as a whole. The passage from the stage of preliminary negotiations to the ratification of a peace treaty may seem to have had a logical evolution for those who look back upon a settlement after the lapse of many years. But logical development, or a pattern of events, is not usually evident to the peacemakers at the time. Multifarious pressures affect their negotiations. Thresholds between phases of peacemaking, or between one issue area and another, may or may not have been crossed. Peacemakers are immersed in the process, perhaps overwhelmed by it; the apparent hopelessness or futility of the peacemaking task, the emotions the war has generated, and the often pressing need for immediate solutions combine to prevent their acquisition of more than a temporally and substantively limited view of what it is possible to achieve. It is conceivable that peacemaking studies may eventually provide standards for a settlement or incline statesmen to adopt multiple perspectives during peace negotiations. Our understanding of peacemaking, an objective of this book, enables us to see relevant events and factors in their relations to each other, to discern additional connections and relations, and to recognize where it might have been possible to follow other courses toward peace.

Peacemakers and their governments not only have the usual human difficulty of being unable to foresee how they must order their future; they also have an incomplete and biased perspective of what it is they must settle, what their war was about. They must not, for example, confuse current issues with those of the early stages of the war; they had better settle the war now being fought—which is not necessarily the same war they began.

A peace settlement is Janus-like. It is both forward-looking and backward-looking: it sets the seal of the belligerents upon decisions made by force of arms; and it lays down rules and structures for interparty relations in the postwar era. The more complex a war and the more it is internationalized, the more far-reaching will its settlement be. In this sense, it becomes a constitution for the state system. Yet, the legacy of a multilateral war is, among other things, a settlement of greater intrinsic inadequacy. The resolution of past troubles is less complete; the provisions for reducing or preventing future conflict less realistic. Certainly for multilateral war, but for simpler wars as well, it is important to understand what a settlement must do in the circumstances, and what it *may* do in order to reinforce its beneficial projection upon the future. For only then may both belligerents and interested parties begin early to plan for a more adequate and lasting settlement.

To the end of *understanding* this book has been written. We summarize its major propositions as an overview of the ground we have covered.

1. The character of the war determines the character of its settlement.

2. A complete settlement comprises both military and political terms. The former includes the cease-fire, technical provisions relating to the disposition of troops, and often supervisory and control mechanisms. The political settlement contains the "elements of a settlement," the provisions relating to territory, security guarantees, persons affected by the war, normalization of relations, adjustment of future disputes, and penalties. The first three elements are invariably present in some form in a peace treaty; the last three are sometimes present.

3. In the phase preliminary to substantive peace negotiations, the parties decide whether they mean to move toward peace or continue the war. They frequently try to reach an accommodation on procedures for peace talks. But in all cases throughout the peacemaking period, the parties strive to satisfy their war aims either by military means (until an armistice comes into effect) or by negotiations.

4. A settlement cannot be complete if de-ideologization (or devaluation) has not proceeded far enough to move the parties across the settlement thresholds.

5. In an external war, each of the belligerents has one or more war aims, usefully categorized as dominance, maintenance of the status quo, consolidation, ideological gains, retribution, or opportunistic gains. In an internal war, the insurgent's war aims are either control of the polity or independence. (A war fought for the exercise of autonomy short of independence—in political, religious, or cultural matters—can be subsumed under this last heading.)

6. Identification of the parties' war aims, particularly those at or near the war's end, is required. The peace policies and plans of the belligerents, and ultimately the provisions of a settlement, embody those aims, transformed during the peacemaking process by the *factors* that affect the parties' bargaining powers. (See the first paragraph of the Epilogue.) Isolation of aims also enables us to determine the condition of belligerent alliances: their cohesiveness, their effectiveness, and the likelihood of their dissolution as a result of incompatible war aims.

7. The involvement of one or more alliances in a war and the intervention of states in an internal war complicate the peacemaking process:

it multiplies decision-making (and hence, peace-policy consideration) centers; and it increases the numbers of possible outcomes and modes of settlement. The intrinsic inadequacy of the settlement is also increased. The parties have the choice of making peace collectively or separately, embodying their agreement in one or more multipartite treaties or in a multiplicity of bilateral treaties.

8. War-oriented actors of various kinds (great powers, nonbelligerent allies, regional states, and international organizations), although non-belligerent, can influence peacemaking, depending upon the character—mainly the power position—of the actor, how effectively it is represented at the peace talks, and whether the state system environment of the war is conducive to the adoption of the war or peace policies the actors espouse.

9. Multilateral wars are extensively internationalized. There are many belligerents, and the wars extend over wide areas. A great number of war-oriented actors usually exist. The settlement of a multilateral war, affecting so many states in fundamental ways and concluding a war that has restratified and transformed the state system, has the character of a con-stitution for that system.

10. Multilateral wars may be settled piecemeal or comprehensively. In the latter case, peace negotiations become a cooperative enterprise of the participating states and take on the character of an *ad hoc* international organization.

11. In discoursing about the settlement process, it is essential to move from the analytical level of interstate (or interfaction) relations to the level of *intraparty* politics: to assess how domestic political forces prevent or induce moves toward peace, how transnational politics or diplomatic techniques affect these domestic forces which, in turn, feed back upon the peacemaking process, and how domestic political matters influence the latter during negotiations. It is at this level, moreover, that we see how critically important in history the individual, idiosyncratic policymaker and the political character of the belligerent polity have often been in influencing peacemaking.

12. Peace plans include any policies the belligerents and war-oriented actors adopt in anticipation of or preparation for peace. They may be formal, prepared by the belligerents individually or in consultation with allies; they might even be the work-products of a specially constituted peace planning commission. The plan according to which the belliger-ents seek to establish rules for their postwar relations and structure the postwar regional or world order is a modification of their war aims tempered by the losses sustained or the gains won during the war, reflect-ing their policymakers' images of the roles their states ought to play after the settlement; and indeed, the plan will be determinative of the direc-tion in which the peacemakers attempt to move the peace talks.

13. Peace settlements can fail when they are inadequate or incomplete;

they may be technically defective, or the war issues might remain intensely ideologized. Settlements also fail for reasons quite beyond the powers of the peacemakers to control, by the actions of third-party states or because events occur that change the political environment of the settlement, modifying or destroying the conditions essential to its implementation and effectiveness. A prospective settlement can be improved by a variety of means, but the most important requisites are the peacemakers' awareness of their differing perspectives upon the structure of the war, an understanding of the peacemaking process and of what it is possible to achieve in the circumstances, and a willingness to perfect the settlement and overcome its intrinsic inadequacies by remedial devices during negotiations and afterwards, in the postwar era.

14. We have established a hierarchy of wars, from the structurally simplest to the most complex. This, in effect, also established a hierarchy of peace settlements. System-transforming multilateral wars have been concluded by correspondingly significant restorations of peace. It is these wars and their settlements that have structured the state system in the modern era: they have provided the matrix for interstate relations, including the context of subsequent wars and their settlements. Indeed, the pacifications of the great wars were precedents for those of future wars. It is to them that peacemakers of "small wars" have looked for patterns of settlement. But more fundamentally, it is to them that students of international relations must refer to trace the evolution of the state system. In this sense, a study of the great pacifications gives us an insight into the nature of international relations. Peace settlements, after all, created the modern state system; they have characterized the relations of states and the international law of those relations; and it is through them, in part, that the modern state became what it is.

Does the systematic analysis presented in this book have any efficacy for prediction and control? It is rather limited in these respects, for the present. However, one could take comfort in being able to apply our concepts for an understanding of the forces preventing or inducing peace, for describing modes of settlement and the probable content of a peace settlement, and for estimating its adequacy and significance. Insofar as our knowledge of the variables enables us to understand the probable direction of the peacemaking process and the probable form of a settlement, an analyst-peacemaker could achieve some small measure of control, particularly if his bargaining strength had given him some flexibility at the peace talks. But regardless of bargaining strength, effective diplomacy could enable even the weakest of parties to direct peacemaking in some ways; and then a systematic overview, together with an appreciation of the ways past wars have ended, may provide the peace planner and peacemaker with analytical tools and models for elaborating the best settlement, in the circumstances, commensurate with their interests. Naturally, it is possible that satisfaction of national (or factional) interests will preclude an adequate settlement. It is not entirely utopian to hope, however, that an acquaintance with war-termination studies will serve to induce peacemakers to arrive at the best settlement in the circumstances (with due allowances for the parties' interests). They should be aware of its limitations and of the terms that are likely to lead to difficulties and conflicts, and sensible of the need to revise or complete their settlement when the cooling of passions permits; but, in any event, they should couple their peacemaking with techniques for keeping the peace in the postwar era.

Men and nations have been waging war—and making peace—for centuries. If they will not learn to prevent wars, we may hope they will at least learn to end them better.

Disagreements over
the Structure of War

Belligerents may differ over the form or structure of the war in which they are involved. Consider an internal war situation in which state A has committed troops in support of faction x and state B has reacted by sending "volunteers" to help faction y. The intervening states recognize the faction each supports as the sole legitimate government of state R. The policymakers of A and B may view the war in different ways, as depicted in Figures 1 and 2:

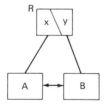

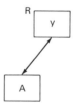

FIGURE A–1. State A's view of the war.   FIGURE A–2. State B's view of the war.

State A insists that B is a belligerent, supporting the rebels y against the government of R (faction x), which consented to the troop support given to R by A. State B, on the other hand, asserts that A is making war upon the legitimate government of R (faction y) through its intervention, and that B is not actively involved in hostilities.[1] If there were a settlement of this war—as opposed to the

1 Until negotiations began in Paris in late 1968, the United States and the Democratic Republic of Vietnam held official views of the Vietnam War similar to the example given here. The U.S. (state A in our example) maintained that the DRVN (state B) had poured cadres into the sovereign Republic of Vietnam (state R) in order to foster rebellion and had later invaded the RVN outright. The National Liberation Front of South Vietnam (faction y, in the

winning of a victory by either faction and the decoupling of the intervenors without negotiations—the form of that settlement would depend upon the structure of the war the belligerents have at least implicitly agreed they were fighting. The parties could amend their views of the war's structure and come to perceive it in about the same way; or they could retain their views and make use of fictions to reconcile their differences, thereby permitting them to achieve a mutually acceptable but probably inadequate settlement.

This is only one instance of disagreement over the structure of war. It is possible for the belligerents to differ in a variety of other situations: if, for example, one state maintains that it is merely war-oriented, while others maintain that it is a belligerent;[2] if there are a multiplicity of factions in an internal war and some of them (or the intervening states) refuse to admit the existence of all the factions that are fighting;[3] if the belligerents in a multilateral war do not agree upon the disposition of the parties to the war;[4] or if the belligerents in the simple war are implicated in a larger war (a multilateral war, perhaps) and are unwilling to treat their conflict as a war within a war.[5]

---

example), according to the U.S. view, was a mere front for the North Vietnamese, without independent existence, wholly a creature of the DRVN. The DRVN official view is similar to the image in Figure 2: The NLF (y) was the only legitimate government in southern Vietnam; DRVN troops were not in the south; the only military forces there were the military arm of the NLF. The U.S. (state A) was making war upon the people of Vietnam. In 1968, the parties in effect agreed to treat the war as an internal-external war in South Vietnam: U.S. and RVN vs. NLF and DRVN. (The reader is referred to Chapter 5 for a discussion of this type of war.) All four parties were invited to the talks; but the U.S. would not recognize the NLF, and the DRVN would not recognize the RVN.

2 This could occur in a simple external war, A vs. B, in which state N was a nonbelligerent ally of B; or in which a great power provided B with assistance of a sort that A would regard as implicating the power as a belligerent.

3 See Chapter 5 for a discussion of internal wars having multiple factions. See, in particular, the Dutch and Greek Revolts (pp. 208–14, 222–5).

4 See Chapter 8. Figures 8–1 and 8–2 show two possible forms of multilateral war. Given the multiplicity of parties and their modes of involvement, it is likely that some of the belligerents will disagree about how they or others were involved.

5 This calls for recognition by the parties of larger issues, tied perhaps to the war aims of the various parties in the multilateral war or recognition by them of the issues affecting vital interests of states other than themselves. In the Thirty Years' War (pp. 379–92), there were several small wars, limited in time and in the number of belligerents involved and relatively independent—at least apparently—of the Central European War: the Danish Intervention, for example, or the War of the Mantuan Succession and the Struggle for the Grisons. These wars were more or less settled through negotiations. But many matters had to be left unsettled because of the larger issues of the central war, which were not resolved at the time—and were settled only at Westphalia in 1648 and in the Peace of the Pyrenees of 1659. Thus, after a series of wars that occur within a limited geographical area or appear to involve common or

There are a number of important consequences of differing views on the structure of war:

1. Not all necessary parties may be in on the settlement process, and hence, not all parties will be obligated.

2. Not all issues can be raised and resolved, particularly those we have called *interconnected questions.*[6]

3. The parties may disagree about the legal and political consequences that follow from their respective images of the war.

4. The belligerents may come to expect different outcomes, some of which neither might have anticipated, which will muddle their policymakers' thinking about ways to move toward peace.

5. The form of the settlement will be different from the form an objective observer would have supposed must be adopted to bring the war to a conclusive end among all belligerents.

The Seven Years' War illustrates this last point.[7] The allies, Britain and Prussia, disagreed about the sort of war they were fighting; and the war was settled through two conferences, one at Paris in which the British participated, the other at Hubertusburg with the Prussians present. There was no liaison between these conferences; consequently, a number of issues were left unresolved.[8]

The results in particular cases depend upon the circumstances and the parties involved. The war might be prolonged, as the parties could refuse to negotiate the issues of a conflict about whose nature they do not agree. If negotiations did begin, they might fail. Or finally, if the parties did reach a settlement, it might be inadequate, based upon fictions that will not last through the first stresses or disagreements of the postwar era.

As a general principle, then, I think we can say that agreement among the belligerents and war-oriented actors in respect of the structure of the war enables the parties to see what solutions are possible. It brings *realism* to peacemaking efforts. The perspectives of each of the parties, after all, will probably give only a partial view of the modes of settlement possible, particularly if policymakers view the conflict through the lenses of their ideologies. In the interests of securing a more adequate settlement, the peace planners of the parties should at least understand how their adversaries (or allies) view the war.

---

analogous issues, the policymaker-analysts must ask: Will it be sufficient to settle one particular war? Should we not seek a general, wide-reaching settlement for all the issues and for all the parties involved in the entire group of wars?

6 *Supra,* pp. 311–6.

7 *Supra,* pp. 374–9.

8 This does show that even among allies there may be differing views as to the structure of the war. Moreover, even among the policymakers within a state or faction such differences often exist. In the former case, divergent perspectives can add to the strains on the coalition and interfere with the efficient coordination of policies for war and for peace. In the latter case, unless the policymakers reconcile their views, they will have difficulty in articulating their war aims, establishing priorities for war aims and other foreign policies, and agreeing upon peace plans (including a plan for moving toward peace and through peace negotiations) .

Relative Compatibility
of War Aims

We hypothesize the simplest case possible for a complex external war: an alliance of states A and B at war with a single state X. Assume that state A and state B each have a single war aim. To compare the relative compatibility of the war aims of states A and B, we could construct a matrix whose columns would represent the possible war aims of state A; the rows would represent the possible war aims of state B. The "possible war aims" are those discussed in Chapter 2: dominance, consolidation of the state, status quo (defense or maintenance of position), ideological gain, retribution, and opportunistic gains. At the intersection of a row and column, the war aim of state A can be compared with the war aim of state B. Because it is inconvenient to insert lengthy comments at matrix intersections, I will take up the possible combinations in linear sequence. It should be emphasized that the following discussion is not (and cannot be) exhaustive. It is meant to be heuristic: to show how kinds of war aims intrinsically place limits upon the cohesiveness and hence the effectiveness of an alliance.

A.   The war aim of state A is dominance.

1. Assume the war aim of the ally, state B, is also dominance. For a given region, two states will not usually be dominant. A condominium is possible, although this form of organization has been notoriously unstable and unsuccessful in the past. Unless A and B can agree to divide a region into spheres of influence, where each has control of a portion of the region or of its resources or markets, a quarrel between them would probably ensue, the least effect of which would be to dissolve the coalition; the most extreme effect, war between the contenders. If B were to accept the predominance of A in the given area, cooperation should be possible. But competition for dominance is not a sign of a healthy coalition. One state is likely to fear and distrust the other and eventually refuse to accept the other's aspirations for predominance.

2. Assume the war aim of state B is its own consolidation. If the consolidation of B were likely to challenge the drive for dominance of A in a given region, there will be disagreement among the allies. If the area B sought to annex were outside of A's sphere of influence, chances for conflict would be reduced. It might be the case that after consolidation, B would not or could not challenge A. Conflict could then arise only if, through fear or distrust, B refused to accept the consequences of a subordinate position in the alliance.

3. Assume the war aim of B is the status quo. If B were fighting a purely defensive war, B's policymakers would probably accept A's assistance, even though A was seeking dominance. When (and if) state B had assured itself that state X (the enemy) no longer constituted a serious threat, B might then refuse to accept A's dominance. Hence, as the threat to B declined, the possibility of disagreement between the allies would increase where the other ally's aim was dominance. But, if state B were at war to maintain its position of predominance in a given region, A's aim for dominance would hardly be compatible with B's war aim, and disagreement would result. Conflict could be avoided by a division of the region into spheres of influence. Even if state B's aim were merely to maintain its position relative to adversary state X and other states, however subordinate that position might be, disagreement between A and B would occur if B were unwilling to accept A's dominance. Or recognizing their state's naturally subordinate power position, B's policymakers might be perfectly prepared to accept their status and the consequences for the war effort and the peace settlement, in which case the alliance would remain viable.

4. Assume B's war aim is ideological (and A's aim is dominance). Clearly, if state A accepted or tolerated state B's ideology *and* state B acquiesced in A's drive for dominance, there would be no disagreement. If the ideology of the one state could not countenance the supremacy (ideological or otherwise) of any associate, conflict would be inevitable. Such is also the case where state A's leaders find state B's ideology distasteful. If these assessments by one state of the other state's aims had been made earlier, there would have been little likelihood of the formation of a coalition. Yet, when in dire need, policymakers are willing to overlook the nature (and implications) of the war aims of a potential alliance partner. Indeed, only in the late stages of the war or in the peace negotiations might the true nature of the allies' war aims become evident. Then, misperceptions will be suddenly cured. Disagreement follows disenchantment; and dissolution of the alliance results.

The specific reasons for conflict in the hypothesized situation would, of course, vary with the facts of the actual situation. The politics of the allies toward a defeated, or nearly defeated state (X) are likely to be in conflict: state B's ideologically motivated desire to convert the citizens of state X or to subordinate them in some way because they are ideological heretics would not be compatible with A's aim of dominance. If A shared B's ideology, or was in sympathy with it, A might permit the subordination of state X by state B as long as the consequences of such a step did not constitute a challenge to A's predominance.

5. Assume state B's war aim is retributive. Cooperation would be possible unless B came to fear A's actual or prospective dominance and refused to acquiesce or unless state B could not obtain tribute from or otherwise punish state X or

remove the provocative cause of the war because A's drive to dominate X denied these values to B.

6. Assume the war aim of B is opportunistic. As in the preceding hypothetical situation, cooperation would be possible unless the allies quarrelled over the particular value that B sought to obtain by going to war with X. State B might also decide to resist A's dominance. In either case, conflict would ensue.

B. State A's war aim is its own consolidation.

1. We have already considered the compatibility of a war aim of dominance and a war aim of consolidation of the state in section A.2. We now assume that both state B and state A have as their war aim their own consolidation. In that event, the allies would be able to cooperate provided that the areas of state X that each sought to annex did not overlap. If they did so, we could expect conflict between them.

2. Assume state B's war aim to be the preservation of the status quo. If fighting a purely defensive war, state B would probably not object to A's consolidation. In fact, B might be willing to purchase A's assistance at the cost of X's territory. If, on the other hand, B had become a belligerent in order to maintain its position in the region, there is apt to be disagreement between the allies if B were dominant and A's consolidation were perceived as a threat to that dominance. Even if state B were only interested in maintaining a non-superior power position vis-à-vis states X, A, and others, A's consolidation could pose what state B's policymakers would see as a threat to B and minimally an undesirable alteration in the balance of power. Disagreement might arise if B sought to moderate A's demands at the peace talks. And it would undoubtedly arise if B opposed A's territorial demands.

3. Assume B's aim is ideological. There is certain to be disagreement if A refuses to accept B's ideology. We could fairly ask how it would have been possible for A to have agreed to form an alliance with B in the first place. In the particular historical situation, B's ideology initially might not have seemed so repugnant to state A's policymakers when their determination to consolidate was pressing and transcended other goals. When this project was seen to be succeeding (or failing), A's policymakers would then be apt to look at B's ideology more critically. State B's leaders, moreover, might be uncomfortable about allying with a state that did not embrace its ideology. But to succeed against state X, they might have been willing temporarily to hide their distaste for the "heretic" A and agree to permit A to annex a part of X's territory. Disagreement would arise at a later stage of the war or during peace negotiations when (and if) B's policymakers decided they need no longer support some or all of A's claims for territory, as A did not accept B's ideology. Even if A and B shared the ideology, disagreement between the allies would be probable if B refused to support A's claims against X or sought to reduce the scope of A's claims.

4. Let us assume state B's war aim is retribution (A's aim remains consolidation). The war aims of the allies would be compatible unless B was to be deprived of the values its leaders sought from X because of state A's territorial demands against X. Of course, if B's leaders had embarked upon the war because of some provocation by X, state A's aim of consolidation at X's expense might fit

in well with B's aim. The annexation of territory by A might automatically in-sure that X would be unable to provoke B in the same way again.

5. Assume B's war aim is opportunistic. In the case where B's war aim was opportunistc, the aims of the allies would be compatible unless B were unable to obtain the values for which its policymakers went to war because of A's territorial demands against state X. In a war either for retribution or for an opportunity value, state B could come into conflict with state A, should the former fear that satisfaction of A's demands would allow it to dominate B.

C. Let us assume that in a third hypothetical situation *state A's war aim is the preservation of the status quo.*

We have analyzed the war-aim pairs of dominance-status quo and consolida-tion of the state-status quo; and we need not repeat that analysis here.

1. Let us then first assume that both state A and state B want to preserve the status quo. If both allies are fighting a defensive war, their war aims would be compatible. Such would also be the case where both states want to maintain their power position relative to other states and to each other. If, during the course of the war or peace negotiations, it appeared that one or the other ally might become dominant in the region, it is conceivable that disagreements would arise as one ally might refuse to acquiesce in the other becoming dominant. Compare this situation with that in section A.3. Now, if one state had initially gone to war against state X in order to maintain its paramount position in a region, pre-sumably another state would not become its ally in a status quo war to maintain its position unless it willingly accepted the first state's predominance. Thus, if state A's war aim were status quo defense and state B's war aim were status quo maintenance of a dominant position, the war aims would probably be compatible, unless and until A's policymakers had become convinced that state B no longer intended to preserve the status quo, but rather intended to increase its dominance in the region, possibly threatening even state A's position. We would have a similar situation where one state was at war to maintain its dominance and the other ally was at war merely to maintain its position relative to state X and others in the region, including state A.

2. Assume state B's war aim is ideological (A's aim remains the status quo). Unless state A came to accept B's ideology or unless the ideologies of the allies A and B were compatible, disagreements would be apt to arise even though the partners might find a basis on which to cooperate before the war or in the war's early stages. Thus, if A were fighting a defensive war, initially it might be will-ing to cooperate with the ideologically alien state B. When and if A's defense succeeded in assuring its leaders of security they might then find grounds for dis-agreement with the ideologically based policy aims of state B's leaders. There is no intrinsic incompatibility between an ideological war aim and a war aim to maintain the ordinary or paramount power position of another state. Hence, cooperation is possible and conceivable. However, an ideologically oriented state B could all too easily be regarded as a challenge to a predominant state A striving to maintain its dominance. The perception by A's policymakers of a challenge of this sort, even if illusory, would certainly lead to disagreement. (Refer to the discussion in section A.4.) State B's ideological aspirations could indeed appear to be a threat to status quo states because the export of an ideology

invariably changes the regional status quo. B's ideological policies relative to state X (should there be victory) might conflict with state A's pragmatic, power political policies; and unless the two allies could work out a *modus vivendi,* disagreement would strain the alliance and might even result in its dissolution.

3. Let us assume state B's war aim is either retributive or opportunistic (A's is the status quo). There would be no disagreement if A were fighting a purely defensive war. If A's war aim was the maintenance of its position, the allies might come to disagree about the kind and quantity of the retributive or opportunity values state B sought. State A might attempt to moderate B's demands; and B's leaders might resent this or regard it as a betrayal of a past commitment. Either state, moreover, might eventually come to fear the other's relative superiority, particularly if the retributive or opportunistic values sought from state X would be thrown into the balance, if acquired by B. It is easy to see that cooperation would be difficult in these situations.

D. For our fourth principal hypothetical situation, let us assume that state A's war aim is ideological.

In the preceding sections, we have compared the consequences of an ideological war aim with the war aims of dominance, consolidation of the state, and preservation of the status quo. We need not repeat that analysis.

1. Let us assume that both state A and state B have ideological war aims. State A and state B must have identical or at least compatible ideologies, or there will eventually be disagreement and conflict. If the ideologies of A and B were clearly incompatible, probably no coalition would have been formed originally (at least to wage solely an ideological war). There is perhaps a large gray area between identity and total incompatibility of ideologies, where policy differences between states can be hidden by rhetoric or the usual self-delusion and misperceptions of the leaders of states. Nevertheless, it is difficult to see how cooperation, let alone the initial formation of the alliance, would be possible if the objects for which A and B were fighting (or will fight) were purely ideological. To embark upon an ideological war implies, of course, that ideology is all-important. Great attention would be paid to ideological considerations, to the ideological purity of the ally, and to the consistency of that ally's policies with the precepts of the ideology.

2. Assume B's war aim is either retributive or opportunistic. In the event state A's ideology conflicted with, or prevented, state B's obtaining the retributive or opportunity values for which state B had waged war, there would be disagreement between the allies. As in the case of the other pairs of war aims just discussed in which ideology was one of the aims, so it is with B's retributive or opportunistic war aims: if the ally B waged the war for a purpose other than an ideological purpose, disagreement would always be possible, particularly if state B refused to adopt or accept the ideology of its coalition partner.

E. Assume that state A's war aim is retribution.

We need consider only two cases: if state B's war aim was also retribution and if it was opportunistic gain. In the former case, cooperation between the allies would be possible (and indeed, probable) unless there were disagreement about the distribution of the particular values sought to be obtained from the mutual enemy state X. Strains would also be placed upon the coalition if the allies differed about the nature of the provocation originally offered by X and how to eliminate that provocation.

If state B's aim was opportunistic gain, A's efforts to punish X might conceivably interfere with B's efforts to obtain its opportunity values. In that event, the allies must reach some agreement about the way they will share the spoils of war.

F.   Finally there is a last hypothetical situation, in which state A's war aim is opportunistic gain.

All other war-aim pairs have been examined except the pair in which state B's war aim is also opportunistic gain. Here, the allies must work out a plan for the distribution of opportunity values. In the event both want the same particular value, disagreement would, of course, ensue.

Bibliography

I. Works dealing with the termination of war and peacemaking

Bloomfield, L. P., and Leiss, A. C. *Controlling Small Wars: A Strategy for the 1970's.* New York: Knopf, 1969.

Calahan, H. A. *What Makes a War End?* New York: Vanguard Press, 1944.

Carr, E. H. *Conditions of Peace.* New York: Macmillan, 1942.

Carroll, B. A. "How Wars End: An Analysis of Some Current Hypotheses." *Journal of Peace Research,* Vol. 4. Oslo, 1969.

Coser, L. A. "The Termination of Conflict." *Journal of Conflict Resolution,* Vol. 5, No. 4, 1961. Pp. 347–53.

Fox, W. T. R. (ed.) *How Wars End. The Annals of the American Academy of Political and Social Science,* Vol. 392, Nov. 1970.

Hemleben, S. J. *Plans for World Peace Through Six Centuries.* Chicago: Univ. of Chicago Press, 1945.

Iklé, F. C. *Every War Must End.* New York: Columbia Univ. Press, 1971.

James, Alan. *The Politics of Peace-Keeping.* New York: Praeger, 1969.

Kahn, Herman, *et al. War Termination: Issues and Concepts.* Harmon-on-Hudson, N.Y.: Hudson Institute, 1968.

Kecskemeti, Paul. *Strategic Surrender.* Stanford: Stanford Univ. Press, 1958.

Klingberg, F. L. "Predicting the Termination of War: Battle Casualties and Population Losses." *Journal of Conflict Resolution,* Vol. 10, No. 2, 1966. Pp. 129–71.

Levi, Werner. "On the Causes of War and the Conditions of Peace." *Journal of Conflict Resolution,* Vol. 4, No. 4, 1960. Pp. 411–20.

———. "On the Causes of Peace." *Journal of Conflict Resolution,* Vol. 8, No. 1, 1964. Pp. 23–35.

Marriott, J. A. R. *Commonwealth or Anarchy? A Survey of Projects of Peace from the Sixteenth to the Twentieth Century.* New York: Columbia Univ. Press, 1939.

Phillimore, W. G. F. *Three Centuries of Treaties of Peace and their Teaching.* London: Murray, 1919.

Phillipson, Coleman. *Termination of War and Treaties of Peace.* New York: Dutton, 1916.

Souleyman, E. V. *The Vision of World Peace in Seventeenth- and Eighteenth-Century France.* New York: G. P. Putnam's Sons, 1941.

Thomson, David *et al. Patterns of Peacemaking.* London: Kegan Paul, 1945.

Wright, Quincy. *A Study of War,* 2 Vols. Chicago: Univ. of Chicago Press, 1942.

——. *The Causes of War and the Conditions of Peace.* London: Longmans, Green & Co. 1935.

II. *Collections containing treaties of peace and related agreements*

Almon, John. *A Collection of all Treaties of Peace, Alliance and Commerce,* 2 Vols. London: J. Almon, 1772.

Bernard, Jacques. *Recueil des Traitez de Paix,* 4 Vols. Amsterdam: Henry et la veuve de T. Boom, 1700.

DuMont, Jean. *Corps Universel Diplomatique du Droit des Gens,* 8 Vols. Amsterdam: Brunel, 1728.

Garden, Guillaume (le Comte de). *Histoire Général des Traités de Paix,* 15 Vols. Paris: Amyot, 1848–87. (An excellent work, analyzing the major European treaties of peace from Westphalia to the Congress of Vienna.)

Great Britain. *A General Collection of Treatys,* 2nd ed., 4 Vols. London: Knapton, Darby *et al.,* 1732.

Hertslet, Edward. *The Map of Europe by Treaty.* 4 Vols. London: Butterworths, 1875–91.

Hertslet, G. E. P. *A Complete Collection of the Treaties and Conventions etc., between Great Britain and Foreign Powers,* 30 Vols. London: Henry Butterworth, 1827–1924.

Israel, F. L. (ed.) *Major Peace Treaties of Modern History, 1648–1967.* 4 Vols. (New York: Chelsea House, 1967).

Jenkinson, Charles. *A Collection of all the Treaties of Peace etc., between Great Britain and other Powers,* 3 Vols. London: J. Debrett, 1785.

Koch, C. G. de. *Abrégé de l'Histoire des Traité de Paix, etc.* 4 Vols. Basle: Chez J. Decker, 1796–97. Revised edition, edited by Schoell, M. S. F., published under the title, *Histoire Abrégé des Traité de Paix.* 15 Vols. Paris: Chez Gide Fils, 1817–18.

Malloy, W. M. *Treaties, Conventions, International Acts, Protocols and Agreements between the U.S.A. and other Powers, 1776–1909,* 4 Vols. Washington, D.C.: Government Printing Office, 1910–38.

Martens, G. F. von. *Recueil de Traités,* 8 Vols. Göttingen: Librairie de Dieterich, 1817–35.

——. *Supplément au Recueil des Traités,* 4 Vols. Göttingen: Dieterich, 1802–8.

——. *Nouveau Recueil de Traités,* 16 Vols. Göttingen: Dieterich, 1817–41.

———. *Nouveau Supplémen au Recueil de Traités*, 3 Vols. Göttingen: Dieterich, 1839–42.

———. *Nouveau Recueil Général de Traités*, 20 Vols. Göttingen: Dieterich, 1843–75.

———. *Nouveau Recueil Général de Traités*, 2° Série, 34 Vols. Göttingen and Leipzig: Dieterich, 1876–1907; 3° Série, 41 Vols. Leipzig & Greifswald: Weicher and Abel, 1909–1969.

Noradounghian, Gabriel. *Recueil d'Actes Internationaux de l'Empire Ottoman*, 4 Vols. Paris: Librairie Cotillon, 1897–1903.

Parry, Clive, *The Consolidated Treaty Series*, 25 Vols. Dobbs Ferry, N.Y.: Oceana, 1969.

Rousset de Missy, Jean. *Recueil d'Historique d'Actes, etc.*, 21 Vols. in 23. The Hague: Chez H. Scheurleer, 1728–55.

Das Staatsarchiv, 86 Vols. Leipzig: Duncker und Humblot, 1861–1919.

de Testa, Ignaz. *Recueil des Traités de la Porte Ottomane*, 10 Vols. Paris: Amyot, 1864–1901.

Wenck, F. A. W. *Codex Iuris Gentium*, 3 Vols. Leipzig: Weidmann, 1781–95.

III. *Historical works dealing with the peace Settlements considered in the text*[1]

SIMPLE EXTERNAL WARS

1. *Russo-Turkish War (1768–1774)*

Hurewitz, J. C. *Diplomacy in the Near and Middle East*, 2 Vols. Princeton: Van Nostrand, 1956. See Vol. 1.

de Keralio, Louis. *Histoire de la Derniére Guerre entre les Russes et les Turcs*, 2 Vols. Paris: Chez la veuve Desaint, 1777.

Sorel, Albert. *The Eastern Question in the Eighteenth Century*. Trans. by Bramwell, F. C. London: Methuen, 1898.

Zinkeisen, J. W. *Geschichte des osmanischen Reiches in Europa*, 7 Vols. Hamburg & Gotha: F. Perthes, 1840–1863. See Vols. 5 & 6.

2. *The War of 1812*

Adams, J. Q. *Documents relating to the Transactions at the Negotiations of Ghent*. Louisville: S. Penn, 1823.

Beirne, F. F. *The War of 1812*. New York: Dutton, 1949.

1. The references collected in this section of the Bibliography include important works in English, French, German, Italian and Spanish, dealing with the settlements of the wars analyzed in Chapters 2, 3, 4, 5 and 9. Inclusion of works relating to the causes and to all the phases and aspects of the named wars would have enlarged the Bibliography beyond manageable proportions. Hence, I have restricted the listing to works that deal with peacemaking only—or to those in which one part of the work contains an important discussion of the peace settlement. The researcher is cautioned to the incompleteness of the list: works in Danish, Dutch, Russian and Swedish (and other languages as well) have been omitted owing to the fact that the author (or his research assistants) did not have competence in these languages.

Engelman, F. L. *The Peace of Christmas Eve.* New York: Brace and World, 1962.
Ford, W. C., "The Treaty of Ghent and After." *Proceedings of the State Historical Society of Wisconsin* (1914). Pp. 78–106.
Ingersoll, C. J. *History of the Second War Between the United States of America and Great Britain,* 2 Vols. Philadelphia: Lippincott, Gramby and Co., 1852.
Melish, John. *Documents relating to the Negotiations for Peace between the United States and Great Britain.* Philadelphia: George Palmer, 1814.
Updyke, F. A. *The Diplomacy of the War of 1812.* Baltimore: Johns Hopkins Press, 1915.
White, P. C. T. *A Nation on Trial: America and the War of 1812.* New York: Wiley, 1965.

3. The Opium War (Anglo-Chinese War of 1841–1842)

Bernard, W. D. *The Nemesis in China, comprising a History of the Late War in that Country.* London: H. Colburn, 1848.
Davis, J. F. *China during the War and since the Peace.* London: Longman *et al.,* 1852.
Holt, Edgar. *The Opium War in China.* Chester Springs: Dufour Editions, 1964.
Kuo Pin-Chia. *A Critical Study of the First Anglo-Chinese War.* Shanghai: Commercial Press, 1935.
Teng Ssu-Yu. *Chang Hsi and the Treaty of Nanking.* Chicago: Univ. of Chicago Press, 1944.

4. The Mexican-American War

Brooks, N. C. *A Complete History of the Mexican War.* Philadelphia: Grigg, Elliot & Co., 1849.
Henry, R. S. *The Story of the Mexican War.* New York: F. Ungar, 1950.
Reeves, J. S. *American Diplomacy under Tyler and Polk.* Baltimore: Johns Hopkins Press, 1907.
Ripley, R. S. *The War with Mexico,* 2 Vols. New York: Harper, 1849.
Rives, G. L. *The United States and Mexico.* New York: C. Scribner's Sons, 1913.
Smith, J. H. *The War with Mexico,* 2 Vols. New York: Macmillan, 1919.

5. Franco-Prussian War

Bismarck, Otto. *Gedanken und Erinnerungen,* 2 Vols. Stuttgart: Cotta, 1921.
Busch, Moritz. *Bismarck: Some Secret Pages of his History,* 2 Vols. New York: Macmillan, 1898.
———. *Bismarck in the Franco-German War,* 2 Vols. New York: C. Scribner's Sons, 1879.
Chodzko, Leonhard (le Comte d'Angeberg). *Recueil des Traités concernant la Guerre Franco-Allemand,* 5 Vols. Paris: Amyot, 1873.
Favre, J. M. *Gouvernement de la Défense Nationale,* 3 Vols. Paris: Plon, 1871–73.
France. *Recueil des Traités, etc. relatifs à la Paix avec L'Allemagne,* 5 Vols. Paris: Imp. Nationale, 1872–79.
Howard, M. F. *The Franco-Prussian War.* New York: Macmillan, 1961.

May, Gaston. *La Traité de Francfort*. Paris: Berger-Levrault, 1909.

O'Farrell, H. H. *The Franco-German War Indemnity and its Economic Results*. London: Harrison & Sons, 1913.

Sorel, Albert. *Histoire Diplomatique de la Guerre Franco-Allemande*, 2 Vols. Paris: Plon, 1875.

Valfrey, Jules. *Histoire du Traité de Francfort et de la Libération du Territoire Français*, 2 Vols. Paris: Amyot, 1874–75.

6. *The Ashanti War*

Brackenbury, Henry. *The Ashanti War*, 2 Vols. Edinburgh: W. Blackwood, 1874.

Claridge, W. W. *A History of the Gold Coast and Ashanti*. London: F. Cass, 1964.

Lloyd, Alan. *The Drums of Kumasi*. London: Longmans, 1964.

7. *The Franco-Tunisian War (1881)*

Constant, P. N. B. (baron d'Estournelles de). *La Politique Française en Tunisie*. Paris: Plon, 1881.

France, Minister of Foreign Affairs. *Documents Diplomatique. Affaires de Tunisie 1881*, Series A, Vol. 113. Paris: Imp. nationale, 1881.

———. *Documents Diplomatiques Français, 1871–1914*, 1° Série, 16 vols. Paris: Imp. nationale, 1929–1954. See Vols. 3 and 4.

Ganiage, Jean. *Les origines du protectorat français en Tunisie (1861–1881)*. Paris: Presses universitaires de France, 1959.

Valet, R. V. *Le conquêt de l'Algérie (1828–1838) et l'Occupation de la Tunisie (1880–1881)*. Algiers: Imp. La typo-litho, 1924.

8. *Italo-Abyssinian War (1894–1896)*

Bellavita, Emilio. *Adua: I Precedenti, La Battaglia, La Conseguenze*. Genoa: Rivista di Roma, 1931.

Cibot, L. J. *L'Éthiopie et la Société des Nations*. Paris: Donat-Montchrestien, 1939.

Conti Rossini, Carlos. *Italia ed Etiopia*. Rome: *Instituto per l'Oriente*, 1935.

Instituto per gli Studi di Politica Internazionale. *Il Conflitto Italo-Etiopico: Documenti*. Milan, 1936.

Italy. *Memoria del Governo Italiano circa la situazione in Etiopia*. Rome (?), 1935.

La Jonquiére, C.E.L.M. *Les Italiens en Érythrée*. Paris: Charles-Lavanzelle, 1897.

9. *The Russo-Polish War (1920–1921)*

Conférence de membres de la constituante de Russie. Comité exécutif. *Mémoire sur la traité de Riga*. Paris, 1921.

Komarnicki, Titus. *Rebirth of the Polish Republic*. London: W. Heinemann, 1957.

Reddaway, W. F., *et al.* (eds.) *The Cambridge History of Poland*, 2 Vols. Cambridge: University Press, 1950–1951. See Vol. 2.

(See also the relevant works collected for the First World War, *infra*.)

10. *The Chaco War*

The Chaco Peace Conference. Washington, D.C.: Government Printing Office, 1940.

Diez de Medina, Eduardo. *Conferencias del Internacionalista boliviano.* La Paz: Imp. Arno hermanos, 1933.

Garner, W. R. *The Chaco Dispute: A Study of Prestige Diplomacy.* Washington, D.C.: Public Affairs Press, 1966.

LaFoy, Margaret. *The Chaco Dispute and the League of Nations.* Ann Arbor: Edwards Bros., 1946.

Mercado Moreira, Miguel. *Historia diplomatica de la Guerra del Chaco.* La Paz, 1966.

Paraguay. Congreso nacional. *La Paz con Bolivia ante el Poder Legislativo.* Asunción: Imp. nacional, 1939.

Proceedings of the Commission of Inquiry and Concilation, Bolivia and Paraguay. Washington, D.C.: Sun Book Co., 1929.

Rodas Eguino, Justo. *La Guerra del Chaco.* Buenos Aires: Libreria y editorial "La Facultad," 1938.

Saavedra, Bautista. *El Chaco y La Conferenza de Paz de Buenos Aires.* Santiago: Talleres de la Editorial Nascimento, 1939.

Urquidi, J. M. *El Uti Possidetis Juris y de Facto.* Cochabamba: Imp. universitaria, 1946.

11. *Russo-Finnish War (1939–1940)*

Dallin, D. J. *Soviet Russia's Foreign Policy, 1939–1942.* Trans. by Leon Dennen. New Haven: Yale Univ. Press, 1942.

Finland. Ministeriet. *Finland reveals secret documents of Soviet Policy, March 1940–June 1941.* New York: W. Funk, 1941.

Jacobson, Max. *The Diplomacy of the Winter War, 1939–1940.* Cambridge, Mass.: Harvard Univ. Press, 1961.

Paasikivi, J. K. *Meine Moskauer Mission, 1939–41.* Hamburg: Holstenverlag, 1966.

Peltier, M. A. *La Finlande dans la Tourmente.* Paris: Éditions France-Empire, 1966.

Tanner, V. A. *The Winter War: Finland against Russia 1939–1940.* Stanford: Stanford Univ. Press, 1957.

Wuorinen, J. H. (ed.) *Finland and World War II.* New York: Ronald Press, 1948.

SIMPLE INTERNAL WARS

1. *Third Huguenot War (1568–1570)*

Armstrong, Edward. *The French Wars of Religion,* 2d ed. Oxford: Blackwell, 1904.

Bailly, Auguste. *La Réforme en France.* Paris: A. Fayard, 1960.

Champion, Pierre. *Charles IX, La France et le contrôle de l'Espagne,* 2 Vols. Paris: B. Grasset, 1939.

Coudy, Julien (ed.). *Die Hugenottenkriege in Augenzeugenberichten*. Düsseldorf: Rauch Verlag, 1965.

Dargaud, J. M. *Histoire de la Liberté Religieuse en France*, 4 Vols. Paris: Charpentier, 1859. See Vol. 3.

Hirschauer, Charles. *La Politique de St. Pie V en France*. Paris: Fontemoing, 1922.

Kervyn de Lettenhove, J.M.B.C. *Les Huguenots et les Gueux*, 6 Vols. Brussels: Beyaert-Storie, 1883–85. See Vol. 2.

Thompson, J. W. *The Wars of Religion in France*. New York: F. Unger, 1957.

2. *The English Revolution of 1688–1689*

Ashley, M. P. *The Glorious Revolution of 1688*. London: Hodder & Stoughton, 1966.

A Collection of State Tracts, published during the Reign of King William III, 3 Vols. London, 1705–7. See Vol. 3.

Great Britain, Parliament. *The Debate at Large between the House of Lords and the House of Commons, in the session of the Convention, anno 1688*. London: J. Wickins, 1695.

The History of the late revolution in England. London, 1689.

Macaulay, T. B. *The History of England from the Accession of James II*, 4 Vols. London: J. M. Dent, 1906. See Vol. 2.

Pinkham, Lucille. *William III and the Respectable Revolution*. Cambridge, Mass.: Harvard Univ. Press, 1954.

Trevelyan, G. M. *The English Revolution, 1688–1689*. London: T. Butterworth, 1938.

3. *The Hungarian Rebellion (1703–1711)*

Fiedler, Joseph (ed.). *Actenstücke zur Geschichte Franz Rákóczy's und seiner Verbindungen mit dem Auslande*, 2 Vols. Vienna: Hof- und Staatsdruckerei, 1855–58.

Hengelmüller von Hengervár, Ladislaus. *Hungary's Fight for National Existence*. London: Macmillan, 1913.

An Historical and Geographical Account of the Ancient Kingdom of Hungary. London: A. Bettesworth, 1717.

Macartney, C. A. *Hungary: A Short History*. Edinburgh: University Press, 1962.

4. *The Texas Revolt (1835–1836)*

Castañeda, C. E., (trans.) *The Mexican Side of the Texan Revolution*. Dallas: P. L. Turner, 1928.

Maillard, N. D. *The History of the Republic of Texas*. London: Smith, Elder & Co., 1842.

Wharton, C. R. *Texas under many Flags*, 5 Vols. Chicago: American Historical Society, 1930.

Wooten, D. G. (ed.). *A Complete History of Texas*, 2 Vols. Dallas: Texas History Co., 1898.

Wortham, C. J. *A History of Texas,* 5 Vols. Fort Worth: Wortham-Molyneaux, 1924.

Yoakum, H. K. *History of Texas,* 2 Vols. Austin: Steck Co., 1935.

5. *The Cuban Revolt (1869–1878)*

Guerra y Sanchez, Ramiro. *Guerra de los diez años, 1868–1878.* Havana: Cultural, 1950.

————. *Historia de la Nacion Cubana,* 10 Vols. Havana: Editorial Historia de la Nacion Cubana, 1952. See Vols. 5, 6, and 7; but principally Vol. 6.

Johnson, W. F. *The History of Cuba,* 4 Vols. New York: B. F. Buck, 1920. See Vol. 3.

Mendez Capote, Domingo. *El pacto del Zanjon.* Havana: Molina, 1929.

Mesa Rodriguez, M. I. *Diez años de guerra.* Havana: Imp. "El Siglo XX," 1954.

6. *The Philippine Insurrection (1898–1902)*

Agoncillo, Teodoro & Milagros, C. G. *History of the Filipino People,* 3d ed. Quezon City: Malaya Books, 1970.

Grunder, G. A. & Livezey, W. E. *The Philippines and the United States.* Norman, Okla.: Univ. of Oklahoma Press, 1951.

Malcolm, G. A. *The Government of the Philippines.* Rochester: Lawyers Cooperative Publishing Co., 1916.

Salamanca, B. S. *The Filipino Reaction to American Rule, 1901–1913.* Hamden, Conn.: Shoe String Press, 1968.

Zaide, G. F. *Philippine Political and Cultural History,* 2 Vols., Rev. ed. Manila: Philippine Education Co., 1957.

7. *The Irish Rebellion (1919–1921)*

Beasley, Pierce. *Michael Collins and the Making of a New Ireland,* 2 Vols. London: G. G. Harrap, 1926.

Bromage, M. C. *De Valera and the March of a Nation.* London: Hutchinson, 1956.

Gallagher, Frank. *Anglo-Irish Treaty.* London: Hutchinson, 1965.

Holt, Edgar. *Protest in Arms: The Irish Troubles, 1916–1923.* New York: Coward-McCann, 1961.

Macardle, Dorothy. *The Irish Republic.* London: Gollancz, 1937.

O'Hegarty, P. S. *A History of Ireland under the Union, 1801–1922.* London: Methuen, 1952.

Pakenham, Frank. *Peace by Ordeal.* London: J. Cape, 1935.

Williams, Desmond (ed.). *The Irish Struggle, 1916–1926.* London: Routledge & Kegan Paul, 1966.

8. *Egyptian Independence (1919–1922)*

Berque, Jacques. *L'Égypte impérialisme et révolution.* Paris: Gallimard, 1967.

Gargour, P. A. *Étapes de l'indépendence égyptienne aperçus d'histoire diplomatique.* Paris: Librairie générale de droit et de jurisprudence, 1942.

Marlowe, John. *A History of Modern Egypt and Anglo-Egyptian Relations*, 2d ed. Hamden, Conn.: Archon Books, 1970.

Symons, M. T. *Britain and Egypt; the Rise of Egyptian Nationalism.* London: Palmer, 1925.

Zayid, M. Y. *Egypt's Struggle for Independence.* Beirut: Khayats, 1965.

9. *Tunisian Independence (1949–1956)*

Bourguiba, Habib. *La Tunisie et la France.* Paris: R. Julliard, 1954.

Debbasch, Charles. *La Républic Tunisienne.* Paris: Librairie générale de droit et de jurisprudence, 1962.

France. *Conventions entre la France et la Tunisie.* Paris: Imp. nationale, 1955.

Garas, Félix. *Bourguiba et la naissance d'une nation.* Paris: R. Julliard, 1956.

Ling, D. L. *Tunisia, from Protectorate to Republic.* Bloomington, Ind.: Indiana Univ. Press, 1967.

10. *The Kurdish Insurrection (1961–1967, 1970+)*

Ghassemlou, A. R. *Kurdistan and the Kurds.* Prague: Czechoslovak Academy of Sciences, 1965.

Iraq and Its North. Baghdad: Dar-al-Jumhuriyah, 1965.

Schmidt, D. A. *Journey Among Brave Men.* Boston: Little, Brown, 1964.

Vanly, I. C. *The Revolution of Iraki Kurdistan, Part I (September, 1961 to December, 1963)*. Lausanne: Committee for the Defense of Kurdish People's Rights, 1965.

COMPLEX EXTERNAL WARS

1. *Last War of the Habsburg-Valois Rivalry (1557–1559)*

Mattingly, Garrett. "No Peace Beyond What Line?" *Transactions of the Royal Historical Society,* 5th Series, Vol. 13. London, 1963. Pp. 145–162.

McElwee, W. L. *The Reign of Charles V, 1516–1558.* London: Macmillan, 1936.

Robertson, William. *The History of the Reign of the Emperor Charles V,* 3 Vols. Philadelphia: Lippincott, 1916.

Ruble, Alphonse. *Le traité de Câteau-Cambrésis.* Paris: Labitte, E. Paul & Cie., 1889.

2. *Second Anglo-Dutch War (1664–1667)*

Comenius, J. A. *The Angel of Peace.* New York: Pantheon, 1944.

Description exacte de tout ce qui s'est passé dans les Guerres entre le roy d'Angleterre, le roy de France, les estats de Provinces Unies du Pays-bas, et l'Évêque de Munster. Amsterdam: Chez Jacques Benjamin, 1668.

Feiling, K. G. *British Foreign Policy, 1660–1672.* London: Macmillan, 1930.

Geyl, Pieter. *The Netherlands in the Seventeenth Century,* 2 Vols. New York: Barnes and Noble, 1964–6. See Vol. 2 (1648–1715).

———. *Orange and Stuart, 1641–1672.* Trans. by Pomerans, Arnold. New York: Scribner, 1970.

Great Britain. *Sovereigns, etc.,* 1660–1685 (Charles II). *His Majesties gracious speech to both houses of Parliament, etc.* London: Bill and Barker, 1673/1674.

Mignet, F.A.M.A. *Négociations relative à la succession d'Espagne, sous Louis XIV,* 4 Vols. Paris: Imp. royale, 1835–42. See Vol. 2.

Rogers, P. G. *The Dutch in the Medway.* London: Oxford Univ. Press, 1970.

3. *Austro-Russian War against Turkey (1787–1792)*

Coxe, William. *History of the House of Austria,* 4 Vols. London: G. Bell, 1893–95. See Vol. 3.

Criste, Oskar. *Kriege unter Kaiser Josef II.* Vienna: L. W. Seidel & Sons, 1904.

Marriott, J. A. R. *The Eastern Question,* 4th ed. Oxford: Clarendon Press, 1940.

Stavrianos, L. S. *The Balkans since 1453.* New York: Holt, Rinehart & Winston, 1958.

Zinkeisen, J. W., *op. cit.,* Vol. 6.

4. *The Crimean War*

"Ancien Diplomate." *Le Traité de Paris.* Paris: Didot, 1856.

Borries, Kurt. *Preussen im Krimkrieg.* Stuttgart: W. Kohlhammer, 1930.

Bowles, T. G. *The Declaration of Paris of 1856.* London: S. Low, Marston & Co., 1900.

Desjardins, Arthur. *Le Congrès de Paris (1856) et la Jurisprudence Internationale.* Paris: Pedone-Lauriel, 1884.

Friedjung, Heinrich. *Der Krimkrieg und die österreichische politik.* Stuttgart: Cotta, 1911.

Gourdon, Édouard. *Histoire de Congrès de Paris.* Paris: Librairie nouvelle, 1857.

Guichen, Eugène. *La guerre de Crimée (1854–1856) et l'attitude des puissances européenes.* Paris: Éditions A. Pedone, 1936.

Hazen, C. D., et al. *Three Peace Congresses of the Nineteenth Century.* Cambridge, Mass.: Harvard Univ. Press, 1917.

Jasmund, Julius von. *Aktenstücke zur orientalischen frage,* 3 Vols. Berlin: F. Schneider, 1855–59.

Piggott, F. T. *The Declaration of Paris, 1856.* London: Univ. of London Press, 1919.

Puryear, V. J. *England, Russia and the Straits Question.* Hamden, Conn.: Archon Books, 1965.

Rein, Adolf. *Die Teilnahme Sardiniens am Krimkrieg und die öffentliche Meinung in Italien.* Leipzig: Voigtländer, 1910.

Sirtema van Grovestins, C. F. (Baron). *Le Congrès de Vienne . . . et le Congrès de Paris en 1856.* Paris: Dentu, 1856.

Temperley, H. W. V. *England and the Near East: The Crimea.* Hamden, Conn.: Archon Books, 1964.

5. *Second War over Schleswig-Holstein (1864)*

Friis, Aage. *L'Europe, le Danemark et le Slesvig du nord,* 4 Vols. Copenhagen: Levin & Munksgaard, 1939–59.

Gasselin, Louis. *La Question du Schleswig-Holstein*. Paris: A. Rousseau, 1909.

Germany. Auswärtiges Amt. *Bismarck und die nordschleswigsche frage, 1864–1879*. Berlin: Deutsche verlagsgesellschaft für politik und geschichte, 1925.

Hotz, Karl. *Politik und Kriegführung auf deutscher Seite im Deutsch-Dänischen Kriege, 1864*. Tübingen: Göbel, 1935.

Steefel, Lawrence. *The Schleswig-Holstein Question*. Cambridge, Mass.: Harvard Univ. Press, 1932.

Stolberg-Wernigerode, Albrecht. *Bismarck und die schleswig-holsteinische Frage*. Kiel: Kieler Zeitung, 1928.

Westergaard, Waldemar. *Denmark and Slesvig*. London: Oxford Univ. Press, 1946.

6. *War of the Pacific (1879–1883)*

Ahumada Moreno, Pascual. *Guerra del Pacífico. Recopilacion completa de todos los documentos oficiales, etc.*, 8 Vols. in 4. Valparaiso: Imp. del Progreso, 1884–89.

Arbitration between Peru and Chile, 2 Vols. and Appendix. Washington, D.C.: National Capitol Press, 1923–25.

Barros Arana, Diego. *Histoire de la Guerre du Pacifique*. Paris: L. Baudoin, 1881.

Benavides, S. A. *Historia Compendiada de la Guerra Pacífica*. Santiago: Soc. imp. y lit. Universo, 1927.

Blanlot Holley, Anselmo. *Historia de la Paz entre Chile y El Peru*. Santiago: Balcells, 1919.

Bulnes, Gonzalo. *Guerra del Pacífico*, 3 Vols. Santiago: Editorial de Pacifico, 1955.

Burr, R. N. *By Reason or Force*. Berkeley: Univ. of California Press, 1967.

Caivano, Tommaso. *Historia de la Guerra de América entre Chile, Peru y Bolivia*. Lima: G. Stolte, 1901.

Dennis, W. J. *Documentary History of the Tacna-Arica Dispute*. Iowa City: University Press, 1927.

———. *Tacna and Arica*. New Haven: Yale Univ. Press, 1931.

Egana, Rafael. *La Cuestion Tacna I Arica*. Santiago: Barcelona Printing Co., 1900.

Garcia Calderon, Francisco. *Mediacion de los Estados Unidos de Norte América en la Guerra de Pacífico*. Buenos Aires: Imp. y libreria de Mayo, 1884.

Garland, Alejandro. *Los Conflictos Sudamericanos en relacion con les Estados Unidos*. Lima: Imp. J. Newton & Co., 1900.

Maúrtua, Anibal. *La Politica Internacional de Chile y la Liquidacion de la Guerra de Pacífico*. Lima: E. Moreno, 1901.

Medina, P. M. *La Controversia Peruano-Chilena*, 2 Vols. Lima: Imp. Torres Aguirre, 1925.

Millington, Herbert. *American Diplomacy and the War of the Pacific*. New York: Columbia Univ. Press, 1948.

United States. President (1881–1885). *Messages from the President of the United States, transmitting papers relating to the war in South America*. Washington, D.C.: Government Printing Office, 1882.

Varas, Carlos. *Tacna y Arica bajo la Soberania Chilena*. Santiago: Imp. de "La Nacion," 1922.

7. The Boer War

De Wet, C. R. *Three Years War*. London: A. Constable, 1902.

Holt, Edgar. *The Boer War*. London: Putnam, 1958.

Galloni d'Istria, Charles. *Le droit des gens dans la Guerre de l'Afrique Australe*. Paris: La Rose, 1903.

Kestell, J. D. & Van Velden, D. E. *The Peace Negotiations between the Governments of the South African Republics and the Orange Free State*. London: R. Clay, 1912.

8. The Boxer Rebellion

Clements, P. H. *The Boxer Rebellion*. New York: Columbia Univ. Press, 1915.

Kelly, J. S. *A Forgotten Conference: The Negotiations at Peking*. Geneva: E. Droz, 1962.

Martin, Christopher. *The Boxer Rebellion*. London: Abelard-Schuman, 1968.

Smith, A. H. *China in Convulsion*, 2 Vols. New York: F. H. Revell Co., 1901.

Steigger, G. N. *China and the Occident; the Origin and Development of the Boxer Movement*. New York: Russell & Russell, 1966.

Tan, C. C. *The Boxer Catastrophe*. New York: Columbia Univ. Press, 1955.

Thomson, H. C. *China and the Powers*. London: Longmans, Green & Co., 1902.

COMPLEX INTERNAL WARS

1. The Dutch Revolt

Geyl, Pieter. *The Netherlands in the Seventeenth Century*, 2 Vols. (Volume 1 was originally entitled, *The Netherlands Divided, 1609–1648*.) New York: Barnes & Noble, 1964–66.

———. *The Revolt of the Netherlands*. New York: Barnes & Noble, 1958.

Grierson, Edward. *The Fatal Inheritance: Philip II and the Spanish Netherlands*. Garden City, N.Y.: Doubleday, 1969.

Lettres sur la pacification du Gand, par un ancien professeur d'histoire. 2d. ed'n. Ghent: C. Poelman, 1876.

Motley, J. L. *History of the United Netherlands*, 4 Vols. New York: Harper, 1861–68.

———. *The Rise of the Dutch Republic*, 3 Vols. London: Frowde, 1906.

Vlekke, B. H. M. *Evolution of the Dutch Nation*. New York: Roy Publishers, 1945.

Wicquefort, Abraham van. *L'histoire de l'éstablissement de la Réplublic des Provinces-Unies*, 3 Vols. London: Aux dépens de la Compagnie, 1749.

2. War of the Polish Succession

Boyé, Pierre. *Stanislas Leszczynski et le troisième traité de Vienne*. Paris: Berger-Levrault, 1898.

Gurlitt, Cornelius. *August der Starke*, 3rd ed., 2 Vols. Dresden: Sibyllen-verlag, 1924.

Roberts, Penfield. *The Quest for Security, 1715–1740.* New York: Harper & Row, 1947.

3. *The War for American Independence*

Bailey, T. A. *A Diplomatic History of the American People,* 7th ed. New York: Appleton-Century-Crofts, 1964.

Fauchille, Paul. *La Diplomatie Française et la Ligue des Neutres.* Paris: Pedone-Lauriel, 1893.

Malcolm-Smith, E. F. *British Diplomacy in the 18th Century, 1700–1789.* London: Williams & Norgate, 1937.

Morris, R. B. *The Peacemakers.* New York: Harper & Row, 1965.

Miller, J. C. *Triumph of Freedom.* Boston: Little, Brown, 1948.

Rose, J. H., *et al. Cambridge History of the British Empire,* 8 Vols. Cambridge: University Press, 1929–36. See Vol. 1.

Warren, Mercy. *History of the Rise, Progress and Termination of the American Revolution,* 3 Vols. Boston: Manning & Loring, 1805.

4. *Greek War for Independence (1821–1830)*

Charnisay, Phillipe. *L'insurrection Hellénique et la diplomatie Européene.* Paris: Montpellier Univ., 1904.

Driault, Édouard and Lhéritier, Michel. *Histoire Diplomatique de la Grèce,* 5 Vols. Paris: Les Presses universitaires de France, 1925–26.

Woodhouse, C. M. *The Greek War of Independence.* London: Hutchinson, 1952.

5. *The First and Second Wars of Mehemet Ali against the Sultan*

Cadalvène, Edmond de, and Barrault, Émile. *Histoire de la guerre Méhémed-Ali contre la Porte Ottomane (1831–1833).* Paris: A. Bertrand, 1837.

Cattaui, J. E. *Histoire des Rapports de l'Égypte avec la Sublime Porte.* Paris: Jouve, 1919.

Dodwell, H. H. *The Founder of Modern Egypt; a Study of Muhammed 'Ali.* Cambridge: University Press, 1931.

Douin, Georges. (ed.) *La Première guerre de Syrie (1831–1832).* 2 Vols. Cairo: Imp. de l'Institut, français d'archéologie orientale du Caire, 1931.

Driault, Édouard. *L'Egypte et L'Europe, La Crise de 1839–1841,* 5 Vols. Cairo: Imp. de l'Institut français d'archéologie orientale du Caire, 1930–34.

Great Britain. Foreign Office. *Correspondence relative to the Affairs of the Levant,* 2 Vols. London: T. R. Harrison, 1841.

Guichen, Eugène. *La Crise d'Orient (1839–1841), et L'Europe.* Paris: Émile-Paul, 1921.

Polites, Athanasios. *Le Conflit turco-égyptienne 1838–1841.* Cairo: Imp. de l'Institut français d'archéologie orientale du Caire, 1931.

Sabry, Mohammed. *L'Empire égyptien sous Mohamed-Ali et la question d'Orient.* Paris: Librairie orientaliste, 1930.

6. *Russo-Turkish War of 1877–1878*

Hayes, C. J. H. *A Generation of Materialism, 1871–1900*. New York: Harper & Row, 1921.

Hellwald, Friedrich & Beck, L. C. (eds.). *Die heutige Türkei*, 2 Vols. Leipzig: O. Spamer, 1878–79.

Hozier, H. M., (ed.). *The Russo-Turkish War*, 5 Vols. London: W. Mackenzie, 1879. See Vol. 5.

Martens, F. F. *La Paix et la Guerre*. Paris: A. Rousseau, 1901.

7. *Korean War (1950–1953)*

Brazda, Jaroslav. *The Korean Armistice Agreement, a Comparative Study*. Gainesville, Fla.: Univ. of Florida, 1956.

Goodrich, L. M. *Korea: A Study of U.S. Policy in the United Nations*. New York: Council on Foreign Relations, 1956.

Great Britain. Foreign Office. *Special Report of the Unified Command on the Korean Armistice Agreement*. Cmnd. Doc. No. 8938. London: H.M.S.O., 1953.

Kim, Myong-whai. *Prisoners of War as a Major Problem of the Korean Armistice, 1953*. New York: New York Univ., 1960.

Leckie, Robert. *Conflict: The History of the Korean War, 1950–1953*. New York: Putnam, 1962.

Rees, David. *Korea: The Limited War*. New York: St. Martin's Press, 1964.

United States Department of State. *Armistice in Korea; Selected Statements and Documents*. Washington, D.C.: Government Printing Office, 1953.

Vatcher, W. H., Jr. *Panmunjom: The Story of the Korean Military Armistice Negotiations*. New York: Praeger, 1958.

Yoo, Tae-ho. *The Korean War and the United Nations*. Louvain: Desbaraz, 1965.

8. *Laotian Civil War (1955–1962)*

Champassak, S. N. *Storm over Laos, A Contemporary History*. New York: Praeger, 1961.

Dommen, A. J. *Conflict in Laos: The Politics of Neutralization*. New York: Praeger, 1964.

Fall, B. B. *Anatomy of a Crisis: The Laotian Crisis of 1960–1961*. Garden City, N.Y.: Doubleday, 1969.

Great Britain. Foreign Office. *Documents relating to British Involvement in the Indo-China Conflict, 1945–1965*. Cmnd. Doc. No. 2834. London: H.M.S.O., 1965.

———. *International Conference on the Settlement of the Laotian Question*. Laos No. 1 (1962), Cmnd. Doc. No. 1828. London: H.M.S.O., 1962.

Langer, P. F., and Zasloff, J. J. *North Vietnam and the Pathet Lao*. Cambridge, Mass.: Harvard Univ. Press, 1970.

Modelski, George. *International Conference on the Settlement of the Laotian Question, 1961–62*. Canberra: Australian National Univ., 1962.

Randle, R. F. *Geneva 1954: The Settlement of the Indochinese War*. Princeton: Princeton Univ. Press, 1969.

Toye, Hugh. *Laos: Buffer State or Battleground.* London: Oxford Univ. Press, 1968.

MULTILATERAL WARS

1. *Thirty Years' War*

Bougeant, G. H. *Histoire des Guerres et des Négociations qui Précéderent le Traité de Westphalie,* 3 Vols. Paris: J. Mariette, 1767.

——. *Histoire du Traité de Westphalie,* 6 Vols. Paris: Didot, 1751.

Braubach, Max. *Der Westfälische Friede.* Münster: Aschendorff, 1948.

Clément, Nicolas. *Mémoires et Négociations Secrets de la Cour de France touchant la Paix de Munster,* 4 Vols. Amsterdam: Frères Chatelain, 1710.

Dickmann, Fritz. *Der Westfälische Frieden,* 2d ed. Münster: Aschendorff, 1965.

Gindely, Anton. *History of the Thirty Years War,* 2 Vols. New York: G. P. Putnam's Sons, 1884. Trans. by Ten Brook, Alfred.

Israel, Friedrich. *Adam Adami und seine Arcana pacis Westphalicae.* Berlin: Ebering, 1909.

Platzhoff, Walter. *Geschichte des Europäischen Staatensystems, 1559–1660.* Munich: R. Oldenbourg, 1967.

Steinberg, S. H. *The Thirty Years' War and the Conflict for European Hegemony.* New York: Norton, 1966.

Turrettini, Robert. *La Signification des Traités de Westphalie dans le Domaine du Droit des Gens.* Geneva: Imp. Genèvoise, 1949.

Wedgewood, C. V. *The Thirty Years' War.* London: J. Cape, 1938.

2. *Franco-Dutch War of 1672–1679*

Actes et Mémoires des Négotiations de la Paix de Nimegue, 4 Vols. Amsterdam: Chez A. Wolfgangk, 1680.

André, Louis. *Louis XIV et l'Europe.* Paris: Michel, 1950.

Immich, Max. *Geschichte des europäischen Staatensystems von 1660 bis 1789.* Munich: R. Oldenbourg, 1905.

Mignet, F. A. M. A., *op. cit.* (under Second Anglo-Dutch War). See Vol. 4.

Nussbaum, F. L. *The Triumph of Science and Reason, 1660–1685.* New York: Harper & Row, 1953.

Picavet, C. G. *La Diplomatie française au temps de Louis XIV, 1661–1715.* Paris: F. Alcan, 1930.

Sirtema van Grovestins, C. F. (Baron). *Guillaume III et Louis XIV: histories des luttes et rivalités,* 8 Vols. Paris: L. Toinon, 1868. See Vol. 3.

Zeller, Gaston. *Les Temps Modernes, II: de Louis XIV à 1789,* 2 Vols. Paris: Hachete, 1955.

3. *The European War of 1683–1700*

Bernard, Jacques. *Actes et mémoires des négociations de la paix de Ryswick,* 2d ed., 5 Vols. The Hague: A. Moetjens, 1707.

Legrelle, Arsène. *Notes et documents sur la Paix de Ryswick.* Lille: Imp. de Desclée *et al.,* 1894.

Morgan, W. T. "Economic Aspects of the Negotiations at Ryswick." *Transactions of the Royal Historical Society,* 4th Series, Vol. 14. London, 1931. Pp. 225–49.

Perkins, J. B. *France under the Regency.* Boston: Houghton, Mifflin & Co., 1892.

Popovič, M. R. *Der Friede von Carlowitz.* Leipzig: O. Schmidt, 1893.

Wolf, J. B. *The Emergence of the Great Powers, 1685–1715.* New York: Harper & Row, 1951.

4. *War of the Spanish Succession*

Actes, Mémoires et autres Pièces Authentiques concernant la Paix d'Utrecht, 6 Vols. Utrecht: G. vande Water *et al.,* 1714.

Courcy, M. R. R. (le Marquis de). *La Coalition de 1701 contre la France.* Paris: Plon, 1886.

Defoe, Daniel. *Peace of Poverty.* London: John Morphew, 1712.

———. *Reasons why this nation ought to put a speedy end to this expensive war.* London: J. Baker, 1711.

Fransen, Petronella. *Leibniz und die Friedensschlüsse von Utrecht und Rastatt-Baden.* Purmerend: J. Muusses, 1933.

Freschot, Casimir. *The compleat history of the treaty of Utrecht,* 2 Vols. London: A. Roper *et al.,* 1715.

Gaedeke, Arnold. *Die Politik Oesterreichs in der spanischen Erbfolgefrage.* Leipzig: Duncker & Humblot, 1877.

Geikie, Roderick, and Montgomery, I. A. *The Dutch Barrier, 1705–1719.* Cambridge: University Press, 1930.

Gerard, J. W. *The peace of Utrecht.* London: G. P. Putnam's Sons, 1885.

Giraud, Charles. *Le Traité d'Utrecht.* Paris: Plon, 1847.

Kamen, H. A. F. *The War of Succession in Spain, 1700–1715.* Bloomington, Ind.: Indiana Univ. Press, 1969.

Legrelle, Arsène. *La Diplomatie française et la succession d'Espagne,* 4 Vols. Paris: Pichon, 1888–93.

———. *L'Europe en 1713 après la guerre de la succession d'Espagne.* Braine-le-Comte: Zech, 1897.

Sixte, Prince de Bourbon-Parma. *Le Traité d'Utrecht et les lois fondementales du royaume.* Paris: Champion, 1914.

Trevelyan, G. M. *Bolingbroke's Defense of the Treaty of Utrecht.* Cambridge: University Press, 1932.

Weber, Ottocar. *Der Friede von Utrecht.* Gotha: F. A. Perthes, 1891.

Wolf, J.B., *op. cit.*

5. *The War of the Austrian Succession*

Austria. Kriegsarchiv. Kriegsgeschichtliche Abteilung. *Oesterreichischer Erbfolgekrieg, 1740–8,* 9 Vols. Vienna: Seidel, 1896–1914 (There is nothing of the Peace of Aix-la-Chapelle in this work; but it does deal with the preliminary settlements.)

Broche, Gaston. *La républic de Gênes et la France pendant la guerre de la succession d'Autriche.* Paris: Société française d'imprimerie et de libraire, 1935.

Broglie, Albert (le duc de). *La Paix d'Aix-la-Chapelle*. Paris: Calmann Levy, 1892.

Dorn, W. L. *Competition for Empire, 1740–1763*. New York: Harper & Row, 1940.

A General view of the present politics and interests of the principal powers of Europe, 2nd ed. London: W. Webb, 1747.

6. *The Seven Years' War*

Beaulieu-Marconnay, Carl. *Der Hubertusburger Friede*. Leipzig: Hirzel, 1871.

Blart, Louis. *Les rapports de la France et de l'Espagne après le pacte de famille*. Paris: F. Alcan, 1915.

Choiseul, E. F. (le duc de). *Mémoire Historique sur la négociation de la France et Angleterre depuis le 26 mars 1761 jusqu'au 20 Septembre 1761*. Paris: Imp. royale, 1761.

Considerations on the Approaching Peace. London: W. Morgan, 1762.

Corbett, J. S. *England in the Seven Years' War*, 2 Vols., 2nd ed. London: Longmans, Green, 1918.

Dorn, W. L., *op. cit.*

Longman, F. W. *Frederick the Great and the Seven Years' War*. London: Longmans, Green, 1898.

Member of Parliament. *An appeal to knowledge; or Candid Discussion of the Preliminaries of Peace, signed at Fontainebleau, Nov. 3, 1762*. London: J. Wilkie, 1763.

Ranke, Leopold von. *Sämmtliche Werke*, 54 Vols. Leipzig; Duncker & Humblot, 1868–1890. See Vol. 29, *Zwölf bücher preussischer geschichte*, Leipzig: 1878–9, and Vol. 30, *Zur geschichte von Oesterreich und Preussen*, Leipzig: Duncker & Humblot, 1875.

Rashed, Z. E. *The Peace of Paris, 1763*. Liverpool: University Press, 1951.

Schaefer, Arnold. *Geschichte des Siebenjährigen Kriegs*, 2 Vols. Berlin: W. Hertz, 1867–74.

Sherrard, O. A. *Lord Chatham: Pitt and the Seven Years' War*. London: Bodley Head, 1955.

Soulange-Bodin, André. *La Diplomatie de Louis XV et le Pacte de famille*. Paris: Perrin, 1894.

7. *The Wars of France against Europe (1792–1815)*

Capefigue, J. B. H. R. *Le Congrès de Vienne*. Paris: Gerdes, 1847.

Chodzko, Leonhart. *Le Congrès de Vienne*, 4 Vols. Paris: Amyot, 1864.

Flassan, Gaetan de Raxis de. *Histoire du Congrès de Vienne*, 3 Vols. Paris: Treuttel et Wurtz, 1829.

Fournier, August. *Der Congress von Châtillon*. Vienna: E. Temsky, 1900.

Hauff, Ludwig. *Die Verträge von 1815*. Bamburg: Buchner, 1864.

Kissinger, H. A. *A World Restored: Metternich, Castlereagh and the Problems of Peace, 1812–1822*. Boston: Houghton, Mifflin, 1957.

Klüber, J. L. *Übersicht der Diplomatischen Verhandlungen des Wiener Congresses*. Frankfort am Main: Andrea, 1816.

Königer, Julius. *Der Krieg von 1815 und die Verträge von Wien und Paris.* Leipzig: Hirzel, 1865.

Rie, Robert. *Der Wiener Kongress und das Völkerrecht.* Bonn: Röhrscheid, 1957.

Schaumann, A. F. H. *Geschichte des zweiten Pariser Friedens.* Göttingen: Vandenhoeck & Ruprecht, 1844.

Webster, C. K. *The Congress of Vienna, 1814–1815.* London: G. Bell, 1945.

Weil, M. H. *Les Dessous du Congrès de Vienne,* 2 Vols. Paris: Payot, 1917.

8. *The First World War*

Albrecht-Carrié, René. *Italy at the Paris Peace Conference.* New York: Columbia Univ. Press, 1938.

Almond, Nina, *et al. The Treaty of St. Germain.* Stanford: Stanford Univ. Press, 1935.

Baker, R. S. *Woodrow Wilson and World Settlement,* 3 Vols. Garden City, N.Y.: Doubleday, 1923.

Berber, Fritz. *Das Diktat von Versailles,* 2 Vols. Essen: Essener verlagsanstalt, 1939.

Bethlen, Stephen. *The Treaty of Trianon and European Peace.* London: Longmans, Green, 1934.

Caldis, C. G. *The Council of Four as a Joint Emergency Authority.* Geneva: Graduate Institute of International Studies, 1953.

Curato, Federico. *La Conferenza della Pace, 1919–1920,* 2 Vols. Milan: Instituto per gli studi di politica internazionale, 1942.

Deak, Francis. *Hungary at the Paris Peace Conference.* New York: Columbia Univ. Press, 1942.

Dimtcheff, K. T. *Le Traité de Neuilly.* Toulouse: Imp. languedocienne, 1930.

Driault, Éduard, *Les traités de 1918–1921.* Paris: Librairie du Recueil Sirey, 1937.

Drost, Pieter. *Contracts and Peace Treaties.* Hague: Martinus Nijhoff, 1948.

Forster, Kent. *The Failures of Peace: The Search for a Negotiated Peace During the First World War.* Washington, D.C.: American Council on Public Affairs, 1941.

Genov, G. P. *Bulgaria and the Treaty of Neuilly.* Sofia: Danov, 1935.

Germany. Deutschen Waffenstillstands Kommission. *Der Waffenstillstand, 1918–1919,* 3 Vols. Berlin: Deutsche verlagsgesellschaft für politik und geschichte, 1928.

Gidel, Gilbert, *et al. Le Traité de Paix, avec l'Allemagne, etc. et les Intérêts Privés.* Paris: Librairie générale de droit et de jurisprudence, 1921.

Grawe, Joachim. *Einwirkungen der Friedensverträge nach dem ersten und zweiten Weltkrieg in die Verfassung der besiegten Staaten.* Darmstadt: Stoytscheff, 1963.

Hankey, Lord. *The Supreme Control of the Paris Peace Conference, 1919.* London: George Allen & Unwin, 1963.

Kraus, Herbert, *et al.,* (eds.). *Urkunden zum Friedensverträge,* 2 Vols. Berlin: F. Vahlen *et al.,* 1920.

Kunz, J. L. *Die Revision der Pariser friedensverträge.* Vienna: Springer, 1932.

Lambert, Margaret. *The Saar.* London: Faber & Faber, 1934.

Lederer, I. J. *Yugoslavia at the Paris Peace Conference.* New Haven: Yale Univ. Press, 1963.

Loewenfeld, William, *et al.* (eds.) . *Die beschlagnahme, liquidation und freigabe deutschen vermögens im auslande,* etc., 5 parts. Berlin: Heymanns verlag, 1924–30.

Luckau, Alma. *The German Delegation at the Paris Peace Conference.* New York: Columbia Univ. Press, 1941.

Mantoux, Paul. *Les Délibérations du Conseil des Quatres,* 2 Vols. Paris: Éditions du Centre Nationale de la Recherche Scientifique, 1955.

Marston, F. S. *The Peace Conference of 1919: Organization and Procedure.* New York: Oxford Univ. Press, 1944.

Maurice, F. B. *The Armistice of 1918.* London: Oxford Univ. Press, 1943.

Mayer, A. J. *Politics and Diplomacy of Peacemaking, 1918–1919.* New York: Knopf, 1967.

Partsch, Josef & Triepel, Heinrich. *Abhandlungen zum Friedensverträge,* 5 Vols. Berlin: A Struycken *et al.,* 1921–23.

Rain, Pierre. *L'Europe de Versailles.* Paris: Payot, 1945.

Rudin, H. R. *Armistice, 1918.* New Haven: Yale Univ. Press, 1944.

Stein, B. E. *Die Russische Frage auf der pariser Friedenskonferenz, 1919–1920.* Leipzig: Kohler & Amelang, 1953.

Temperley, H. W. V. (ed.) . *A History of the Peace Conference of Paris,* 6 Vols. London: Frowdy *et al.,* 1920–24.

Thompson, J. M. *Russia, Bolshevism, and the Versailles Peace.* Princeton: Princeton Univ. Press, 1966.

Ullein-Reviczky, Antal. *La Nature Juridique des Clauses Territoriales du Traité de Trianon.* 2d ed. Paris: A. Pedone, 1936.

United States. Department of State. *The Treaty of Versailles and after; Annotations of the Text of the Treaty.* Washington, D. C., Government Printing Office, 1947.

Wheeler-Bennett, J. W. *Brest-Litovsk: The Forgotten Peace.* New York: St. Martin's Press, 1966.

General references

The Cambridge Modern History, 13 Vols. Cambridge: University Press, 1902–12.

The New Cambridge Modern History, 12 Vols. Cambridge: Cambridge Univ. Press, 1957–60.

Index

Adjustment of disputes, 48–50, 156–57,
  492; *see also* Elements of settlement
Adrianople, Convention of (1878),
  229–30
Adrianople, Treaty of (1829), 223–24
Agenda, 25t., 322–23
Agents of war-oriented actors, 272–73
Agreements, pre-determining, 459–60;
  see also Treaties
Aix-la-Chapelle, Treaty of
  (1668), 345
  (1748), 367f.
Algeria, 71
Alliances
  cohesiveness, 116f., 511f.
  condition of, 118f.
  effectiveness, 124f.
  effects of defeat, 123f.
  neutralization, 31
  peacemaking generally, 9–10, 116f.,
    192f., 502–5
  peace talks, 485
  politics of peace, 127f.
  structures of war, 2

Allies, *see also* War-oriented actors
  non-belligerent, 15, 257–59, 289f.
  war aims, 290–91
  war-oriented, 289f.
Alliance-faction internal war, 192f.;
  see also Internal Wars
Alsace, 68–70, 354, 388–89, 392, 412,
  414, 416
Ambiguities in a peace treaty, 488–89
American Independence, War for, 3t.,
  121, 126
  summary of settlement, 217–22
Ancon, Treaty of, 172–73
Anglo-Chinese War; *see* Opium War
Anglo-Dutch War, Second
  summary of settlement, 160–63
Argentina
  Chaco War, 76–79
  War of the Pacific, 171
Armed forces
  disposition of, 86, 87–88t., 95
  security of, 29
Armenia, 405, 409, 425
Armistice; *see also* Cease-fire

Armistice (cont.)
  agreement, 86, 88–89
    with Germany (1918), 411–13
  supervisory commission, 86–88
  violations, 86–88, 91
Ashanti
  Conferedation, 70–71
  War, summary of settlement, 70–71
Augsburg
  Peace of (1555), 22, 383, 390, 391
  War of the League of, 119, 347–57
Austria, 3, 15, 61–62, 68, 73, 118, 124–
    126, 163f., 169f., 222, 225f., 341f.,
    347f., 357f., 366f., 374f., 380f.,
    392f.; see also Holy Roman Em-
    pire; Habsburg, House of
Austria-Hungary, 175, 228–30, 405f.,
    420f.
Austrian Succession, War of, 126
  summary of settlement, 366–74
Austro-Russian War against Turkey
  summary of settlement, 163–65
Autonomy, wars for; see Independence,
    wars for

Baden, Peace of (1714), 366
Balkan War, First (1912), 15
Bardo, Treaty of, 71–72, 111
Bargaining
  position, 44f., 51–52
  strength, 52f., 81–82n., 90, 95f., 245–
    46, 502
Barrier, The, 359f.
Bavaria, 222, 224, 348f., 357f., 366f.,
    380f., 393, 396
Belgium, 175,, 405f.
Berlin
  Congress of (1878), 228f.
  Peace of (1742), 367, 371, 378
  Treaty of (1918), 408
Boer War
  summary of settlement, 173–75
Bohemia, 380f.
  Palatine War, 380
Bolivia, 76–79, 171f., 405
Bolsheviks, 406–408
Boundary Commissions, 98–99

Boxer Rebellion
  summary of settlement, 175–177
Brandenburg, 119–20, 160f., 341, 343,
    348f., 380; see also Prussia
Brandenburg-Prussia, 357f.
Brazil, 76–79, 405
Breda
  Peace of, 160f.
  Treaty of (1667), 344
Breslau
  Peace of (1742), 367, 369, 378
  Treaty of (1813), 396
Brest-Litovsk, Treaty of, 407, 408, 414
Britain; see Great Britain
Bucharest, Treaty of, 407, 414
Buffer zone, 90
Bulgaria, 15, 62, 228f., 405f., 423f.

Cambodia, 16, 238–39
Canada, 63–64, 362, 373, 377
Carlowitz, Treaty of, 348, 355f.
Catalonia, 353, 361, 364, 380, 392
Câteau-Cambrésis, Treaty of, 157f., 211
Catholicism, Roman, 12–13; see also
    Papacy; Thirty Years War, 380f.
Cease-fire, 27f., 86, 87–88t., 89f., 95,
    137f., 327–28, 483; see also Ar-
    mistice
  agreement, 40–42
    defects in, 485–86
    violation, 30–31
  commission, 30
  condition of, 29f.
  war-oriented actors, 275–76, 281
Chaco War
  summary of settlement, 76–79
Changed conditions, · 489; see also
    Treaties of peace
Chaumont, Treaties of (1814), 396
Chile, 76–79, 171f.
China, 64–66, 175f., 405
  People's Republic of, 16, 236f.
Civil rights, 42, 92–93
Coalition governments, 89f.
Coalitions; see also Alliances; Allies
Collective defense, 145f., 149f.
Cologne, 340f., 357

Colonies, Thirteen, 217f.

Commissions
  peace planning, 460–61
  resolution of disputes, 48–49

Complex external wars; *see* Chapter 4;
  see also External wars
  aims of allies, 122f.
  modes of settlement, 128–29
  peacemaking, 116f.
  settlement summaries, 157f.

Complex internal wars, 181f.; *see* Chapter 5; *see also* Internal wars
  settlement summaries, 208f.
  stalemated, 189f.

Compliance with settlement terms, 201f.

Comprehensive settlement of multilateral wars, 320f.; *see also* Multilateral Wars; Piecemeal settlements

Conferences of war-oriented actors, 297f.; *see also* Peace conferences

Congress of Vienna (1814–15), 8f., 394f., 399f.

Consolidation of the state (as a war aim), 56–57, 511f.; *see also* External wars; War aims

Constantinople, Peace of (1879), 233

Constitutions
  settlement of internal war, 92–93, 96
  state system, 317, 331f., 506

Control of polity (as a war aim), 89f., 182f.; *see also* Internal wars; War aims

Context of peace negotiations, 23; *see* generally Chapter 1 and Epilogue

Crimea, 61–62, 165f., 357

Crimean War, 3t., 117, 124
  summary of settlement, 165–69

Cuban Rebellion of 1869–78
  summary of settlement, 107–08

Czechoslovakia, 406, 409f.

Danubian Principalities, 165f., 223f.; *see also* Moldavia; Wallachia

Decision-makers; *see* policymakers; Chapter 10

De-escalation, 475f.

Defeat; *see also* Outcomes of wars
  effect on allies, 123f.
  outcome of complex internal wars, 182f., 186f., 193, 195–96

De-ideologization, 11, 43–44, 89, 430, 467f., 504; *see also* Devaluation; Ideologies

Demilitarization, 31, 44–45

Demobilization, 478

Denmark, 118, 160f., 163, 169f., 219, 341f., 359, 375, 379f., 393, 394, 411

De-valuation, 11f., 43–44; *see also* De-ideologization

Diplomatic relations, resumption of; *see* Resumption of relations

Directorate of peace conference, 321f.

Disarmament, 31, 44–45

Disengagement from internal wars, 187f., 194, 195–96; *see also* Internal wars

Disputes, adjustments of; *see* Elements of settlement; Adjustment of disputes

Domestic politics
  desire for peace, 445
  factors of, in settlement, 9
  during negotiations, 449f.
  influences upon, generally 431f.
  legislatures, 433f., 452f.
  military situation, 442f.
  military elites, 449–52
  non-military elites, 436f.
  peacemaking generally, 430f., 505
  peace plans, 463, 478, 479–80
  perceptions of policymakers, 441–42
  preparations for peace, 478f.
  propaganda, 445f.
  public opinion, 432–33, 479–80
  reorganization of government, 480
  war-oriented actors, 246

Dominance (as a war aim), 54–55, 511f.; *see also* War aims

Dresden, Peace of (1745), 367, 369, 370, 371, 379
Dutch Revolt
    summary of settlement, 208–14
Dynastic principle, 33

Economic elements of political settlement, 83n.
Egypt, 110–11, 225f., 406, 417
Egyptian Independence, struggle for
    summary of settlement, 110–11
English Revolution of 1688–89; see also Great Britain
    summary of settlement, 103–4
Elections, 91
Elements of political settlement, 82–83, 490f., 504
    adjustment of disputes, 48–50, 156–57, 492
    guarantees of security, 44–48, 56, 491
    penalties, 50–52, 153–54, 493
    persons, 40–42, 97f., 141–42, 278, 490
    resumption of relations, 42–44, 154–56, 279, 491–92
    security guarantees, 145f., 278–79, 332–33, 469f.
    territory, 37–40, 44, 52, 54f., 139f., 277–78, 332–33, 490
Elites, 436f., 449–52, 455–56
England; see Great Britain
English Revolution
    summary of settlement, 103–4
Escalation; see De-escalation
Ethiopia, 72–73
European War of 1683–1700, 120
    summary of settlement, 347–57
External (foreign) wars, 1f.
    complex, 116f., 122f., 128–29, 157f.; see Chapter 4
    peace plans for, 469f.
    simple, 24f.; see Chapter 2
Extrinsic problems, 488
    causes of settlement failure, 484–85

Factions, 2, 181f.; see also Internal war; and Chapters 3 and 5

Factors for peace, 432–33; see generally Chapters 7 and 10, and refer to particular summaries of settlements
Failure of settlements, 481f., 497f.; see Chapter 12
Finland, 79–81, 406; see also Russo-Finnish War
First World War; see World War I
Fountainebleau, Peace of
    (1679), 341f.
    (1762), 376
Fourteen Points, 412–13
France, 15–16
    American Independence, 121, 126
    Anglo-Dutch War, Second, 160f.
    Austrian Succession, War of, 126, 366f.
    Austro-Russian War against Turkey, 163
    Boer War, 173
    Boxer Rebellion, 175f.
    Crimean War, 124, 165f.
    Dutch Revolt, 208f.
    English Revolution, 103
    European War of 1683–1700, 120, 347f.
    France against Europe (1792–1815), 392–405
    Franco-Dutch War, 340f.
    Franco-Prussian War, 68–70
    Franco-Tunisian War, 71–72
    Greek Revolt, 222f.
    Habsburg-Valois Rivalry, 157f.
    Italo-Abyssinian War, 73
    Mehemet Ali Wars, 225f.
    Napoleonic Wars, 121, 392–405
    Opium War, 65
    Pacific, War of the, 171
    Polish Succession, 119, 214f.
    Russo-Finnish War, 77–78
    Russo-Turkish War
        (1768), 61–62
        (1877), 228
    Schleswig-Holstein War, 169
    Seven Years War, 374f.
    Spanish Succession, war of, 357f.

France (*cont.*)
Thirty Years War, 379f.
Tunisian Independence, 111–12
World War I, 405f.
France against Europe, wars of 1792–
1815; *see* Napoleonic wars
Franco-Dutch War of 1672–79, 119–20
summary of settlement, 340–47
Franco-Prussian War
summary of settlement, 68–70
Franco-Tunisian War
summary of settlement, 71–72
Frankfort, Peace of, 68–70
Frederick the Great, 118–19, 126, 366f.
French Revolution, 392f.
Free territory, 40
Füssen, Peace of (1745), 367, 369

Geneva Conference
Indochina, 8, 238
Laos, 238–40
Genoa, 366f.
German Confederation, 169f., 400–401
Germany, 12–13, 15, 68–70, 79–81, 171,
173, 175f., 228, 374f., 379f., 389f.,
393f., 405f., 414f.; *see also* Holy
Roman Empire
Gertruydenberg, Conference of, 361
Ghent, Treaty of, 63–64
Gibraltar, 219f., 364
Glorious Revolution; *see* English Rev-
olution
Great Britain (this entry includes ref-
erences to England and Britain),
15
American Independence, War for,
121, 126, 217–22
Anglo-Dutch War, 160f.
Ashanti War, 70–71
Austrian Succession, War of the,
366–74
Austro-Russian War against Turkey,
163
Boer War, 173f.
Boxer Rebellion, 175f.
Crimean War, 124, 165–69
Dutch Revolt, 208–14

Great Britain (*cont.*)
Egyptian Independence, 110–11
English Revolution, 103–4
European War of 1683–1700, 347–57
Franco-Dutch War of 1672–79, 340f.
Franco-Prussian War, 68
Greek Revolt, 222f.
Habsburg-Valois War (Last), 157f.
Huguenot War, Third, 102
Irish Rebellion, 109–10
Italo-Abyssinian War, 73
Mehemet Ali Wars, 225–28
Napoleonic Wars, 125, 392–405
Opium War, 64–66
Pacific, War of the, 17
Parliament, 103–4, 110, 218f.
Polish Succession, War of the, 215
Russo-Finnish War, 77–80
Russo-Turkish War
(1768), 61–62
(1877), 228
Schleswig-Holstein, 169
Seven Years War, 119–20, 374–79
Spanish Succession, War of the, 121,
124, 357–66
Thirty Years War, 380
Tunisian Independence, 111
War of 1812, 63–64
World War I, 405–28
Great Northern War, 359
Great powers, 466
peace plans, 469f.
war-oriented, 15, 247f., 252–54, 255f.,
283f., 286f.
Greco-Turkish War, 405, 424–25
Greece, 15, 222–25, 228, 405f., 424–25
Greek Revolt
summary of settlement, 222–25
Guadelupe Hidalgo, Treaty of, 66–68
Guarantees of security, 44–48, 56, 491;
see also Elements of settlement

Habsburg, House of, 104–5, 210f., 214f.,
357f., 367f., 380f., 420f.
Habsburg-Valois Rivalry, Last War of,
13
summary of settlement, 157–60

Hamburg, Treaty of (1762), 374
Hanover, 3, 104, 348f., 361f., 367, 368, 374f.
Convention of (1745), 367
Holy Alliance, 22, 403
Holy League, War of the; see European War of 1683–1700
Holy Roman Empire, 119–20, 209f., 216f., 219, 341f., 357f., 368f., 374f., 380f., 393; see also Habsburg, House of; Austria; Germany
Holy See; see Papacy
Hubertusburg, Treaty of, 374, 379
Huguenot War, Third
summary of settlement, 101–3
Hungary, 77–80, 104–5, 355f., 405f.; see also Austria-Hungary
Hungarian Rebellion (1703–11), 104–5, 359

Ideological values, 10f.
Ideological war aims, 57–59, 511f.; see also War aims
Ideologies, 21, 50, 467–69
Images; see Perceptions
Inadequacies of a settlement
intrinsic, 481–82
kinds of, 483f.
India, 3, 16, 221, 237f., 374, 379
Incumbent faction, 84f., 181f., see generally Chapters 3, 5, and 6
Independence, wars for, 95f., 182f.; see generally Chapters 3 and 5
Insurgent faction, 11, 84f., 181f., see generally Chapters 3, 5, and 6
Interconnected questions, 318, 320, 331–32, 334–36, 510
Internal affairs, questions relating to, 207–8
Internal wars, 1f., 84f.; see Chapters 3, 5, and 6
internal-external wars, 194f., 199f.
complex, 181f.
peace plans, 470f.
political settlement, 89f., 92–93
proxy, 302f.

Internal wars (cont.)
simple, 84–89, 100f.
types, 1f., 84f.
war-oriented states, 279
International organizations, 203
collective security, 146f., 264f.
membership, 268–69
military forces, 292
plans for peace, 464–65
political settlements, 293f.
war aims, 265f.
war-oriented actor, as a, 15, 264f., 291f., 295–96
Internationalization of war, 3, 20–21
Intervention, 7, 189–91, 250f., 493–94
Irish Rebellion
summary of settlement, 109–10
Italo-Abyssinian War
summary of settlement, 72–73
Italy, 7–8, 68, 71–73, 171, 175, 215f., 228, 359f., 372f., 380–81, 384f., 392f.; see also Savoy; Sicily

Japan, 7, 175f., 405
Jassy, Peace of, 163f.

Kalisch, Treaty of, 396
Kasr-Said, Treaty of, 71–72
Kleinschnellendorf, Convention of, 367
Korea, 233f.
Korean War, 4, 14
summary of settlement, 233–36
Kurdish Insurrection, 3, 112–13
Kutchuk-Kainarji, Treaty of, 61, 62, 165

Laos, 8, 16
Laotian Civil War
summary of settlement, 236–40
London
Conference
Balkan Wars, 15
Greek Revolt, 223f.
Schleswig-Holstein, 169f.
Treaty of
(1604), 212–13
(1827), 222f.
(1840), 227

Leadership (factor in domestic politics), 439–41

League of Nations, 76–80, 408, 413, 416f.

Legislatures (and peace negotiations), 452f.

Levant, 62, 222f.; see also Ottoman Empire; Turkey

Lorraine, 68–70; see also Alsace

Louis XIV, 120–21, 124, 161, 341f., 347f., 358f., 389

Lund, Peace of (1679), 341f.

Lyons, Peace of (1601), 212

Mandates, 409, 427

Mediation, 49; see Chapter 7

Mehemet Ali, Wars of
summary of settlements, 225–28

Mexico
Mexican-American War, 66–68
Texas Revolt, 106

Mexican-American War
summary of settlement, 66–68

Military Administration, 30, 139

Military elites in domestic politics, 449–52

Military operations, 8–9, 473–75

Military settlement phase, 7f.
cease-fire, 137f.
complex external wars, 137f.
complex internal wars, 205–6
military administration, 30, 139
simple external wars, 27f.
simple internal wars, 85–89
troop dispositions, 138–39
war-oriented actors, 275–77

Modes of settlement; see also Peace settlements; Political settlements
alliance-faction internal wars, 192–94
internal-external wars, 195f.

Moldavia, 62, 165f., 306

Montenegro, 15, 228f., 405

Morocco, 71, 111, 416

Multilateral wars, 337f., 505–6; see generally Chapters 8 and 9
analysis, 308–12

Multilateral wars (cont.)
characteristics, of, 307f.
classification, 2, 4, 307f.
interconnected questions, 318f., 331f.
military settlement, 327f.
modalities of settlement, 319f.
peace plans, 471, 473
preliminaries of peace, 327f.
small states, 312
stages of negotiations, 327f.
summaries of settlements, 337f.
system transformation, 315f.
termination, 318f.

Münster, 160f., 340f., 385–86
Treaties of (1648), 209, 214, 354, 382f., 386f.

Muscovy; see Russia

Nanking, Treaty of, 64–66

Naples, 359f., 392

Napoleon, 125, 392f.

Napoleonic Wars, 22
summary of settlement, 392–405

Nationality, 42, 97f., 141–42

Netherlands, 175, 402, 411, 416; see also United Provinces of the Netherlands; Dutch Revolt
Spanish, 159f., 344f., 347f., 358f.

Netherlands Revolt; see Dutch Revolt

Neuilly, Treaty of (1919), 407, 423–24

Neutralization, 31, 46

Nijmegen, Peace of (1679), 119, 341f., 354, 355, 365

Non-belligerent allies, 15, 257–59, 289f.;
see generally Chapters 6 and 7;
see also Alliances; War-oriented actors

Non-obligated parties, 486–87

Obligatory force of peace treaties, 201f., 486–87

Occupation zone; see Territory

Opportunity (as a war aim), 60–61, 511f.

Opium War
summary of settlement, 64–66

Orientation of states to wars, 14f.; *see*
    Chapters 6 and 7; *see also* War-
    oriented actors
Osnabrück, 385–86
    Treaty of (1648), 382f., 387f.
Ottoman Empire, 9, 61–62, 165f., 225f.,
    228f., 343, 384, 405f.; *see also*
    Turkey
Outchalé (Uccialli), Treaty of, 73
Outcomes of wars, 5f., 502
    alliance-faction internal wars, 192–94
    bargaining strength, 8
Outcomes of wars
    complex internal wars, 182f., 192f.
    internal-external wars, 195f.
    state-faction internal wars, 182f.
Order, inter-state, 458f., 461f.

Pacific, War of the
    summary of settlement, 171–73
Palatinate, 380f.
Palestine, 408, 427
Papacy, 157f., 212f., 348f., 359, 384f.,
    393f.
Paraguay, 76–79
Parties, necessary, 510
Partition solution, 89f.
Parent state (in wars for independ-
    ence), 95f., 198
Paris
    Congress (Crimean War), 165f.
    Peace of, (1763), 374f.
    Peace of, (1814, 1815), 394, 397–99
    Peace Conference (1919), 409, 413f.
Peace conferences, 320f., 325f.; *see also*
    Peace settlements; Peacemaking
    process; Political settlements
Peace feelers, 24f., 85, 87–88, 129–30,
    443–44
Peacekeeping, 292, 497–98
Peacemaking process, vii, 4–5, 502f.;
    see also Elements of settlement;
    Peace settlements; Political set-
    tlements; War-oriented actors
    alliances, 116f., 502, 504–5
    domestic politics, 430f., 505
    factors affecting, 9f.

Peacemaking process
    military settlements, 137f.
    political settlements, 139f.
    pre-condition to talks, 133f.
    preliminary phase, 129f.
    procedural questions, 25, 26t., 133f.,
        135f., 202f.
    stages, 7f.
Peace plans, 457f., 461f., 482, 498f., 505
    allies, 458–59
    de-escalation, 475f.
    domestic politics, 463
    ideologies, 467f.
    external wars, 469f.
    internal wars, 470f.
    military operations, 473–75
    multilateral wars, 471–73
    preparations, 478f.
    security guarantees, 469f.
Peace settlements, 4–5, 502; *see also*
    Elements of settlement; Peace-
    making process; Political settle-
    ments
    acceptability, 502
    constitution for the state system, 317,
        331f., 506
    failure, 481f., 493f., 497f.
    improving, 498f.
    inadequacies, 481f., 505–6
    modes of settlement, 128–29, 182f.
    multilateral wars, 307f., 325f., 337f.
    preliminaries, 24f., 504
Peace treaties; *see* Treaties
Penalties (element of settlement), 50–
    52, 153–54, 493
Peoples' Republic of China; *see* China
Perceptions of policymakers, 20, 317,
    441–42
Persons affected by the war (element
    of settlement), 40–42, 97f., 141–
    42, 278, 490
Peru, 76–79, 171f., 405
Philippine Insurrection
    summary of settlement, 108
Piecemeal settlements, 487f.; *see also*
    Multilateral wars
Piedmont-Savoy; *see* Savoy

Plans for peace; *see* Peace Plans

Plebiscites, 38–39, 57

Poland, 73–76, 214f., 343, 348f., 356, 359, 380–81, 401–2, 406f., 426

Polish Succession, War of the, 119
summary of settlement, 214–17

Policymakers, 438f., *see* generally Chapter 10

Political settlement, 7f., 83n.; *see also* Elements of settlement; Peace settlements
adjustment of disputes, 48–50, 156–57
bargaining strength, 52f.
elements of, 36f., 192, 206–8, 504
external wars, 36f., 139f.
inadequacies, 490f.
internal wars, 89f., 95f., 206–8
multilateral wars, 314–15, 331f.
penalties, 40–42, 50–52, 144–45, 153–54
resumption of relations, 42–44, 154–56

Political settlement
security guarantees, 44–48, 145f.
territory, 37–40, 139f.
war aims, 52f.
war-oriented actors, 282f.

Polity, preparation for peace, 478f., *see also* Internal wars; Domestic politics

Portugal, 124, 219, 357f., 374f., 380, 393f., 403, 405

Power position, 10f., 18–19

Post-war world, 457f.; *see* generally Chapters 11 and 12

Pragmatic Sanction (1713), 368f.

Prague, Peace of (1635), 381, 384

Preliminary phase of settlement, 95, 129f., 280, 504; *see also* Peacemaking; Peace settlements

Pre-conditions to negotiations, 85, 187–88

Presence of war-oriented actors, 270f.

Prisoners of war, 42, 95

Propaganda, 422f.

Prussia, 3, 61–62, 68–70, 118, 124–26, 163, 165f., 169f., 215, 219, 222, 302f., 366f., 374f., 393f.

Public opinion, 432–33, 452f.; *see* Chapter 10

Pyrenees, Treaty of (1659), 351, 381–82, 384

Rastadt, Peace of, 357f.

Ratification of peace treaty, 486–87

Realism, 476f.

Regional states (as war-oriented actors), 15, 260f., 283f., 286f., 497f.

Reparation, 43, 50, 51–52

Resumption of relations (element of settlement), 42–44, 154–56, 279, 491–92

Retribution (as war aim), 59–60, 511f.

Reunions, 347f.

Rhine, 347f., 393, 400–401, 414–15

Riga, Treaty of, 74–76

Roumania, 228f., 405f.; *see also* Danubian Principalities

Rumelia, Eastern, 228f.

Russia, 3, 9, 15, 61–62, 63–64, 68, 117, 118, 124, 125, 163f., 165f., 169, 175f., 214f., 217f., 222f., 225f., 228f., 348f., 356–57, 359, 372, 374f., 381, 392f., 405f.; *see also* Soviet Union

Russian Civil Wars, 406

Russian Revolution, 406–8; *see also* World War I

Russo-Finnish War (Winter War), 3
summary of settlement, 79–81

Russo-Polish War
summary of settlement, 73–76

Russo-Turkish Wars
summary of settlement
war of 1768, 61–62
war of 1877–78, 228–33

Ryswick, 120
Clause, 354
Peace of, 348f.

Saar, 417

San Stefano, Treaty of (1878), 228f.

Sardinia, 119, 165f., 214f., 366f., 392f., 402; *see also* Italy; Savoy

Savoy, 120, 348f., 357f., 380–81

Saxony, 3, 214f., 348f., 359, 366f., 374f., 380f., 393, 401; *see also* Germany; Holy Roman Empire; Poland

Schleswig-Holstein, Second War over summary of settlement, 169–71

Schmalkaldic League, 12–13

SEATO, 237f.

Security guarantees (element of settlement), 145f., 278–79, 332–33, 469f.

Self-determination, 410, 412

Settlements; *see* Peace settlements; Political settlements

Settlement summaries of wars

   Anglo-Dutch, Second, 160–63

   American Independence, 217–22

   Ashanti, 50–71

   Austro-Russian against Turkey, 163–65

   Austrian Succession, 366–74

   Boer, 173–75

   Boxer Rebellion, 175–77

   Chaco, 76–79

   Crimean, 165–69

   Cuban Revolt, 107–8

   Dutch Revolt, 208–14

   Egyptian Independence, Struggle for, 110–11

   English Revolution, 103–4

   European, of 1683–1700, 347–57

   Franco-Dutch, of 1672–79, 340–47

   Franco-Prussian, 68–70

   Franco-Tunisian, 71–72

   French, against Europe (1792–1815), 392–405

   Greek Independence, 222–25

   Habsburg-Valois, Last, 157–60

   Huguenot, Third, 101–3

   Hungarian Rebellion, 104–5

   Irish Rebellion, 109–10

   Italo-Abyssinian, 72–73

   Korean War, 233–36

   Kurdish Insurrection, 112–13

   Laotian Civil War, 236–40

Settlement summaries of wars (*cont.*)

   Mehemet Ali Wars, 225–28

   Mexican American, 66–68

   Napoleonic, 392–405

   Opium, 64–66

   Pacific, 171–73

   Philippine Insurrection, 108

   Polish Succession, 214–17

   Russo-Finnish, 79–81

   Russo-Polish, 73–76

   Russo-Turkish, of 1768, 61–62

   Russo-Turkish, of 1877, 228–33

   Schleswig-Holstein, Second, 169–71

   Seven Years War, 374–79

   Spanish Succession, 357–66

   Texas Revolt, 106–7

   Thirty Years War, 379–92

   Tunisian Independence, 111–12

   War of 1812, 63–64

   World War I, 405–28

Serbia, 15, 228f., 405f.

Seven Years War, 3, 118–19, 510 summary of settlement, 374–79

Sèvres, Treaty of (1920), 407

Sicily, 216, 219, 359f., 372

Silesia, 366f., 374f.

Simple internal wars; *see* Internal wars

Sistova, Peace of, 164–65

Soviet Union, 16, 73–76, 79–81, 234, 236f., 407f.; *see also* Russia

South African War; *see* Boer War

Spain, 3, 71, 102–3, 107–8, 111, 119–21, 157f., 175, 208f., 214, 218f., 341f., 347f., 366f., 374f., 380f., 392f., 411

Spanish Succession, War of the, 120, 121, 124 summary of settement, 357–66

State-faction internal wars; *see* Internal wars

Status quo (as war aim), 18f., 55–56, 511f.

St. Germain

   Edict, 102

   Peace of

      (1679), 341f.

      (1919), 407, 421f.

St. Petersburg, Treaty of, (1762), 374

Straits, 424–25
Convention of (1841), 228
Structure of wars, viii, 1f., 508f.
Successor States, 95f., 199
Summaries of settlements; see Settlement summaries
Surrender, 6–7
Sweden, 3, 77–80, 160, 163, 165, 169, 219, 340f., 348f., 359, 374f., 379f., 393, 399, 411
Switzerland, 355, 389, 393f., 402, 411
Syria, 225f., 409, 418, 427
Szatmar, Peace of, 104–5

Territory (as element of settlement), 37–40, 44, 52, 54f., 139f., 277–78, 332–33, 490
Texas, 66
Revolt, summary of, 106–7
Thirty Years War, 209
summary of settlements, 379–92
Thresholds of settlement, 4–5, 14
Transnational factors in peacemaking, 442f.
Treaties of peace
ambiguities, 485f., 488–89, 498–99
changed conditions, 489
non-obligated parties, 486–87
preliminaries, 483–84
ratification, 486–87
secret treaties, 459–60
Trianon, Treaty of (1920), 407, 421f.
Troop disposition, 29f., 86f., 138–39; see also military settlement
Tunisia
summary of settlements of
Franco-Tunisian War, 71–72
Struggle for Tunisian Independence, 111–12
Turin, Peace of (1696), 120, 348, 354
Turkey, 15, 61–62, 113, 117, 163f., 165f., 222f., 347f., 359, 393, 424f.; see also Ottoman Empire
Twelve Years Truce (1609), 213–14
Two Sicilies, Kingdom of; see Sicily

Ukraine, 74f.
United Kingdom; see Great Britain

United Nations, 16, 48–49, 68, 111, 233f.
United Provinces of the Netherlands, 103, 119–21, 124, 160f., 163, 218, 340f., 348f., 357f., 372f., 379f., 392f.; see also Netherlands, Spanish
United States, 8, 16, 63–64, 65, 66–68, 76–79, 106f., 111, 121, 171f., 173, 175f., 233f., 236f., 395, 405f.
Unkiar-Iskelessi, Treaty of, 255f.
Uruguay, 76–79
Utopianism, 467–68; see also realism
Utrecht, Peace of, 120, 347, 357f.

Values, 10f., 430–31
Velasco, Treaties of, 106
Venice, 348f., 356, 385, 391
Vereeniging, Peace of, 174
Versailles
Armistice (1871), 68–69
Treaty (1919), 406, 415f.
Vervins, Peace of (1598), 210–11
Vienna
Conference of
Mehemet Ali Wars, 227
Crimean War, 165f.
Congress of, 63, 347f.
Conventions of (1736), 216–17
Peace of
(1738), 217
(1864), 170–71
Vietnam, 16
DRVN, 16, 236f.
RVN, 237
War, 508–509n
Vigevano, Treaty of, 348, 351–52
Violations, 48–49; see also Cease-fire; Military settlement; see generally Chapter 12

Wallachia, 62, 165f.
Wars; see also War aims
classification, 1f.
legal consequences, 43–44
outcome, 5f., 502
types, 131–32, 140f., 147f., 151f.

War aims, 20, 32f., 495–96n.
  after settlement, 485–86
  allies, 121f.
  bargaining strength, 52f., 502
  change of, 35
  classification of, 32f., 504
  compatibility of, 245–46, 257f., 304,
    458–59, 511f.
    intrinsic incompatibility, 121f.
    matrix analysis of, 510f.
  great powers, 247f.
  non-belligerent allies, 257f.
  preliminary phase of settlement,
    130f.
  political settlement phase, 140f.
  security, 462n.
  war-oriented actors, 147f., 151f., 282f.
War crimes, 52t.
War guilt, 51
War-oriented actors, 3, 15f., 20–21,
  244f., 270f., 505
  belligerents negotiating for peace,
    272f.
  belligerents not negotiating, 280f.
  conferences of, 297f.
  great powers, 247f., 283f., 286f.

War-oriented actors (cont.)
  international organizations, 264f.
    291–96
  military settlements, 275–77
  non-belligerent allies, 257f., 289f.
  promote or prevent negotiations,
    252, 272f.
  regional states, 15, 260f., 283f., 286f.,
    497f.
  war aims, 245–46, 282f.
War of 1812
  summary of settlement, 63–64
Washington Conference (Chaco War),
  77–79
Westminster, Treaty of, 341f.
Westphalia, Peace of (1648), 311,
  345f., 354, 355, 362, 365, 382f.,
  386f.
Winter War; see Russo-Finnish War
World War I, 4, 120
  summary of settlement, 405–28

Yugoslavia, 409f.

Zanjon, Treaty of, 107–8
Zell, Peace of (1679), 341f.